The Lancashire Parish Register Society

Vol 159

The Registers of

All Saints

Newton Heath

ISBN: 1 85445 153 7

The Lancashire
Parish Register Society

The Lancashire Parish Register Society

The registers of

All Saints

Newton Heath

Part 2: 1797 - 1837

Transcribed and edited by

George C. Cadman

Printed and published by permission of
The Parochial Church Council

Printed by the Advertiser Printing Works, Newport, Shropshire
2005

Introduction

Newton Chapel, later becoming the Parish Church of All Saints Newton Heath, began its days as early as 1556, a time of great turbulent religious upheaval, the inhabitants being mainly Puritan in their sympathies. It was built of wattle and daub: the first of some eight Chapels of Ease under the Manchester Collegiate Church, the nearest other Chapel of Ease being at Gorton (later St. James'). Lands owned at Newton formed part of the historic estates of the Manchester Collegiate Church.

Newton Chapel stood on a wild heath (Newton Heath), on the highest ground and on the site of the ancient Roman Road from Chester to Manchester and on to York, at its junction with the roads connecting the townships of Moston and Droylsden. Close by is the road linking the townships of Manchester, Failsworth and Oldham.

Newton Chapel was rebuilt in 1598 and an old timber found in the rubble when rebuilding in 1814 was found to have the date '1556' carved upon it, thus 1556 being the probable date of the first building.

The first permanent Curate at Newton Chapel was appointed in 1598, those before 1598 being clergy sent from the Manchester Collegiate Church. This 1598 chapel was built of oak stanchions and small branches plastered with mud, and whitewashed. The gallery was reached by a stone stairway on the outside of the building. The floor of the chapel was bare earth, and being of clay was very cold. Rushes were strewn over the floor in winter, brought in by the rush carts. There were stocks close to the chapel for the use of male offenders, and from the centre of the gallery projected a circular stall where female offenders were made to stand through services as a penance.

In 1738 the mud walls were replaced with brick, and interior repairs were carried out. In 1795 the building was declared unsafe as a place of worship. On Sunday 1st May 1808 an anniversary service was held in the chapel and the next morning, at 6 am, the building finally collapsed. Apparently it had been repaired some 4 years earlier, and the reason for its final collapse was said to be that the repairs had been carried out during the winter season. Services continued amidst the dereliction, as no effort towards rebuilding was made for the next 5 years.

The present neo-classical gothic building of 1814 was built to a design by William Atkinson, architect, of Manchester. An Act of Parliament authorised £3500 to be raised by church rates on the chapelry property, a supplemental Act authorised a further £3300, and pews were rented out to raise further money. The cracked bell from the old building was moved to the new chapel of 1814, and in 1860 a new bell was installed.

Newton was made up of village greens upon which cattle were grazed, and the chapel, parsonage and school were built on the heath, which was otherwise wild. Farmers from Failsworth, not being residents of Newton, were fined for grazing their cattle on the heath, as the Authorities had declared that "No Person other than a Resident of Newton shall graze his cattle on Newton Heath."

Industries include coalmining from the 17th century meeting the needs of Manchester, handloom weaving in the 17th century, and cotton spinning and silk weaving in the 18th and 19th centuries. Heavy engineering became prominent in the 19th century, and with this huge industrialisation the population of Newton increased from a few hundred in the late 1700s to over 30,000 a century later. These later industries include soap, matches, glassmaking, cable manufacture, and iron and steel industries.

Newton Heath became part of one of the most industrialised areas in the land, with manufacturers Mather and Platt, A.V. Roe, Matthew Swain & Co. and others - indeed Blackpool Tower was manufactured here.

Formerly owning land in Newton, the Manchester Collegiate Church used Newton Chapel as a means of coping with a massive increase in burials. This had resulted from the rapid increase in population and a shortage of ground for burials at Manchester, hence the numerous people from Manchester being buried at Newton from the year 1790.

Of particular interest are the burial entries of the late 17th century: affidavits relating to the compulsary burial of corpses in woollen cloth, unusually giving details of witnesses.

For further reading see H.T.Crofton; *A History of Newton Chapelry, vols 1 & 2*; Chetham Society; 1904.

The Parish Registers are deposited in the Diocesan Record Office at Manchester Central Library, with the following designations:

Volume 1 (M362/1/1/1) baptisms 7 January 1655 - 13 March 1722, burials 1672*(gravestone inscription)* - 7 March 1727, marriages 1682 - 3 Sept 1727
The earlier whereabouts of this first known register is unknown, but in 1862 the register was given to John Higson (see below), consisting of about 49 surviving fragments, and after some were pieced together in assumed chronological order there are now 39 fragments, most of which are only three-quarters or less of the original page size, which measured 35.5 cm high x 16.5 cm wide, the top, bottom and sides having perished, with loss of many entries and information. The covers (very delapidated), have a rectangular black inlay.

In 1862 John Owen and John Higson attempted to date, arrange in chronological order, and transcribe the fragments (part of the 'Owen Manuscripts') but the arrangement was sometimes faulty. John Higson writes: "On the 5th December 1862 I received from Mrs. Pegge of Newton Heath an oblong tin Box measuring 9¼ in x 4¼ in x 4¼ in (23.5 x 11 x 11 cm) &

labelled on a strip of paper "Old Registers of Baptisms, Burials & Marriages prior to 1666(*sic*) (signed) W. Hutchinson March 21 1862." Mr. Pegge Surgeon (*see also Miscellaneous Items*) had borrowed them from the Rector Mr. Hutchinson in order that I might arrange, copy, and insert them in a parchment book to be purchased by him, and presented to Newton Church. Mr. Pegge then lay ill in bed, & died a few days afterwards, so that his design could not be executed. I copied the Marriages & Deaths, Mr. Owen the Baptisms, and I carefully collated the copies, & returned the originals to Mr. Hutchinson on the 21 March 1863.

On opening the box I found two remnants of old calf-leather which had once formed part of the covering of the Register Book. The leaves had all been ruthlessly torn out, and then stowed away in some damp place, the edges of the leaves gradually frittering away until in many places the Christian names of the beginning, and the dates at the end of the lines are illegible. I straightened them with my penknife, and smoothed them with a hot iron, and thereby rescued many a name, and many a date, which seemed to have passed for ever into oblivion.

(i) The Marriages number 36 and range from March 7th 1698 to about April 1715 and are written on a slip & a half or three pages of paper.
(ii) The Baptisms number — (*as written*) & extend from January 7th 1655 to May 1722, and are written on 35 fragmentary slips of 70 pages (*70 sides*), but which originally have only constituted some 20 to 30 leaves of the Book; these are in bad order indeed, and there is considerable uncertainty about the years of some of them, owing to the scandalous mutilation which they have undergone. There are only five baptisms inserted by the Church officials in mistake amongst the internments of the year 1727.
(iii) The Burials number 749 and stretch from about the year 1678 to March 7th 1728 (*1727*) and are recorded on 11½ slips or 23 pages, more or less fragmentary. These leaves, however, are in much better order than those on which the baptisms are inserted, at least as regards their not being torn up into so many pieces. John Higson."

In 1938 Bertram William Tuff Norman, historian, presented transcriptions of the fragments and noted further possible resolutions. The transcription presented here results from a further study in the light of these earlier attempts.

Whilst it must be noted that entries are lost from the top and bottom of almost every page, and also details from both edges of the pages, many entries are supplemented by the Owen Manuscripts and the B.W.T. Norman transcripts, having been copied at earlier times when the fragments were less worn away than today, and these supplements, now unverifiable, are recorded here in brace brackets { }. The use of round brackets ( ) indicates assumed completion of names both from the Owen Manuscripts and the present transcriber.

There are no known extant Bishop's Transcripts prior to the year 1721. From 1721 the Bishop's Transcripts have been collated and differences noted using square brackets [ ].

Entries from the BTs which are lost from the upper or lower edges of the fragments of this register and thus which cannot be ascertained as to which page they were written upon, have been entered between broken lines in this transcript; these entries also give some indication of the extent of losses of entries from the earlier pages of this register. A child's name so incomplete that it cannot be ascertained is transcribed as seen but is indexed as NXN.

5 gravestone inscriptions between 1672 and 1720, supplementing the burials in Volume 1, are recorded in the Chetham Society History of Newton Chapelry, presented in italics in this transcript.

Volume 2 (M362/1/1/2) baptisms 31 March 1723 – 25 December 1755, burials 25 March 1728 – 24 December 1755, marriages 15 June 1729 – 23 March 1754
    Size 30cm high x 15cm wide, 62 leaves.
    Written on spine: Burials from 1729 (*sic*) to 1755 (*remainder faded*)
    Brown velvet-covered covers, parchment pages. Completely intact; in good condition.

Volume 3 (M362/1/1/3) baptisms 4 Jan 1756 – 22 Sep 1782, burials 9 Jan 1756 – 10 Dec 1782
    Size 36cm high x 19½cm wide, 54 leaves.
    Front cover entitled: Baptisms 1756 to 1782 & Burials 1756 to 1782
    Brown velvet-covered covers, ribbed spine, cover & spine partially damaged and coming loose, parchment pages in good condition.

Volume 4 (M362/1/6/3&4) This register, containing further baptisms of 1782 plus baptisms 5 Jan 1783 – 25 Nov 1792 and burials 16 Jan 1783 – 6 Dec 1792, known as the 'Small Register', was apparently mislaid subsequent to microfilming at Manchester Central Library in 1958 and all that remains is the microfilm and a transcript taken by B.W.T. Norman, historian, dated 14 Nov 1938.
Although some readings of the microfilm are difficult, some are complemented by the transcripts of B.W.T. Norman which cover Volume 1 and Volume 4.
It is interesting to note however, that an inspection of the microfilm of the 'Small Register' reveals perfect uniformity, written entirely in one hand, and thus suggesting that the 'Small Register' was itself an early transcript of a missing original register. Also, the date 1787 at the head of the Burials for that year had originally read 1887.

Volume 5 (M362/1/2/1) baptisms 1 Jan 1793 – 25 Dec 1812
    Size 39cm high x 17½ cm wide, 88 leaves.
    Front cover entitled Baptisms 1792 (*sic*) to 1812
    Red and gold-edged label on spine inscribed CHRISTENINGS
    Fully leather-bound cover, parchment pages. Completely intact; in good condition.

Volume 6 (M362/1/4/1) burials 6 May 1793 – 18 Dec 1812 plus further baptisms of 1812 and baptisms 1813 – 1816 prior to use of 'George Rose' register Volume 7.
    Size 39cm high x 17½cm wide, 94 leaves, 5 unused.

Red and gold-edged label on front cover inscribed (*in capitals*): Edmund Newton Samuel Beswick William Booth Thomas Corns Churchwardens 1795

On inside of front cover is written: Abt 6,500 entries

Handwritten label on spine reads: Burials 1793 – 1812 (*baptism label fragmented*).

Fully leather-bound cover, parchment pages. In reasonable condition but fading.

The following are the standard 'George Rose' registers – all are in good condition M362/1/2/2 to 1/2/4 (baptisms) and M362/1/4/2 to 1/4/4 (burials)

Volume 7   baptisms 10 Jan 1813 – 14 Sep 1823
Volume 8   burials 1 Jan 1813 – 24 Aug 1823
Volume 9   baptisms 14 Sep 1823 – 4 Dec 1831
Volume 10 burials 25 Aug 1823 – 21 Sep 1831
Volume 11 baptisms 11 Dec 1831 – Dec 1842
Volume 12 burials 22 Sep 1831 – Nov 1842

From 1783 to 1792 (the 'Small Register') spinner and spinr are recorded as spinster in the BT.

From 1783 to 1792 (the 'Small Register') Jos'h is recorded as Joseph in the BT.

From 1793 to 1811 occupations are not given in the BT.

From 1793 to 1812 date of birth, cause of death, age at death, and 'poor' are not given in the BT, except [poor] when thus indicated.

Age at death is given in the BT from 1813.

Please note that all Miscellaneous Items were published in Part 1 (L.P.R.S. Volume 158).

Officiating Clergy

1598	Mr Medcalf	1704	Griffith Swinton
1609	Randle Bate	1717	William Perkins
1615	Humphrey Barnett	1729	Thomas Wroe
1617	George Gee	1730	William Shrigley
1637	Mr Bernard	1756	William Purnell
1642	Robert Symond	1764	Richard Millward
1646	William Walker	1772	Matthew Sedgwick
1650	John Walker	1789	William Jackson
1662	Thomas Lawton	1792	Abraham Ashworth
1678	William Coulbourne	1818	Thomas Gaskell
1695	James Lawton	1834	William Hutchinson

Names of Ministers, Curates, Assistant Curates, Clerks, and Wardens can be located in the Miscellaneous Index.

Abbreviations

bo	born
B T	Bishop's Transcript
d(s)	daughter(s) of, or day(s) in context
m	month(s)
M	Manchester
n.d.	no date
n.m.	no month
NSN	no surname
NXN	no Christian name
p.	parish of
PR	Parish Register
s(s)	son(s) of
w.	wife of
wdw.	widow of
wk(s)	week(s)
y	year(s)

Hon. General Editor's Note

The Society continues to enjoy the generosity of a number of donors, whose contributions are helping towards the cost of publications this year. We would like to thank:

Miss Penny S.K. Bell

J. Bonnell

Mrs Joan Hamilton

Prof. Larry Hibbert

Miss Margaret Irvine

Mr Stephen Reid

Baptisms

Baptisms in 1797
[Account of Baptisms and Burials at Newton Heath Chapel]

Jan	1	John s. John & Elizabeth Mather, inn-keeper, Manchester
"	1	Betty d. Peter & Mary Wildblood, waggoner, Newton
"	1	Joseph s. Samuel & Mary Berry, cordwainer, Failsworth
"	1	John s. John & Mary Williamson, labourer, Failsworth
"	1	Jane d. James & Mary Crossley, weaver, Failsworth
"	6	Thomas s. James & Susannah Taylor, farmer, Moston
"	8	Jonas Lancashire s. Thomas & Alice Stafford, collier, Bradford
"	15	Mary d. William & Nancy Hanes, weaver, Newton
"	15	William s. William & Hannah Pritchard, husbandman, Newton
"	15	George s. William & Martha Sanderson, sawyer, Manchester, bo Jun 1796
"	22	James s. John & Tabitha Brierley, weaver, Failsworth
"	22	Thomas spu. s. Alice Kershaw, Newton
"	29	Alice spurious s. [d.] Hannah Etchels, Failsworth
"	29	William s. Samuel & Mary Matley, dyer, Newton
"	31	Isabel d. Daniel & Mary Smith, weaver, Failsworth
"	31	William s. George & Sarah Etchels, weaver, Failsworth
"	31	Robert s. Richard & Mary Richardson, weaver, Newton
Feb	5	James s. Thomas & Alice Hulton, farmer, Moston
"	5	Alice d. John & Betty Rothwell, dyer, Ashton pari
"	5	Alexander s. James & Betty Clough, weaver, Failsworth
"	8	William s. John & Esther Taylor, miner, Failsworth
"	8	Betty spu d. Anne Clough, weaver, Failsworth
"	12	Nancy spu d. Betty Whitehead, Failsworth
"	19	Nancy d. James & Mary Tetlow, weaver, Newton
"	19	Sarah d. Jeremia & Martha Kemp, warper, Newton
"	19	David s. William & Anne Tervins, taylor, Failsworth
"	19	Anne spu d. Betty Grane, Droylsden
"	26	Martha d. John & Mary Bates, shoe-maker, Failsworth
"	26	Anne d. Edmund & Ellen Chadderton, weaver, Moston
"	26	Sarah d. William & Ellen Hibbert, weaver, Failsworth
"	28	Mary spu d. Martha Burton, Newton
Mar	5	Betty [Elizth] d. John & Sarah Ogden, weaver, Failsworth
"	12	William s. Jonathan & Esther Slater, merchant, Newton
"	15	Elizabeth d. John & Elizabeth Clarkson, sawyer, Manchester
"	23	Matty [Martha] d. James & Alice Ogden, weaver, Failsworth

"	26	Joshua s. Ralph & Betty Burchill, weaver, Failsworth	(1796)
"	26	Jane d. John & Sarah Clough, weaver, Failsworth	
Apr	2	Esther d. John & Anne Watts, farmer, Newton	
"	2	John s. Thomas & Mary Fallows, gardener, Failsworth	
"	9	Jane d. Edmund & Ellen Schofield, hatter, Failsworth	
"	11	Thomas s. John & Mary Burgess, husbandman, Failsworth	
"	14	Elizabeth d. Robert & Jane Isherwood, printer, Ashton pari	
"	16	Susannah [Susannah Barker] d. John & Elizabeth Brown, sawyer, Failsworth	
"	16	George s. William & Mary Brown, weaver, Newton	
"	16	Hugh s. Thomas & Jane Bickley, sawyer, Manchester	
"	16	Betty d. George & Sarah Bardsley, weaver, Newton	
"	19	Maria d. James & Mary Whittaker, printer, Ashton-pari	
"	21	Mary d. Ralph & Hannah Chatherton [Chadderton], collier, Manchester	
"	23	Samuel s. Samuel & Hannah Robinson, weaver, Newton	
["	23	Esther d. John & Mary Higham, Failsw (entry in BT only)	]
"	30	Nancy spu d. Sarah Greave, Failsworth	
"	30	William s. James & Catharine Brown, weaver, Newton	
May	7	Joseph s. John & Sarah Tetlow, warehouseman, Newton	
"	7	Jane d. Robert & Betty Whitehead, weaver, Failsworth	
"	7	John s. John & Mary Pollit, weaver, Newton	
"	7	James spu s. Alice Makin, Moston	
"	14	Isabel d. Isaac & Margaret Dean, husbandman, Failsworth	
"	14	Jane d. James & Mary Ogden, farmer, Manchester	
"	14	William s. James & Betty [Elizth] Smith, weaver, Failsworth	
"	20	Thomas s. James & Mary Rogers, printer, Ashton-par	
"	20	Amelia d. Joshua & Olive Wild, labourer, Failsworth	
"	21	Damaris d. James & Mary Etchels, weaver, Failsworth	
"	21	John s. James & Hannah Wilkinson, weaver, Failsworth	
"	21	Joseph s. John & Elizabeth Blackshaw, cotton spinner, Hollinwood	
Jun	4	Sarah d. John & Elizabeth Houghton, innholder, Newton	
"	4	Mary d. James & Alice Wilde, weaver, Newton	
"	4	James s. William & Mary Stevenson, weaver, Failsworth	
"	11	Joseph s. Thomas & Anne Collinson, weaver, Failsworth	
"	11	Thomas s. Thomas & Alice Fletcher, taylor, Ashton paris	
"	15	Jenny [Jane] d. Thomas & Alice Walmsley, farmer, Droylsden	
"	25	Betty [Elizth] d. William & Mary Crowder, waggoner, Newton	
"	25	James s. John & Elizabeth Wyatt, weaver, Newton	
"	25	Martha d. Austin & Martha Anderton, weaver, Moston	
"	25	Ralph s. Joseph & Mary Bradley, weaver, Failsworth	
"	25	Thomas s. Thomas & Elizabeth Dickens, weaver, Newton	
"	25	Miles s. John & Sarah Hibbert, weaver, Failsworth	
"	25	Esther d. Samuel & Elizabeth Hoyle, labourer, Bradford	
"	25	Anne d. James & Phebe Hulme, weaver, Failsworth	
"	25	Betty [Elizth] d. Richard & Anne Johnson, innkeeper, Newton	
"	26	Sarah spu d. Jane Walmsley, Newton	

Jul	2	John s. James & Nancy Rydings, weaver, Failsworth	(1796)
"	2	James s. William & Jane Barrow, innkeeper, Failsworth	
"	2	Sarah d. James & Anne Allen, weaver, Failsworth	
"	4	Nancy d. Thomas & Jane Smith, weaver, Failsworth	
"	9	Betty [Elizth] d. John & Mary Hulme, weaver, Newton	
"	9	Elizabeth d. Adam & Mary Dawson, dyer, Failsworth	
"	10	John spu s. Sarah Smith, Failsworth	
"	10	John spu s. Anne Rayner, Failsworth	
"	16	Sarah d. John & Hannah Lees, weaver, Failsworth	
"	24	Jane spu d. Margaret Hibbert, Failsworth	
"	30	William s. James & Mary Hooley, husbandman, Failsworth	
"	30	Phineas s. John & Alice Makin, weaver, Failsworth	
"	30	John s. John & Betty [Elizth] Herriot, printer, Ashton paris	
"	30	Thomas s. David & Martha Ogden, weaver, Moston	
Aug	6	Sally [Sarah] d. Jacob & Hannah Etchels, weaver, Newton	
"	6	Anne spu d. Sally [Sarah] Taylor, Droylsden	
"	9	Maria d. William & Elizabeth Barrett, farmer, Newton	
"	9	Mary d. John & Mary Hibbert, printer, Ashton paris	
"	13	Edward s. John & Jane Yates, weaver, Failsworth	
"	13	Sally d. James & Sarah Whittaker, weaver, Failsworth	
"	13	George s. James & Margaret Booth, cordwainer, Manchester	
"	17	Sarah d. John & Sarah Thorp, surgeon, Manchester	
"	20	Esther d. Robert & Sarah Berry, carpenter, Manchester	
"	20	Sarah d. James & Morica [Monica] Smith, weaver, Newton	
"	25	William s. John & Alice Williamson, weaver, Failsworth	
Sep	3	Richard s. James & Martha Kemp, weaver, Manchester	
"	3	Thomas s. James & Sarah Wilson, farmer, Moston	
"	3	Samuel s. Jonathan & Mary Taylor, weaver, Moston	
"	3	Ashton s. Thomas & Elizabeth Shepley, weaver, Failsworth	
"	7	John s. Samuel & Ann Barker, Culcheth Newton, bo Jul 20	
"	7	Thomas s. John & Mary Robinson, taylor, Failsworth	
"	7	Betty spu d. Anne Clough, Failsworth	
"	10	Hannah d. Robert & Anne Glossop, weaver, Failsworth	
"	11	Betty d. John & Phebe Lancaster, weaver, Failsworth	
"	17	Mary d. James & Mary Thorp, weaver, Failsworth	
"	17	Mary d. James & Mary Schofield, weaver, Failsworth	
"	17	Mary d. James & Mary Barlow, weaver, Failsworth	
"	24	Mary d. Edward & Mary Hughs, labourer, Hollinwood	
"	25	Thomas s. Thomas & Mary Hyde, farmer, Failsworth	
Oct	8	Anne d. Philip & Alice Dunkerley, whitster, Moston	
"	15	Mary d. Ralph & Nancy Smethurst, weaver, Failsworth	
"	22	Lucy d. Thomas & Betty [Elizth] Tetlow, weaver, Newton	
"	22	John spu s. Hannah Lees, Failsworth	
"	22	Mary d. Thomas & Alice Gorton, joiner, Failsworth	
"	25	Peter Joseph s. Jeremiah & Dorothy Buxton, butcher, Manchester	

"	29	Mary d. Robert & Jane Stott, weaver, Failsworth
"	29	Agnes d. John & Anne Hulton, weaver, Failsworth
Nov	5	Maria d. Robert & Martha Hulton, weaver, Failsworth
"	12	James spu s. Jane Simister, Failsworth
"	12	Hannah d. John & Alice Brown, weaver, Failsworth
"	12	John s. William & Elizabeth Goodyear, weaver, Newton
"	12	John s. Joseph & Anne Clough, weaver, Newton
"	19	Anne d. Robert & Mary Walmsley, innkeeper, Failsworth
"	19	Martha d. James & Jane Allen, weaver, Newton
"	19	John s. John & Elizabeth Pollit, weaver, Failsworth
"	19	Robert s. Thomas & Mary Clegg, joiner, Failsworth
"	19	Alice d. William & Anne Ratcliffe, weaver, Newton
"	19	Betty [Elizth] d. Ashton & Betty [Mary] Shepley, weaver, Failsworth
Dec	1	Anne d. Samuel & Betty [Elizth] Lees, blacksmith, Failsworth
"	3	Sarah d. John & Elizabeth Mather, innkeeper, Manchester
"	3	Samuel s. Samuel & Ellen Irvine, manufacturer, Manchester
"	3	Phebe d. William & Elizabeth Glossop, weaver, Moston
"	10	Joseph s. Joshua & Betty [Elizth] Swift, weaver, Failsworth
"	10	Mary d. William & Anne Whitehead, weaver, Failsworth
"	10	Sarah d. James & Alice Lees, weaver, Failsworth
"	10	William s. Richard & Margaret Whitehead, weaver, Moston
"	17	John s. Samuel & Phebe Ainsworth, hatter, Newton
"	25	Mary d. William & Jenny [Jane] Clegg, joiner, Failsworth
"	25	Simeon s. Philip & Jane Smith, farmer, Failsworth
"	28	Thomas spu s. Anne Goodyear, Newton

Baptisms in 1798

Jan	1	Samuel s. Jonathan & Martha Shelmerdine, weaver, Newton
"	3	George s. Philip & Sarah Schofield, weaver, Droylsden
"	7	Mary d. William & Rebecca Worral, farmer, Failsworth
"	10	Robert s. John & Alice Thorp, weaver, Failsworth
"	11	Alice d. William & Alice Lane, innkeeper, Manchester
"	14	Joseph s. James & Anne Hulton, weaver, Failsworth
"	21	Anne d. John & Susannah Wardley, weaver, Moston
"	21	Robert s. John & Alice Hulton, weaver, Failsworth
"	21	Mark s. George & Bridget Clough, weaver, Failsworth
"	21	Edward s. Thomas & Sarah Walmsley, farmer, Failsworth
"	28	Nancy d. Thomas & Peggy [Margt] Wright, smith, Failsworth
Feb	4	Samuel s. Thurstan & Mary Smethurst, weaver, Failsworth
"	4	Anne d. Miles & Mary Schofield, dyer, Newton
"	4	Mary d. John & Alice Kershaw, weaver, Failsworth
"	4	Charles s. James & Mary [Sarah] Tomlinson, weaver, Failsworth
"	4	Charles s. John & Martha Booth, shop-keeper, Failsworth
"	11	John s. Charles & Mary Trussel, printer, Newton

"	11	Thomas s. Abraham & Jane Ashworth, Minister of Newton, bo Jan 4
"	11	Anne d. Thomas & Betty Knott, weaver, Failsworth
"	11	Charles s. Edward & Mary Hampson, basket-maker, Pendleton
"	13	Thomas s. John & Hannah Heslop, labourer, Newton, bo May 24 1795
"	13	John s. John & Hannah Heslop, labourer, Newton
"	18	Mary d. Isaac & Martha Ford, weaver, Failsworth
"	25	John s. William & Sarah Daltry, husbandman, Newton
"	25	Maria d. John & Alice Clough, weaver, Failsworth
"	25	Alice spu. d. Anne Boardman, Failsworth
Mar	4	Samuel s. Samuel & Mary Mellor, weaver, Newton
"	5	Thomas s. James & Martha Slater, farmer, Failsworth
"	11	Sarah d. Edmund & Alice Walmsley, joiner, Manchester
"	11	Sarah d. James & Elizabeth Brammell, labourer, Failsworth
"	11	Alice d. James & Esther Allen, weaver, Newton
"	18	Joseph s. Samuel & Mary Hulme, weaver, Newton
"	18	Sally d. Abraham & Betty [Elizth] Mather, weaver, Droylsden
"	18	Joseph s. John & Sally [Sarah] Whitehead, weaver, Failsworth
"	18	William s. James & Alice Eckersley, weaver, Failsworth
"	25	John s. John & Esther Etchels, weaver, Failsworth
"	25	Alice d. Joshua & Alice Wyatt, weaver, Newton
Apr	1	Sarah d. James & Sarah Lord, wheelwright, Failsworth
"	1	Robert s. George & Betty [Elizth] Hardy, weaver, Failsworth
"	8	Jane d. Thomas & Mary Brown, weaver, Newton
"	9	Betty [Elizth] d. Joseph & Alice Hulme, weaver, Newton
"	22	John spu s. Anne Watson, Newton
"	22	James s. Benjamin & Mary Howarth, farmer, Droylsden
"	23	John s. James & Martha Richardson, weaver, Newton
"	23	Sarah d. James & Marah [Mary] Tetlow, weaver, Newton
"	29	Solomon s. Thomas & Susannah Etchels, weaver, Failsworth
"	29	Mary d. James & Margaret Crossley, labourer, Moston
May	2	Samuel s. Thomas & Alice Hall, brickmaker, Newton
"	7	Anne d. Thomas & Sarah Walmsley, weaver, Failsworth
"	13	Moses s. John & Hannah Ford, weaver, Failsworth
"	20	Jonathan s. Jonathan & Peggy [Margt] Grimshaw, weaver, Droylsden
"	21	William s. James & Mary Tetlow, farmer, Newton
"	27	Betty [Elizth] d. Joseph & Mary Smethurst, weaver, Failsworth
Jun	3	Joseph s. John & Mary Smith, weaver, Failsworth
"	10	George s. Robert & Isabel Hulton, weaver, Failsworth
"	10	Matty [Martha] d. Richard & Annis [Agnes] Unsworth, Failsworth
"	10	Sarah d. John & Betty [Elizth] Berrington, tanner, Failsworth
"	10	Anthony Lane s. Robert & Mary Ryder, grocer, Newton
"	10	Betty [Elizth] d. John & Betty [Elizth] Tervin labourer, Ashton Pari
"	17	Hannah d. James & Betty [Elizth] Wild, weaver, Droylsden
"	17	Nancy d. John & Betty [Elizth] Howard, weaver, Failsworth
"	24	Charlotte d. Joseph & Charlotte Greenwood, weaver, Failsworth

Jul	1	Anne spu. d. Mary Ormrod, Moston
"	1	Mary d. Thomas & Betty Wyld, weaver, Failsworth
["	1	Maria d. John & Hannah Rogers, Newton (*entry in BT only*)]
"	15	John s. George & Grace Howles, weaver, Newton
"	15	William spu. s. Anne Whittaker, Failsworth
"	22	William s. John & Mary Brundrett, weaver, Failsworth
"	22	Susannah d. Joseph & Mary Hope, carpenter, Bradford
"	22	Anne spu. d. Jane Edge, Failsworth
"	29	Mary d. James & Phillis Thorp, weaver, Failsworth
"	29	William s. Matthew & Betty [Elizth] Thorp, weaver, Failsworth
"	29	John s. John & Peggy [Margt] Lees, warper, Newton
Aug	12	Hannah d. William & Mary Whitehead, weaver, Moston
"	12	William s. Charls & Betty [Elizth] Garlick, weaver, Failsworth
"	27	Sally [Sarah] d. James & Nancy Woolstencroft, whitster, Failsworth
Sep	2	Sarah d. William & Sarah Robinson, slater, Newton
"	2	Nancy d. John & Mary Thornley, weaver, Failsworth
"	2	John s. John & Betty [Elizth] Clough, weaver, Failsworth
"	4	Martha spu. d. Betty [Elizth] Hardy, Failsworth
"	5	Esther d. Richard & Sarah Simister, weaver, Failsworth
"	5	Hannah d. Nathan & Sarah Hibbert, weaver, Failsworth
"	5	Mary d. Matthew & Anne Howles, weaver, Newton
"	16	Mark s. Thomas & Martha Goodyear, weaver, Failsworth
"	16	Jane d. John & Alice Hall, carpenter, Failsworth
"	16	Anne d. George & Mary Hibbert, cordwainer, Failsworth
"	16	Elizabeth d. Edward & Martha Whitehead, bricklayer, Droylsden
"	23	Anne d. William & Anne Haynes, weaver, Newton
"	30	Joseph s. Elias & Sarah Whiteley, weaver, Droylsden
Oct	7	Samuel s. Henry & Rachel Scowcroft, printer, Failsworth
"	7	Isabel d. Luke & Anne Smith, weaver, Failsworth
"	14	Robert s. John & Anne Taylor, weaver, Failsworth
"	14	Nancy d. James & Sarah Clough, weaver, Failsworth
"	19	Betty [Elizth] d. John & Mary Booth, weaver, Failsworth
"	21	Sally d. John & Sally [Sarah] Pendleton, whitster, Newton
"	28	James s. James & Mary Etchels, weaver, Failsworth
"	28	William s. John & Anne Eckersley, weaver, Failsworth
"	28	Lucy d. Edmund & Mary Taylor, weaver, Droylsden
"	28	Jenny d. Samuel & Betty [Elizth] Clough, weaver, Failsworth
"	28	Joseph s. James & Hannah Wilkinson, weaver, Failsworth
"	28	David s. John & Sarah Harrison, weaver, Newton
Nov	4	Sarah d. James & Mary Waters, weaver, Failsworth
"	4	Joseph s. Samuel & Hannah Robinson, weaver, Newton, aged 9 weeks
"	4	Anne d. Joseph & Lettice Tomlinson, weaver, Failsworth
"	11	William s. George & Mary Lane, innholder, Failsworth
"	18	Hannah d. George & Anne Etchels, weaver, Failsworth
"	25	John s. Benjamin & Mary Butterworth, weaver, Moston

"	25	Mary d. Joseph & Mary Clough, husbandman, Failsworth
"	27	Alice d. James & Mary Gradwell, weaver, Failsworth
"	29	Nancy spu. d. Betty [Elizth] Leech, Failsworth
Dec	2	John s. Joseph & Betty [Elizth] Ogden, weaver, Failsworth
"	2	Thomas s. Joseph & Mary Schofield, weaver, Moston
"	9	Charles s. John & Sally [Sarah] Taylor, weaver, Failsworth
"	25	Alice d. James & Jane Allen, weaver, Newton
"	25	Sarah d. David & Martha Ogden, weaver, Moston
"	25	Hannah d. William & Ellen Hibbert, weaver, Newton
"	25	Jane d. James & Mary Simister, whitster, Newton
"	30	Betty [Elizth] d. Robert & Mary Barlow, weaver, Failsworth

Baptisms in 1799

Jan	1	Margaretta d. Samuel & Anne Barker, Newton, bo Aug 8 1798
"	2	Mary d. Joseph & Mary Turner, slater, Newton
"	6	Betty [Elizth] d. Edmund & Olivia Schofield, weaver, Failsworth
"	6	James s. Thomas & Elizabeth Barlow, weaver, Failsworth
"	6	Sarah d. John & Frances Goodyear, weaver, Failsworth
"	10	Thomas s. John & Betty [Elizth] Robinson, slater, Newton
"	10	Samuel s. Thomas & Martha Clegg, weaver, Failsworth
"	20	Sally [Sarah] d. James & Alice Howarth, carter, Failsworth
"	20	Joseph s. Thomas & Esther Tomkinson, hatter, Newton
"	20	Jonas s. Joseph & Mary Cowling, sawyer, Failsworth
"	27	Samuel s. Elias & Jane Bethell, labourer, Newton
"	27	Sally [Sarah] d. James & Mary Crossley, weaver, Failsworth
Feb	3	Joseph s. Miles & Sally [Sarah] Mayo, weaver, Newton
"	3	James s. Joseph & Elizabeth Taylor, weaver, Failsworth
"	3	Jane d. Joseph & Tabitha Tinker, weaver, Moston
"	10	Robert s. Robert & Betty [Elizth] Whitehead, weaver, Failsworth
"	15	John Pollit s. James & Anne Whitehead, weaver, Failsworth
"	17	George s. George & Sarah Barsley, weaver, Newton
"	17	John s. Jacob & Hannah Etchels, weaver, Newton
"	24	Thomas s. John & Margaret Whitehead, weaver, Moston
"	27	Joseph s. John & Mary Bates, cordwainer, Failsworth
"	27	Mary d. Thomas & Mary Houghton, hatter, Manchester
Mar	3	Joseph s. John & Esther Taylor, cordwainer, Failsworth
"	3	Thomas s. John & Sarah Ogden, weaver, Failsworth
"	10	John s. Joseph & Sarah Berry, smith, Failsworth
"	10	Anne d. William & Alice Taylor, weaver, Failsworth
"	10	Jane d. James & Nancy Morris, printer, Newton
"	10	Anne d. Abraham & Jane Beswick, miller, Newton
"	17	Mary d. Daniel & Alice Watkins, weaver, Newton, bo Oct 19 1796
"	17	Daniel s. Daniel & Alice Watkins, weaver, Newton, bo Dec 12 1798
"	18	Sarah d. Thomas & Sarah Walmsley, farmer, Failsworth

"	24	Anne & Jane ds. John & Hannah Lees, weaver, Failsworth	(*1799*)
"	24	Martha d. James & Margaret Howarth, weaver, Newton	
"	24	Hannah d. William & Mary Stevenson, weaver, Failsworth	
"	24	John s. George & Sarah Etchels, weaver, Failsworth	
"	24	Charles s. James & Nancy Rydings, weaver, Failsworth	
"	30	William s. William & Anne Middleton, weaver, Failsworth	
"	31	Maria d. John & Tabitha Brierley, weaver, Failsworth	
"	31	Elizabeth d. William & Alice Lane, innholder, Manchester	
Apr	2	Nancy [Anne] d. Matthew & Nanny [Anne] Gradwell, weaver, Failsworth	
"	3	Mary d. Samuel & Mary Etchels, weaver, Failsworth	
"	3	Alexander s. George & Mary Smith, weaver, Failsworth	
"	7	Matthew s. Samuel & Phebe Ainsworth, hatter, Newton	
"	7	Martha d. Robert & Anne Glossop, weaver, Failsworth	
"	7	James s. James & Sarah Whittaker, weaver, Failsworth	
"	7	William s. Thomas & Mary Brown, weaver, Manchester	
"	7	George s. Thomas & Alice Fletcher, taylor, Ashton Pari	
"	8	Maria d. John & Ellen Berry, weaver, Failsworth	
"	14	James Horatio Nelson s. David & Betty Hulton, sergeant, Failsworth	
"	14	Robert s. James & Phebe Hulme, weaver, Failsworth	
"	14	Robert s. John & Anne Richardson, carpenter, Werneth	
"	15	Betty [Elizth] d. Joseph & Sarah Wylde, weaver, Failsworth	
"	19	James s. William & Mary Wilde, weaver, Droylsden	
"	19	Robert s. John & Mary Wilkinson, weaver, Failsworth	
[		The above is a true Copy taken from the Register at Newton Heath Chapel]	
[		A. Ashworth Minister	]
[		Willm Booth John Booth Ch. Wardens	]
"	21	James s. Thomas & Mary Whitehead, weaver, Failsworth	
"	21	Sarah d. William & Sarah Wood, farmer, Newton	
"	28	Ellen d. John & Mary Robinson, taylor, Failsworth	
May	5	Jenny d. James & Sarah Wilson, farmer, Moston	
"	5	Elizabeth d. Joseph & Jane Harding, farmer, Newton	
"	12	Sarah d. Peter & Mary Wildblood, waggoner, Newton	
"	12	John s. John & Anne Haslem, schoolmaster, Failsworth	
"	12	Robert s. William & Betty [Elizth] Glossop, weaver, Moston	
"	12	Mary d. James & Anne Allen, weaver, Hollinwood	
"	13	Lissey d. Richard & Mary Richardson, weaver, Newton	
"	26	Maria d. James & Anne Hulton, weaver, Failsworth	
"	26	Nathanuel s. James & Mary Clough, weaver, Failsworth	
"	26	Mary d. George & Ruth Dunkerley, weaver, Chadderton	
Jun	2	Elizabeth d. Thomas & Mary Fallows, gardener, Failsworth	
"	9	Robert s. Robert & Jane Stott, manufacturer, Failsworth	
"	9	Sally [Sarah] d. William & Jane Barrow, innkeeper, Failsworth	
"	9	Sally [Sarah] d. Daniel & Betty [Elizth] Ashton, weaver, Failsworth	
"	9	Mary d. John & Rachel Gradwell, weaver, Newton	
"	9	John s. John & Anne Hulton, weaver, Failsworth	

"	9	Joseph s. Richard & Nancy Darlington, labourer, Failsworth (*1799*)
"	9	Anne d. Samuel & Phebe Clough, weaver, Failsworth
"	24	Joseph s. John & Alice Brown, weaver, Failsworth
"	30	Betty [Elizth] d. James & Mary Thorp, weaver, Failsworth
Jul	7	John s. John & Agnes Lowe, Failsworth
"	17	John s. Edward & Anne Eckersley, weaver, Failsworth
"	22	Anne spu. d. Sarah Smith, Failsworth
"	24	Anne d. William & Alice Wroe, weaver, Newton
Aug	4	Anne d. Charles & Betty [Elizth] Walmsley, bleacher, Newton
"	11	Martha d. James & Catharine Brown, weaver, Newton
"	18	Jane d. Henry & Mary Forester, Newton
"	18	Thomas Morris s. Samuel & Ellen Irvine, manufacturer, Newton, bo May 11 1799
"	25	Anne d. John & Alice Hulton, weaver, Failsworth
"	25	Samuel s. John & Sarah Holland, weaver, Droylsden
Sep	1	James s. William & Sarah Daltry, farmer, Newton
"	8	Ellen d. James & Jane Schofield, weaver, Failsworth
"	22	Anne d. John & Martha Kershaw, weaver, Failsworth
"	26	John s. Thomas & Elizabeth Shepley, weaver, Failsworth
"	29	Jeremiah s. Jeremiah & Martha Kemp, warper, Manchester
"	29	Hannah d. John & Mary Higham, weaver, Failsworth
"	29	Hannah d. James & Mary Berry, weaver, Failsworth
"	29	Charles s. Samuel & Hannah Robinson, weaver, Newton
Oct	4	Sarah d. Samuel & Mary Berry, shoemaker, Failsworth
"	6	Alice d. Thomas & Alice Walmsley, farmer, Droylsden
"	6	John s. Thomas & Jane Robinson, weaver, Failsworth
"	6	Sarah d. James & Hannah Hibbert, weaver, Newton
"	11	Anne d. Robert & Anne Wilson, weaver, Moston
"	13	Sally [Sarah] d. Joseph & Margaret Ogden, weaver, Failsworth
"	13	William s. Joseph & Anne Fildes, farmer, Newton
"	20	Matty [Martha] d. George & Mary Hibbert, cordwainer, Failsworth
"	20	David s. John & Sarah Ogden, weaver, Moston
"	20	Joshua s. Joshua & Betty [Elizth] Swift, weaver, Failsworth
"	20	Peggy [Margt] d. John & Betty [Elizth] Smith, weaver, Failsworth
"	20	Maria d. James & Mary Hooley, husbandman, Failsworth
"	20	Dan s. James & Nancy Woolstencroft, whitster, Failsworth
"	27	Robert s. John & Elizabeth Stott, weaver, Failsworth
"	27	John s. Adam & Mary Dawson, dyer, Failsworth
Nov	3	Mary spu. d. Jane Barlow, weaver, Failsworth
"	3	Elizabeth d. Thomas & Elizabeth Dickens, weaver, Newton
"	3	Mary d. William & Anne Ratcliffe, weaver, Newton
"	3	Robert s. James & Anne Allen, weaver, Failsworth
"	3	Mary d. Thomas & Jane Smith, weaver, Failsworth
"	10	John s. Ashton & Mary Shepley, weaver, Failsworth
"	10	Jonathan s. William & Elizabeth Goodier, weaver, Newton

"	24	Thomas s. Daniel & Anne Smith, weaver, Newton
Dec	1	Sarah d. Ralph & Nancy [Anne] Smethurst, weaver, Failsworth
"	1	Hannah d. George & Betty [Elizth] Hardy, weaver, Failsworth
"	1	Hannah d. Robert & Mary Allen, innholder, Newton
"	15	Hannah d. Thomas & Elizabeth Berry, farmer, Failsworth
"	20	Joseph s. Abraham & Betty [Elizth] Mather, weaver, Droylsden
"	22	Philip s. Philip & Alice Dunkerley, whitster, Failsworth
"	22	Moses spu. s. Jane Berry, Failsworth
"	25	Mary d. Joseph & Mary Smethurst, weaver, Failsworth
"	25	John s. Thomas & Peggy [Mary] Wright, smith, Failsworth
"	25	Jonas (*altered; original unclear*) [Jonas] s. John & Sarah Tetlow, weaver, Newton
"	25	George s. Obadiah & Sarah Bradshaw, husbandman, Failsworth
"	29	Hannah d. Andrew & Emy Berry, carpenter, Manchester

Baptisms in 1800

[Account of Baptisms and Burials at Newton Heath Chapel in the Year 1800]

Jan	5	Joshua s. Thomas & Anne Collinson, weaver, Failsworth
"	12	Hannah d. John & Peggy [Margt] Brown, farmer, Newton
"	19	Samuel s. Thomas & Hannah Tetlow, weaver, Newton
"	19	William s. William & Mary Brown, weaver, Newton
"	19	Richard s. John & Betty [Elizth] Pollit, weaver, Failsworth
"	19	Anne d. Edmund & Olivia Schofield, weaver, Failsworth
"	22	Alice d. Josiah & Elizabeth Brown, weaver, Failsworth
"	22[26]	Joseph & David ss. John & Alice Makin, weaver, Failsworth (*separate entries in BT*)
"	22[26]	Philip s. James & Betty [Elizth] Berry, weaver, Failsworth
Feb	2	Joel s. Thomas & Susannah Etchels, weaver, Failsworth
"	7	William s. Richard & Sarah Simister, weaver, Failsworth
"	9	Anne d. Joseph & Anne Clough, weaver, Newton
"	9	James & Thomas spu. ss. Anne Rayner, Failsworth (*separate entries in BT*)
"	10	Robert spu. s. Jane Walmsley, Failsworth
"	16	Maria d. George & Bridget Clough, weaver, Failsworth
"	16	Jonathan s. Jonathan & Mary Schofield, weaver, Ashton Par
"	16	Maria d. James & Susannah Mills, joiner, Ashton Pa
"	17	Daniel s. John & Alice Clough, weaver, Failsworth
"	23	Alice d. Edmund & Alice Walmsley, joiner, Manchester
"	23	Mary d. James & Martha Kemp, weaver, Manchester
"	23	Mary Anne d. Richard & Margaret Whitehead, weaver, Manchester
"	23	Martha d. Thomas & Mary Hyde, farmer, Failsworth
"	23	Horsefall s. John & Alice Oldham, husbandman, Newton
"	25	Elizabeth d. John & Alice Parry, miner, Manchester
"	26	Elizabeth d. James & Mary Aspell, shopkeeper, Newton
Mar	2	Margaret d. William & Ellen Caldwell, farmer, Newton

"	9	Sarah d. John & Isabel Pugh, husbandman, Newton
"	9	Betty [Elizth] d. Joseph & Mary Bardsley, weaver, Newton
"	16	Alice & Elizabeth twin ds. Thomas & Catherine Barns, innkeeper, Ashton Parish (*separate entries in BT*)
"	16	William s. Thurstan & Mary Smethurst, weaver, Failsworth
"	25	Alice d. John & Prudence Hodgen, weaver, Failsworth
"	30	Mary d. James & Martha Ashton, weaver, Moston
"	30	Esther d. John & Betty [Elizth] Clough, weaver, Failsworth
"	30	Anne d. John & Martha Booth, shopkeeper, Failsworth
"	30	Betty [Elizth] d. Matthew & Anne Howles, husbandman, Failsworth
"	30	Matty d. Jacob & Hannah Etchels, weaver, Newton
Apr	6	Betty [Elizth] d. William & Bella Bolton, printer, Newton
"	6	Joseph spu. s. Anne Watson, Failsworth
"	13	John s. Joseph & Elizabeth Taylor, weaver, Failsworth
"	13	John s. John & Hannah Taylor, husbandman, Failsworth
"	13	Luke s. James & Alice Eckersley, weaver, Failsworth
"	13	James s. Jonathan & Esther Schofield, weaver, Moston
"	13	Anne d. Joseph & Mary Schofield, farmer, Moston
"	15	Hannah d. Robert & Isabella Hulton, weaver, Failsworth
"	15	Betty [Elizth] spu. d. Mary Wood, Newton
"	24	George s. Samuel & Elizabeth Lees, blacksmith, Failsworth
"	27	Benjamin s. James & Mary Tetlow, farmer, Newton
"	27	Samuel s. James & Mary Etchels, weaver, Failsworth
"	27	Maria d. John & Mary Smith, weaver, Failsworth
"	27	John s. Thomas & Betty [Elizth] Wyld, weaver, Failsworth
"	27	Esther d. Robert & Martha Hulton, weaver, Failsworth
May	4	John s. Robert & Sarah Berry, carpenter, Manchester
"	4	Abraham s. Jonathan & Mary Taylor, weaver, Moston
"	5	Sally [Sarah] d. Samuel & Betty [Elizth] Clough, weaver, Failsworth
"	11	Hannah d. Joshua & Alice Wyatt, weaver, Newton
"	11	Mary d. Thomas & Sarah Walmsley, farmer, Failsworth
"	18	George s. Thomas & Alice Hall, bricklayer, Newton
"	18	Betty [Elizth] d. William & Hannah Pritchard, husbandman, Newton
"	18	Martha d. Benjamin & Mary Howarth, farmer, Droylsden
"	20	William Heathcoate s. John & Anne Hulton, weaver, Failsworth
"	22	Jane d. Abraham & Jane Ashworth, Minister of Newton
"	25	Sarah d. Jonathan & Margaret Grimshaw, weaver, Droylsden
"	28	Elizabeth d. William & Elizabeth Barrett, farmer, Newton
Jun	1	John s. James & Margaret Crossley, husbandman, Moston
"	1	Mary Anne d. James & Mary Hardy, weaver, Newton
"	1	Samuel s. William & Anne Whitehead, weaver, Failsworth
"	1	William s. George & Grace Howles, weaver, Newton
"	1	Thomas s. Francis & Sarah Wood, weaver, Newton
"	8	Isabel d. Giles & Anne Eckersley, weaver, Failsworth
"	8	Mary d. Thomas & Betty [Elizth] Knott, weaver, Failsworth

"	15	Mary Anne d. Peter & Hannah Wood, weaver, Oldham
"	15	Sarah d. John & Peggy [Margt] Whitehead, weaver, Moston
"	15	John s. William & Anne Thornley, weaver, Failsworth
"	15	William s. John & Hannah Ford, weaver, Failsworth
"	15	Sarah d. George & Peggy [Margt] Booth, weaver, Newton
"	16	Anne d. James & Elizabeth Johnson, weaver, Newton
"	20	Sarah d. John & Mary Slater, manufacturer, Newton, bo Feb 7 1800
"	22	Joseph s. John & Sarah Taylor, weaver, Failsworth
"	22	Martha d. Thomas & Mary Clegg, joiner, Failsworth
"	29	Joseph s. James & Mary Ogden, whitster, Newton
"	29	Peter s. Samuel & Mary Wolstenhulme (Worsley *struck through*) [Worsley], sawyer, Failsworth
Jul	6	Mary d. John & Peggy [Margt] Lees, putterout, Failsworth
"	6	Mary d. John & Elizabeth Mather, manufacturer, Manchester
"	9	James s. John & Elizabeth Tervin, labourer, Ashton Parish
"	13	George s. Joseph & Jane Heath, tanner, Newton
"	20	Hannah d. John & Alice Kershaw, weaver, Failsworth
"	20	Sarah spu. d. Jane Simister, Failsworth
"	20	Margaret d. John & Elizabeth Barrington, tanner, Failsworth
"	22	Mary d. Richard & Anne Johnson, whitster, Newton
"	27	James s. James & Jane Pilkington, weaver, Failsworth
"	27	Anne d. James & Anne Whittaker, bricklayer, Moston
"	27	Elijah s. John & Mary Pollit, weaver, Newton
"	27	John spu. s. Mary Barlow, Failsworth
"	27	Hannah d. Thomas & Sarah Walmsley, weaver, Failsworth
Aug	3	William Collinson s. James & Nancy Rydings, weaver, Failsworth
"	10	William s. Samuel & Mary Hulme, weaver, Newton
"	17	John s. John & Mary Hulme, weaver, Newton
"	20	William s. William & Alice Lane, innholder, Manchester
"	31	Alice d. Thomas & Alice Hulton, weaver, Moston
Sep	7	James s. George & Mary Lane, innholder, Failsworth
"	7	Matty [Martha] d. James & Esther Aldred, weaver, Failsworth
"	14	Alice d. Joseph & Alice Hulme, weaver, Newton
"	14	John s. Edward & Martha Whitehead, bricklayer, Droylsden
["	15	Dessemona Harold d. Geo. & Hannah Bedson, Manchester (*entry in BT only*)]
["	15	Eliza d. Geo. & Hannah Bedson, Manchester (*entry in BT only*)]
"	21	Mary d. John & Esther Etchels, weaver, Failsworth
Oct	9	Thomas spu. s. Elizabeth Holt, Manchester
"	12	Hannah spu. d. Elizabeth Tomlinson, Moston
"	12	Anne d. James & Betty [Elizth] Barritt, farmer, Droylsden
"	12	Alice d. James & Elizabeth Bethell, whitster, Droylsden
"	12	Phebe d. Thomas & Mary Brown, weaver, Newton
Nov	16	Mary Anne d. William & Mary Galloway, joiner, Newton
"	23	Sally [Sarah] d. Peter & Anne Clough, weaver, Failsworth
"	30	James s. Isaac & Martha Butterworth, weaver, Failsworth

Dec	14	William s. Thomas & Mary Thorp, weaver, Failsworth
"	21	Betty [Elizth] d. Joseph & Mary Cowling, sawyer, Failsworth
"	25	Isaiah s. John & Sarah Crossley, weaver, Newton
"	25	William spu. s. Sarah Farrand, Failsworth

Baptisms in 1801
[Account of Baptisms and Burials at Newton Heath Chapel in the Year 1801]

Jan	4	John s. John & Mary Thornley, weaver, Failsworth
"	4	Betty [Elizth] spu. d. Anne Wolstenholme, Failsworth
"	4	Joel spu. s. Martha Taylor, Failsworth
"	4	Anne d. Miles & Hannah Rigley, weaver, Failsworth
"	18	Samuel s. Jonathan & Nancy Leech, weaver, Failsworth
"	25	Joel spu. s. Betty [Elizth] Holt, Failsworth
"	25	James s. James & Mary Gradwell, weaver, Failsworth
"	25	Samuel s. John & Alice Hall, carpenter, Failsworth
"	25	Thomas s. James & Jane Allen, weaver, Newton
"	25	Hannah d. Joseph & Lettice Tomlinson, weaver, Failsworth
Feb	1	Agnes d. Edward & Olive Schofield, weaver, Failsworth
"	1	Samuel s. Joseph & Elizabeth Seel, printer, Newton
"	8	Anne spu d. Elizabeth Booth, Newton
"	8	Benjamin s. William & Jane Barrow, innkeeper, Failsworth
"	15	Samuel s. John & Susannah [Susan] Moore, weaver, Failsworth
"	22	Nancy d. James & Phebe Smethurst, weaver, Failsworth
"	22	Thomas s. William & Anne Thornley, weaver, Failsworth
"	27	Sarah d. Joseph & Sarah Wylde, weaver, Failsworth
Mar	1	Hannah d. John & Elizabeth Wyatt, weaver, Newton
"	1	George s. William & Sarah Daltry, farmer, Newton
"	1	John s. John & Martha Herod, printer, Failsworth
"	8	Anne d. John & Esther Taylor, shoe-maker, Failsworth
"	8	Hannah d. Richard & Mary Richardson, weaver, Newton
"	8	Joseph s. James & Sally [Sarah] Whittaker, weaver, Failsworth
"	15	Thomas s. Peter & Mary Wildblood, husbandman, Newton
"	15	Betty [Elizth] d. John & Nancy Howard, weaver, Failsworth
"	15	Betty [Elizth] d. John & Ruth Jackson, husbandman, Failsworth
"	15	Maria Greenwood d. James & Anne Boardman, printer, Newton
"	17	John s. John & Catharine Harrop, hatter, Openshaw
"	18	Mark spu. s. Mary Smith, Failsworth
"	25	Thomas s. Thomas & Elizabeth Barlow, weaver, Failsworth
"	29	Jane d. Robert & Jane Stott, manufacturer, Failsworth
"	29	Anne d. Joseph & Agnes Slater, weaver, Failsworth
"	29	James spu s. Alice Ratcliffe, Newton
Apr	1	Philip s. John & Betty [Elizth] Houghton, innholder, Newton
"	5	Joel s. Joseph & Mary Brown, weaver, Woodhouses A.P.
"	5	Thomas s. Robert & Mary Collins, farmer, Moston

"	19	Betty [Elizth] d. James & Sarah Wilson, farmer, Moston
"	26	Thomas s. James & Mary Andrew, print-cutter, Newton
"	26	James s. James & Mary Thorp, weaver, Failsworth
May	3	Matty [Martha] d. Joseph & Betty [Elizth] Ogden, weaver, Failsworth
"	3	Mary d. Edmund & Jane Whitehead, weaver, Moston
"	3	James s. William & Jane Butterworth, weaver, Failsworth
"	3	Henry s. James & Mary Crossley, weaver, Failsworth
"	6	Mary spu. d. Elizabeth Allen, Failsworth
"	17	John s. Jonathan & Esther Schofield, weaver, Moston
"	24	Robert s. William & Mary Stevenson, weaver, Failsworth
"	24	William s. James & Phebe Hulme, weaver, Failsworth
"	24	William s. William & Mary Tomlinson, weaver, Moston
"	24	William s. James & Mary Clough, weaver, Failsworth
"	31	Andrew s. George & Mary Smith, weaver, Failsworth
Jun	7	Sally [Sarah] d. James & Alice Ogden, weaver, Failsworth
"	14	Edward s. John & Alice Hulton, weaver, Failsworth
"	14	James s. John & Sarah Ogden, weaver, Failsworth
"	21	Maria d. John & Martha Kershaw, weaver, Newton
"	21	John s. William & Mary Crowther, husbandman, Newton
"	28	Thomas s. Thomas & Sarah Walmsley, farmer, Failsworth
"	28	Nancy d. William & Elizabeth Glossop, weaver, Moston
"	28	Hannah d. Luke & Anne Smith, weaver, Failsworth
Jul	5	Betty [Elizth] d. Joseph & Margaret Ogden, weaver, Failsworth
"	6	Betty [Elizth] d. Robert & Mary Hulme, whitster, Droylsden
"	12	Sarah d. Samuel & Betty [Elizth] Ogden, weaver, Failsworth
"	12	Elizabeth d. Samuel & Betty [Elizth] Taylor, weaver, Oldham
"	13	George s. John & Mary White, printer, Clayton
"	19	John s. Joseph & Martha Clough, weaver, Woodhouses
"	19	Dan s. Ashton & Mary Shepley, weaver, Newton
"	19	Thomas s. Thomas & Elizabeth Tetlow, warper, Newton
"	19	Lydia d. Isaac & Margaret (*altered*) [Mary] Dean, husbandman, Failsworth
"	26	Martha d. James & Betty [Elizth] Wilde, weaver, Droylsden
"	26	James s. Samuel & Betty [Elizth] Hoyle, labourer, Bradford
"	26	William spu s. Anne Barnes, Failsworth
"	26	Phebe d. Samuel & Phebe Clough, weaver, Failsworth
Aug	2	Hannah sp d. Anne Whitaker, Failsworth
"	9	Betty [Elizth] d. John & Hannah Lees, weaver, Failsworth
"	9	Joseph s. John & Mary Wilkinson, weaver, Failsworth
"	16	Martha d. William & Sarah Robinson, slater, Newton
"	16	John s. John & Phebe Taylor, weaver, Moston
"	16	Samuel Thomason spu s. Mary Bardsley, Failsworth
"	23	Thomas s. James & Nancy Hulton, weaver, Failsworth
"	23	Alice d. John & Mary Slater, manufacturer, Newton
"	23	Charles s. John & Sarah Harrison, weaver, Newton
"	30	James s. William & Anne Haynes, weaver, Newton

Sep	6	Elizabeth spu d. Mary Williamson, Failsworth
"	13	Ellen d. Thomas & Elizabeth Berry, farmer, Gorton
"	13	James s. Robert & Mary Walmsley, farmer, Newton
"	13	Martha d. Robert & Mary Walmsley, farmer, Newton

(*last 2 entries bracketed together and the word* twins *entered in margin*)

"	13	Richard s. Ralph & Betty [Elizth] Birchell, weaver, Failsworth
"	13	Thomas s. David & Nancy Rawlinson, printer, Failsworth
"	13	Elizabeth d. Robert & Elizabeth Hall, weaver, Newton
"	13	Mary d. James & Mary Simister, bleacher, Newton
"	20	Hannah d. James & Sarah Lord, wheelwright, Failsworth
"	21	Jane d. Thomas & Anne Etchels, weaver, Droylsden
"	27	Abraham s. Joseph & Elizabeth Taylor, weaver, Failsworth
"	27	Margaret d. Joseph & Anne Taylor, weaver, Failsworth
"	27	William s. Obadiah & Sarah Bradshaw, husbandman, Failsworth
"	30	Thomas s. James & Mary Hooley, labourer, Failsworth
"	30	Sally d. William & Rebecca Worral, farmer, Failsworth
Oct	8	William s. John & Mary Bates, cordwainer, Failsworth
"	18	John spu. s. Anne Mather, Droylsden
"	25	Eli s. Joshua & Betty [Elizth] Swift, weaver, Failsworth
"	25	Anne d. James & Mary Etchels, weaver, Failsworth
Nov	1	Mary d. George & Sarah Etchels, weaver, Failsworth
"	5	John s. William & Ellen Hibbert, weaver, Failsworth
"	10	George spu s. Anne Watts, Newton
"	13	Betty [Elizth] d. James & Mary Waters, weaver, Failsworth
"	17	Anne d. Robert & Betty [Elizth] Whitehead, weaver, Failsworth
"	22	Joseph s. Ralph & Nancy Smethurst, weaver, Failsworth

Baptisms in 1802

[Baptized at Newton-Heath Chapel in the Year of Our Lord 1802]

Jan	3	Thomas s. William & Sarah Walker, weaver, Newton
"	5	Joshua s. James & Anne Pilkington, spinner, Manchester
"	10	Nancy spu. d. Milley Gradwell, Failsworth
"	12	Joel s. William & Betty Goodier, weaver, Newton
"	12	Daniel s. Daniel & Mary Wild, farmer, Newton
"	17	John s. James & Margaret [Mary] Howarth, weaver, Newton
"	22	Isabel d. Edmund [Edward] & Anne Eckersley, weaver, Failsworth
"	22	James s. Thomas & Mary Smith, weaver, Failsworth
"	22	James s. Joseph & Elizabeth Wrigley, weaver, Failsworth
"	29	Joseph s. John & Fanny Goodyear, weaver, Failsworth
"	31	John spu. s. Elizabeth Ditchfield, Failsworth
"	31	Jane d. Philip & Esther Berry, shopkeeper, Newton (*entry not in BT*)
Feb	7	William s. John & Betty Stott, weaver, Failsworth
"	14	James s. John & Anne Hulton, weaver, Failsworth
"	16	Jane d. James & Esther Beswick, blacksmith, Manchester

"	21	Robert s. John & Peggy Lees, warehouseman, Failsworth *(1802)*
"	21	Anne spu. d. Violet Simister, Failsworth
"	21	William s. William & Alice Taylor, weaver, Failsworth
"	28	Matthew s. James & Catherine Brown, weaver, Newton
Mar	1	John s. James & Betty Riddel, printer, Newton
"	14	Simeon s. Thomas & Jane Smith, weaver, Failsworth
"	14	George s. Edmund & Olive Schofield, weaver, Failsworth
"	14	Betty d. Matthew & Nancy Field, cordwainer, Manchester
"	14	Robert s. Joseph & Anne Fildes, farmer, Newton
"	21	Betty d. John & Mary Robinson, taylor, Failsworth
"	25	Jane d. Robert & Anne Glossop, weaver, Failsworth
"	28	Sarah d. Joseph & Sarah Berry, blacksmith, Failsworth
Apr	4	Betty & Nancy twin ds. Matthew & Nancy Gradwell, weaver, Failsworth
"	9	Robert s. Joseph & Mary Clough, Failsworth, weaver
"	9	Mary spu. d. Anne Rayner, Failsworth
"	18	John s. William & Maria Hamner, farmer, Droylsden
"	18	Martha d. John & Martha Booth, shopkeeper, Failsworth
"	18	Sally d. John & Betty Clough, weaver, Failsworth
"	25	Mary d. James & Sarah Clough, weaver, Failsworth
"	25	James s. James & Mary Tetlow, farmer, Newton (*entry apparently inserted at a later time; not in BT*)
"	25	James s. Joseph & Mary Bardsley, weaver, Failsworth
"	25	Mary d. John & Betty Pollit, weaver, Failsworth
May	2	Sarah d. Adam & Mary Dawson, dyer, Failsworth
"	2	Lydia d. George & Elizabeth Prince, warehouseman, Newton
"	2	Jane d. James & Jane Schofield, hatter, Failsworth
"	5	Elizabeth d. Joseph & Mary Brown, weaver, Woodhouses A.P.
"	9	Edward s. Moses & Betty Preston, weaver, Failsworth
"	16	George s. William & Mary Brown, manufacturer, Manchester
"	23	John s. Thurstan & Mary Smethurst, weaver, Failsworth
"	23	Thomas s. James & Nancy Woolstencroft, whitster, Failsworth
"	24	Lucretia d. Jonathan & Margaret Grimshaw, weaver, Droylsden
"	27	Sarah d. Thomas & Martha Goodier, weaver, Failsworth
"	30	Hannah d. John & Mary Booth, weaver, Failsworth
Jun	6	Alice d. John & Sally Pendleton, weaver, Manchester
"	6	Sally d. Thomas & Susannah Etchels, weaver, Failsworth
"	6	Betty d. John & Sarah Taylor, weaver, Failsworth
"	6	Sally d. Josiah & Elizabeth Brown, weaver, Failsworth
"	6	Jane d. Benjamin & Mary Howarth, farmer, Droylsden
"	6	Nathanael s. John & Peggy Whitehead, weaver, Moston
"	6	Catharine d. John & Ellen Plant, calenderer, Newton
"	6	John s. Robert & Mary Barlow, weaver, Newton (*entry not in BT*)
"	9	Richard spu. s. Anne Pollit, Newton [Richard s. Joseph & Ann Pollet, Newton]
"	20	Jacob s. Jacob & Hannah Etchels, weaver, Newton
"	20	Maria d. James & Betty Bythell, weaver, Droylsden

"	20	Elizabeth d. Thomas & Mary Dawson, dyer, Newton	(*1802*)
"	21	Betty d. John & Mary Smith, weaver, Failsworth	
"	21	Elizabeth spu. d. Mary Taylor, Failsworth	
"	22	Sarah d. James & Jane Thornley, weaver, Droylsden	
"	22	John s. William & Sarah Berry, weaver, Failsworth	
Jul	4	Joseph spu. s. Martha Squire, Failsworth	
"	4	Matty d. James & Alice Thorpe, weaver, Failsworth	
"	4	Anne d. Thomas & Betty Wyld, weaver, Failsworth	
"	4	James s. Edward & Martha Whitehead, bricklayer, Droylsden	
"	9	Abraham s. Ralph & Anne Mather, weaver, Droylsden	
"	11	Joseph s. Matthew & Sarah Brown, weaver, Newton	
"	11	James s. James & Alice Ogden, weaver, Failsworth	
"	11	Ellen d. Thomas & Anne Collinson, weaver, Failsworth	
"	11	William s. George & Betty Hardy, weaver, Failsworth	
"	18	Elizabeth d. Robert & Isabella Hulton, weaver, Failsworth	
"	18	Sally d. John & Alice Oldham, husbandman, Newton	
"	18	William spu. s. Mary Garlick, Failsworth [William s. Henry & Mary Garlick, Failsworth]	
"	18	Peter s. Charles & Betty Walmsley, whitster, Newton	
"	25	George s. George & Betty Hudson, weaver, Newton	
"	28	Ellen d. John & Elizabeth Smith, farmer, Newton	
Aug	1	Joseph s. John & Anne Richardson, joiner, Hollinwood	
"	1	Esther d. Joseph & Anne Clough, weaver, Newton	
"	2	John s. Abraham & Betty Mather, weaver, Droylsden	
"	6	Joseph s. John & Hannah Williamson, labourer, Cutler Hill	
"	8	Anne d. James & Jane Pilkington, labourer, Failsworth	
"	15	Nancy d. John & Betty Tervin, labourer, Newton	
"	15	Thomas s. John & Mary Lord, cotton manufacturer, Bolton	
"	15	Hannah d. James & Margaret Crossley, husbandman, Moston	
"	15	Anthony s. George & Mary Lane, inn-holder, Failsworth	
"	15	John spu. s. Anne Ramsbotham, Newton	
"	22	Ellen d. Anthony & Elinor Welsh, carrier, Newton, bo May 27 1802	
"	23	David s. John & Hannah Taylor, weaver, Failsworth	
"	23	Hannah d. John & Elizabeth Whittaker, weaver, Failsworth	
"	25	James s. John & Mary Simister, weaver, Failsworth	
"	29	William s. Isaac & Ellen Beesley, calico printer, Failsworth	
"	29	Thomas s. William & Mary Wild, weaver, Droylsden	
Sep	5	John s. Samuel & Betty Ogden, weaver, Failsworth	
"	10	Mary d. Edward & Sarah Jackson, weaver, Newton	
"	12	Lissey d. Matthew & Elizabeth Thorpe, weaver, Moston	
"	12	William s. Joseph & Alice Shelmerdine, weaver, Newton	
"	19	Hannah d. Matthew & Anne Howles, weaver, Bradbury	
"	27	Mary d. Philip & Jane Smith, farmer, Failsworth	
"	27	Elizabeth spu. d. Jane Collinson. Failsworth	
Oct	3	Alice d. John & Alice Hall, carpenter, Failsworth	

"	3	Betty d. Robert & Betty Clough, weaver, Failsworth
"	3	William s. Robert & Sarah Berry, carpenter, Manchester
"	7	Thomas s. Philip & Alice Dunkerley, weaver, Failsworth
"	10	Sarah d. James & Hannah Berry, whitesmith, Failsworth
"	11	Lissey d. John & Anne Eckersley, weaver, Failsworth
"	11	Robert s. Joseph & Alice Hulme, weaver, Newton
"	17	Matthew s. John & Hannah Ford, weaver, Failsworth
"	17	Samuel s. Abraham & Jane Beswick, crofter, Droylsden
"	17	Mary d. Samuel & Betty Clough, weaver, Failsworth
"	18	Mary d. David & Anne Etchels, weaver, Failsworth
"	18	Mary d. Luke & Ellen Etchels, weaver, Failsworth
"	22	Esther (spu. *not in BT*) d. Agnes Hulton, Failsworth
"	22	Richard s. Thomas & Mary Thorpe, weaver, Failsworth
"	24	Zachariah s. Thomas & Jane Robinson, weaver, Failsworth
"	30	Sebastian s. Sebastian & Sarah Nash, callico-printer, Failsworth
"	31	Alice d. John & Rachel Bythel, weaver, Newton
Nov	2	Mary d. James & Hannah Ashton, weaver, Failsworth
"	3	Thomas s. John & Betty Houghton, innholder, Newton
"	7	Mary Anne d. James & Alice Howarth, labourer, Failsworth
"	7	Anne d. James & Sarah Lord, wheelwright, Failsworth
"	7	Mary Aldred d. William & Alice Lane, innholder, Manchester
"	8	John s. Peter & Hannah Lomax, dyer, Newton
"	14	David s. James & Sarah Ogden, weaver, Failsworth
"	14	John s. Luke & Hannah Etchels, weaver, Failsworth
"	14	Thomas spu. s. Hannah Stott, Failsworth
"	15	Richard s. Thomas & Mary Brown, weaver, Failsworth
"	15	Elizabeth d. James & Martha Pollit, weaver, Newton
"	21	Harriett d. John & Mary Robinson, printcutter, Newton
"	28	George s. John & Elizabeth Robinson, slater, Newton
"	28	Anne d. Thomas & Elizabeth Shepley, weaver, Failsworth
Dec	5	John s. John & Mary Higham, weaver, Failsworth
"	12	William s. John & Sarah Tetlow, warehouseman, Newton
"	12	James s. John & Sarah Ogden, weaver, Moston
"	17	Isabel d. Thomas & Elizabeth Knott, weaver, Failsworth
"	19	Sarah d. Robert & Martha Hulton, weaver, Failsworth
"	25	Elijah s. James & Nancy Rydings, weaver, Failsworth
"	25	Susan d. Robert & Frances Mills, dyer, Ashton Pari
"	26	William s. William & Maria Bond, wheelwright, Failsworth

[A. Ashworth Minister   ]
[James Kenyon William Brown Ch Wardens   ]

Baptisms in 1803
[Baptisms at Newton Heath Chapel in 1803]
(*each page in the BT for this year is signed* A. Ashworth Minister)

Jan	6	Mary d. John & Susan Moore, weaver, Failsworth
"	6	Jane d. Thomas & Alice Hulton, farmer, Moston
"	7	Margaret d. John & Anne Clough, drawer, Droylsden
"	9	Thomas Wroe s. Thomas & Esther Tomkinson, hatter, Newton
"	9	James s. Peter & Anne Fletcher, weaver, Failsworth
"	12	John s. Thomas & Nancy Whittaker, weaver, Manchester
"	16	William s. William & Mary Bentley, printer, Ashton Parish
"	16	Samuel s. Jonathan & Mary Shelmerdine, weaver, Newton
"	16	Betty d. Thomas & Sarah Walmsley, farmer, Failsworth, bo Oct 4 1802
"	17	Maria d. Joseph & Elizabeth Seel, printer, Newton
"	23	Sarah d. John & Hannah Wright, weaver, Failsworth
"	23	Anne spu d. Betty Berry, Failsworth
"	30	Mary d. Joseph & Sarah Hibbert, printer, Newton
"	30	Mary d. John & Anne Hulton, weaver, Failsworth
"	30	John s. James & Phebe Hulme, weaver, Failsworth
Feb	4	Betty spu d. Matty Kershaw, Failsworth
"	5	Mary d. William & Mary Heywood, dyer, Newton
"	6	Esther d. Richard & Sarah Simister, weaver, Newton
"	6	Henry s. John & Martha Etchels, weaver, Droylsden
"	13	John s. Joseph & Jane Heath, tanner, Newton
"	20	David spu. s. Elizabeth Holt, Failsworth
"	20	Elizabeth d. Joseph & Agnes Slater, weaver, Failsworth
"	20	James s. George & Grace Howles, weaver, Newton
"	27	Esther d. John & Mary Robinson, weaver, Droylsden
"	27	Abraham s. James & Margaret Dronsfield, weaver, Failsworth
Mar	6	Samuel s. James & Sarah Whittaker, weaver, Failsworth
"	13	Hannah d. James & Anne Thorneley, weaver, Failsworth
"	13	Absalom s. Samuel & Elizabeth Taylor, weaver, Moston
"	13	Thomas s. Jonathan & Esther Schofield, weaver, Moston
"	20	John s. William & Bella Bolton, engraver, Newton
"	20	Samuel s. Samuel & Sarah Hilton, shopkeeper, Failsworth
"	20	Joseph s. James & Hannah Hibbert, labourer, Newton
"	21	John s. John & Elizabeth Thorp, weaver, Moston
"	27	John s. Joseph & Elizabeth Ogden, weaver, Failsworth
"	27	John s. Edmund & Mary Taylor, weaver, Droylsden
"	27	Charles s. John & Alice Hulton, weaver, Failsworth
"	27	John s. Thomas & Mary Brown, weaver, Newton
"	27	Mary d. Thomas & Mary Smith, weaver, Failsworth
"	28	James s. John & Sarah Howarth, weaver, Droylsden
Apr	3	John s. James & Martha Kemp, weaver, Manchester
"	3	John s. John & Sarah Dean, labourer, Newton

"	3	Thomas s. James & Betty Johnson, weaver, Failsworth	*(1803)*
"	3	Alice d. John & Ellen Ramsbotham, dyer, Newton	
"	3	Sarah d. William & Anne Thorneley, weaver, Failsworth	
"	10	Sarah d. John & Mary Thornley, weaver, Failsworth	
"	10	Mary d. George & Alice Smith, weaver, Failsworth	
"	10	Hannah d. Thomas & Elizabeth Mather, weaver, Newton	
"	17	James spu. s. Sarah Clough, Failsworth	
"	19	Thomas s. William & Maria Hamner, farmer, Droylsden	
"	24	Hannah d. John & Martha Ogden, weaver, Failsworth	
"	24	Elizabeth d. John & Mary Slater, manufacturer, Newton	
May	1	Mary d. William & Mary Daltry, farmer, Newton	
"	1	William s. John & Alice Thorpe, weaver, Failsworth	
"	8	Betty d. Robert & Mary Clough, weaver, Failsworth, aged 13y 8m 1w	
"	8	Joseph s. Joseph & Elizabeth Taylor, weaver, Failsworth	
"	8	John s. Thomas & Alice Horrocks, weaver, Failsworth	
"	8	John s. Joseph & Betty Wrigley, weaver, Failsworth	
"	22	Nancy d. William & Sarah Robinson, slater, Newton	
"	23	Samuel s. James & Mary Andrew, printcutter, Newton	
"	29	John s. John & Betty Berrington, tanner, Failsworth	
"	29	Samuel s. Joseph & Anne Taylor, weaver, Failsworth	
"	29	James s. Hugh & Betty Garvey, taylor, Failsworth	
"	29	Mark spu. s. Sarah Mather, Droylsden	
"	29	Betty d. William & Anne Radcliffe, weaver, Moston	
"	29	Elizabeth d. James & Mary Holt, weaver, Failsworth	
Jun	5	Miles s. Miles & Elizabeth Slater, weaver, Failsworth	
"	5	Matthew s. John & Alice Williamson, weaver, Failsworth	
"	5	Ellen d. Miles & Mary Schofield, labourer, Newton	
"	5	James s. Eli & Sarah Whiteley, weaver, Droylsden, aged 6 weeks	
"	5	James s. Edmund & Olivia Schofield, weaver, Failsworth	
"	12	Esther d. Robert & Betty Taylor, weaver, Failsworth	
"	19	William s. Ralph & Isabella Ramshaw, waggoner, Newton	
"	26	Mary d. Moses & Betty Berry, farmer, Failsworth	
"	26	Thomas s. Joseph & Margaret Ogden, weaver, Failsworth	
"	26	Alice d. George & Mary Hibbert, shoe maker, Failsworth	
"	26	Elizabeth d. Thomas & Elizabeth Barlow, weaver, Failsworth	
"	26	Mary Anne d. Samuel & Mary Mellor, weaver, Newton	
"	27	Thomas s. Joseph & Mary Turner, slater, Newton	
Jul	3	John s. Joseph & Mary Schofield, weaver, Moston	
"	3	Nancy d. James & Mary Thorpe, weaver, Failsworth	
"	4	Mary d. George & Mary Smith, weaver, Failsworth	
"	10	Mary d. James & Mary Rydings, weaver, Failsworth	
"	16	John s. John & Betty Smith, weaver, Failsworth	
"	17	Mary Anne d. William & Anne Clarke, weaver, Newton	
"	17	John s. James & Anne Grindrod, weaver, Newton	
"	17	Anne d. George & Elizabeth Harris, butler, Failsworth	

"	17	Elizabeth d. James & Betty Fletcher, labourer, Droylsden (*1803*)
"	24	Richard (Samuel *struck through*) [Saml] s. John & Mary Stansfield, hatter, Newton
"	24	George s. Richard & Mary Walker, weaver, Newton
"	24	Jonathan s. Thomas & Esther Dawson, whitster, Failsworth
"	24	Ellen d. John & Ellen Taylor, printer, Ashton Parish
"	31	Joseph s. William & Jane Barrow, innkeeper, Failsworth
"	31	William s. James & Jane Allen, weaver, Newton
"	31	James s. James & Sarah Wilson, weaver, Moston
"	31	Mary d. James & Phebe Smethurst, weaver, Failsworth
Aug	3	Sarah d. William & Hannah Middleton, weaver, Failsworth
"	6	James s. Thomas & Elizabeth Gossilton, weaver, Newton
"	7	Thomas s. John & Martha Kershaw, weaver, Newton
"	7	Alice d. Robert & Anne Lord, labourer, Droylsden
"	7	Betty d. Jonathan & Betty Swift, weaver, Newton
"	8	Susannah d. John & Sarah Clough, weaver, Failsworth
"	14	James s. Edmund & Jane Whitehead, weaver, Chadderton
"	14	James s. Thomas & Martha Smith, weaver, Failsworth
"	14	Ellen d. William & Sarah Walker, weaver, Newton
"	14	Sarah d. James & Hannah Wilkinson, weaver, Failsworth
"	18	Sarah d. Nehemiah & Mary Heap, weaver, Droylsden
"	21	Nancy d. Henry & Jane Bolton, navigator, Newton
"	23	Martha d. James & Mary Berry, weaver, Newton
"	23	Elias s. Thomas & Anne Whittaker, bleacher, Newton
"	28	Alice d. James & Betty Wyld, weaver, Droylsden
"	28	Susannah d. Joseph & Lettice Tomlinson, weaver, Failsworth
"	28	John s. Samuel & Anne Pollit, weaver, Failsworth
"	28	Martha d. Joseph & Sarah Berry, blacksmith, Failsworth
"	30	William s. John & Mary Whitehead, innkeeper, Newton
Sep	3	Elizabeth d. James & Francis (*sic*) [Frances] Barret, labourer, Failsworth
"	4	Edmund s. Philip & Esther Houghton, farmer, Newton
"	4	John s. David & Sarah Ogden, weaver, Failsworth
"	4	Nancy d. George & Mary Tomlinson, weaver, Failsworth
"	4	James s. George & Sarah Etchels, weaver, Failsworth
"	4	Ralph s. Ralph & Nancy Smethurst, weaver, Failsworth
"	4	Nancy d. Ralph & Nancy Smethurst, weaver, Failsworth
		(*last 2 entries bracketed together and the word* twins *entered in margin*)
"	11	Robert spu. s. Anne Rowe, Failsworth
"	11	Jinny d. John & Sarah Ogden, book-keeper, Failsworth
"	18	Thomas s. Thomas & Mary Ashworth, weaver, Newton
"	18	Luke spu. s. Mary Swift, Newton
"	18	John s. Anne d. twins of Samuel & Mary Scholes, soldier, Failsworth (*separate entries in BT*)
"	20	John spu. s. Jane Walmsley, farmer, Failsworth
"	20	Anne d. James & Hannah Ashton, weaver, Failsworth

"	25	Elizabeth d. James & Jane Fitton, cotton spinner, Manchester
"	25	Sarah d. Joseph & Martha Clough, weaver, Woodhouses A.P.
"	25	Joseph s. Joseph & Mary Bardsley, weaver, Failswoprth
"	25	Elizabeth d. John & Susannah Ward, weaver, Moston
"	27	Alice d. Daniel & Mary Wild, farmer, Newton
Oct	9	Abraham s. Thomas & Mary Dawson, printer, Newton
"	16	Phebe d. Richard & Anne Johnson, labourer, Ardwick M.P.
"	16	James Rutherford s. Richard & Mary Hartley, innholder, Failsworth
"	16	Hannah d. Thomas & Peggy Wright, blacksmith, Failsworth
"	23	Benjamin s. John & Hannah Lees, weaver, Failsworth
"	23	Betty d. James & Anne Thorpe, weaver, Failsworth
"	23	Mary d. John & Elizabeth Robinson, weaver, Woodhouses A.P.
"	23	John s. William & Hannah Drinkwater, bricklayer, Newton
"	23	John s. John & Mary Whittaker, weaver, Failsworth
"	23	Thomas s. Samuel & Betty Ainsworth, hatter, Newton
"	23	Hannah d. George & Mary Wolstenholme, weaver, Newton
"	23	John s. Peter & Mary Wild, waggoner, Newton
"	25	Samuel s. Samuel & Elizabeth Lees, blacksmith, Failsworth
"	30	James spu. s. Milley Gra(a)dwell, Failsworth
Nov	13	Hannah d. John & Fanny Goodyear, weaver, Failsworth
"	13	Sarah d. Ashton & Mary Shepley, weaver, Newton
"	13	Joseph s. John & Jane (Mary *struck through*) [Mary] Standring, bar-keeper, Failsworth
"	20	William s. Robert & Mary Barlow, weaver, Failsworth
"	20	Olive d. William & Jane Butterworth, weaver, Failsworth
"	20	George s. John & Margaret Lees, warehouseman, Failsworth
"	27	Frederick s. John & Elizabeth Stott, weaver, Failsworth
"	27	John s. Benjamin & Violet Hulton, weaver, Failsworth
"	27	John s. William & Rebecca Worral, farmer, Failsworth
Dec	22	Mary d. Abraham & Mary Briscoe, printdrawer, Newton
"	25	Anne spu. d. Mary Whitehead, Moston
"	25	John s. William & Catherine Gradwell, weaver, Failsworth
"	25	Jane d. Jacob & Hannah Etchels, weaver, Newton
"	25	James s. Joseph & Mary Brown, farmer, Woodhouses A.P.
"	25	Sarah d. Samuel & Alice Tonge, weaver, Failsworth
"	25	Joseph s. James & Frances Clough, farmer, Droylsden

Baptisms in 1804
[Christenings at Newton Heath Chapel Anno 1804]

Jan	1	Samuel s. Abraham & Nancy Lee, dyer, Newton
"	1	Samuel s. James & Sarah Berry, weaver, Failsworth
"	1	Hannah d. John & Mary Thor(n)ley, weaver, Failsworth
"	1	Mary d. Robert & Ellen Avenson, miller, Moston
"	1	John s. John & Anne Beswick, labourer, Failsworth

"	8	Alice d. William & Alice Taylor, weaver, Failsworth
"	8	Mary d. Jonathan & Mary Hooley, bleacher, Newton
"	15	Richard s. William & Sarah Harrison, weaver, Moston
"	15	Thomas s. William & Sarah Harrison, weaver, Moston
		(*last 2 entries bracketed together and the word* twins *entered in margin; entries combined in BT*)
"	22	Betty d. Samuel & Betty Smith, weaver, Failsworth
"	29	Mary d. Richard & Betty Wilkinson, joiner, Newton
Feb	5	James s. Thomas & Betty Berry, farmer, Gorton
"	5	Mary d. Josiah & Betty Brown, weaver, Failsworth
"	5	Betty d. James & Jane Schofield, weaver, Failsworth
"	5	Rose d. James & Mary Etchels, weaver, Failsworth
"	5	Henry s. Matthew & Sarah Brown, weaver, Failsworth
"	5	John s. Joseph & Martha Wylde, weaver, Newton
"	12	Betty d. John & Mary Bates, cordwainer, Failsworth
"	12	James s. John & Sarah Taylor, weaver, Failsworth
"	12	Anne d. Charles & Hannah Heywood, weaver, Newton
"	16	Joseph s. Philip & Esther Berry, shopkeeper, Newton
"	19	James spu. s. Anne Wrigley, Failsworth
"	24	James s. Launcelot & Mary Hulton, weaver, Failsworth
Mar	4	Charles s. James & Hannah Miller, print-cutter, Newton
"	4	Jonah s. William & Elizabeth Goodier, weaver, Newton
"	5	Joseph s. Thomas & Anne Etchels, weaver, Droylsden
"	11	Sarah d. Robert & Elizabeth Hall, weaver, Newton, bo Jan 29
"	11	Jane d. Robert & Penelope Whitehead, weaver, Failsworth
"	11	Sarah d. John & Margaret Whitehead, weaver, Moston
"	18	Philis d. James & Nancy Rydings, weaver, Failsworth
"	18	Margaret d. Philip & Sarah Martin, printer, Newton
"	18	Jonathan s. Edmund & Alice Walmsley, joiner, Manchester
Apr	1	Joseph s. John & Anne Hulton, weaver, Failsworth
"	1	Charles s. James & Margaret Clough, weaver, Failsworth
"	1	William s. Abel & Mary Tomlinson, weaver, Failsworth
"	1	John s. James & Hannah Timmis, weaver, Failsworth
"	1	Olive d. John & Anne Whitaker, weaver, Failsworth
"	1	Alice d. Moses & Elizabeth Preston, weaver, Failsworth
"	1	Charles s. Samuel & Elizabeth Ogden, weaver, Failsworth
"	4	Esther d. Robert & Betty Whitehead, weaver, Failsworth
"	5	Robert s. Robert & Anne Glossop, weaver, Failsworth
"	5	Jonas s. Thomas & Jane Smith, weaver, Failsworth
"	8	Elizabeth d. James & Mary Gradwell, weaver, Failsworth
"	15	Anne d. Robert & Martha Rydings, weaver, Failsworth
"	15	James s. John & Anne Howarth, colour maker, Newton
"	22	Abraham s. Robert & Frances Mills, dyer, Waterside A.P.
"	24	William s. William & Ellen Hibbert, weaver, Failsworth
"	29	Thomas s. John & Esther Taylor, cordwainer, Failsworth

"	29	Betty d. Jame[s] & Anne Whitehead, weaver, Failsworth	*(1804)*
"	29	Fanny d. Jonathan & Peggy Grimshaw, weaver, Droylsden	
"	29	James s. Joseph & Anne Fildes, farmer, Newton	
"	30	Jane d. John & Catherine Harrop, hatter, Openshaw	
May	2	Ophelia d. Thomas & Jane [Anne] Collinson, weaver, Failsworth	
"	6	Mary d. John & Sarah Prince, weaver, Newton	
"	13	Anne d. William & Anne Whitehead, weaver, Failsworth	
"	13	James s. John & Sarah Taylor, weaver, Failsworth	
"	13	Samuel s. Robert & Mary Grimshaw, weaver, Newton	
"	14	Robert s. James & Mary Tetlow, farmer, Newton	
"	14	Joseph s. James & Anne Kershaw, weaver, Failsworth	
"	16	George s. George & Mary Lane, innkeeper, Failsworth	
"	17	William s. James & Nancy Woolstencroft, bleacher, Failsworth	
"	17	James s. George & Betty Hardy, weaver, Failsworth	
"	20	William Lucas s. James & Elizabeth Riddell, printer, Newton	
"	20	Charles s. John & Anne Mills, farmer, Newton	
"	20	John s. John & Sarah Whitehead, cotton manufacturer, Failsworth	
"	20	Joseph s. James & Mary Barnes, printer, Failsworth	
"	20	Elizabeth d. John & Margaret Brown, gardener, Ashton Parish	
"	23	Robert s. Luke & Anne Smith, farmer, Failsworth	
"	23	Hannah d. James & Mary Simister, bleacher, Newton	
"	25	Sarah d. John & Sarah Holland, weaver, Droylsden, bo Jan 1	
Jun	3	Joseph s. Joseph & Mary Hope, carpenter, Bradford	
"	3	Joseph s. Adam & Mary Dawson, dyer, Failsworth	
"	3	David s. Robert & Isabel Hulton, weaver, Failsworth	
"	3	Daniel s. John & Mary Smith, warehouseman, Failsworth	
"	8	Thomas s. James & Alice Thorp, weaver, Failsworth	
"	10	Jenny d. Thomas & Susannah Etchels, weaver, Failsworth	
"	10	Sarah d. James & Anne Thornaley, weaver, Failsworth	
"	12	Betty d. Robert & Anne Taylor, printer, Newton	
"	13	Frances d. William & Alice Lane, innholder, Manchester	
"	24	Edward s. James & Jane Pilkington, labourer, Failsworth	
"	24	Joseph s. Jonathan & Esther Schofield, weaver, Moston	
"	24	Benjamin s. John & Mary Wilkinson, weaver, Failsworth	
"	26	James s. Robert & Mary Ogden, weaver, Newton	
Jul	1	Ellen d. James & Hannah Berry, smith, Failsworth	
"	4	John s. Matthew & Elizabeth Thorp, weaver, Moston	
"	4	Joseph s. Joseph & Mary Tinker, weaver, Moston, bo Apr 19	
"	8	John spu s. Martha Barlow, Failsworth	
"	8	Elizabeth d. Charles & Anne Hall, bricklayer, Manchester	
"	11	Alice d. Edward & Anne Eckersley, weaver, Failsworth	
"	15	Jonas s. William & Mary Brown, manufacturer, Manchester	
"	15	Mary d. John & Ruth Jackson, husbandman, Failsworth	
"	16	Mary d. James & Mary Whitehead, weaver, Failsworth	
"	16	John s. Thomas & Mary Smith, weaver, Failsworth	

"	19	Anne d. Robert & Betty Clough, weaver, Failsworth *(1804)*
"	20	Esther d. John & Betty Houghton, innholder, Newton
"	22	John s. Edward & Mary Andrew, weaver, Newton
"	22	James s. John & Betty Ashton, weaver, Moston
"	30	James s. John & Elizabeth Whitaker, weaver, Failsworth
Aug	12	John s. Thomas & Mary Brown, weaver, Failsworth
"	12	Anne spu. d. Betty Fildes, Failsworth
"	19	William s. Edward & Martha Whitehead, bricklayer, Droylsden
"	19	James s. Christian & Sarah Miller, husbandman, Newton
"	26	William s. James & Elizabeth Bethell, whitster, Droylsden
Sep	2	Eliza d. William & Mary Winder, taylor, Newton
"	2	Robert s. George & Alice Smith, weaver, Failsworth
"	9	Mary d. Thomas & Mary Sidebottom, weaver, Moston
"	16	David s. David & Betty Potter, Moston
"	16	Joel spu. s. Mary Whittaker, Failsworth
"	16	Abraham s. James & Mary Clough, weaver, Failsworth
"	16	Thomas s. George & Margaret Ayres, cordwainer, Failsworth
"	17	Robert s. Joshua & Alice Stott, weaver, Newton
"	23	Robert s. John & Mary West, soldier, Manchester
"	23	James s. Edward & Sarah Jackson, weaver, Newton
"	30	Eli s. James & Martha Swift, weaver, Failsworth
"	30	George s. James & Catherine Brown, weaver, Newton
Oct	14	George s. George & Grace Howles, weaver, Newton
"	14	Elizabeth d. Richard & Mary Richardson, weaver, Newton
"	14	Mary d. John & Hannah Wright, weaver, Failsworth
"	21	Sarah spu. d. Betty Preston, Failsworth
Nov	11	Mary spu. d. Hannah Walmsley, Newton
"	18	Samuel s. William & Mary Wild, weaver, Openshaw
"	18	Alice d. John & Betty Tervin, husbandman, Newton
"	25	William s. Abraham & Martha Whitehead, weaver, Failsworth
"	25	Josiah s. John & Helen Davis, labourer, Failsworth
"	25	Rebecca d. Michael & Isabella Patten, labourer, Failsworth
Dec	2	Mary d. John & Ellen Taylor, printer, Ashton Parish
"	2	John s. John & Elizabeth Whitehead, weaver, Newton
"	2	Anne d. John & Mary Slater, manufacturer, Newton
"	9	Anne d. Alexander & Isabella Glashen, weaver, Failsworth
"	9	John s. John & Sarah Ogden, weaver, Moston
"	9	Ellen d. Joseph & Ellen Caldwell, farmer, Newton
"	9	Sarah d. Thomas & Margaret Holden, printer, Newton
"	11	Hannah d. George & Elizabeth Staton, weaver, Newton (*entry not in BT*)
"	16	William s. Ralph & Mary Bradley, labourer, Failsworth
"	17	Thomas s. Thomas & Elizabeth Mather, weaver, Newton
"	18	Jonathan s. Thomas & Anne Whitaker, bleacher, Newton
"	19	Thomas s. John & Alice Hall, carpenter, Failsworth
"	25	Mary d. John & Anne Clough, print drawer, Droylsden

"	25	Anne d. Joseph & Anne Berry, weaver, Failsworth
"	25	James s. Joseph & Mary Taylor, weaver, Failsworth
"	25	Sarah d. Joseph & Mary Turner, slater, Newton
"	25	John s. David & Anne Etchels, weaver, Failsworth
"	25	Jane d. Joseph & Mary Pott, manufacturer, Newton
[		A. Ashworth Minister]

Baptisms in 1805
[Baptized at Newton Heath Chapel in the year 1805]

Jan	1	Maria d. John & Martha Etchels, weaver, Droylsden
"	6	Mary Anne d. James & Margaret Crossley, husbandman, Moston
"	6	Betty d. James & Mary Schofield, weaver, Moston
"	13	William s. Joseph & Sarah Rydings, weaver, Failsworth
"	27	Thomas s. Joseph & Elizabeth Ogden, weaver, Failsworth
"	27	Sarah d. John & Mary Simister, weaver, Failsworth
Feb	3	Peter s. Matthew & Anne Gradwell, weaver, Failsworth
"	4	Anne d. Samuel & Anne Pollit, weaver, Failsworth
"	10	William s. Joseph & Martha Booth, shopkeeper, Failsworth
"	17[19]	Joseph s. John & Sarah Berry, weaver, Failsworth
"	17[19]	Jane d. Ralph & Jane Smethurst, weaver, Failsworth
"	17	Thomas s. John & Sarah Dean, weaver, Newton (*entry not in BT*)
"	18	Daniel s. Thomas & Elizabeth Knott, weaver, Failsworth
"	24	George s. Alexander & Margaret Noble, navigator, Newton
Mar	3	Mary Anne d. Samuel & Elizabeth Hyde, collier, Bradford
"	4	William s. Samuel & Mary Birtles, taylor, Failsworth
"	4	Betty d. Richard & Sarah Simister, weaver, Newton
"	10	Hannah d. Abraham & Elizabeth Mather, weaver, Droylsden
"	10	William s. William & Sarah Robinson, slater, Newton
"	10	Edmund s. Edmund & Olivia Schofield, weaver, Failsworth
"	10	Mary spu. d. Martha Whitehead, Failsworth
"	11	Joel s. Luke & Anne Smith, weaver, Failsworth
"	11	James s. William & Mary Stevenson, weaver, Failsworth
"	15	Joseph s. John & Mary Nash, bo Jul 22 1795, Failsworth
"	15	Eliza d. John & Mary Nash, bo Jun 12 1797, Failsworth
"	15	Mary Maria Sarah d. Sebastian & Sarah Nash, bo Jan 25 1805, Failsworth
"	17	Henry s. Daniel & Hannah Hulton, weaver, Failsworth
"	17	Benjamin spu. s. Betty Hulton, Failsworth
"	17	Isabella d. William & Isabella Bolton, calico printer, Newton
"	24	William (spu. *not in BT*) s. Sarah Riley, Failsworth
"	24	Sally d. James & Alice Ogden, weaver, Failsworth
"	30	Alice d. Peter & Anne Fletcher, weaver, Failsworth
"	30	Betty d. James & Sarah Swift, weaver, Newton
"	31	Thurstan s. Thurstan & Mary Smethurst, weaver, Failsworth
"	31	John s. Peter & Betty Smith, weaver, Failsworth

"	31	Esther d. Joseph & Alice Hulme, weaver, Newton
Apr	7	George s. John & Ellen Plant, weaver, Newton
"	7	John s. Isaac & Ellen Beesley, calico printer, Failsworth
"	7	Joseph (spu. *not in BT*) s. Betty Blackshaw, Failsworth
"	12	Eliza d. Joseph & Elizabeth Seel, printer, Newton
"	14	William s. John (& Mary *not in BT*) Billinge, hatter, Newton
"	14	William s. James & Sarah Whitaker, weaver, Failsworth
"	14	Maria d. George & Mary Wolstenhulme, weaver, Failsworth
"	14	Sarah d. James & Martha Allen, labourer, Failsworth
"	14	Mary (spu. *not in BT*) d. Martha Greenwood, Failsworth
"	14	John (spu. *not in BT*) s. Sarah Thorpe, Manchester
"	14	Sarah d. John & Sarah Ogden, weaver, Failsworth
"	14	John s. William & Hannah Etchels, weaver, Failsworth
"	21	John s. Launcelot & Mary Hulton, weaver, Failsworth
"	21	Jane d. John & Elizabeth Arrandale, weaver, Droylsden
"	28	Sarah d. Miles & Mary Schofield, bleacher, Newton
May	5	John s. Robert & Sarah Berry, carpenter, Manchester
"	5	Sarah d. John & Jane Fitton, cotton spinner, Manchester
"	5	Alice d. James & Phebe Smethurst, weaver, Failsworth
"	5	Sally d. Thomas & Betty Wylde, weaver, Failsworth
"	12	Ellen d. Samuel & Ellen Smith, weaver, Failsworth
"	12	William s. William & Sarah Walker, weaver, Newton
"	19	Jonathan s. James & Mary Thorpe, weaver, Failsworth
"	22	Joseph Moores s. James & Phebe Hulme, weaver, Failsworth
"	26	Hannah d. Thomas & Betty Gosilton, weaver, Newton
"	26	Mary d. George & Mary Tomlinson, dyer, Failsworth
"	26	John s. George & Nancy Bramell, blacksmith, Newton
Jun	2	Jane d. Samuel & Betty Ainsworth, hatter, Newton
"	2	Samuel s. James & Hannah Timmis, wheelwright, Failsworth
"	2	Jenny d. Richard & Anne Pollit, weaver, Failsworth
"	2	John s. John & Betty Whitehead, weaver, Moston
"	2	Richard s. William [Richard] & Nancy Robinson, weaver, Failsworth
"	5	Sarah d. Philip & Elizabeth Smith, weaver, Failsworth
"	5	Mary d. Philip & Elizabeth Smith, weaver, Failsworth
"	5	Betty d. James & Hannah Hibbert, weaver, Newton
"	6	Elizabeth d. George & Elizabeth Prince, warehouseman, Newton
"	7	Thomas s. William & Mary Bentley, calico printer, Failsworth
"	9	Elizabeth d. Thomas & Anne Ryder, farmer, Moston
"	12	Richard s. Joseph & Martha Clough, weaver, Woodhouses A.P.
"	16	Hannah d. Robert & Martha Hulton, weaver, Failsworth
"	21	Thomas (spu. *not in BT*) s. Mary Smith, Failsworth
"	23	Elizabeth d. William & Jenny Barrow, innholder, Failsworth
"	23	Mary d. John & Sarah Tetlow, warehouseman, Newton
"	23	William s. Edmund & Jane Whitehead, weaver, Hollinwood
"	25	James s. James & Jane Allen, weaver, Newton

"	30	Thomas s. Joseph & Elizabeth Taylor, weaver, Failsworth (*1805*)
"	30	Sarah d. James & Martha Kemp, weaver, Manchester
"	30	Robert s. William & Sarah Daltry, farmer, Newton
"	30	Betty d. James & Mary Smith, weaver, Failsworth
"	30	Lettice d. William & Anne Ratcliffe, weaver, Moston
"	30	Elizabeth d. James & Sarah Nuttall, dyer, Newton
Jul	3	Andrew s. Samuel & Elizabeth Clough, weaver, Failsworth
"	7	Mary d. John & Hannah Lord, weaver, Failsworth
"	7	Catharine d. Abraham & Jane Ashworth, Minister of Newton, bo Jun 7
"	12	Anne d. Issachar & Elizabeth Thorpe, weaver, Failsworth
"	14	Philip (spu. *not in BT*) s. Tabby Berry, Failsworth
"	14	Betty d. John & Alice Williamson, weaver, Failsworth
"	14	Alice d. Andrew & Amy Berry, carpenter, Manchester
"	14	Elizabeth d. Austin & Mary Chadwick, weaver, Newton
"	15	Matilda d. William & Elizabeth Aldred, weaver, Ashton Paris[h]
"	18	Elizabeth d. John & Sarah Summers, whitesmith, Newton
"	21	Samuel (spu. *not in BT*) s. Nanny Smith, Failsworth
"	21	Mary d. John & Sarah Smith, weaver, Failsworth
"	22	Joshua s. William & Nancy Whitaker, weaver, Newton
"	31	Robert s. John & Sarah Walmsley, warehouseman, Failsworth
Aug	4	Sarah d. John & Betty Robinson, farmer, Woodhouses A.P.
"	4	Jane d. Benjamin & Violet Hulton, weaver, Failsworth
"	4	Joseph s. George & Betty Hulton, weaver, Failsworth
"	11	Mary d. Luke & Hannah Etchels, weaver, Failsworth
"	11	Sarah d. (*blank; entry not in BT*)
"	11	Samuel s. William & Hannah Prichard, husbandman, Newton
"	15	Sally Mather d. John & Sarah Mason, weaver, Droylsden
"	18	Eliza (spu. *not in BT*) d. Sarah Jenning, Manchester
"	18	Jonathan s. Samuel & Anne Etchels, weaver, Failsworth
"	25	William s. Richard & Mary Walker, weaver, Newton
"	25	James s. Samuel & Mary Lowe, weaver, Newton
"	25	Joseph s. Peter & Mary Wylde, waggoner, Newton
"	25	Esther d. Thomas & Mary Houghton, hatter, Manchester
"	25	Elizabeth d. Thomas & Mary Houghton, hatter, Manchester
		(*last 2 entries bracketed together and the word* twins *entered in margin*)
"	28	Daniel s. James & Martha Wolstencroft, bleacher, Failsworth
Sep	1	Robert s. William & Elenor Harrison, printcutter, Newton
"	1	John s. Samuel & Jane Mather, weaver, Newton
"	1	John s. Samuel & Sarah Berry, weaver, Failsworth
"	1	Mary Anne (spu. *not in BT*) d. Elizabeth Barlow, Newton
"	1	William s. James & Frances Clough, husbandman, Newton
"	8	John s. John & Phebe Stevenson, weaver, Failsworth
"	8	Jonathan s. Joshua & Betty Swift, weaver, Newton
"	8	David spu. s. Agnes Hulton, Failsworth
"	8	James s. David & Betty Pollet, weaver, Failsworth

"	8	Nancy d. Alexander & Margaret Hague, mason, Failsworth *(1805)*
"	15	William s. Ashton & Mary Shepley, manufacturer, Newton
"	15	Mary d. Thomas & Margaret Wright, blacksmith, Failsworth
"	22	Elizabeth d. Richard & Alice Mills, joiner, Newton
"	22	Hannah d. James & Elizabeth Coffen, labourer, Newton
"	23	Joseph s. Thomas & Mary Schofield, weaver, Failsworth
"	29	John s. John & Martha Kershaw, weaver, Failsworth
"	29	Ralph s. Jonathan & Ellen Taylor, weaver, Moston
"	29	Mary d. William & Jane Allen, weaver, Failsworth
"	29	Peter s. Robert & Mary Holroyd, husbandman, Newton
"	29	Betty d. James & Mary Etchels, weaver, Failsworth
"	30	John s. James & Elizabeth Johnson, weaver, Failsworth
Oct	6	James (spu *not in BT*) s. Jane Collinson, Failsworth
"	6	Sarah d. James & Mary Viney, spinner, Failsworth
"	6	William s. James & Esther Gillies, mason, Newton
"	20	Thomas s. John & Mary Thornily, weaver, Failsworth
"	20	Elizabeth d. Peter & Hannah Wood, weaver, North-moor
"	20	George s. James & Betty Wyld, weaver, Droylsden
"	23	Mary d. William & Elizabeth Atkinson, innholder, Failsworth
"	27	John s. Thomas & Alice Horridge, weaver, Failsworth
"	27	David s. John & Rachel Bythell, weaver, Newton
"	27	Mary d. Abel & Mary Tomlinson, weaver, Failsworth
Nov	3	Thomas s. John & Mary Whitaker, weaver, Failsworth
"	3	Sarah d. John & Hannah Williamson, joiner, Cutler hill
"	3	Margaret d. George & Elizabeth Parkinson, tanner, Failsworth
"	3	William s. John & Susannah Wardley, weaver, Moston
"	10	Mary d. Joseph & Anne Clough, weaver, Newton
"	10	Elizabeth d. Charles & Hannah Heywood, weaver, Newton
"	10	Mary d. John & Sarah Harrison, weaver, Newton
"	10	John s. Joseph & Alice Berry, weaver, Failsworth
"	12	William s. Thomas & Martha Hooley, bleacher, Newton
"	17	Betty d. Thomas & Jane Robinson, weaver, Newton
"	24	Sarah d. William & Maria Hamner, farmer, Droylsden
"	24	Elizabeth d. Henry & Mary Holland, weaver, Failsworth
Dec	1	Joseph s. John & Elizabeth Stott, manufacturer, Failsworth
"	1	William s. Thomas & Mary Brown, weaver, Newton
" '	1	William s. Joseph & Margaret Ogden, weaver, Failsworth
"	15	William s. William & Anne Wilson, weaver, Moston
"	15	Joseph s. Joshua & Olivia Wylde, bleacher, Failsworth
"	22	Rebecca d. Nathaniel & Anne Thorley, gardener, Failsworth, bo Jun 3 1800
"	22	Mary Anne d. Thomas & Hannah Allen, weaver, Failsworth
"	22	Joseph s. John & Mary Thorley, weaver, Failsworth
"	25	Horatio s. James & Nancy Rydings, weaver, Failsworth
"	25	Betty d. George & Alice Smith, weaver, Failsworth
"	25	Susan d. James & Sarah Wilson, weaver, Moston

"	25	David s. James & Anne Kershaw, weaver, Failsworth
"	25	Sarah Anne d. Looklean & Mary Bine, navigator, Newton
"	25	Elizabeth d. Thomas & Sarah Moore, weaver, Manchester
"	29	Jonathan s. John & Hannah Taylor, weaver, Droylsden

Baptisms in 1806
[Baptisms at Newton-Heath-Chapel in the year 1806]

Jan	5	John s. Thomas & Mary Walmsley, farmer, Failsworth
"	5	Samuel s. John & Esther Schofield, weaver, Moston
"	19	Joseph s. William & Mary Pendleton, weaver, Failsworth
"	19	Philip s. Matthew & Sarah Arrandale (Andrew *struck through*) [Andrew], weaver, Droylsden
"	24	Nancy spu. d. Anne Goodyear [Goodier], Failsworth
"	26	Samuel s. Joseph & Mary Turner, slater, Newton
"	26	William spu. s. Mary Scholes, Stockport
Feb	2	Joseph s. John & Sarah Taylor, weaver, Failsworth
"	9	Edward s. George & Sarah Etchels, weaver, Failsworth
"	16	Anne d. William & Sarah Thorley, weaver, Failsworth
"	16	Matthew spu. s. Anne Barnes, Failsworth
"	16	Ellen spu. d. Betty Clare, Failsworth
"	16	Hannah spu. d. Anne Pollit, Failsworth
"	16	Andrew s. James & Martha Hulton, weaver, Failsworth
"	16	William s. William & Jane Butterworth, weaver, Failsworth
"	16	Joseph s. John & Anne Hulton, weaver, Failsworth
"	23	Elizabeth spu d. Hannah Smith, Failsworth
"	23	Thomas spu s. Martha Smith, Failsworth
"	23	Job s. William & Betty Goodyear [Goodier], weaver, Newton
Mar	2	Thomas s. William & Mary Tomlinson, weaver, Moston
"	2	Thomas s. William & Martha Cordingley, weaver, Failsworth
"	2	William s. John & Mary Robinson, weaver, Droylsden
"	2	Ashton s. William & Rebecca Worrall, farmer, Failsworth
"	9	William s. Jacob & Hannah Etchels, weaver, Newton
"	9	John s. Joseph & Mary Brown, weaver, Wood-houses A.P.
"	9	Peter s. John & Hannah Ford, weaver, Failsworth
"	16	John s. James & Mary Holt [Hall], weaver, Failsworth
"	16[9]	Levi s. William & Anne Whitehead, weaver, Failsworth
"	16	Maria d. Joshua & Alice Stott, manufacturer, Newton
"	16	William s. George & Margaret Hare, shoe maker, Failsworth
"	23	Elizabeth d. George & Elizabeth Staton, weaver, Newton
"	30	Anne d. Abraham & Martha Pollit, weaver, Failsworth
"	30	Anne d. James & Mary Gradwell, weaver, Failsworth
Apr	6	Henry s. James & Anne Thorp, weaver, Failsworth
"	6	Thomas s. William & Hannah Drinkwater, bricklayer, Newton
"	6	John s. Robert & Mary Ogden, weaver, Newton

"	6	James s. John & Anne Whitaker, weaver, Failsworth
"	13	Hannah d. William & Anne Thorniley [Thorley], weaver, Failsworth
"	13	John s. James & Mary Tetlow, farmer, Newton
"	13	Hannah d. Moses & Clarissa Gradwell, weaver, Newton
"	13	James s. John & Elizabeth Whitehead, weaver, Newton
"	20	George s. Joseph & Elizabeth Wrigley, weaver, Failsworth
"	20	Ellen d. George & Elizabeth Ripley, weaver, Moston
"	20	Samuel s. Samuel & Anne Pollit, weaver, Failsworth
"	27	Henry s. Thomas & Sarah Shepley, weaver, Failsworth
"	27	Hannah d. William & Anne Clarke, weaver, Newton
May	4	John s. Eli & Sarah Whiteley, weaver, Droylsden
"	4	Margaret d. John & Margaret Brown, gardener, Ashton Pari
"	11	Henry s. John & Anne Eckersley, weaver, Failsworth
"	11	Esther d. Edmund & Olive Schofield, weaver, Failsworth
"	18	Joseph s. Jonathan & Mary Hooley, Newton
Jun	1	Joseph s. Richard & Elizabeth Wilkinson, joiner, Hollinwood
"	1	Charles s. John & Anne Howarth, collier, Failsworth
"	1	James s. Joseph & Mary Schofield, weaver, Moston
"	8	James s. Peter & Jane [Ann] Ogden, weaver, Moston
"	8	Samuel s. John & Fanny Goodier, weaver, Hollinwood
"	15	Benjamin s. James & Sarah Ogden, weaver, Failsworth
"	15	William spu s. Mary Sharples, Failsworth
Jul	6	John s. William & Mary Brown, weaver, Manchester
"	6	Jane d. Thomas & Sarah Walmsley, farmer, Failsworth
"	6	John s. James & Betty Ogden, weaver, Failsworth
"	6	Joseph s. Josiah & Elizabeth Brown, weaver, Oldham
"	6	John s. Samuel & Mary Robinson, slater, Newton
"	6	James s. John & Elizabeth Barrington, tanner, Failsworth
"	6	Anne d. Ralph & Elizabeth Ramshaw, husbandman, Newton
"	6	William spu. s. Mary Horrocks, Failsworth
"	13	Sally d. Thomas & Mary Smith, weaver, Failsworth
"	20	Milley d. John & Lydia Marsden, labourer, Bradford
"	20	Samuel s. William & Mary Clayton, labourer, Failsworth
"	20	William spu. s. Elizabeth Barlow, Failsworth
"	27	Thomas s. John & Elizabeth Walker, weaver, Failsworth
"	27	Hannah d. James & Mary Smith, weaver, Failsworth
"	27	Elizabeth d. James & Margaret [Mary] Clough, weaver, Failsworth
Aug	3	Thomas s. Edmund & Alice Walmsley, joiner, Manchester
"	10	John s. William & Mary Lee, labourer, Droylsden
"	10	Mary d. James & Hannah Berry, blacksmith, Failsworth
"	10	Asshton s. Matthew & Sarah Brown, weaver, Newton
"	10	William s. James & Jane Pilkington, labourer, Failsworth
"	10	Frederick s. Luke & Ellen Etchels, weaver, Failsworth
"	17	Olive d. Thomas & Anne Collinson, weaver, Failsworth
"	24	Anne d. Charles & Anne Hall, bricklayer, Newton

"	24	Lucy d. Thomas & Susannah Etchels, weaver, Failsworth
"	24	James s. Samuel & Elizabeth Taylor, weaver, Failsworth
"	31	Mary d. John & Hannah Lees, weaver, Failsworth
Sep	7	William s. Samuel & Milley Simister, weaver, Failsworth
"	7	Mary d. John & Sarah Taylor, weaver, Failsworth
"	7	William s. Thomas & Frances Robinson, weaver, Newton
"	7	Jane d. Robert & Isabel Hulton, weaver, Failsworth
"	7	Joseph s. John & Esther Taylor, cordwainer, Failsworth
"	7	Robert s. William & Alice Taylor, weaver, Failsworth
"	7	James s. James & Elizabeth Bithell [Bythel], weaver, Droylsden
"	14	Maria d. John & Mary Stansfield, hatter, Newton
"	21	John s. Austin & Mary Chadwick, weaver, Newton
"	21	Hannah d. George & Mary Hibbert, cordwainer, Failsworth
"	28	Martha d. Richard & Anne Johnson, weaver, Ardwick
"	28	Edmund s. John & Anne Mills, farmer, Newton
"	28	Samuel s. Jonathan & Margaret Grimshaw, weaver, Droylsden
Oct	5	John Buckleton s. George & Elizabeth Robinson, slater, Newton
"	5	James s. Samuel & Ellen Clough, weaver, Failsworth
"	5	Joseph s. David & Hannah Hulton, weaver, Failsworth
"	5	Sarah d. John & Peggy Lees, weaver, Failsworth
"	5	William s. George & Elizabeth Parkinson, tanner, Failsworth
"	19	Phebe d. Robert & Elizabeth Clough, weaver, Failsworth
"	19	Betty d. Peter & Hannah Lomax, dyer, Newton
"	19	John spu s. Martha Etchels, Failsworth
"	19	John s. John & Ellen Davis, husbandman, Failsworth
"	19	Charlotte d. Samuel & Elizabeth Ogden, weaver, Newton
"	19	John s. Robert & Martha Rydings, weaver, Failsworth
"	26	Thomas s. George & Grace Howles, weaver, Newton
Nov	2	Mary d. Thomas & Sarah Chadwick, weaver, Newton
"	5	Robert s. Edward & Anne Eckersley, weaver, Failsworth
"	9	Mary d. James & Anne Ashton, weaver, Failsworth
"	16	William s. John & Mary Slater, manufacturer, Newton
"	16	Violet d. Ralph & Mary Bradley, husbandman, Failsworth
"	23	Hannah d. John & Mary Smith, weaver, Newton
"	23	Jane d. William & Catherine Gradwell, weaver, Failsworth
"	23	Anne d. Edward & Sarah Jackson, weaver, Newton
"	30	John s. James & Catherine Brown, weaver, Newton
"	30	Thomas s. Joseph & Anne Taylor, weaver, Failsworth
"	30	John s. Thomas & Elizabeth Berry, farmer, Gorton
Dec	7	John spu. s. Elizabeth Pollit, Failsworth
"	14	George s. Alexander & Elizabeth Telashen, weaver, Failsworth
"	14	John s. Joseph & Martha Booth, shop keeper, Failsworth
"	14	John s. William & Sarah Wood, weaver, Newton
"	14	Elizabeth spu d. Esther Taylor, Failsworth
"	14	Roger & Richard twin ss. Richard & Mary Richardson, weaver, Newton

"	14	Elizabeth d. Robert & Alice Barlow, weaver, Newton
"	21	James spu s. Sarah Smith, Failsworth
"	21	Elizabeth d. John & Grace Blackshaw, smith, Failsworth
"	21	Elizabeth d. George & Anne Brandon, smith, Newton
"	25	Mary d. Thomas & Margaret [Mary] Brown, weaver, Failsworth
"	25	Thomas s. Thomas & Mary Sidebottom, weaver, Moston
"	25	Elizabeth d. Joseph & Sarah Wylde, weaver, Failsworth
"	25	Thomas s. David & Anne Etchels, weaver, Failsworth
"	25	William s. John & Elizabeth Worsley, weaver, Newton
"	28	Catharine spu d. Mary Mather, Droylsden
"	28	Anne d. Launcelot & Mary Hulton, weaver, Failsworth
[		A. Ashworth Minister]
[		James Kenyon Joseph Bertenshaw William Brown John Moore Wardens]

Baptisms in 1807

[A true Copy of the Register at Newton Heath Chapel in the Parish of Manchester in the County
of Lancaster for the Year 1807]

Jan	4	Nancy d. Peter & Mary Wylde, waggoner, Newton
"	4	Mary d. John & Elizabeth Ashton, bricklayer, Moston
"	11	Edmund s. Thomas & Hannah Ogden, weaver, Failsworth
"	18	Ellen d. Thomas & Mary Schofield, weaver, Failsworth
"	18	Joseph s. John & Sarah Ogden, weaver, Moston
"	25	Jonathan s. George & Mary Lane, innholder, Failsworth
"	25	James s. John & Elizabeth Robinson, weaver, Woodhouses A.P.
"	25	John s. Joseph & Mary Potts, manufacturer, Newton
"	26	Sarah d. William & Sarah Walker, weaver, Newton
Feb	1	Olivia & Nancy twin ds. Philip & Esther Berry, shopkeeper, Newton (*separate entries in BT*)
"	1	Mary d. James & Anne Thornley, weaver, Failsworth
"	1	William s. John & Mary Daxon, labourer, Newton
"	8	Lucy d. Joseph & Mary Berry, weaver, Failsworth
"	8	Joseph s. John & Elizabeth Fletcher, weaver, Failsworth
"	8	Esther d. Joseph & Alice Berry, weaver, Failsworth
"	8	Joseph s. Joseph & Anne Fildes, farmer, Newton
"	8	Israel s. John & Elizabeth Clough, weaver, Failsworth
"	8	Thomas s. John & Sarah Walmsley, husbandman, Failsworth
"	8	Aaron s. Thomas & Mary Taylor, weaver, Moston
"	8	John s. Joseph & Sarah Rydings, weaver, Failsworth
"	11	James Richard s. Jeremiah & Martha Hopwood, weaver, Newton
"	15	Mary Anne d. David & Martha Mercey, shoe maker, Manchester
"	15	Sarah d. John & Anne Clough, weaver, Woodhouses A.P.
"	15	John s. William & Sarah Robinson, slater, Newton
"	15	Timothy s. John & Martha Etchels, weaver, Droylsden
"	22	Sarah d. Thomas & Anne Ryder, farmer, Moston

"	22	Anne d. Joseph & Jane Ogden, weaver, Failsworth	*(1807)*
"	22	Mary d. John & Sarah Ogden, weaver, Failsworth	
"	22	Anthony s. William & Elizabeth Aldred, weaver, Newton	
"	22	William s. James & Sarah Nuttall, dyer, Newton	
Mar	1	Jane d. Robert & Sarah Berry, carpenter, Manchester	
"	1	Jane d. Thomas & Anne Whittaker, bleacher, Newton	
"	1	Betty d. Jonathan & Ellen [Anne] Taylor, weaver, Moston	
"	1	Betty d. John & Sarah Berry, weaver, Failsworth	
"	1	John s. Thomas & Mary Howard, weaver, Failsworth	
"	15	Robert s. Thomas & Mary Walmsley, farmer, Failsworth	
"	19	John s. George & Mary Wolstenholme, weaver, Newton	
"	22	Edward s. Thomas & Mary Shaw, joiner, Failsworth	
"	22	Hannah d. Adam & Mary Dawson, dyer, Failsworth	
"	22	Luke s. James & Mary Etchels, weaver, Failsworth	
"	22	Joseph s. James & Jane Griffith, labourer, Woodhouses A.P.	
"	22	James spu s. Elizabeth Pendleton, Fa[i]lsworth	
"	29	Daniel s. George & Elizabeth Hulton, weaver, Failsworth	
"	29	Sally d. Joseph & Martha Ogden, shop keeper, Failsworth	
"	29	John s. Shadrack & Mary Ashton, collier, Droylsden	
"	29	Sarah d. John & Sarah Smith, weaver, Newton	
"	29	John s. William & Elinor Woolley, weaver, Newton	
"	29	Frances d. Samuel & Elizabeth NSN, collier, Droylsden	
"	31	Anne d. Joseph & Alice Hulme, weaver, Newton	
Apr	12	Joseph s. Samuel & Ellen Smith, weaver, Hollinwood	
"	12	Mary d. Thurstan & Mary Smethurst, weaver, Failsworth	
"	12	Alice d. Ralph & Jane Smethurst, weaver, Failsworth	
"	12	Robert s. John & Mary Wilson, weaver, Blackley	
"	12	Anne d. William & Mary Wallcroft, weaver, Newton	
"	17	Peter s. Peter & Rachel Nightingale, cotton dealer, Manchester, bo Jan 10 1807	
"	19	Dorcas d. Samuel & Hannah Worrall, weaver, Woodhouses A.P.	
"	19	Violet d. James & Sarah Clough, weaver, Failsworth	
"	19	Abraham spu s. Mary Wolstencroft, Failsworth	
"	21	James s. James & Hannah Timmins, wheelwright, Failsworth	
"	26	Elizabeth d. John & Sarah Whitehead, manufacturer, Failsworth	
"	26	Mary d. James & Sarah Swift, weaver, Failsworth	
"	26	Elizabeth d. Robert & Elizabeth Clegg, joiner, Failsworth	
"	29	Elizabeth d. John & Sarah Hilton, weaver, Newton, bo Mar 31	
May	3	Betty d. Andrew & Anne Clegg, joiner, Failsworth	
"	3	Anne d. Thomas Wroe & Anne Beswick, weaver, Failsworth	
"	3	Thomas s. Isaac & Ellen Beesley, printer, Failsworth	
"	10	Ellen d. Peter & Nancy Ferries, collier, Bradford	
"	10	Joshua s. Peter & Elizabeth Smith, weaver, Failsworth	
"	10	Anne d. Richard & Sarah Simister, weaver, Newton	
"	17	Jonathan s. John & Mary Whitaker, weaver, Failsworth	
"	17	Alice d. John & Jane Smith, farmer, Failsworth	

"	17	Mary d. Matthew & Jane Wyatt, weaver, Newton *(1807)*
"	17	James s. James & Phebe Hulme, weaver, Failsworth
"	17	Mary d. Abraham & Martha Whitehead, weaver, Little moss
"	17	Rosa d. James & Hannah Wilkinson, weaver, Failsworth
"	20	George s. Samuel & Mary Smith, engraver, Newton
"	20	Thomas s. John & Martha Hulme, bleacher, Droylsden
"	24	Sarah d. Thomas & Mary Ashworth, weaver, Newton
"	27	James s. John & Mary Billenge, hatter, Newton
"	27	Ellen d. Thomas & Mary Walmsley, smith, Failsworth
"	27	Joseph spu s. Jane Stott, Failsworth
"	31	William s. John & Sarah Dean, husbandman, Newton
Jun	2	Joseph s. Joseph & Mary Grimshaw, innholder, Failsworth
"	7	Anne spu d. Martha Kershaw, Failsworth
"	7	David spu s. Jane Whitehead, Moston
"	7	Joseph s. Edmund & Olivia Schofield, weaver, Failsworth
"	7	Mary d. Peter & Anne Fletcher, weaver, Failsworth
"	7	Hannah d. James & Phebe Smethurst, weaver, Failsworth
"	14	Joshua s. Joshua & Esther Brown, weaver, Moston
"	14	Milissa d. William & Alice Smith, weaver, Newton, bo Dec 9 1806
"	21	Robert s. Robert & Elizabeth Hall, weaver, Newton, bo Apr 22
"	21	Elizabeth d. John & Hannah Williamson, boatswain, Cutler hill
"	21	Josephus s. Benjamin & Violet Hulton, weaver, Failsworth
"	21	Mary spu d. Agnes Hulton, Failsworth
"	21	Hannah d. John & Sarah Taylor, weaver, Failsworth
"	21	William s. John & Ellen Plant, calenderer, Newton
"	21	James s. John & Betty Whitehead, weaver, Moston
"	28	Betty d. John & Hannah Wright, weaver, Failsworth
"	28	Mary d. Joseph & Elizabeth Ogden, weaver, Failsworth
Jul	5	John s. Richard & Anne Pollit, weaver, Failsworth
"	5	Martha d. William & Jane Barrow, innholder, Failsworth
"	5	Ellen d. Roger & Ellen Leather, weaver, Newton
"	12	Elizabeth d. Miles & Elizabeth Slater, weaver, Failsworth
"	19	Aaron s. John & Alice Hall, carpenter, Failsworth
"	19	Jane d. Thomas & Betty Tetlow, weaver, Gorton
"	26	John s. George & Anne Travis, weaver, Newton
"	26	Anne d. Joseph & Elizabeth Seel, printer, Newton
"	26	Luke s. Thomas & Mary Clegg, joiner, Failsworth
Aug	2	William s. Richard & Hannah Gorton, weaver, Failsworth
"	2	William s. Jonathan & Mary Schofield, weaver, Moston
"	2	Mary Anne d. James & Alice Wild, weaver, Newton
"	9	Betty d. Samuel & Phebe Clough, weaver, Failsworth
"	16	Nancy d. Samuel & Martha Clough, weaver, Failsworth
"	16	Henry s. Joseph & Martha Clough, weaver, Failsworth
"	16	Ralph s. Samuel & Jane Mather, weaver, Newton
"	19	James s. James & Mary Clegg, joiner, Ashton

"	23	James s. Thomas & Anne Fletcher, weaver, Failsworth, bo Nov 19 1797
"	23	John s. James & Lucy Greaves, weaver, Failsworth
"	23	John s. William & Mary Bentley, printer, Failsworth
"	23	Rachel d. Robert & Frances Mills, dyer, Ashton
"	23	Mary d. William & Sarah Sudworth, collier, Manchester
"	23	Benjamin s. John & Betty Whitaker, weaver, Failsworth
"	30	John s. Thomas & Mary Dawson, dyer, Newton, bo Jun 27
Sep	6	John spu s. Jenny Smith, Failsworth
"	6	Betty d. Thomas & Milley Heald, weaver, Failsworth
"	13	Elizabeth d. John & Martha Kershaw, weaver, Failsworth
"	13	Joseph s. William & Mary Wilde, weaver, Droylsden
"	13	John spu s. Anne Wroe, Failsworth
"	20	John s. John & Mary Thorley, weaver, Failsworth
"	20	Edwin & Emma s. & d. Thomas & Barbara Hughes, innholder, Newton, bo Sep 5 (twins *entered in margin; separate entries in BT*)
"	27	Thomas s. Thomas & Alice Hulton, farmer, Moston
"	27	Joseph s. George & Alice Smith, weaver, Failsworth
"	27	Sarah d. James & Margaret Crossley, labourer, Harpurhey
Oct	4	Joseph s. Ratcliffe & Sarah Potts, weaver, Newton
"	4	Edmund s. Thomas & Sarah Gorton, joiner, Failsworth
"	4	John s. Francis & Martha Brown, farmer, Woodhouses A.P.
"	11	Joel s. Samuel & Anne Pollit, weaver, Failsworth
"	11	Maria d. Abraham & Betty Mather, weaver, Droylsden
"	11	Mary d. Edmund & Anne Unsworth, weaver, Moston
"	18	Benjamin s. John & Mary Brierley, weaver, Failsworth
"	18	Lavinia d. James & Nancy Rydings, weaver, Failsworth
"	18	Mary spu. d. Martha Ashton, Failsworth
"	18	Sally d. Joseph & Elizabeth Taylor, weaver, Failsworth
Nov	1	Betty d. John & Sarah Lees, hostler, Newton
"	1	Solomon s. Robert & Anne Rydings, weaver, Failsworth
"	1	William s. Matthew & Nancy Gradwell, weaver, Failsworth
"	8	Jane d. Joshua & Elizabeth Swift, weaver, Newton
"	8	Thomas s. Samuel & Mary Moore, weaver, Moston
"	15	Mary d. John & Anne Hulton, weaver, Failsworth
"	15	James sp s. Mary Moors, weaver, Manchester
"	22	Sarah d. Joseph & Annis [Agnes] Slater, weaver, Failsworth
"	22	Hannah d. Robt. & Elizabeth Ogden, small ware weaver, Newton
"	29	Hannah d. George & Elizabeth Parkinson, tanner, Failsworth
"	29	Betty d. Saml. & Sarah Berry, weaver, Failsworth
"	29	Hannah d. Willm. & Anne Ratcliffe, weaver, Newton
Dec	6	Margaret d. Thos. & Elizth. Nuttall, bleacher, Newton
"	20	Benjamin s. George & Margt. Hare, shoe-maker, Failsworth
"	21	Robert s. Joseph & Mary Tinker, weaver, Moston
"	21	Jenny d. John & Mary Anderton, weaver, Moston
"	25	Maria d. John & Betty Whitehead, weaver, Newton

"	27	Betty d. Saml. & Anne Etchels, weaver, Failsworth
"	27	Anne sp d. Hannah Etchels, weaver, Failsworth
"	27	William s. Luke & Hannah Etchels, weaver, Failsworth
"	27	Mary d. Thos. & Mary Worsley, weaver, Moston
"	29	Robert sp s. Jane Whitaker, Manchester
"	29	Mary d. John & Lydia Marsden, labourer, Bradford (*entry struck through; see next entry*)

Baptisms in 1808
[Baptisms at Newton Heath Chapel in 1808]

Jan	3	Mary d. John & Lydia Marsden, labourer, Bradford (*see previous entry*)
"	3	Benjamin s. Thos. & Sarah Walmsley, farmer, Failsworth
"	17	Lucy d. John & Alice Williamson, weaver, Failsworth
"	24	Nancy d. James & Betty Wild [Wyld], weaver, Droylsden
"	24	John s. Charles & Hannah Heywood, weaver, Newton
"	27	Nancy d. John & Mary Etchels, weaver, Droylsden
"	31	Joseph spu s. Betty Schofield, Failsworth
"	31	Jane d. James & Jane Allen, weaver, Newton
Feb	7	Joel sp s. Anne Knowles, Failsworth
"	7	Isaiah s. James & Martha Hulton, weaver, Failsworth
"	7	Henry s. James & Anne Kershaw, weaver, Newton
"	7	Sarah d. John & Anne Hulton, weaver, Failsworth
"	14	Henry s. Saml. & Mary Robinson, slater, Newton
"	14	William s. James & Margt. Makin, weaver, Newton
"	14	Joseph s. Jacob & Hannah Etchels, weaver, Newton
"	14	Sally sp d. Mary Cheetham, weaver, Failsworth
"	14	Frances d. James & Frances Clough, husbandman, Newton
"	14	Esther d. Robt. & Mary Hulme, bleacher, Droylsden
"	21	Lucy d. John & Betty Tarvin, husbandman, Newton
"	28	Joseph s. John & Elizabeth Stott, manufacturer, Failsworth
"	28	Samuel s. Thos. & Elizth. Wild, weaver, Failsworth
"	28	Thomas s. Joseph & Mary Horrocks, labourer, Failsworth
"	28	Edmund s. Richd. & Jane Travis, weaver, Newton
"	28	Hannah d. John & Anne Whitaker, weaver, Failsworth
Mar	6	Sarah d. Christopher & Sarah Miller, husbandman, Newton
"	10	Sally d. Richd. & Hannah Barrow, manufacturer, Failsworth
"	13	John sp s. Betty Walmsley, Failsworth
"	13	Maria d. John & Mary Hulton, weaver, Failsworth
"	13	Edward s. James & Mary Tetlow, farmer, Newton
"	20	Betty d. Sampson & Alice Farrand, weaver, Newton
"	27	Charles s. John & Mary Thorniley, weaver, Failsworth
"	27	Anne d. Joseph & Mary Stott, weaver, Failsworth
"	31	James s. Willm. & Alice Lane, innkeeper, Manchester
Apr	3	John s. Robt. & Alice Whitehead, weaver, Wood houses Ashton Parish

"	3	Sally sp d. Mary Taylor, Failsworth	*(1808)*
"	3	Ellen d. Abrm. & Martha Pollit, weaver, Failsworth	
"	10	Joseph s. John & Mary Simister, weaver, Failsworth	
"	17	Joseph s. Aaron & Hannah Gradwell, weaver, Newton	
"	17	Elizabeth (sp *not in BT*) d. Alice Dunkerley, Failsworth	
"	17	Hannah d. Robt. & Betty Wright, weaver, Failsworth	
"	17	Mary d. John & Mary Thorp, weaver, Moston	
"	17	Elizabeth d. John & Mary Thorp, weaver, Moston	
"	17	Maria d. Willm. & Maria Hamner, husbandman, Failsworth	
"	17	Mary d. James & Elizth. Birch; weaver, Newton	
"	17	Joseph s. Robt. & Martha Hulton, weaver, Failsworth	
"	17	Mary d. Jas. & Margt. Clough, weaver, Failsworth	
"	24	Sarah d. James & Sarah Wilson, weaver, Moston	
"	25	Esther d. Nicholas & Jane Simister, weaver, Newton	
"	27	Andrew s. George & Sarah Etchels, weaver, Failsworth	
May	1	Sarah d. Willm. & Mary Pendleton, weaver, Failsworth	
"	1	Horatio s. Willm. & Sarah Harrison, weaver, Moston	
"	1	Mary d. James & Martha Wylde, farmer, Newton	
"	8	Thomas s. Joseph & Mary Brown, weaver, Failsworth	
"	8	Isabel Anne d. John & Betty Worsley, weaver, Newton	
"	8	Mary d. Thos. & Elizth. Berry, farmer, Gorton	
"	8	John s. David & Betty Ogden, weaver, Failsworth	
"	8	Matty d. James & Mary Wright, weaver, Failsworth	
"	8	William s. Henry & Elizth. Pearpoint, gardener, Waterside A.P.	
"	15	James s. John & Elizth. Walker, weaver, Failsworth	
"	15	Hannah sp d. Martha Barlow, Failsworth	
"	15	James s. Jas. & Jane Schofield, weaver, Failsworth	
"	22	Thomas s. Ashton & Mary Shepley, manufacturer, Newton	
"	22	Joseph s. Saml. & Mary Holland, weaver, Failsworth	
"	22	George s. Henry & Mary Holland, weaver, Failsworth	
"	24	Catharine d. David & Elizth. Hudson, millwright, Newton	
"	29	Judith d. John & Anne Dean, farmer, Newton	
"	29	Henry s. John & Sarah Sommers, lock keeper, Newton	
"	29	Elizabeth d. Danl. & Mary Whitehead, weaver, Newton	
"	29	Elizabeth d. Joseph & Mary Berry, weaver, Failsworth	
"	31	Elizabeth d. Thos. & Peggy Wright, smith, Failsworth	
Jun	12	Edward s. Thos. & Mary Brown, weaver, Newton	
"	12	Joseph s. James & Jane Pilkington, husbandman, Failsworth	
"	13	John sp s. Anne Pollit, Failsworth	
"	19	Richard s. Richd. & Mary Walker, weaver, Newton	
"	19	Hannah d. James & Hannah Berry, smith, Failsworth	
"	23	Nancy d. John & Mary Stansfield, hatter, Newton	
"	26	Anne d. James & Mary Smith, weaver, Failsworth	
"	26	Sarah d. Joseph & Mary Wild, weaver, Droylsden	
Jul	10	Ophelia d. James & Anne Thorp, weaver, Failsworth	

"	10	Jeremiah s. James & Martha Kemp, weaver, Manchester	(*1808*)
"	17	Robert s. Thos. & Sarah Wyatt, weaver, Failsworth	
"	17	Benjamin s. Saml. & Ellen Clough, weaver, Failsworth	
"	17	Jane d. Saml. & Hannah Barritt, farmer, Droylsden	
"	18	Mary d. Thos. & Martha Hooley, bleacher, Newton	
"	18	Harriett sp d. Anne Dunkerley, Failsworth	
"	24	Jane d. John & Margt. Lees, weaver, Failsworth	
"	24	Hannah d. David & Anne Etchels, weaver, Failsworth	
"	24	Jonathan s. Joshua & Alice Stott, weaver, Failsworth	
"	24	Mary d. Saml. & Betty Taylor, weaver, Failsworth	
"	24	Samuel s. Nathl. & Betty Taylor, weaver, Failsworth	
"	24	Samuel s. Thos. & Mary Smith, weaver, Failsworth	
"	30	Sally d. Jas. & Mary Gradwell, weaver, Failsworth	
"	31	John sp s. Anne Chadderton, Failsworth	
"	31	Mary d. Ralph & Mary Bradley, husbandman, Failsworth	
"	31	Hannah d. Thos. & Elizth. Knott, weaver, Newton	
Aug	7	David s. Jonathn. & Mary Hooley, brewer, Newton	
"	7	Hannah d. Josiah & Elizth. Brown, weaver, Hollinwood	
"	14	Margaret Mary d. George & Margt. [Mary] Sykes, manufacturer, Manchester, bo Aug 15 1801	
"	14	Mary Chorlton d. George & Margt. [Mary] Sykes, manufacturer, Manchester, bo Apr 27 1804	
"	14	Elizabeth Smyth d. George & Margt. [Mary] Sykes, manufacturer, Mancheser, bo Nov 3 1805	
"	14	Lucinda Forster d. George & Margt. [Mary] Sykes, manufacturer, Manchester, bo Apr 26 1807	
"	14	William Forster s. George & Margt. [Mary] Sykes, manufacturer, Manchester, bo Jul 17 1808	
"	14	Alice d. Jas. & Alice Ogden, weaver, Failsworth	
"	14	Maria d. Thos. & Susannah Etchels, weaver, Failsworth	
"	14	Mary Anne d. Ralph & Jane Smethurst, weaver, Hollinwood	
"	19	John s. Saml. & Jane Rydings, weaver, Failsworth	
"	21	Charles s. Dan & Hannah Hulton, weaver, Failsworth	
"	21	Ruth d. Jonathan & Anne Clough, weaver, Newton	
"	21	Anne d. Jonat[ha]n & Esther Etchels, weaver, Failsworth	
"	21	John s. James & Anne Howarth, labourer, Failsworth	
"	21	Tabitha d. Joseph & Sarah Rydings, weaver, Failsworth	
"	21	James s. Thos. & Anne Dunkerley, weaver, Failsworth	
"	23	Mary Anne d. Willm. & Sarah Walker, weaver, Newton	
"	28	Anne d. Jonathan & Peggy Grimshaw, weaver, Drysden, bo Jul 17	
Sep	10	Alice d. Joseph & Alice Taylor, printer, Newton	
"	11	Betty d. Robt. & Betty Whitehead, weaver, Failsworth	
"	18	William s. James & Elizth. Whitehead, weaver, Newton, bo Jul 1(?)	
"	18	Anne d. Willm. & Elizth. Pickles, shoe maker, Failsworth	
"	19	Thomas s. George & Elizth. Prince, warehouseman, Newton	

"	26	Anne d. Jonathan & Hannah Glossop, weaver, Failsworth
Oct	7	Richard s. Thos. & Mary Prenton, sawyer, Failsworth
"	9	James s. Joseph & Martha Booth, shopkeeper, Failsworth, bo Sep 5
"	24	Samuel sp s. Mary Newton, Failsworth
"	30	Thomas s. Joseph & Anne Fildes, farmer, Newton
"	30	Hannah d. Matthew & Sarah Brown, weaver, Newton
"	30	Esther d. John & Betty Robinson, weaver, Woodhouses Ash par
"	30	Mary d. John & Sarah Walmsley, labourer, Failsworth
"	30	Thomas s. Austin & Mary Chadwick, weaver, Newton
"	30	Samuel s. George & Grace Howles, weaver, Newton
Nov	6	Ann d. John & Jane Turner, weaver, Openshaw
"	6	Mary d. Joseph & Betty Wrigley, weaver, Failsworth
"	6	Mary d. William & Martha Cordhingley, weaver, Failsworth
"	6	Jane d. James & Betty Bythell [Bithell], weaver, Droylsden
"	15	William s. James & Mary Etchels, weaver, Failsworth
"	15	Nancy d. Thos. & Betty Barlow, weaver, Failsworth
Dec	25	John s. Matthew & Jane Wyatt, weaver, Newton
"	25	Hannah d. Jos'h [Joseph] & Sarah Rogers, weaver, Newton
"	25	Hannah d. John & Sarah Tetlow, warehouseman, Newton
[		A true Copy from the Register of Newton Chapel from Jany 3rd to Dec 25th 1808 both inclusive.

R.A. Singleton Curate

William Brown Jos'h Bertenshaw John Moore   ]

1809
[Baptisms at Newton Heath Chapel in 1809]

Jan	1	Edmund s. Will. & Mary Wallcroft, weaver, Newton
"	16	Samuel s. John & Mary Smith, weaver, Newton
"	16	Peter s. Peter & Mary Wild [Wyld], waggoner, Newton
"	16	Richard s. Moses & Clarissa Gradwell, weaver, Newton
"	22	Martha d. Robert & Betty Clough, weaver, Failsworth
"	29	Harriot d. William & Elizah. Hibbert, weaver, Failsworth
"	29	Elizabeth d. Alice Clough (, single woman *not in BT*), weaver, Failsworth (*surname struck through in PR*)
"	29	Sarah d. Joseph & Ann Taylor, weaver, Failsworth
"	29	Elizabeth d. Thomas & Jane Taylor, weaver, Failsworth
"	30	John s. Edmd. & Olivia Scholfield, weaver, Failsworth
Feb	5	Andrew s. Andrew & Hannah Clegg, joiner etc, Failsworth
"	9	Jane d. Thos. & Jane Moores, weaver, Manchester
"	19	Abraham s. Joseph & Martha Ogden, shopkeeper, Failsworth
"	19	James Booth s. Elizabeth Pendleton, single woman, Failsworth
"	26	Abraham s. Abraham & Mary Briscoe, innkeeper, Newton
Mar	5	Sarah d. Thomas & Mary Walmsley, farmer, Failsworth
"	26	George s. George & Elizabeth Parkinson, tanner, Failsworth

"	26	Isaiah Robinson s. George & Elizabeth Robinson, slater, Newton
"	26	Philip s. Thomas & Mary Houlton, hatter, Manchester
"	29	Mary d. George & Elizabeth Hilton, weaver, Failsworth
Apr	2	Andrew s. George & Mary Lane, innkeeper, Failsworth
"	2	Elizabeth d. Mary Kershaw, singlewoman, Failsworth
"	23	Robert Ogden s. John & Sarah Ogden, weaver, Failsworth
"	23	Mary d. John & Sarah Taylor, weaver, Failsworth
"	23	Ann d. John & Mary Whittaker, weaver, Failsworth
"	23	Joseph s. Joseph & Alice Hulme, weaver, Newton
May	8	Robert s. Robert & (*blank in PR & BT*) Whitehead, weaver, Failsworth
"	8	Elizabeth d. William & Ann Thorneley, weaver, Failsworth
"	8	Mary d. Ino. [John] & Grace Blackshaw, blacksmith, Failsworth
"	8	James s. Geoe. & Mary Hibbert, cordwainer, Failsworth
"	8	Mary d. Ino. [John] & Sarah Whitehead, manufacturer, Failsworth
"	10	Elizabeth d. Willm. & Alice Taylor, weaver, Failsworth
"	10	John s. Ino. [John] & Esther Moreton, book-keeper, Manchester
"	10	Elizabeth d. Jos'h & Alice Berry, weaver, Failsworth
		(*BT faded for the next two entries, which cannot therefore be fully verified.*)
"	14	Alice d. James & Phebe Hulme, weaver, Failsworth
"	19	Hannah d. Willm. & Elizabeth Goodier, weaver, Newton
"	24	Ellis s. Thos. & Ann Whittaker, husbandman, Newton
Jun	4	John s. Thos. & Mary Ashworth, weaver, Newton
"	4	Samuel s. Saml. & Eliza. Hyde, labourer, Bradford
"	4	Ralph s. John & Sarah Ogden, weaver, Newton
"	23	Lucy d. Elizah. Worsley, singlewoman, Newton
"	25	Sarah d. Wm. & Mary Clayton, husbandman, Failsworth
"	25	Joseph s. Geo. & Mary Tomlinson, weaver, Failsworth
Jul	2	Susanah d. James & Martha Wylde, husbandman, Newton
"	2	James s. Peter & Hanah Lomas, dyer, Newton
"	2	Sarah d. Luke & Ellen Etchels, weaver, Failsworth
"	16	Mary d. Richd. & Ann Kenyon, calico printer, Failsworth
"	23	Susannah d. John & Mary Whitehead, inn-keeper, Newton
"	30	Joshua s. Joseph & Sarah Ogden, school master, Newton
"	30	Samuel s. Aaron & Hannah Gradwell, weaver, Newton
"	30	Martha d. John & Hannah Wright, weaver, Failsworth
"	31	Esther d. Esther Whitehead, single, weaver, Failsworth
Aug	6	Ann d. Elias & Sarah Whiteley, weaver, Droylsden
"	8	Joseph s. Robt. & Alice Barlow, crofter, Newton
"	13	Joseph s. Geoe. & Elizah. Hardy, weaver, Failsworth
"	13	Mary d. Jos'h & Martha Clough, weaver, Woodhouses, Ashton
"	13	William s. Willm. & Hannah Drinkwater, bricklayer, Newton
"	27	Joseph s. Joseph & Mary Grimshaw, publican, Failsworth
Sep	6	Luke s. James & Martha Swift, weaver, Failsworth
"	26	Eliza d. Abrahm. & Mary Taylor, weaver, Failsworth
"	26	James s. Richd. & Sarah Simister, weaver, Newton

"	26	Sarah d. John & Martha Kershaw, weaver, Failsworth
Oct	9	James s. Will. & Elizabeth Booth, hatter, Newton
"	17	Mary d. John & Ann Mills, farmer, Newton
"	17	Absalom s. Benjn. & Violet Hilton, weaver, Failsworth
"	19	George s. Geoe. & Elizah. Taylor, weaver, Droylsden
"	20	Alice d. Benn. & Mary Lees, weaver, Failsworth
"	22	Ann d. Isaac & Ellen Beezely, farmer, Failsworth
"	30	John s. John & Betty Smith, husbandman, Failsworth
Nov	5	Elizabeth d. Joseph & Elizah. Taylor, weaver, Failsworth
"	5	Ann d. Will. & Mary Bentley, calico-printer, Newton
"	5	Mary Ann d. Sarah Brierly (, single-woman *not in BT*), Failsworth
"	19	Joseph s. Abrahm. & Martha Whitehead, weaver, Moston
"	19	Edward s. Ashton & Mary Shepley, manufacturer, Newton
Dec	6	Hannah d. Ann Stott (, singlewoman *not in BT*), Newton
"	10	Thomas s. Thos. & Elizabeth Smith, labourer, Newton
"	10	Robert s. James & Martha Butterworth, weaver, Failsworth
"	24	William s. Robt. & Elizah. Hall, small ware weaver, Newton
"	24	Henry s. William & Jenny Barrow, inn-keeper, Failsworth
"	24	Lucy d. Jos'h & Elizah. Seel, calico printer, Newton
"	29	Thomas s. Edwd. & Ann Eckersley, weaver, Failsworth

[A Copy of all the Baptisms from The Baptism: at Register of the Chapel of Newton in the Parish of Manchester, in the County of Lancaster, & in the Diocese of Chester, from the 1. Januy. 1809 to the 29th Decr. 1809 both inclusive.   ]

[R.A. Singleton Curate   ]

[John Stott Warden   John Moore   Joseph Bertenshaw   William Brown   ]

Janry. 1810
[Baptisms at Newton Heath Chapel 1810]

Jan	7	Mary Anne d. Jno. [John] & Elizah. Stott, manufacturer, Failsworth
"	17	Jane d. Thos. & Isabella Smith, print-cutter, Newton
"	21	Benjamin s. Jno. [John] & Esther Taylor, shoe-maker, Failsworth
"	21	Elizabeth d. Jno. [John] & Mary Hooley, hatter, Newton
"	21	James s. Jno. [John] & Alice Hall, carpenter, Failsworth
"	28	Helen d. Chas. & Hannah Heywood, weaver, Newton
"	28	William s. Edwd. & Sarah Jackson, small-ware weaver, Manchester
Feb	11	Mary d. Robt. & Frances Mills, dyer, Ashton
"	12	Hannah d. John & Mary Smith, weaver, Newton
"	12	Simeon s. Samuel & Ann Pollit, weaver, Failsworth
"	12	Isaiah s. Geo. & Sarah Etchels, weaver, Failsworth
"	13	Thomas s. Saml. & Martha Berry, weaver, Newton
"	18	Robert s. Jonan. & Betty Partington, weaver, Alkrington
"	21	Elizabeth d. John & Alice Haycock, calico-printer, Newton
"	21	Mary d. Robt. & Alice Whitehead, weaver, Woodhouses
Mar	5	Ralph s. Thurston & Mary Smethurst, weaver, Failsworth

"	16	Martha d. Thos. & Hannah Ogden, weaver, Failsworth
"	25	Hushaiah d. William & Maria Hamner, farmer, Failsworth
"	25	Susannah d. William & Betty Aldred, weaver, Newton
Apr	1	Maria d. Luke & Hannah Etchells, weaver, Failsworth
"	2	Jane d. Philip & Jane Smith, farmer, Failsworth
"	2	Ellen d. Joseph & Mary Berry, weaver, Failsworth
"	2	Josep[h] s. William & Mary Hampson, weaver, Newton
"	8	John s. John & Jane Smith, weaver, Failsworth
"	8	Maria d. Joseph & Sarah Dyson, calico-printer, Droylsden
"	9	James s. Nicholas & Jane Simmester, weaver, Failsworth
"	11	Mary d. William & Mary Daltry, weaver, Newton
"	13	John s. John & Mary Hulton, weaver, Failsworth
"	22	John s. John & Mary Brierley, weaver, Failsworth
"	22	Elizabeth d. David & Ann Etchels, weaver, Failsworth
"	22	Samuel s. Thos. & Amelia Heald, crofter, Newton
"	22	Jane d. John & Sarah Hilton, weaver, Newton
"	22	Mary d. John & Mary Tetlow, weaver, Newton
"	22	Helen d. Geoe. & Mary Wolstenholme, weaver, Newton
"	22	William s. Jas. & Elizabeth Tetlow, warper, Failsworth
"	24	John s. Hannah Bardsley, singlewon., Failsworth
"	24	Ann d. Richd. & Ann Pollit, weaver, Failsworth
"	24	Olive d. Mary Fildes, singlewon, Failsworth
"	25	Anne d. James & Hannah Timmis, wheelwright, Failsworth
"	25	John s. Saml. & Helen Clough, weaver, Failsworth
"	29	Samuel s. James & Mary Tetlow, farmer, Newton
"	30	Charles s. William & Jane Allen, weaver, Failsworth
"	30	James Sykes s. John & Mary Thorley, weaver, Failsworth
May	21	Edmund s. James & Mary Simister, labourer, Newton
"	22	Moses s. Thos. & Elizabeth Berry, farmer, Gorton
"	27	Wilson s. James & Sarah Wilson, weaver, Moston
"	27	James s. Jacob & Hannah Etchels, weaver, Newton
Jun	11	Martha d. Henry & Mary Holland, weaver, Newton
"	11	Sarah d. Nathl. & Betty Taylor, weaver, Failsworth
"	17	Jonathan s. John & Elizah. Whitehead, weaver, Newton
"	17	Matthew s. Matthew & Nanny Gradwell, weaver, Failsworth
"	17	Anne d. Samuel & Jenny Wild, weaver, Failsworth
"	19	Hannah d. Martha Etchels, wdw. the late Jonathan Etchels, Failsworth
Jul	15	Martha d. James & Nanny Kershaw, weaver, Manchester
"	22	Mary d. Peter & the late Mary Wild, husbandman, Newton
"	24	Sally d. Thos. Wyat & Sally, weaver, Failsworth
"	24	Martha d. David & Betty Ogden, weaver, Failsworth
"	24	Richard s. Josiah & Elizabeth Brown, weaver, Hollinwood
"	27	Ellen d. John & Ellen Berry, weaver, Failsworth
"	27	Elizabeth d. John & Alice Dawson, cordwainer, Moston
Aug	5	Sarah d. Elizabeth Ashton, singlewoman, Failsworth

Jul	31	Omitted Thomas s. Thomas & Olivia Scholfield, weaver, Failsworth (*order correct in BT*)
Aug	24	Jonathan s. John & Ann Hilton, weaver, Failsworth
"	24	Esther d. Daniel & Sarah Whitehead, weaver, Failsworth
Sep	2	Daniel s. James & Martha Wilde, weaver, Newton
"	2	Jeremiah s. Peter & Hannah Lomax, dyer, Newton
"	5	Mary d. Joseph & Sally Ridings, weaver, Failsworth
"	6	James s. Abraham & Martha Pollitt, weaver, Failsworth
"	9	Sarah d. Thomas & Martha Hooley, crofter, Newton
"	9	Joseph s. John & Helen Plant, calenderer, Newton
"	16	John s. George & Elizah. Parkinson, tanner, Failsworth
"	16	Phebe d. James & Phebe Smethurst, weaver, Failsworth
"	16	Hannah d. William & Phebe Gradwell, weaver, Newton
"	26	John Dixon s. Sebastian & Sarah Nash, bo 3 Jan 1807, Failsworth
Oct	8	Eliza d. William & Elizabeth Hibbert, weaver, Failsworth
"	24	Francis s. Joseph & Mary Brown, weaver, Failsworth
Nov	18	Anne d. Richard & Jane Travis, weaver, Newton
"	18	Thomas s. Esther Haddock, singlewoman, Failsworth
"	18	Anne d. James & Jane Allen, weaver, Newton
"	18	Sarah d. Elizabeth Diggles, singlewoman, Newton
"	25	Nancy d. John & Ann Whittaker, weaver, Failsworth
Dec	2	Mary d. Meshec & Betty Ashton, collier, Droylsden
"	23	Elizabeth d. William & Mary Pendleton, weaver, Failsworth
"	23	William s. John & Jane Turner, weaver, Openshaw
[		A true Copy of the Baptismal Register of Newton Chapel in the Parish of Manchester & Diocese of Chester for the year 1810. R.A. Singleton Curate Joseph Bertenshaw William Brown Thos Hulton Wardens]

Janry. 1811
(*edge of BT faded; dates cannot be verified upto May 24*)

Jan	9	Thomas s. Thomas & Jane Smith, weaver, Failsworth
"	9	Martha d. Martha Hilton, single-woman, Failsworth
Feb	5	Jane d. Thomas & Mary Walmsley, farmer, Failsworth
Mar	1	Anne d. Thomas & Hannah Allen, weaver, Failsworth
"	12	Richard [spu.] s. Betty Walmsley (, singlewoman *not in BT*), Failsworth
"	12	Elizabeth d. Thomas & Betty Wilde, weaver, Failsworth
"	12	Anne d. Mary Geofrey (, singlewoman *not in BT*), Oldham
"	21	Samuel s. Joseph & Mary Grimshaw, inn-keeper, Failsworth
"	21	Sally d. John & Anne Clough, weaver, Failsworth
"	24	Mark s. George & Grace Howles, weaver, Newton
"	24	Esther d. John & Esther Moreton, book-keeper, Manchester
"	24	John s. William & Jane Barrow, inn-keeper, Failsworth
"	24	Hellen [Helena] d. Thomas & Peggy Wright, blacksmith, Failsworth

"	24	Mary d. James & Betty Ogden, weaver, Failsworth
"	24	Elizabeth d. Joseph & Anne Taylor, weaver, Failsworth (*BT faded; entry cannot be verified*)
Apr	12	Elijah s. Philip & Sarah Scho(r)field, weaver, Droylsden
"	12	Lois d. Philip & Sarah Scho(r)field, weaver, Droylsden
"	14	Sidney s. James & Mary Smith, weaver, Failsworth
"	14	Margaret d. Joshua & Alice Stott, weaver, Failsworth
"	14	Nancy d. Robert & Elizabeth Whitehead, weaver, Failsworth
"	14	Charles s. George & Betty Hilton, weaver, Failsworth
"	14	Samuel s. Robert & Betty Clough, weaver, Failsworth
"	14	Richard s. James & Mary Gradwell, weaver, Failsworth
"	14	Elizabeth [spu.] d. Mary Gradwell (, single-woman *not in BT*), Failsworth
"	14	William s. John & Elizabeth Butterworth, weaver, Newton
"	25	Rolando s. Thomas & Alice Collinson, weaver, Failsworth
"	28	Thomas s. James & Martha Hulton, weaver, Failsworth
"	28	Thomas s. Matthew & Sarah Brown, weaver, Newton
"	30	John s. John & Sarah Taylor, weaver, Failsworth
"	30	Anne d. Thomas & Mary Thorp, weaver, Failsworth
May	15	Elizabeth d. Joseph & Sarah Rogers, weaver, Failsworth
"	23	George s. Ratcliffe & Sarah Potts, weaver, Newton
"	26	Thomas s. John & Martha Turner, weaver, Failsworth
"	26	Hannah d. George & Elizabeth Prince, warehouseman, Newton
"	26	John s. Thomas & Hannah Dunkerley, weaver, Failsworth
"	26	Anne d. Samuel & Milly Simister, weaver, Failsworth
"	26	Jane d. John & Jane Smith, husbandman, Failsworth
"	26	Mary d. Peter & Betty Smith, weaver, Failsworth
"	26	Ralph s. Ralph & Mary Bradley, husbandman, Failsworth
Jun	2	Thomas s. James & Alice Ogden, weaver, Failsworth
"	2	Richard s. Ralph & Jane Smethurst, weaver, Hollinwood
"	2	John s. Thomas & Jane Taylor, weaver, Failsworth
"	2	William s. Thomas & Nancy Chatterton, weaver, Failsworth
"	2	Martha d. John & Elizabeth Whittaker, weaver, Failsworth
"	10	Esther d. Will. [John] & Ann Thornley, weaver, Failsworth
"	10	Hannah d. John & Mary Simister, weaver, Failsworth
"	23	Esther d. John & Grace Blackshaw, blacksmith, Failsworth
"	23	Joseph s. Joseph & Martha Ogden, shop-keeper, Failsworth
"	23	Enoch s. William & Sarah Robinson, slater, Newton
"	23	Garside s. Moses & Clarissa Gradwell, weaver, Newton
"	30	Hellen d. John & Mary Whittaker, weaver, Failsworth
"	30	Alice d. David & Anne Etchells, weaver, Failsworth
"	30	Mary d. John & Sarah Walmsley, labourer, Failsworth
"	30	Betty d. Samuel & Mary Ogden, weaver, Failsworth
"	30	Nancy d. Samuel & Jane Mather, weaver, Newton
Jul	28	Helen[a] d. Robert & Alice Whitehead, weaver, Ashton
"	28	Thomas s. George & Anne Travis, bo 28 Mar, crofter, Newton

"	28	Joseph s. George & Mary Lane, innkeeper, Failsworth
"	28	Robert s. Thos. & Barbara Hughes, innkeeper, Newton
Aug	6	Mary d. Richard & Mary Richardson, weaver, Newton
"	25	Thomas s. John & Sarah Ogden, detail labourer, Newton
"	25	Mary d. Thomas & Mary Dawson, dyer, Newton
"	25	Mary d. Thomas & Mary Ashworth, weaver, Newton
"	25	Ann d. John & Betty Barrow, shopkeeper, Failsworth
"	25	Ann d. Elijah & Sarah Whitehead, weaver, Failsworth
"	26	(altered from 25)[26] John s. John & Mary Smith, weaver, Newton
"	29	Hannah d. John & Peggy Lees, warehouseman, Failsworth
Sep	12	Edward s. Thomas & Mary Brown, weaver, Newton
"	12	Ann d. Jno. [John] & Betty Smith, labourer, Failsworth
"	29	James s. John & Martha Kershaw, weaver, Failsworth
"	29	Robert s. Elizabeth Whittaker (, single woman *not in BT*), Failsworth
"	29	Henry [spu.] s. Betty Ditchfield (, single woman *not in BT*), Failsworth
Oct	31	Hannah d. James & Martha Swift, weaver, Failsworth
"	31	Mary d. William & Elizabth. Goodier, weaver, Newton
Nov	10	Henry s. John & Sarah Tetlow, warehouseman, Newton
"	24	Betty d. Saml. & Milley Simister, weaver, Failsworth, bo Feb 13 1808
"	24	John s. Thos. & Anne Whitaker, bleacher, Newton
"	24	John s. Joseph & Alice Hulme, weaver, Newton
Dec	1	Samuel s. James & Alice Mason, weaver, Manchester, bo Aug 22 1811
"	1	William s. Joseph & Martha Bardsley, weaver, Failsworth, bo Oct 19 1811
"	8	Mark s. James & Lucy Greaves, spinner, Hollinwood, bo Jul 10 1811
"	8	Mary Anne d. Mary Smith, weaver, Failsworth, bo Oct 19 1811
"	22	Esther Rosina d. John & Anne Hulton, weaver, Failsworth, bo Nov 11
"	22	Sarah d. Joseph & Anne Fildes, farmer, Newton, bo Aug 9 1811
"	22	John s. Sarah Wolstencroft, Failsworth, bo Nov 12
"	23	Edward s. Saml. & Elizabeth Lees, farmer, Failsworth, bo Jan 20 1810
"	25	Sarah d. George & Elizabeth Parkinson, tanner, Failsworth, bo Oct 21 1811
"	25	Andrew s. Joseph & Mary Berry, blacksmith, Failsworthrh, Nov 30
"	25	James s. Robt. & Betty Lees, weaver, Failsworth, Nov 12
"	25	Alice d. Mary Blakley [Blackshaw], Failsworth, Nov 5
"	29	Mary Gee d. James & Anne Howarth, carter, Bradford, bo Sep 17 1811
"	29	Ellen [Helena] d. John & Anne Holland, weaver, Failsworth
"	29	Elizabeth d. Isaac & Ellen Beesley, farmer, Failsworth, bo Nov 16 1811
[		A. Ashworth Minister
		Joseph Bertenshaw John Brundrett Wardens]

(1812)
(*year omitted*)
[Baptisms at Newton Heath Chapel 1812]

| Jan | 5 | George s. Geo. & Anne Yates, bleacher, Newton, bo Dec 6 1811 |
| " | 5 | Benjamin s. Benjn. & Mary Barrow, manufacturer, Failsworth, bo Nov 4 1811(*?*) |

"	26	Eliza d. Philip & Elizth. Smith, weaver, Failsw
"	26	Harriett d. Richd. & Mary Walker, small ware weaver, Newton, bo 1 Jan
Feb	2	Martha d. Thos. & Sarah Barlow, weaver, Moston
"	2	John s. Thos. & Milley Yeald, weaver, Failsw, aged 6 wks
"	9	John s. David & Elizth. Taylor, shopkeeper, Hollinwood
"	9	Lucy d. John & Elizth. Robinson, weaver, Manchr.
"	9	Joseph s. Richd. & Anne Hulme, distiller, Waterside A.P.
"	9	Daniel s. Wm. & Mary Walker, sm ware weaver, Newton
"	23	Elizabeth sp. d. Hannah Bardsley, Failsw
"	27	Jane d. Luke & Hannah Etchels, weaver, Failsw
Mar	2	George s. Joseph & Elizth. Ogden, weaver, Failsw
"	15	Daniel s. Wm. & Mary Bentley, cal printer, Moston
"	22	James s. Saml. & Hannah Robinson, weaver, Failsw
"	29	Joseph s. Joseph & Elizth. Seel, printer, Newton
"	29	James s. John & Mary Tetlow, weaver, Failsw
"	29	Joseph s. John & Martha Holland, weaver, Failsw
"	30	William s. Alexander & Isabel Jellashan, weaver, Failsw (*see burial same date*)
Apr	5	Betty d. Jas. & Martha Wild, weaver, Newton
"	5	Esther d. Geo. & Jane Hulton, weaver, Failsw
"	12	Eliza d. Joseph & Jane Ogden, weaver, Failsw
"	15	Mary d. Chas. & Alice Taylor, weaver, Newton, bo Jan 22
"	15	Mary d. John & Jane Howarth, bleacher, Newton, bo Mar 6
"	26	Fanny d. Rigby & Susannah Stanton, Newton, calenderer
May	3	Esther d. Saml. & Anne Pollit, weaver, Failsw, bo Shrove Tuesday, Failsw

Continued in the burials Register

(*inside back cover:*) Transfer to the Register of Burials marked 1795, where the Baptisms are continued for the remainder of the year 1812. See opposite side of the Book, not among the Burials

(*The following baptisms for the year 1812 are entered in the Burials Register.*)

May	17	Samuel s. Robt. & Alice Mills, weaver, Hollinwood, bo Apr 15
"	17	Jane d. Robt. & Alice Barlow, bleacher, Newton
"	24	James s. Nathl. & Elizth. Taylor, weaver, Failsworth, ag 6 wks
"	24	Samuel s. John & Betty Whitehead, weaver, Newton, 7 wks
"	24	Elizabeth d. Wm. & Cathne. Gradwell, weaver, Failsworth, bo Feb 23(*?*)
"	28	Nicholas s. Richd. & Sarah Simister, weaver, Newton, bo Apr 1
"	31	William s. Thos. & Isabella Smith, print cutter, Newton, bo Apr 28
Jun	1	James s. John & Sarah Hilton, weaver, Newton, bo May 24
"	14	Frederick s. Luke & Ellen Etchels, weaver, Failsworth, 3 wks (*?*)
"	21	Peter s. Edmd. & Olivia Schofield, weaver, Failsworth, 5 wks (*?*)
"	21	Edward (Edmund *struck through*) [Edward] s. Jas. & Hannah Berry, smith, Failsworth, 6 wks

Jul	19	William s. Joseph & Sarah Lees, weaver, Failsworth, ag 8 wks
"	19	Jonathan [sp.] s. Mary Unsworth, weaver, Moston, bo Jul 2
"	20	Maria d. John & Sarah Taylor, weaver, Failsworth, bo Jun 19
"	20	Thomas s. Richd. & Martha Pollit, weaver, Failsworth
"	21	John s. Saml. & Sarah Livsley, coal miner, Manchester, bo Jun 20
"	21	Hannah d. Saml. & Mary Robinson, slater, Newton, bo Jun 6
"	26	Leah s. Leah & Mary Foden, farmer, Failsworth, bo May 21
"	28	Samuel s. George & Betty Hardy, weaver, Failsworth, bo Apr 29
"	30	Elizabeth d. Francis & Martha Brown, farmer, Failsworth, bo May 24
Aug	16	Thomas s. George & Sarah Etchels, weaver, Failsworth, bo Jun 27
"	23	Mary d. George & Anne Morris, bleacher, Failsworth, bo Jul 21
"	30	John s. Henry & Mary Holland, weaver, Newton, bo Jun -
"	30	Elizabeth d. Saml. & Ellen Clough, weaver, Failsworth, bo Jul 24
Sep	2	Mary d. James & Sarah Wilson, weaver, Moston, bo Jun 29
"	2	Mary d. James & Anne Ogden, clerk, Newton, bo Jun 4 1810
"	2	William s. Jas. & Anne Ogden, clerk, Newton
"	6	John s. Joseph & Hannah Stansfield, hatter, Newton, bo Jun 30
"	13	Ellen d. Robert & Anne Banks, farmer, Failsworth, bo Feb 19
"	20	Sarah d. Jas. & Sarah Swift, weaver, Failsworth, bo Jul 19
"	20	William s. Joseph & Martha Clough, weaver, Wood Houses Ashton Parish, bo Aug 16
"	27	Oliver s. Abrm. & Martha Whitehead, weaver, Newton, bo Jul 13
Oct	4	Richard s. John & Esther Taylor, shoe maker, Failsworth, bo Jul 16
"	4	Joseph s. Joseph & Mary Pott, manufacturer, Newton, bo Sep 3
"	4	Susannah d. Elias & Sarah Whitley, weaver, Droylsden, bo Apr 18
"	4	Elizabeth d. Giles & Mary Eckersley, weaver, Failsworth, bo Jul 9
"	7	Margaret d. John & Elizabeth Tervin, labourer, Newton, bo Sep 23
"	11	Harriett d. John & Anne Whitaker, weaver, Failsworth, bo Sep 20
"	11	Nancy d. Jonathan & Esther Etchels, weaver, Failsworth, bo Sep 5
"	11	John s. John & Alice Hall, carpenter, Failsworth, bo Sep 13
"	11	Tabitha d. Robert & Esther Brierley, weaver, Failsworth, bo Aug 11
"	11	John s. Willm. & Mary Hampson, slater, Newton, bo Sep 15
"	18	Elizabeth d. Joseph & Mary Stott, weaver, Hollinwood, bo Sep 24
"	18	Elizabeth d. Willm. & Nancy Robinson, weaver, Failsworth, bo Sep 18
"	21	William s. Thos. & Anne Horrocks, weaver, Failsworth, bo Jul 24
"	25	Henry s. Willm. & Sarah Crossley, weaver, Failsworth, bo Sep 4
"	25	Luke s. John & Jane Smith (Crossley *struck through*), weaver, Failsworth, bo Sep 16
"	28	Hannah d. John & Mary Leigh, weaver, Manchester, bo Oct 4
Nov	12	Joseph s. Joseph & Mary Brown, weaver, Wood Houses, bo Oct 1
"	12	Betty d. Thos. & Mary Walmsley, farmer, Failsworth, bo Nov 3
"	15	Richard s. Richd. & Hannah Barrows, manuf, Failsworth, bo Sep 15
"	19	Anne d. Joseph & Mary Wild, weaver, Audenshaw, bo Sep 14
"	29	Jenny d. Richd. & Alice Mills, bleacher, Newton, bo Oct 18
"	29	Mary d. John & Mary Brierley, weaver, Failsworth, bo Oct 20

Dec	6	John s. Thos. & Mary Ogden, weaver, Failsworth, bo Nov 2
"	13	James s. Thos. & Mary Caunce, gardener, Failsworth, bo Oct 27
"	13	Anne d. Joseph & Hannah Williamson, weaver, Newton, bo Oct
"	18	William s. James & Anne Clough, weaver, Failsworth, bo Nov 8
"	25	Anne d. Joseph & Nancy Ogden, weaver, Failsworth, bo Oct 19
"	25	Hannah d. Jonathn. & Anne Clough, dyer, Newton, bo Dec 4

[The above is a true Copy taken from the Register at Newton Heath Chapel
A. Ashworth Minister
Robert Berry   James Tetlow   Wardens   ]
(new register commences: volume 7 - George Rose format)

(Baptisms continue to be entered in the Burials Register, upto Oct 13 1816. Almost all give dates of birth and the entries were apparently transferred to the George Rose Baptism Register without birth dates. Birth dates are thus recorded from the original entries. Differences between the two are shown by editorial notes)

1813
[Newton Heath Chapel Baptisms 1813]
(birth dates are within 12 months unless otherwise stated)
(BT faded; most entries cannot be verified upto March 31)

Bapt.		Born		
Jan	10	Nov	30	Caleb s. Joseph & Martha Ogden, Failsworth, shopkeeper
"	15	Dec	24	Henry s. James & Sarah Smith, Newton, innholder
"	24	Jan	17	John s. John & Elizabeth Barrow, Failsworth, shopkeeper
Feb	1			Nancy d. George & Mary Wolstenholme, Newton, weaver
"	7	Jul	5	Louisa d. William & Maria Hamner, Failsworth, weaver
"	7	Nov	14	Richard s. Richard & Jenny Travis, Newton, weaver
"	21			Joel s. Samuel & Elizabeth Wild, weaver, Droylsden
"	21	Nov	2	Robert s. Thomas & Elizabeth Smith, labourer, Newton
"	22	Nov 8 1811		Elizabeth d. Nicholas & Jane Simister, Failsworth (*George Rose register reads* Newton) [Failsworth], weaver
"	28	Feb	15	John spu. s. Mary Fildes, Failsworth, weaver
"	28	"	20	John s. James & Betty Ogden, Failsworth, weaver
"	28	Dec	19	Sarah d. Samuel & Betty Taylor, Failsworth, weaver
"	28	Jan	5	William s. William & Mary Pendleton, Failsworth, weaver
Mar	7	Feb	4	Nanny d. George & Betty Hulton, Failsworth, weaver
"	7	"	9	Thomas s. John & Mary Brundrett, Failsworth, weaver
"	7	Jan	5	Eliza spu. d. Nancy Swift, Newton, weaver
"	14	Feb	16	Elizabeth d. George & Elizabeth Parkinson, Failsworth, tanner
"	14	"	7	Anne spu. d. Mary Cheetham, Failsworth, weaver
"	17	"	16	Harriett d. Andrew & Hannah Clegg, Failsworth, joiner
"	28	"	28	Frances d. Mary Williamson, Failsworth, weaver
"	28	Oct	1	Hannah d. Thomas & Mary Houghton, Manchester, hatter

"	28	Feb	20	John s. George & Mary Haire, Failsworth, cordwainer (?)
				(*occupation blank in George Rose register*)
"	31			Sarah d. John & Sarah Walmsley, Failsworth, labourer
Apr	11	Mar	11	Mary d. John & Mary Smith, Newton, manufacturer
"	11	"	19	John s. Robert & Frances Mills, Water-side, dyer
"	11	"	31	Francis s. Samuel & Millicent Simister, Failsworth, weaver
"	12	Jan	21	Sally d. James & Mary Etchels, Failsworth, weaver
"	18	Mar	10	Susannah d. Joseph & Hannah Thornley, Failsworth, weaver
"	18	Feb	17	Martha d. Joseph & Sarah Rydings, Failsworth, weaver
"	18	Apr	12	Joseph sp. s. Martha Hulton, Failsworth, weaver
"	18	Feb	24	Reuben s. John & Anne Holt, Failsworth, weaver
May	9	Apr	10	James s. Thomas & Mary Allanson, Newton, warehouseman
"	9	Jan	23	Mary Anne d. Ratcliffe & Sarah Pott, Newton, weaver
"	16	May 11 1811		Sarah d. Robert & Elizabeth Ogden, Newton, weaver
"	16	Aug	1(?)	Sarah d. David & Anne Etchels, Failsworth, weaver
"	23	May	20	James sp. s. Jane Pollit, Failsworth, weaver
"	23	Apr	18	James s. William & Elizabeth Goddier, Newton, weaver
"	23	Mar	20	Anne d. John & Betty Robinson, Manchester, weaver
"	30	"	26	Benjamin s. Edward & Anne Eckersley, Failsworth, weaver
"	30	Apr	18(?)	Mary d. Benjamin & Maria Barrow, Failsworth, manufacturer
Jun	6	Apr	9	Robert s. Joseph & Rebecca Hulton, Failsworth, weaver
"	6	May	10	Mary d. Richard & Sarah Worswick, Failsworth, farmer
"	6	Apr	18(?)	John s. Margaret Mellor, Newton, weaver
"	6	May	8	James s. John & Grace Blackshaw, Failsworth, smith
"	6	"	6	Betty d. John & Anne Hilton, Failsworth, weaver
"	6	Apr	23	Eliza d. Samuel & Elizabeth Bradshaw, Newton, weaver
"	6	May	15(?)	Alice d. Charles & Anne Winstanley, Manchester, coal-miner
"	6	Mar	30(?)	George s. Matthew & Anne Gradwell, Blackley, weaver
"	13	May	10	Mary d. Joseph & Elizabeth Higham, Failsworth, weaver
"	13	"	11	John s. Robert & Anne Banks, Failsworth, farmer
"	20	Mar	26	Anne d. Ralph & Mary Bradley, Failsworth, weaver
"	20	"	27	Mary d. Matthew & Sarah Brown, Newton, weaver
"	20	"	3	Joseph s. Joseph & Anne Taylor, Failsworth, weaver
Jul	4	May	18	Joseph s. David & Elizabeth Ogden, Failsworth, weaver
"	4	"	6	Violet d. John & Mary Simister, Failsworth, weaver
"	10	Apr	24	Jane d. James & Phebe Smethurst, Failsworth, weaver
"	11	Jun	11	William s. William & Alice Taylor, Failsworth, weaver
"	18	May	20	Margaret d. Samuel & Mary Dean, Failsworth, weaver
"	18	Apr	16	George s. James & Anne Kershaw, Manchester, weaver
"	25	Jun	31(*sic*)	Hannah d. William & Elizabeth Ashworth, Manchester,
weaver				
"	25	Jul	21	Christiana & Eliza twin ds. James & Elizabeth Hulton,
				Failsworth, weaver (*separate entries in George Rose register*)
Aug	1	Jun	16	Jane spu. d. Anne Wilkinson, Failsworth, weaver
"	1	May	27	Olive d. John & Anne Clough, Failsworth, weaver

"	22	Jun	21	Elizabeth d. Richard & Anne Kenyon, Newton, printer
Sep	2			Anne Eliza (*?*) d. Wm. Embury & Mary Anne Edwards, seaman (*entry in pencil; not in BT and not in George Rose*)
"	5	Jun	10	Matty d. James & Hannah Timmis, Failsworth, wheelwright
"	12	"	2	Alfred s. Thomas & Alice Collinson, Failsworth, weaver
"	12	"	4	William s. William & Sarah Wallcroft, Newton, weaver
Oct	3	Aug	23	Nancy d. William & Mary Bentley, Newton, printer
"	3	Sep	26(*?*)	Henry sp. s. Anne Walton, Newton
"	3	Aug	20	Matthew s. George & Grace Howles, Newton, weaver
"	10	Mar	18	Thomas s. Matthew & Mary Wright, Failsworth, weaver
"	10	Sep	16	Anne (*George Rose register reads* Anne (Mary *struck through*)) d. Joseph & Sarah Rogers, Failsworth, weaver (*BT reads* Anne d. Joseph & Sarah Rogers, weaver, Failsworth)
"	31	"	16	Mary d. John & Sarah Ogden, Newton, weaver
Nov	7	Oct	15	Sarah d. Joseph & Mary Shaw, Failsworth, labourer
"	7	Jan	29	Mary d. John & Jane Greenhalgh, Newton, calico-printer
"	18	Feb	19	John s. Matthew & Mary Thornicroft, Irlam, farmer
"	18	Sep	13	James s. Leah & Jane Foden, Newton, farmer
"	21	"	14	Betty spu. d. Anne Stott, Newton
"	28	Oct	26	John sp. s. Martha Ogden, Failsworth, weaver
Dec	19	Dec	11	Mary Greaves spu. d. Sutcliffe Hulton, Failsworth, weaver
"	19	Oct	6	Alice d. Elijah & Sarah Whitehead, Failsworth, weaver
"	26	Sep	25	Thomas s. Thomas & Hannah Allen, Failsworth, weaver
"	26	Nov	4	Anne d. William & Sarah Robinson, Newton, slater
"	27	Aug	1	Hannah d. Thomas & Mary Bradbury, Thornham, collier
[				A. Ashworth Minister]

1814

[Newton Heath Baptisms 1814]
(*date of birth not given in BT*)

Jan	9	Nov	10	David s. John & Elizabeth Taylor, Newton, weaver
"	9	Dec	5	Thomas s. Thomas & Mary Dawson, Newton, dyer
"	16	Jan	14	Mary d. Dan & Hannah Hulton, Failsworth, weaver
"	16	Nov	17	Charles spurious s. Mary Thorpe, Failsworth, weaver (*burials register reads* Charles s. Thos. (*struck through*) & Mary Thorpe, Failsworth, weaver)
"	16	"	23	Sarah d. Robert & Betty Lees, Failsworth, weaver
"	30	Jan	7	Hannah d. John & Nancy Halliwell, Newton, bleacher
"	30	"	1	Sarah d. Jonathan & Elizabeth Lees, Newton, warehouseman
Feb	6	"	31	Nathaniel s. Samuel & Mary Robinson, Newton, slater
"	6	Dec	26	Eliza d. Thomas & Elizabeth Berry, Gorton, farmer
"	13	Jan	3	Isaac s. Isaac & Ellen Beesley, Failsworth, printer
"	13	Dec	18	Elizabeth d. Moses & Clarissa Gradwell, Newton, weaver
"	13	Nov	21	Jonathan s. Thomas & Mary Thorpe, Failsworth, weaver

"	13	Oct	10	Betsey d. Thomas & Martha Hooley, Newton, bleacher
"	20	Nov	21	Nancy d. William & Anne Thornley, Failsworth, weaver
"	20	Jan	9	Betty d. John & Jane Blackshaw, Newton, manufacturer
"	20	"	8	Reuben s. Samuel & Anne Pollet, Failsworth, weaver
"	20	Dec	19	Mary d. William & Sarah Thornley, Failsworth, weaver
Mar	6	Jan	29	Samuel s. Abraham & Martha Pollit, Failsworth, weaver
"	13	Feb	14	Eliza d. Nicholas & Jane Simister, Failsworth, weaver
"	20	Jan	29	Joseph s. James & Martha Swift, Failsworth, weaver
"	30	Feb	6	Robert s. Thomas & Jane Taylor, Manchester, weaver
Apr	10	Jan	2	Thomas s. William & Nancy Walker, Droylsden, hatter
"	10	"	29	William s. Benjamin & Mary Hulton, Failsworth, weaver
"	10	Feb	17	Jane d. Thomas & Mary Ashworth, Newton, weaver
"	10	"	25	Esther d. John & Martha Kershaw, Newton, weaver
"	10	"	9	Elizabeth d. Joshua & Alice Stott, Failsworth, weaver
"	10	Apr	3	Abraham s. James & Mary Tetlow, Newton, farmer
"	10	Dec	21	Mary d. Peter & Hannah Lomax, Newton, print dyer
"	10	Feb	21	Sally d. Samuel & Hannah Smith, Hollinwood, weaver
"	10	Sep	25	Hannah d. John & Alice Taylor, Failsworth, weaver
"	10	Dec	15(?)	David s. Thomas & Mary Ogden, Failsworth, weaver
"	10	Sep	4	Mary d. Thomas & Betty Fletcher, Failsworth, weaver
May	1	Apr	13	James s. James & Elizabeth Tetlow, Newton, weaver
"	1	Feb	24	Hannah d. William & Anne Preston, Failsworth, weaver
"	1	Apr	4	Alice d. John & Anne Berry, Failsworth, weaver
"	1	Feb	29(sic)	Andrew spurious s. Hannah Gorton, Failsworth, weaver
"	1	Apr	16	Sarah d. George & Sarah Etchels, Failsworth, weaver
"	10	Jan	20	Samuel s. John & Sarah Taylor, Failsworth, weaver
"	15	Apr	25	John s. Thomas & Mary Wright, Manchester, hatter
"	15	"	5	Anne d. James & Hannah Berry, Failsworth, blacksmith
"	22	"	3	Absalom spurious s. Mary Travis, Newton, weaver
"	23	"	3	Isaac s. Thomas & Hannah Dunkerley, Failsworth, weaver
"	29	"	30	Mary d. George & Anne Yates, Newton, whitster
"	29	"	1	Charles s. John & Peggy Lees, Failsworth, warehouseman
"	29	"	20	James spurious s. Sarah Ogden, Failsworth, weaver
"	29	"	30	James s. Richard & Martha Pollit, Failsworth, weaver
"	29	"	28	Rachel d. James & Mary Smith, Failsworth, weaver
"	29	Mar	23	Betty d. John & Matty Holland, Newton, weaver
Jun	2	"	22	Isaac s. John & Sarah Hilton, Newton, s.w. weaver
"	5	Apr	29	Elizabeth d. Thomas & Anne McIlvenna, Newton, navigator
"	5	"	1	John spurious s. Martha Berry, Newton, weaver
"	5	Sep 11 1812		Rosanna d. John & Sarah Haworth, Newton, cal. printer
"	5	Apr	17	William s. John & Sarah Haworth, Newton, cal. printer
"	12	Dec	5	Nancy d. Charles & Alice Taylor, Newton, small ware weaver
"	13	May	11	James s. Edmund & Elizabeth Shaw, Newton, husbandman
"	19	Apr	5	Anne d. Joseph & Anne Fildes, Newton, farmer
"	19	May	7	Thomas s. James & Martha Wild, Newton, weaver

"	19	"	9	Luke s. John & Sarah Williamson, Failsworth, weaver (*1814*)
"	19	"	12	Nanny d. George & Nanny Morris, Woodhouses Ash. par., bleacher
"	26	"	24	Edwin s. Joseph & Martha Clough, Woodhouses Ash. par., weaver
"	27	"	14	Hannah d. James & Mary Gradwell, Failsworth, weaver
Jul	3	"	14	Edwin s. John & Mary Thorley, Failsworth, weaver
"	3	"	15	Mary d. Edward & Betty Wild, Failsworth, weaver
"	3	Apr	16	Hannah d. Daniel & Hannah Etchels, Failsworth, weaver
"	7	Jun	12	John s. James & Sarah Smith, Newton, innholder
"	10	"	3	Benjamin s. Edmund & Olivia Schofield, Failsworth, weaver
"	10	Apr	17	William s. John & Sarah Wild, Newton, bleacher
"	10	"	29	Mary spurious d. Hannah Gillibrand, Failsworth, weaver
"	10	Jun	14	Martha d. Charles & Hannah Heywood, Newton, weaver
"	31	Apr	11	James s. John & Jane Rydings, Failsworth, weaver
Aug	7	Jun	17	John s. Jacob & Hannah Etchels, Newton, weaver
"	14	May	11	Thomas s. Francis & Martha Brown, Failsworth, farmer
"	19	Jun	15	Ambrose s. James & Ellen Ogden, Failsworth, weaver
"	21	Jul	16	James s. John & Elizabeth Whitehead, Newton, weaver
"	21	"	14	Jane spurious d. Betty Whitaker, Failsworth, weaver
"	21	"	27	Martha d. James & Betty Clough, Manchester, weaver
"	21	"	18	Joseph spurious s. Mary Booth, Failsworth, weaver
"	21	Mar	5	Betty spurious d. Martha Hardy, Failsworth, weaver
"	21	Aug	12	James s. John & Jane Crossley, Failsworth, weaver
"	28	Jul	4	Mary d. Samuel & Alice Brundret, Failsworth, weaver
"	28	Aug	24	Jane d. Thomas & Mary Ashton, Failsworth, weaver
Sep	4	"	9	Mary d. Thomas & Mary Allanson, Newton, bleacher
"	10	Feb	17	Alice d. Adam & Alice Mortin, Bradshaw Hedge Derbyshire, carrier
"	11	Aug	3	Alice d. James & Sarah Wilson, Moston, weaver
"	11	"	7	Sarah d. Joseph & Mary Horrocks, Failsworth, weaver
"	11	Jul	24	John s. William & Mary Smith, Failsworth, weaver
"	11	Sep	5	Alice d. Samuel & Jane Mather, Newton, weaver
"	18	Apr	23	John s. Edmund & Anne Unsworth, Moston, weaver
"	25	Jul	27	Mary d. John & Alice Booth, Failsworth, weaver
"	25	Aug	19	Hannah d. Richard & Hannah Barrow, Failsworth, manufacturer
Oct	2	Sep	1	Jane d. John & Mary Wilson, Hollinwood, weaver
"	2	"	30	Mally d. John & Anne Whitaker, Failsworth, weaver
"	16	"	10	Henry s. George & Elizabeth Parkinson, Failsworth, tanner
"	16	"	12	Lucy d. Joseph & Mary Berry, Failsworth, weaver
"	24	"	11	Mary d. Samuel & Jane Wood, Newton, printer
"	30	"	19	Anne d. Thomas & Isabella Smith, Newton, print cutter
"	30	Aug	17	Edwin s. Launcelot & Mary Hulton, Failsworth, weaver
"	30	Sep	12	Alice d. Thomas & Hannah Whitaker, Newton, bleacher

"	30	"	23	Alice d. John & Mary Smith, Newton, manufacturer
Nov	6	Oct	10	Susan spurious d. Martha Taylor, Failsworth, weaver
"	6	Sep	24	James s. James & Betty Marsden, Newton, bleacher
"	6	"	12	Harriet d. John & Betty Dickenson, Newton, stay-maker
"	20	Oct	21	Mary d. Joseph & Elizabeth Cheetham, Failsworth, weaver
"	20	"	23	William s. Joseph & Hannah Williamson, Newton, weaver
"	27			Thomas s. Jacob & Sarah Simpson, Newton, bleacher
"	27	Oct	19	John s. Joseph & Elizabeth Higham, Failsworth, weaver
"	27	"	11	Mary spurious d. Sarah Hodgson, Failsworth, weaver
"	27	"	15	Samuel spurious s. Elizabeth Smith, Failsworth, weaver
"	27	"	24	John spurious s. Mary Smith, Failsworth, weaver
"	30	"	23	James s. John & Nanny Holt, Failsworth, weaver
Dec	4	Nov	9	Betty d. George & Sarah Hulton, Failsworth, weaver
"	11	Dec	10	Samuel s. Richard & Margaret Whitehead, Woodhouses Ash. par., weaver
"	18	Nov	15	Thomas s. Leah & Mary Foden, Newton, labourer
"	18	Sep	19	Alice d. Thomas & Anne Brooks, Manchester, weaver
"	18	Oct	19	Elizabeth d. Benjamin & Maria Barrow, Failsworth, manufacturer
"	25	Nov	19	Samuel s. William & Betty Ashworth, Manchester, weaver
"	25	"	4	Luke s. John & Sarah Taylor, Failsworth, weaver
"	25	Oct	19	Isabel d. Luke & Ellen Etchels, Failsworth, weaver
"	26	Dec	25	William s. Joseph & Catharine Fletcher, Failsworth, weaver
"	29	Oct	27	Anne d. Abraham & Martha Whitehead, Newton, weaver
"	30	Mar 13	1812	Anne d. Richd. & Anne (?) Johnson, weaver, Ardwick (*entry struck through; entry not in George Rose Register or BT*)
[				A. Ashworth Curate of Newton
				Robert Berry Warden]

1815
(date of birth not given in BT)

Jan	1	Sep	30	Anne d. Thomas & Anne Horrocks, Droylsden, dyer
"	8	Nov	25	Anne d. John & Mary Brundret, Failsworth, weaver
"	8	Dec	4	Anne d. John & Dolly Knott, Newton, weaver
"	29	"	17	Matty d. Joseph & Martha Booth, shopkeeper, Failsworth
Feb	5	Nov	15	Hugh s. James & Anne Tomlinson, Newton, bleacher
"	5	Dec	23	William s. John & Sarah Marsden, Newton, bleacher
"	5	Nov	1	Benjamin s. Henry & Susannah Etchels, Ashton under Lyne, weaver
"	7	"	15	Henry s. Joseph & Isabella Grimshaw, Failsworth, hatter
"	12	Oct	28	James s. William & Sarah Pollit, Failsworth, weaver
"	19	Feb	13	Mary Anne d. Joseph & Betty Brown, Failsworth, weaver
"	19	Dec	26	Mary d. Samuel & Hannah Robinson, Failsworth, weaver
"	22			Joseph s. Robert & Esther Brierley, Failsworth, weaver
"	22			Anne d. Robert & Esther Brierley, Failsworth, weaver
"	26	Jan	4	Mary d. Thomas & Mary Walmsley, Failsworth, farmer

"	26	Dec	31	Joseph spurious s. Betty Hibbert, Newton
Mar	5	Jan	23	William s. Richard & Jenny Travis, Newton, weaver
"	5	Nov	19	Anne spurious d. Betty Tinker, Failsworth, weaver
"	19	"	30	John s. John & Mary Hooley, Failsworth, hatter
"	20	Mar	12	Mariah d. Elijah & Charlotte Hulton, Failsworth, weaver
"	25	Feb	25	Susannah d. Joseph & Agnes Slater, Failsworth, weaver
"	26	Jan	15	Robert s. Thomas & Martha Winterbottom, Failsworth, weaver
"	26	"	14	Amelia d. Edward & Anne Worrall, Failsworth, weaver
"	26	Feb	24(?)	Isabel spurious d. Anne Glossop, Failsworth, weaver
"	26	"	8	Nanny d. George & Betty Hulton, Failsworth, weaver
"	26	Jan	14	Betty d. Joseph & Rebecca Hulton, Failsworth, weaver
"	26	Mar	4	Joseph spurious s. Hannah Bardsley, Failsworth, weaver
"	26	Jan	16	William s. William & Nancy Robinson, Failsworth, weaver
Apr	9	Feb	13	Henry s. Nathaniel & Grace Campbell, Newton, book keeper
"	9	Jan	12	Thomas s. Thomas & Sarah Wyatt, Failsworth, weaver
"	9	Feb	14	James s. James & Betty Ogden, Failsworth, weaver
"	9	"	19	Esther d. Joseph & Jane Ogden, Failsworth, weaver
"	11	Mar	30	John s. Henry & Elizabeth Radcliffe, Failsworth, wheelwright
"	23	"	22	William s. Aaron & Mary Anne Gradwell, Newton, weaver
"	23	Feb	9	David s. Thomas & Nancy Ogden, Failsworth, weaver
"	24	Apr	17	Ellen d. Robert & Sarah Berry, Failsworth, farmer
"	30	Mar	5	Richard s. George & Mary Lane, Failsworth, innholder
"	30	"	1	Samuel s. William & Sarah Wallcroft, Newton, weaver
May	7	Feb	9	Philip s. John & Esther Taylor, Failsworth, shoe maker
"	7	"	18	Lavinia d. John & Betty Robinson, Manchester, weaver
"	7	Apr	9	Sarah d. James & Alice Fletcher, Newton, weaver
"	14	Mar	3	Betty d. William & Sarah Knott, Failsworth, weaver
"	14	Apr	27	Anne d. John & Mary Brierley, Failsworth, weaver
"	14	Mar	19	Nathaniel s. William & Elizabeth Hibbert, Manchester, weaver
"	14	Apr	3	Charles spurious s. Hannah Smith, Failsworth, weaver
"	14	Mar	19	James s. Jonathan & Anne Clough, Newton, dyer
"	15	May	3	Jenny d. Andrew & Hannah Clegg, Failsworth, joiner
"	15	Mar	20	Ashton s. James & Betty Hulton, Failsworth, weaver
"	21	"	10	Abraham s. Abraham & Mary Horrocks, Woodhouses Ashton Par. (*burial register reads* Woodhouses (Cutler Hill *struck out*) Ash. Par.) [Woodhouses Ashton Par], dyer
"	21	"	22	William s. Joshua & Alice Taylor, Failsworth, hatter
"	28	Feb	26	Martha d. Samuel & Mary Holland, Failsworth, weaver
"	28	Mar	27	John spurious s. Anne Dawson, Droylsden, weaver
"	28	"	14	Hannah d. Ratcliffe & Sarah Potts, Newton, manufacturer
"	28	"	24	Rachel d. Samuel & Elizabeth Pollit, Failsworth, weaver
"	29	Mar 13	1812	Anne d. Richard & Anne Johnson, Ardwick, weaver
Jun	11	"	28	Emanuel s. Jonathan & Martha Leech, Failsworth, weaver
"	11	Apr	17	Harriet d. Robert & Betty Whitehead, Failsworth, weaver
"	11	May	9	Edwin s. John & Mary Collin, Failsworth, weaver

"	11	Apr	2-	Anne d. John & Mary Simister, Failsworth, weaver (*1815*)
"	11	"	7	Abraham spurious s. Jenny Pollit, Failsworth, weaver
"	11	May	4	Abraham spurious s. Anne Pollit, Failsworth, weaver
"	12	"	18	James s. Joseph & Priscilla Hadfield, Newton, weaver
"	18	Feb	16	John s. Matthew & Sarah Brown, Newton, weaver
"	18	May	5	Mary spurious d. Anne Linn, Failsworth, weaver
"	18	Apr	15	Joseph s. Joseph & Hannah Stansfield, Newton, hatter
"	18	May	25	Maria spurious d. Mary Stansfield, Newton, weaver
"	25	"	21	Anne spurious d. Mary Ogden, Failsworth, weaver
"	25	Apr	7	Joseph s. John & Elizabeth Taylor, Newton, weaver
"	25	May	6	James spurious s. Mary Terven, Newton, weaver
Jul	2	"	11	Edwin s. Thomas & Jane Lord, Newton, wheelwright
"	2	Mar	17	Anne d. James & Mary Lord, Newton, joiner
"	2	Jun	29	Emanuel s. Joseph & Alice Robinson, Failsworth, weaver
"	2	Aug	8	Sarah d. Thomas & Jane Wood, Newton, skinner
"	2	Apr	28	John s. James & Mary Ashworth, Newton, bleacher
"	2	Jun	18	Sarah spurious d. Martha Greaves, Failsworth, weaver (*burials register reads* Sarah d. (John *struck through*) & Martha Greaves, Failsworth, weaver)
"	2	Jan	10	William Robinson s. John & Sarah Crossley, Ault Hill Ashton Par, farmer
"	9	Mar	25	Edwin s. James & Anne Winstanley, Manchester, weaver
"	16	Jun	27	William s. Benjamin & Anne Bayley, Failsworth, weaver (*surname written in a different hand in George Rose register*)
"	16	Apr	28	Eliza d. James & Alice Ogden, Failsworth, weaver
"	16	May	28	William s. James & Jane Taylor, Failsworth, weaver
"	16	Mar	15	Eliza d. Thomas & Mary Ogden, Failsworth, farmer
"	16	Jun	14(?)	Esther d. Elijah & Sarah Whitehead, Failsworth, weaver
"	17	Nov	17	Esther d. James & Elizabeth Hall, Newton, dyer
"	24	Jun	1	Hannah d. John Boardman & Hannah Etchels, Failsworth, weaver
"	30	Jul	8	James s. James & Martha Wild, Newton, weaver
"	30	May	25	Nancy d. Thomas & Alice Collinson, Failsworth, weaver
"	30	Jun	22	William s. Thomas & Elizabeth Fotheringham, Failsworth, weaver
"	30	"	11	Anne d. William & Ellen Greenhalgh, Newton, tailor
Aug	6	"	29	David s. George & Margaret Eyre, Failsworth, cordwainer
"	13	"	15	Thomas s. Thomas & Peggy Hulme, Failsworth, farmer
"	13	Jul	2	Nancy d. Joseph & Hannah Thornley, Failsworth, weaver
"	20	"	21	Maria d. Robert & Frances Mills, Water Side Ashton Par, dyer
"	20	"	12	Hannah d. William & Mary Hampson, Newton, slater
"	20	May	17	James s. James & Sarah Swift, Failsworth, weaver
"	20	Jun	13	James s. William & Sarah Crossley, Failsworth, weaver
"	20	"	5	David s. Luke & Hannah Etchels, Failsworth, weaver
"	20	Nov 16	1812	William s. Samuel & Margaret Beswick, Droylsden, weaver
"	20	May	24	Thomas s. William & Elizabeth Worrall, Failsworth, weaver

"	20	Aug	5	Hannah d. William & Betty Valentine, Newton, crofter
"	20	Jun	22	Harriet d. Samuel & Mary Dean, Failsworth, weaver
"	22	Apr	20	Jane d. David & Elizabeth White, Newton, calico printer
"	27	Jul	28	Samuel s. William & Mary Pendleton, Failsworth, weaver
Sep	3	"	7	John s. Henry & Anne Crowther, Droylsden, weaver
"	3	Aug	7	James s. George & Alice Smith, Failsworth, weaver
"	3	Jul	31	Mary d. George & Mary Wolstenholme, Newton, weaver
"	3	May	20	Mary d. Samuel & Mary Holland, Failsworth, weaver
"	4	"	16	Joel s. Thomas & Mary Smith, Failsworth, weaver
"	10	Jun	12	Sarah d. George & Elizabeth Smith, Droylsden, hatter
"	10	"	18	Lydia d. James & Elizabeth Barlow, Water Side Ashton Par, bleacher
"	10	Jul(?)	27	Richard s. James & Anne Kershaw, Manchester, warehouseman
"	11	Jul	10	James s. William & Anne Wilson, Chadderton, weaver
"	17	Aug	15	Edwin spurious s. Mary Hibbert, Failsworth, weaver
"	17	"	20	Elizabeth d. John & Martha Thomason, Failsworth, weaver
"	18	Jun	19	Anne d. Joseph & Anne Taylor, Failsworth, weaver
"	19	Jul	1(?)	Sarah d. John & Sarah Taylor, Failsworth, weaver
"	19	May	30	Susannah d. Joseph & Elizabeth Taylor, Failsworth, weaver
"	24	Aug	20	Thomas s. Joseph & Betty Baguley, Failsworth, cotton spinner
"	26	"	19	Abel s. Peter & Mary Wright, Failsworth, weaver
"	27	Sep	26	Mary Anne d. John & Phebe Taylor, Newton, weaver
Oct	1	Jul	29	Richard s. John & Mary Howard, Woodhouses, weaver
"	8	Oct(?)	7	James spurious s. Anne Stott, Newton, weaver
"	8	Sep	8	George s. Joseph & Elizabeth Seel, Newton, printer
"	8	"	29	Elizabeth d. NSN Brought by John Hulton
"	9	Aug	2	Elizabeth d. Joseph & Sarah Lees, Failsworth, weaver
"	9	Oct	2	Anne spurious d. Catharine Tomlinson, Moston, farmer
"	15	Aug	29	John s. Thomas & Jane Bates, Waterside, bleacher
"	15	Sep	4	Alice spurious d. Mary Whitehead, Waterside, weaver
"	22	Aug	27	Edwin s. Charles & Anne Winstanley, Manchester, collier
"	22	Oct	10(?)	Betty d. William & Elizabeth Goodyear, Newton, weaver
"	23	"	23	William s. James & Jane Blake, Failsworth, cal printer
"	29	Aug	21	John s. Moses & Elizabeth Preston, Failsworth, weaver
"	29	Sep	30	Peggy d. Robert & Mary Allen, Newton, bleacher
"	29	Aug	30	Thomas William spurious s. Deborah Fox, Moston, farmer
Nov	5	Jun	4	Joseph Slater spurious s. Sarah Ogden, Newton, weaver
"	5	Nov	2	Alice d. William & Catharine Gradwell, Failsworth, weaver
"	12	Oct	7	Thomas s. David & Betty Ogden, Failsworth, weaver
"	12	Aug	24	Sarah d. Thomas & Mary Bradbury, Chadderton, collier
"	12	Oct	30	Anne d. William & Mary Pickering, Newton, weaver
"	12	Sep	3	Joseph s. Thomas & Hannah Allen, Failsworth, weaver
"	12	Aug	20	Joshua spurious s. Jane Collinson, Failsworth, weaver
"	19	Nov	15	Lavinia d. Peter & Anne Fletcher, Failsworth, weaver

"	19	Aug	12	William Perry s. William & Maria Hamner, Manchester, farmer
"	19	Oct	23	Jenny d. Thomas & Mary Dawson, Newton, dyer
"	19	Jul	20	Andrew s. Abraham & Mary Wood, Failsworth, weaver
"	19	Aug 12 1793		Elizabeth d. James & Mary (*blank in PR & BT*), farmer (*the words* See the old book *appear in the margin of the George Rose register*; *burials register reads* Elizabeth d. James & Mary Bowering, Wood Radwell Norfolk, farmer)
"	26	Aug	21	Benjamin s. Samuel & Anne Pollit, Failsworth, weaver
"	26	Nov	29(?)	Nancy Maria spurious d. Maria Barlow, Failsworth, weaver (*burials register reads* Nancy sp d. Maria Barlow, Failsworth, weaver)
Dec	3	"	24(?)	Mary d. John & Elizabeth Barrow, Failsworth, farmer
"	3	Oct	26	James s. Joseph & Elizabeth Mills, Waterside Ashton Par, printer
"	24	Nov	26	Nancy d. David & Elizabeth Potter, Failsworth, weaver
"	24	Sep	24	John s. Jonathan & Sarah Boardman, Failsworth, weaver
"	24	Oct	24	Harriet d. Thomas & Jane Smith, Failsworth, weaver
"	24	Sep	21	Mary Anne d. James & Jane Kemp, Newton, musician (weaver *struck through in burials register*)
"	25	Aug	12	Joseph s. Robert & Elizabeth Lees, Failsworth, weaver
"	31	Jun	4	Hannah d. Samuel & Betty Jones, Newton, bleacher
"	31	Nov	5	Isaac s. Robert & Alice Barlow, Newton, bleacher
[				Signed. John Piccop]

1816

(date of birth not given in BT)

Jan	7	Nov	13	Samuel s. Joseph & Nancy Ogden, Failsworth, weaver
"	7	Dec	7	Nancy d. Edmund & Olivia Schofield, Failsworth, weaver
"	8	Nov	31(*sic*)	Sydney s. Samuel & Mary Robinson, Newton, slater
"	10	Dec	7	Anne d. Samuel & Alice Brundret, Failsworth, weaver
"	14	Oct	14	Mary d. John & Jenny Taylor, Failsworth, weaver
"	14	Nov	8	William s. John & Anne Haslem, Failsworth, weaver
"	28	Dec	27	James s. John & Anne Berry, Failsworth, weaver
"	28	"	16	John s. Daniel & Hannah Knott, Failsworth, weaver
"	28	Jan	21	James s. John & Jane Smith, Failsworth, farmer
"	28	Dec	8	John s. Richard & Martha Pollit, Failsworth, weaver
"	31	Oct	6	Joseph s. Thomas & Nanny Berry, Failsworth, weaver
Feb	4	Jan	6	Alice spurious d. Mary Etchels, Failsworth, weaver
"	7	Nov	17	Thomas spurious s. Alice Clough, Failsworth, weaver
"	11	Jan	4	Andrew s. John & Martha Turner, Failsworth, weaver
"	12	Feb 6 1815		Mary d. John & Martha Hulme, Droylsden, whitster
"	21	Nov	26	Martha d. John & Mary Ellinson, Failsworth, carpenter
"	25	Jan	11	John Clare s. James & Hannah Berry, Failsworth, blacksmith
"	25	Dec	30	Lettice d. George & Elizabeth Tomlinson, Failsworth, weaver

"	25	Jan	11	John s. Joseph & Sarah Rogers, Failsworth, weaver
Mar	3	Oct	31	James s. Samuel & Mary Hyde, Newton, weaver
"	3	Jan	2	George s. Samuel & Jennett Wood, Droylsden, printer
"	3	Feb	25	Lucy d. Nicholas & Jane Simister, Failsworth, weaver
"	10	Mar 10 1797		Joseph s. John & Hannah Haslem, Failsworth, weaver
"	10	Feb	9	James s. William & Elizabeth Glossop, Failsworth, weaver
"	10	Jan	22	Eliza d. John & Anne Clough, Failsworth, weaver
"	10	Feb	7	James s. Joseph & Elizabeth Higham, Failsworth, weaver
"	12	Jan	18	Elizabeth spurious d. Sarah Ogden, Failsworth, weaver
"	17	Dec	19	Mary d. Robert & Anne Rydings, Failsworth, weaver
"	17	Feb	18	Jonathan s. Jacob & Hannah Etchels, Newton, shopkeeper
"	17	Dec 20 1814		Hannah spurious d. Anne Hardy, Failsworth, weaver
"	17	Jan	3	Mary d. Samuel & Milley Simister, Failsworth, weaver
"	24	Feb	8	John s. Thomas & Mary McIlvenna, Newton, labourer
"	24	Jan	29	Mary d. John & Isabella Mills, Woodhouses Ashton Par, print cutter
"	24	Sep	17	Peter s. Adam & Margaret Horrocks, Droylsden, printer
"	27	Jan	3	Mary d. Benjamin & Anne Wright, Failsworth, weaver
"	31	Dec	15	Mary Anne d. John & Mary Smith, Newton, manufacturer
"	31	Mar	19	Nancy d. James & Peggy Higham, Newton, weaver
"	31	"	9	John spurious s. Esther Higham, Newton, weaver
"	31	Oct 14 1814		John s. James & Alice Scholfield, Manchester, coal miner
Apr	14	Feb	13(?)	James s. James & Phebe Smethurst, Failsworth, weaver
"	14	Mar	28	James spurious s. Hannah Whitaker, Failsworth, weaver
"	14	Apr	8	Olive spurious d. Jane Whitaker, Failsworth, weaver
"	14	Mar	23	John s. John & Jenny Blackshaw, Newton, manufacturer
"	14	"	22	Henry s. John & Jenny Crossley, Failsworth, weaver
"	15	Jan	21	Thomas s. John & Mary Blackley, Failsworth, blacksmith
"	28	Apr	1	Henry s. Thomas & Elizabeth Berry, Gorton, farmer
"	28	May	17	John s. William & Elizabeth Lees, Manchester, weaver
May	5	Mar	28	Ellen d. Thomas Wroe & Hannah (Elizabeth *struck through in George Rose register*) [Hannah] Beswick, Failsworth, weaver
"	5	"	10	Martha d. Richard & Martha Worsick, Harpurhey, farmer
"	12	Feb	8	Anne d. Samuel & Anne Dawson, Failsworth, weaver
"	12	Apr	27	Elizabeth d. Elias & Elizabeth Lomax, Newton, weaver
"	16	"	27	Kirby s. James & Sarah Smith, Newton, innholder
"	19	Mar	5	Wilson s. John & Mary Wilson, Hollinwood, weaver
"	19			Mary d. Thomas & Mary Thorpe, Failsworth, weaver
"	20	Mar	31	Joseph s. Joseph & Sarah Rydings, Failsworth, weaver
"	26	Apr	16	John spurious s. Mary Brundrett, Failsworth, weaver
"	26	Mar	17	James s. John & Matty Holland, Moston, weaver
"	26	May	14	Hannah d. Abraham & Martha Pollit, Failsworth, weaver
Jun	2	"	31	Sarah Anne d. Edmund & Jane Whitehead, Moston, weaver
"	2	Feb	25	John s. Joseph & Elizabeth Wrigley, Failsworth, weaver
"	2	Apr	10	Mary d. Luke & Rachel Hulton, Failsworth, weaver

"	2	"	10	Martha d. Luke & Rachel Hulton, Failsworth, weaver
"	2	Mar	9	Thomas s. John & Anne Holt, Failsworth, weaver
"	5	"	25	George s. John & Mary Barlow, Millhouses, cal. printer
"	7	Apr	26	Edward s. John & Esther Whitehead, Newton, farmer
"	7	Mar	10	Christopher s. Christopher & Sarah Miller, Newton, labourer
"	9	May	15	Richard s. Robert & Elizabeth Hall, Newton, weaver
"	9	Mar	29	Mary Anne d. John & Mary Thorley, Failsworth, weaver
"	16	Apr	25	Joshua s. Charles & Alice Collinson, Failsworth, weaver
"	16	Mar	30	John s. Josiah & Elizabeth Brown, Hollinwood, weaver
"	16	May	3	Samuel s. Thomas & Milley Yeld, Failsworth, weaver
"	16	Mar	28	William s. Samuel & Mary Lees, Failsworth, weaver
"	16	Apr	28	John spurious s. Alice Mills, Failsworth, weaver
"	23	May	6	John s. David & Elizabeth Whitaker, Newton, wheelwright
"	23	Feb	20	William s. Samuel & Anne Butterworth, Manchester, coal miner
"	23	May	13	Elizabeth d. Ralph & Sarah Ogden, Failsworth, weaver
"	23	Jun	9	James s. James & Rachel Hough, bleacher, Newton
"	30	Feb	13	Anne d. William & Anne Preston, Failsworth, weaver
"	30	May	8	Anne d. Benjamin & Maria Barrow, Failsworth, weaver
Jul	10	Jun	14	Hannah spurious d. Nancy Rogers, Newton, weaver
"	14	"	6	John s. Aaron & Mary Anne Gradwell, Newton, weaver
"	14	"	15	Edwin s. Joseph & Sarah Marshall, Moston, bricklayer
"	21	"	9	William s. William & Lydia Thornicroft, Newton, labourer
"	21	May	22	Jane d. William & Maria Blundret, Bradford, dyer
"	28	Jun	29	William spurious s. Charlotte Taylor, Newton, weaver
Aug	4	May	6	Thomas s. Thomas & Mary Schofield, Failsworth, weaver
"	4	"	25	John s. John & Anne Webb, Newton, cal. printer
"	5	Jul	24	Sally d. Elijah & Charlotte Hilton, Failsworth, weaver
"	11	May	14	Eliza d. Ratcliffe & Sarah Pott, Newton, manufacturer
"	14	Mar	14	John s. George & Mary Hibbert, Failsworth, cordwainer
"	18	Jun	16	Robert s. Edward & Anne Worrall, Failsworth, weaver
"	18	Aug	10	William s. James & Elizabeth Taylor, Moston, farmer
"	25			Esther d. Thomas & Hannah Dawson, Newton, dyer
"	25	Aug	14	Elizabeth d. Richard & Mary Walker, Newton, smallware weaver
"	25	Jun	11	William s. James & Anne Livsey, Manchester, coal miner
"	27	Aug	3	William s. James & Elizabeth Bardsley, Failsworth, weaver
Sep	2	May	22	Henry s. Ralph & Mary Bradley, Newton, carter
"	8	Jul	28	Edwin s. Dan & Hannah Hulton, Failsworth, weaver
"	15	Jun	6	Hannah Booth d. Mary Heath, Newton, weaver
"	15	"	15	Daniel s. Joseph & Martha Clough, Woodhouses, weaver
"	15			Catharine d. John & Elizabeth Whitehead, Newton, weaver
"	22	Aug	18	Mary d. Joseph & Hannah Williamson, Newton, weaver
"	29	Sep	16	Betty d. James & Sarah Worrall, Failsworth, farmer
"	29	"	26	John s. Sally Chatterton, Newton, weaver
"	30	May	8	John s. James & Jane Blake, Failsworth, printer
Oct	6	Sep	2	Alexander s. Thomas & Mary Allanson, Newton, bleacher

"	6	"	10	Alice d. Charles & Hannah Heywood, Newton, weaver
"	6	Jun	5	James s. Thomas & Martha Winterbottom, Failsworth, weaver
"	7	Aug	29	Alice d. George & Anne Yates, Newton, whitster
"	12	Sep	5	John s. Phebe Allen, Failsworth, weaver
"	13	Aug	11	Alice d. William & Jane Bythill, Failsworth, weaver
"	28			James of Thomas & Mary Ashworth, Newton, weaver
"	28			Matilda of Peter & Hannah Lomax, Newton, printer
Nov	3			William of Thomas & Ann Brundrett, Failsworth, weaver
"	3			Ann of John & Mary Brierley, Failsworth, weaver
"	3			Thomas of Thomas & Elizabeth Lancashire, Moston, dyer
"	3			Mary of Robert & Betty Stansfield, Medlock Vale, carter
"	3			Thomas of Thomas & Jane Wood, Newton, fellmonger
"	6			Ann of Joseph & Mary Bury, Failsworth, weaver
"	10			Peter natural child of Mary Hall, Newton, weaver
"	10			Sarah of George & Ann Morris, Newton, crofter
"	10			Elizabeth of Thomas & Charity Healey, Newton, weaver
"	10			Mary natural child of Ann Spencer, Failsworth, weaver
"	17			Agnes of William & Hannah Winn, Newton, excise officer
"	17			Frances of William & Sarah Robinson, Newton, slater
Dec	8			Cato of Joseph & Catherine Fletcher, Failsworth, weaver
"	8			Abraham of Samuel & Jane Mather, Newton, weaver
"	8			David of Thomas & Ann Whitaker, Newton, crofter
"	15			Robert of John & Ann Payton, Newton, crofter
"	16			Alexander Newall of Richard & Ann Molloy, Manchester, weaver
"	16			Frances of John & Mary Chatterton, Manchester, collier
"	22			Sarah of Matthew & Sarah Brown, Newton, weaver
"	22			John of James & Sarah Wilson, Moston, weaver
"	25			Peter of James & Ann Marsden, Newton, crofter
"	29			John of Robert & Esther Brierly, Failsworth, weaver
[				Signed John Piccop]

1817

Jan	5	Mary of Joseph & Priscilla Fletcher, Newton, weaver
"	12	Hannah of Thomas & Jane Lord, Newton, wheelwright
"	12	Azariah of Joseph & Alice Robinson, Newton, weaver
"	12	Agnes of Edmund & Olivia Schofield, Failsworth, weaver
"	19	Eliza of Isaac & Mary Whitehead, Newton, printer
"	19	Mary of John & Ann Thorneley, Droylsden, weaver
"	26	Thomas natural child of Jane Bury, Failsworth, weaver
"	26	Hannah of Richard & Elizabeth Makin, Moston, weaver
"	27	Sarah of Matthew & Susannah Gradwell, Newton, weaver, bo Sep 1800
"	27	Thomas of Matthew & Susannah Gradwell, Newton, weaver, bo Dec 1802
"	27	Mark of Matthew & Susannah Gradwell, Newton, weaver, bo Feb 1805
"	27	Ann of Matthew & Susannah Gradwell, Newton, weaver, bo Nov 1808

"	27	Samuel of Matthew & Susannah Gradwell, Newton, weaver, bo Dec 1810
"	27	Daniel of Matthew & Susannah Gradwell, Newton, weaver, bo Jan 1816
"	27	Joseph of Thomas & Jane Wild, Newton, farmer
Feb	2	Alice of Samuel & Mary Kenyon, Failsworth, weaver
"	9	Ann of William & Martha Cordinley, Failsworth, weaver
"	9	Alice of George & Sarah Hulton, Newton, weaver
"	9	Mary Ann natural child of Betty Whitehead, Droylsden, weaver
"	9	Lavinia of George & Elizabeth Smith, Droylsden, hatter
"	16	Elizabeth of James & Alice Fletcher, Newton, weaver
"	16	Benjamin of Benjamin & Mary Hulton, Failsworth, weaver
"	16	William of John & Sarah Taylor, Failsworth, weaver
"	16	John of William & Ann Clegg, Failsworth, joiner
Mar	2	Mary of John & Elizabeth Taylor, Newton, weaver
"	2	Fanny of John & Martha Thomason, Failsworth, weaver
"	2	Alfred natural child of Sally Simister, Failsworth, weaver
"	4	Mary of George & Elizabeth Parkinson, Failsworth, tanner
"	7	Jenny of Samuel & Hannah Smith, Hollinwood, weaver
		(*written in margin:*) This Child was privately baptized by Mr. Ashworth
"	9	Elizabeth of John & Sarah Smith, Newton, weaver
"	23	Robert of Samuel & Sarah Garside, Newton, butcher
"	23	Robert of James & Betty Marsden, Newton, crofter
"	30	Betty of Abraham & Martha Whitehead, Moston, farmer
"	30	Edwin natural child of Mary Stott, Failsworth, weaver
"	30	Nancy natural child of Esther Robinson, Ashton, weaver
"	30	James natural child of Hannah Hulton, Failsworth, weaver
Apr	6	Mary Ann of Robert & Ann Ramsden, Newton, labourer
"	6	Ann of Thomas & Mary Ryder, Moston, farmer
"	6	James of Robert & Betty Ogden, Oldham, blacksmith
"	6	Thomas of James & Ann Taylor, Failsworth, weaver
"	6	Lettice Whitehead of Robert & Betty Clough, Failsworth, weaver
"	6	William of James & Hannah Swindells, Newton, weaver
"	6	Sarah of James & Mary Smith, Failsworth, weaver
"	13	Eliza of James & Frances Clough, Newton, labourer
"	20	Margaret of Jeremiah & Alice Etchels, Droylsden, dyer
"	25	Mary Ann of George & Mary Ann Travis, Newton, crofter, bo Feb 28 1814
"	25	George of George & Mary Ann Travis, Newton, crofter
"	27	Damaris of Henry & Lucy Etchels, Failsworth, weaver
"	27	Sarah of James & Martha Wild, Newton, weaver
May	4	Daniel of George & Grace Howles, Newton, weaver
"	4	Hannah of Samuel & Margaret Cheetham, Manchester, innkeeper
"	4	Alice of William & Mary Kershaw, Oldham, weaver
"	11	Hannah of John & Sarah Crossley, Alt Hill in Ashton Parish, farmer
"	18	Esther of Thomas & Mary Walmsley, Failsworth, farmer
"	18	Ann of Joseph & Sally Tomlinson, Newton, crofter
"	25	Mary of George & Betty Ramsbottom, Newton, printer

"	25	Hannah of Samuel & Ann Bottomley, Newton, labourer *(1817)*
"	25	Elizabeth of Daniel & Hannah Wolsencroft, Manchester, innkeeper
"	25	Selina natural child of Mary Nailor, Newton, weaver
"	25	Mary of George & Mary Lane, Failsworth, innkeeper
"	25	Francis s. Joseph & Rebecca Hulton, Failsworth, weaver
"	25	Thomas of Samuel & Hannah Robinson, Failsworth, weaver
"	25	Martha of Samuel & Susannah Thornely, Droylsden, weaver
"	25	Mary of William & Elizabeth Ashworth, Manchester, weaver
"	25	Charles of Joseph & Isabella Grimshaw, Failsworth, hatter
"	25	James of James & Mary Lord, Newton, joiner
Jun	1	Lavinia of John & Martha Turner, Failsworth, weaver
"	1	Joseph of Robert & Alice Whitehead, Woodhouses p. Ashton under Lyne, weaver
"	1	Samuel of John & Ann Clough, Newton, dyer
"	5	Robert of John & Mary Thorley, Failsworth, weaver
"	8	Robert of Robert & Frances Mills, Medlock Vale, dyer (*occupation altered; original rubbed out*) [dyer]
"	8	Margaret of William & Jane Mather, Droylsden, weaver
"	10	Thomas of Daniel & Hannah Wolsencroft, Manchester, innkeeper, bo May 8 1808
"	12	Mary Ann d. Sarah Booth, Newton, natural child
"	15	Benjamin of Joseph & Rebecca Barret, Failsworth, farmer
"	15	Veturia d. John & Betty Robinson, Manchester, weaver
"	18	Thomas of Thomas & Isabella Smith, Newton, print block cutter
"	22	Richard of Richard & Sally Worsick, Harpurhey, farmer
"	24	James of William & Elizabeth Lees, Manchester, small ware weaver
"	25	Sarah of Joseph & Mary Brown, Failsworth, weaver
"	26	Sarah of Francis & Martha Brown, Failsworth, farmer
"	29	John natural child of Ann Thorp, Failsworth, weaver
"	29	John of James & Margaret Miller, Wood Houses p. Ashton under Lyne, weaver
"	29	Mary of Eli & Ann Crowder or Crowther (*thus in PR & BT*), Droylsden, weaver
Jul	1	Rosanna d. John & Mary Etchells, Failsworth, weaver
"	6	Violet d. Samuel & Ann Pollit, Failsworth, weaver
"	6	Hannah of James & Elizabeth Clough, Manchester, weaver
"	6	Ann of John & Ann Wild, Wood houses p. Ashton, printer
"	6	John of Miles & Mary Ann Mason, Failsworth, blacksmith
"	6	John of James & Jane Taylor, Failsworth, weaver
"	13	Joel of Joseph & Hannah Thornely, Failsworth, weaver
"	13	John of Jonathan & Phoebe Handley, Droylsden, collier
"	13	Ann d. Edmund & Elizabeth Shaw, Newton, labourer
"	20	Mary of William & Sarah Walcraft, Newton, smallware weaver
"	20	Mary of Jonathan & Ann Chadwick, Droylsden, printer
"	25	Mary of Thomas & Elizabeth Todd, Culcheth Cottage, merchant, bo Dec 18 1801
"	27	John of James & Lucy Berry, Newton, labourer
"	27	Sidney of John & Mary Smith, Newton, manufacturer
"	27	Samuel of Benjamin & Jane Howarth, Droylsden, labourer

Aug	10	Mary of Garside & Alice Blomeley, Newton, weaver
"	16	John of James & Rachel Hough, Newton, bleacher, bo Jun 16 1799 (*entry placed between Aug 17 & 24 in PR & BT*)
"	17	Henry of George & Anne Brandon, Failsworth, blacksmith
"	17	James of Thomas & Alice Horrocks, Newton, labourer, aged 16 years
"	17	Anne of John & Elizabeth Bardsley, Droylsden, dyer, aged 15 years
"	17	Alice of Thomas & Sarah Gorton, Failsworth, joiner
"	17	John natural child of Mary Berry, Failsworth, weaver
"	24	Charles of Joseph & Betty Whitaker, Failsworth, weaver
"	24	Robert of James & Sarah Hunter, Newton, stone mason
"	24	John of John & Martha Ogden, Failsworth, weaver
"	24	Alice of Samuel & Mary Robinson, Newton, flagger
"	31	Ashton of George & Sarah Etchells, Failsworth, weaver
Sep	7	John of John & Nancy Halliwell, Newton, crofter
"	7	Joseph of Adam & Mary Consterdine, Blackley, dyer
"	14	John of Benjamin & Nancy Worsick, Failsworth, farmer
"	21	Anne of Edward & Nancy Robinson, Failsworth, weaver
"	21	Thomas of Thomas & Jane Yates, Newton, crofter
"	21	Elizabeth of Abraham & Mary Horrocks, Woodhouses in Ashton Parish, dyer
"	28	Mary of Joseph & Margaret Ogden, Failsworth, weaver
"	28	James of Joseph & Jane Ogden, Failsworth, weaver
"	28	William of John & Mary Duckworth, Newton, printer
"	30	Mary of Robert & Sarah Branton, Newton, weaver
"	30	Hannah of Robert & Sarah Branton, Newton, weaver
Oct	5	John of William & Mary Fenton, Medlock Vale Ashton Parish, dyer
"	5	Andrew of Joseph & Jane Ellor, Newton, dyer
"	5	Jane of James & Ann Kershaw, Manchester, warehouseman
"	12	Hannah of Jonathan & Martha Leech, Newton, weaver
"	12	Hannah of George & Charlotte Smethurst, Newton, dyer
"	26	Susannah of Joseph & Alice Slater, Failsworth, weaver
"	26	John of Lee & Mary Foden, Newton, labourer
"	26	Elizabeth of John & Esther Taylor, Failsworth, shoe maker
"	31	William of Lauflane & Mary Boyne, Newton, labourer
Nov	2	Jonathan of Joseph & Martha Booth, Failsworth, shopkeeper
"	2	Samuel of John & Mary Howard, Woodhouses, weaver
"	2	Elizabeth natural child of Mary Whitehead, Failsworth, weaver
"	2	Jane of Thomas & Elizabeth Cash, Newton, blacksmith
"	9	Eliza of John & Sarah Wild, Newton, crofter
"	16	Elizabeth of John & Mary Simister, Failsworth, weaver
"	16	Arthur of Thomas & Margaret Hulme, Failsworth, farmer
"	16	James of Thomas & Mary Dawson, Newton, dyer
"	16	George of George & Elizabeth Wade, Newton, printer
"	16	Thomas of Joseph & Elizabeth Higham, Failsworth, weaver
Dec	7	Robert natural child of Mary Smith, Failsworth, weaver
"	7	Thomas of Samuel & Mary Hyde, Newton, weaver

"	11	Joseph of William & Hannah Drinkwater, Newton, bricklayer
"	14	John of Peter & Hannah Tomlinson, Failsworth, printer
"	16	Lucy of James & Ellen Howarth, Newton, pattern drawer
"	16	Rosanna of James & Ellen Howarth, Newton, pattern drawer
"	23	George John s. John & Elizabeth Rachel Piccop, officiating curate of Newton
"	25	Ellen of John & Martha Kershaw, Newton, weaver
"	25	Maria of Peter & Ann Fletcher, Failsworth, weaver
[		Signed John Piccop]

1818

Jan	8	Jane of John & Jane Blackshaw, Newton, manufacturer
"	11	Samuel of Samuel & Mellicent Simister, Failsworth, weaver
"	11	Sarah of Samuel & Mellicent Simister, Failsworth, weaver
"	11	Benjamin of James & Esther Chadderton, Failsworth, weaver
"	23	John of William & Betty Valentine, Newton, crofter
Feb	1	James of Daniel & Sarah Knott, Failsworth, weaver
"	11	John of Joshua & Betty Wood, Newton, labourer
"	22	Eliza natural child of Sarah Wyatt, Newton, weaver
"	22	Andrew of Joseph & Martha Bardsley, Failsworth, weaver
Mar	1	James natural child of Agnes Hulton, Failsworth, weaver
"	1	David of John & Sarah Hilton, Newton, weaver
"	8	Samuel of James & Mary Burton, Newton, weaver
"	8	Thomas of Joseph & Sally Rydings, Failsworth, weaver
"	8	Joseph of Joseph & Sally Rydings, Failsworth, weaver
"	10	Henry of John & Isabella Mills, Medlock Vale, printer
"	15	Mary of Joseph & Sarah Rogers, Failsworth, weaver
"	15	John of Peter & Nancy Travis, Manchester, collier
"	22	Samuel of George & Anne Clarke, Newton, weaver
"	22	James of Eli & Jane Rydings, Failsworth, weaver
"	22	William of Thomas & Alice Featherstone, Failsworth, tanner
"	22	Sarah natural child of Susannah Nicholson, Failsworth, weaver
"	22	James of John & Mary Blackley, Newton, blacksmith
"	22	John of John & Mary Bowker, Newton, crofter
"	22	Harriot natural child of Mary Schofield, Failsworth, weaver
"	22	Robert of Lancelot & Mary Hilton, Failsworth, weaver
"	22	Martha of George & Elizabeth Hulton, Failsworth, weaver
"	22	Mary of James & Martha Swift, Failsworth, weaver
Apr	5	James of Robert Pollit, Newton, labourer & Sarah Charlsworth, Failsworth, weaver
"	5	James of John & Sarah Kenyon, Manchester, collier
"	12	Sarah of John & Elizabeth Whitehead, Moston, weaver
"	19	William of James & Anne Taylor, Failsworth, weaver
"	19	Mary of Joseph & Hannah Williamson, Newton, weaver
May	3	Robert of John & Jane Crossley, Failsworth, weaver

"	3	Anne of Thomas & Jane Wood, Newton, skinner	*(1818)*
"	10	Ellen of William & Elizabeth Glossop, Failsworth, weaver	
"	10	Kirby s. Joseph & Martha Ogden, Failsworth, shopkeeper	
"	10	James of Thomas & Sarah Taylor, Failsworth, weaver	
"	10	Ellen of William & Mary Pendleton, Failsworth, weaver	
"	10	Charles of Charles & Elizabeth Walmsley, Newton, crofter	
"	10	Jemima of Charles & Elizabeth Walmsley, Newton, crofter	
"	10	Sarah of Charles & Elizabeth Walmsley, Newton, crofter	
"	10	Mary of James & Elizabeth Kenyon, Failsworth, weaver	
"	17	James of William & Maria Hamner, Manchester, labourer	
"	17	Jane of Ralph & Sarah Ogden, Failsworth, weaver	
"	17	Eliza of William & Nancy Robinson, Failsworth, weaver	
"	17	Ann of Thomas & Martha Hooley, Newton, labourer	
"	17	Mary of Joshua & Sarah Eckersley, Failsworth, weaver, bo Mar 16	
"	17	Sarah of Andrew & Hannah Clegg, Failsworth, joiner	
"	17	Eliza of Andrew & Hannah Clegg, Failsworth, joiner	
"	17	Joshua of George & Margaret Eyre, Failsworth, shoe maker	
"	17	James of Isaac & Amelia Moors, Manchester, warehouse man	
"	17	John of William & Mary Greenhalgh, Failsworth, tailor	
"	17	John of James & Sarah Robinson, Failsworth, tailor	
"	31	Robert of John & Anne Berry, Failsworth, weaver	
"	31	John of Joseph & Sarah Lees, Failsworth, weaver	
"	31	Jane of William & Nancy Walker, Droylsden, hatter	
"	31	Mary of Thomas & Elizabeth Futteringham, Failsworth, weaver	
Jun	7	Ellen of Joseph & Rachel Yarwood, Manchester, spinner	
"	7	James of Thomas & Anne Hamer, Newton, maker up, bo Oct 22 1813	
"	7	John of Thomas & Anne Hamer, Newton, maker up, bo Sep 29 1815	
"	7	Thomas of Thomas & Anne Hamer, Newton, maker up	
"	7	Obadiah of Edward & Jane Tipton, Droylsden, collier	
"	7	William of William & Sarah Pollit, Failsworth, weaver	
"	10	William Grime of William Christopher & Hannah Chew, Newton, attorney	
"	14	Christiana of Samuel & Mary Dean, Failsworth, weaver	
"	14	Elizabeth natural child of Hannah Brindle, Failsworth, milliner	
"	28	George of George & Mary Wolstenholme, Newton, weaver	
"	28	Hannah of John & Alice Heap, Manchester, weaver	
"	28	William of Richard & Martha Pollit, Failsworth, weaver	
"	28	Thomas of Adam & Margaret Horrocks, Droylsden, labourer	
Jul	3	Isach of William & Nancy Whitaker, Newton, weaver	
"	5	Jane of Mary Taylor & Joel Hodson, Failsworth, weavers	
"	12	Mary of Jonathan & Elizabeth Lees, Newton, warper	
"	12	Ratcliffe of Ratcliffe & Sarah Pott, Newton, manufacturer	
"	12	John of Jacob & Sarah Simpson, Newton, crofter	
"	12	Mary of James & Margaret Higham, Failsworth, crofter	
"	15	Phoebe of Peter & Jane Done, Manchester, labourer	
"	19	John of Thomas & Ann Hanson, Longwood p. Huddersfield Yorkshire, clothier	

"	19	John of Thomas & Sarah Lamb, Newton, labourer
"	19	Edward of George & Mary Hall, Manchester, spinner
"	19	Esther of James Quin, late of Failsworth, printer & Susannah Nuttall, Failsworth, weaver
"	21	Emma of Charles & Anne Winstanley, Manchester, collier
"	26	Thomas of John & Betty Knott, Failsworth, weaver
"	26	Anne natural child of Anne Collinson, Failsworth, weaver
"	26	James of Joseph & Anne Etchells, Hollinwood, weaver
"	26	Dan of John & Anne Haslam, Failsworth, weaver
"	26	William of Joseph & Sarah Marshall, Failsworth, weaver
"	26	William of John & Jane Slater, Moston, labourer
"	29	Mareus of Robert & Mary Heymer, Culcheth Hall, manufacturer, bo Oct 23 1808
[		*written in margin of BT*: Mr (Robert) Heymer's six chldren had been Privately baptized by Mr Singleton of Blackley - John Piccop]
"	29	Theophilus of Robert & Mary Heymer, Culcheth Hall, manufacturer, bo Nov 28 1809
"	29	John of Robert & Mary Heymer, Culcheth Hall, manufacturer, bo Feb 22 1811
"	29	Emma Anne of Robert & Mary Heymer, Culcheth Hall, manufacturer, bo Jul 5 1812
"	29	Nathaniel of Robert & Mary Heymer, Culcheth Hall, manufacturer, bo Feb 4 1814
"	29	Thomas Issachar of Robert & Mary Heymer, Culcheth Hall, manufacturer, bo Dec 15 1816
Aug	2	Martha of David & Betty Potter, Failsworth, weaver
"	9	Hannah of George & Betty Tomlinson, Failsworth, weaver
"	9	John of Joseph & Nancy Ogden, Failsworth, weaver
"	9	Sarah of William & Elizabeth Goodier, Newton, weaver
"	13	Joseph of Samuel & Hannah Barrett, Manchester, shopkeeper
"	16	William of Abraham & Elizabeth Mather, Failsworth, weaver
"	16	Jane of Thomas & Mary Allanson, Culcheth, shopkeeper
"	16	Elizabeth of Joseph & Alice Tetlow, Newton, weaver
"	19	Martha of Elijah & Charlotte Hilton, Failsworth, weaver
"	23	James of John & Hannah Wyatt, Newton, weaver
"	23	Robert of William & Anne Dobson, Ashton Parish, labourer
"	23	Thomas of Richard & Jane Travis, Newton, weaver
"	23	James of John & Frances Howarth, Failsworth, dyer
"	23	Henry of Joseph & Betty Mills, Ashton Parish, calico printer
"	23	William of John & Anne Thornley, Droylsden, weaver
"	23	Hannah of John & Mary Hay, Newton, calico printer
"	23	Francis s. Samuel & Mary Holland, Failsworth, weaver
"	23	Sarah of William & Betty Worrall, Failsworth, labourer
"	30	Matilda of Joseph & Mary Berry, Failsworth, weaver
Sep	1	Sarah of Luke & Rachel Hulton, Failsworth, weaver
"	6	Hannah of William & Ellen Smith, Hollinwood, weaver
"	6	Ellen of Isaac & Anne Butler, Hollinwood, dresser

"	6	Anne of Aaron & Mary Anne Gredwell, Newton, weaver
"	6	Esther of George & Elizabeth Smith, Droylsden, labourer
"	13	Anne of Robert & Anne Ridings, Failsworth, weaver
"	13	Joseph of William & Anne Ware, Failsworth, calico printer
"	13	Francis s. Joseph & Rebecca Hulton, Failsworth, weaver
"	13	Sarah of William & Hannah Winn, Newton, excise officer
"	20	James of David & Elizabeth Ogden, Failsworth, weaver
"	20	Richard of Nicholas & Jane Simister, Failsworth, weaver
"	20	Mary Anne of Thomas & Jane Wild, Newton, publican
"	24	Anne of John & Anne Holt, Failsworth, weaver
"	27	William natural child of Martha Barrington, Moston, weaver
"	27	Jonathan of Jonathan & Esther Etchels, Failsworth, weaver
"	27	Eliza of John & Anne Bradbury, Manchester, shoe maker
"	28	Joseph of Thomas & Amelia Yeld, Failsworth, crofter
Oct	4	John of Robert & Sarah Branton, Newton, weaver
"	4	Esther of James & Sarah Simister, Newton, weaver
"	4	James of James & Sarah Simister, Newton, weaver
"	4	John of James & Sarah Simister, Newton, weaver
"	4	John of John & Anne Grime, Droylsden, farmer
"	11	Anna of Richard & Anne Hulme, Droylsden, farmer
"	11	Jane of James & Jane Aldred, Newton, shoe maker
"	16	Hannah of Ashton & Betty Ashton, Failsworth, weaver
"	18	Richard of Richard & Mary Walker, Newton, smallware weaver
"	18	Anne of John & Martha Holland, Moston, weaver
"	25	Joel of Joel & Martha Brown, Moston, farmer
Nov	1	Eliza of Joseph & Alice Tetlow, Newton, warehouse man
"	8	Enoch of Henry & Sarah Roginson, Newton, blacksmith
"	8	Abraham of David & Betty Whitaker, Newton, wheelwright
"	8	Alice of Thomas & Mary Bredbury, Oldham, collier
"	8	Thomas of John & Mary Thorley, Failsworth, weaver
"	15	John of John & Esther Whitaker, Blackley, farmer
"	15	Timothy of Samuel & Mary Haughton, Manchester, fustian cutter
"	15	Elizabeth of Samuel & Betty Jones, Newton, crofter
"	22	John of Joseph & Maria Arrondale, Droylsden, weaver
"	29	Thomas of John & Anne Brown, Newton, dyer
"	29	Sarah of Charles & Anna Heywood, Newton, weaver
Dec	6	James of Samuel & Martha Barton, Droylsden, dyer
"	13	Alice of John & Sarah Williamson, Failsworth, weaver
"	25	Elizabeth Rachel d. John & Elizabeth Rachel Piccop, officiating curate of Newton
"	25	Jane of James & Hannah Swindells, Newton, weaver
"	25	Margaret of Charles & Alice Taylor, Newton, weaver
"	25	Thomas Joseph s. Charles & Alice Taylor, Newton, weaver
"	25	George of Charles & Eliza Ekersley, Newton, weaver
"	27	Hannah d. William & Hannah Drinkwater, Newton, bricklayer
"	27	George s. William & Hannah Drinkwater, Newton, bricklayer

"	27	Ann d. James & Sarah Wilson, Moston, weaver
"	27	John s. Elizabeth Bradshaw, Moston, spinster

1819

Jan	3	John s. James & Sarah Worral, Failsworth, farmer
"	3	Joseph s. James & Ann Taylor, Failsworth, weaver
"	3	Sarah d. John & Mary Allen, Newton, labourer
"	10	Samuel s. Samuel & Sarah Grimshaw, Failsworth, hatter
"	10	Joseph s. John & Diana Tongue, Failsworth, weaver
"	10	Ann d. Oliver & Martha Ogden, Failsworth, weaver
"	17	Frederic s. George & Elizabeth Parkinson, Failsworth, tanner
"	17	William s. Thomas & Mary Whitehead, Failsworth, weaver
"	17	Ann d. Charles & Alice Collinson, Failsworth, weaver
"	17	William s. John & Ann Tipton, Droylsden, collier
"	24	Simeon s. John & Betty Fletcher, Failsworth, weaver
"	24	Thomas s. George & Ann Yates, Newton, whitster
"	24	Joseph s. James & Betty Marsden, Newton, whitster
"	31	John s. Joseph & Jenny Thornley, Failsworth, weaver
Feb	7	Ellen d. John & Mary Linley, Newton, weaver
"	7	Martha d. John & Mary Linley, Newton, weaver
"	7	Samuel s. Samuel & Jane Mather, Newton, weaver
"	7	Ann d. Dan & Hannah Hulton, Failsworth, weaver
"	14	Mary d. Shettle & Esther Chorlton, Failsworth, innkeeper
"	21	Samuel s. Samuel & Mary Robinson, Newton, slater
"	21	Marianne d. Sarah Schofield, Failsworth, spinster
"	21	Alice d. John & Ann Whittaker, Failsworth, weaver
"	21	William s. James & Sarah Wilson, Moston, farmer
"	21	Sarah d. Hannah Brown, Newton, spinster
"	26	Thomas s. William & Elizabeth Lees, Manchester, weaver
"	28	Joseph s. James & Alice Fletcher, Failsworth, weaver
"	28	Samuel s. Garside & Alice Blomiley, Newton, weaver
"	28	John s. Daniel & Hannah Berrington, Manchesr., labourer
"	28	Mary d. John & Margaret Wood, Failsworth, weaver
Mar	4	Isabella d. John & Mary Smith, Newton, manufacturer
"	5	Samuel s. Joseph & Mary Horrocks, Failsworth, bricklayer
"	5	Robert s. John & Mary Garlick, Failsworth, labourer
"	7	Thomas s. Christopher & Sarah Miller, Newton, labourer
"	7	Jeremy s. Samuel & Ann Dawson, Failsworth, weaver
"	7	John s. Joshua & Sarah Ann Swift, Manchester, dyer
"	14	Harriet d. William & Hannah Ferrent, Newton, designer
"	14	Ann d Joseph & Priscilla Fletcher, Newton, weaver
"	14	Martha d. Mary Fletcher, Failsworth, spinster
"	14	John s. Joseph & Rebecca Barrat, Newton, labourer
"	14	Maria d. Robert & Mary Drinkwater, Newton, bricklayer

" 21 John (George *struck through*) [John] s. George & Sarah Hulton, Newton, weaver *(1819)*

" 21 Henry s. James & Abigail Blackshaw, Failsworth, hatter

Apr 4 Alice d. James & Martha Wyld, Droylsden, weaver

" 4 Martha d. Elizabeth Wolstencroft, Failsworth, weaver

" 11 Joseph s. Joseph & Elizabeth Seel, Newton, printer

" 11 Betty d. Robert & Esther Brierly, Failsworth, weaver

" 11 Abraham s. Thomas & Mary Ashworth, Newton, weaver

" 11 Elizabeth d. Ashton & Ann Shepley, Newton, weaver

" 11 Elizabeth d. Samuel & Ann Bottomley, Manchesr., labourer

" 11 Alice d. Sarah Makin, Moston, spinster

" 11 Sarah d. Richard & Betty Makin, Moston, weaver

" 25 William s. Elias & Elizabeth Lomax, Newton, weaver

" 25 Elizabeth d. William & Mary Council, Newton, weaver

" 25 Edward s. William & Mary Council, Newton, weaver

" 25 John s. William & Mary Council, Newton, weaver

" 25 Charles s. William & Mary Council, Newton, weaver

May 2 Abraham s. John & Mary Gredwell, Newton, weaver

" 2 William s. Joseph & Betty Mills, Medlock Ashton Parish, printer

" 2 Mary d. James & Ann Ogden, Oldham, blacksmith

" 2 Alice d. Thomas & Margaret Horrocks, Newton, bleacher

" 9 David s. William & Betty Davenport, Failsworth, weaver

" 9 James s. Samuel & Sarah Garside, Newton, innkeeper

" 9 Samuel s. Thomas & Mary Hutton [Hulton], Failsworth, weaver

" 9 Matthew s. Matthew & Sarah Brown, Newton, weaver

" 13 Mary d. Joseph & Ann Fildes, Newton, farmer

" 13 Joseph s. John & Elizabeth Fildes, Newton, innkeeper

" 16 Ann Frances d. John & Ann Webb, Audenshaw, printer

" 16 Ruth d. John & Mary Chatterton, Manchester, collier

" 16 Hannah d. John & Betty Whitehead, Newton, weaver

" 16 Richard s. Jonathan & Ann Clough, Newton, dyer

" 16 Thomas s. Richard & Alice Whitehead, Woodhouses, weaver

" 16 Luke s. William & Mary Williamson, Failsworth, weaver

" 16 William s. Joshua & Betty Wood, Newton, farmer

" 23 James s. William & Ann Booth, Failsworth, weaver

" 23 William s. Thomas & Jane Yates, Newton, crofter

" 30 Joseph s. William & Mary Hulton, Failsworth, weaver

" 30 Joseph s. William & Betty Crossley, Failsworth, shopkeeper

" 30 Mary d. Joseph & Ann Robinson, Failsworth, weaver

" 30 Sarah d. John & Nancy Whittaker, Failsworth, weaver

Jun 6 Hannah d. Robert & Alice Stanfield, Newton, hatter

" 6 Frances d. James & Alice Swift, Failsworth, weaver

" 6 Esther d. Samuel & Mary Kenyon, Hollinwood, weaver

" 6 Mary d. John & Mary Howard, Woodhouses, weaver

" 6 John s. Edward & Ann Worral, Failsworth, weaver

"	6	Benjamin s. Benjamin & Jane Howarth, Droylsden, farmer
"	8	James s. James & Mary Gradwell, Failsworth, weaver
"	10	Hannah d. Robert & Elizabeth Clough, Failsworth, weaver
"	13	Abraham s. James & Hannah Ogden, Failsworth, weaver
"	13	Ann d. Thomas & Nancy Ogden, Failsworth, weaver
"	20	Jane d. Thomas & Jane Wood, Newton, felmonger
"	20	Harriet d. James & Nancy Kershaw, Manchester, warehouseman
"	20	Sally d. Edmund & Olive Schofield, Failsworth, weaver
"	20	Philip s. Robert & Frances Mills, Medlock Vale, dyer
"	23	Margaret d. James & Margaret Jackson, Manchester, weaver
"	23	Ann d. James & Margaret Jackson, Manchester, weaver
"	27	Sarah d. Joseph & Elizabeth Tonkinson, Newton, weaver
"	27	Mary d. Joseph & Hannah Thornley, Failsworth, weaver
"	27	Mary d. Henry & Betty Ratcliff, Failsworth, wheelwright
"	27	Marianne d. Robert & Mary Gorton, Chadderton, farmer
"	27	Lot s. William & Mary Hampson, Newton, slater
Jul	4	Robert s. John & Elizabeth Taylor, Woodhouses, weaver
"	4	Mary d. Samuel & Ann Barnes, Manchester, weaver
"	11	Eliza d. Joseph & Hannah Sutcliff, Manchester, weaver
"	18	Joseph s. William & Phoebe Jackson, Droylsden, collier
"	18	Robert s. James & Ann Tomlinson, Newton, crofter
"	25	Elizabeth d. Richard & Hannah Barrow, Failsworth, weaver
"	25	Elizabeth d. Ann Clough, Failsworth, spinster
"	25	Hannah d. Robert & Jane Mills, Failsworth, weaver
"	25	William s. William & Sarah Ramsden, Failsworth, weaver
"	25	Elizabeth d. Sally Wolstencroft, Failsworth, spinster
Aug	1	Joseph s. James & Alice Taylor, Failsworth, weaver
"	1	Ann d. Jonathan & Martha Leech, Newton, weaver
"	8	William s. William & Catherine Gradwell, Newton, weaver
"	8	Sarah d. Thomas & Ann Wilson, Failsworth, weaver
"	15	Edward s. William & Elizabeth Ashworth, Manchester, weaver
"	15	James s. John & Mary Porter, Newton, crofter
"	15	Tryphena d. Benjamin & Ann Bayley, Newton, weaver
"	22	James Hall s. William & Marianne Barnes, Manchester, weaver
"	22	John s. James & Elizabeth Hale, Manchester, weaver
"	22	Ann d. James & Sarah Hunter, Ashton under Line Parish, stonemason
"	22	Jane d. Adam & Alice Martin, Manchester, labourer
"	22	Benjamin s. Benjamin & Mary Hulton, Failsworth, weaver
"	22	James s. Jonah & Mary Greaves, Ashton under Line Parish, weaver
"	27	Catherine d. William & Betty Valentine, Manchester, labourer
"	29	Edwin s. John & Ann Clough, Failsworth, weaver
"	29	Benjamin s. Jane Pollit, Failsworth, spinster
Sep	5	Jane d. John & Sarah Goodier, Newton, packer
"	5	Elizabeth d. George & Ann Morris, Ashton under Line Parish, packer
"	5	Betty d. Samuel & Ann Lowe, Manchester, weaver

"	5	Samuel s. Thomas & Ann Hamer, Newton, packer
"	5	Elizabeth d. Thomas & Jane Wyld, Newton, inn keeper
"	12	John s. Samuel & Mary Hyde, Newton, weaver
"	12	Elizabeth d. Mary Thorpe, Failsworth, spinster
"	12	Martha d. John & Sarah Hulton, Newton, weaver
"	19	Sarah d. James & Betty Bardsley, Failsworth, weaver
"	19	Elizabeth d. William & Mary Greenhalgh, Failsworth, tailor
"	26	Samuel s. Joseph & Sarah Wright, Newton, saddler
"	26	Hannah d. Thomas & Mary Walmsley, Failsworth, farmer
"	26	John s. Joseph & Ann Taylor, Newton, weaver
"	26	Martha d. Thomas & Elizabeth Lancashire, Blackley, dyer
Oct	3	John s. Joseph & Sarah Brandon, Medlock Vale, labourer
"	3	Elizabeth d. Thomas & Betty Fletcher, Failsworth, weaver
"	3	William s. Daniel & Sarah Clayton, Manchester, collier
"	10	Joseph s. James & Jane Taylor, Failsworth, weaver
"	10	Richard s. Richard & Esther Thorpe, Moston, weaver
"	10	Janette d. John & Grace Bradshaw, Newton, printer
"	17	Eliza d. Mary Smethurst, Hollinwood, spinster
"	17	Thomas s. Joseph & Sarah Tomlinson, Newton, crofter
"	24	James s. Joseph & Sarah Rogers, Failsworth, weaver
"	31	Robert s. Margaret McVenom, Newton, spinster
"	31	Jane d. Abraham & Martha Whitehead, Chadderton, farmer
"	31	Elizabeth d. William & Mary Walker, Manchester, collier
Nov	7	Mary d. John & Mary Smith, Failsworth, weaver
"	7	Ellen d. Edward & Sarah Caldwell, Newton, farmer
"	7	William s. Leah & Mary Foden, Newton, labourer
"	14	Lemuel s. William & Mary Smith, Ashton Parish, printer
"	14	Robert s. Robert & Mary Allen, Newton, printer
"	28	William Houghton s. John & Sarah Caldwell, Newton, wheelwright
"	28	Hannah d. Edward & Nancy Robinson, Failsworth, weaver
Dec	5	John s. Samuel & Mary Lees, Failsworth, weaver
"	5	Henry s. John & Sarah Rothwell, Newton, printer
"	12	Elizabeth d. Thomas & Elizabeth Cash, Newton, blacksmith
"	12	Sidney s. William & Mary Smith, Woodhouses, weaver
"	12	Abraham s. William & Jane Mather, Droylsden, weaver
"	19	George s. William & Ann Ware, Failsworth, calico printer
"	19	Maria d. Peter & Nancy Travis, Manchester, collier
"	25	William s. James & Mary Lees, Failsworth, weaver
"	25	Jane Townsend d. Charles & Eliza Eckersley, Newton, weaver
"	25	William s. William & Nancy Booth, Newton, innkeeper
"	26	William s. James & Hannah Brierly, Failsworth, weaver
[		Thos Gaskell Incumbent of Newton]
[		Jas Hough Chapelwarden of Newton]

1820

Jan	2	Joseph s. Joseph & Elizabeth Higham, Newton, weaver
"	2	George s. William & Hannah Brandon, Newton, dyer
"	16	John s. Moses & Clarissa Gradwell, Newton, weaver
"	16	William s. Moses & Clarissa Gradwell, Newton, weaver
"	23	Ralph s. William & Mary Rutter, Newton, bleacher
"	30	Hannah d. Ralph & Sarah Ogden, Failsworth, weaver
"	30	John s. James & Ellen Howarth, Failsworth, draughtsman
"	30	Mary d. John & Mary Blakeley, Newton, blacksmith
Feb	13	Sarah d. James & Mary Burton, Newton, weaver
"	13	Richard s. John & Alice Worsick, Failsworth, farmer
"	13	Marianne d. William & Mary Cliffe, Newton, collier
"	13	William s. David & Ann Ogden, Failsworth, weaver
"	16	James s. William & Elizabeth Sutcliff, Failsworth, cordwainer
"	20	William s. Thomas & Betty Coupe, Droylsden, draughtsman
"	20	Margaret d. Thomas & Betty Coupe, Droylsden, draughtsman
"	20	Esther d. John & Jane Slater, Moston, labourer
"	27	Judith d. Joseph & Alice Tetlow, Newton, weaver
"	27	Sarah d. John & Jane Blackshaw, Newton, manufacturer
"	27	Violet d. Joseph & Mary Bury, Failsworth, weaver
"	27	James s. Betty Brindle, Failsworth, spinster
"	27	Elizabeth d. William & Elizabeth Phillips, Bradford, bricklayer
Mar	7	William s. John & Hannah Etchels, Failsworth, weaver
"	12	Sarah d. Isaac & Elizabeth Heapy, Droylsden, hatter
"	13	Sarah d. Mary Jinks, Ashton Parish, spinster
"	13	Veloma d. John & Betty Robinson, Manchester, labourer
"	19	James s. Ann Taylor, Failsworth, spinster
"	22	Mary d. Robert & Betty Lees, Failsworth, weaver
"	22	Alice d. Robert & Betty Lees, Failsworth, weaver
"	25	Mary d. Mary Walmsley, Failsworth, spinster
"	26	Elizabeth d. Thomas & Elizabeth Berry, Moston, farmer
Apr	2	Charles s. Betty Whittaker, Newton, spinster
"	2	Mary d. James & Sally Whittaker, Failsworth, weaver
"	2	William s. William & Martha Cordingly, Failsworth, weaver
"	2	Joseph s. Jane Berry, Failsworth, spinster
"	2	Joseph s. John & Jane Crossley, Failsworth, weaver
"	2	John s. Samuel & Jane Bethel, Newton, calenderer
"	2	Rosina d. Benjamin & Nancy Worsick, Failsworth, farmer
"	2	Mary d. John & Sarah Marsden, Newton, bleacher
"	9	William s. Joseph & Jane Ogden, Failsworth, weaver
"	9	Sarah d. Hannah Richardson, Newton, spinster
"	16	Elizabeth d. William & Betty Lees, Hollinwood, labourer
"	16	Henry s. Joseph & Catherine Fletcher, Failsworth, weaver
"	23	Esther d. William & Mary Counsell, Newton, weaver

"	23	Jane d. Luke & Rachel Hulton, Failsworth, weaver	*(1820)*
"	24	Ralph s. Samuel & Hannah Robinson, Failsworth, weaver	
"	30	Richard s. Richard & Sarah Worsick, Medlock Vale, farmer	
May	7	William s. Richard & Ann Pollitt, Newton, weaver	
"	7	Sarah d. Richard & Ann Pollitt, Newton, weaver	
"	7	Sarah d. Samuel & Mary Haughton, Manchester, fustian cutter	
"	8	Ann d. John & Sarah Wyld, Newton, weaver	
"	14	Henry s. James & Sarah Mather, Failsworth, weaver	
"	17	John s. Joseph & Sarah Holland, Moston, innkeeper	
"	21	Mary d. William & Lucy Seel, Newton, maker up	
"	21	Sarah d. James & Betty Kenyon, Failsworth, weaver	
"	21	Mary Anne d. Alice Brown, Hollinwood, spinster	
"	21	Thomas s. James & Martha Swift, Failsworth, weaver	
"	21	Mary d. Thomas & Mary Aston, Failsworth, weaver	
"	21	John s. Alice Collin, Failsworth, spinster	
"	21	Francis s. James & Anne Taylor, Failsworth, weaver	
"	21	Alice d. Thomas & Sarah Taylor, Failsworth, weaver	
"	21	Amelia d. Peter & Mary Pilling, Newton, labourer	
"	21	Elizabeth d. Ratliff & Sarah (*blank*) [Pott], Newton, manufacturer	
"	21	William s. John & Alice Heap, Manchester, weaver	
"	23	Abraham s. Abraham & Mary Lee, Manchester, weaver	
"	28	Elizabeth d. John & Sarah Newton, Droylsden, joiner	
"	28	Thomas s. William & Ann Mosdel, Medlock Vale, labourer	
Jun	4	Mary Anne d. Elisha & Charlotte Hulton, Failsworth, weaver	
"	4	Betty d. Samuel & Phoebe Travis, Newton, labourer	
"	4	James s. John & Anne Thornley, Droylsden, weaver	
"	4	Abigail d. Nancy Naylor, Newton, spinster	
"	11	David s. James & Ellen Hulton, Failsworth, weaver	
"	11	Edward s. John & Betty Whitehead, Moston, weaver	
"	11	James s. Jonathan & Phoebe Handley, Clayton, collier	
"	18	Edward s. William & Lydia Thornycroft, Newton, labourer	
"	18	James s. John & Mary Wilson, Moston, dyer	
"	25	Ann d. William & Agnes Hulton, Failsworth, weaver	
"	25	Samuel s. James & Martha Wild, Droylsden, weaver	
Jul	2	Martha d. John & Mary Warburton, Droylsden, labourer	
"	2	Elizabeth d. Phoebe Glossop, Moston, spinster	
"	2	Nancy d. George & Betty Tomlinson, Failsworth, weaver	
"	2	Josias s. Betty Wolstenholme, Failsworth, spinster	
"	9	John s. Martha Garlick, Failsworth, spinster	
"	16	Elizabeth d. William & Sarah Bradshaw, Newton, weaver	
"	16	Samuel s. Garside & Alice Blomely, Newton, weaver	
"	23	James s. Joseph & Ann Etchels, Hollinwood, weaver	
"	23	George s. Richard & Jenny Travis, Newton, weaver	
"	23	Ellen d. Joshua & Sarah Eckersley, Failsworth, weaver	
"	30	James s. Mally Booth, Failsworth, spinster	

Aug	6	Elizabeth d. William & Elizabeth Collinson, Failsworth, weaver
"	6	Elizabeth d. Thomas & Sarah Lamb, Newton, labourer
"	6	John Harrison s. John & Mary Smith, Newton, manufacturer
"	6	Peter s. William & Ellen Smith, Oldham, weaver
"	6	Margaret d. Shekel & Esther Chorlton, Failsworth, shopkeeper
"	9	Alexander s. Thomas & Elizabeth Fotheringham, Failsworth, weaver
"	11	Richard Charles s. John & Martha Thomason, Failsworth, weaver
"	13	John s. Thomas & Ann Allen, Failsworth, labourer
"	13	Thomas s. John & Ann Berry, Failsworth, weaver
"	16	Alice d. William & Elizabeth Glossop, Failsworth, weaver
"	20	Sarah Ireland d. Thomas & Ann Hamson, Longwood near Huddersfield, clothier
"	20	Mary d. Robert & Alice Stansfield, Newton, hatter
"	20	Ellen d. Ashton & Betty Ashton, Failsworth, weaver
"	20	Thomas s. James & Sarah Marshal, Failsworth, bricklayer
"	20	James s. William & Esther Summers, Newton, dyer
"	20	Elizabeth d. William & Mary Whitehead, Manchester, weaver
"	20	Betty d. James & Isabella Wild, Failsworth, weaver
"	20	Maria d. George & Elizabeth Hulton, Failsworth, weaver
"	20	William s. William & Hannah Wynne, Newton, excise officer
"	27	James s. James & Jane Aldred, Newton, cordwainer
"	27	Robert s. Ann Hulton, Failsworth, spinster
Sep	3	John s. James & Nancy Renshaw, Failsworth, blacksmith
"	10	Charles s. Samuel & Ann Pollit, Failsworth, weaver
"	17	Elizabeth d. Joseph & Sarah Swift, Collyhurst, dyer
"	17	Margaret d. Joseph & Sarah Swift, Collyhurst, dyer
"	17	Ann d. Hannah Brindle, Failsworth, spinster
"	24	William s. Joseph & Alice Robinson, Failsworth, weaver
"	24	Sarah d. James & Alice Mills, Medlock Vale, printer
Oct	8	Mary d. Solomon & Betty Etchels, Failsworth, weaver
"	15	Joseph s. James & Elizabeth Barker, Newton, smallware manufacturer
"	16	Thomas Cranmer s. Rev. John & Elizabeth Rachel Piccop, Manchester, bo 24 Nov 1819
"	22	Mary d. John & Mary Newton, Failsworth, publican
"	22	Sarah Ann d. Peter & Nancy Travis, Manchester, collier
"	25	Martha d. John & Mary Howard, Ashton, weaver
"	29	Rosalind d. George & Elizabeth Parkinson, Failsworth, tanner
Nov	5	John s. George & Sarah Garlick, Failsworth, weaver
"	12	Elias s. John & Mary Hay, Newton, print cutter
"	12	William s. Simon & Martha Dearden, Newton, printer
"	12	Amelia d. Simon & Martha Dearden, Newton, printer
"	12	Mary d. Joseph & Maria Arrundale, Droylsden, labourer
"	19	Thomas s. Joseph & Priscilla Fletcher, Newton, weaver
"	19	James s. Mary Fitton, Moston, spinster
"	26	Elizabeth d. John & Anne Garner, Droylsden, farmer
Dec	3	John s. John & Betty Knott, Failsworth, weaver

"	3	John s. James & Sarah Wilson, Moston, weaver
"	10	Sarah d. Thomas & Jane Bates, Waterside, labourer
"	10	Ellen d. William & Elizabeth Davenport, Failsworth, weaver
"	24	James s. James & Mary Blomiley, Newton, weaver
"	24	Robert s. Betty Barlow, Failsworth, spinster
"	24	John Horatio Nelson s. William & Ann Booth, Failsworth, weaver
"	24	Ellen d. Thomas & Mary Allanson, Newton, bleacher
"	25	Rosanna d. Sarah Robinson, Newton, spinster
"	25	Nancy d. George & Margaret Eyre, Failsworth, shoemaker
"	25	Mary Lancashire d. Samuel & Martha Hulton, Moston, farmer
"	25	Marianne d. James & Betty Whitehead, Failsworth, weaver
"	25	Emanuel s. James & Alice Swift, Failsworth, weaver
"	28	James s. Elizabeth Clegg, Failsworth, spinster
"	28	Hannah d. Samuel & Martha Smethurst, Salford, porter
"	31	James s. John & Mary Bowker, Newton, whitster
"	31	Betty d. Thomas & Hannah Horrocks, Newton, dyer

1821

[Register of Baptisms & Burials at Newton Chapel in 1821] (*written in hand-drawn ornamental design on inside front cover of BT*)

Jan	7	Ann d. Benjamin & Jane Howarth, Droylsden, labourer
"	7	Thomas Whitehead s. Sarah Berry, Failsworth, spinster
"	7	Nancy d. William & Mary Greenhalgh, Ashton Parish, farmer
"	14	William s. Robert & Sarah Branton, Newton, weaver
"	14	Elizabeth d. William & Elizabeth Howarth, Droylsden, lock keeper
"	14	Phoebe d. James & Sarah Worral, Failsworth, carter
"	25	James s. Samuel & Jane Wyld, Failsworth, weaver
"	28	William s. Mary Whitehead, Failsworth, spinster
"	28	Sarah d. Eli & Jane Ridings, Failsworth, weaver
"	28	Jane d. Joseph & Mary Davies, Newton, weaver
Feb	4	Elizabeth d. Samuel & Mary Dean, Failsworth, weaver
"	7	William s. Mary Collinson, Failsworth, spinster
"	7	Elizabeth d. John & Sarah Taylor, Failsworth, weaver
"	11	Esther d. Joseph & Betty Tomkinson, Newton, weaver
"	11	Elizabeth d. Ann Knott, Failsworth, spinster
"	11	James s. Thomas & Margaret Horrocks, Failsworth, bleacher
"	16	George s. Joseph & Sarah Lees, Failsworth, weaver
"	18	Nancy d. William & Phoebe Jacks, Droylsden, collier
"	18	George s. Joshua & Sarah Anne Swift, Collyhurst, dyer
"	18	Thomas Squire s. Joseph & Martha Booth, Failsworth, shopkeeper
"	25	Elizabeth d. Miles & Marianne Mason, Failsworth, blacksmith
"	25	Eli s. Samuel & Mary Robinson, Newton, slater
"	25	Sarah d. Richard & Anne Hulme, Droylsden, farmer
"	25	John s. James & Alice Fletcher, Failsworth, weaver

"	25	Anne d. Thomas & Mary Winterbotham, Failsworth, weaver
"	25	James s. William & Mary Pendlebury, Newton, weaver
Mar	4	Edmund s. Nicholas & Jane Simister, Newton, weaver
"	18	Mary d. Joseph & Sarah Tomlinson, Newton, bleacher
"	18	William Sykes s. John & Mary Thorley, Failsworth, weaver
"	23	Mary d. William & Betty Lee, Newton, weaver
Apr	1	Matilda d. Andrew & Hannah Clegg, Failsworth, joiner
"	3	Frederic s. James & Mary Shepley, Newton, weaver
"	8	James s. David & Ann Ogden, Failsworth, weaver
"	8	Catherine d. Thos. & Jane Yates, Newton, bleacher
"	8	Marianne d. Richard & Mary Walker, Newton, weaver
"	8	Alice d. Daniel & Sarah Clayton, Manchesr., soldier
"	13	John s. John & Elizabeth Fildes, Newton, innkeeper
"	13	Daniel s. Thomas & Jane Wyld, Newton, innkeeper
"	15	John s. Richard & Betty Bee, Manchesr., weaver
"	18	Betty Sarah d. Charles & Alice Taylor, Newton, weaver
"	22	John s. John & Mary Smith, Newton, blockcutter
"	22	John s. Joseph & Anne Greaves, Failsworth, carter
"	22	William s. James & Anne Barnes, Newton, weaver
"	22	Joseph s. Thomas & Martha Whitelegg, Droylsden, weaver
"	22	John s. Samuel & Mary Moore, Failsworth, weaver
"	22	Edwin s. Josiah & Alice Etchels, Failsworth, weaver
"	22	Joseph s. George & Sarah Hilton, Newton, weaver
"	22	Joseph s. George & Anne Yates, Newton, whitster
"	22	Anne d. James & Betty Marsden, Manchesr., whitster
"	22	Esther d. Michael & Esther Smith, Manchesr., calico printer
"	22	James s. Robert & Jane Mills, Failsworth, weaver
"	22	William s. Michael & Elizabeth Waring, Newton, blockcutter
"	22	Elizabeth d. Michael & Elizabeth Waring, Newton, blockcutter
"	22	James s. Alice Mills, Failsworth, spinster
"	22	Betty d. George & Betty Travis, Newton, bleacher
"	22	Charles s. James & Anne Kershaw, Manr., warehouse man
"	29	Henry s. William & Lydia Dean, Gorton, hatter
May	6	Andrew s. Andrew & Rebekah Horrocks, Ashton, printer
"	6	Elizabeth d. Jonathan & Esther Naylor, Newton, weaver
"	13	John s. William & Betty Crossley, Failsworth, shopkeeper
"	20	Ann d. John & Mary Whitehead, Failsworth, weaver
"	20	Edwin s. Joseph & Rebecca Hulton, Failsworth, weaver
"	22	Elizabeth d. John & Hannah Wood, Droylsden, farmer
"	22	John s. Charles & Alice Collinson, Failsworth, weaver
"	22	Jenny d. John & Ann Clough, Failsworth, weaver
"	28	Jane d. William & Nancy Whittaker, Newton, weaver
Jun	10	Samuel s. Samuel & Mary Ward, Failsworth, weaver
"	10	John s. Betty Wroe, Failsworth, spinster
"	10	Sarah d. James & Anne Ogden, Hollinwood, blacksmith

"	12	Anne d. Jonathan & Anne Glossop, Failsworth, weaver
"	12	Anne d. John & Jane Blackshaw, Newton, weaver
"	17	Matilda d. Thomas & Mary Johnson, Newton, weaver
"	17	Hannah d. Jenny Pollitt, Failsworth, spinster
"	17	Betty d. Joseph & Nancy Ogden, Failsworth, weaver
"	17	William s. Abraham & Mary Horrocks, Ashton Parish, bleacher
"	17	Joseph s. Samuel & Jane Mather, Newton, weaver
"	17	Joseph & Elizabeth children of Samuel & Sarah Grimshaw, Failsworth, farmer
"	17	John s. William & Jane Mather, Droylsden, weaver
"	17	Joshua s. John & Sarah Newton, Droylsden, wheelwright
"	24	Ann d. Alfred & Martha Bertenshaw, Droylsden, hatter
"	24	Maria d. Ellen Kay, Blackley, spinster
Jul	1	Alice d. Jonathan & Sarah Boardman, Chadderton, weaver
"	1	Matthew s. Robert & Anna Richardson, Failsworth, hatter
"	8	Elizabeth Houghton d. John & Sarah Caldwell, Newton, wheelwright
"	8	Elizabeth Scott d. William Middleton & Anne Scott Laurie, Failsworth, schoolmaster
"	8	Nancy d. Joseph & Mary Bardsley, Failsworth, weaver
"	8	Betty d. Joseph & Mary Bardsley, Failsworth, weaver
"	8	Jane d. George & Anne Morris, Ashton Parish, bleacher
"	11	Matthew s. Richard & Esther Thorpe, Moston, weaver
"	15	Samuel s. Joseph & Rebekah Barritt, Newton, labourer
"	22	William s. Thomas & Mary Bagnal, Newton, weaver
"	29	Job s. John & Mary Ellison, Newton, carpenter
"	29	Thomas s. Betty Allen, Failsworth, spinster
"	29	Robert s. James & Mary Hilton, Newton, weaver
Aug	12	Sarah d. Joseph & Hannah Thornley, Failsworth, weaver
"	15	Anne d. Willey & Nancy Booth, Newton, inn keeper
"	17	Townley s. William Christopher & Hannah Chew, Newton, solicitor
"	19	Philip s. Thomas & Elizabeth Lancashire, Blackley, dyer
"	19	John s. James & Sarah Bradbury, Newton, labourer
"	19	Henry s. John & Hannah Wyatt, Newton, weaver
"	19	Sabrine d. Samuel & Mary Hyde, Newton, weaver
"	19	James Walker s. Elizabeth Dobs, Alfreton Derbyshire, spinster
"	19	Joseph s. Thomas & Martha Shires, Manchester, iron-founder
"	19	James s. Martha Thorpe, Failsworth, spinster
"	19	Ellen d. William & Elizabeth Wood, Manchester, painter
"	19	Mally d. William & Mally Hulton, Failsworth, weaver
"	19	John s. Martha Ravenscroft, Failsworth, spinster
"	19	William s. Frank & Martha Brown, Failsworth, farmer
"	19	James s. William & Lucy Seel, Newton, packer
"	19	Henry s. Samuel & Ann Dawson, Failsworth, weaver
"	26	Hannah d. James & Jane Aldred, Failsworth, weaver
"	26	Mary d. William & Mary Brown, Failsworth, sawyer
Sep	2	Elizabeth d. Samuel & Anne Barnes, Manchester, weaver

"	2	Betty d. James & Anne Taylor, Failsworth, weaver
"	9	Elizabeth d. James & Betty Wyld, Failsworth, weaver
"	9	James s. John & Anne Hall, Failsworth, weaver
"	9	Hannah d. Robert & Anne Ridings, Failsworth, weaver
"	9	Hannah d. John & Sarah Goodier, Newton, packer
"	9	Nancy d. John & Mary Stott, Failsworth, weaver
"	16	Abraham s. James & Ellen Clough, Failsworth, weaver
"	16	Joseph s. Jonathan & Sarah Titter, Newton, dyer
"	16	Mary d. James & Mary Wilkinson, Failsworth, weaver
"	16	Elizabeth d. George & Jane Robinson, Droylsden, dyer
"	16	Emma d. James & Elizabeth Clough, Manchester, weaver
"	30	Maria Albiston d. Catherine Newton, Manchester
"	30	Hannah d. James & Hannah Blackshaw, Failsworth, hatter
"	30	William s. James & Mary Burton, Newton, weaver
"	30	John s. Margaret Berrington, Moston, spinster
Oct	7	William s. Robert & Betty Clough, Failsworth, weaver
"	7	Nancy d. Samuel & Elizabeth Jones, Newton, bleacher
"	7	Anne d. John & Mary Porter, Newton, bleacher
"	11	William Norton s. Revd. John & Elizabeth Rachel Piccope, Manchester, clerk
"	14	Elizabeth d. Sarah Lees, Failsworth, spinster
"	14	James s. Joseph & Maria Wilkinson, Failsworth, weaver
"	21	Thomas s. John & Betty Fletcher, Failsworth, weaver
"	21	Frances d. William & Hannah Stopford, Droylsden, weaver
"	21	James s. Frances Finley, Pendleton, spinster
"	21	James s. William & Mary Smith, Woodhouses, weaver
"	28	Sarah d. Joseph & Anne Higham, Newton, weaver
"	28	Mary d. Samuel & Jane Bethel, Newton, calenderer
Nov	4	Joseph s. Nancy Rogers, Newton, spinster
"	4	Anne d. James & Esther Brierly, Failsworth, weaver
"	11	Anne d. Charles & Anne Winstanly, Manchester, collier
"	18	Charles s. William & Betty Makin, Newton, dyer
"	25	Paul & Silas twin ss. Martha Greaves, Failsworth, spinster
"	25	Thomas s. John & Mary Gradwell, Newton, weaver
"	25	Edmund s. Thomas & Mary Dawson, Newton, dyer
"	25	Hannah d. Robert & Susanna Marsden, Newton, bleacher
Dec	2	Mary d. David & Mary Knott, Failsworth, weaver
"	25	Isabella d. James & Betty Whitehead, Failsworth, weaver
"	25	John s. Joseph & Alice Tetlow, Newton, weaver
"	30	Thomas Orlando s. Charles & Elizabeth Ridings, Newton, weaver
"	30	Benjamin s. William & Mary Howarth, Droylsden, labourer

1822

Jan	1	Richard s. Joseph & Sarah Wright, Newton, saddler
"	6	Elizabeth d. Nancy McVenom, Newton, spinster

"	6	Anne d. John & Anne Clough, Failsworth, weaver	*(1822)*
"	6	Elizabeth d. William & Jenny Bethel, Failsworth, weaver	
"	6	Jane d. William & Hannah Brandon, Medlock Vale, dyer	
"	6	John s. James & Margaret Higham, Medlock Vale, dyer	
"	6	Richard & John ss. John & Frances Howarth, Medlock Vale, dyer	
"	6	Margaret d. Adam & Margaret Horrocks, Droylsden, labourer	
"	13	William Hopwood s. Thomas & Mary Ashworth, Newton, weaver	
"	20	Edward s. Isaac & Betty Heapy, Droylsden, hatter	
"	27	Anne d. Martha Garlick, Failsworth, spinster	
"	27	Betty d. John & Mary Duckworth, Failsworth, calico printer	
"	29	John s. John & Betty Robinson, Newton, weaver	
Feb	3	Emma d. Moses & Clarissa Gradwell, Newton, weaver	
"	3	Elizabeth d. Ratliff & Sarah Pott, Newton, manufacturer	
"	3	Lee s. Lee & Mary Foden, Newton, labourer	
"	10	Maria d. Joseph & Betty Mills, Medlock Vale, calenderer	
"	11	Caroline d. James & Hannah Dennis, Medlock Vale, gardener	
"	14	John s. John & Mary Simister, Failsworth, weaver	
"	17	Anne d. James & Sarah Mather, Failsworth, weaver	
"	17	Jane d. William & Alice Walton, Newton, calico printer	
"	17	Betty d. Jane Whittaker, Failsworth, spinster	
"	17	Hannah d. Joseph & Sally Marshal, Failsworth, bricksetter	
"	17	Mary d. John & Esther Wood, Newton, farmer	
"	17	William s. John & Mary Wilson, Moston, weaver	
"	21	Joseph s. Elijah & Charlotte Hilton, Failsworth, weaver	
"	21	Charlotte d. Thomas & Mary Berry, Failsworth, weaver	
"	24	Mary d. Benjamin & Mary Hulton, Failsworth, weaver	
Mar	10	William s. John & Betty Taylor, Woodhouses, weaver	
"	10	Elizabeth d. Robert & Alice Whitehead, Woodhouses, weaver	
"	17	Joseph s. Joseph & Sarah Rogers, Failsworth, weaver	
"	24	Joseph s. Samuel & Ellen Clough, Failsworth, weaver	
"	26	Eliza d. Anne Wroe, Newton, spinster	
"	31	Lucy d. John & Sarah Williamson, Failsworth, weaver	
Apr	7	David s. John & Sarah Wyld, Newton, bleacher	
"	7	Peter s. Robert & Mary Allen, Newton, dyer	
"	7	William s. John & Alice Lees, Failsworth, weaver	
"	7	Ann d. Betty Bold, Failsworth, spinster	
"	7	Richard s. John & Jane Taylor, Chadderton, weaver	
"	7	James s. Clarissa Kenyon, Hollinwood, spinster	
"	7	Thomas s. James & Elizabeth Kenyon, Hollinwood, weaver	
"	7	Jane d. John & Mary Blackley, Newton, blacksmith	
"	7	Susan d. Joseph & Catherine Fletcher, Failsworth, weaver	
"	7	Mary d. John & Ann Robinson, Failsworth, weaver	
"	7	Ellen d. James & Sarah Whittaker, Failsworth, weaver	
"	17	James s. Thomas & Anne Wilson, Moston, weaver	
"	21	Hannah d. Joseph & Jenny Thornley, Failsworth, weaver	

"	21	Ellen d. William & Peggy Waters, Moston, weaver	*(1822)*
"	21	William s. Ann Harrison, Newton, spinster	
"	28	Thomas s. Ashton & Ann Shepley, Newton, weaver	
May	5	James s. Mary Chadderton, Failsworth, spinster	
"	12	Eliza d. John & Mary Smith, Newton, manufacturer	
"	12	Caroline d. James & Hannah Dennis, Ashton Parish, gardener	
"	17	Marianne d. James & Sarah Simister, Newton, labourer	
"	19	Lavinia d. James & Ruth Whitehead, Failsworth, weaver	
"	23	Mary d. James & Elizabeth Barker, Newton, smallware manufacturer	
"	26	Sarah Anne d. James & Hannah Swindels, Newton, weaver	
"	26	Susanna d. Peter & Hannah Thomason, Failsworth, calico printer	
"	26	Marianne d. Benjamin & Anne Bailey, Newton, weaver	
"	26	George s. William & Anne Ware, Failsworth, calico printer	
"	26	John s. Robert & Alice Stansfield, Newton, hatter	
"	26	John s. George & Elizabeth Smith, Droylsden, bricksetter	
"	26	Thomas s. James & Elizabeth Wyld, Failsworth, weaver	
"	26	Benjamin s. John & Elizabeth Ridings, Failsworth, weaver	
"	26	Mary d. James & Jane Hesketh, Failsworth, weaver	
"	29	Edwin s. George & Grace Howles, Newton, weaver	
Jun	2	Henry s. Luke & Rachel Hilton, Failsworth, weaver	
"	2	Phoebe d. William & Phoebe Smethurst, Newton, weaver	
"	3	Samuel s. William & Mary Greenhalgh, Woodhouses, farmer	
"	4	Betty d. Peter & Betty Rider, Failsworth, farmer	
"	4	Peter s. Peter & Betty Rider, Failsworth, farmer	
"	5	Peter s. Peter & Mary Pilling, Newton, carter	
"	9	James s. William & Mary Fenton, Medlock Vale, dyer	
"	9	William s. John & Martha Consterdine, Newton, labourer	
"	9	Sarah d. James & Elizabeth Barlow, Medlock Vale, bleacher	
"	13	James s. James & Anne Tomlinson, Newton, bleacher	
"	14	Anne d. William Christopher & Hannah Chew, Newton, solicitor	
"	14	Eliza d. James & Betty Aspell, Newton, innkeeper	
"	16	William s. Jonathan & Anne Glossop, Failsworth, weaver	
"	16	Alice d. Richard & Alice Mills, Newton, dyer	
"	17	Alice d. William & Betty Valentine, Manchester, calenderer	
"	23	James s. Mary Ridings, Failsworth, spinster	
"	23	Henry s. Edward & Nancy Robinson, Failsworth, weaver	
"	23	Ellen d. John & Alice Worsick, Failsworth, farmer	
"	23	Mary d. Thomas & Anne Allen, Failsworth, labourer	
"	23	Sarah d. Martha Berry, Failsworth, spinster	
"	30	Margaret d. James & Sarah Smith, Newton, weaver	
"	30	Joseph s. James & Sarah Smith, Newton, weaver	
"	30	Matty d. Thomas & Mally Ashton, Failsworth, weaver	
"	30	Elizabeth d. Joseph & Jane Ogden, Failsworth, weaver	
Jul	7	Sarah Anne d. John & Sarah Crossley, Ashton Parish, farmer	
"	7	Betty d. Oliver & Martha Ogden, Failsworth, weaver	

"	7	Anne d. John & Dinah Tongue, Failsworth, weaver
"	14	Mary d. John & Nancy Whittaker, Failsworth, weaver
"	14	Thomas s. Thomas & Elizabeth Cash, Newton, blacksmith
"	21	John s. James & Anne Howarth, Newton, farmer
"	21	Charles s. George & Sarah Garlick, Hollinwood, weaver
"	23	Hannah d. Samuel & Mary Lees, Failsworth, weaver
"	23	John s. William & Betty Lees, Hollinwood, weaver
"	23	Violet d. Samuel & Milly Simister, Failsworth, weaver
"	23	William s. Robert & Betty Lees, Failsworth, weaver
"	28	William s. Ashton & Betty Ashton, Failsworth, weaver
"	28	James s. Joseph & Martha Ogden, Failsworth, shopkeeper
Aug	1	Thomas s. John & Sarah Houlton, Manchester, hatter
"	4	Richard Carlisle s. John & Margaret Clark, Failsworth, weaver
"	4	Elizabeth d. Thomas & Elizabeth Smith, Manchester, labourer
"	5	Henry s. John & Jane Slater, Moston, labourer
"	11	Thomas s. John & Martha Whitehead, Failsworth, weaver
"	11	Henry s. Joseph & Sarah Whitehead, Failsworth, weaver
"	11	Anne d. John & Anne Berry, Failsworth, weaver
"	18	Elizabeth d. Joseph & Hannah Stansfield, Newton, hatter
"	18	Hannah d. William & Lydia Thornicroft, Newton, porter
"	18	William s. John & Esther Dean, Failsworth, labourer
"	18	Elizabeth d. Richard & Sarah Worsick, Failsworth, farmer
"	25	Thomas s. Alice Bent, Failsworth, spinster
"	25	William s. William & Mary Barnes, Manchester, labourer
"	25	Phoebe d. George & Betty Tomlinson, Failsworth, weaver
"	25	John s. William & Sarah Brundritt, Failsworth, weaver
"	25	James s. Joseph & Mary Davies, Newton, weaver
"	25	Esther d. Ann Collinson, Failsworth, spinster
"	25	William s. William & Sarah Knott, Failsworth, weaver
"	25	John s. James & Sarah Hunter, Ashton Parish, stone mason
"	25	Edmund Walmsley s. Thomas & Sarah Taylor, Failsworth, weaver
"	25	Emma d. William & Hannah Davies, Medlock Vale, labourer
"	25	Elizabeth d. James & Anne Taylor, Failsworth, weaver
"	25	Mary d. Samuel & Betty Smethurst, Moston, weaver
"	25	George s. Robert & Sarah Whitehead, Clayton, weaver
"	25	Hannah d. James & Mary Lees, Failsworth, weaver
"	25	Emma d. William & Mary Walker, Manchester, collier
"	25	Amelia d. Ralph & Jane Smethurst, Failsworth, weaver
"	25	Ann d. John & Martha Tetlow, Newton, carter
"	25	Hannah d. John & Maria Taylor, Newton, weaver
"	25	Harriet d. Robert & Jane Ralston, Medlock Vale, engraver
"	25	James s. Robert & Jane Ralston, Medlock Vale, engraver
Sep	27	William s. William & Agnes Allen, Failsworth, weaver
"	27	James s. Thomas & Mary Taylor, Failsworth, weaver
"	29	John s. Joseph & Alice Tetlow, Manchester, manufacturer

"	29	David Hague s. John & Mary Lomas, Salford, draper
"	29	David Hague s. John & Sarah Brooke, Huddersfield, drysalter, bo 20 Sep 1807
"	29	Alice d. James & Jenny Taylor, Failsworth, weaver
"	29	Ruth d. Thomas & Jane Wood, Manchester, fellmonger
Oct	3	John s. Thomas & Sarah Chadwick, Manchester, dyer
"	13	Nancy d. Thomas & Margaret Hulme, Failsworth, farmer
"	13	Margaret d. David & Sally Horrocks, Failsworth, labourer
"	20	Thomas s. Betty Bardsley, Failsworth, spinster
"	27	Marianne d. James & Mary Newton, Harpurhey, dyer
"	27	Robert s. John & Anne Thornley, Droylsden, weaver
"	27	Thomas s. Thomas & Jane Lord, Newton, wheelwright
Nov	3	John Ashton s. Mary Oliver, Hyde, bo 28 May 1815
"	3	Crispin s. William & Anne Aldred, Failsworth, shoemaker
"	3	Anne d. John & Anne Speakman, Droylsden, labourer
"	3	Richard s. David & Hannah Harrison, Newton, weaver
"	3	John s. George & Mary Whittaker, Failsworth, hatter
"	10	Joseph s. Benjamin & Jane Howarth, Droylsden, labourer
"	12	Sarah Anne d. John & Sarah Marsden, Newton, bleacher
"	17	William s. William & Sarah Barlow, Newton, blockcutter
"	24	Henry s. Richard & Martha Drinkwater, Newton, printer
"	24	Robert s. William & Betty Glossop, Failsworth, weaver
"	24	Joseph s. William & Sarah Shelmerdine, Newton, weaver
Dec	1	John s. Peter & Mary Stott, Moston, weaver
"	1	Matty d. Thomas & Martha Winterbottom, Failsworth, weaver
"	12	John s. James & Jenny Allen, Newton, bleacher
"	12	John s. James & Anne Allen, Failsworth, weaver
"	15	Esther d. William & Elizabeth Davenport, Failsworth, weaver
"	16	Alice d. James & Alice Hough, Culcheth, bleacher, bo 10 Sep 1820
"	22	Sarah d. Jane Taylor, Droylsden, spinster
"	22	Hannah d. James & Alice Fletcher, Failsworth, weaver
"	25	Margaret d. James & Jane Higginbottom, Failsworth, calico printer
"	25	Mary d. Joseph & Mary Berry, Failsworth, weaver
"	25	William Stanley s. Charles & Eliza Eckersley, Newton, weaver
"	25	Richard s. Richard & Anne Hulme, Droylsden, farmer
"	29	Michael s. John & Mary Smith, Newton, blockcutter
"	29	Ellen d. Robert & Susanna Marsden, Newton, calenderer

1823

Jan	5	Mary d. William & Esther Whitehead, Failsworth, weaver
"	12	Nancy d. Thomas & Sarah Lamb, Culcheth, labourer
"	12	Philip s. James & Hannah Berry, Failsworth, farmer
"	12	Edward Henry s. John & Elizabeth Shepley, Newton, joiner
"	12	Andrew s. Andrew & Sarah Lane, Manchester, carter
"	19	Thomas s. James & Mary Cooke, Manchester, weaver

"	19	Joseph s. James & Alice Mills, Ashton Parish, calico printer	*(1823)*
"	19	Catherine d. William & Ellen Smith, Hollinwood, weaver	
"	24	Hannah d. Thomas & Jane Wild, Newton, innkeeper	
"	26	Anne d. Thomas & Ellen Shawcross, Manchester, labourer	
Feb	2	Sarah d. Thomas & Margaret Horrocks, Failsworth, bleacher	
"	5	Jane d. William & Elizabeth Goodier, Newton, weaver	
"	9	Henry s. John & Esther Whitehead, Blackley, farmer	
"	9	Eliza d. James & Martha Wild, Droylsden, weaver	
"	9	James s. John & Elizabeth Eaton, Medlock Vale, farmer	
"	9	Ellen d. William & Elizabeth Hall, Droylsden, farmer	
"	13	Marianne d. James & Betty Ogden, Moston, weaver	
"	13	Mary d. Abraham & Anne Ogden, Manchester, weaver	
"	13	Sarah d. William & Marianne Gould, Moston, weaver	
"	16	John s. Michael & Elizabeth Waring, Newton, print cutter	
"	16	Anne d. Daniel & Hannah Knott, Failsworth, weaver	
"	16	Anne d. Levi & Ellen Clough, Failsworth, weaver	
"	23	Joseph s. James & Mary Smith, Droylsden, weaver	
Mar	2	Thomas s. Betty Gillibrand, Failsworth, spinster	
"	2	David s. David & Elizabeth Whittaker, Newton, wheelwright	
"	9	James s. James & Ellen Howarth, Droylsden, pattern drawer	
"	9	Esther d. Dan & Hannah Hulton, Newton, weaver	
"	16	James s. Jonathan & Esther Etchels, Failsworth, labourer	
"	16	Abraham s. Abraham & Matty Whitehead, Chadderton, weaver	
"	16	Jane d. James & Elizabeth Wilson, Newton, weaver	
"	16	Rebecca d. William & Betty Worral, Failsworth, weaver	
"	19	Robert s. Willy & Nancy Booth, Newton, innkeeper	
"	30	Joseph s. William & Betty Makin, Newton, dyer	
"	30	Mary d. James & Martha Makin, Moston, dyer	
"	30	Alice d. Joseph & Priscilla Fletcher, Newton, weaver	
"	30	Martha d. Charles & Elizabeth Sydebotham, Newton, weaver	
"	30	James s. Philip & Mary Taylor, Failsworth, weaver	
"	30	Marianne d. James & Anne Etchels, Failsworth, weaver	
"	30	Alice d. John & Sarah Tomlinson, Moston, weaver	
"	30	David s. Jesse & Ellen Barber, Newton, shoemaker	
"	30	Hannah d. Sarah Fletcher, Newton, spinster	
"	30	Samuel s. Samuel & Mary Dean, Failsworth, weaver	
"	30	Anne d. Edmund & Anne Tetlow, Failsworth, weaver	
"	30	Nancy d. James & Mary Blomily, Newton, weaver	
"	30	Sarah Wilson d. Robert & Jenny Mills, Chadderton, weaver	
"	30	Sarah d. Joseph & Maria Wilkinson, Failsworth, weaver	
"	30	John s. David & Anne Ogden, Failsworth, weaver	
"	30	Jane d. Thomas & Jane Yates, Newton, bleacher	
"	30	James s. James & Anne Taylor, Failsworth, weaver	
Apr	6	James s. Richard & Sarah Chorlton, Failsworth, innkeeper	
"	6	Susanna d. Josiah & Alice Etchels, Failsworth, weaver	

"	13	Andrew s. James & Anne Kershaw, Manchester, warper	*(1823)*
"	20	Matthew s. William & Catherine Gradwell, Failsworth, weaver	
"	27	William s. Nicholas & Jane Simister, Newton, weaver	
"	27	Thomas s. George & Jane Robinson, Medlock Vale, labourer	
May	11	Thomas Dewhurst s. Sarah Ridings, Failsworth, spinster	
"	18	Dan s. Samuel & Mary Robinson, Newton, stonemason	
"	18	Ann d. Josiah & Jane Garlick, Failsworth, weaver	
"	18	Jane d. Richard & Jane Travis, Newton, weaver	
"	18	Robert s. Samuel & Mary Etchels, Failsworth, weaver	
"	18	Thomas s. Thomas & Martha Tomlinson, Newton, dyer	
"	18	James s. Elizabeth Allen, Newton, spinster	
"	18	Sarah d. George & Margaret Eyre, Failsworth, cordwainer	
"	25	Daniel s. Daniel & Sarah Clayton, Manchester, sho(o)pkeeper	
"	25	William s. Benjamin & Mary Barrow, Failsworth, weaver	
"	25	Hannah d. Thomas & Martha Whitelegg, Manchester, labourer	
"	25	James Berry s. Elijah & Charlotte Hilton, Failsworth, weaver	
"	25	Olive d. John & Mary Berry, Newton, innkeeper	
"	27	Sidney s. John & Mary Whitehead, Failsworth, weaver	
Jun	1	William Alfred s. William & Betty Crossley, Failsworth, shopkeeper	
"	1	John s. James & Ellen Clough, Failsworth, weaver	
"	5	Josephina Anne d. Charles Roberts & Sarah Hooley, Newton, calico printer	
"	5	Ellen d. Nancy Turvin, Newton, spinster	
"	8	Marianne Elizabeth d. James & Anne Clough, Manchester, weaver	
"	8	William s. Thomas & Betty Hayes, Failsworth, blockcutter	
"	8	John Crossley s. John & Mary Travis, Rusholme, manservant	
"	8	Martha d. Mary Cairns, Newton, spinster	
"	10	Daniel s. John & Sarah Syddal, Manchester (*entry struck through; in PR only; see entry in Burials*)	
"	12	Mary & Sarah twin ds. John & Hannah Wood, Droylsden, farmer	
"	13	Marianne d. Joseph & Hannah Smith, Newton, weaver	
"	15	Selina d. James & Mary Ashworth, Holkhome near Bury [Hockhulme near Bury], dyer	
"	15	Catherina d. John & Mary Clough, Failsworth, weaver	
"	15	John s. James & Ellen Hulton, Failsworth, weaver	
"	15	Joel s. Maria Robinson, Newton, spinster	
"	15	Elizabeth d. Joseph & Alice Robinson, Failsworth, weaver	
"	15	Phoebe d. William & Phoebe Jacks, Clayton, collier	
"	22	Robert s. Joseph & Elizabeth Seel, Newton, calico printer	
"	22	Anne d. George & Anne Yates, Newton, bleacher	
"	22	John s. John & Sarah Keen, Failsworth	
"	22	Joseph s. Hannah Gray, Moston, spinster	
"	22	Sarah d. Wright & Martha Crompshaw, Newton, weaver	
"	23	Joseph s. Robert & Sarah Branton, Newton, weaver	
"	26	Betty d. William & Betty Crompton, Manchester, weaver	
"	29	Marianne d. Daniel & Anne Berrington, Marple, farmer	

Jul	4	John s. Mary Etchels, Failsworth, spinster	*(1823)*
"	6	Alice d. John & Elizabeth Smith, Newton, weaver	
"	6	Mary d. James & Jenny Aldred, Failsworth, weaver	
"	6	Joseph s. Betty Kershaw, Failsworth, spinster	
"	6	Samson s. Mary Gradwell, Newton, spinster	
"	9	Alice d. Thomas & Mary Livesey, Manchester, collier	
"	13	James s. Isaac & Ellen Hyde, Newton, weaver	
"	13	Martha d. John & Elizabeth Robinson, Newton, weaver	
"	13	Mary d. Samuel & Hannah Lees, Failsworth, weaver	
"	13	Robert s. Jonathan & Sarah Boardman, Chadderton, weaver	
"	13	Anne d. Robert & Mary Richardson, Hollinwood, hatter	
"	20	Anne d. William & Jane Mather, Droylsden, weaver	
"	24	Eliza d. John & Sarah Mather, Newton, hatter	
"	27	Joseph s. Joseph & Anne Etchels, Hollinwood, weaver	
"	27	Margaret d. Charles & Hannah Heywood, Newton, weaver	
"	27	John s. James & Jane Aldred, Newton, shoemaker	
"	27	Anne d. John & Alice Pilkington, Failsworth, labourer	
"	27	Alice d. Joseph & Anne Higham, Newton, weaver	
"	27	Thomas s. John & Nanny Holt, Failsworth, weaver	
"	29	James s. Leah & Mary Foden, Newton, labourer	
"	30	Andrew s. Joseph & Rebekah Hulton, Failsworth, weaver	
"	30	Mary d. Robert & Elizabeth Wilkinson, Failsworth, weaver	
Aug	3	David s. John & Elizabeth Taylor, Ashton Parish, weaver	
"	3	Martha d. Matthew & Sarah Brown, Newton, weaver	
"	10	Joseph s. Samuel & Mary Moore, Failsworth, weaver	
"	17	Matty d. Edmund & Olive Schofield, Failsworth, weaver	
"	24	Alice d. John & Mary Hulton, Failsworth, weaver	
"	24	Harriet d. William & Mary Dalton, Manchester, fustian cutter	
"	24	Caroline d. John & Martha Shedwick, Newton, blockcutter (*see second entry below*)	
"	24	Eliza d. James & Alice Swift, Failsworth, weaver	
"	24	James s. John & Martha Shedwick, Newton, blockcutter	
"	24	Sarah d. William & Anne Leigh, Manchester, collier	
"	24	Anne d. Samuel & Anne Barnes, Manchester, weaver	
"	24	William s. John & Mary Cooper, Manchester, weaver	
"	24	John s. Samuel & Anne Bottomly, Manchester, brewer	
"	24	Robert s. Isaac & Elizabeth Heppy, Droylsden, hatter	
"	24	Edward s. Joseph & Maria Arrundale, Droylsden, bricksetter	
"	24	Mary d. William & Anne Booth, Failsworth, weaver	
"	24	James s. Thomas & Sarah Dawson, Newton, dyer	
"	24	James s. William & Mary Pendleton, Newton, weaver	
"	24	James s. Joseph & Mary Whittaker, Newton, weaver	
"	24	John s. Sally Jackson, Newton, spinster	
"	24	Jane d. James & Betty Brown, Manchester, joiner	
"	25	William s. George & Anne Clarke, Newton, weaver	

	25	Joseph s. Charles & Elizabeth Walmsley, Newton, weaver	*(1823)*
"	31	Ellen d. George & Anne Morris, Medlock Vale, calico printer	
"	31	Nancy d. Joseph & Mally Smethurst, Failsworth, weaver	
"	31	Ruth d. Jane Kay, Failsworth, spinster	
"	31	James s. Sarah Brown, Hollinwood, spinster	
Sep	7	Alfred s. Ratcliff & Sarah Potts, Newton, cotton manufacturer	
"	7	Robert s. John & Maria Stott, Failsworth, weaver	
"	14	Anne d. Elias & Betty Whittaker, Newton, weaver	
"	14	Horsefall s. Robert & Marianne Hulme, Newton, calenderer	
"	14	Sarah d. William & Mary Greenhalgh, Woodhouses, tailor	

(new register commences: volume 9)

Sep	14	Nancy d. John & Esther Brierly, Failsworth, weaver
"	14	Sarah d. George & Sarah Bardsley, Newton, weaver
"	14	Samuel s. Edmund & Betty Shaw, Newton, labourer
"	14	Rachel d. William & Elizabeth Wood, Manchester, painter
"	19	Benjamin s. Daniel & Hannah Etchels, Failsworth, weaver
"	19	Sarah d. Daniel & Hannah Etchels, Failsworth, weaver
"	21	Alice Thorpe d. Luke & Catherine Eckersley, Failsworth, weaver
"	21	Joseph s. John & Mary Whitehead, Failsworth, weaver
"	21	James s. Joseph & Anne Greaves, Failsworth, weaver
"	21	Isaiah s. James & Sarah Williamson, Droylsden, weaver
"	21	Eliza d. Betty Wroe, Failsworth, spinster
"	28	John s. Luke & Jane Wharmby, Failsworth, weaver
"	28	Betty d. Thomas & Jane Bates, Failsworth, bleacher
"	28	William Cooper s. William & Anne Johnson, Manchester, cutter
"	28	John s. John & Ellen O`Neal, Failsworth, weaver
"	28	James s. Philip & Anne Berry, Failsworth, weaver
"	28	Mary d. Thomas & Mary Howard, Failsworth, weaver
"	28	Nancy d. Mary Schofield, Failsworth, spinster
Oct	3	Robert s. Mary Williams, Newton, spinster
"	5	Mary d. Isaac & Elizabeth Andrew, Failsworth, calico printer
"	5	Anne d. Betty Brindle, Ashton Parish, spinster
"	5	Alice d. James & Betty Fallows, Newton, labourer
"	5	Lavinia d. Thomas & Mary Ogden, Failsworth, weaver
"	12	Percy Bradshaw s. Charles & Isabella Ridings, Newton, weaver
"	12	Margaret d. Joseph & Rebecca Barrett, Newton, labourer
"	15	James s. Thomas & Mary Robinson, Droylsden, dyer
"	15	Mary d. Joseph & Hannah Bardsley, Droylsden, block cutter
"	19	Sarah Anne d. John & Sarah Twimlow, Newton, labourer
"	19	Anne d. James & Sarah Worral, Failsworth, farmer
"	19	Elizabeth d. George & Esther Higham, Newton, labourer
"	19	Sarah d. William & Lucy Sale, Newton, bleacher
"	22	John s. Mary Turvin, Newton, spinster

"	26	John s. Sarah Wyld, Failsworth, spinster
"	26	Robert s. James & Mary Burton, Newton, weaver
"	26	Eliza d. Edmund & Sarah Walmsley, Failsworth, farmer
"	27	Elizabeth d. John & Alice Chadwick, Newton, dyer
Nov	2	Abigail d. Anne Dunkerly, Failsworth, spinster
"	2	Richard William s. John & Mary Lomas, Salford, draper
"	2	Sarah d. John & Martha Higham, Newton, weaver
"	16	John s. Philip & Nancy Ashton, Failsworth, weaver
"	16	Olive d. James & Mary Butterworth, Newton, weaver
"	23	William s. Jonathan & Phoebe Brown, Newton, weaver
"	23	Mary d. John & Mary Allen, Newton, farmer
"	23	James s. Robert & Esther Brierly, Failsworth, weaver
"	24	John s. Thomas & Mary Yeald, Failsworth, bleacher
"	30	Fanny d. Jonathan & Anne Glossop, Failsworth, weaver
"	30	Sarah Anne d. Miles & Marianne Mason, Failsworth, blacksmith
Dec	11	Anne d. Abraham & Anne Collins, Farnworth nr. Bolton, carter
"	11	Nancy d. John & Mary Howard, Woodhouses, weaver
"	14	Henry s. William & Mary Smith, Failsworth, weaver
"	14	Sarah d. David & Alice Winstanley, Manchester, collier
"	14	John s. George & Charlotte Smethurst, Newton, dyer
"	14	William s. George & Charlotte Smethurst, Newton, dyer
"	14	Betty d. Robert & Bathsheba Boardman, Manr., weaver
"	21	Anne d. James & Ruth Whitehead, Failsworth, weaver
"	25	Betty d. James & Sarah Whittaker, Failsworth, weaver
"	25	Jane d. John & Betty Consterdine, Newton, labourer
"	28	Alice d. Joshua & Sarah Anne Swift, Collyhurst, dyer
"	31	James s. John & Sarah Wyld, Newton, labourer

1824

Jan	1	Maria d. John & Mary Duckworth, Saddleworth, calico printer
"	1	Samuel s. Joseph & Jane Berry, Newton, weaver
"	2	Jemima d. Robert & Mary Drinkwater, Newton, carter
"	4	Anne d. James & Anne Ogden, Hollinwood, blacksmith
"	11	William s. William & Hannah Stopford, Droylsden, weaver
"	11	John s. Eli & Jenny Swift, Failsworth, weaver
"	18	Richard s. Samuel & Mary Lord, Ashton Parish, labourer
"	18	Betty d. George & Sarah Garlick, Hollinwood, weaver
"	25	Thomas s. Alice Taylor, Failsworth, spinster
"	25	Elizabeth d. William & Sarah Ridings, Failsworth, weaver
"	25	Elizabeth & Sarah twin children of Ashton & Sarah Worral, Failsworth, carter
"	30	Olive d. James & Sarah Bradbury, Newton, labourer
Feb	1	Hannah d. John & Betty Whitehead, Moston, weaver
"	1	Hannah d. Joseph & Alice Tetlow, Manchester, weaver
"	1	William s. Susan Clough, Failsworth, spinster

"	8	Thomas s. Thomas & Mary Allanson, Newton, bleacher
"	8	Sarah d. William & Mary Fenton, Medlock Vale, dyer
"	15	Anne d. John & Fanny Hall, Medlock Vale, dyer
"	15	John s. James & Anne Ogden, Failsworth, weaver
"	15	Anne d. Philip & Betty Wagstaff, Newton, weaver
"	15	Squire s. Henry & Betty Ratcliff, Failsworth, wheelwright
"	15	Anne d. Thomas & Jane Lancashire, Newton, shopkeeper
"	15	Anne d. Garside & Alice Blomiley, Newton, weaver
"	15	Hannah d. Samuel & Mary Holland, Failsworth, weaver
"	22	George s. John & Grace Bradshaw, Medlock Vale, calico printer
"	22	Thomas s. John & Alice Chadwick, Newton, dyer
"	23	Maria d. William & Nancy Butterworth, Newton, weaver
"	29	Benjamin s. Thomas & Mary Prenton, Failsworth, sawyer
"	29	Edward s. Thomas & Anne Potter, Newton, weaver
Mar	7	Joseph s. John & Betty Fletcher, Failsworth, weaver
"	14	Henry s. William & Betty Sutcliff, Newton, shoemaker
"	14	Elias s. Samuel & Jane Bethel, Newton, glazier
"	14	Sarah d. George & Betty Ramsbotham, Middleton, calico printer
"	14	Betty d. John & Hannah Walmsley, Newton, labourer
"	21	Anne d. John & Mary Hay, Newton, print cutter
"	21	Anne d. William & Jenny Bethel, Failsworth, weaver
"	28	John s. Robert & Mary Berry, Failsworth, weaver
Apr	4	Thomas s. Joseph & Betty Tomkinson, Newton, weaver
"	4	Elizabeth d. Jonathan & Elizabeth Lees, Hollinwood, innkeeper
"	4	Caroline d. Ashton & Betty Ashton, Failsworth, weaver
"	9	Sarah d. John & Sarah Wilson, Manchester, collier
"	11	Mary Anne d. George & Elizabeth Smith, Droylsden, bricklayer
"	15	James s. Bold Bagshaw & Elizabeth Robinson, Newton, innkeeper
"	18	Olivia d. William & Agnes Allen, Failsworth, weaver
"	18	Marianne d. David & Sally Makin, Moston, weaver
"	18	Ralph s. Ralph & Mary Darbyshire, Droylsden, dyer
"	18	Richard s. William & Esther Whitehead, Failsworth, weaver
"	18	Hannah d. Peter & Margaret Later, Moston, farmer
"	18	Margaret d. George & Mary Whittaker, Failsworth, hatter
"	18	Mary d. Richard & Damaris Etchels, Manchester, weaver
"	18	Sarah d. William & Alice Hibbert, Failsworth, weaver
"	18	Mary d. John & Anne Clough, Failsworth, weaver
"	18	David s. Thomas & Margaret Horrocks, Failsworth, bleacher
"	18	Joseph s. Jane Milner, Newton, spinster
"	18	Nancy d. John & Anne Hall, Failsworth, weaver
"	18	Frances d. John & Mary Blackley, Newton, blacksmith
"	18	John s. James & Hannah Burgess, Manchesr., weaver
"	25	Elizabeth d. John & Isabella Goodier, Newton, calenderer
"	25	Joseph s. Joseph & Nancy Ogden, Failsworth, weaver
May	2	Samuel Seddon s. Samuel & Mary Hyde, Failsworth, weaver

"	9	Thomas s. John & Anne Tonge, Newton, calenderer *(1824)*
"	9	Peter s. Peter & Mary Stott, Moston, weaver
"	16	John s. Thomas & Mary Taylor, Failsworth, weaver
"	16	Elizabeth d. William & Sarah Brundrett, Failsworth, weaver
"	20	Cornelius s. Alice Clough, Failsworth, weaver
"	23	Elizabeth d. James & Margaret Higham, Failsworth, dyer
"	23	Mary d. Joseph & Anne Whitehead, Failsworth, dyer
"	23	John s. James & Elizabeth Barker, Newton, smallware manufacturer
"	30	Marianne Clarissa d. Moses & Clarissa Gradwell, Newton, weaver
"	30	John s. Thomas & Rachel Bottomley, Bradford, labourer
Jun	6	Hannah d. John & Alice Worsick, Failsworth, labourer
"	6	James s. John & Mary Wylde, Failsworth, weaver
"	6	Alice d. John & Anne Robinson, Failsworth, weaver
"	6	Eliza d. John & Jane Blackshaw, Newton, warper
"	6	Emma d. John & Jane Blackshaw, Newton, warper
"	6	Thomas s. David & Anne Ogden, Failsworth, weaver
"	6	John s. Ralph & Mary Ogden, Failsworth, weaver
"	6	James s. Joseph & Olive Needham, Failsworth, bricklayer
"	6	Henry s. John & Esther Dewhurst, Hollinwood, labourer
"	6	Olive d. John & Maria Taylor, Failsworth, weaver
"	6	Mary d. John & Anne Gardner, Droylsden, farmer
"	6	Marianne d. Sarah Lancashire, Failsworth, spinster
"	6	Mary d. John & Jane Crossley, Failsworth, weaver
"	6	Alice d. James & Elizabeth Kenyon, Hollinwood, weaver
"	6	Mary d. John & Ellen O'Neale, Failsworth, weaver
"	10	Sarah Anne d. Anne Ashworth, Newton, spinster
"	13	Thomas Sidney s. William & Phoebe Smethurst, Failsworth, weaver
"	13	*(date altered; original unclear)* [13] Kirkley s. John & Anne Clough, Failsworth, weaver
"	13	Thomas s. Ralph & Sarah Ogden, Failsworth, weaver
"	13	William s. Ralph & Sarah Ogden, Failsworth, weaver
"	20	Anne d. Thomas & Mary Kay, Moston, farmer
"	21	Betty d. John & Mary Bowker, Newton, bleacher
"	27	Samuel s. John & Jane Holding, Manchester, collier
Jul	4	William s. James & Abigail Blackshaw, Failsworth, hatter
"	11	Elizabeth d. James & Sarah Mather, Newton, weaver
"	11	Catherine d. James & Sarah Mather, Newton, weaver
"	11	Robert s. John & Alice Lees, Failsworth, weaver
"	11	Elizabeth d. Thomas & Matty Winterbotham, Failsworth, weaver
"	11	Sarah Anne d. William & Mary Anne Robinson, Newton, flagger
"	14	Thomas s. Joseph & Mary Brown, Ashton Parish, farmer
"	18	Marianne d. William & Hannah Brandon, Failsworth, engineer
"	18	Susan d. Joseph & Betty Nuttal, Medlock Vale, calenderer
"	18	George s. George & Sarah Hulton, Newton, weaver
"	18	Betty d. Thomas & Hannah Taylor, Newton, weaver

"	19	James s. John & Anne Linley, Hyde, shoemaker (*1824*)
"	25	Anne d. Luke & Isabella Smith, Failsworth, weaver
"	25	John s. James & Elizabeth Davenport, Medlock Vale, gardener
"	25	William s. James & Elizabeth Davenport, Medlock Vale, gardener
"	25	Elizabeth Ellen d. William & Mary Anne Holt, Newton, blacksmith, bo Jun 24 1824
"	25	Hannah d. Sarah Berry, Failsworth, spinster
"	25	Richard s. Richard & Sarah Rogers, Newton, weaver
"	27	Sarah Anne d. William & Hannah Kay, Stockport, dyer
Aug	1	Betty d. James & Matty Ogden, Failsworth, weaver
"	1	Alice d. Moses & Phoebe Holland, Chadderton, weaver
"	1	Eliza d. Thomas & Mary Allen, Newton, calenderer
"	5	Ellen d. James & Margaret Peat, Medlock Vale, pattern drawer
"	8	Anne d. John & Nancy Whittaker, Failsworth, weaver
"	8	Robert s. James & Alice Taylor, Failsworth, weaver
"	8	John s. Anne Bradshaw, Failsworth, spinster
"	10	John s. Robert & Betty Lees, Failsworth, weaver
"	11	Joseph s. William & Sarah Shelmerdine, Newton, weaver
"	11	Joseph s. Samuel & Betty Jones, Newton, bleacher
"	15	Lavinia Ridings d. Benjamin & Nancy Worsick, Droylsden, farmer
"	15	Isabella Anne d. Peter & Anne Stone, Newton, silversmith
"	22	Thomas s. John & Esther Bradley, Droylsden, labourer
"	22	Joseph s. John & Esther Bradley, Droylsden, labourer
"	22	James s. James & Anne Harrison, Manchester, bleacher
"	22	Susanna d. Solomon & Betty Etchels, Macclesfield, weaver
"	22	Sarah Anne d. James & Eleanor Bardsley, Newton, weaver
"	22	Jane d. William & Alice Walton, Newton, calico printer
"	22	Thomas s. John & Sarah Drinkwater, Manchester, bricklayer
"	22	Elizabeth d. Christopher & Hannah Jeffries, Newton, labourer
"	22	Edward s. Joseph & Mary Tetlow, Manchester, shopkeeper
"	22	Samuel s. Samuel & Mary Grimshaw, Droylsden, weaver
"	22	Sarah d. James & Anne Barnes, Newton, weaver
"	22	Elizabeth d. John & Elizabeth Whitehead, Manchester, collier
"	22	Thomas s. George & Ruth Bottomley, Manchester, blacksmith
"	22	Nancy d. George & Betty Travis, Newton, bleacher
"	22	John s. Joseph & Maria Wilkinson, Failsworth, weaver
"	22	George s. William & Anne Aldred, Failsworth, shoemaker
"	29	Jane d. John & Anne Pattison, Newton, labourer
"	29	Sarah d. William & Mary Gradwell Hamson, Newton, slater
Sep	12	Joseph s. James & Hannah Pilkington, Failsworth, labourer
"	12	Mary d. Mary Berry, Failsworth, spinster
"	12	Thomas s. Robert & Susanna Marsden, Newton, calenderer
"	14	Handel s. John & Mary Thorley, Failsworth, weaver
"	19	Mary d. James & Anne Howarth, Newton, labourer
"	19	Hannah d. John & Sarah Whitehead, Failsworth, weaver

"	19	Mary & Sarah ds. James & Hannah Etchels, Failsworth, weaver
"	26	Samuel s. Richard & Nancy Trover, Newton, engineer
"	26	Eliza d. John & Betty Walker, Ashton, weaver
Oct	3	William s. William & Anne Waire, Failsworth, calico printer
"	17	Jane d. John & Betty Shepley, Newton, joiner
"	17	John s. Samuel & Mary Kenyon, Hollinwood, weaver
"	17	Richard s. Joseph & Hannah Richardson, Newton, weaver
"	17	Elizabeth d. Edward & Nancy Robinson, Failsworth, weaver
"	17	Alice d. Rebecca Horrocks, Failsworth, spinster
"	17	Samuel s. James & Mary Newton, Harpurhey, dyer
"	20	Alice d. George & Elizabeth Hilton, Failsworth, weaver
"	20	Sarah d. George & Elizabeth Hilton, Failsworth, weaver
"	24	Betty d. George & Anne Yates, Newton, bleacher
"	24	William s. Joseph & Mary Davies, Newton, weaver
"	24	Mary Holmes d. Abraham & Anne Mills, Failsworth, cordwainer
"	24	Marianne d. James & Mary Walmsley, Failsworth, weaver
"	24	Jenny d. Joseph & Martha Walmsley, Failsworth, weaver
"	31	Ellen d. Matthew & Anne Gradwell, Newton, weaver
"	31	Henry s. Fanny Etchels, Droylsden, spinster
"	31	Mary d. John & Sarah Williamson, Newton, weaver
"	31	Betty d. Mary Hulme, Droylsden, spinster
Nov	7	Elizabeth d. Mary Taylor, Newton, spinster
"	7	William s. Benjamin & Jane Howarth, Droylsden, labourer
"	7	Matty d. Peter & Anne Fletcher, Failsworth, weaver
"	7	Nancy d. Edward & Maria Hulton, Failsworth, weaver
"	7	Daniel s. James & Alice Smith, Droylsden, weaver
"	14	George s. Samuel & Mary Lees, Failsworth, weaver
"	21	Elizabeth d. Joseph & Olive Wyld, Newton, weaver
"	21	Hannah d. James & Jane Hesketh, Failsworth, weaver
"	21	Elizabeth d. Joseph & Catherine Fletcher, Newton, weaver
"	26	John Ashton s. Willy & Nancy Booth, Newton, innkeeper
"	28	Mary d. Mary Whitehead, Failsworth, spinster
"	28	Hannah d. John & Elizabeth Smith, Newton, weaver
Dec	5	Ellen d. Robert & Jane Railston, Droylsden, engraver
"	5	Ellen d. Joseph & Jane Ellor, Gorton, hatter
"	5	John s. Sarah Oldham, Newton, spinster
"	8	Emmanuel s. Abraham & Martha Pollitt, Failsworth, weaver
"	8	Henry s. Abraham & Martha Pollitt, Failsworth, weaver
"	8	Robert s. Thomas & Alice Hough, Failsworth, weaver
"	14	Sophia d. Thomas & Jane Wyld, Newton, innkeeper
"	19	Thomas s. Thomas & Betty Coupe, Medlock Vale, pattern drawer
"	25	Samuel s. James & Betty Whitehead, Failsworth, weaver
"	25	John s. James & Isabel Wyld, Failsworth, weaver
"	25	Edwin s. William & Mary Booth, Failsworth, weaver
"	25	Elizabeth d. John & Martha Tetlow, Failsworth, weaver

"	26	Joseph s. Edmund & Betty Ridings, Failsworth, weaver
"	26	Mary d. Thomas & Elizabeth Hadfield, Droylsden, bricklayer
"	26	Mary d. Betty Gillibrand, Failsworth, spinster
"	26	John s. Sarah Dawson, Failsworth, spinster
[		T. Gaskell, Incumbent Of Newton
		Jas Hough Chapelwarden]

1825

Jan	2	Sarah Anne d. Richard & Mary Walker, Newton, weaver
"	2	Robert s. Philip & Mary Taylor, Failsworth, weaver
"	7	Elizabeth d. Aaron & Marianne Gradwell, Newton, weaver
"	9	Elizabeth d. Joseph & Sarah Whitehead, Failsworth, weaver
"	9	Emma d. Maria Riley, Failsworth, spinster
"	9	James s. Robert & Anne Berry, Failsworth, joiner
"	9	Samuel s. Robert & Anne Whitehead, Failsworth, weaver
"	9	Hannah d. Christopher & Anne Jefferies, Newton, brickmaker
"	16	Betty d. Jane Chapman, Failsworth, spinster
"	16	Sarah d. Ann Dawson, Droylsden, spinster
"	16	James s. John & Hannah Ridings, Failsworth, weaver
"	16	Joseph s. John & Mary Smith, Newton, block cutter
"	16	Mary d. Joseph & Jane Ogden, Failsworth, weaver
"	17	Sarah d. John & Anne Thornley, Droylsden, weaver
"	23	Marianne d. John & Sarah Bentley, Newton, weaver
"	23	William s. Matty Etchels, Droylsden, spinster
"	23	Benjamin s. Sarah Ogden, Failsworth, spinster
"	25	Elizabeth d. Thomas & Elizabeth Lancashire, Manchesr., dyer
"	26	John s. Samuel & Hannah Robinson, Failsworth, weaver
"	30	Thomas s. Joseph & Sarah Rogers, Failsworth, weaver
"	30	James s. John & Anne Speakman, Clayton, labourer
Feb	6	William s. Joseph & Nanny Greaves, Failsworth, labourer
"	13	Alfred s. Benjamin & Mary Hulton, Failsworth, weaver
"	13	Samuel s. Thomas & Sarah Taylor, Failsworth, weaver
"	13	Harriet d. Joseph & Martha Clough, Woodhouses, weaver
"	13	Joseph s. John & Hannah Berry, Failsworth, weaver
"	13	John s. William & Martha Eyre, Failsworth, weaver
"	13	Selina d. James & Sally Tweadale, Newton, schoolmaster
"	13	Cornelius s. Thomas & Jane Yates, Newton, bleacher
"	20	George & John twin ss. John & Mary Thornley, Failsworth, weaver
"	20	Mary Gee d. Thomas & Elizabeth Cash, Newton, blacksmith
"	27	John s. James & Anne Taylor, Failsworth, weaver
Mar	3	Peggy d. John & Mary Howard, Woodhouses, weaver
"	3	John Thomason s. Benjamin & Jenny Hulton, Failsworth, weaver
"	3	William s. John & Hannah Thornley, Failsworth, weaver
"	6	Sarah d. Anne Wilkinson, Failsworth, spinster

"	6	Edmund s. Joseph & Anne Higham, Failsworth, weaver	*(1825)*
"	6	Mary d. John & Matty Higham, Newton, weaver	
"	6	John s. James & Jane Schofield, Manchester, labourer	
"	10	Abraham s. Robert & Sarah Whitehead, Newton, weaver	
"	16	Robert s. John & Hannah Allen, Newton, calico printer	
"	17	Robert s. Robert & Anne Allen, Failsworth, weaver	
"	20	Joseph s. Hannah Tomlinson, Failsworth, spinster	
"	20	Sarah d. John & Violet McNamee, Newton, bleacher	
"	20	Kay s. David & Mary Knott, Failsworth, weaver	
"	21	Hannah d. Joseph & Mary Butterworth, Manr., weaver	
"	27	Betty d. Thomas & Ann Wilson, Moston, weaver	
Apr	1	John s. John & Sarah Marsden, Newton, bleacher	
"	1	William s. James & Anne Tomlinson, Newton, engineer	
"	1	Thomas s. Samuel & Betty Hardman, Newton, weaver	
"	1	John & Mary children of Samuel & Betty Hardman, Newton, weaver	
"	3	Joseph s. James & Jane Higginbotham, Mill houses, calico printer	
"	3	Alice d. William & Jane Mather, Droylsden, weaver	
"	3	Mary d. James & Mary Burton, Newton, weaver	
"	3	James s. John & Anne Wood, Failsworth, weaver	
"	3	William s. Sarah Chadderton, Newton, spinster	
"	3	John s. James & Anne Taylor, Failsworth, weaver	
"	3	Robert s. Thomas & Sarah Bradshaw, Failsworth, weaver	
"	3	William s. William & Anne Moulsdale, Medlock Vale, labourer	
"	3	Sarah d. James & Sarah Hunter, Ashton Parish, stone mason	
"	10	James s. John & Mary Whitehead, Failsworth, weaver	
"	10	James s. Sarah Howarth, Droylsden, spinster	
"	10	Hannah d. Isaac & Elizabeth Andrew, Newton, calico printer	
"	10	John s. James & Sarah Bradbury, Newton, labourer	
"	17	William s. Samuel & Betty Barlow, Medlock Vale, bleacher	
"	17	Samuel s. Charles & Lydia Walker, Gorton, hatter	
"	17	Mary d. George & Jane Robinson, Failsworth, dyer	
"	17	Samuel s. Samuel & Betty Barlow, Medlock Vale, bleacher	
"	17	Sarah d. William & Lydia Thornycroft, Manr., porter	
"	24	Samuel s. Jonathan & Esther Dawson, Newton, weaver	
"	24	William s. Joseph & Hannah Smith, Newton, warper	
May	1	Anne d. Nicholas & Jane Simister, Newton, weaver	
"	1	James s. Isaac & Elizabeth Schofield, Failsworth, weaver	
"	1	Mary d. Hannah Wolstenholme, Failsworth, spinster	
"	1	Anne d. James & Eliza Gradwell, Blackley, bleacher	
"	6	James s. David & Elizabeth Whittaker, Newton, wheelwright	
"	15	John s. John & Anne Gradwell, Failsworth, weaver	
"	15	James s. Susanna Caton, Newton, spinster	
"	15	William s. William & Elizabeth Worral, Failsworth, farmer	
"	18	Frederic Daniel s. Daniel & Lucy Speakman, Hulme, cotton spinner	
"	22	Thomas s. John & Mary Hughes, Newton, slater	

"	22	Samuel s. James & Mary Blomiley, Newton, weaver
"	22	Alice d. Jeremiah & Alice Etchels, Droylsden, weaver
"	22	James s. Thomas & Mary Berry, Failsworth, weaver
"	22	Lavinia d. Elijah & Charlotte Hilton, Failsworth, weaver
"	22	Martha d. William & Anne Booth, Chorlton row, collier
"	22	Luke s. William & Hannah Eckersley, Failsworth, weaver
"	22	James s. William & Susanna Horrocks, Ashton underline, dyer
"	22	Robert s. Robert & Alice Bradshaw, Newton, calico printer
"	22	Ellis s. Joseph & Rebekah Hulton, Failsworth, weaver
"	22	Andrew s. Daniel & Hannah Etchels, Failsworth, weaver
"	22	Sarah d. Margaret Smith, Newton, spinster
"	22	Nancy d. John & Mary Ramsden, Manchesr., carter
"	25	Emma & Elizabeth ds. John & Anne Bateman, Newton, warehouse man
"	29	James s. Robert & Mary Berry, Failsworth, weaver
"	29	William s. James & Alice Fletcher, Failsworth, weaver
"	29	Joel s. William & Hannah Hulme, Newton, porter
"	29	Sarah d. Edmund & Anne Tetlow, Failsworth, weaver
"	29	Elizabeth d. Isaac & Elizabeth Heapey, Droylsden, hatter
"	29	John s. Samuel & Mary Lord, Failsworth, labourer
Jun	5	Hannah d. Joseph & Mary Smethurst, Failsworth, weaver
"	5	Robert s. John & Elizabeth Eaton, Medlock Vale, labourer
"	12	John s. John & Martha Owen, Blackley, farmer
"	12	Thomas s. John & Anne Gardner, Droylsden, farmer
"	12	Robert s. Robert & Sarah Branton, Newton, weaver
"	12	John s. Leah & Mary Foden, Newton, labourer
"	12	Martha d. Robert & Elizabeth Wilkinson, Failsworth, weaver
"	12	Jane d. Samuel & Anne Bottomley, Manchesr., brewer
"	12	Martha d. William & Betty Glossop, Failsworth, weaver
"	15	William s. John & Elizabeth Howles, Newton, bleacher
"	16	Eliza d. Samuel & Jane Mather, Newton, dyer (*entry placed between June 19 & 22 in PR & BT*)
"	19	John s. John & Ruth Bottomley, Manchesr., blacksmith
"	19	Maria d. Hannah Whittaker, Failsworth, spinster
"	22	Anne d. Thomas & Anne Hamer, Failsworth, bleacher
"	22	Robert s. John & Sarah Whitehead, Newton, calico printer
"	22	Elizabeth d. Elijah & Jane Pollitt, Newton, dyer
"	26	Mary Jane Shepley d. Josiah & Mary Barnes Holt, Failsworth, manufacturer
"	26	Hannah d. Henry & Elizabeth Hulton, Failsworth, weaver
Jul	3	Robert s. Luke & Rachel Hilton, Failsworth, farmer
"	3	James s. Philip & Nancy Ashton, Failsworth, weaver
"	3	Margaret d. Adam & Margaret Horrocks, Droylsden, dyer
"	3	Sarah d. Thomas & Mary Hall, Manchester, labourer
"	10	Edwin s. John & Hannah Thorpe, Newton, weaver
"	17	Elizabeth d. John & Martha Tervin, Newton, labourer
"	17	William s. John & Alice Gannon, Newton, calico printer

"	17	Rosanna d. Radcliff & Sarah Potts, Newton, manufacturer
"	17	Thomas s. Joseph & Maria Arrandale, Droylsden, bricklayer
"	17	Jane d. Thomas & Jane Taylor, Manchester, labourer
"	24	Anne d. Joseph & Priscilla Fletcher, Newton, weaver
"	24	Alice d. Josiah & Alice Etchels, Failsworth, weaver
"	31	Robert s. James & Alice Mills, Medlock Vale, calico printer
"	31	Cockshut s. George & Mary Whittaker, Failsworth, hatter
"	31	Alfred s. John & Mary Standring, Droylsden, weaver
"	31	Daniel s. Daniel & Hannah Berrington, Manchesr., farmer
"	31	Anne d. Edmund & Sarah Walmsley, Failsworth, farmer
Aug	7	George s. Joseph & Sally Eckersley, Failsworth, weaver
"	7	Sarah Anne d. Thomas & Mally Hyde, Failsworth, weaver
"	14	Philip s. John & Mary Berry, Newton, brewer
"	21	Jane d. Ashton & Anne Shepley, Newton, weaver
"	21	Henry s. James & Esther Chadderton, Ashton underlyne, weaver
"	21	Isaac s. James & Esther Chadderton, Ashton underlyne, weaver
"	21	Sarah d. James & Elizabeth Wilson, Newton, weaver
"	21	Henry s. David & Anne Ogden, Failsworth, weaver
"	21	Elizabeth d. Robert & Elizabeth Taylor, Failsworth, weaver
"	21	Mary d. Samuel & Mary Dean, Failsworth, weaver
"	21	William s. Thomas & Sarah Dawson, Newton, dyer
"	21	Elizabeth d. Thomas & Mary Livesey, Manchester, collier
"	21	Thomas s. William & Betty Makin, Newton, dyer
"	21	Benjamin s. James & Esther Brierly, Failsworth, weaver
"	21	Jane d. Charles & Anne Winstanley, Manchesr., collier
"	21	John s. James & Hannah Seel, Droylsden, bleacher
"	21	James s. William & Sarah Walmsley, Failsworth, weaver
"	21	Amelia d. John & Mary Wilkinson, Failsworth, weaver
"	21	Anne d. George & Sarah Tomlinson, Moston, weaver
"	21	Alice d. John & Alice Thorpe, Failsworth, weaver
"	21	William s. John & Elizabeth Goodier, Newton, calenderer
"	21	Sarah Anne d. Samuel & Ellen Clough, Failsworth, weaver
"	21	John s. Thomas & Jane Jones, Newton, labourer
"	21	Alice d. Anne Hulton, Failsworth, spinster
"	21	John s. William & Sarah Knott, Failsworth, weaver
"	21	Betty d. Daniel & Hannah Knott, Failsworth, weaver
"	21	Betty d. Nathaniel & Betty Taylor, Failsworth, weaver
"	21	Richard s. Isaac & Anne Barratt, Newton, bleacher
"	21	Elizabeth d. William & Elizabeth Wood, Manchester, painter
"	21	Henry s. John & Alice Pilkington, Failsworth, labourer
"	21	Thomas s. Richard & Sarah Worsick, Failsworth, brickmaker
"	28	Thomas s. Thomas & Jane Wood, Manchester, skinner
Sep	4	Anne d. William & Sarah Barlow, Newton, block cutter
"	4	Rebekah d. James & Anne Hooley, Newton, cotton manufacturer
"	4	Harriet d. John & Caroline Mercer, Newton, glazier

"	11	Nancy d. Mary Tonge, Failsworth, spinster
"	11	Charles s. Josiah & Jane Garlick, Failsworth, weaver
"	11	James s. John & Betty Davenport, Levenshulme, weaver
"	13	Abraham s. Samuel & Mary Moorhouse, Failsworth, weaver
"	18	Isaac s. John & Anne Bailey, Manchester, collier
Oct	2	Sarah d. Mary Taylor, Newton, spinster
"	9	Alice d. James & Alice Swift, Failsworth, weaver
"	9	Mary d. David & Hannah Harrison, Newton, weaver
"	9	William s. George & Mary Bardsley, Newton, dyer
"	9	Thomas Cooper s. John & Esther Whitehead, Newton, farmer
"	16	James s. Thomas & Betty Hodgin, Failsworth, weaver
"	16	Jane d. William & Marianne Whitehead, Failsworth, weaver
"	16	James s. John & Mary Whitehead, Failsworth, weaver
"	16	Thomas s. John & Mary Whitehead, Failsworth, weaver
"	23	John s. John & Betty Taylor, Failsworth, weaver
"	23	Elizabeth d. Mary Tomlinson, Moston, spinster
"	30	John s. Joseph & Mary Richardson, Failsworth, joiner
"	30	Abraham s. James & Ellen Clough, Failsworth, weaver
"	30	William s. John & Anne Hibbert, Newton, weaver
Nov	6	Joseph s. Philip & Anne Berry, Failsworth, weaver
"	13	Jane d. Thomas & Mary Robinson, Droylsden, labourer
"	13	Sarah d. Richard & Alice Dawson, Failsworth, dyer
"	20	John s. Mary Swift, Failsworth, spinster
"	20	Anne d. James & Mary Yates, Newton, calenderer
"	20	Mary d. George & Anne Grimshaw, Chadderton, farmer
"	27	Mary d. John & Ellen Taylor, Failsworth, weaver
Dec	4	Alice d. John & Anne Clough, Failsworth, weaver
"	11	Charles Peter s. Peter & Anne Stone, Newton, jeweller
"	11	Thomas s. James & Ruth Whitehead, Failsworth, weaver
"	25	Betty d. James & Jane Aldred, Failsworth, weaver
"	25	George s. Thomas & Betty Fletcher, Failsworth, weaver
"	25	Betty d. John & Mary Wyld, Newton, weaver
"	25	Martha d. John & Jane Smith, Failsworth, weaver
"	25	Alice d. Samuel & Hannah Lees, Failsworth, weaver
"	25	Jane d. John & Mary Blakeley, Newton, blacksmith
"	25	Lucy d. Joseph & Esther Kershaw, Newton, weaver
"	25	Joseph s. Thomas & Hannah Taylor, Newton, weaver
"	27	Henry s. William & Anne Hibbert, Failsworth, weaver

1826

Jan	1	James s. James & Hannah Berry, Failsworth, blacksmith
"	1	William s. William & Mary Smith, Failsworth, weaver
"	1	William s. William & Lucy Seel, Newton, bleacher
"	1	William s. Ashton & Sarah Worral, Failsworth, carter

"	1	Nancy d. Thomas & Mary Howard, Failsworth, weaver	*(1826)*
"	1	George Frederick s. John & Mary Lomas, Manchester, wollen draper	
"	1	Caroline d. Anne Sykes, Newton, spinster	
"	1	Jane d. Jane Wyld, Droylsden, spinster	
"	8	Charles s. James & Elizabeth Walmsley, Newton, labourer	
"	15	James Ridings s. Benjamin & Nancy Worsick, Droylsden, farmer	
"	22	Samuel s. James & Anne Clough, Newton, weaver	
"	22	Alice d. William & Mary Fenton, Medlock Vale, dyer	
"	24	William s. Levi & Ellen Clough, Newton, weaver	
Feb	5	Ann d. Samuel & Mary Etchels, Newton, weaver	
"	5	Hannah d. Richard & Agnes Higginson, Reddish, blacksmith	
"	5	Mary d. Charles & Betty Sydebotham, Newton, dyer	

(BT faded; next 8 entries cannot be verified)

"	12	James s. Uriah & Hannah Booth, Newton, labourer
"	12	Robert s. John & Hannah Walmsley, Newton, labourer
"	12	William s. Thomas & Mary Ogden, Hollinwood, weaver
"	12	Nancy d. Thomas & Nancy Johnson, Failsworth, weaver
"	12	Amelia d. Charles & Isabella Ridings, Newton, weaver
"	19	James s. Abel & Nancy Whatmough, Newton, mason
"	19	John s. John & Margaret Burns, Newton, cotton spinner
"	26	William s. Matthew & Sarah Brown, Newton, weaver
"	26	Mary d. Joseph & Sarah Whitehead, Failsworth, weaver
"	26	Caroline d. Oliver & Matty Ogden, Failsworth, weaver
"	26	John s. Robert & Susanna Marsden, Newton, calenderer
"	27	Eliza d. James & Hannah Berry, Failsworth, blacksmith, bo Feb 11 1818
"	27	Janet Martha d. James & Hannah Berry, Failsworth, blacksmith, bo 12 Nov 1821
Mar	4	Joseph s. John & Martha Shadwick, Failsworth, blockcutter
"	5	Anne d. Joseph & Alice Tetlow, Manchester, weaver
"	5	Sarah Anne d. Samuel & Martha Hulton, Moston, labourer
"	5	Lydia d. John & Mary Hoyle, Manchester, weaver
"	12	Hannah d. Samuel & Mary Pollitt, Failsworth, weaver
"	12	John s. Edmund & Elizabeth Wylde, Manchester, joiner
"	19	Jonathan s. James & Sarah Whittaker, Failsworth, weaver
"	19	Frederick s. John & Maria Stott, Failsworth, weaver
"	26	Benjamin s. Joseph & Anne Whitehead, Failsworth, dyer
"	26	Matthew s. John & Mary Newton, Failsworth, inn keeper
"	26	Richard s. William & Esther Whitehead, Failsworth, weaver
"	26	Alice d. Thomas & Mary Dunkerly, Failsworth, weaver
"	26	Peggy d. George & Mary Lees, Failsworth, weaver
"	26	Hannah d. William & Phoebe Smethurst, Failsworth, weaver
Apr	9	James s. George & Charlotte Smethurst, Newton, dyer
"	9	George s. William & Alice Walton, Newton, calico printer
"	10	Joseph s. James & Anne Ogden, Woodhouses, weaver
"	16	Nancy d. Samuel & Jane Bethel, Newton, bleacher

"	16	James s. Abel & Grace Sharples, Failsworth, tailor *(1826)*
"	16	Sarah Anne d. Anne Kershaw, Newton, spinster
"	23	John s. Adam & Betty Dodson, Newton, bleacher
"	23	Hannah d. William & Sarah Pollitt, Failsworth, weaver
"	26	John s. James & Agnes Ashton, New Mill Derbyshire, engraver
"	30	Anne d. Henry & Mary Rogerson, Newton, blacksmith
"	30	Edward s. John & Betty Allen, Failsworth, weaver
May	7	Robert s. John & Anne Pattison, Newton, shopkeeper
"	7	Henry s. John & Esther Ditchfield, Newton, calenderer
"	7	James s. Samuel & Mary Grimshaw, Droylsden, weaver
"	11	William Bagshaw s. Bold Bagshaw & Elizabeth Robinson, Manchester, innkeeper
"	14	Mary d. Benjamin & Betty Lees, Failsworth, weaver
"	14	Anne d. James & Anne Taylor, Failsworth, weaver
"	14	Brutus s. William & Martha Ford, Failsworth, weaver
"	14	Nancy d. Anne Thorpe, Failsworth, spinster
"	14	Isaac s. Samuel & Mary Hyde, Failsworth, weaver
"	16	Rachel d. John & Maria Taylor, Failsworth, weaver
Jun	1	William s. John & Hannah Benson, Manchester, weaver
"	4	Martha d. Thomas & Nancy Ogden, Newton, weaver
"	4	Mary d. Jonathan & Esther Etchels, Failsworth, labourer
"	4	Noah s. Samuel & Mary Robinson, Newton, stonemason
"	11	William s. John & Sarah Mather, Failsworth, hatter
"	11	Mary Anne d. John & Mary Duckworth, Stayley wood, calico printer
"	11	Joseph s. James & Elizabeth Kenyon, Hollinwood, weaver
"	11	Elizabeth d. Thomas & Elizabeth Cooper, Droylsden, pattern designer
"	18	Elizabeth d. James & Mary Butterworth, Newton, weaver
"	18	James s. William & Eliza Hardy, Failsworth, bleacher
"	18	Joseph s. John & Martha Whitehead, Failsworth, weaver
"	18	James s. Thomas & Alice Pollitt, Newton, dyer
"	18	Emma d. John & Jane Blackshaw, Newton, warehouseman
"	18	Sarah d. William & Betty Sutcliff, Newton, shoemaker
"	18	Mark s. John & Mary Hay, Newton, print cutter
"	21	Susan d. Thomas & Anne Wilson, Chadderton, weaver
"	28	Ellen d. James & Ellen Travis, Manchester, hatter
Jul	2	James s. Joseph & Matty Ogden, Moston, weaver
"	9	Thomas s. John & Elizabeth Robinson, Newton, weaver
"	10	Joseph s. William & Alice Thorpe, Failsworth, weaver
"	16	William s. Peter & Margaret Slater, Newton, labourer
"	16	Mary d. John & Mary Travis, Moston, footman
"	16	Betty d. William & Anne Whitehead, Failsworth, hatter
"	16	Peter s. John & Betty Abbot, Newton, labourer
"	16	William s. John & Betty Abbot, Newton, labourer
"	18	Sarah d. Robert & Susanna Cheetham, Ashton Parish, calico printer, bo 20 Dec 1804

"	23	William s. Thomas & Mary Taylor, Failsworth, weaver
"	23	Thomas s. Thomas & Mary Kay, Moston, farmer
"	26	Thomas s. James & Martha Ogden, Failsworth, weaver
"	30	Joseph s. David & Sally Makin, Moston, weaver
"	30	John s. Thomas & Maria (Betty *struck through*) [Maria] Robinson, Clayton Vale, dyer
"	30	William s. Joseph & Mary Hilton, Newton, weaver
"	30	Sarah d. Abraham & Nancy Taylor, Newton, dyer
Aug	3	Mary d. James & Sarah Houlton, Newton, farmer
"	4	Edward s. Elizabeth Williams, Newton, spinster
"	6	James s. Peter & Mary Stott, Moston, weaver
"	6	John s. John & Hannah Wood, Droylsden, farmer
"	6	Marianne d. Philip & Elizabeth Wagstaff, Chorlton row, weaver
"	10	Edmund s. Robert & Alice Whitehead, Newton, weaver
"	10	Robert s. Joseph & Hannah Williamson, Newton, weaver
"	13	Thomas s. John & Anne Horrocks, Newton, bleacher
"	20	John s. Edward & Maria Hulton, Failsworth, warper
"	20	Elizabeth d. William & Mary Hulton, Failsworth, weaver
"	20	Elizabeth d. Joshua & Sarah Swift, Newton, dyer
"	20	James s. James & Margaret Higham, Failsworth, gardener
"	20	Joel s. Robert & Anne Whitehead, Failsworth, weaver
"	20	Sarah Anne d. William & Mary Barnes, Manchester, labourer
"	20	Betty d. Sarah Clough, Failsworth, spinster
"	20	Elizabeth d. William & Anne Brandon, Ashton underlyne, engineer
"	20	Samuel s. William & Sarah Brown, Openshaw, weaver
"	20	Thomas s. James & Anne Ogden, Hollinwood, blacksmith
"	20	Anne d. William & Elizabeth Whitelegg, Droylsden, weaver
"	20	Thomas s. William & Sarah Prescott, Strangeways, labourer
"	20	Mary d. Benjamin & Jane Howarth, Droylsden, farmer
"	25	Joseph Brunkart s. Joseph & Maria Wilkinson, Failsworth, weaver
"	27	James s. James & Anne Allen, Failsworth, weaver
"	31	Margaret d. Thomas & Sarah Ratcliffe, Denton, bricklayer
Sep	3	Anne d. Joseph & Eliza Jane Coop, Newton, joiner
"	10	Emma d. Charles & Anne Wilson, Newton, weaver
"	15	William s. William & Mary Greenhalgh, Failsworth, tailor
"	17	Thomas s. Thomas & Margaret Horrocks, Millhouses, bleacher
"	20	Joseph s. Robert & Alice Stansfield, Newton, hatter
"	24	Susan d. Joel & Mary Smith, Failsworth, weaver
"	24	Mary d. Eli & Sarah Swift, Failsworth, weaver
"	24	Phoebe d. Jonah & Betty Goodier, Newton, bleacher
"	24	James s. Ralph & Mary Ogden, Failsworth, weaver
Oct	1	Jane d. Joseph & Sarah Wilkinson, Hollinwood, weaver
"	1	Sarah d. John & Betty Hyde, Newton, weaver
"	1	Thomas s. James & Alice Robinson, Newton, weaver
"	8	John s. Joseph & Elizabeth Tomkinson, Newton, weaver

"	8	Esther d. Thomas & Jane Lancashire, Newton, shopkeeper
"	8	Mary d. Thomas & Marianne Allen, Newton, packer
"	15	John s. Thomas & Mary Ogden, Moston, dyer
"	15	Robert s. Obadiah & Alice Bradshaw, Manchester, calico printer
"	22	Sarah d. James & Mary Newton, Harpurhey, dyer
"	22	William s. Thomas & Jane Bates, Failsworth, bleacher
"	22	Elizabeth d. Thomas & Mary Printon, Failsworth, sawyer
"	23	John s. William & Jane Robinson, Failsworth, calico printer
"	29	George s. John & Betty Holds, Newton, bleacher
"	29	William s. James & Anne Thorpe, Failsworth, weaver
"	29	John s. John & Grace Bradshaw, Strangeways, calico printer
Nov	5	James s. John & Alice Timmis, Failsworth, weaver
"	12	Elizabeth d. Samuel & Mary Kenyon, Hollinwood, weaver
"	12	James s. Joseph & Jenny Thornley, Failsworth, weaver
"	12	Anne d. Edward & Jane Tipton, Droylsden, collier
"	12	Thomas s. James & Betty Moston, Moston, miller
"	12	Martha d. William & Mary Holt, Newton, blacksmith
"	12	Sarah Anne d. James & Sarah Tweedale, Newton, schoolmaster
"	19	Mary d. Henry & Elizabeth Hulton, Failsworth, warehouseman
"	19	Catherine d. Frances Garside, Droylsden, spinster
"	26	Elizabeth Seddon d. Thomas & Jane Wyld, Newton, innkeeper
"	26	John s. George & Anne Morris, Medlock Vale, calico printer
Dec	3	Sarah d. James & Jane Hesketh, Failsworth, weaver
"	3	James s. George & Esther Wood, Newton, farmer
"	7	Mary d. Edward & Nancy Robinson, Failsworth, weaver
"	10	Thomas s. George & Elizabeth Smith, Droylsden, bricklayer
"	10	Anne & Ellen twin ds. James & Anne Howarth, Newton, labourer
"	10	John s. James & Elizabeth Fallows, Culcheth, labourer
"	17	Sarah d. Moses & Clarissa Gradwell, Newton, weaver
"	24	Thomas s. William & Mary Booth, Failsworth, weaver
"	24	Ellen d. Robert & Anne Berry, Failsworth, joiner
"	24	Marianne d. James & Martha Bray, Newton, cordwainer
"	24	Sally d. Thomas & Matty Winterbotham, Failsworth, weaver
"	24	Mary d. Elijah & Jane Pollitt, Newton, weaver
"	31	Enoch s. Garrick & Isabella Brown, Failsworth, baker
"	31	William Worral s. William & Sally Lane, Failsworth, innkeeper
"	31	John s. John & Sarah Whitehead, Newton, calico printer
"	31	William s. James & Sarah Worral, Failsworth, farmer
"	31	Sarah Anne d. Thomas & Sarah Eyre, Failsworth, shoemaker
"	31	William s. John & Mary Burgess, Newton, book keeper
[		Tho Gaskell, Incumbent of Newton]

1827

Jan	7	Amelia d. John & Alice Worsick, Failsworth, farmer

"	7	Jane d. John & Martha Tetlow, Newton, labourer *(1827)*
"	7	John Dickenson s. John & Marianne Lomas, Salford, wollen draper
"	7	Samuel s. Isaac & Ellen Hyde, Newton, weaver
"	7	Elizabeth d. James & Anne Barnes, Newton, weaver
"	21	Lavinia d. Thomas & Sarah Barlow, Failsworth, weaver
"	21	Mary d. Joseph & Anne Boon, Newton, shoemaker
"	28	Anne d. Abraham & Anne Mills, Failsworth, shoemaker
Feb	4	Martha d. Miles & Marianne Mason, Failsworth, blacksmith
"	4	Sarah d. Jonathan & Phoebe Handley, Droylsden, collier
"	18	John s. Samuel & Sarah Trevor, Medlock Vale, labourer
"	18	Margaret d. Richard & Nancy Trevor, Newton, engineer
"	20	Catherine Anne d. John & Caroline Mercer, Newton, glazier
"	25	Hannah d. John & Anne Gardner, Droylsden, farmer
"	25	Daniel s. Joseph & Mary Tetlow, Manchester, calico manufacturer
"	25	Phoebe d. Jonathan & Hannah Chadderton, Failsworth, weaver
"	25	Mary d. Samuel & Mary Lord, Failsworth, labourer
"	25	Hannah d. William & Anne Aldred, Failsworth, shoemaker
"	25	William s. George & Anne Haywood, Droylsden, bleacher
"	25	William s. David & Mary Knott, Failsworth, weaver
"	25	Mary d. Luke & Anne Clegg, Failsworth, joiner
"	25	Mary d. James & Sarah Mather, Newton, weaver
"	25	Samuel s. Ashton & Betty Ashton, Failsworth, weaver
Mar	11	Elijah s. Elijah & Charlotte Hilton, Failsworth, weaver
"	11	Jane d. Joseph & Alice Robinson, Newton, weaver
"	11	Thomas s. John & Sarah Twimlow, Newton, labourer
"	18	Anne d. Thomas & Jane Yates, Newton, bleacher
"	25	Dan s. George & Sarah Hilton, Newton, weaver
"	25	Joseph s. Joseph & Betty Mills, Failsworth, calenderer
"	25	John s. Richard & Mary Whitehead, Manchester, collier
Apr	1	Jane d. Philip & Elizabeth Schofield, Newton, cordwainer
"	1	Benjamin s. Sarah Wyld, Failsworth, spinster
"	8	Thomas s. Richard & Sarah Clough, Woodhouses, weaver
"	11	Nancy d. John & Mary Thornley, Failsworth, weaver
"	15	Sidney s. Mark & Alice Smith, Newton, weaver
"	15	Hannah d. Joseph & Anne Higham, Newton, weaver
"	15	Charles Richard s. Benjamin & Nancy Worsick, Droylsden, farmer
"	15	Alice d. James & Jane Higginbotham, Newton, calico printer
"	15	James s. Robert & Sarah Hulme, Newton, calenderer
"	15	Anne d. William & Jane Harrison, Ardwick, weaver
"	15	Betty d. Betty Collinson, Failsworth, spinster
"	15	James s. John & Elizabeth Smith, Newton, weaver
"	15	Jonas s. John & Anne Hilton, Chadderton, weaver
"	15	Edward s. John & Esther Dewhurst, Hollinwood, labourer
"	15	John s. William & Jenny Bethel, Failsworth, weaver
"	15	John s. John & Sarah Tomlinson, Moston, weaver

"	15	James s. Betty Etchels, Failsworth, spinster	*(1827)*
"	15	Mary d. James & Anne Lee, Newton, weaver	
"	15	Esther d. William & Mary Wilson, Moston, weaver	
"	15	Hannah d. Sally Wyatt, Failsworth, spinster	
"	15	Elias s. Isaac & Elizabeth Heapy, Droylsden, hatter	
"	15	Rabbina d. Jonathan & Mary Hooley, Newton, labourer	
"	15	Joseph s. William & Hannah Eckersley, Failsworth, weaver	
"	18	Ellen d. John & Martha Turvin, Hollinwood, labourer	
"	22	Charles s. James & Alice Mills, Ashton Parish, calico printer	
"	22	Sarah d. Richard & Susanna Thomas, Manchester, cotton spinner	
"	22	Eliza d. Richard & Susanna Thomas, Manchester, cotton spinner	
"	22	Margaret d. Abraham & Anne Collinge, Newton, dyer	
"	22	Robert s. William & Deborah Davies, Medlock Vale, gardener	
"	22	Marianne & Margaret twin ds. Elisha & Anne Hibbert, Droylsden, weaver	
"	29	Elizabeth d. John & Betty Wormald, Oldham, cotton spinner	
May	13	Elizabeth d. Samuel & Susanna Bagnal, Newton, weaver	
"	13	Thomas s. John & Sarah Gammel, Droylsden, stone mason	
"	13	Ellen d. Thomas & Mary Cole, Failsworth, warehouseman	
"	13	Heber s. Heber & Elizabeth Whittingham, Newton, miller	
"	13	Marianne d. William & Ellen Sutliff, Newton, colour mixer	
"	16	Elizabeth & Jemima ds. John Michael & Elizabeth Higgins, Newton, officer-of excise	
"	20	Abraham s. Thomas & Anne Ogden, Duckinfield, collier	
"	20	James s. William & Margaret Allen, Newton, weaver	
"	21	Jane d. Samuel & Mary Lees, Failsworth, weaver	
"	21	Elizabeth d. George & Alice Senior, Manchester, collier	
"	24	Samuel s. Samuel & Anne Lowe, Manchester, weaver	
"	27	Samuel s. John & Mary Smith, Newton, blockcutter	
"	27	Sarah d. James & Sarah Fildes, Droylsden, bookkeeper	
"	27	Catherine d. Thomas & Sarah Taylor, Failsworth, weaver	
"	28	John s. Joseph & Mary Davies, Chorlton row, weaver	
Jun	3	Elizabeth d. James & Mary Burton, Newton, weaver	
"	3	Nancy d. Joseph & Nancy Ogden, Failsworth, weaver	
"	3	Joseph s. Joseph & Alice Whitehead, Failsworth, porter	
"	3	James s. Thurston & Jane Smethurst, Newton, labourer	
"	3	John s. Hannah Haslam, Failsworth, spinster	
"	3	Betty d. William & Martha Eyre, Failsworth, weaver	
"	3	Olive d. Hannah Whittaker, Failsworth, spinster	
"	3	Mary d. Samuel & Sarah Oaksley, Droylsden, labourer	
"	3	Sarah Anne d. Mark & Marianne Mather, Salford, manufacturer	
"	3	James s. Sarah Fletcher, Newton, spinster	
"	3	Mary d. James & Anne Kirk, Failsworth, baker	
"	10	Mary d. Ellen Bury, Failsworth, spinster	
"	10	Kitty d. Isaac & Elizabeth Andrew, Stayley wood, calico printer	
"	17	Matthew s. John & Violet McNamee, Newton, bleacher	

"	17	James s. George & Anne Grimshaw, Chadderton, labourer	*(1827)*
"	17	Jane d. Betty Wroe, Failsworth, spinster	
"	17	William s. Joseph & Maria Hallady, Fairfield, bricksetter	
"	17	William s. Hannah Royle, Hollinwood, spinster	
"	19	Harriet d. John & Anne Hilton, Failsworth, weaver (*altered from the original* labourer) [weaver]	
"	24	John s. James & Anne Hodgin, Failsworth, weaver	
"	24	George s. James & Alice Fletcher, Woodhouses	
"	24	Ellen d. James & Alice Smith, Droylsden, weaver	
Jul	1	Thomas s. Richard & Esther Thorpe, Moston, weaver	
"	3	John s. Nicholas & Margaret Edge, Failsworth, blockcutter	
"	3	James s. George & Jane Robinson, Failsworth, dyer	
"	8	James s. William & Harriet Allen, Newton, calenderer	
"	8	James s. James & Susan Hilton, Chadderton, weaver	
"	19	Jane Goodier d. Thomas & Mary Rubery, Manchester, agent, aged 15 years	
"	19	William s. John & Martha Turner, Stockport, land surveyor	
"	22	Ellen d. James & Mary Lees, Failsworth, weaver	
"	22	Anne d. Thomas & Anne Hardman, Newton, throwster	
"	29	Henry s. David & Anne Ogden, Newton, weaver	
"	30	Anne d. Joseph & Mary Whittaker, Newton, weaver	
Aug	5	Thomas s. John & Elizabeth Taylor, Failsworth, weaver	
"	5	Alice d. Garside & Alice Blomily, Newton, weaver	
"	9	James s. Matthew & Hannah Gradwell, Newton, weaver	
"	12	Elizabeth d. John & Anne Tonge, Newton, calenderer	
"	13	John & Elizabeth s. & d. John & Jane Baker, Droylsden, bookkeeper	
"	13	John s. James & Jane Pendlebury, Droylsden, bleacher	
"	13	Sarah d. James & Mary Yates, Newton, maker up	
"	13	Mary d. George & Jane Walker, Droylsden, weaver (*entry placed after 5th entry below; same in BT*)	
"	19	John s. Charles & Mary Hulton, Manchester, weaver	
"	19	Hannah d. Robert & Betty Taylor, Failsworth, weaver	
"	19	Joseph s. John & Matty Higham, Newton, weaver	
"	19	Sarah d. Elizabeth Rogers, Newton, spinster	
"	19	Mary d. John & Esther Brierly, Failsworth, weaver	
"	19	Elizabeth d. John & Maria Stott, Newton, weaver	
"	19	James s. Luke & Jane Wharmby, Newton, weaver	
"	19	Mary d. John & Anne Clough, Failsworth, weaver	
"	26	Mary d. Luke & Isabel Smith, Failsworth, weaver	
"	26	James s. Joseph & Anne Bradbury, Bradford, collier	
"	26	Fanny d. William & Anne Howard, Chadderton, weaver	
"	26	Nathan s. Lee & Mary Foden, Newton, labourer	
"	26	Marianne d. Hannah Richardson, Failsworth, spinster	
Sep	2	James s. Robert & Margaret Taylor, Failsworth, weaver	
"	9	John s. Thomas & Mary Dunkerly, Newton, weaver	
"	16	Sally d. Elizabeth Taylor, Failsworth, spinster	

"	23	James s. Richard & Sarah Worsick, Failsworth, farmer	*(1827)*
"	23	William s. John & Mary Allen, Newton, labourer	
"	23	Mary d. Thomas & Betty Wolstencroft, Newton, whitster	
"	23	Andrew s. Joseph & Sarah Rogers, Failsworth, weaver	
"	23	Marianne d. Charles & Lydia Walker, Gorton, hatter	
"	23	Anne d. James & Anne Taylor, Failsworth, weaver	
"	30	John s. Charles & Anne Dootson, Hooley Hill, crofter	
"	30	John s. James & Eliza Gradwell, Droylsden, crofter	
Oct	7	Martha d. Thomas & Elizabeth Cash, Newton, blacksmith	
"	7	Thomas s. Henry & Mary Rogerson, Newton, blacksmith	
"	10	Charles Francis s. Josiah & Mary Barnes Holt, Newton, shopkeeper	
"	14	Hugh s. Thomas & Mary Parr, Clayton, bleacher	
"	14	Marianne d. Richard & Alice Dawson, Clayton, dyer	
"	21	Benjamin s. William & Mary Howarth, Newton, shopkeeper	
"	21	John s. John & Anne Berry, Failsworth, weaver	
"	21	Thomas s. James & Alice Taylor, Failsworth, weaver	
"	21	James s. John & Sarah Marsden, Newton, bleacher	
"	21	Anne d. John & Betty Eaton, Medlock Vale, labourer	
"	28	James s. John & Hannah Allen, Newton, block printer	
"	28	Hannah d. Luke & Rachel Hilton, Failsworth, weaver	
"	28	Thomas s. Daniel & Hannah Knott, Failsworth, weaver	
"	28	Elizabeth d. James & Mary Blomiley, Newton, weaver	
"	28	Marianne d. William & Betty Makin, Newton, dyer	
"	29	John s. Joseph & Hannah Smith, Newton, warper	
Nov	2	George s. Isaac & Elizabeth Schofield, Failsworth, weaver	
"	4	Marianne d. Thomas & Martha Kemp, Newton, warehouseman	
"	4	Joseph s. Samuel & Elizabeth Smith, Failsworth, fustian cutter	
"	4	Anne d. Alexander & Mary Galashan, Failsworth, weaver	
"	4	Robert s. Robert & Elizabeth Lees, Failsworth, weaver	
"	4	Elizabeth d. Adam & Margaret Horrocks, Droylsden, bleacher	
"	11	Elizabeth d. Ashton & Anne Shepley, Newton, weaver	
"	11	John s. James & Betsey Moston, Moston, miller	
"	11	William s. James & Betty Bracegirdle, Failsworth, bricksetter	
"	18	Eliza d. George & Mary Whittaker, Failsworth, hatter	
"	18	Elizabeth d. Robert & Elizabeth Wilkinson, Failsworth, weaver	
"	18	Mary d. Robert & Elizabeth Grimston, Failsworth, toll collector	
"	18	Hannah d. Charles & Anne Winstanley, Manchesr., collier	
"	18	Elizabeth d. Daniel & Hannah Berrington, Newton, carter	
Dec	2	James s. Joseph & Mary Richardson, Failsworth, joiner	
"	2	Mary d. Thomas & Elizabeth Buckley, Newton, shoemaker	
"	2	Martha d. Thomas & Jane Taylor, Newton, silk throwster	
"	6	Sarah d. John & Esther Dichfield, Newton, calenderer	
"	9	Anne d. Edward & Martha Allen, Failsworth, weaver	
"	16	Margaret d. John & Anne Speakman, Newton, labourer	
"	25	Mary d. Alexander & Mary Smith, Failsworth, weaver	

"	25	Martha d. John & Mary Wilkinson, Failsworth, weaver
"	25	Dan s. Nicholas & Jane Simister, Newton, weaver
"	25	Robert s. William & Esther Whitehead, Failsworth, weaver
"	25	James Bardsley s. Thomas & Nancy Johnson, Failsworth, weaver
"	25	Henry s. John & Sarah Bentley, Newton, weaver
"	25	James s. John & Martha Consterdine, Newton, labourer
"	25	Thomas s. Joseph & Mary Butterworth, Manr., weaver
"	25	James s. John & Anne Bailey, Manchester, collier
"	30	James s. John & Anne Dewhurst, Failsworth, joiner
"	30	John s. Thomas & Sarah Thornley, Failsworth, weaver
"	30	John s. William & Sarah Stanfield, Newton, hatter
"	30	Andrew s. Thomas & Mary Pollitt, Failsworth, weaver
"	30	Betty d. James & Hannah Etchels, Failsworth, weaver
"	30	John s. Joseph & Priscilla Fletcher, Newton, weaver

1828

Jan	1	William s. Abel & Nancy Whatmouth, Newton, stonemason
"	6	James s. Mary Hyde, Newton, spinster
"	6	Thomas s. Mark & Elizabeth Brown, Failsworth, weaver
"	6	Eliza d. John & Hannah Wyatt, Newton, weaver
"	13	Hannah d. William & Martha Ford, Failsworth, weaver
"	13	Elizabeth d. John & Ellen Taylor, Failsworth, weaver
"	13	James s. Thomas & Jane Wood, Manchester, fellmonger
"	20	Anne d. Simeon & Hannah Smith, Failsworth, weaver
"	20	Mary d. Adam & Betty Doodson, Newton, bleacher
"	22	John s. James & Jane Taylor, Newton, silk manufacturer
"	26	Phoebe d. John & Alice Pilkington, Failsworth, labourer
"	26	Thomas s. Thomas & Hannah Taylor, Failsworth, weaver
"	27	Alice d. Jane Thorpe, Manchester, spinster
"	27	Charles s. James & Mary Radcliffe, Newton, warehouseman, bo 29 Aug 1824
"	27	Ellen d. James & Mary Radcliffe, Newton, warehouseman
Feb	10	William s. John & Mary Ramsden, Newton, bleacher
"	10	James s. Matthew & Sarah Smith, Newton, dyer
"	10	Jane d. William & Marianne Fenton, Newton, dyer
"	14	Richard s. James & Mary Butterworth, Newton, weaver
"	14	Marianne d. Joseph & Jane Ellor, Droylsden, hatter
"	17	Anne d. Benjamin & Mary Hulton, Failsworth, weaver
"	17	Elizabeth d. Thomas & Mary Ogden, Moston, dyer
"	17	Joseph s. John & Mary Wyld, Newton, weaver
"	17	John s. Samuel & Esther Corns, Manchester, dyer
"	17	Samuel s. John & Amelia Corns, Failsworth, shopkeeper
"	17	Frederick s. Sarah Robinson, Newton, spinster
"	17	Elizabeth d. Charles & Elizabeth Sydebotham, Newton, dyer

"	17	John s. James & Alice Swift, Manchester, weaver
"	17	Thomas s. James & Anne Ogden, Woodhouses, weaver
"	24	John s. William & Lucy Seel, Newton, bleacher
"	26	Sarah d. John & Anne Whitehead, Failsworth, weaver
"	28	Elizabeth d. John & Elizabeth Barton, Manchester, engineer
"	28	Samuel s. William & Sarah Barlow, Newton, blockcutter
Mar	2	Anne d. James & Anne Tomlinson, Culcheth, bleacher
"	2	Mary d. William & Phoebe Smethurst, Failsworth, weaver
"	5	Benjamin s. James & Sarah Goodier, Manchester, labourer
"	9	Anne d. Alice Robinson, Manchester, spinster
"	9	Maria d. Edward & Hannah Radcliff, Manchester, warehouseman
"	9	Alice d. Samuel & Alice Winstanley, Newton, collier
"	16	Emma & Martha Elizabeth ds. Joseph & Sarah Lees, Newton, shopkeeper
"	16	Robert s. William & Hannah Barlow, Failsworth, weaver
"	16	Louisa d. John & Margaret Jones, Moston, dyer
"	16	John Thomas Joseph & Elizabeth children of John & Margaret Jones, Moston, dyer
"	23	James s. James & Anne Hague, Newton, calico printer
"	23	Isabella d. John & Mary Whitehead, Failsworth, weaver
"	23	Mary Williams d. Joel & Mary Goodier, Newton, bleacher
"	25	Thomas s. Samuel & Martha Hulton, Moston, labourer
"	25	Mary d. Daniel & Elizabeth Wyld, Newton, labourer
"	30	Cato s. Joseph & Sarah Whitehead, Failsworth, weaver
Apr	6	George s. William & Anne Yates, Newton, packer
"	6	Robert s. Robert & Jenny Mills, Chadderton, weaver
"	6	William s. Peter & Mary Stott, Moston, labourer
"	6	Richard Corns s. James & Ellen Haslam, Manchesr., calico printer
"	6	Thomas s. John & Anne Dean, Newton, skinner
"	6	Nancy d. Christopher & Margaret Mayo, Manchester, weaver
"	6	Rebekah d. Isaac & Anne Barratt, Failsworth, bleacher
"	6	Elizabeth d. Edward & Mary Hulton, Failsworth, weaver
"	6	Nancy d. Joseph & Mary Hilton, Newton, weaver
"	6	Thomas William s. William & Elizabeth Wood, Manchester, painter
"	6	Sarah d. Joseph & Betty Mills, Failsworth, calenderer
"	6	Betty d. Zechariah & Anne Robinson, Manchesr., weaver
"	6	Joseph s. Uriah & Hannah Booth, Ashton, engineer
"	6	Rebekah d. Thomas & Jane Nelson, Newton, weaver
"	13	Henry s. James & Hannah Whitehead, Failsworth, bricksetter
"	15	James s. James & Mary Hilton, Newton, weaver
"	20	Anne d. Henry & Betty Thorpe, Failsworth, weaver
"	20	Anthony s. Thomas & Alice Hough, Failsworth, weaver
"	20	James s. Benjamin & Martha Tetlow, Newton, labourer
"	24	Elizabeth d. Joseph & Sarah Kenyon, Newton, dyer
"	27	Samuel s. George & Sarah Garlick, Hollinwood, weaver
"	27	Simeon s. George & Sarah Garlick, Hollinwood, weaver

"	27	William s. William & Jane Mather, Droylsden, weaver (*1828*)
"	27	Marianne d. Thomas & Margaret Horrocks, Millhouses, crofter
"	27	Drusilla d. Martha Booth, Millhouses, spinster
May	4	Mary d. James & Elizabeth Walmsley, Newton, labourer
"	4	Olive d. John & Lydia Barlow, Newton, dyer
"	4	Mary d. Samuel & Elizabeth Barlow, Medlock Vale, bleacher
"	11	Benjamin s. James & Jane Aldred, Failsworth, weaver
"	22	Ruth Richards d. Bold Bagshaw & Elizabeth Robinson, Manchester, innkeeper
"	25	Alfred s. Sarah Clough, Failsworth, spinster
"	25	George s. James & Ophelia Berrington, Newton, dyer
"	25	John s. William & Alice Walton, Newton, calico printer
"	25	Nancy d. John & Mary Hughes, Newton, slater
"	25	Sarah d. James & Mary Schofield, Failsworth, weaver
"	25	Nancy d. George & Betty Hilton, Failsworth, weaver
"	25	Elizabeth d. George & Betty Hilton, Failsworth, weaver
"	25	Richard s. Richard & Mary Walker, Newton, weaver
"	25	John s. Joseph & Martha Walmsley, Failsworth, weaver
"	25	Robert s. John & Betty Wolstencroft, Moston, weaver
"	25	Immanuel s. William & Mary Smith, Failsworth, weaver
"	25	Sarah d. John & Mary Whitehead, Failsworth, weaver
"	25	Henry s. Andrew & Sarah Smith, Failsworth, weaver
Jun	1	William s. William & Hannah Brown, Newton, blockcutter
"	1	James s. William & Anne Hibbert, Newton, weaver
"	1	Betty d. James & Mary Whitehead, Chadderton, weaver
"	1	Thomas s. Philip & Sarah Dunkerly, Failsworth, weaver
"	1	Ellen d. James & Sally Whittaker, Failsworth, weaver
"	6	Anne d. Joseph & Olive Wyld, Newton, weaver
"	6	Anne d. Thomas & Sarah Barlow, Failsworth, weaver
"	6	Nancy d. Samuel & Mary Moore, Failsworth, weaver
"	8	Anne d. David & Mary Knott, Failsworth, weaver
"	8	Betty d. John & Hannah Cheetham, Failsworth, carter
"	8	Benjamin s. George & Anne Yates, Newton, bleacher
"	15	John Bowes s. John Bowes & Isabella Wilson, Newton, sea captain
"	15	Betty d. Abraham & Sally Knott, Failsworth, weaver
"	17	Marianne d. James & Isabel Lomas, Newton, weaver
"	22	Sarah d. Charles & Martha Tomlinson, Newton, dyer
"	22	Elizabeth d. John & Elizabeth Butterworth, Newton, weaver
"	22	Elizabeth d. Joseph & Hannah Williamson, Newton, weaver
"	22	James s. Joshua & Sarah Eckersley, Failsworth, weaver
"	22	James s. Thomas & Jane Heywood, Newton, bleacher
"	29	Sarah Anne d. William & Elizabeth Mellor, Newton, labourer
"	29	Harriet d. Joshua & Sarah Hill, Newton, brickmaker
"	29	Martha d. John & Ellen Smith, Newton, cotton spinner
Jul	6	Jonathan s. Jonah & Elizabeth Goodier, Newton, bleacher
"	6	Anne d. Anne Smith, Newton, spinster

"	6	Mary d. John & Esther Marsden, Newton, bleacher	(*1828*)
"	20	John s. James & Hannah Collinson, Failsworth, weaver	
"	20	William s. Thomas & Mary Robinson, Droylsden, labourer	
"	20	Sarah d. Matthew & Matty Smith, Failsworth, weaver	
"	27	Josiah s. Josiah & Alice Etchels, Failsworth, weaver	
"	27	Sarah d. Peter & Jane Whitehead, Newton, cotton spinner	
Aug	3	Thomas s. James & Esther Brierly, Failsworth, weaver	
"	10	Sarah d. Launcelot & Mary Hilton, Newton, weaver, aged 19ys & 11mos	
"	10	Mary d. Launcelot & Mary Hilton, Newton, weaver, aged 17ys & 6 mos	
"	10	Frederick s. Peter & Anne Stone, Newton, jeweller	
"	10	John & Mary s. & d. James & Alice Bardsley, Failsworth, weaver	
"	10	Mary d. Abel & Grace Sharples, Failsworth, tailor	
"	10	Alice Wilson d. John & Alice Ridings, Newton, weaver	
"	14	Thomas s. Samuel & Sarah Garside, Newton, innkeeper	
"	17	Mary d. Thomas & Alice Jamison, Manchesr., joiner	
"	17	Joshua s. Joshua & Mary Stonier, Newton, shoemaker	
"	24	Anne d. Saml. & Mary Dean, Failsworth, weaver	
"	24	Charlotte d. James & Marianne Taylor, Oldham, weaver	
"	24	Eliza d. James & Helena Bardsley, Newton, weaver	
"	24	Anne d. Robert & Alice Stansfield, Newton, hatter	
"	24	Jane d. Thomas & Jane Wilkinson, Failsworth, weaver	
"	24	Richard s. Richard & Sarah Hall, Newton, labourer	
"	24	John s. William & Mary Anne Holt, Newton, blacksmith, bo Aug 1 1828	
"	24	Mary d. Samuel & Mary Salt, Newton, tailor	
"	24	Jane d. Thomas & Betty Buckley, Manchester, shoemaker	
"	24	Joseph s. Levi & Ellen Clough, Newton, weaver	
"	24	Sarah d. Thomas & Anne Thornley, Droylsden, labourer	
"	24	John s. Thomas & Alice Pollitt, Newton, dyer	
"	24	Marianne d. John Taylor & Elizabeth Walmsley, Newton, blockcutter	
"	24	Thomas s. Thomas & Mary Jones, Newton, labourer	
"	24	Anne d. William & Deborah Davies, Medlock Vale, gardener	
"	24	Joseph s. Thomas & Maria Robinson, Newton, dyer	
"	24	John s. David & Sally Makin, Moston, weaver	
"	24	Sarah d. James & Mary Dyson, Newton, dyer	
"	24	Samuel s. Thomas & Catherine Lloyd, Newton, collier	
"	24	George s. John & Anne Gardner, Droylsden, farmer	
"	24	Marianne d. Joseph & Betty Needham, Failsworth, bricksetter	
"	24	Esther d. James & Anne Ogden, Hollinwood, blacksmith	
"	31	Hannah d. Sarah Hamson, Newton, spinster	
"	31	Sarah d. Samuel & Anne Bottomly, Manchester, labourer	
Sep	7	Marianne d. Thomas & Hannah Langford, Newton, engineer	
"	21	John s. John & Sally Mather, Newton, hatter	
"	21	John s. George & Mary Bardsley, Newton, dyer	
"	28	Robert s. John & Grace Ridings, Failsworth, weaver	
"	28	Sarah d. John & Jane Smith, Failsworth, labourer	

"	28	Edward s. Maria Stockport, Failsworth, spinster
"	28	Ellen d. John & Nancy Whittaker, Failsworth, weaver
"	28	Mary d. James & Mary Wood, Newton, tailor
"	28	Alice d. Abraham & Nancy Taylor, Newton, dyer
"	28	Jane d. Edmund & Sarah Walmsley, Failsworth, farmer
Oct	5	James s. James & Hannah Chadderton, Failsworth, weaver
"	6	William s. John & Anne Bailey, Manchester, collier
"	12	James s. Henry & Mary Hyde, Failsworth, weaver
"	12	Anne d. Henry & Mary Hyde, Failsworth, weaver
"	12	Jane d. Robert & Sarah Hilton, Newton, weaver
"	16	Charles s. John & Anne Hibbert, Newton, weaver
"	19	Thomas s. Samuel & Alice Penlington, Newton, bleacher
"	19	James s. John & Mary Travis, Ardwick, servantman
"	19	Joel s. John & Mary Standring, Droylsden, weaver
"	19	Charles Roberts s. Daniel & Mary Knott, Newton, sawyer
"	21	Esther d. James & Anne Allen, Failsworth, weaver
"	26	Sarah d. Edward & Nancy Robinson, Failsworth, weaver
"	26	David s. William & Marianne Loughhead, Newton, weaver
Nov	2	Anne d. Thomas & Mary Dunkerly, Newton, weaver
"	2	Henry s. Robert & Anne Whitehead, Failsworth, weaver
"	2	Marianne d. Robert & Betty Brookes, Manchester, dyer
"	2	George s. Thomas & Nancy Ogden, Newton, weaver
"	2	Esther d. John & Anne Clough, Failsworth, weaver
"	6	Marianne d. John & Anne Berry, Newton, labourer
"	9	William s. Israel & Sally Clough, Failsworth, weaver
"	9	Ellen d. Josiah & Mary Barnes Holt (Barnes *struck through*), Newton, shopkeeper
"	9	Henry s. John & Mary Burgess, Manchester, bookkeeper
"	16	Thomas s. James & Anne Allen, Newton, weaver
"	16	Sarah d. Thomas & Elizabeth Johnson, Moston, carpenter
"	19	George Briscoe s. George & Mary Clay, Manchester, pawnbroker
"	19	Jane Barbara d. George & Mary Clay, Manchester, pawnbroker
"	19	Abraham s. George & Mary Clay, Manchester, pawnbroker
"	23	Charles s. James & Sally Tweedale, Newton, schoolmaster
"	23	Emma d. Joseph & Alice Tetlow, Newton, weaver
"	23	Mary d. Thomas & Anne Brundrit, Failsworth, weaver
"	30	Anne d. Joel & Mary Smith, Failsworth, weaver
"	30	Hannah d. Samuel & Hannah Entwisle, Newton, cotton spinner
Dec	7	Alfred s. John & Elizabeth Smith, Newton, weaver
"	7	John s. Henry & Hannah Hamnet, Newton, calico printer
"	14	Robert s. Betty Walmsley, Moston, spinster
"	14	David s. Jesse & Hannah Knott, Failsworth, farmer
"	14	Edward s. James & Ruth Whitehead, Failsworth, weaver
"	21	James s. Daniel & Hannah Smethurst, Manchester, cotton spinner
"	25	Elizabeth d. John & Mary Hay, Droylsden, blockcutter

"	25	Joseph s. Joseph & Nanny Greaves, Failsworth, weaver
"	25	Kezia d. John Michael & Elizabeth Higgins, Newton, excise officer
"	28	Elizabeth d. Samuel & Elizabeth Hall, Newton, dyer

1829

Jan	1	Jane Elizabeth d. Henry & Elizabeth Hilton, Manchester, manufacturer
"	4	Elizabeth d. John & Martha Higham, Newton, weaver
"	4	Charles William s. Charles & Isabella Ridings, Newton, weaver
"	4	John s. William & Betty Whitelegg, Newton, dyer
"	4	Matilda d. William & Mary Walker, Newton, weaver
"	4	Elizabeth d. Edward & Jane Tipton, Clayton, collier
"	4	Luke s. Joseph & Anne Higham, Newton, weaver
"	4	Thomas s. Joseph & Mary Aldred, Clayton, collier
"	4	Susanna d. Samuel & Mary Lord, Failsworth, labourer
"	18	James s. James & Jane Hesketh, Failsworth, weaver
"	18	Elizabeth d. William & Sarah Lane, Failsworth, innkeeper
"	18	John s. Robert & Sarah Whitehead, Newton, calico printer
"	18	Samuel s. Joseph & Judith Smith, Chadderton, cotton spinner
"	18	Hannah d. Joseph & Judith Smith, Chadderton, cotton spinner
"	25	James s. John & Catherine Cadman, Newton, cotton spinner
Feb	1	Hannah d. Thomas & Jane Lancashire, Newton, shopkeeper
"	1	James Edwards s. James Edwards & Elizabeth Hancock, Newton, pattern designer
"	1	Phoebe d. Jonathan & Phoebe Handley, Clayton, collier
"	8	Elisha & Hannah children of Elisha & Ann Hibbert, Droylsden, weaver
"	8	Elizabeth d. William & Betty Sutliffe, Reddish, shoemaker
"	8	Marianne d. John & Christiana Gregory, Gorton, bleacher
"	8	Anne d. Mary Whitehead, Failsworth, spinster
"	15	William s. William & Mary Clough, Failsworth, butcher
"	22	Nancy Collinson d. Benjamin & Nancy Worsick, Droylsden, farmer
"	22	Elizabeth d. James & Hannah Pilkington, Newton, labourer
"	24	James s. Henry & Martha Burgess, Manchester, weaver
"	27	James s. Joseph & Isabel Grimshaw, Failsworth, hatter
Mar	1	Cockshot s. Thomas & Susanna Whittaker, Failsworth, hatter
"	1	Mary d. Nanny Berry, Failsworth, spinster
"	1	Samuel s. Moses & Clarissa Gradwell, Newton, weaver
"	1	Mary d. Luke & Nancy Etchels, Newton, weaver
"	1	Robert s. Elijah & Charlotte Hilton, Failsworth, weaver
"	1	Henry s. James & Mary Yates, Newton, bleacher
"	1	Martha d. Hannah Bracegirdle, Failsworth, spinster
"	1	James Whitehead s. Isaac & Elizabeth Heapy, Droylsden, hatter
"	8	James s. Samuel & Jane Bethel, Newton, bleacher
"	8	Francis s. Jonathan & Sarah Clough, Newton, dyer

"	8	Peggy d. James & Anne Taylor, Failsworth, weaver	*(1829)*
"	15	John s. John & Jane Nightingale, Newton, bleacher	
"	15	Elizabeth d. William & Marianne Curd, soldier	
"	16	Catherine d. James Smale & Jane Thornly, Newton, surgeon	
"	18	Ellen d. John & Elizabeth Robinson, Newton, weaver	
"	22	William s. John & Martha Turvin, Newton, farmer	
"	22	Thomas s. Richard & Margaret Taylor, Newton, dyer	
"	29	David s. William & Hannah Grindley, Newton, silk spinner	
"	29	James s. John & Mary Smith, Newton, blockcutter	
"	29	James s. Joseph & Alice Robinson, Failsworth, weaver	
"	29	Alice d. Peter & Margaret Later, Newton, engineer	
"	29	Joel s. James & Alice Schofield, Failsworth, weaver	
"	29	Thomas s. John & Elizabeth Howles, Newton, bleacher	
Apr	2	Thomas & Mary twin children of Willey & Nancy Booth, Newton, innkeeper	
"	12	John s. Joseph & Sarah Kay, Newton, dyer	
"	19	Nancy d. William & Hannah Brandon, Ashton underline, engineer	
"	19	Wright s. James & Margaret Higham, Ashton underline, gardener	
"	19	Rachel d. Thomas & Jane Yates, Reddish, bleacher	
"	19	Betty d. Joseph & Susanna Hilton, Chadderton, weaver	
"	19	Anne d. John & Hannah Hilton, Newton, weaver	
"	19	John s. Richard & Martha Drinkwater, Newton, labourer	
"	19	Robert s. Richard & Martha Drinkwater, Newton, labourer	
"	19	James s. Richard & Martha Drinkwater, Newton, labourer	
"	19	Mary d. Edward & Esther Whitehead, Failsworth, bleacher	
"	19	Olive d. Henry & Mary Rogerson, Newton, blacksmith	
"	23	James s. James & Jane Taylor, Newton, silk manufacturer	
"	26	Joseph s. John & Jane Lancashire, Newton, warehouseman	
"	26	Jane d. Isaac & Elizabeth Andrew, Newton, calico printer	
"	26	Sarah d. William & Jane Mather, Droylsden, weaver	
"	26	James s. Samuel & Hannah Lees, Failsworth, weaver	
May	3	Joseph s. Elizabeth Hibbert, Manchester, spinster	
"	10	Esther d. Matthew & Sarah Brown, Newton, weaver	
"	10	James s. Samuel & Susanna Wharmby, Droylsden, weaver	
"	10	Marianne d. John & Jane Baker, Droylsden, book keeper	
"	17	Mary d. John & Hannah Thornley, Failsworth, weaver	
"	17	John s. John & Anne Pattison, Newton, shopkeeper	
"	20	Samuel s. Thomas & Deborah Bentley, Newton, weaver	
"	24	Jane d. James & Esther Rose, Newton, weaver	
"	24	Emma d. John & Anne Dean, Newton, skinner	
"	31	John s. Joseph & Mary Hulton, Failsworth, weaver	
"	31	Henry s. Richard & Jane Travis, Newton, weaver	
Jun	7	Sarah Ann & Marianne ds. Robert & Esther Brierly, Failsworth, weaver	
"	7	George s. William & Martha Eyre, Failsworth, weaver	
"	7	Thomas s. John & Betty Lomax, Failsworth, shoemaker	
"	7	William s. David & Sarah Hulton, Newton, weaver	

| " | 7 | Anne d. John & Anne Horrocks, Newton, ostler | (1829) |

" 7 Anne d. John & Anne Horrocks, Newton, ostler (1829)
" 7 Edward s. Richard & Anne Aaron, Newton, paper maker
" 7 William s. Thomas & Mary Ogden, Failsworth, weaver
" 7 Alton s. William & Sally Middleton, Failsworth, weaver
" 7 Jane d. Samuel & Anne Gradwell, Newton, weaver
" 7 Samuel s. John & Harriet Simpson, Newton, silk spinner
" 7 Jane d. John & Sarah Twimlow, Newton, carter
" 7 Mary d. Robert & Sarah Hulme, Newton, calenderer
" 7 Emma d. Samuel & Martha Hulton, Failsworth, servantman
" 7 George s. George & Mary Whittaker, Failsworth, hatter
" 7 John s. James & Alice Fletcher, Newton, calico printer
" 7 Mary d. William & Anne Aldred, Failsworth, shoemaker
" 7 Amelia d. Richard & Sarah Worsick, Failsworth, farmer
" 9 Anne d. Betty Wroe, Failsworth, spinster
" 10 Charles s. John & Mary Egerton, Newton, shoemaker
" 12 John s. David & Anne Harrison, Newton, weaver
" 14 Anne d. Eli & Sarah Swift, Failsworth, weaver
" 14 Nancy d. Ralph & Betty Smethurst, Hollinwood, weaver
" 14 John s. William & Jane Harrison, Ardwick, weaver
" 14 Emma Anne d. John & Anne Thornley, Droylsden, weaver
" 14 William s. Thomas & Mary Allen, Newton, calenderer
" 14 John s. William & Alice Thorpe, Failsworth, weaver
" 14 Phoebe d. Thomas & Elizabeth Whitehead, Failsworth, weaver
" 21 John s. William & Hannah Bowyer, Newton, blockcutter
" 21 Sarah d. Thomas & Sarah Lamb, Newton, labourer
" 21 John s. Joseph & Elizabeth Johnson, Newton, silk throwster
" 28 John s. Joseph & Betty Nichols, Failsworth, blacksmith
Jul 5 Thomas s. Thomas & Betty Coupe, Newton, pattern designer
" 8 James s. Thomas & Anne Brooks, Newton, dyer
" 12 Emma d. John & Alice Worsick, Failsworth, farmer
" 19 John s. James & Mary Newton, Harpurhey, dyer
" 19 Meshech Ashton s. James & Mary Kenyon, Droylsden, collier
" 26 Robert s. Joseph & Sarah Ogden, Failsworth, weaver
" 26 Mary d. Thomas & Sarah Thornley, Failsworth, weaver
" 28 William s. Joseph & Elizabeth Tomkinson, Newton, weaver
" 28 William s. John & Anne Gradwell, Newton, weaver
Aug 2 Thomas s. Charles & Lavinia Barnes, Chorlton Row, leather dealer
" 2 Samuel s. John & Sarah Sydebotham, Newton, labourer
" 5 Beky d. John & Sarah Ogden, Failsworth, weaver
" 9 Henry & Frederick ss. John & Anne Tongue, Newton, calenderer
" 9 John s. Benjamin & Jane Howarth, Droylsden, labourer
" 9 Sarah d. Joseph & Hannah Bardsley, Failsworth, weaver
" 16 Thomas s. John & Sarah Warhurst, Newton, cotton spinner
" 23 John s. John & Ellen Lees, Failsworth, weaver
" 23 John s. William & Phoebe Smethurst, Failsworth, weaver

"	23	Wright s. John & Mary Standring, Droylsden, labourer
"	23	George s. William & Sarah Bardsley, Newton, bleacher
"	23	Elizabeth d. William & Jane Lomax, Failsworth, blacksmith
"	23	Elizabeth d. George & Anne Grimshaw, Oldham, farmer
"	23	Ellen d. Elizabeth Smith, Failsworth, spinster
"	23	John s. Joseph & Anne Whitehead, Failsworth, dyer
"	23	William Walter s. David & Anne Ogden, Newton, weaver
"	23	Barbara d. Joseph & Anne Copeland, Failsworth, shoemaker
"	30	Mary d. William & Mary Howarth, Newton, shopkeeper
"	30	Hannah d. Horatio & Anne Ridings, Newton, weaver
"	30	Sarah Margaret d. Joseph & Mary Tetlow, Newton, warehouseman
Sep	3	Betty d. John & Hannah Booth, Hollinwood, weaver
"	3	Hannah d. Thomas & Mary Hyde, Failsworth, weaver
"	13	Alice d. Andrew & Sarah Smith, Failsworth, weaver
"	13	Robert s. Sally Knott, Failsworth, spinster
"	13	John s. Anne Travis, Newton, spinster
"	13	Sarah Anne d. Samuel & Mary Pollitt, Failsworth, weaver
"	13	Mary d. George & Mary Simister, Droylsden, bleacher
"	14	Sarah d. Sarah Radford, Manchester, spinster
"	16	Jane d. Thomas & Jane Wild, Newton, innkeeper
"	20	Alice d. James & Mary Thorpe, Failsworth, weaver
"	20	Robert s. James & Mary Burton, Newton, weaver
"	20	John s. John & Lydia Barlow, Newton, dyer
"	26	Charles John s. Charles & Matilda Addy, Droylsden, calico printer
"	27	John s. Isaac & Elizabeth Schofield, Failsworth, weaver
"	27	William s. James & Jane Higginbotham, Newton, calico printer
"	27	Joseph s. Abraham & Mary Ogden, Failsworth, weaver
"	30	Thomas s. Thomas & Mary Taylor, Failsworth, weaver
Oct	4	Margaret d. Samuel & Sarah Trevor, Medlock Vale, labourer
"	4	Hannah d. John & Alice Timmis, Failsworth, weaver
"	4	Sarah d. John & Grace Bradshaw, Strangeways, calico printer
"	4	John s. Jonathan & Hannah Schofield, Newton, calico printer
"	4	Amelia d. James & Eliza Gradwell, Newton, bleacher
"	4	Sarah d. Nicholas & Margaret Edge, Failsworth, print cutter
"	11	Sarah Anne d. Benjamin & Maria Thornley, Droylsden, weaver
"	11	James s. Joseph & Maria Bates, Newton, shopkeeper
"	13	Elizabeth d. Isaac & Sarah Clough, Failsworth, weaver
"	18	John s. Robert & Mary Hope, Newton, dyer
"	25	Thomas s. John & Mary Wild, Newton, weaver
"	25	Hannah d. John & Violet McNamee, Newton, bleacher
"	25	James s. William & Mary Greenhalgh, Failsworth, tailor
"	25	Silas s. William & Sarah Pollitt, Failsworth, weaver
"	25	Anne d. John & Mary Lindley, Newton, dyer
"	25	Elizabeth d. John & Mary Lindley, Newton, dyer
Nov	1	Henry s. Josiah & Jane Garlick, Failsworth, weaver

"	1	James s. John & Anne Greenwood, Failsworth, bricklayer
"	2	Sarah Catherine d. Obadiah & Alice Bradshaw, Manr., calico printer
"	8	William Loyd s. John & Mary Lomas, Manchester, woollen draper
"	15	David s. Joseph & Sarah Rogers, Failsworth, weaver
"	15	Mary d. John & Betty Hyde, Newton, farmer
"	15	Betty d. Thomas & Hannah Allen, Failsworth, weaver
"	15	Henry & John ss. John & Rachel Hodson, Manchester, calenderer
"	15	Ralph s. William & Mary Rutter, Newton, bleacher
"	15	Hannah d. Richard & Susanna Thomas, Manchester, cotton spinner
"	22	Sarah d. John & Betty Royle, Hollinwood, weaver
"	22	Joel s. Joel & Mary Brown, Hollinwood, labourer
Dec	6	Helvia d. William & Martha Ford, Failsworth, weaver
"	6	Thomas s. Philip & Rebekah Lancashire, Moston, farmer
"	13	Anne d. John & Esther Dewhurst, Hollinwood, weaver
"	13	Marianne d. William & Anne Egerton, Bradford, calico printer
"	15	John s. Elijah & Jane Pollitt, Newton, weaver
"	20	Sarah d. James & Hannah Hibbert, Failsworth, weaver
"	20	Elizabeth d. John & Mary Gradwell, Newton, bleacher
"	20	Sarah Anne d. Joseph & Betty Consterdine, Newton, printcutter
"	25	George s. Nicholas & Jane Simister, Newton, weaver
"	27	Violet d. Josephus & Marianne Hulton, Failsworth, weaver
"	27	Margaret d. Michael & Mary Armstrong, Failsworth, weaver
"	27	Nancy d. William & Mary Whitehead, Newton, weaver
"	29	Sarah d. William & Martha Berry, Manchester, blacksmith
"	29	Anne d. James & Mary Lees, Failsworth, weaver
"	29	Elizabeth d. Thomas & Sarah Taylor, Failsworth, weaver

1830

Jan	3	Hannah d. George & Anne Heywood, Droylsden, bleacher
"	3	Anne d. James & Mary Schofield, Failsworth, weaver
"	3	Richard s. Joseph & Mary Wyatt, Newton, calico printer
"	10	William s. Adam & Sarah Horrocks, Failsworth, labourer
"	10	Edmund s. George & Jane Robinson, Failsworth, labourer
"	17	James s. Elizabeth Wright, Newton, spinster
"	25	Elizabeth d. John & Sarah Whitehead, Failsworth, weaver
"	31	Eliza d. Miles & Marianne Mason, Failsworth, blacksmith
Feb	2	John s. Thomas & Mary Ogden, Hollinwood, weaver
"	7	Mary d. Robert & Susanna Marsden, Newton, bleacher
"	9	Sarah d. Joseph & Jane Thornley, Failsworth, weaver
"	14	James s. Edward & Maria Hulton, Failsworth, shopkeeper
"	14	Hannah d. Thomas & Rachel Bottomly, Bradford, labourer
"	21	James s. Thomas & Betty Wolstencroft, Newton, bleacher
"	21	Elizabeth Alice d. James & Abigail Blackshaw, Failsworth, hatter
"	21	Sarah d. James & Isabel Hyde, Newton, farmer

"	28	Sarah d. George & Hannah Wright, Failsworth, weaver	*(1830)*
"	28	John s. John & Sarah Marsden, Newton, bleacher	
Mar	7	Anne d. Joshua & Nancy Robinson, Failsworth, calico printer	
"	7	Thomas s. James & Alice Mills, Ashton, calico printer	
"	7	James s. John & Anne Berry, Failsworth, weaver	
"	10	Eliza d. Samuel & Mary Holland, Failsworth, weaver	
"	10	Ellen d. Joseph & Mary Whittaker, Newton, weaver	
"	14	William s. Adam & Betty Dootson, Audenshaw, bleacher	
"	14	Thomas s. Matthew & Sarah Smith, Newton, dyer	
"	21	Betty d. William & Jane Shepley, Newton, joiner	
"	21	Robert s. John & Betty Johnson, Failsworth, weaver	
"	21	Alice d. Abraham & Anne Collinge, Newton, dyer	
"	21	John & Samuel ss. Thomas & Jane Heywood, Newton, bleacher	
"	22	Joseph s. Betty Hulme, Newton, spinster	
"	22	Hannah d. John & Martha Higham, Newton, weaver	
"	28	Robert s. Peter & Mary Stott, Moston, weaver	
Apr	4	John s. Maria d. Robert & Marianne Tattersal, Newton, shopkeeper	
"	4	Anne d. James & Hannah Collinson, Failsworth, weaver	
"	4	John s. Robert & Elizabeth Wilkinson, Failsworth, weaver	
"	4	Elizabeth d. Joel & Mary Goodier, Newton, bleacher	
"	11	Mary d. Joshua & Mary Collinson, Failsworth, weaver	
"	11	James s. Thomas & Charlotte Hale, Newton, shoe maker	
"	11	Hannah d. Charles & Anne Winstanley, Manchester, collier	
"	11	Mary d. Samuel & Mary Lees, Failsworth, weaver	
"	11	John s. Philip & Mary Berry, Newton, dyer	
"	11	Sarah d. John & Martha Tetlow, Newton, weaver	
"	11	Harriet d. John & Christiana Gregory, Gorton, bleacher	
"	11	Joseph s. Robert & Anne Lees, Failsworth, weaver	
"	11	Martha d. Mary Whitehead, Failsworth, spinster	
"	11	Elizabeth d. William & Eliza Hardy, Newton, dyer	
"	11	James s. Thomas & Jane Bates, Failsworth, bleacher	
"	11	James s. William & Mary Clough, Failsworth, weaver	
"	11	Ralph s. Thurston & Jane Smethurst, Hollinwood, bricklayer	
"	18	Martha d. John & Olivia Bardsley, Newton, dyer	
"	18	Elizabeth d. Joseph & Mary Fletcher, Newton, calico printer	
"	22	Joseph s. Daniel & Hannah Berrington, Newton, labourer	
"	25	Elizabeth d. Samuel & Hannah Entwisle, Newton, cotton spinner	
"	25	Marianne d. Thomas & Jane Jones, Newton, labourer	
"	25	Reuben s. Thomas & Susanna Whittaker, Failsworth, hatter	
May	2	Mary d. James & Betty Marsden, Newton, bleacher	
"	9	Thomas s. William & Hannah Barlow, Failsworth, weaver	
"	23	Mary d. George & Sarah Garlick, Failsworth, weaver	
"	23	John s. Robert & Martha Eckersley, Failsworth, weaver	
"	24	Isabella Carter d. John Bowes & Isabella Wilson, Newton, master mariner	
"	30	Edward s. John & Sally Whitehead, Newton, calico printer	

"	30	William s. John & Sarah Bentley, Newton, weaver (*1830*)
"	30	James s. John & Mary Smith, Newton, weaver
"	30	James s. David & Mary Knott, Failsworth, weaver
"	30	Daniel s. Daniel & Hannah Knott, Failsworth, weaver
"	30	Samuel s. Richard & Martha Richardson, Newton, tailor
"	30	Mary d. Benjamin & Martha Tetlow, Newton, farmer
"	30	Anne d. William & Rosa Simister, Newton, weaver
"	30	George s. Zechariah & Nanny Robinson, Manchester, weaver
"	30	George s. Joseph & Sarah Kenyon, Newton, dyer
Jun	4	Edwin & Anne children of Joseph & Hannah Bardsley, Failsworth, weaver
"	4	George s. Joseph & Sarah Kay, Newton, engineer
"	6	Nancy d. John & Martha Whitehead, Failsworth, weaver
"	6	Martha d. Abraham & Mary Moore, Moston, weaver
"	6	Hannah d. Hannah Ogden, Chadderton, spinster
"	6	Isabel d. Isaiah & Sarah Etchels, Failsworth, weaver
"	6	John s. John & Anne Thornley, Chadderton, weaver
"	6	Anne d. George & Anne Morris, Medlock Vale, calico printer
"	6	Robert s. Joseph & Hannah Brown, Newton, labourer
"	6	James s. Henry & Betty Brown, Newton, labourer
"	6	Sarah d. Ashton & Anne Brown, Newton, weaver
"	6	Eliza Anne d. John & Mary Swift, Manchester, weaver
"	6	Margaret d. George & Esther Wood, Newton, shopkeeper
"	11	Sarah d. Willy & Nancy Booth, Newton, innkeeper
"	20	William s. Samuel & Sarah Huxley, Droylsden, labourer
"	20	Andrew s. Thomas & Jane Nelson, Newton, weaver
"	20	Martha d. William & Harriet Allen, Newton, bleacher
"	20	John s. James & Mary Dyson, Newton, weaver
"	20	James Horatio s. John & Ellen Taylor, Failsworth, weaver
"	20	Matthew s. John & Mally Whitehead, Failsworth, weaver
"	22	Sarah & Anne ds. Thomas & Anne Thornley, Droylsden, labourer
"	27	John s. Abel & Nancy Whatmough, Newton, stonemason
"	27	Robert s. Benjamin & Mary Lees, Failsworth, weaver
"	27	Anne d. James & Jenny Aldred, Failsworth, weaver
"	27	Jane d. John & Mary Burgess, Manchester, manager of a silk mill
Jul	4	Eliza Jane d. Bold Bagshaw & Elizabeth Robinson, Manchester, innkeeper
"	4	Henry s. Robert & Mary Heywood, Medlock Vale, distiller
"	4	Joshua s. William & Dorothy Cheadle, Newton, gardener
"	4	Daniel s. George & Anne Yates, Reddish, bleacher
"	4	Betty d. Mary Etchels, Failsworth, spinster
"	4	Jonathan s. James & Sarah Whittaker, Failsworth, weaver
"	6	William s. James & Hannah Etchels, Failsworth, weaver
"	6	Mary d. Thomas & Alice Hough, Failsworth, weaver
"	11	Sarah d. William & Mary Robinson, Failsworth, calico printer
"	18	George s. Thomas & Mary Cole, Failsworth, warehouseman
"	18	William s. James & Mary Hulton, Newton, weaver

"	18	Robert s. Abraham & Agnes Younge Mills, Medlock Vale, blockcutter
"	18	Thomas s. Richard & Sarah Hall, Newton, servant man
"	18	Ellen d. Nancy Moores, Failsworth, spinster
"	18	John s. Philip & Sarah Dunkerly, Failsworth, weaver
"	18	Thomas s. William & Sarah Lane, Failsworth, innkeeper
"	21	Esther d. James & Sarah Houghton, Newton, coach proprietor
"	25	Elizabeth d. John & Jane Wroe, Failsworth, weaver
"	25	Jane d. Ashton & Betty Ashton, Failsworth, weaver
"	25	Jane d. James & Martha Bray, Newton, shoemaker
"	25	George s. John & Anne Dewhurst, Failsworth, joiner
Aug	1	Ellen d. Thomas & Elizabeth Cash, Newton, blacksmith
"	1	Robert s. James & Anne Ogden, Woodhouses, weaver
"	2	Anne d. James & Rosa Taylor, Failsworth, weaver
"	15	Sarah d. Thomas & Jane Hay, Failsworth, blockcutter
"	15	James s. John & Mary Whitehead, Failsworth, weaver
"	22	William s. William & Elizabeth Wood, Manchester, painter
"	22	Elizabeth d. Mary Smith, Failsworth, spinster
"	22	Mary d. Henry & Martha Burgess, Manchester, weaver
"	22	Elizabeth d. Emanuel & Mary Fletcher, Failsworth, weaver
"	22	Mary d. Thomas & Sarah Barlow, Failsworth, weaver
"	22	Alfred s. Joseph & Elizabeth Pott, Manchester, warehouseman
"	22	Sarah d. James & Alice Swift, Failsworth, weaver
"	22	Jane d. Thomas & Anne Wilson, Moston, weaver
"	22	John s. James & Betty Bracegirdle, Failsworth, bricklayer
"	22	John s. Joseph & Ellen Dawson, Failsworth, weaver
"	22	Samuel s. James & Margaret Higham, Ashton underlyne, gardener
"	22	Esther d. Jonathan & Hannah Chadderton, Failsworth, weaver
"	22	Joseph s. John & Anne Wright, Newton, bleacher
"	22	William s. William & Mary Manley, Newton, sawyer
"	22	Thomas s. Luke & Anne Clegg, Failsworth, carpenter
"	22	Alice d. William & Anne Eckersley, Failsworth, weaver
"	22	James s. Joseph & Sarah Gradwell, Newton, weaver
"	22	Fanny d. Joseph & Anne Boon, Newton, shoemaker
"	22	Jane d. Thomas & Nancy Gillibrand, Failsworth, weaver
"	22	Charles s. Jesse & Hannah Knott, Failsworth, farmer
"	22	Maria d. Joshua & Mary Mason, Newton, manager of a silk mill
"	22	Nancy d. John & Mary Ramsden, Newton, bleacher
"	29	Esther d. James & Ruth Whitehead, Failsworth, weaver
"	29	Edmund s. James & Mary Whitehead, Chadderton, weaver
Sep	5	Elizabeth d. Thomas & Alice Brown, Hollinwood, tailor
"	5	Isabel d. Joshua & Sarah Eckersley, Failsworth, weaver
"	12	Robert s. Peter & Lucy Maria Holroyd, Failsworth, tailor
"	12	Thomas s. Peter & Mary Wyld, Failsworth, labourer
"	14	Elizabeth d. Samuel & Sarah Garside, Clayton Bridge, butcher
"	14	Mary Jane d. James Smale & Jane Thornley, Newton, surgeon

"	19	William Henry s. Alice Birchal, Stockport, spinster (*1830*)
"	19	Jane d. James & Hannah Whitehead, Chadderton, bricklayer
"	19	James s. James & Margaret Smith, Failsworth, weaver
"	26	Samuel s. Samuel & Mary Salt, Newton, tailor
"	26	Harriet d. William & Mary Walker, Newton, weaver
"	26	Thomas s. Thomas & Jane Taylor, Newton, silk throwster
"	26	James s. James & Betty Barlow, Medlock Vale, crofter
"	26	Jane d. James & Betty Davenport, Medlock Vale, gardener
"	26	James s. James & Betty Davenport, Medlock Vale, gardener
"	27	Martha d. John & Mary Waddilove, Newton, calico printer
Oct	3	William s. John & Anne Dean, Newton, skinner
"	3	Jane d. Edward & Elizabeth Hancock, Newton, designer
"	3	Peter s. James & Alice Schofield, Failsworth, weaver
"	8	Hannah d. Joseph & Alice Robinson, Failsworth, weaver
"	10	Joseph s. Luke & Rachel Hilton, Failsworth, weaver
"	17	Anne d. James & Alice Fletcher, Newton, calico printer
"	17	Elizabeth d. George & Elizabeth Smith, Droylsden, bricklayer
"	17	Thomas s. Sarah Wyld, Droylsden, spinster
"	24	Betty d. Samuel & Mary Moore, Failsworth, weaver
"	24	Samuel s. William & Esther Whitehead, Failsworth, weaver
"	26	James s. Bartholomew & Alice Brown, Failsworth, hatter
"	26	William s. Thomas & Deborah Bentley, Newton, weaver
"	26	Samuel s. Paul & Sarah Clough, Failsworth, weaver
"	26	William John & Eliza children of James & Betty Whitehead, Failsworth, weaver
"	31	William s. Thomas & Sarah Thornley, Failsworth, weaver
"	31	John Brundritt s. Hannah Brown, Newton, spinster
Nov	7	Eliza d. Sarah Whitehead, Failsworth, spinster
"	7	John s. Barnard & Mary Fishwick, Newton, calico printer
"	14	Robert s. John & Martha Consterdine, Newton, labourer
"	14	William s. Joseph & Elizabeth Stone, Newton, silkspinner
"	14	Jane d. William & Lucy Seel, Newton, bleacher
"	14	Elizabeth d. Joseph & Hannah Bardsley, Droylsden, blockcutter
"	14	Elizabeth d. George & Anne Heywood, Droylsden, bleacher
"	21	Eliza Whittaker d. William & Hannah Brown, Newton, blockcutter
"	23	Ellen Jane d. James & Jane Taylor, Newton, silk manufacturer
Dec	12	Elizabeth d. Joseph & Priscilla Fletcher, Newton, weaver
"	12	Edmund s. William & Elizabeth Makin, Newton, dyer
"	12	Thomas s. Thomas & Hannah Langford, Newton, millwright
"	12	Anne d. Elizabeth Lee, Newton, spinster
"	19	Joseph s. John & Esther Ditchfield, Newton, calenderer
"	19	Elizabeth d. James Horatio Nelson & Esther Hulton, Failsworth, labourer
"	26	James s. John & Martha Tervin, Newton, farmer
"	26	Anne d. Mark & Millicent Gradwell, Newton, silk printer

1831

Jan	2	Joseph s. Isaac & Anne Barrow, Newton, bleacher
"	2	Sarah d. Thomas & Maria Robinson, Newton, dyer
"	9	Martha d. William & Anne Hibbert, Failsworth, weaver
"	9	Sarah d. William & Alice Thorpe, Failsworth, weaver
"	9	Richard s. Joseph & Mary Hilton, Failsworth, weaver
"	9	George Abraham s. Joseph & Mary Ramsbottom, Newton, calico printer
"	16	William s. John & Hannah Evans, Newton, servant man
"	23	Joseph s. Joseph & Elizabeth Johnson, Failsworth, silk manufacturer
"	23	Eliza d. Thomas & Jane Wyld, Newton, innkeeper
"	23	Jane d. Joseph & Olive Wyld, Newton, weaver
"	30	James Ogden s. John & Jane Stafford, Newton, cotton spinner
"	30	Edwin s. John & Anne Gardner, Droylsden, farmer
"	30	Eliza d. Richard & Alice Dawson, Failsworth, dyer
"	30	John s. Thomas & Sarah Heywood, Newton, crofter
"	30	Thomas s. Thomas & Mary Robinson, Droylsden, bleacher
Feb	1	William s. Thomas & Mary Tomlinson, Moston, weaver
"	6	Margaret d. John & Elizabeth Lytle, Newton, labourer
"	6	John s. James & Elizabeth Jones, Newton, dyer
"	10	Samuel s. Joseph & Hannah Smith, Newton, warper
"	11	Henry s. Jonathan & Mary Ratliff, Newton, calico printer
"	13	Bridget d. Levi & Ellen Clough, Newton, weaver
"	13	Marianne d. Peter & Esther Boardman, Newton, labourer
"	20	Anne d. Henry & Mary Eckersley, Failsworth, weaver
"	20	Frances d. John & Esther Schofield, Failsworth, weaver
"	27	Hannah d. William & Hannah Brindley, Failsworth, silk throwster
"	27	Samuel s. Joseph & Anne Copeland, Failsworth, shoemaker
"	27	Sarah & William children of Isaac & Maria Jones, Newton, cotton spinner
"	27	Caroline d. John & Jane Nightingale, Newton, bleacher
"	28	Henry s. James & Eliza Gradwell, Droylsden, bleacher
Mar	6	Emma d. Matthew & Elizabeth Lamb, Newton, calico printer
"	6	Mary d. Hannah Ogden, Failsworth, spinster
"	13	George s. John & Elizabeth Robinson, Newton, weaver
"	13	Elizabeth d. Edmund & Sarah Walmsley, Failsworth, farmer
"	13	James s. Martha Ogden, Failsworth, spinster
"	13	Daniel s. Jonathan & Phoebe Handley, Droylsden, collier
"	20	Joseph s. James & Mary Thorpe, Failsworth, weaver
"	20	Edward s. William & Betty Worral, Failsworth, weaver
"	22	Edwin s. James & Sally Mather, Newton, weaver
"	27	Joshua s. James & Hannah Buckley, Newton, clothier
Apr	3	Sarah d. Charles & Betty Sydebotham, Newton, dyer
"	3	Ellen d. James & Mary Yates, Newton, bleacher
"	3	Jane d. Abel & Grace Sharples, Failsworth, tailor
"	3	Ellen d. Thomas & Alice Pollitt, Newton, dyer

"	3	James s. James & Mary Ramsden, Manchester, carter
"	3	Mary d. George & Mary Whittaker, Failsworth, hatter
"	3	John s. James & Phoebe Howard, Woodhouses, weaver
"	3	Mary d. Peter & Margaret Later, Newton, labourer
"	3	Hannah d. William & Jenny Simister, Failsworth, weaver
"	3	John s. Thomas & Anne Cordingly, Failsworth, weaver
"	6	Aaron s. John & Mary Dutton, Failsworth, calico printer
"	6	Marianne d. William & Eliza Hardy, Newton, dyer
"	6	Sarah Anne d. William & Alice Walton, Newton, calico printer
"	10	James s. Joseph & Betty Hilton, Failsworth, weaver
"	10	Hannah d. John & Mary Smith, Newton, blockcutter
"	10	Jane d. Martha Smith, Failsworth, spinster
"	10	John s. John & Sarah Sydebotham, Newton, labourer
"	19	Andrew s. Thomas & Harriet Ogden, Hollinwood, weaver
"	21	Marianne d. George & Mary Clay, Newton, innkeeper
"	24	Mary d. Jonah & Elizabeth Goodier, Newton, bleacher
"	24	William Henry s. William & Ellen Hesketh, Failsworth, shoemaker
May	1	John s. Joseph & Jenny Ogden, Collyhurst, dyer
"	8	Thomas s. James & Sally Tweedale, Newton, schoolmaster
"	12	Elizabeth d. George & Mary Bardsley, Newton, dyer
"	15	Joseph s. Peter & Jane Whitehead, Newton, cotton spinner
"	22	Thomas s. Cornelius & Rachel Yates, Gorton, bleacher
"	22	Mary d. Samuel & Alice Pendleton, Droylsden, farmer
"	22	Joseph s. Luke & Nancy Etchels, Newton, weaver
"	22	Esther d. Mary Hulton, Failsworth, spinster
"	22	George s. James & Jane Hesketh, Failsworth, weaver
"	22	Richard s. Richard & Ellen Hill, Manchester, collier
"	22	Edmund s. John & Sarah Whitehead, Failsworth, weaver
"	29	Rebekah d. Joseph & Rebekah Hilton, Ashton Parish
"	29	John & Sarah children of John & Anne Hall, Failsworth, weaver
"	29	Angelina d. Benjamin & Nancy Worsick, Clayton, farmer
Jun	2	Caroline d. James & Leonora Bardsley, Newton, weaver
"	5	James s. Edmund & Anne Royle, Failsworth, weaver
"	12	Anne d. William & Phoebe Smethurst, Failsworth, weaver
"	12	Phoebe d. Joseph & Betty Nicholls, Failsworth, blacksmith
"	12	William s. Edward & Anne Worral, Failsworth, weaver
"	12	William s. Isaac & Elizabeth Andrew, Clayton Bridge, calico printer
"	19	George s. John & Charlotte Ramsbottom, Newton, cotton spinner
"	19	Samuel s. John & Mary Hay, Droylsden, blockcutter
"	26	John s. Joel & Mary Smith, Failsworth, weaver
"	26	Rosina d. Joseph & Mary Aldred, Droylsden, collier
"	26	Sarah d. Charles & Isabella Ridings, Newton, shopkeeper
"	26	Olive Hooley d. Charlotte Whitehead, Newton, spinster
"	26	James s. Charles & Lavinia Barnes, Newton, leather dealer
Jul	3	Emma d. Hannah Stott, Newton, spinster

"	3	William s. Joseph & Anne Higham, Newton, weaver
"	3	William s. Samuel & Martha Hulton, Failsworth, labourer
"	3	Elizabeth d. John & Mary Allen, Newton, labourer
"	3	James Bowers s. James & Esther Rose, Newton, weaver
"	10	Thomas Clarke s. Thomas & Esther Kershaw, Manchester, hatter
"	10	Elisha s. Richard & Betty Rostern, Droylsden, weaver
"	17	George s. Andrew & Sarah Smith, Failsworth, weaver
"	17	Edward s. James & Mary Allen, Failsworth, weaver
"	21	William s. George & Mary Walker, Newton, schoolmaster
"	24	James s. Jonathan & Sarah Goodier, Newton, bleacher
"	24	Jane d. Josiah & Alice Etchels, Failsworth, weaver
"	24	William s. Joel & Hannah Pollitt, Failsworth, weaver
"	24	Elihu s. John & Mary Standring, Droylsden, labourer
"	24	Nancy d. James & Ophelia Berrington, Newton, dyer
"	31	Jane d. John & Mary Brierly, Failsworth, weaver
"	31	Mary d. Samuel & Anne Bottomley, Manchester, shopkeeper
"	31	Charles s. Benjamin & Alice Thorpe, Failsworth, weaver
Aug	7	William s. Joseph & Hannah Stansfield, Newton, hatter
"	7	Thomas s. John & Sarah Swindels, Droylsden, weaver
"	7	James s. James & Alice Smith, Droylsden, weaver
"	7	Barbara Jane d. John & Mary Hughes, Newton, slater
"	14	Frederic s. John & Mary Lomas, Manchesr., draper
"	14	Ellen d. Hannah Wright, Failsworth, spinster
"	15	Betty d. Robert & Martha Eckersley, Failsworth, weaver
"	15	Anne d. Israel & Sarah Clough, Failsworth, weaver
"	21	William s. James & Mary Ratcliff, Newton, warehouseman
"	21	Alexander s. James & Anne Ogden, Hollinwood, blacksmith
"	21	Jane d. Thomas & Mary Hopwood, Newton, cotton spinner
"	21	Anne d. George & Anne Grimshaw, Newton, farmer
"	21	Sarah d. Thurston & Jane Smethurst, Hollinwood, bricklayer
"	21	John s. Thomas & Mary Whitehead, Moston, weaver
"	21	Stephen s. Thomas & Anne Brookes, Newton, dyer
"	21	Mary d. James & Sarah Whitehead, Moston, weaver
"	21	Hannah d. John & Betty Lomax, Failsworth, cordwainer
"	21	William s. Robert & Jane Taylor, Failsworth, weaver
"	21	Ellen d. Richard & Eliza Barlow, Newton, dyer
"	21	Mary d. James & Hannah Hibbert, Failsworth, weaver
"	21	Thomas s. Launcelot & Anne Hogg, Newton, cotton spinner
"	21	Henry s. William & Mary Clough, Failsworth, weaver
"	21	James s. Martha Wright, Hollinwood, spinster
"	21	Henry s. William & Sarah Bardsley, Newton, bleacher
"	21	Jane d. Thomas & Mary Allen, Newton, bleacher
"	21	William s. Thomas & Martha Whitelegg, Manchester, labourer
"	22	Marianne d. Joseph & Anne Ogden, Newton, weaver
"	28	John s. John & Ellen Warhurst, Newton, cotton spinner

Sep	4	Alice Stafford d. Ratliff & Elizabeth Fielding, Droylsden, dyer
"	4	Sarah d. James & Elizabeth Brierly, Failsworth, weaver
"	4	Anne d. Nathaniel & Anne Wolstencroft, Droylsden, engineer
"	9	John s. Henry & Betty Thorpe, Failsworth, weaver
"	11	Matthew s. John & Hannah Wyatt, Newton, weaver
"	11	James s. William & Sarah Ridings, Failsworth, weaver
"	18	Betty d. John & Anne Hibbert, Newton, weaver
"	18	George s. John & Alice Heap, Collyhurst, machine maker
"	21	Jane d. James & Alice Robinson, Newton, weaver
"	25	Hannah d. John & Elizabeth Still, Bradford, weaver
"	25	John s. Josiah & Jane Garlick, Failsworth, weaver
"	25	Sarah d. Mary Whitehead, Failsworth, spinster
Oct	2	Sarah Anne d. Benjamin & Mary Hulton, Failsworth, weaver
"	2	Mary d. Jonathan & Hannah Schofield, Manchester, calico printer
"	9	William s. Sarah Wolstenholme, Newton, spinster
"	16	Alice d. Joseph & Martha Walmsley, Failsworth, weaver
"	16	William s. Thomas & Jane Welch, Droylsden, crofter
"	16	Elizabeth d. Edward & Mary Tetlow, Newton, labourer
"	16	Cornelius s. Richard & Martha Drinkwater, Newton, labourer
"	16	Nicholas s. William & Rosa Simister, Newton, weaver
"	16	Lydia d. Jonathan & Sarah Clough, Newton, dyer
"	17	John s. William & Elizabeth Houlton, Manchester, innkeeper
"	23	Ellen d. James & Jane Middleton, Newton, cotton spinner
"	30	Maria d. John & Anne Wyld, Woodhouses, calico printer
"	30	Mary d. James & Anne Tomlinson, Newton, bleacher
"	30	Alice d. John & Jane Blackshaw, Newton, warehouseman
"	30	John s. William & Hannah Brandon, Ashton underline, engineer
Nov	6	William s. Elizabeth Kaye, Newton, spinster
"	13	Maria d. Garside & Alice Blomeley, Newton, weaver
"	13	Jane d. Adam & Betty Doodson, Hooley Hill, bleacher
"	13	Maria d. James & Anne Allen, Failsworth, weaver
"	20	Edward s. Edward & Maria Hulton, Failsworth, shopkeeper
"	29	Harriet d. Henry & Betty Brown, Newton, labourer
"	20	Samuel s. James & Alice Bardsley, Failsworth, weaver
"	27	Harriet d. Henry & Elizabeth Robinson, Newton, slater
Dec	4	Anne Heathcot d. William & Mary Hulton, Failsworth, weaver
"	4	William s. Robert & Susanna Marsden, Newton, bleacher

(new register commences: volume 11)

"	11	Sarah d. John & Mary Gradwell, Newton, bleacher
"	18	James s. John & Betsey Holt, Newton, silk manufacturer
"	19	Martha d. John & Violet McNamee, Newton, bleacher
"	25	James s. James & Sarah Houlton, Newton, coach proprietor
"	25	Robert s. Luke & Isabel Smith, Failsworth, farmer

" 25 Joseph s. William & Hannah Bowyer, Newton, blockcutter

1832

Jan	1	Marianne d. Alexander & Mary Cairns, Newton, millwright
"	1	Elizabeth d. James & Mary Butterworth, Newton, weaver
"	1	Selina d. Joseph & Ellen Dawson, Failsworth, weaver
"	1	Edward s. William & Mary Butterworth, Newton, weaver
"	1	Elizabeth d. Philip & Rebekah Lancashire, Moston, farmer
"	1	Marianne d. Joseph & Sarah Kenyon, Newton, dyer
"	1	Joseph s. James & Anne Clough, Failsworth, weaver
"	1	William Rostern s. Mary Hooles, Newton, spinster
"	1	Margaret d. Abraham & Esther Heywood, Woodhouses, blacksmith
"	1	John s. Abraham & Agnes Mills, Ashton, cotton spinner
"	1	James s. Thomas & Jane Hay, Failsworth, printcutter
"	8	Christiana d. James & Betsey Wyld, Droylsden, weaver
"	8	Sarah d. George & Anne Heywood, Droylsden, bleacher
"	22	Sarah d. John & Anne Dean, Newton, skinner
"	22	Martha d. Thomas & Sarah Dean, Newton, farmer
"	22	Joseph s. Robert & Sarah Hilton, Newton, porter
"	25	Joseph s. Joseph & Sarah Lees, Newton, shopkeeper
"	29	Nancy d. Frederick & Anne Collinson, Failsworth, weaver
Feb	5	Ellen d. John & Jane Booth, Failsworth, weaver
"	12	Margaret d. Nicholas & Margaret Edge, Failsworth, printcutter
"	12	Thomas s. William & Anne Egerton, Bradford, calico printer
"	19	Mary d. Henry & Mary Rogerson, Newton, blacksmith
"	19	Phoebe d. Betty Clough, Failsworth, spinster
"	26	Alice d. Thomas & Anne Thornley, Droylsden, labourer
"	26	Betty d. William & Jane Mather, Audenshaw, weaver
Mar	4	Mary d. Thomas & Jane Bates, Failsworth, bleacher
"	4	Mary d. George & Nancy Worral, Failsworth, weaver
"	4	James s. Mally Whitehead, Chadderton, spinster
"	4	James s. John & Elizabeth Howles, Newton, bleacher
"	4	James s. Hannah Barlow, Newton, spinster
"	4	James s. John & Alice Lees, Newton, weaver
"	4	Sarah d. David & Harriet Hulton, Failsworth, weaver
"	4	John s. Hannah Pollitt, Failsworth, spinster
"	11	Charles s. Samuel & Mary Etchels, Newton, weaver
"	11	Edward s. Samuel & Mary Etchels, Newton, weaver
"	11	Eliza d. Richard & Martha Richardson, Newton, tailor
"	11	James s. William & Sarah Lane, Failsworth, innkeeper
"	11	Enoch s. Thomas & Anne Aldred, Newton, weaver
"	15	Mary d. Benjamin & Mary Lees, Failsworth, weaver
"	15	Hannah d. Samuel & Hannah Lees, Failsworth, weaver
"	15	John s. James & Jane Aldred, Failsworth, weaver

"	18	Martha d. Robert & Sarah Whitehead, Newton, dyer
"	18	Betty d. Robert & Sarah Whitehead, Newton, dyer
"	18	Nancy d. Edward & Nancy Robinson, Failsworth, weaver
"	18	Sarah d. William & Betty Rider, Failsworth, innkeeper
"	18	Alice d. Daniel & Hannah Berrington, Newton, carter
"	21	Mary d. Joseph & Sarah Bentley, Newton, weaver
"	25	William Henry Vincent s. Josiah & Mary Barnes Holt, Manchester, tobacconist
"	25	Thomas s. John & Harriet Hulme, Medlock Vale, carter
"	25	Aaron s. Thomas & Susanna Whittaker, Failsworth, hatter
"	25	Susanna d. Richard & Susanna Thomas, Manchester, cotton spinner
Apr	1	William Primrose s. Joseph & Mary Tetlow, Newton, warehouseman
"	1	Sarah d. Nanny Schofield, Failsworth, spinster
"	1	Launcelot s. John & Hannah Hilton, Newton, weaver
"	1	Jane d. James & Sarah Whittaker, Failsworth, weaver
"	1	Esther d. Robert & Anne Whitehead, Failsworth, weaver
"	15	Jacob & Eliza children of William & Sarah Etchels, Newton, calico printer
"	15	Sarah Jane d. Lucy Walker, Newton, spinster
"	22	Sally d. William & Mary Berry, Failsworth, weaver
"	22	John s. Charles & Hannah Collinge, Fasilsworth, weaver
"	22	James s. John & Martha Tetlow, Newton, weaver
"	22	Dinah d. Henry & Mary Hyde, Failsworth, weaver
"	22	James s. John & Esther Dewhurst, Failsworth, labourer
"	22	John s. George & Jane Robinson, Failsworth, dyer
"	22	George & Ellen children of Robert & Mary Jackson, Newton, calico printer
"	22	Sarah d. Samuel & Mary Moores, Failsworth, weaver
"	22	William s. Samuel & Mary Hyde, Failsworth, weaver
"	22	Marianne d. Thomas & Jane Howard, Newton, crofter
"	22	Olivia d. James & Mary Schofield, Failsworth, weaver
"	22	Thomas s. Isaiah & Sarah Etchels, Failsworth, weaver
"	22	Elizabeth d. James & Lucy Hay, Failsworth, labourer
"	22	Thomas s. Thomas & Elizabeth Buckley, Manchester, shoemaker
"	22	Elizabeth d. James & Jane Peel, Newton, labourer
"	22	William s. Samuel & Susanna Smith, Manchester, wheelwright
"	22	George s. Samuel & Sarah Traver, Ashton Parish, labourer
"	22	William s. John & Betty Hyde, Newton, farmer
"	22	Anne d. William & Anne Tates, Newton, labourer
"	22	Sarah d. Samuel & Mary Lord, Failsworth, labourer
"	29	Sarah d. William & Susanna Horrocks, Blackley, dyer
"	29	Sarah d. Elijah & Jane Pollitt, Newton, weaver
May	13	Elizabeth d. Thomas & Jane Lancashire, Newton, shopkeeper
"	13	Marianne d. John & Maria Stott, Newton, weaver
"	13	Sarah d. John & Hannah Cheetham, Failsworth, carter
"	13	Lucy d. John & Betty Robinson, Newton, weaver
"	16	Anne d. James & Jane Taylor, Newton, silk manufacturer

"	27	Benjamin s. Robert & Jenny Taylor, Failsworth, weaver *(1832)*
Jun	4	John Briscoe s. James Smale & Jane Thornley, Oldham, surgeon
"	10	William Hulme s. James & Anne Leigh, Newton, weaver
"	10	Miles s. Miles & Lydia Taylor, Newton, farmer
"	10	Thomas s. Thomas & Anne Wilson, Moston, weaver
"	10	Edwin s. Joseph & Hannah Brown, Failsworth, farmer
"	10	Jane d. Alice Hill, Failsworth, spinster
"	10	Eliza d. Joseph & Mally Smethurst, Hollinwood, weaver
"	17	James s. John & Olive Bardsley, Newton, dyer
"	17	Jane d. John Owen & Anne Harrop, Manchester, chairmaker
"	17	James s. John & Hannah Thornley, Chadderton, weaver
"	24	William s. John & Mary Wyld, Newton, weaver
"	24	James s. James & Hannah Ogden, Newton, weaver
"	24	Joseph s. Joseph & Elizabeth Wilson, Newton, silk throwster
Jul	1	Anne d. Joseph & Martha Smethurst, Newton, collier
"	1	Henry s. George & Sarah Hilton, Newton, weaver
"	1	Margaret & Jane twin ds. Joshua & Margaret Bent, Droylsden, bleacher
"	8	John s. Samuel & Anne Gradwell, Newton, dyer
"	15	John s. Robert & Anne Hulme, Newton, bleacher
"	15	Eliza d. James & Anne Pomfrit, Newton, cotton spinner
"	22	Joseph s. William & Dorothy Cheadle, Newton, gardener, bo Oct 25 1831
"	22	Mary d. Benjamin & Anne Worsick, Droylsden, farmer
"	22	James s. Abraham & Nancy Taylor, Clayton Bridge, dyer
"	22	Sarah Elizabeth d. Christopher & Hannah Gregory, Ardwick, bleacher
"	22	Elizabeth d. Robert & Anne Lees, Failsworth, weaver
"	22	Robert & John ss. Thomas & Margaret Horrocks, Failsworth, bleacher
"	22	William & Ellen children of John & Anne Pattison, Newton, milkman
"	22	George s. George & Betty Smith, Droylsden, bricklayer
"	22	Henry s. John & Sarah Marsden, Newton, bleacher
"	24	Thomas s. Joseph & Jenny Thornley, Failsworth, weaver
"	24	Ralph s. Jane Greenwood, Failsworth, spinster
"	24	Eliza d. Samuel & Mary Pollitt, Failsworth, weaver
"	29	Thomas s. Thomas & Sarah Taylor, Newton, weaver
"	29	Charles Edward s. John & Elizabeth Bradbury, Droylsden, agent
Aug	5	Olivia d. James & Anne Ogden, Woodhouses, weaver
"	5	James s. James & Sarah Mather, Newton, weaver
"	12	John s. Robert & Elizabeth Grimston, Newton, tollbar keeper
"	19	Samuel s. John & Anne Hilton, Failsworth, weaver
"	19	Samuel s. Adam & Sarah Horrocks, Medlock Vale, print cutter
"	19	Jane d. John & Sarah Bentley, Newton, weaver
"	19	William s. Samuel & Elizabeth Haslam, Failsworth, bricklayer
"	19	John s. Joseph & Hannah Berry, Failsworth, weaver
"	19	Charles s. John & Hannah Thornley, Failsworth, weaver
"	19	William s. Daniel & Mary Knott, Failsworth, sawyer
"	19	Joseph s. James & Isabel Hyde, Newton, farmer

"	19	Joseph s. Eli & Sarah Swift, Failsworth, weaver	*(1832)*
"	19	Hannah d. Robert & Sarah Hulme, Newton, calenderer	
"	19	Thomas s. Joseph & Betty Robinson, Ashton underlyne, labourer	
"	19	Henry s. John & Charlotte Ramsbotham, Newton, cotton spinner	
"	19	John Grey s. Robert & Hannah Edmiston, Newton, warper	
"	19	William Berry s. Elijah & Charlotte Hilton, Failsworth, weaver	
"	19	James s. John & Elizabeth Taylor, Newton, blockcutter	
"	19	Elijah s. James & Mary Whitehead, Moston, weaver	
"	26	Dan s. William & Jane Shipley, Newton, joiner	
"	26	Jane d. Zechariah & Anne Robinson, Manchester, weaver	
"	26	Thomas s. James & Ruth Whitehead, Failsworth, weaver	
Sep	2	Eliza d. Sarah Horrocks, Newton, spinster	
"	9	Alice d. Joseph & Ellen Howard, Newton, bookkeeper	
"	9	Violet d. Thomas & Anne Thorpe, Failsworth, weaver	
"	9	Ellen d. Jonah & Betty Goodier, Newton, bleacher	
"	9	Anne d. Jane Smith, Failsworth, spinster	
"	10	Ellen d. Charles & Anne Winstanley, Manchester, collier	
"	16	Thomas s. Philip & Mary Berry, Newton, labourer	
"	16	Jane d. John & Hannah Slater, Failsworth, weaver	
"	16	George s. William & Mary Holt, Newton, blacksmith	
"	18	Richard s. Matthew & Betty Thorpe, Moston, weaver	
"	23	William s. John & Sally Whitehead, Newton, calico printer	
"	23	Anne d. Thomas & Alice Pollitt, Newton, dyer	
"	23	Thomas s. William & Hannah Brindley, Newton, silk throwster	
"	23	Mary d. Richard & Betty Rostern, Droylsden, weaver	
"	23	John s. Richard & Phoebe Allen, Failsworth, labourer	
"	23	Maria d. Levi & Ellen Clough, Newton, weaver	
"	23	Ellen & Eliza ds. John & Betty Redfern, Newton, dyer	
"	30	John William s. Sarah Schofield, Droylsden, spinster	
Oct	3	Amelia d. Matthew & Harriet Broadbent, Newton, weaver	
"	7	Sarah d. Thomas & Martha Kemp, Newton, warehouseman	
"	7	Anne d. Thomas & Sarah Thornley, Failsworth, weaver	
"	7	John Hulme s. John & Elizabeth Smith, Newton, weaver	
"	7	Robert & William ss. John & Mary Whitehead, Moston, farmer	
"	14	Thomas s. John & Mary Burgess, Manchester, silk manufacturer	
"	14	Thomas s. George & Esther Wood, Newton, shopkeeper	
"	14	John s. James & Jane Taylor, Newton, labourer	
"	14	Joseph s. Richard & Phillis Brown, Hollinwood, weaver	
"	14	John Williams s. James & Betty Barlow, Medlock Vale, crofter	
"	21	Elizabeth d. Thomas & Charlotte Hall, Newton, shoemaker	
"	21	William s. Joshua & Nancy Robinson, Newton, calico printer	
"	21	Henry John Gratrix s. Samuel & Martha Rostern, Newton, calico printer	
"	21	Dinah d. William & Alice Walton, Newton, calico printer	
"	25	Eliza d. John & Isabella Wilson, Newton, master mariner	
"	25	John s. Joel & Elizabeth Taylor, Failsworth, weaver	

"	28	Peter s. Thomas & Sarah Heywood, Newton, bleacher
Nov	4	Mary d. Thomas & Susan Etchels, Failsworth, weaver
"	7	Michael s. Michael & Elizabeth Waring, Newton, printcutter
"	7	Alice d. John & Ellen Mills, Newton, pattern drawer
"	8	Benjamin s. Robert & Elizabeth Wilkinson, Failsworth, weaver
"	11	Henry s. Bernard & Mary Fishwick, Newton, calico printer
"	11	Samuel s. Matthew & Sarah Smith, Newton, dyer
"	18	Selina d. James & Elizabeth Brierly, Failsworth, weaver
"	18	James s. James & Martha Bray, Newton, shoemaker
"	25	Josiah s. James Edwards & Elizabeth Hancock, Newton, designer
"	25	Samuel s. Joseph & Sarah Bentley, Newton, warper
"	25	Mary d. Jonathan & Betty Hilton, Failsworth, weaver
"	25	Margaret d. William & Esther Whitehead, Failsworth, weaver
"	25	Sarah Anne d. Thomas & Hannah Hogg, Ashton, cotton spinner
Dec	2	William & James ss. William & Nancy Dawson, Newton, warper
"	2	Elizabeth Jane d. Charles & Sarah Cook, Failsworth, carter
"	2	Matilda d. Thomas & Jane Taylor, Newton, silk manufacturer
"	2	George s. Richard & Sarah Hall, Newton, labourer
"	2	Anne d. Absalom & Harriet Hulton, Failsworth, weaver
"	9	Hannah d. Edward & Jane Tipton, Clayton, collier
"	9	Betty d. Peter & Jane Whitehead, Newton, cotton spinner
"	9	John s. William & Susan Waine, Newton, hatter
"	9	Sarah Anne d. Thomas & Jane Wild, Newton, innkeeper
"	9	Ellen d. Samuel & Jane Bithel, Newton, bleacher
"	10	Aaron s. Joel & Hannah Pollitt, Failsworth, weaver
"	16	William s. Charles & Lavinia Barnes, Newton, leather dealer
"	16	Robert s. Benjamin & Martha Tetlow, Failsworth, labourer
"	16	Hannah d. John & Elizabeth Crossley, Manchester, weaver
"	16	Hannah d. Samuel & Anne Goodier, Denton, farmer
"	23	Nancy d. Thomas & Betty Wolstencroft, Newton, bleacher
"	23	Mary d. Robert & Hannah Davies, Newton, cotton spinner
"	30	Mary d. Robert & Martha Walmsley, Failsworth, weaver
"	30	Eliza d. Samuel & Mary Salt, Newton, tailor
"	30	Mary d. Thomas & Rachel Bottomly, Bradford, farmer
"	30	Priscilla d. John & Jenny Howarth, Clayton, bleacher
"	30	Joseph s. William & Sarah Stansfield, Newton, hatter

1833

Jan	6	Phoebe d. Thomas & Jane Jones, Newton, labourer
"	13	Sarah d. Peter & Maria Lucy Holroyd, Failsworth, tailor
"	13	Mary d. Joseph & Elizabeth Pott, Newton, warehouseman
"	20	Marianne d. John & Anne Gardner, Droylsden, farmer
"	20	Anne d. John & Sarah Arrandale, Clayton, dyer
"	20	William s. Joseph & Elizabeth Selby, Openshaw, hatter

"	27	Anne d. George & Mary Mills, Newton, labourer
"	27	Joseph s. George & Mary Bardsley, Newton, dyer
"	31	Abraham s. William & Sarah Hilton, Failsworth, weaver
Feb	1	Benjamin s. Peter & Mary Stott, Moston, weaver
"	3	Mary d. John Rogers & Mary Siddall, Newton, bookkeeper
"	17	Anne d. James & Alice Schofield, Failsworth, weaver
"	17	Mary d. Peter & Mary Wyld, Failsworth, labourer
"	17	James s. James & Alice Mills, Medlock Vale, calico printer
"	17	John s. Joseph & Anne Taylor, Failsworth, weaver
"	17	Jane d. William & Sarah Walmsley, Failsworth, weaver
"	17	Thomas s. John & Marianne Yates, Manchester, bleacher
"	24	Mary d. John & Alice Worsick, Droylsden, farmer
"	24	James s. Andrew & Sally Smith, Failsworth, weaver
"	24	Emma d. Samuel & Olive Taylor, Newton, weaver
"	24	Elizabeth d. Ashton & Anne Brown, Newton, labourer
"	24	Thirza d. Thomas & Mary Hopwood, Newton, cotton spinner
Mar	3	Mary d. Thomas & Mary Dunkerley, Newton, weaver
"	7	Samuel s. William & Eliza Hardy, Newton, dyer
"	10	James s. James & Betsey Moston, Moston, miller
"	10	James s. Anne Kershaw, Failsworth, spinster
"	24	William Winn s. George & Hannah Robinson, Manchester, grocer
"	24	Sarah d. Joshua & Sarah Eckersley, Failsworth, weaver
"	26	Lavinia d. Charles & Alice Collinson, Failsworth, weaver
"	31	Jane d. Benjamin & Jane Howarth, Droylsden, labourer
"	31	Ellen d. John & Anne Hibbert, Newton, weaver
Apr	3	Marianne d. Maria Mather, Newton, spinster
"	5	Elizabeth d. William & Lucy Seel, Newton, bleacher
"	5	Mary d. James & Margaret Higham, Ashton, gardener
"	7	Jane d. James & Mary Allen, Failsworth, weaver
"	7	Sarah d. Abel & Nancy Watmouth, Newton, stonemason
"	7	Edmund s. Edmund & Sarah Walmsley, Failsworth, labourer
"	7	Abraham s. Edward & Margaret Lewis, Newton, wheelwright
"	7	Elizabeth d. Thomas & Jane Hay, Failsworth, printcutter
"	7	Marianne d. William & Mary Walker, Newton, weaver
"	7	James Whittaker s. Thomas & Nancy Gillibrand, Failsworth, weaver
"	7	William s. James & Anne Allen, Failsworth, weaver
"	7	Elizabeth d. Jonathan & Esther Dawson, Failsworth, weaver
"	7	Robert s. Joseph & Esther Kershaw, Failsworth, weaver
"	9	Sarah d. John & Martha Chadwick, Failsworth, blockcutter
"	14	Nancy d. William & Martha Eyre, Failsworth, weaver
"	14	Thomas s. William & Mary Robinson, Failsworth, calico printer, bo Mar 19 1833
"	14	Thomas s. Matthew & Elizabeth Lamb, Newton, tawer
"	21	Esther d. Launcelot & Anne Hogg, Newton, cotton spinner
"	21	William s. David & Hannah Hamson, Failsworth, weaver
"	28	Martha d. Samuel & Martha Hulton, Moston, labourer

"	30	Jane d. Robert & Anne Thorley, Failsworth, weaver	*(1833)*
"	30	Elizabeth d. Peter & Margaret Later, Newton, labourer	
May	5	James s. John & Anne Sykes, Droylsden, collier	
"	5	Sarah d. Philip & Mary Houghton, Newton, farmer	
"	5	Elizabeth d. Thomas & Maria Robinson, Newton, dyer	
"	8	Anne d. Joseph & Anne Etchels, Failsworth, weaver	
"	10	James s. Benjamin & Jane Hilton, Failsworth, weaver	
"	12	James s. John & Mary Gee Berry, Droylsden, collier	
"	12	Marianne d. Ratliff & Elizabeth Fielding, Droylsden, dyer	
"	19	Frances Twyford d. Richard & Charlotte Renshaw, Newton, bookkeeper	
"	23	George s. George & Mary Clay, Manchester, innkeeper	
"	26	Isaac s. Isaac & Maria Jones, Newton, cotton spinner	
"	26	James s. Henry & Elizabeth Robinson, Newton, slater	
"	26	Jane d. James & Anne Hilton, Failsworth, weaver	
"	26	John s. John & Jane Nightingale, Newton, bleacher	
"	26	John s. Syers & Prudence Haslam, Failsworth, bricklayer	
Jun	2	Septimus s. John & Mary Lomas, Newton, draper	
"	2	Lawrence s. Thomas & Elizabeth Cash, Newton, blacksmith	
"	9	William s. John & Esther Ditchfield, Newton, bleacher	
"	16	Betty d. David & Betty Knott, Failsworth, labourer	
"	16	Esther Anne d. Samuel & Sarah Huxley, Droylsden, labourer	
"	16	William s. John & Anne Birch, Failsworth, bleacher	
"	16	John s. Thomas & Mary Robinson, Droylsden, dyer	
"	23	William s. Mary Gradwell, Newton, spinster	
"	23	Esther d. John & Mary Smith, Newton, blockcutter	
"	23	Anne d. James & Anne Forest, Newton, weaver	
"	30	Marianne d. John & Maria Heywood, Newton, cotton spinner	
"	30	Abel s. John & Sarah Whitehead, Failsworth, weaver	
"	30	Mary d. Samuel & Alice Oakes, Newton, labourer	
"	30	James s. Ashton & Betty Ashton, Failsworth, weaver	
"	30	Anne d. Thomas & Sarah Dean, Newton, farmer	
Jul	7	Elizabeth d. Joseph & Anne Ogden, Newton, weaver	
"	7	Elizabeth d. Richard & Alice Dawson, Failsworth, dyer	
"	7	Mary d. John & Nancy Smethurst, Hollinwood, labourer	
"	7	Betty d. Levi & Mary Pendleton, Newton, weaver	
"	12	Harriet d. James & Betty Whitehead, Failsworth, weaver	
"	12	Edwin s. Anne Pollitt, Failsworth, spinster	
"	14	Sarah d. John & Mary Ramsden, Newton, labourer	
"	14	Thomas s. William & Mary Smith, Salford, labourer	
"	14	Robert s. Thomas & Catherine Hulme, Droylsden, bleacher	
"	14	James s. James & Betty Jones, Newton, dyer	
"	19	Mary d. John & Elizabeth Johnson, Failsworth, weaver	
"	19	Thomas s. Edward & Anne Worral, Failsworth, weaver	
"	21	Ellen d. John & Elizabeth Robinson, Newton, slater	
"	21	John s. John & Phillis Barnes, Newton, saddler	

"	21	Jane d. Nicholas & Margaret Edge, Failsworth, blockcutter *(1833)*
"	28	Charles s. Thomas & Anne Brookes, Newton, dyer
"	28	Marianne d. Edward & Alice Berry, Failsworth, weaver
Aug	8	Charlotte d. James & Mary Newton, Harpurhey, dyer
"	4	William James s. Richard & Martha Lees, Staley Bridge, carter
"	4	Samuel s. Thomas & Margaret Smith, Newton, blockcutter
"	11	Anne Buckley d. Joseph & Sarah Barnes, Newton, calico printer
"	11	Matthew s. Joseph & Maria Arrandale, Droylsden, bricklayer
"	16	John s. Israel & Sarah Clough, Failsworth, weaver
"	16	Mary d. Edward & Anne Pimlot, Failsworth, weaver
"	18	Marianne James & William children of Joseph & Margaret Etchels, Droylsden, bleacher
"	18	David s. David & Sarah Makin, Newton, weaver
"	18	David William John & Jane children of David Winstanley, Manchester, collier
"	25	Nancy d. Thomas & Deborah Bentley, Newton, weaver
"	25	Mary d. John & Anne Wright, Openshaw, bleacher
"	25	Alice d. William & Alice Thorpe, Failsworth, weaver
"	25	Richard s. Thomas & Mary Moss, Millhouses, glazier
"	25	Joseph s. John & Betty Allen, Failsworth, weaver
"	25	James s. James & Jane Hesketh, Failsworth, carter
"	25	John s. Luke & Nancy Etchels, Newton, weaver
"	25	Richard s. Richard & Elizabeth Smethurst, Failsworth, weaver
"	25	George s. Richard & Ellen Wolstenholme, Newton, crofter
"	25	Ellen d. Sarah Buckley, Newton, spinster
"	25	James s. Peter & Betty Whitehead, Newton, engineer
"	25	William s. James & Mary Yates, Newton, bleacher
"	25	Marianne d. Henry & Alice Wright, Newton, saddler
"	25	Sarah Anne d. Robert & Elizabeth Ratliff, Newton, calico printer
"	25	John s. James & Sarah Whitehead, Moston, weaver
"	25	Sarah Anne d. John & Sarah Sydebotham, Newton, dyer
"	25	Mary Anne d. Mark & Rebekah Williamson, Moston, weaver
"	25	Daniel s. John & Harriet Hulme, Newton, labourer
"	25	Edward s. James & Anne Allen, Failsworth, weaver
"	25	Christiana & Martha ds. John & Esther Brierley, Failsworth, weaver
"	25	James s. Henry & Betty Thorpe, Failsworth, weaver
"	25	William s. John & Elizabeth Little, Newton, shopkeeper
"	25	Robert s. William & Elizabeth Williamson, Newton, labourer
"	25	William Henry s. William & Elizabeth Wood, Manchester, painter
"	25	Hannah d. John & Sarah Tomlinson, Moston, weaver
"	25	Sarah d. David & Sarah Makin, Newton, weaver
"	25	James s. Mary Schofield, Newton, spinster
Sep	1	Jane d. Joseph & Sarah Whitehead, Failsworth, weaver
"	8	George s. Thomas & Hannah Langford, Newton, engineer
"	15	Mary d. John & Anne Bentham, Newton, labourer
"	15	Mary d. John & Jane Ashworth, Newton, weaver

"	15	Elizabeth d. William & Marianne Davies, Failsworth, cotton spinner
"	15	George s. William & Sarah Drinkwater, Newton, bricksetter
"	15	Eliza d. Thomas & Sarah Dawson, Newton, warper
"	15	Olive d. John & Marianne Egerton, Newton, shoemaker
"	22	Maria d. Bold Bagshaw & Elizabeth Robinson, Manchester, innkeeper
"	22	Luke s. Joel & Mary Smith, Failsworth, weaver
"	22	William s. Francis & Esther Broadbent, Newton, weaver
"	22	Mary d. Thomas & Betty Hudson, Failsworth, boatman
"	29	James s. William & Elizabeth Reid, Newton, weaver
"	29	Anne d. Robert & Betty Glossop, Failsworth, weaver
"	29	John s. Isaac & Elizabeth Heppy, Droylsden, hatter
"	29	Henry Hunt s. Isaac & Betty Andrew, Newton, calico printer
"	29	Eliza d. James & Jane Middleton, Newton, cotton spinner
Oct	6	John s. John & Martha Taylor, Newton, labourer
"	6	Mary d. John & Betty Lomax, Failsworth, shoemaker
"	6	Jane d. John & Betty Robinson, Newton, weaver
"	8	Maria d. William & Elizabeth Still, Newton, weaver
"	13	John s. John & Nancy Whittaker, Failsworth, weaver
"	13	Isaac s. Isaac & Anne Butler, Chadderton, farmer
"	13	Phoebe d. James & Mary Johnson, Moston, farmer
"	13	Eliza d. John & Mary Hughes, Newton, slater
"	20	Sarah Anne d. James & Anne Pomfret, Newton, cotton spinner
"	20	Sarah Anne d. (Thomas & *struck through; does not appear in BT*) Sarah Ridings, Failsworth, spinster
"	27	Ellen d. John & Mary Whitehead, Failsworth, weaver
"	27	Ellen d. Matthew & Ellen Howarth, Newton, shopkeeper
"	30	John Booth s. Stephen & Anne Grundy, Liverpool, landwailer
"	30	William s. James & Sarah Houghton, Newton, coachman
Nov	3	Elizabeth d. Luke & Mary Crossley, Failsworth, weaver
"	3	Samuel s. Thomas & Hannah Brundritt, Failsworth, weaver
"	3	Hannah d. Martha Wright, Failsworth, spinster
"	3	John s. John & Anne Dean, Newton, skinner
"	7	Sarah d. James & Elizabeth Walmsley, Newton, carter
"	10	Amelia d. Joseph & Betty Berry, Failsworth, labourer
"	10	Phoebe d. John & Jane Hulme, Manchester, warper
"	10	Martha Moss d. James & Esther (Sarah*struck through*) [Sarah] Rose, Newton, weaver
"	10	Alice d. George & Anne Grimshaw, Newton, farmer
"	11	James s. James Smale & Jane Thornley, Newton, surgeon
"	17	Anne d. Adam & Betty Dudson, Ashton Parish, bleacher
"	17	William s. John & Anne Thorley, Failsworth, weaver
"	17	Anne d. Levi & Alice Whitehead, Failsworth, weaver
"	17	Jane d. John & Betsey Holt, Newton, silk manufacturer
"	24	Luke s. William & Jane Etchels, Newton, joiner
"	24	Margaret Elizabeth d. William & Sarah Ridings, Failsworth, weaver

"	24	Robert s. William & Sarah Bardsley, Newton, dyer
Dec	1	Anne d. Dan & Martha Hilton, Moston, weaver
"	1	Sarah Anne d. Samuel & Sarah Schofield, Moston, labourer
"	1	Robert s. James & Phoebe Howard, Woodhouses, weaver
"	3	Mary d. Abel & Grace Sharples, Newton, tailor
"	5	Sarah Hannah d. William & Mary Butterworth, Manchester, grocer
"	5	Anne d. Thomas & Martha Smith, Newton, dyer
"	8	Rosanna d. Richard & Matty Drinkwater, Newton, calico printer
"	8	Sarah d. Robert & Susanna Marsden, Newton, bleacher
"	8	Mary John & William children of Samuel & Sarah Garside, Newton, innkeeper
"	8	Selina d. George & Mary Whittaker, Failsworth, hatter
"	8	Jane d. John & Ellen Taylor, Failsworth, weaver
"	9	Mary d. Joseph & Maria Bates, Newton, shopkeeper
"	15	Jonathan s. William & Sarah Lane, Failsworth, innkeeper
"	15	John s. William & Hannah Barlow, Failsworth, weaver
"	22	Joseph s. Robert & Sarah Southwell, Newton, hatter
"	22	James s. Enoch & Esther Robinson, Newton, slater
"	22	Hannah d. James & Matty Robinson, Failsworth, weaver
"	22	Edmund s. Robert & Jane Taylor, Failsworth, weaver
"	22	Anne d. Joseph & Betty Nichols, Oldham, blacksmith
"	22	Esther d. John & Esther Lindley, Newton, dyer
"	25	Sarah Anne d. Jonathan & Sarah Goodier, Newton, bleacher
"	25	Hannah d. Thomas & Mary Allen, Newton, bleacher
"	29	Sarah & Anne ds. Richard & Sarah Worsick, Failsworth, farmer
"	29	Amelia d. Benjamin & Nancy Worsick, Clayton, farmer

1834

Jan	1	Sarah d. James & Hannah Hibbert, Newton, weaver
"	5	Joseph Jane Martha & Mary children of George & Elizabeth Tomlinson, Failsworth, weaver
"	5	James s. Thomas & Anne Thorpe, Failsworth, weaver
"	5	John s. James & Mary Thorpe, Failsworth, weaver
"	5	Sarah d. Philip & Jane Wyatt, Failsworth, weaver
"	5	Thomas s. Abraham & Elizabeth Fletcher, Newton, dyer
"	5	Eliza d. Henry & Betty Brown, Newton, labourer
"	12	Mary d. William & Elizabeth Middleton, Newton, cotton spinner
"	12	James s. William & Matty Clough, Failsworth, weaver
"	12	Higham s. Job & Mary Travis, Newton, weaver
Feb	9	Marianne d. Alexander & Sarah Watson, Ashton Parish, bleacher
"	9	Priscilla d. Richard & Esther Thorpe, Moston, weaver
"	9	Elizabeth d. Daniel & Mary Smith, Salford, warehouseman
"	9	James Bradshaw s. Charles & Isabella Ridings, Newton, shopkeeper
"	9	Elizabeth d. Daniel & Hannah Knott, Failsworth, weaver
"	9	George s. George & Esther Wood, Newton, shopkeeper

"	11	Anne d. Thomas & Mary Fildes, Newton, packer (*1834*)
"	11	Robert s. Jonathan & Betty Hilton, Failsworth, weaver
"	16	Hannah d. William & Martha Bern, Manchester, blacksmith
"	16	Jane d. John & Elizabeth Still, Bradford, weaver
"	16	Sarah Anne d. Joseph & Sarah Kenyon, Newton, dyer
"	16	Ellen d. Abraham & Anne Collinge, Newton, dyer
"	16	James s. Thomas & Sarah Fairhurst, Manchester, silk manufacturer
"	16	Hamlet s. Thomas & Elizabeth Marsden, Newton, calico printer
"	16	Jesse s. Jesse & Hannah Knott, Failsworth, farmer
"	16	Henry s. Betty Hilton, Failsworth, spinster
"	16	Elizabeth d. William & Mary Dawson, Failsworth, blockcutter
"	18	Robert s. John & Martha Whitehead, Failsworth, weaver
"	23	Maria d. Richard & Martha Richardson, Newton, tailor
"	23	John s. Joseph & Sarah Wylde, Newton, labourer
Mar	2	Samuel s. William & Anne Egerton, Bradford, calico printer
"	2	Henry s. James & Margaret Simister, Newton, baker
"	2	Robert s. Joseph & Martha Walmsley, Failsworth, weaver
"	9	Alice d. Anne Whitehead, Failsworth, spinster
"	11	Simeon s. Mark & Anne Smith, Newton, weaver
"	12	Samuel s. Reuben & Sarah Holt, Medlock Vale, labourer
"	16	Joseph s. Thomas & Jane Welsh, Bradford, bleacher
"	16	Eliza d. Samuel & Hannah Bottomley, Manchester, shopkeeper
"	16	Thomas s. Robert & Catherine Brookes, Newton, dyer
"	24	Robert s. James & Alice Lees, Failsworth, weaver
"	28	James s. James & Anne Ogden, Hollinwood, blacksmith
"	30	Philip Lancashire s. John & Anne Greaves, Crompton, cotton spinner
"	30	Dennis s. Joseph & Mary Ramsbottom, Newton, calico printer
"	30	Sarah Jane d. Elizabeth Kaye, Newton, spinster
"	30	Anne d. Edward & Anne Pomfret, Manchester, fustian cutter
"	30	Violet d. Thomas & Anne Cordingly, Failsworth, weaver
"	30	James s. John & Betty Wolstencroft, Failsworth, labourer
"	30	Marianne d. Joseph & Anne Boon, Newton, shoemaker
"	30	James s. Joseph & Elizabeth Howard, Newton, bookmaker
"	30	Anne d. Charles & Betty Sydebotham, Newton, weaver
"	30	Richard & Sarah children of Mark & Elizabeth Brown, Failsworth, weaver
"	30	Nanny d. William & Anne Bates, Failsworth, cordwainer
"	30	Samuel s. John & Alice Heald, Newton, bleacher
"	30	William s. James & Judith Williamson, Droylsden, dyer
"	30	James Hulme s. James & Anne Leigh, Newton, weaver
"	30	George s. William & Sarah Gradwell, Failsworth, bleacher
"	30	James & Phillis children of Robert & Elizabeth Taylor, Failsworth, weaver
"	30	William s. Thomas & Alice Hough, Failsworth, weaver
"	30	Joseph s. John & Sarah Tomlinson, Moston, weaver
"	30	Mary d. George & Hannah Wright, Failsworth, weaver
Apr	6	Thomas s. James & Jane Peel, Newton, farmer

"	6	Betty d. James & Alice Robinson, Newton, weaver	(*1834*)
"	13	James s. Thomas & Sarah Thornley, Failsworth, weaver	
"	13	William s. Frederick & Anne Collinson, Failsworth, weaver	
"	13	Ellen d. William & Anne Yates, Newton, labourer	
"	16	Elizabeth d. Jonathan & Sarah Clough, Newton, dyer	
"	20	Thomas William s. James & Betty Moston, Moston, farmer	
"	20	Mary d. John & Betty Wolstenholme, Failsworth, weaver	
"	20	Anne d. Cornelius & Rachel Yates, Newton, bleacher	
"	20	Robert s. Robert & Alice Stansfield, Newton, hatter	
"	20	Sarah d. William & Charlotte Hooley, Newton, hatter	
"	27	Elizabeth d. William Heathcot & Mary Hulton, Moston, weaver	
May	4	Benjamin s. Josephus & Marianne Hulton, Moston, weaver	
"	4	Nelson s. Thomas & Susanna Whittaker, Failsworth, hatter	
"	4	George s. George & Jane Robinson, Failsworth, dyer	
"	11	Anne d. Robert & Hannah Edmondson, Newton, warper	
"	11	Emma d. John & Elizabeth Whitehead, Moston, weaver	
"	18	Alice d. Samuel & Alice Pendleton, Droylsden, farmer	
"	18	Benjamin s. James & Anne Clough, Failsworth, weaver	
"	18	Mary d. John & Alice Hyde, Moston, weaver	
"	18	Mary d. John & Violet Mack, Newton, bleacher	
"	18	Thomas Henry s. William & Alice Finch, Newton	
"	18	Mary & Hannah ds. William & Alice Walton, Newton, calico printer	
"	25	Sarah d. James & Sally Whittaker, Failsworth, weaver	
"	25	Nancy d. Jonathan & Hannah Chadderton, Failsworth, weaver	
"	25	Thomas s. Jonathan & Hannah Chadderton, Failsworth, weaver	
"	25	Charles s. John & Hannah Thornley, Chadderton, weaver	
"	25	Margaret d. George & Anne Heywood, Newton, bleacher	
"	25	Mary d. Isaac & Betty Whittaker, Failsworth, hatter	
"	25	Elizabeth d. Joseph & Hannah Barlow, Newton, cotton spinner	
"	26	Benjamin s. John & Mary Anne Brierly, Failsworth, weaver	
"	26	Thomas s. Thomas & Sarah Barlow, Failsworth, weaver	
Jun	1	Martha d. Philip & Rebecca Lancashire, Moston, farmer, bo 18 Feb 1834	
"	1	William s. William & Jane Bythill, Failsworth, weaver	
"	1	Nancy d. Gideon & Elizabeth Sykes, Newton, weaver	
"	8	Anne d. Hugh & Mary Coupe, Crumpsal, farmer	
"	8	Ellen d. Jeremiah & Alice Etchels, Droylsden, dyer	
"	8	Robert s. Thomas & Sarah Taylor, Failsworth, weaver	
"	8	Anne d. Jane Wilkinson, Moston, weaver	
"	8	Mary Jane d. Joseph & Hannah Hooley, Manchester, painter	
"	8	Thomas s. Richard & Sarah Anne Hinks, Droylsden, collier	
"	8	James s. Thomas & Sarah Bern, Newton, labourer	
"	8	John s. Thomas & Anne Wilson, Ashton, weaver	
"	15	Maria d. Edward & Maud Hulton, Failsworth, shopkeeper	
"	15	Philip s. John & Sally Whitehead, Newton, calico printer	
"	22	Joseph s. Thomas & Jane Lancashire, Newton, shopkeeper	

	22	Abram s. James & Ann (Jane *struck through*) [Anne] Taylor, Failsworth, weaver
	22	Hannah d. Matthew & Matty Kershaw, Failsworth, weaver
	22	Thomas s. Susanna Taylor, Failsworth, illegitimate
	22	Willm. s. John & Sarah Pelling, Clayton, laborer
	22	Richard s. John & Ann Speakman, Smedley, laborer
	22	William s. Joseph & Ann Copeland, Failsworth, shoemaker
	23	Byron s. John & Isabella Wilson, Newton, mariner
	29	Charles s. Job & Mary Ogden, Failsworth, silk weaver
	29	Thomas s. William & Jane Mather, Droylsden, cotton weaver
Jul	6	Ann d. John & Mary Gredwell, Newton, bleacher
	6	Nancy d. Horatio & Ann Ridings, Newton, weaver
	6	Esther d. Thomas & Ann Holt, Newton, spinner
	6	Emma d. Ann Hague, Newton, house servant, illegitimate
	6	Jane d. Joseph & Hannah Bardsley, Droylsden, block cutter
	6	Cornelius s. William & Mary Whitehead, Newton, weaver
	13	Sarah d. Henry & Prudence Whitaker, Manchester, puker maker (*sic in BT also*)
	13	Esther d. Miles & Lydia Taylor, Manchester, milk dealer
	13	Thomas s. Robert & Ann Hulme, calendar maker, Newton
	13	Ann d. James & Ophelia Berrington, Droylsden, calico dyer
	13	Samuel s. James & Sally Smith, Failsworth, farmer
	20	Mary Ann d. Zechariah & Ann Robinson, Manchester, weaver
	20	John s. Alfred & Lucy Collinson, Failsworth, laborer
	20	William s. James & Isabella Hyde, Newton, farmer
	20	Thomas s. William & Nancy Bouker, bleacher, Newton
	27	Benjamin s. John & Alice Lee, Droylsden, laborer
	27	Sarah Ann d. Thomas & Susan Etchells, Failsworth, weaver
Aug	3	Alice d. Violet Simister, Failsworth, weaver
	3	Ann d. John & Ann Robinson, Failsworth, weaver
	3	Robert s. David & Sarah Hulton, Failsworth, laborer
	3	Helen d. John & Maria Heywood, Newton, cotton spinner
	3	Alice d. James & Hannah Buckley, Newton, cotton weaver
	3	Mary d. James & Mary Allen, Failsworth, weaver
	3	Emma d. Thomas & Jane Nelson, Newton, silk weaver
	10	Sarah d. Joseph & Alice Booth, Failsworth, cotton spinner
	10	Thomas s. James & Sarah Robinson, Newton, porter
	17	Henry s. Benjamin & Sarah Thornley, Droylsden, laborer
	17	Robert s. Thomas & Betty Coupe, Newton, pattern designer
	24	Mary Ann d. Samuel & Ann Gredwell, Newton, weaver
	24	Jane d. Adam & Sarah Horrocks, Clayton Bridge, printer
	24	Ann d. George & Mary Ashworth, Newton, bleacher
	24	Joseph s. James & Lucy Hay, Newton, bleacher
	24	Emma d. John & Sarah Marsden, Newton, bleacher
	24	Thomas s. Mary & Samuel Salt, Newton, taylor
	24	Mary d. John & Anne Latham, Newton, weaver (draper *struck through*) [weaver]

"	24	Sarah d. Joseph & Hannah Brown, Failsworth, farmer (*1834*)
"	24	Thomas s. Ann Barnes, Newton
"	24	Mary d. William & Susanna Horrocks, Crumpsall, laborer
"	24	Henry s. Thomas & Eliz. Buckley, Manchester, shoemaker
"	24	Walter s. James & Hannah Ogden, Newton, silk weaver
"	24	Ann d. Mary Murray, illegitimate, Newton
"	31(24 *struck through*) [31]	John Whitmore s. John Rogers & Mary Siddall, Culcheth
"	31	Susanna d. John Rogers & Mary Siddall, Culcheth
Sep	5	(Aug 24 *struck through*) [Sep 5] Mary d. John & Hannah Hilton, Moston, silk weaver
"	7	Nancy d. Richard & Nancy Treaver, Haughton Green, engineer
"	14	Elizabeth d. Jonathan & Phoebe Handley, Clayton, coal miner
"	14	Alice d. James & Ruth Whitehead, Failsworth, silk weaver
"	14	Thomas s. Robert & Mary Jackson, Newton, silk dyer
"	14	Ellen d. Anne Schofield, Moston, illegitimate
"	21	Mary Ann d. Joseph & Elizabeth Wright, Newton, weaver
"	21	John s. James & Sarah Wright, Newton, sacker
"	21	Sarah d. Joseph & Elizabeth Hall, Newton, weaver
"	21	Martha d. Henry & Betty Robinson, Newton, mason
"	21	James s. Hannah Gredwell, Failsworth, illegitimate
"	28	John s. John & Hannah Wyatt, Newton, weaver
"	28	William s. Robert & Elizabeth Groamston, Newton, toll keeper
"	28	William s. Henry (William *struck through*) [Henry] & Mary Eckersley, Failsworth, weaver
"	29	Joseph s. John & Ann Beswick, Failsworth, weaver
Oct	5	Charles Henry s. Charles & Lavinia Barns, Newton, leather dealer
"	5	Mary d. John & Ann Walmsley, Failsworth, weaver
"	5	Violet d. William & Jane Smith, Newton, weaver
"	12	Esther d. Peter & Mary Stott, Moston, weaver
"	12	Lavinia d. James & Betty Whitehead, Failsworth, weaver
"	12	John s. George & Sarah Hardman, Openshaw, wheelwright
"	12	Thomas s. Samuel & Hannah Taylor, Failsworth, weaver
"	19	Hannah d. James & Patience Carter, Newton, spinner
"	19	James s. Samuel & Ann Williamson, Droylsden, dyer
"	19	William s. Samuel & Ann Williamson, Droylsden, dyer
"	19	Eliza d. David & Alice Williamson, Droylsden, dyer
"	19	Caleb s. Daniel & Hannah Barrington, Newton, farmer
"	19	Betty d. William & Helen Winter, weaver, Failsworth
"	19	Joseph s. Jonathan & Nanny Needham, weaver, Failsworth
"	23	John s. Laurence & Grace Wering, Newton, taylor
"	24	John s. James Edwards & Elizabeth Hancock, Newton, pattern designer
"	24	Robert Newton s. James & Esther Barnes, Newton, block printer
"	26	Joseph s. Elizabeth Bond, illegitimate, Newton
"	26	William s. Robert & Elizabeth Wilkinson, Failsworth, weaver
"	26	Edwin s. James & Rebecca Jemima Taylor, Newton, weaver

Nov	2	Mary d. Thomas & Catharine Hulme, Droylsden, bleacher
"	2	Elizabeth d. John & Olivia Bardsley, Newton, blue dyer
"	2	John s. Thomas & Sarah Simpson, Failsworth, hatter
"	2	William s. Joseph & Sarah Chadderton, Newton, laborer
"	3	Ann d. William & Elizabeth Davenport, Failsworth, weaver, bo 1825 Aug 7
"	3	Jane d. William & Elizabeth Davenport, Failsworth, weaver, bo 1830 Nov 26
"	3	Alice d. William & Elizabeth Davenport, Failsworth, weaver, bo 1833 Sep 16
"	9	Mary d. James (Joseph *struck through*) [James] & Mary Schofield, Failsworth, weaver
"	9	Joseph s. Matthew & Sarah Smith, Newton, dyer
"	9	Henry s. John & Ann Hulme, Newton, dyer
"	9	Mary d. Duke & Isabella Smith, Failsworth, manufacturer
"	9	William Henry s. Eliza Dean, Failsworth, illegitimate
"	9	Ann d. William & Sarah Woodall, Newton, laborer
"	16	Esther d. William & Hannah Brandom, Newton, engineer
"	16	Mary d. Joel & Agnes Berry, Failsworth, shoemaker
"	16	Joseph s. James & Margaret Higham, gardener
"	21	Robert s. Thomas & Ann Thornley, Droylsden, laborer
"	23	Thomas s. James & Elizabeth Milner, Newton, laborer
"	23	Joseph s. Peter & Jane Whitehead, Newton, spinner
"	30	Emma d. Joseph & Ruth Hibbert, Failsworth, hatter
"	30	Elizabeth d. George & Maria Ashton, Droylsden, crofter
"	30	Ann d. Esther & William Whitehead, weaver, Failsworth
"	30	Leah d. Richard & Ellen Whitaker, Failsworth, hatter
"	30	Peter s. Robert & Hannah Hardman, Manchester, warper
"	30	Isaac s. Edward & Margaret Lavis, Newton, wheelwright
"	30	William s. Samuel & Alice Oaks, Newton, farmer
Dec	7	Elizabeth d. William & Elizabeth Williamson, Newton, hawker
"	7	Elizabeth d. John & Sarah Arendale, Droylsden, dyer
"	7	Robert s. George & Mary Bardsley, Newton, dyer
"	7	James s. Elijah & Jane Pollitt, Newton, weaver
"	9	Alexander s. James & Isabella Lomas, Newton, silk weaver
"	14	James s. William & Rose Simister, Newton, weaver
"	14	Betty d. William & Rose Simister, Newton, weaver
"	14	Luke s. John & Sarah Pollitt, Failsworth, weaver
"	21	Edward s. William & Alice Hull, Ashton, printer
"	21	Peter s. Agrayman & Elizabeth Ryder, Failsworth, farmer
"	21	Susan d. Henry & Ann Flemming, Failsworth, gardener
"	22	Thomas s. Benjamin & Matty Tetlow, Failsworth, laborer
"	24	Esther d. John & Mary Smith, Newton, (*occupation blank in PR & BT*)
"	25(24 *struck through*) [25] Elizabeth d. John & Hannah Traver, Newton, crofter
"	25	Joseph Primrose s. Joseph & Mary Tetlow, Newton, warehouseman
"	28	Mary d. Thomas & Sarah Wild, Newton, warehouseman

1835

Jan	4	Robert s. William & Lucy Seel, Newton, bleacher
"	4	Emma d. Eliza Simister, Newton, illegitimate
"	4	Julia d. William & Martha Ford, Failsworth, weaver
"	4	Mary d. James & Phoebe Hurd, Failsworth, weaver
"	4	Henry s. Susan Mosdale, Droylsden, illegitimate
"	4	Jane d. Samuel & Mary Lord, Failsworth, laborer
"	7	Phoebe d. John & Ann Hilton, Failsworth, weaver
"	7	James s. James & Ann Ogden, Failsworth, weaver
"	8	James s. Mary Whitehead, Failsworth, illegitimate
"	8	Elizabeth d. David & Harriett Hulton, Failsworth, weaver
"	8	George s. Levi & Ellen Clough, Newton, weaver
"	8	Ann d. Abel & Nancy Watmough, Newton, stonemason
"	11	Reuben s. Hannah Tomlinson, Failsworth, illegitimate
"	11	Samuel s. Samuel & Hannah Lees, Failsworth, weaver
"	11	James s. John & Betty Redfern, Newton, calenderer
"	18	Sarah d. Thomas & Alice Pollitt, Newton, dyer
"	18	Mary d. Shadrach & Martha Ashton, Droylsden, miner, bo Feb 2 1815
"	18	William s. Shadrach & Martha Ashton, Droylsden, miner, bo Aug 16 1817
"	18	Thomas s. Shadrach & Martha Ashton, Droylsden, miner, bo Mar 9 1824
"	18	Betty d. William & Mary Gloster, Openshaw, dyer, bo Nov 2 1834
"	18	Rob[er]t s. Rob[er]t & Jenny Taylor, Failsworth, weaver
"	25	Matthew s. William & Mary Grimshaw, Newton, laborer
"	25	Thomas s. Robert & Ann Lees, Failsworth, weaver
"	25	Ann d. Jonathan & Elizabeth Hilton, Failsworth, weaver
"	29	Amelia d. John & Betty Robinson, Newton, weaver
Feb	1	Jane d. Joseph & Alice Ogden, Failsworth, farmer
"	1	John s. Jonathan & Elizabeth Lees, Newton, laborer
"	1	James s. James & Ellen Clough, Failsworth, weaver
"	8	William s. Tabitha Ridings, Failsworth, illegitimate
"	13	John s. Thomas & Martha Smith, Mostyn, dyer
"	15	Joseph s. John & Ann Sykes, Droylsden, miner
"	15	Mary d. John & Hannah Cheetham, Failsworth, porter
"	15	Robert s. Bernard & Mary Fishwick, Newton, calico printer
"	16	John s. William & Ann Marsden, Newton, calenderer
"	18	Robert s. Robert & Sarah Whitehead, Droylsden, painter
Mar	1	Sarah d. James & Elizabeth Brown, Manchester, joiner
"	1	Emma d. John & Sarah Bentley, Newton, weaver
"	1	Mary Ann d. Thomas & Jane Jones, Newton, laborer
"	1	John s. John & Alice Heap, Manchester, mechanic
"	1	Ann d. Ellis & Amelia Whitaker, Newton, spinner
"	12	James s. Joseph & Alice Whitehead, Newton, porter
"	12	Luke s. Robert & Sarah Hilton, Newton, porter, bo 6 Mar 1834
"	15	Nancy d. John & Phillis Barnes, Newton, saddler

"	15	Thomas s. Thomas & Sarah Dean, Newton, farmer *(1835)*
"	15	John s. Robert & Elizabeth Ratcliff, Newton, collar maker
"	15	John s. Thomas & Jane Hay, Failsworth, printer
"	18	John George s. George & Mary Clay, Manchester, publican
"	24	Thomas s. Bartholomew John & Alice Brown, Failsworth, hatter
"	29	John s. Samuel & Mary Pollitt, Failsworth, weaver
"	29	John s. John & Esther Dewhurst, Failsworth, weaver
"	31	Arthur s. John & Elizabeth Webster, Newton, solicitor, bo Nov 24 1834
Apr	5	Margaret d. Philip & Mary Hulton, Newton, farmer
"	5	Ellen d. Charles & Sarah Lees, Failsworth, hatter
"	12	John s. Richard & Mary Rosthern, Newton, printer
"	12	Abednego Ashton, Droylsden, bo 27[17] Nov 1812 (*no occupation in PR or BT*)
"	19	Sarah Jane d. Matthew & Elizabeth Lamb, printer, Newton
"	19	Jos[h]ua s. James & Alice Smith, Manchester, weaver
"	19	William s. Martha Ellison, illegitimate
"	19	Jane d. Joshua & Sarah Swift, Colley Hurst, dyer
"	19	Sidney s. Eliza Smith, bo 14 Jan 1835
"	19	Emily d. Edward & Ann Johnson, Newton, silk spinner
"	19	Ellen d. Samuel & Ann Bottomley, Manchester, shopkeeper
"	19	William Henry s. William & Mary Smith, Salford, calenderer
"	19	Elizabeth d. Peter & Mary Wylde, Failsworth, carter
"	19	Charles s. John & Ann Bateman, Culceth, bookkeeper
"	19	Joseph s. James & Margaret Simister, Newton, carter
"	19	Alice d. Horatio Nelson & Mary Collinson, Failsworth, weaver
"	19	Sarah d. James & Elizabeth Brierley, Failsworth, weaver
"	19	Charles s. Charles & Ann Winstanley, Manchester, collier
"	19	William s. James & Ann Hill, Newton, bricklayer
"	19	Rachel d. William & Nanny Dawson, Newton, warper
"	19	William s. John & Ann Garner, Droylsden, farmer
"	19	Thomas s. Joshua & Margaret Bent, Droylsden, bleacher
"	19	John s. James & Ann Etchells, Droylsden, dyer
"	19	Martha d. Joseph & Ann Taylor, Failsworth, carter
"	19	Enoch s. Thomas & Mary Hopwood, Newton, cotton spinner
"	19	Martha d. Joseph & Hamanah (*sic*) [Hannah] Collier, Newton, watchman
"	19	James s. Cyrus & Prudence Haslam, Failsworth, (bricklayer *struck through*) [bricklayer]
"	21	Eliza d. Mark Robinson & Ellen Carter, Newton, tinplate worker
"	25	John s. George Foster & Sarah Twedale, Bolton Lancashire, millwright
"	29	Mary d. John & Esther Ditchfield, Newton, calenderer
"	29	Sarah Ann d. Isaac & Ann Barratt, Newton, bleacher, bo 17 Nov 1833
"	29	Sarah Ann d. Joseph & Betty Consterdine, Newton, blockcutter
May	3	James s. Samuel & Martha Hulton, Newton, laborer
"	3	Hannah d. Joseph & Mary Hulton, Failsworth, weaver
"	3	Joseph s. William & Harriet Wellock, Newton, cattle dealer
"	10	Sarah Ann d. William & Sally Lane, Failsworth, publican

"	10	Sarah Ann, Susan, Kezia & Jemima ds. William & Mary Barker, Newton, laborer; Sarah Ann bo 10 Feb 1826, Susan bo 27 Jul 1828, Kezia bo 21 May 1831, Jemima bo 24 May 1834
"	11	Joseph s. Peter & Lucy Maria Holroyd, Failsworth, taylor
"	17	Sarah d. John & Elizabeth Robinson, Newton, slater
"	17	Hannah d. Thomas & Maria Robinson, Newton, dyer
"	17	Sarah d. Joseph & Maria Arundale, Droylsden, bricklayer
"	17	John s. James & Mary Ann Proctor, Blakeley, dyer
"	24	Samuel s. John & Betty Lees, Newton, weaver
"	24	Martha d. William & Charlotte Hooley, Droylsden, hatter
"	24	George s. William & Mary Robinson, Failsworth, printer
"	24	William s. George & Sarah Watson, Salford, book keeper
"	26	Ann d. William & Mary Ann Horrocks, Newton, laborer
"	26	Robert s. John & Elizabeth Whitehead, Moston, weaver
"	31	William s. Isaac & Elizabeth Heappeay, Woodhouses Ashton, hatter
Jun	7	Mary d. Thomas & Mary Moss, Newton, printer
"	7	Alice d. Eli & Sarah Swift, Failsworth, weaver, bo 30 Aug 1834
"	7	James s. John & Hannah Thornley, Failsworth, weaver
"	7	Elizabeth d. William & Mary Pendleton, Failsworth, weaver
"	7	Rachel d. Joseph & Betty Hilton, Failsworth, weaver
"	7	Thomas s. Charles & Hannah Collinge, Failsworth, weaver
"	7	Sophia d. John & Hannah Slater, Failsworth, weaver
"	7	Hannah d. Thomas & Mary Ann Barratt, Newton, finisher
"	7	Mary d. Alice Etchells, Failsworth, illegitimate, bo 16 Mar 1835
"	7	Samuel s. John & Christiana Gregory, Ardwick, laborer
"	7	Jane d. John & Nancy Whittaker, Failsworth, weaver, bo 23 Jan 1835
"	7	Elizabeth d. William & Mary Platt, Newton, book keeper, bo 24 Apr 1835
"	7	Grace d. John & Jane Richards, fustian cutter, bo 30 Sep 1834
"	7	Joseph s. John & Jane Richards, fustian cutter, bo Apr 15 1835
"	7	Eliza d. John & Mary Stanley, Droylsden, weaver
"	14	Jane d. John & Sarah Mather, Newton, hatter
"	14	Mary Ann d. Mark & Millicent Gradwell, Raynor Macclesfield, calico printer
"	14	Ellen Adelah d. Joseph & Mary Ramsbotham, Newton, calico printer
"	21	Mary d. Joseph & Sarah Simister, laborer, Failsworth
"	21	Ann d. Abel & Nancy Watmough, Newton, stone mason, bo 24 Dec 1834
"	25	Maria d. Richard & Alice Dawson, Failsworth, dyer
"	25	Ruth d. Ralph & Elizabeth Garner, Newton, farmer, bo 20 Apr 1818
"	28	Mary d. Robert & Betty Glossop, Failsworth, weaver
"	28	Nancy d. Joseph & Elizabeth Pott, Newton, warehouseman
Jul	5	Mary Harrison d. John & Ann Greaves, Newton, innkeeper
"	5	Jane d. Henry & Mary Rogerson, Newton, blacksmith
"	12	Elizabeth d. Robert & Elizabeth Wilson, Newton, calico printer
"	15	Abraham s. James & Sarah Mather, Newton, weaver
"	19	Ann d. Joseph & Ann Higham, Newton, silk weaver
"	19	John s. John & Jane Pollitt, Newton, laborer

	19	James s. Thomas & Mary Whitehead, Moston, silk weaver	(*1835*)
"	19	Robert s. John & Ann Ward, Newton, printer	
"	19	Esther Emma d. Josiah & Mary Barnes Holt, Manchester, tobacconist	
"	26	George Elder s. Finlay & Helen Ross, Newton, book keeper	
"	26	Sarah Ann d. Thomas & Esther Kershaw, Manchester, hatter	
"	26	Elizabeth d. Thomas & Esther Kershaw, Manchester, hatter	
"	26	Joseph s. Samuel & Eliza Smith, Failsworth, weaver	
Aug	2	Elizabeth d. Jonah & Ann Goodier, Newton, bleacher	
"	2	John s. John & Maria Heywood, Newton, spinner	
"	9	James s. Joseph & Sarah Whitehead, Failsworth, weaver	
"	9	Ann d. Joel & Betty Taylor, Failsworth, weaver	
"	9	Thomas s. John & Elizabeth Smith, Collyhurst, weaver	
"	16	Mary Ann d. Edward & Jane Tipton, Droylsden, coalminer	
"	16	Esther d. Benjamin & Hannah Taylor, Failsworth, weaver	
"	16	Eliza d. Thomas & Rachel Bottomley, Bradford, farmer	
"	16	Rachel d. Thomas & Mary Ogden, Manchester, brewer	
"	16	Moses s. John & Mary Duckworth, Failsworth, calico printer	
"	16	William s. Edward & Alice Whitehead, Newton, dyer	
"	23	Simeon s. Emmanuel & Mary Fletcher, Hyde, overlooker, bo Oct 10 1834	
"	23	Sarah Ann d. Henry & Alice Wright, Newton, saddler	
"	23	Henry s. Robert & Caroline Roberts, Hyde, joiner	
"	23	Joseph s. James & Mary Lees, Failsworth, weaver	
"	23	Mary Ann d. William & Jane Etchells, Newton, joiner	
"	23	Thomas s. Joshua & Ann Robinson, Newton, calico printer	
"	23	Amelia d. Charles & Alice Collinson, weaver, Failsworth	
"	23	Thomas s. Samuel & Elizabeth Gradwell, Newton, weaver, bo Jun 22 1833	
"	23	Robert s. John & Mary Smith, Newton, weaver	
"	23	Sarah Ann d. John & Mary Smith, Newton, weaver	
"	23	Joseph s. Joel & Hannah Pollitt, Failsworth, weaver	
"	23	Peter s. Peter & Margaret Later, Newton, laborer	
"	23	Jane d. Thomas & Jane Taylor, Newton, overlooker	
"	23	Elizabeth d. Rolando & Ellen Collinson, Newton, silkweaver, bo Nov 15 1834	
"	23	Samuel s. Robert & Hannah Taylor, Newton, crofter	
"	23	Sarah d. Mary Rylands, illegitimate	
"	23	Margaret d. Robert & Sarah Barritt, traveller, bo 29 Dec 1834	
"	23	Elizabeth d. John & Elizabeth Taylor, Newton, block cutter	
"	30	Fanny Emma d. Daniel & Mary Smith, Salford, warehouseman	
"	30	Jenny d. Job & Mary Ogden, Failsworth, weaver	
"	30	Mary Elizabeth d. James & Mary Johnson, Moston, farmer	
"	30	Martha d. Ashton & Ann Brown, Newton, laborer	
Sep	9	Elizabeth d. John & Alice Pilkington, Failsworth, laborer	
"	9	John s. John & Alice Pilkington, Failsworth, laborer	
"	9	Sarah Ann d. Jonathan & Hannah Chadderton, Failsworth, weaver	
"	13	Richard s. Josiah & Alice Etchells, Failsworth, weaver	
"	13	Phebe d. William & Phebe Wolsendale, Newton, spinner	

"	20	Ann d. James & Martha Bird, Newton, engineer	*(1835)*
"	20	Alice d. William & Sarah Hibbert, Failsworth, weaver	
"	24	Sabina d. Isaac & Betty Whittaker, Failsworth, hatter	
"	25	John Thomas s. James & Sally Leigh, Newton, cotton spinner, bo 1 Sep 1835	
"	27	Jane d. Thomas & Jane Lancashire, Newton, shopkeeper	
"	27	Jane d. William & Mary Ann Davies, Newton, spinner	
"	27	Andrew s. Joseph & Sarah Bardsley, Failsworth, weaver	
Oct	4	Sarah Ann d. Henry & Margaret Raby, Newton, dyer	
"	4	James s. Jonathan & Louisa Taylor, Newton, crofter	
"	4	James Washington s. Isaac & Betty Andrew, Newton, printer	
"	4	Mary Ann d. William & Eliza Hardy, Failsworth, dyer	
"	7	Nancy d. Joseph & Sarah Bentley, Newton, warper	
"	11	Catharine d. Thomas & Betty Hatfield, Newton, bricklayer	
"	11	Thomas s. Daniel & Mary Davies, Failsworth, laborer	
"	11	Alice d. William & Martha Hare, Failsworth, weaver	
"	12	Jane d. John & Elizabeth otherwise Elizabeth Mercy Ashworth, Newton, silk manufacturer	
"	18	Elizabeth d. John & Betty Hyde, Newton, farmer	
"	18	Isabella d. James & Jane Taylor, Newton, dyer	
"	25	Elizabeth d. George & Mary Ramsbottom, Newton, carder	
"	25	Mary d. Samuel & Elizabeth Berry, Failsworth, weaver	
"	25	William s. William & Mary Walker, Newton, weaver	
"	25	Robert s. Joseph & Ann Whitehead, Failsworth, laborer	
Nov	1	Thomas s. John & Sarah Sidebottom, Newton, farmer	
"	1	John s. James & Mary Yates, Newton, maker up	
"	1	Martha d. James & Mary Newton, Harpurhey, laborer	
"	1	James s. Benjamin & Jane Nichols, Failsworth, weaver	
"	8	Mary Ann d. John & Mary Ann Smith, Newton, blockcutter	
"	8	Edwin s. John & Martha Tervin, Newton, farmer	
"	8	Harriett d. John & Elizabeth Foulks, Manchester, laborer	
"	8	James s. Thomas & Martha Kemp, Newton, warehouseman	
"	8	Elizabeth d. John & Elizabeth Still, Bradford, weaver	
"	8	Mary d. Elizabeth Booth, Newton, illegitimate	
"	8	James s. William & Mary Kirkland, Moston, husbandman	
"	15	Sarah d. Jonathan & Ann Robinson, Failsworth, mason	
"	15	Sophia d. Joseph & Mary Aldred, Droylsden, collier	
"	15	Mary d. William & Sarah Bardsley, Newton, dyer	
"	15	Mary d. Joseph & Sarah Kenyon, Newton, dyer	
"	22	Mary d. Henry & Betty Brown, Newton, laborer	
"	22	John s. Matthew & Hannah Howarth, Newton, warehouseman	
"	22	Michael s. George & Mary Mills, Failsworth, laborer	
"	22	Martha d. Samuel & Hannah Entwistle, Newton, spinner	
"	24	Nancy d. Nanny Gradwell, Blakeley, illegitimate	
"	29	Samuel s. Thomas & Ann Thorpe, Failsworth, silk weaver	
"	29	Alfred s. George & Mary Whittaker, Failsworth, hatter, bo Sep 18 1835	

"	29	George s. Ralph & Elizabeth Garner, Newton, farmer, bo Jun 14 1813
"	29	Joseph s. Ralph & Elizabeth Garner, Newton, farmer, bo Apr 10 1815
Dec	6	Sarah d. James & Sarah Robinson, Newton, porter
"	6	Elizabeth d. Thomas & Hannah Sumner, Openshaw, engineer
"	6	Thomas s. Joseph & Elizabeth Berry, Failsworth, laborer
"	6	John Bell s. Joseph & Harriett Lees, Newton, cotton stretcher
"	6	Rachel d. James & Eliza Bell, Manchester, spinner
"	6	John s. Robert & Mary Allen, Newton, tawer
"	6	Thomas s. William & Betty Ryder, Failsworth, butcher
"	10	Charlotte d. Thomas & Charlotte Hall, cordwainer (*abode blank in PR & BT*)
"	10	Louisa d. Job & Mary Travis, Newton, weaver
"	13	Samuel s. Samuel & Betty Haslam, Failsworth, bricklayer
"	13	Margaret d. Thomas & Jane Longworth, Newton, clogger
"	13	Sarah d. Francis & Esther Broadbent, Newton, weaver
"	13	Ann d. John & Alice Boardman, Collyhurst, laborer
"	13	Hannah d. Charles & Lavinia Barnes, Newton, traveller
"	17	Hannah d. Samuel & Ann Lowe, Manchester, bo 21 Dec 1832
"	20	Joseph Horsfall s. Joseph & Elizabeth Tomkinson, Newton, weaver
"	27	Robert s. Joel & Mary Smith, Failsworth, silk weaver
"	27	Eliza d. James & Mary Wolstencroft, Failsworth, joiner
"	27	Mary d. Andrew & Sarah Smith, Failsworth, silkweaver
"	27	John s. John & Alice Hyde, Moston, silkweaver
"	27	William s. Robert & Sarah Hulme, Manchester, laborer
"	27	Joseph s. John & Jane Hulme, Manchester, laborer

1836

(BT faded; most entries up to May 8 cannot be verified .)

Jan	3	William s. William & Mary Lamb, Newton, laborer
"	3	James s. John & Elizabeth Holme, Newton, calenderer
"	3	Henry s. Joshua & Frances Royle, Newton, shoemaker
"	3	Sarah Ann d. Joseph & Hannah Barlow, Newton, slater
"	3	Sarah Ann d. Jabez & Ellen Hamer, Newton, lock keeper
"	3	John Armitage s. James & Mary Ann Whitworth, Newton, warper
"	3	James s. James & Mary Ann Whitworth, Newton, warper
"	3	Samuel s. Thomas & Elizabeth Forrest, Newton, weaver
"	3	James s. William & Martha Fletcher, Newton, weaver
"	3	John Evans s. John & Ellen Lindley, Newton, silk thrower
"	3	Sarah d. Thomas & Sarah Thornley, Failsworth, weaver
"	3	Sarah d. Samuel & Martha Roston, Newton, calico printer
"	10	John s. John & Elizabeth Stevenson, book keeper
"	10	William s. Joseph & Mary Whittaker, Newton, weaver
"	10	John Standring s. Mary Ann Whitehead, Moston, illegitimate
"	17	Henry s. Thomas & Margaret Perch, Manchester, engraver
"	17	Sarah Ann d. Samuel & Amelia Pimlott, Newton, weaver

"	17	Elizabeth d. Joseph & Margaret Etchells, Newton, weaver
"	24	Jane d. Ann Ogden, illegitimate
"	24	Martha d. Robert & Susanna Marsden, Newton, laborer
"	31	Sarah d. James & Jane Middleton, Newton, silk weaver
"	31	Robert s. John & Isabella Morris, Newton, dyer
"	31	James s. John & Betty Gregson, Newton, printer
"	31	William s. Thomas & Betty Wolstencroft, Newton, bleacher
"	31	Robert Yates s. Thomas & Jannett Worsley, Manchester, joiner
"	31	Joseph Hooley s. Daniel & Mary Knott, Newton, sawyer
Feb	14	William s. William & Mary Clough, Failsworth, weaver
"	14	Sarah d. James & Elizabeth Taylor, Failsworth, weaver
"	14	William s. Henry & Betty Thorpe, Failsworth, weaver
"	14	Martha d. Samuel & Mary Etchells, Newton, weaver
"	14	Samuel John s. John & Mary Siddall, Droylsden, collier
"	14	Susanna d. John & Sarah Payling, Droylsden, laborer
"	14	Sarah d. John & Betty Lomax, Failsworth, shoemaker
"	14	Alice d. Mary Robinson, Failsworth, illegitimate
"	14	Mary d. Robt. & Martha Eckersley, Failsworth, weaver
"	14	Harriett d. Jane Hargreaves, Newton
"	14	Jane Catharine d. Samuel & Sarah Garside, Newton, publican
"	21	Hannah d. James & Hannah Hibbert, Newton, weaver
"	21	Ann d. James & Eliza Ann Richardson, Failsworth, joiner
"	21	Margaret d. James & Sarah Farrand, Ashton, bleacher
"	21	William Walter s. Benjamin & Nancy Worsick, Droylsden, publican
"	28	Amelia d. James & Esther Barnes, Newton, block printer
Mar	10	Susanna d. Samuel & Mary Salt, Newton, taylor
"	13	William Robinson s. Samuel & Ann Tetlow, Newton, slater
"	13	Sarah d. John & Martha Chadwick, Newton, block cutter
"	13	Thomas s. James & Ann Allen, weaver, Failsworth
"	17	Martha d. William & Hannah Barlow, weaver, Failsworth
"	20	Hannah d. James & Ann Pomfritt, Newton, spinner
"	20	Alice d. James & Alice Schofield, Failsworth, weaver
"	20	Wright s. Benjamin & Jane Howarth, Droylsden, laborer
"	23	Samuel s. William & Ann Entwistle, Newton, warehouseman
"	27	Joseph s. Mary Ridings, Failsworth, illegitimate
"	27	Thomas s. James & Elizabeth Jones, print dyer, Newton
"	27	William Philip s. Sarah Berry, illegitimate, Newton
Apr	3	Edward s. John & Hannah Hulton, Moston, weaver
"	3	Jane d. Charles & Ann Wilson, weaver, Newton
"	3	Harriett d. John & Ann Wright, Bradford, bleacher
"	3	Richard Henry s. William & Elizabeth Wood, Manchester, painter
"	3	John s. James & Catharine Clerk, Failsworth, weaver
"	3	Robert s. Robert & Mary Berry, Failsworth, weaver
"	3	Ellen d. Nathan & Ellen Dale, Failsworth, weaver
"	3	Mary d. William & Martha Howard, Failsworth, weaver

"	3	Sarah d. James & Ann Ogden, Failsworth, weaver	*(1836)*
"	3	John Allen s. William & Ann Bates, Droylsden, cordwainer	
"	3	Mary d. John & Mary Hughes, Newton, stonemason	
"	3	Sarah d. Robert & Sarah Barritt, Newton, book keeper	
"	3	George s. George & Ann Scholes, Newton, dairyman	
"	3	James s. Joseph & Sarah Chadderton, Newton, laborer	
"	3	Lucy Matilda d. Jonathan & Nanny Needham, Failsworth, weaver	
"	3	Samuel s. Joseph & Mary Barrett, Droylsden, printer	
"	7	Charles s. Joseph & Hannah Smith, Newton, warper	
"	10	Ann d. Joseph & Betsy Moston, Moston, farmer	
"	10	George Octavus s. John & Mary Lomas, Newton, draper	
"	10	Thomas s. Adam & Betty Dootson, Audenshaw, bleacher	
"	10	Mary Ann Jane d. James & Alice Mills, Ashton, printer	
"	10	Thomas s. Richard & Agnes Whittle, Newton, weaver	
"	24	Robert s. Samuel & Susan Smith, Manchester, wheelwright	
"	24	Jane d. Job & Ann Goodier, Newton, laborer	
"	24	James s. Peter & Lucy Maria Holroyd (Holcroft *struck through*) [Holcroft], Failsworth (Newton *struck through*) [Newton], tailor	
May	8	Nancy d. Peter & Mary Stott, Moston, weaver	
"	22	Ruth d. John & Sarah Whitehead, Failsworth, weaver	
"	22	Samuel s. Thomas & Ann Bromhead, Failsworth, weaver	
"	22	Annabella d. John & Alice Bagnall, Newton, weaver	
"	22	Jane d. Philip & Mary Berry, dyer, Newton	
"	22	Robert s. Daniel & Hannah Knott, Failsworth, laborer	
"	22	John s. John & Mary Hallison, Manchester, coalminer	
"	22	Elizabeth d. John & Martha Tetlow, Newton, weaver	
"	22	Sarah d. Samuel & Hannah Tailor, Failsworth, weaver	
"	22	Robert s. James & Mary Allen, Failsworth, weaver	
"	22	Jane d. Thomas & Jane Welch, Clayton, crofter	
"	22	Phebe d. Joseph & Phebe Nichols, Oldham, smith	
"	22	Sarah Ann d. William & Caroline Maloney, Failsworth, laborer	
"	22	Eliza d. Garside & Sarah Rose Gradwell (Rose *struck through*), Newton, shopman	
"	22	Noah s. Ellen Berry, Failsworth, illegitimate	
"	22	Benjamin s. Samuel & Alice Pendleton, Clayton, groom	
"	22	Mary d. John & Mary Whitehead, Failsworth, weaver	
"	29	Martha d. Thomas & Catharine Hulme, Droylsden, crofter	
"	29	Alfred s. Thomas & Susan Etchells, Failsworth, weaver	
"	29	Jane d. Mary Pollitt, Failsworth, illegitimate	
"	29	Amos s. Mark & Ann Clough, Failsworth, weaver	
"	29	Samuel s. John & Betty Haslam, Failsworth, bricksetter	
"	29	Mary Ann d. John & Ann Hibbert, Moston, weaver	
"	29	Jane d. Levi & Alice Whitehead, Failsworth, weaver	
Jun	5	Henry s. Joel & Agnes Berry, Failsworth, shoemaker	
"	5	Samuel s. Nathaniel & Charlotte Robinson, Newton, stonemason	

"	5	Isaac s. Frederick & Ann Collinson, Failsworth, weaver (*1836*)
"	5	Sarah Ann s. Egrayman & Elizabeth Ryder, Failsworth, farmer
"	5	Amelia, Sarah, Jacob, Abraham children of Isaac & Amelia Moors, Manchester Amelia bo Feb 19 1819 Sarah bo May 25 1820 Jacob bo May 21 1821 Abraham bo Jul 4 1826
"	13	Elizabeth d. John & Mary Ramsden, Newton, laborer
"	19	James s. William & Mary Mucklestone, Newton, bricklayer
"	26	Eliza d. Edward & Maria Hulton, Failsworth, shopkeeper
"	26	Samuel s. Benjamin & Sarah Thornley, Droylsden, laborer
"	26	John s. John & Alice Worsick, Newton, laborer
"	26	Elizabeth d. Horatio & Ann Ridings, Newton, weaver
"	26	John Thomas s. John & Betsy (Elizabeth *struck through*) [Elizabeth] Holt, Newton, silk manufacturer, bo May 4 1836
"	26	James s. Joseph & Elizabeth Selby, Droylsden, hatter
"	26	Susanna d. Joseph & Maria Bates, Newton, shop keeper
"	26	Robert s. James & Mary Thorpe, Failsworth, weaver
"	26	James s. James & Hannah Etchells, Failsworth, weaver
"	29	James s. John & Ann Gradwell, Newton, laborer, bo 6 Feb 1828
"	29	John s. John & Ann Gradwell, Newton, laborer, bo 31 Mar 1835
"	29	Mary Ann d. Thomas & Elizabeth Marsden, calico printer, bo Jun 11 1835
Jul	3	Rebecca d. John & Ann Hulme, Newton, dyer
"	3	Lucy Matilda d. William & Ellen Winterbottom, Failsworth, weaver
"	6	Samuel Dixon s. John Dixon & Ellen Nash, Clayton, captain in E.J. Service
"	10	Jonas s. John & Mary Thornley, Chadderton, weaver
"	17	Philip Smith s. Samuel & Jane Greaves, Newton, laborer
"	17	Mary Ann d. Mark & Alice Smith, Newton, weaver
"	17	Sarah d. Richard & Sarah Ann Hinks, Droylsden, coalminer
"	17	Ann d. William & Sarah Walmesley, Failsworth, weaver
"	17	William, Mary, Abraham children of James & Ann Taylor, Failsworth, weaver
"	17	Edward s. William & Mary Robinson, Failsworth, fustian cutter
"	20	Lucy d. George & Mary Clay, Manchester, gentn.
"	24	Martha d. John & Betty Wolstencroft, Failsworth, laborer
"	24	Sarah d. Peter & Ann Scholes, Failsworth, weaver
"	24	Sarah d. James & Olivia Rydings, Failsworth, weaver
"	24	Hannah d. James & Martha Bray, Newton, shoemaker
"	24	Ellen d. Abel & Grace Sharples, Newton, taylor
"	24	Samuel s. George & Jane Robinson, Failsworth, dyer
"	25	Benjamin s. John & Jane Roe, Failsworth, weaver
"	25	Jane d. John & Jane Roe, Failsworth, weaver
"	31	Henry Barrett s. Stephen & Ann Rothwell, Droylsden, calico printer, bo 11 May 1836
"	31	Elizabeth d. Thomas & Mary Allen, Newton, maker up
"	31	Joseph s. Enoch & Mary Ann Kershaw, Failsworth, weaver
"	31	Mary d. Jonas & Sarah Bostock, Newton, silk worker

"	31	Susan d. Thomas & Sarah Taylor, Failsworth, weaver	*(1836)*
Aug	3	Ann d. Robert & Ann Whitehead, Failsworth, weaver	
"	4	Benjamin s. James & Ann Ogden, Ashton, weaver	
"	4	Agnes d. James & Mary Schofield, Failsworth, weaver	
"	7	Sidney s. William & Alice Jackson, Newton, engineer	
"	7	John s. John & Ann Robinson, Failsworth, weaver	
"	10	James s. James & Jane Aldred, Failsworth, weaver	
"	18	George Daniel s. John Bowes & Isabella Wilson, Newton, master mariner	
"	7	misplaced Jane d. Ann Tomlinson, Newton, illegitimate (*order thus also in BT*)	
"	21	Mary d. James & Lucy Hay, Newton, bleacher	
"	21	Thomas s. Cornelius & Rachel Yates, Newton, bleacher	
"	21	John s. Thomas & Mary Gillebrand, Failsworth, weaver	
"	21	James s. Luke & Elizabeth Williamson, Moston, weaver	
"	21	Mary d. Reuben & Alice Jackson, Newton, bricklayer	
"	21	Elizabeth d. John & Martha Whitehead, Failsworth, weaver	
"	21	John s. Mark & Rebecca Williamson, Moston, weaver	
"	21	Ann d. Edwin & Mary Hilton, Manchester, dyer	
"	21	Mary Ann d. John & Mary Ann Parkinson, Manchester, engineer	
"	21	Jonathan s. Matthew & Elizabeth Lamb, Newton, calico printer	
"	21	Mary d. James & Esther Rose, Newton, weaver	
"	25	Mary Ann d. William & Amelia Wylde, Newton, laborer	
"	28	John s. James & Mary Butterworth, Newton, weaver	
"	28	John s. William & Nancy Bowker, Newton, bleacher	
"	28	Mary Helen d. John & Alice Lee, Droylsden, husbandman	
"	28	Henry s. Richard & Caroline Farmer, Failsworth, gardener	
"	31	Ann d. John & Ann Thornley, Droylsden, weaver, bo 24 Dec 1830	
"	31	Elizabeth d. John & Ann Thornley, Droylsden, weaver, bo 23 Jul 1828	
Sep	4	John s. Charles & Mary Partington, Manchester, weaver, bo 13 Feb 1823	
"	4	Hannah d. Ann Dummelow, Manchester, illegitimate, bo 6 Jan 1819	
"	4	Hannah d. David & Alice Williamson, Droylsden, dyer	
"	4	Nancy d. John & Ann Walmesley, Failsworth, weaver	
"	4	Amelia d. Samuel & Sarah Schofield, Moston, engineer	
"	11	Mary Ann d. John & Elizabeth Hulme, Newton, calenderer	
"	11	Eliza Jane d. Ann Ogden, Newton, illegitimate	
"	18	Matthew s. John & Hannah Draper, Newton, crofter	
"	21	John s. Thomas & Mary Fildes, Newton, laborer, bo Jun 23 1836	
"	25	Edward s. John & Mary Wylde, Failsworth, weaver	
"	25	Horatio s. John & Sarah Pollitt, Newton, weaver	
"	25	Elizabeth d. James & Sarah Smith, Failsworth, weaver	
"	25	Joseph s. Matthew & Martha Kershaw, Failsworth, weaver	
Oct	2	Mary d. John & Sally Whitehead, Newton, calico printer	
"	2	Nancy d. Alexander & Sarah Watson, Droylsden, laborer	
"	2	Elizabeth d. William & Alice Walton, Droylsden, calico printer	
"	2	Nancy d. John & Ann Pattison, Newton, laborer	
"	2	Maria d. Thomas & Ann Thornley, laborer, Droylsden	

"	9	George s. James & Mary Whitehead, Moston, weaver	(*1836*)
"	9	Elizabeth Taylor d. James & Mary Lees, Failsworth, weaver	
"	9	John s. Luke & Mary Crossley, Failsworth, weaver	
"	9	Robert s. John & Ann Heywood, Droylsden, blacksmith	
"	9	Ann d. Thomas & Sarah Wylde, Newton, porter	
"	16	Elizabeth d. Joseph & Ann Boon, Newton, shoemaker	
"	16	Robert s. Joseph & Elizabeth Hilton, Failsworth, weaver	
"	16	Robert s. Laurence & Priscilla Clegg, Bradford, carder	
"	16	James s. George & Mary Bardsley, Newton, dyer	
"	16	John s. John & Elizabeth Lytle, Newton, shopkeeper	
"	20	Samuel s. Richard & Esther Thorpe, Moston, weaver	
"	23	Hannah d. Benjamin & Susanna Etchells, Failsworth, weaver	
"	23	Mary Ann d. James & Isabella Hyde, Culcheth, laborer	
"	23	Zachariah s. William & Lucy Seel, Culcheth, bleacher	
"	23	George s. Hannah Lee, Saddleworth, illegitimate	
"	30	George s. James & Alice Swift, Manchester, weaver	
"	30	Robert s. Adam & Sarah Horrocks, Newton, block cutter	
"	30	Philip s. Thomas & Mary Dunkerley, Newton, weaver	
"	30	Ann d. James & Betty Whittaker, Failsworth, weaver	
"	31	Margaret Burdekin d. Willm. & Sarah Boardman, Blackburn, bo 28 Mar 1798	
"	31	Sarah Brierley d. Willm. & Sarah Boardman, Blackburn, bo 28 Jun 1804	
"	31	Mary Jane d. Benjamin & Sarah Brierley, Newton, gentn., bo Sep 18 1836	
Nov	6	Ann d. Joseph & Betty Lancashire, Failsworth, shopkeeper	
"	6	George s. William & Sarah Woodall, Newton, laborer	
"	13	Enoch s. Richard & Ellen Whittaker, Failsworth, hatter	
"	13	Mary d. George & Mary Ann Ogden, Failsworth, weaver	
"	13	Mary d. Joseph & Ann Bell, Failsworth, farmer	
"	13	Edward s. Catharine Waite, Gorton, illegitimate	
"	13	Sarah d. John & Elizabeth Tipton, joiner, Clayton	
"	20	Henry s. Matthew & Maria Phathain, Turton in Bolton , tinplate worker	
"	20	Eliza d. Joseph & Ann Nuttall, Clayton, crofter	
"	23	Joseph s. John & Esther Dawson, Newton, warper	
"	27	Martha d. John & Sarah Birch, Failsworth, coachman	
"	27	Luke s. James & Hannah Collinson, Failsworth, weaver	
"	29	Joseph s. Joseph & Hannah Smith, Newton, warper, bo Jan 21 1833	
"	29	Emma d. Joseph & Hannah Smith, warper, bo 6 Jan 1821	
Dec	4	Thomas Ramsden s. Willm. & Mary Ann Rawlinson, Manchester, screw (shoe *struck through*) maker [screw maker]	
"	9	Thomas s. Thomas & Mary Ridings, Newton, bricklayer	
"	11	Philip s. Philip & Sarah Dunkerley, Failsworth, weaver	
"	11	Ellen d. Willm. & Nancy Fisher, Failsworth, laborer	
"	11	Mary d. Henry & Betty Robinson, Failsworth, slater	
"	11	David s. Thomas & Maria Etherington, Newton, reed maker	
"	11	James s. Robt. & Hannah Taylor, Newton, dyer	
"	18	John s. James & Jane Allen, Failsworth	

"	18	Samuel s. Elizabeth Taylor, Newton, illegitimate
"	18	Sarah Ann d. James & Hannah Ogden, Newton, weaver
"	25	John Willm. s. John & Ann Greaves, Newton, publican, bo Oct 13 1836
"	25	Hannah d. Miles & Lydia Taylor, Manchester, shopkeeper
"	25	John s. Robt. & Elizabeth Wilkinson, Failsworth, weaver
"	25	Henry s. Jane Clegg, illegitimate
[		Signed in the presence of me Willm Hutchinson Incumbent of Newton Heath July 1ˢ 1837
		Abraham Taylor Chapel Warden of Newton]

1837

Jan	1	Eliza d. Henry & Margaret Raby, Newton, dyer
"	1	Christiana d. Rolando & Ellen Collinson, Newton, weaver, bo Sep 10 1836
"	1	Isabella d. John & Ann Latham, Newton, weaver
"	1	James s. John & Ann Stones, Newton, silk throwster
"	1	William Thomas s. John & Sarah Booth, Newton, book keeper
"	1	Alice d. James & Hannah Blomeley, Newton, weaver
"	1	Joseph s. Sarah Johnson, Newton, illegitimate
"	1	Joseph Henry s. Samuel & Nancy Summerfield, Openshaw, laborer
"	1	William Lee s. Willm. & Elizabeth Davenport, Failsworth, weaver
"	8	Charles Edward s. William & Elizabeth Bradbury, Clayton, book keeper
"	8	Thomas s. Willm. & Mary Horrocks, Newton, crofter
"	8	Jane d. Edward & Margaret Lewis, Newton, wheelwright
"	8	Sarah d. James & Ellen Clough, Failsworth, weaver
"	8	Joseph s. Joseph & Hannah Hesford, Newton, dyer
"	10	Sarah Whittaker d. Robert & Grace Clegg, Newton, laborer
"	12	George Haigh s. Henry Henshaw & Susannah Sarah Hadfield, Chorlton upon Medlock, artist
"	15	Mary d. Edward & Ann Winstanley, Manchester, collier
"	15	Frederick s. Samuel & Mary Moore, Failsworth, weaver
"	15	Hannah Haigh d. Joseph & Mary Hulme, Droylsden, laborer
"	15	Sarah Ann d. John & Mary Bradbury, Staley Bridge, spinner
"	22	Henry s. William & Mary Pendleton, Failsworth, weaver
"	29	Thomas s. Thomas & Jane Hay, Failsworth, laborer
"	29	Margaret d. Ann Turner, Newton, illegitimate
"	29	Joseph s. William & Mary Fletcher, Collyhurst, laborer
Feb	2	John s. Reuben & Sarah Holt, Medlock, laborer
"	3	Alice d. David & Hannah Harrison, Droylsden, laborer
"	5	Mary d. William & Hannah Fishwick, Droylsden, laborer (*entry placed after next in PR & BT*)
"	8	Abraham Briscow s. James & Jane Thornley, Newton, printer
"	12	(8 *struck through*) [12] Harriett d. Henry & Alice Wright, Newton, saddler
"	15	(12 *struck through*) [15] Mary Ann d. Martha Stewart, illegitimate (*abode & occupation blank in PR & BT*)

"	19	(15 *struck through*) [19] James s. Richard & Ellen Bradwell (*abode & occupation blank in PR & BT*)
"	19	Thomas s. James & Elizabeth Alford, Newton, dyer
"	19	John s. William & Mary Minshull, cotton spinner
"	19	Mary d. James & Ann Ogden, Failsworth, weaver
"	21	Jane d. William & Martha Berry, Manchester, mechanic
"	21	Elizabeth d. William & Elizabeth Livesey, Manchester, collier
"	26	Robert s. Absalom & Harriett Hulton, Failsworth, weaver
"	26	George s. Thomas & Ann Wright, Failsworth, weaver
"	26	Elizabeth d. John & Mary Ann Jones, Droylsden, engineer
"	26	Andrew s. Thomas & Jane Nelson, Newton, weaver
"	26	William s. Elizabeth Hall, Newton, illegitimate
"	26	Sarah Ann d. Gideon & Elizabeth Sykes, Newton, weaver
"	26	Sarah d. John & Hannah Warren, Manchester, clogger
"	26	Jane d. James & Henrietta Fletcher, Failsworth, weaver
"	26	Peter s. James & Henrietta Fletcher, Failsworth, weaver
"	28	Joseph s. John & Ellen Stansfield, Manchester, weaver
"	28	Hannah d. Levi & Ellen Clough, Newton, weaver
Mar	5	Alice d. James & Betsey Moston, Moston, farmer
"	5	Sarah d. Joseph & Olive Wylde, Newton, weaver
"	5	Mary d. Thomas & Alice Pollitt, Newton, dyer
"	5	Joshua s. Jonah & Ann Goodier, Newton, shopkeeper
"	6	Mary Wilson d. Robert & Jane Mills, Failsworth, weaver
"	6	James s. James & Ruth Whitehead, Failsworth, weaver
"	16	Mary d. Joseph & Ann Coupland, Newton, shoemaker
"	19	Sarah Ann d. William & Sarah Lane, Failsworth, publican
"	19	Richard s. John & Eliza Brownells, Newton, laborer
"	26	Mary d. John & Elizabeth Walsh, Clayton, dyer
"	26	Mary d. Sally & James Tweedale, Newton, schoolmaster
"	26	James Lees s. Charles & Mary Cordy, Clayton, dyer
"	26	Robert s. Charles & Mary Cordy, Clayton, dyer
"	26	John s. Charles & Betty Sidebottom, Newton, laborer
"	26	Joseph s. William & Alice Butterworth, Manchester, leatherdresser
"	26	Esquire s. John & Betty Gregson, Newton, block printer
"	26	Thomas s. John & Ann Stafford, Clayton, miner
Apr	2	Elizabeth d. Jonathan & Ann Robinson, Failsworth, slater
"	2	Mary Ann d. Bold Bagshaw & Elizabeth Robinson, Manchester, publican
"	2	Elizabeth d. Edward & Alice Berry, Hollinwood, weaver
"	9	Olive d. John & Olive Bardsley, Newton, dyer
"	9	Elizabeth d. Abraham & Ann Collins, Newton, dyer
"	16	Mary d. Abednego & Elizabeth Ashton, Clayton, collier
"	16	John s. James & Mary Darbyshire, Failsworth, fustian cutter
"	18	Isaac s. Isaac & Elizabeth Steele, Clayton, collier
"	23	William s. John & Mary Robinson, Newton, crofter
"	23	James s. Thomas & Mary Steele, Newton, laborer

"	23	Sarah Matilda d. Thomas & Alice Brown, Moston, laborer	*(1837)*
"	30	James s. James & Ann Allen, Newton, laborer	
"	30	Emma d. Edward & Mary Tetlow, Newton, laborer	
May	8	Sarah Ann d. David & Hannah Taylor, Newton, laborer	
"	14	Jane d. William & Mary Butterworth, Newton, weaver	
"	14	Martha d. Peter & Margaret Later, Newton, laborer	
"	14	Charles s. John & Sarah Sidebottom, Newton, laborer	
"	14	William s. Obadiah & Sarah Tippon, Salford, laborer	
"	14	Elizabeth d. Obadiah & Sarah Tippon, Salford, laborer	
"	14	Hannah d. William & Catharine Etchells, Droylsden, bricklayer	
"	14	William s. James & Mary Ann Brown, Newton, bricklayer	
"	16	Jane d. Mark Robinson & Ellen Carter, Newton, tinplate worker	
"	18	William Hardy s. John & Elizabeth Mercy Ashworth, Newton, silk manufacturer, bo Mar 30 1837	
"	21	Matthew s. Henry & Betty Brown, Newton, laborer	
"	21	Peter s. James & Patience Carter, Newton, cotton spinner	
"	21	Elizabeth d. Daniel & Alice Chadderton, Failsworth, navigator	
"	21	Solomon s. Josiah & Alice Etchells, Failsworth, weaver	
"	21	Henry s. Thomas & Mary Ann Barrett, Newton, printer	
"	24	Agnes d. John & Elizabeth Webster, Newton, attorney at law	
"	24	Henry s. William & Sarah Marsden, Newton, bleacher	
"	25	Frances d. Joseph & Frances Gawkroger, Newton (*occupation blank in PR & BT*)	
"	25	Joseph s. Joseph & Sarah Whitehead, Failsworth, weaver	
Jun	2	Ann d. Charles & Sarah Fletcher, Culcheth, book keeper	
"	4	Joseph s. Joseph & Eliza Smethurst, Manchester, currier	
"	4	John s. David & Sarah Hilton, Failsworth, bleacher	
"	4	Sarah d. James & Alice Bardsley, Failsworth, weaver	
"	4	Mary d. Joseph & Ann Andrews, Failsworth, weaver	
"	4	Elizabeth d. James & Phebe Howard, Failsworth, weaver	
"	4	Ellen d. Benjamin & Ann Ogden, Failsworth, dyer	
"	4	Mary Ann d. Robert & Mary Jackson, Newton, printer	
"	4	Ann d. John & Mary Higham, Newton, wheelwright	
"	4	Mary d. Robert & Martha Minshull, Newton, cotton spinner	
"	5	John s. Richard & Alice Dawson, Failsworth, dyer	
"	5	Ann d. William & Sarah Bardsley, Failsworth, dyer	
"	5	Martha d. Samuel & Sarah Hardy, Newton, dyer	
"	11	Josiah Borlase s. Josiah & Mary Barnes Holt, Manchester, tobacconist	
"	11	Philip s. John & Esther Hammersley, Newton, fustian cutter	
"	11	Mary Ann d. William & Prudence Lockett, fustian cutter, Failsworth	
"	11	Joseph s. George & Sarah Ogden, Droylsden, bricklayer	
"	11	Eliza d. James & Elizabeth Hall, Newton, skein dyer	
"	16	Joseph Todd s. James & Mary Ann Orrell, Culcheth, bleacher	
"	18	Alice d. Joseph & Ann Taylor, bo 21 May 1837 (*abode & occupation blank in PR & BT*)	
"	18	Edward s. John & Sarah Marsden (*abode & occupation blank in PR & BT*)	

"	18	Esther Maria d. Thomas & Martha Prest (*abode & occupation blank in PR & BT*)
"	18	John s. James & Ellen Lister, Christened at the age of about five years (*abode & occupation blank in PR & BT*)
"	25	Abel s. George & Mary Andrews, Newton, baker
"	25	Rachel d. Cornelius & Rachel Yates, Newton, bleacher
"	25	Eli s. Samuel & Martha Rostron, Newton, printer
"	25	Margaret d. Matthew & Hannah Howarth, Newton, shopkeeper
"	25	Hannah d. Joseph & Hannah Bardsley, block cutter, Droylsden
"	25	Richard Thomas s. Charles & Sarah Cooke, farmer, Ashton
"	25	Sarah Ann d. James & Rebecca Yates, laborer, Manchester
"	25	Samuel s. John & Hannah Smith, weaver, Failsworth
"	25	Elizabeth d. Jonathan & Hannah Chadderton, weaver, Failsworth
"	25	James s. Samuel & Mary Lord, Failsworth, block cutter
"	25	Martha d. Isaac & Elizabeth Heapey, Ashton, hatter
"	25	Elizabeth d. John & Elizabeth Smith, Newton, slater
Jul	2	William s. Robert & Elizabeth Ratcliff, Newton, dyer
"	2	Samuel s. William & Nanny Dawson, Newton, warper
"	2	Jane d. William & Jane Etchells, Newton, joiner
"	2	Samuel s. Joel & Agnes Berry, Failsworth, shoemaker
"	2	Jane d. William & Jane Etchells, Newton, joiner
"	2	Joseph s. Joseph & Mary Scott, Newton, boatman
"	2	John s. Joseph & Mary Scott, Newton, boatman
"	2	Nancy d. John & Martha MacInvenna, Gorton, overlooker
"	2	Ann d. William & Mary Ann Holt, Newton, blacksmith, bo May 28 1837
"	2	Priscilla d. Joseph & Priscilla Fletcher, Newton, weaver
"	2	Sarah Ann d. Richard & Sarah Tetlow, Newton, laborer
"	9	Emily Jane d. Thomas & Esther Kershaw, Manchester, hatter
"	9	Elizabeth d. John & Nancy Whittaker, Failsworth, weaver
"	9	Sarah Ann d. Joseph & Betty Berry, Failsworth, weaver
"	9	Sarah Ann d. John & Mary Duckworth, Newton, printer
"	9	Sarah d. James & Hannah Wright, Openshaw, saddler
"	16	Eliza d. Ophelia Holland, Failsworth, illegitimate
"	16	Joseph s. Hannah Etchells, Failsworth
"	16	Francis s. Thomas & Sarah Greene, Droylsden, shoemaker
"	23	Alice d. John & Hannah Smith, Newton, laborer
"	23	James s. William & Elizabeth Williamson, Newton, weaver
"	23	Ebenezer Williams s. Thomas & Ann Logan, Newton, weaver
"	23	John Williams s. Thomas & Ann Logan, Newton, weaver
"	23	Susanna d. John & Ann Sykes, Droylsden, miner
"	26	James s. Joseph & Mary Entwistle, weaver, bo Dec 12 1819
"	26	Martha d. Joseph & Mary Entwistle, bo Aug 5 1822
"	30	William s. George & Sarah Parkinson, Droylsden, warehouseman, bo Apr 19 1835
"	30	Alice d. Joseph & Phebe Barlow, Failsworth, brickmaker

"	30	Samuel s. James & Betty Derby, Hollinwood, miller (*1837*)
"	30	Charles s. Horatio Nelson & Mary Collinson, Failsworth, weaver
"	31	John Collin s. Samuel & Ann Williamson, Droylsden, dyer, bo 19 Jul 1837
Aug	4	John Alexander s. Walter & Cherry Young, Salford, engineer
"	6	Ann d. Elijah & Jane Pollitt, Newton, weaver
"	6	Thomas s. William & Charlotte Hooley, Hooley Hill, hat maker
"	6	Sarah d. Thomas & Mary Whitehead, Moston, weaver
"	6	James Bishop s. David & Charlotte Miller, Failsworth, plasterer
"	6	Lavinia d. James & Esther Barnes, Newton, laborer
"	6	William s. Ann Wilson, Moston, illegitimate
"	6	George s. Ann Travis, Newton, illegitimate
"	6	William s. Sarah Heywood, Moston, illegitimate
"	6	Mary Ann d. Charles & Elizabeth Hesford, Clayton, dyer
"	13	Betty d. James & Sarah Robinson, Newton, porter
"	13	William Thomas s. John & Jane Ashworth, Chorlton upon Medlock, weaver
"	13	Susanna d. Mark & Millicent Gradwell, Stockport, calico printer
"	13	Esther Ann d. William & Ann Spence, Droylsden, coachman
"	13	Thomas s. John & Ann Ward, laborer, Newton
"	13	Elizabeth d. Jonathan & Sarah Goodier, laborer, Culcheth
"	13	George s. James & Sarah Wilson, weaver, Newton
"	20	Elizabeth d. John & Esther Dewhurst, weaver, Failsworth
"	20	John s. Richard & Susan Taylor, warper, Failsworth
"	20	Dan s. Luke & Nancy Etchells, weaver, Failsworth
"	20	Jane d. Thomas & Sally Schofield, weaver, Failsworth
"	20	Sarah d. Peter & Mary Wylde, laborer, Failsworth
"	20	William s. Edwin & Ann Makin, Moston, bleacher
"	20	Ellen d. John & Martha O'Neile, Failsworth, laborer
"	20	Sarah d. Zachariah & Ann Robinson, Manchester, weaver
"	20	Mary d. John & Lucy Bateman, Newton, joiner
"	20	Robert s. Sarah Lees, Newton, illegitimate
"	27	Robert s. Richard & Mary Rostron, Newton, printer
"	27	David s. John & Emma Schofield, Manchester, laborer
Sep	6	Joseph s. James & Jemima Taylor, Failsworth
"	7	William s. Richard & Veluria Fishwick, Newton
"	10	Selina d. George & Mary Whittaker, Failsworth, hatter
"	10	Edward s. John & Ann Owen, Newton, engraver
"	10	John s. William & Mary Robinson, Failsworth, printer
"	10	Ann d. John & Olive Brown, Newton (*occupation blank in PR & BT*)
"	10	Betty d. James & Jane Hesketh, Failsworth, laborer
"	10	Sarah Anne d. Joseph & Jane Gibson, Newton, laborer
"	17	Sidney Samuel s. Charles & Isabella Ridings, Newton, shopkeeper
"	17	Edwin s. Charles & Lavinia Barnes, Manchester, traveller
"	17	James s. Joseph & Elizabeth Kenworthy, Newton (*occupation blank in PR & BT*)
"	17	Thomas s. William & Alice Hall, Hollinwood, silk weaver
"	17	Sarah Ann d. Samuel & Ann Schofield, Hollinwood, weaver, bo 25 Feb 1818

"	22	William s. Ann Kershaw, illegitimate	(*1837*)
"	24	John s. John & Esther Ditchfield, Newton, laborer	
"	24	Edward s. Samuel & Mary Royle, Newton, weaver	
"	24	Emma d. William & Mary Harris, Failsworth, laborer	
"	24	Eliza d. William & Mary Harris, Failsworth, laborer	
"	24	Elizabeth d. William & Mary Harris, Failsworth, laborer	
"	29	Elizabeth d. James & Mary Ogden, Failsworth, weaver	
Oct	1	Nicholas s. Nicholas & Margaret Edge, Failsworth, block cutter	
"	1	George s. Isabella Bown, Newton, illegitimate	
"	1	Thomas s. Levi & Charlotte Sudworth, Manchester, laborer	
"	8	William s. James Horatio Nelson & Ann Hulton, Failsworth, laborer	
"	13	Joseph s. John & Jane Hulme, Colleyhurst, shopkeeper	
"	15	John s. William Heathcote & Mary Hulton, Failsworth, weaver	
"	15	Thomas Ashton s. Thomas & Jane Bates, Failsworth, bleacher	
"	15	Edwin s. Joseph & Mary Arundale, Droylsden, bricklayer	
"	19	Agnes d. George & Hannah Robinson, Salford, grocer	
"	22	John s. Elizabeth Haywood, Failsworth	
"	22	Elizabeth d. William & Harriett Wellock, Newton, farmer	
"	22	William s. William & Eliza Harding, Failsworth, bleacher	
"	22	Samuel s. Samuel & Elizabeth Gradwell, Newton, weaver	
"	22	Frances d. James & Elizabeth Howarth, Newton, shopkeeper	
"	22	Emma d. Samuel & Ann Tetlow, Culcheth, mason	
"	31	Samuel s. James & Sarah Mather, Newton, weaver	
Nov	2	James s. Philip & Mary Houlton, Newton, farmer	
"	5	Thomas s. Thomas & Sarah Thornley, Failsworth, publican	
"	19	Joseph s. John & Betty Hyde, Newton, farmer	
"	26	William Bland s. Joseph & Mary Barrow, Newton, farmer	
"	26	James s. Robert & Helen Percival, Failsworth, weaver	
"	26	Thomas s. Thomas & Hannah Hogg, Newton, spinner	
"	26	Elizabeth d. John & Mary Ann Smith, Failsworth, weaver	
Dec	3	William s. James & Jane Hancock, Salford, pattern designer	
"	3	Martha d. James & Mary Brown, Newton, bricklayer	
"	10	Elizabeth Sarah d. John & Isabella Morris, Culcheth, laborer	
"	10	James s. Samuel & Jane Graves, Newton, farmer	
"	10	John s. Matthew & Sarah Smith, Newton, laborer	
"	10	John Henry s. James & Mary Trevor, Failsworth, taylor	
"	10	Elijah s. John & Alice Hyde, Moston, weaver	
"	10	Emma d. William & Mary Ann Davies, Newton, laborer	
"	17	Alfred s. James & Judith Williamson, Openshaw, dyer	
"	24	Mary d. James & Mary Johnson, Moston, farmer	
"	25	Martha d. John & Ann Stones, Newton, silk throwster	
"	31	Samuel s. Samuel & Mary Lees, Failsworth, weaver	
"	31	Elizabeth d. Lancelot & Ann Hogg, Droylsden, cotton spinner	
"	31	Robert William s. Johnathan & Amelia Taylor, Culcheth, bleacher	
"	31	Joseph s. John & Jane Smith, Newton, weaver	

"   31   Richard s. William & Hannah Wilson, Newton, spinner
"   31   Ann d. Betty Ogden, Hollinwood, illegitimate
[Wm Hutchinson Minister April 27 1838.   ]
               Witness Abr Taylor Chapel Warden   ]

(The following entries record births prior to 1838, searching to December 1842:)

1838

Bapt.		Born	
Apr	15	Feb 14 1822	Harry s. John & Mary Barber, miller (*place blank in PR & BT*)
"	15	Mar 27 1820	Thamar d. John & Mary Barber, miller (*place blank in PR & BT*)
"	29	Dec 1 1822	Hannah d. Alexander & Mary Smith (*place & occupation blank in PR & BT*)
May	20	Jun 21 1832	Jane d. James & Ann Coe, Manchester, hatter (*place blank in PR & BT*)
Jun	8	Dec 5 1837	Julianne d. John & Ann Coupe, pattern designer (*place blank in PR & BT*)
Jul	18	May 7 1835	Samuel s. John & Elizabeth Howles, Newton printer
Sep	4	Jan 30 1837	Amos Ezekiel s. Amos Ezekiel & Sarah Jackson, Newton (*occupation blank in PR & BT*)

1839

Jan	13	Sep 8 1823	Mary Anne d. Richard & Esther Thorpe, Moston, weaver
May	30	Jan 22 1837	Sarah Anne d. William & Mary Anne Lees, Newton, publican
Jul	21	Mar 25 1831	Anne d. John & Sarah Wood, Failsworth, silk weaver

1841

Sep	19	Oct 17 1822	Mary d. Edwd. & Mary Rothwell, Newton, joiner
Oct	10	Aug n.d. 1824	Sarah d. Edwd. & Mary Rothwell, Newton, joiner

Burials

Burials in 1797

Jan	1	Thomas s. John & Barbara Burgess, labourer, fits, M., 5 m
"	1	Mary w. John Williamson, labourer, child bed, Failsworth, 25 y
"	2	William s. William & Ellen Cliffe, spinner, fever, M., 19 y
"	6	Charlotte d. Nancy Davies, fits, Newton, 22 y
"	8	Robert s. John & Mary Fishburne, worm fever, M., 7 y
"	11	Elizabeth d. Bernard & Anne Rice, weaver, small pox, M., 1 y 4 m
"	15	Martha w. William Sanderson, sawyer, weak, M., 39 y
"	16	Sarah Orrit, widow, Failsworth, 83 y
"	21	Peter s. Isaac & Margaret Dean, husbandman, weak, Failsworth, 4 y 4 m
"	26	Sarah d. Richard & Mary Thorp, farmer, swelling of lungs, (Woodhouses *not in BT*) Ashton Parish, 2 y 14 days
"	27	John Walmsley, farmer, Moston, 76 y
"	31	John s. John & Elizabeth Mather, innkeeper, weak, M., 2 m
"	31	Sarah d. Joseph & Abigail Rigley, gardener, Newton
"	31	Mary d. Jonathan & Mary Schofield, weaver, Failsworth
"	31	Betty d. Samuel & Betty Yeld, weaver, Failsworth
Feb	6	Thomas s. John & Martha Hulton, weaver, Failsworth
"	8	John Berry, farmer, consumption, Failsworth, 56 y
"	12	Betty d. James & Betty Jammenson, cotton weaver, decline, M., 2 y 9 m
"	26	Samuel s. James & Sarah Warren, weaver, fits, M., 6 m
"	26	Sarah d. William & Mary Patten, weaver, weak, M., 5 y 3 m
"	26	Mary d. Thomas & Anne Gaunt, farmer, weak, M., 36 y
"	27	William Sudworth, M., 83 y
Mar	3	Betty d. John & Sarah Fletcher, smith, convulsions, M., 4 m 14 days
"	5	John s. John & Betty Walker, weaver, swelling of throat, M., 4 y 5 m
"	5	Elizabeth d. David & Anne Ainsworth, weaver, small pox, M., 3 y
"	5	Mary d. William & Sarah Taylor, husbandman, tooth fever, M., 1 y
"	6	Theophilus Ogden, weaver, Cutler Hill Ashton Parish, 78 y

"	8	William s. Philip [&] Amy Newall, weak, M., 5 m
"	8	Mary Hulme [, widow], weaver, 66 y
"	9	Anne Rothwell, widow, Newton, 83 y
"	10	Jane d. Joseph & Anne Horrocks, calico printer, accident, Coroner's Wart., M., 4 y
"	10	William s. James & Anne Allen, weaver, Coroner's Warrant, Failsworth, 4 y
"	13	Margaret d. James & Betty Montgomery, weaver, weak, M., 1 y
"	14	Richard s. James & Anne Allen, weaver, Failsworth
"	14	Mary d. George & Anne Willis, spinner, weak, M., 9 m
"	15	William s. Richard & Frances Sheldon, sawyer, small pox, M., 2 y
"	15	John s. Richard & Jane Smith, weaver, fever, M., 12 y
"	17	Thomas s. John & Anne Ridd [Rudd], cotton spinner, weak, Failsworth, 15 y 1 m
"	22	Jane w. James Wardley, weaver, weak, M., 31 y
"	23	Mary w. James Tomlinson, weaver, weak, Failsworth, 37 y
"	26	Elizabeth w. Edward Walker, husbandman, Newton, 75 y
"	27	Lydia d. Joseph & Alice Kirkham, weaver, small pox, M., 1 y 3 m
"	28	William s. John & Mary Lister, collier, fits, M., 6 m
"	29	Alice d. James & Alice Walmsley, farmer, weak, Failsworth, 24 y
"	29	John s. Ashton & Mary Shepley, weaver, swelling of lungs, Failsworth, 1 y 6 m
Apr	2	Esther d. Alexander & Mary Graves, weaver, Failsworth
"	5	Sarah d. John & Susannah Crook, dyer, Coroner's Warrant, M., 3 y
"	5	John s. John & Sarah Cunningham, fustian cutter, fever, M., 1 y 4 m
"	8	Samuel s. Thomas & Sally Frost, cotton spinner, small pox, Holt Town M., 3 y
"	8	Anne d. John & Catharine Morgan, sawyer, swelling of lungs, M., 9 m
"	9	William s. Mary Fish, swelling of lungs, M., 7 m
"	11	John Chadderton, weaver, Failsworth, 92 y 2 m
"	12	Martha d. Thomas & Sarah Randles, spinner, tooth fever, M., 1 y
"	14	Edward s. William & Catharine Nixon, cabinet-maker, teeth, M., 1 y 7 m
"	14	Felicia w. Thomas Boote, brickmaker, consumption, M., 42 y
"	16	Thomas s. Anthony & Ruth Myers, dyer, M., 2 y 9 m
"	18	Anne Dawson, widow, M., 80 y
"	19	Thomas s. James & Ellen Taylor, weaver, consumption, (Woodhouses *not in BT*) Ashton Parish, 33 y
"	19	Thomas s. John & Anne Jacks, collier, swelling of lungs, Oldham, 2 y
"	21	James s. Ralph & Hannah Chatterton, collier, M., 1 y 10 m
"	22	Hannah w. Robert Bowker, weaver, decline, M., 63 y
"	27	James s. Michael & Nancy Russel, spinner, small pox, M., 2 y 6 m
[		The above is an accurate Copy of the Register at Newton Heath Chapel]
[		Witness A. Ashworth Minister]
[		(*blank*) Ch. Wardens]

May	2	Mary d. John & Mary Bell, weaver, small pox, M., 1 y
"	3	Joseph Wolstenhulme, well sinker, M., 32 y
"	7	Elizabeth w. Matthew Field, shoemaker, decline, M., 26 y
"	7	William spurious s. Hannah Gillibrand, Failsworth, 21 days
"	7	Martha d. Samuel & Mary Wyatt, weaver, weak, M., 17 y
"	7	Sarah d. David & Hannah Ainsworth, weaver, small pox, M., 1 y 10 m
"	7	James s. John & Elizabeth Barlow, weaver, Failsworth, 6 m
"	15	William s. Thomas & Mary Manfield, decline, M., 7 m
"	15	Hannah d. Joseph & Nancy Taylor, blacksmith, fits, M., 3 y 8 m
"	17	Elizabeth d. Thomas & Hannah Gradwell, weaver, meazles, M., 6 y
"	20	Theophilus Wolstenholme, weaver, surfeit, M., 66 y
"	22	George s. Joseph & Anne Priestnall, warehouseman, blister'd lung, M., 2 y 3 m
"	26	George Barlow, weaver, Coroners Warrant, Failsworth, 61 y
"	30	Anne Booth (wdw. William Booth *not in BT*), Failsworth, 77 y
"	31	Hannah w. Jonathan Butterworth, weaver, M., 60 y
"	31	Betty [Elizth] d. Thomas & Nancy Higson, weaver, convulsions, M., 4 m
Jun	4	Edward O'Brian [O'Bryan], taylor, Coroner's Wart., M., 40 y
"	4	William Clough, weaver, consumption, Failsworth, 56 y
"	6	Thomas s. Thomas & Alice Stafford, collier, Coroner's Wart., M., 2 y 1 m 15 days
"	11	Robert s. John & Nancy Carr, spinner, small pox, M., 10 m
"	13	Mary d. Thomas & Agnes Jameson, joiner, weak, M., 3 y 10 m
"	13	Elizabeth d. William & Anne Inman, weaver, measles, M., 1 y 2 m
"	13	Martha d. William & Mary Blackshaw, whitster, weak, Openshaw, 20 y 1m
"	16	Samuel s. James & Anne Watson, husbandman, Bradford, 1 y 2 m
"	25	Anne d. Bartholomew & Sarah Reed, weaver, small pox, M., 1 y 10 m
"	25	Elizabeth d. Thomas & Judith Hancock, weaver, small pox, M., 2 y 7 m
"	25	James Lees, weaver, paral., M., 63 y
"	26	James s. Isaac & Sarah Fitton, weaver, consumption, Failsworth, 26 y
"	29	Mary d. Thomas & Elizabeth Robinson, weaver, weak, Newton, 5 y 9 m
Jul	1	Nancy w. Robert Williamson, gardener, weak, Failsworth, 30 y
"	4	Jennett d. Gilbert & Greswell McKay, consumption, M., 25 y
"	7	Catharine d. Abraham & Elizabeth Robinson, warper, Droylsden, 1 day
"	7	George s. George & Sarah Firth, cotton spinner, water in brain, M., 2 y 6m
"	9	James s. James & Mary Whitehead, weaver, decline, M., 19 y
"	13	Alice d. John & Elizabeth Lees, cotton spinner, small pox, M., 2 y
"	15	Mary d. John & Mary Medcalf, carder, small pox, M., 2 y 5 m
"	17	Mary Shore, consumption, Newton, 22 y
"	23	Joseph Whitehead, blacksmith, weak, M., 55 y
"	24	Elizabeth d. Thomas Travis, weaver, fever, Culcheth Newton, 15 y
"	25	Charles Clue s. William & Margaret Fletcher, smith, measles, M., 1 y 5 m
"	30	Alice O'Nield sp. d. Betty Whitworth, fits, M., 6 m

Aug	7	Mary Walker, widow, M., 70 y (*1797*)
"	9	Agnes w. Rowland Wilson, cotton spinner, weak, M., 54 y
"	10	Anne d. James & Anne Blackley, consumption, M., 20 y
"	10	James Connor spurious s. Anne Hall, weak, M., 5 m
"	13	John McClue, consumption, M., 31 y
["	13	Joseph s. Thos & Charlotte Gallymore, M. (*entry in BT only*)]
"	19	Anne d. Andrew & Elizabeth Lane, cotton manufacturer, dropsy, M.,7 y 1m
"	20	Henry s. William & Isabella Sherratt, mule spinner, tooth fever, M., 9 m
"	25	Charles s. Edmund McKay, small pox, M., 7 m
"	25	Alice d. John & Betty [Elizth] Mills, labourer, fits, Newton, 1 y 8 m
"	27	Sarah d. James & Mary Butterworth, weaver, weak, M., 7 m
"	27	John s. John & Elizabeth Smith, weaver, fits, Failsworth, 18 y 1 m 7 days
"	27	John Haslam, harness knitter, weak, Failsworth, 77 y
"	28	Alice w. Robert Finch, labourer, cancer, Failsworth, 45 y
"	30	William s. James & Elizabeth Hall, spinner, M., 2 m 21 days
Sep	7	William Torrins, (weaver *struck through*) tailor, consumption, Failsworth, 24 y
"	10	James s. William & Catharine Taylor, smith, fits, M., 7 y 6 m
"	11	Margaret d. Joseph & Anne Horrocks, calico printer, weak, M., 9 m
"	11	Esther w. John Clough, weaver, child bed, Failsworth, 36 y
"	18	Mary Lancaster, widow, weak, Droylsden, 72 y 6 m
"	20	James s. William & Alice Entwisle, weaver, small pox, M., 8 m
"	23	James s. James & Sarah Tomlinson, weaver, dropsy, Moston, 4 y
"	24	Anne d. Joseph & Barbara Burgess, labourer, weak, M., 16 y
"	25	Joseph s. James & Alice Ruddock, weaver, small pox, M., 9 m
"	27	Elizabeth d. Levi & Mary Whitehead, writer, weak, M., 9 m
Oct	4	Robert s. Robert & Catharine Jones, filer, small pox, M., 1 y 6 m
"	8	Mary d. Edward & Martha Whitehead, bricklayer, weak, Droylsden, 6 m
"	9	John s. Thomas & Frances Andrew, cotton spinner, small pox, M., 10 m
"	9	William s. James & Jane Whitehead, weaver, decline, M., 11 m
"	22	Nancy w. Henry Richardson, drysalter, fever, M., 23 y
"	23	Hannah d. William & Anne Orme, spinner, M., 13 days
"	23	Mary d. Robert & Christian Robinson, weaver, weak, M., 1 y
"	25	Joseph s. Jeremiah & Dorothy Buxton, butcher, accident, M., 13 y
"	27	Mary d. James & Elizabeth Moors, labourer, swelling of lungs, M., 9 m
"	28	Amelia w. Edward Allen, asthma, Collyhurst, 61 y
"	30	Mary d. John & Hannah Whittaker, small pox, M., 1 y 1 m
"	31	Mary d. John & Mary Davidson, cotton spinner, M., 3 days
Nov	1	Sarah d. Jeremiah & Dorothy Buxton, butcher, small pox, M., 2 y
"	2	William s. Henry & Elizabeth Finch, forgeman, small pox, M., 7 y 6 m
"	6	William s. Richard & Mary Smaller, weaver, M., 1 m 7 days
"	6	Ruth w. John Crossley, farmer, dropsy, Newton, 34 y
"	7	Hannah d. James & Elizabeth Moors, labourer, swelling of lungs, M., 2 y 9
"	10	David s. William & Anne Torrins, taylor, fits, Failsworth, 10 m

"	12	Whitnall s. James & Mary Bradley, founderer, weak, M., 2 y
"	13	Margaret d. Samuel & Sarah Taylor, cotton spinner, small pox, M., 7 m
"	19	Thomas s. Thomas & Martha Ashton, weaver, swelling of lungs, Failsworth, 5 y
"	19	Samuel s. Samuel & Sarah Taylor, cotton spinner, small pox, M., 2 y 8 m
"	19	Deborah d. Thomas & Charlotte Gallymore, weaver, small pox, M., 5 m
"	21	Mary d. James & Mary Whittaker, weaver, small pox, Failsworth, 3 y
"	21	Alice w. Thomas Rydings, weaver, child bed, Failsworth, 30 y
"	26	Catharine w. Patrick Plunket, cotton weaver, decline, M., 38 y
"	26	Mary d. David & Alice Foden, weaver, consumption, M., 5 m
"	29	Philip Berry, cotton spinner, fever, M., 32 y
"	30	Harriet d. Thomas & Mary Dean, husbandman, Failsworth
"	30	Israel s. James & Phebe Hulme, weaver, meazles, Failsworth, 1 y 7 m
"	30	Henry s. Joseph & Grace Goose, husbandman, small pox, M., 7 m
Dec	1	Frances d. John & Mary Plimmer, collier, measles, M., 1 y 6 m
"	3	Sarah d. Jeremiah & Martha Kemp, warper, swelling of lungs, M., 11 m
"	3	Sarah d. James & Martha Kemp, weaver, swelling of lungs, M., 5 y
"	6	Mary d. William & Mary [Margt] Crompton, weaver, small pox, M., 1 y 9 m
"	8	Anne d. James & Esther Ogden, farmer, Moston, 3 days
"	8	Lemuel s. Joshua & Mary Smith, weaver, small pox, Failsworth, 4 y 6 m
"	10	Hannah d. Robert & Mary Inman, joiner, small pox, M., 1 y 8 m
"	11	Abraham s. Abraham & Margaret Ogden, weaver, small pox, M., 2 y 11 m
"	12	Alexander s. James & Betty [Elizth] Clough, weaver, small pox, Failsworth, 11 m 21 days
"	15	Mary w. John Robinson [, Droylsden]
"	15	Jane d. Philip & Margaret Forshaw, joiner, measles, M., 2 y 5 m
"	17	Daniel s. Daniel & Betty [Elizth] Ashton, weaver, small pox, Failsworth, 1 y 9 m
"	17	Joseph s. Daniel & Anne Knott, weaver, small pox, M., 1 y 3 m
"	19	Margaret w. Philip Forshaw, joiner, fever, M., 34 y
"	19	John s. Joseph & Sarah Berry, blacksmith, swelling of lungs, Failsworth, 7y
"	20	John s. John & Mary Williamson, swelling of lungs (Cutler Hill *not in BT*) Ashton Parish, 1 y 8 days
"	22	George s. Luke & Catharine Weatherbed, cotton spinner, quinsey, M., 1 y 7 m
"	23	Nancy d. James & Alice Howarth, weaver, small pox, Failsworth, 1 y 3 m
"	24	Isabella w. Peter Fegan, dyer, bowels, M., 46 y
"	24	Rhoda Anne d. William & Anne Harlow, taylor, quinsey, M., 4 y 6 m
"	24	Mary Anne d. Thomas & Dorothy Orme, cotton-spinner, weak, M., 3 m
"	24	Jane d. Robert & Betty [Elizth] Whitehead, weaver, weak, Failsworth, 6 m
"	28	James s. John & Peggy [Margt] Holt, farmer, consumption, Failsworth, 14 y 6 m
"	28	Betty [Elizth] w. John Mills, labourer, consumption, Newton, 27 y 11 m
"	29	James s. Thomas & Alice Rydings, weaver, small pox, Failsworth, 4 y 6 m

" 31   Jacob s. Jacob & Betty [Elizth] Wolsencroft, weaver, surfeit, M., 16 y

" 31   John s. Samuel & Mary Etchells, weaver, small pox, Failsworth, 1 y 9 m

Burials in 1798

Jan	2	Catharine w. Luke Weatherill, cotton spinner, child bed, M., 26 y
"	3	Betty [Elizth] d. William & Anne Schofield, weaver, fits, Droylsden, 7 m
"	7	John s. James & Sarah Warren, weaver, measles, M., 4 y
"	7	Mary d. John & Esther Etchells, weaver, small pox, Failsworth, 2 y
"	10	Abraham s. John & Sarah Clough, weaver, small pox, Failsworth, 2 y 3 m
"	12	Mary d. Joseph & Sarah Fish, weaver, swelling of lungs, M., 1 y 8 m
"	14	John Taylor, weaver, dropsy & jaundice, Cheetham, 63 y
"	14	Mary d. John & Jane Rydings, weaver, small pox, Failsworth, 9 m
"	14	Mary Spencer, widow, Culcheth Newton, 80 y
"	14	James s. James & Esther Beswick, labourer, swelling of lungs, M., 1 y 2 m
"	15	John s. James & Anne Whitehead, weaver, small pox, Failsworth, 3 y 6 m
"	23	John s. Samuel & Phebe Ainsworth, hatter, fits, Newton, 2 m 21 days
"	24	Joseph s. Charles & Mary Watson, painter, worm fever, M., 1 y 3 m
"	24	Anne d. James & Ellen Makin, weaver, small pox, M., 10 m
"	28	Samuel s. Samuel & Ellen Rigby, engineer, chincough, Bradford, 5 y
"	28	Benjamin s. Samuel & Jane Thomas, cotton spinner, fits, M., 5 m
"	28	George s. John & Jane McClen, cotton spinner, fever, M., 4 y 4 m
"	31	Martha d. John & Anne Goulding, husbandman, fever, M., 6 y
Feb	4	Joshua s. Ralph & Elizabeth Burchell, weaver, small pox, Failsworth, 11 m 7 days
"	8	Joseph s. James & Betty [Elizth] Smith, weaver, small pox, Failsworth, 3 y
"	12	Peter s. Peter & Sarah Owen, labourer, small pox, Ardwick, 8 m
"	13	Joseph Ogden, weaver, Failsworth, 88 y 11 m
"	13	George s. Joseph & Tabitha Tinker, weaver, Moston, 5 days
"	22	Barbara w. John Greenhough, collier, child bed, M., 42 y
"	22	Sarah Clough, widow, weakness, Failsworth, 49 y
"	24	Mary d. John & Sarah Whitehead, collier, fits, M., 9 m
"	24	Robert Ogden, weaver, Woodhouses, 51 y
Mar	4	John s. James & Mary Harrison, cotton manufacturer, weak, M., 1 y 10 m
"	4	James s. Bridget Ramsbottom [Ramsbotham], weak, M., 10 m
"	4	William Smethurst, husbandman, Failsworth, 77 y
"	5	Grace w. Henry Dunn, cotton spinner, consumption, M., 30 y
"	7	James Wroe, weaver, palsy, Failsworth, 63 y
"	18	Joseph s. Thomas & Susannah Smith, dyer, scurvy, M., 19 y
"	18	Thomas s. James & Alice Eckersley, weaver, small pox, Failsworth, 2 y
"	20	Sarah d. John & Anne Eckersley, weaver, small pox, Failsworth, 2 y
"	21	George s. Meredith & Fanny [Frances] McConnell, Coroners Warrant, M., 10 y
"	21	Ellen d. William & Mary Patten, brewer, decline, M., 21 y
"	22	George s. James & Dorothy Coe, cotton carder, weakness, M., 2 y

"	23	Edward s. Thomas & Sarah Walmsley, farmer, weakness, Failsworth, 2 m 14 days *(1798)*
"	23	James s. John & Sarah Ogden, weaver, small pox, Failsworth, 3 y 2 m 14 days
"	27	Sarah Walmsley, widow, consumption, Newton, 65 y
Apr	1	Mary Anne d. Robert & Anne Williams, blacksmith, weak, M., 9 m
"	1	Mary Anne d. John & Hannah Gregory, cotton spinner, weak, M., 1 y 1 m
"	3	Elizabeth w. Thomas Cunliffe, labourer, consumption, Newton, 33 y
"	4	David Roberts, dyer, consumption, M., 35 y
"	6	John s. John & Mary Thorp, weaver, decline, Moston, 1 y 7 m 21 days
"	8	Alice d. Joseph & Elizabeth Chambers, copperplate printer, teeth, M., 1 y 4 m
"	8	William s. William & Sarah Dean, dyer, M., 3 y
"	12	Samuel s. Joseph & Sarah Berry, smith, small pox, Failsworth, 2 y
"	12	Eleanora d. Alexander & Ellen Sloan, shoe maker, M., 9 m
"	15	George s. Benjamin & Anne Ridgard, joiner, weak, M., 13 y
"	15	Anne spu. d. Martha Lee, small pox, M., 2 y
"	15	John s. Joseph & Betty [Elizth] Sharpe, taylor, decline, Failsworth, 7 y
"	15	Alice Wood, widow, fever, M., 59 (*or* 69) y
"	16	Rose d. Edward & Susannah Campbell, taylor, teeth, M., 10 m
"	17	Thomas s. Thomas & Elizabeth Dickens, weaver, inflamation, Culcheth [Newton], 10 m
[		Copied from the Register at Newton Heath]
[		A. Ashworth Minister]
[		(*blank*) Chapel Wardens]
"	23	Joseph Wilkinson, cotton spinner, accident, Coroner's Wart., M., 45 y
"	23	Martha d. John & Elizabeth Clarkson, sawyer, consumption, M., 14 y
"	25	Anne d. John & Mary Dawson, printer, weakness, M., 13 y
"	25	Jonathan s. Jonathan & Ellen Thorp, weaver, small pox, Failsworth, 4 y
"	30	Hannah d. William & Rhoda Friend, weaver, weak, M., 1 y 3 m
May	2	Mary d. Richard & Ellen Atkin, joiner, consumption, M., 11 y
"	2	George s. George & Sarah Harrison, whitster, weak, Newton, 2 m 7 days
"	2	Mary d. Thomas & Alice Gorton, joiner, small pox, Failsworth, 7 m
"	6	Martha d. Edward & Mary Williams, hatter, tooth fever, M., 1 y
"	6	James spu. s. Martha Smith, Failsworth, 1 y 5 days
"	6	William s. John & Esther Taylor, small pox, Failsworth, 1 y 1 m
"	10	John & Thomas twin ss. Thomas & Hannah Elli[n]son, miner, weak, M., 14 days
"	11	Edward s. John & Jane Yates, weaver, weak, Failsworth, 1 y
"	13	Sarah w. George Lamb, calico printer, child bed, Newton, 24 y
"	13	Margaret d. Thomas & Mary Roberts, collier, weak, M., 3 days
"	16	Mary Butterworth, consumption, M., 75 y
"	20	John s. Ralph & Anne Mather, weaver, weak, Droylsden, 2 y
"	23	Elizabeth w. James Beswick, whitster, weak, Newton, 78 y
"	28	William s. William & Catharine Taylor, smith, small pox, Salford, 1 y

"	29	Thomas Wood, small ware weaver, asthma, M., 38 y (*1798*)
"	29	Margaret w. Peter Downs, labourer, dropsy, M., 49 y
Jun	5	Anne d. James & Sarah Boardman, weaver, fever, M., 5 y 3 m
"	12	Elizabeth d. John & Judeth Leigh, weaver, fits, M., 1 y 4 m
"	14	William Crabtree, dyer, typhis fever, M., 63 y
"	15	Benjamin Thornally, weaver, weakness, Droylsden, 26 y
"	17	Mary d. William & Mary Pendleton, tailor, Newton
"	19	Hannah d. John & Hannah Clough, weaver, weak, Failsworth, 15 y
"	21	William s. Thomas & Mary Portes, cotton spinner, fits, M., 9 m
"	24	Mary d. John & Mary Nedin, miner, fever, M., 12 y
"	27	John s. Matthew & Nanny Gradwell, weaver, swelling of lungs, Failsworth, 1 y 8 m
"	28	Sarah Houghton, widow, paral., Newton, 63 y
"	28	Edward s. Thomas & Sidney Pierce, labourer, weak, M., 1 m 7 days
Jul	3	Mary d. Henry & Grace Dunn, shoe maker, decline, M., 10 m
"	6	Sarah d. John & Jane Bailey, weaver, accident, M., 6 y
"	8	Robert s. John & Alice Hulton, weaver, swelling of lungs, Failsworth, 6 m
"	8	Mary d. Joseph & Martha Whitehead, blacksmith, dropsy, M., 20 y
"	8	Peter s. Thomas & Mary Grice, husbandman, interni. fever, M., 9 y
"	8	Isaac s. Joseph & Anne Burnley, cotton spinner, weak, M., 10 m
"	8	Samuel s. Samuel & Mary Matley, printer, small pox, Newton, 8 y 4 m
"	13	Elizabeth d. John & Anne Fogg, smith, small pox, M., 2 y 9 m
"	15	Elizabeth d. John & Alice Syddal, coal miner, fits, M., 8 m
"	21	Edmund s. John & Anne Jones, weaver, fits, M., 52 y
"	22	Alice d. John & Betty Lees, bricklayer, small pox, M., 5 y 3 m
"	24	Robert s. William & Jane Bell, weaver, small pox, M., 4 y
"	25	John s. James & Susannah Kemp, weaver, Newton, 36 y
"	26	John s. Samuel & Mary Beswick, whitster, Coroner's Wart., Levenshulme, 26 y
Aug	1	John spus. s. Ruth Bowker, weak, M., 1 m 21 days
"	1	James s. Joshua & Alice Wyatt, weaver, small pox, Newton, 1 y 4 m
"	3	Elizabeth d. Charles & Mary Watson, painter, small pox, M., 5 m 7 days
"	5	Henry s. Henry & Mary Forster, printer, small pox, Newton, 8 m
"	8	James spus. s. Sarah Bowker, weakness, M., 1 y 10 m
"	13	David s. William & Jane Bell, weaver, small pox, M., 2 y
"	14	William s. Thomas & Catharine Thorp, weaver, small pox, Moston, 8 m
"	14	Joseph s. James & Mary Hulme, bricklayer, fits, M., 5 m
"	15	William s. James & Martha Wood, husbandman, small pox, M., 3 y 10 m
"	16	Mary d. William & Esther Naden, collier, small pox, M., 4 y
"	17	James spus. s. Nancy Percivall, small pox, M., 10 m
"	19	Sarah w. George Storer, cotton carder, decline, M., 40 y
"	19	Mary d. Thomas & Mary Roberts, miner, small pox, M., 3 y
"	26	Mary d. James & Jane Wardley, weaver, weakness, M., 8 y
"	26	Alice Mills, widow, weakness, M., 68 y
"	27	Bridget d. John & Anne Sloane, spinner, small pox, M., 1 y 6 m

"	30	John s. Marlow & Mary Magill, weaver, nervous, M., 3 m
Sep	5	Sarah d. William & Ellen Hibbert, weaver, chincough, Newton, 1 y 8 m
"	6	Betty [Elizabeth] d. William & Mary Crowther, farmer, small pox, Newton, 1 y 4 m
"	9	Margaret d. George & Margaret Clayton, hatter, fits, M., 1 m 7 days
"	9	Harriett spu. d. Elizabeth Shaw, small pox, M., 1 y 5 m
"	12	William Fleetwood, clockmaker, M., 30 y
"	14	Mary d. James & Mary Barlow, weaver, small pox, Newton, 1 y 1 m 14d
"	16	Abraham s. John & Alice Shepton [Sephton], cordwainer, small pox, M., 1 y 4 m
"	17	James s. James & Anne Robinson, weaver, fits, M., 9 m
"	25	William s. James & Mary Blackshaw, dyer, small pox, M., 1 y 7 m
"	25	Joseph s. Issachar & Anne Thorp, printer, small pox, M., 5 y 9 m
Oct	1	Robert s. Richard & Mary Forster, M., 10 m
"	1	Sarah Whitehead spu. d. Anne Bradbury, weak, Newton, 1 m
"	5	Anne d. William & Anne Inman, weaver, M., 8 m
"	9	John s. George & Jenny [Jane] Hudson, spinner, consumption, M., 19y 3m
"	14	Anne d. John & Nancy Shuttleworth, weaver, chincough, M., 5 y
"	14	Ellen d. James & Mary Linn, weakness, M., 19 y
"	14	Samuel s. James & Mary Simister, whittster, small pox, Newton, 2 y
"	26	Thomas s. William & Anne Ormand, spinner, small pox, M., 4 y 6 m
"	26	Robert s. John & Alice Thorp, weaver, weak, Failsworth, 6 m
"	26	James Walmsley, decline, Failsworth, 29 y
"	28	Susannah Barker d. John & Betty Brown, sawyer, swelling of lungs, M., 1 y 8 m
"	28	Joseph Darlington, fever, M., 76 y
"	28	Ellen d. Thomas & Ellen Simpson, smith, small pox, M., 2 y 6 m
"	29	Richard s. Thomas & Jane Smart, clerk, decline, M., 2 y
"	30	Anne w. Thomas Martin, weaver, child bed, M., 23 y
Nov	3	Margaret d. John & Ellen Ormerod, weaver, dropsy, M., 19 y
"	4	John s. James & Mary Richmond, cotton spinner, weak, M., 6 m
"	14	Jane d. Henry & Mary Etchels, weaver, weak, Failsworth, 17 y 9 m
"	20	Isaac s. Isaac & Betty [Elizth] Hall, brewer, small pox, M., 2 y 6 m
"	23	Samuel s. Samuel & Martha Johnson, weaver, fever, M., 1 y 3 m
"	23	Richard s. Thomas & Anne Smith, brickmaker, small pox, M., 6 m
"	23	B. Wo[o]lstenholme, widow, M., 76 y
"	25	Humphrey s. Jervis & Alice Marsh, spinner, weak, M., 3 m
"	25	Elizabeth w. William Whitaker, weaver, decline, Failsworth, 55 y
"	28	Anne d. Christian & Anne Pennell, blacksmith, decline, M., 21 y
"	29	Ephraim s. William & Hannah McWilliam, weaver, weak, M., 3 m
"	30	Sarah d. John & Anne Preston, weaver, consumption, Failsworth, 18 y
Dec	2	John s. Philip & Alice Dunkerley, whitster, weak, Failsworth, 5 days
"	4	Margaret d. Richard & Elizabeth Lonsdale, manufacturer, small pox, M., 1 y 8 m
"	6	Martha d. Jacob & Elizebeth Woolsencroft, weaver, weak, Ardwick, 20 y

"   9   James s. Thomas & Elizabeth Upton, painter, small pox, M., 8 m

"   11   Robert s. George & Betty Hardy, weaver, swelling of lungs, Failsworth, 9 m

"   13   Mary d. Charles & Hannah Swindels, labourer, weak, Culcheth Newton [Newton], 7 days

"   13   Martha d. Richard & Fanny Sheldon, sawyer, small pox, M., 1 y 6 m

"   16   Anne d. Samuel & Betty [Elizth] Procter, dyer, small pox, M., 1 y 4 m

"   17   James Rothwell, whitster, consumption, Newton, 49 y 10(?) m

"   17   Mary w. Richard Andrew, whitster, consumption, M., 57 y

"   20   Samuel s. James & Nancy Woolstencroft, whitster, swelling of lungs, Failsworth, 3 y

"   22   Mary d. Michael & Margaret Leary, weak, M., 8 y

"   25   Sarah d. George & Betty [Elizth] Matthewson, weaver, small pox, M., 1 y 1 m

"   25   Mary w. James Richmond, spinner, consumption, M., 33 y

"   25   Mary d. Martha Wyatt, swelling, Newton, 12 y

"   25   John s. John & Elizabeth Smith, manufacturer, teeth, M., 7 m

"   26   Martha sp. d. Elizabeth Syddal, weak, M., 9 m

"   26[27]   Richard Andrew, bleacher, fever, M., 60 y

"   27   Mary d. Bernard & Phebe Laverty, small pox, M., 9 m (*entry not in BT*)

"   28   Elizabeth d. John & Betty [Elizth] Clarkson, sawyer, weak, M., 1 y 6 m

"   28   John s. William & Mary Allen, dyer, small pox, Salford, 2 y

"   30   Samuel s. Jonathan & Martha Shelmerdine, weaver, Culcheth Newton [Newton]

Burials in 1799

Jan   1   Sarah d. Sarah Shawl, weak, M., 2 y

"   1   Mary d. James & Anne Hulme, collier, small pox, M., 4 y 6 m

"   2   James s.Primrose & Jane Robinson, book keeper, fever, M., 13 y

"   2   Charlotte d. John & Nancy Duckworth, dyer, chincough, M., 1 y 5 m

"   3   Elizabeth d. James & Ann Smith, book keeper, fever, M., 13 y

"   6   Thomas s. William & Mary Patten, brewer, fits, M., 4 y

"   7   John s. George & Mary Willcox, spinner, weak, M., 3 days

"   9   John s. John & Elizabeth Paul, clock maker, small pox, M., 1 y 11 m

"   13   Mar[i]a d. Richard & Mary Brown, weaver, decline, M., 33 y

"   13   John s. William & Alice Wilkinson, shoemaker, small pox, M., 3 y

"   13   William s. James & Anne Hulme, miner, fever, M., 2 y 6 m

"   13   Elizabeth w. Lud Wroe, weaver, weak, Failsworth, 70 y

"   13   Martha w. Thomas Clegg, weaver, child bed, Failsworth, 40 y

"   20   Charles s. John & Catherine Morgan, spinner, chincough, M., 1 y

"   23   Margaret d. William & Mary Hall, weaver, small pox, M., 1 y 9 m

"   24   Eliza d. James & Anne Smith, silk spinner, accident, M., 2 y 1 m

"   27   William s. John & Martha Waterhouse, fustian dresser, small pox, M., 1 y 6 m

"   31   Samuel Lees, weaver, paral, Failsworth, 58 y

Feb	3	John Coe, weaver, M., 71 y	(1799)
"	12	John s. Nick McCoffrey, M.	
"	13	Sarah d. William & Margaret Carson, baker, small pox, M., 1 y 3 m	
"	15	James s. Samuel & Mary Newton, copperas maker, swelling of lungs, Ashton, 4 y	
"	17	Samuel Rothwell, fustian cutter, asthma, M., 61 y	
"	18	Benjamin s. Joshua & Hannah Holdroyd, smith, small pox, M., 2 y 9 m	
"	20	Samuel McDowell, consumption, M., 26 y	
"	24	Charles Garlick, weaver, fever, Failsworth, 44 y 10 m	
"	24	William s. James & Elizabeth Thorp, calico printer, M., 3 m	
"	24	James s. William & Anne Harlow, taylor, small pox, M., 1 y 8 m	
"	24	Robert Lees, M., 75 y	
"	25	John s. James & Mary Kirkham, weaver, fever, M., 1 y 6 m	
"	25	Edward s. Samuel & Anne Travis, weaver, consumption [,M.], 21 y 9 m	
"	27	Betsy [Elizth] w. John Houghton, innkeeper, decline, Newton, 23 y	
"	27	William s. Thomas & Nancy Higson, weaver, fits, M., 4 m	
Mar	2	John s. Robert & Ellen Fernon, weaver, fits, M., 4 m	
"	3	Sarah d. Charles & Elizabeth McCullough, spinner, small pox, M., 1 y	
"	7	Margaret d. Henry & Mary Forster, printer, consumption, Newton, 5 y	
"	10	Sarah d. Edmund & Betty [Elizth] Whitehead, weaver, consumption, Ashton Parish, 24 y	
"	10	Anne d. Thomas & Mary Gillebrand, weaver, consumption, Failsworth,21y	
"	14	Mary d. John & Jane Barwick, joiner, decline, M., 10 y	
"	15	Joseph s. Thomas & Hannah Kinder, hatter, small pox, M., 1 y 2 m	
"	17	John s. Benjamin & Jane Thornley, weaver, small pox, Droylsden, 1 y 5 m	
"	17	William s. Henry & Anne Slater, clock maker, small pox, M., 1 y 8 m	
"	17	Bernard s. Patrick & Anne Sloane, weaver, worm fever, M., 2 y 5 m	
"	17	John Coe, M., 72 y	
"	18	Betty [Elizth] w. James Robinson, consumption, Failsworth, 56 y	
"	18	Margaret w. Richard Hardy, velvet dresser, consumption, M., 46 y	
"	24	Robert Henry s. Benjamin & Dorothy Birtles, weaver, small pox, M., 11m	
"	24	Elizabeth d. Thomas & Ellen Edge, shoe maker, small pox, M., 8 m	
"	24	Maria d. John & Betty Barlow, cotton spinner, weakness, M., 1 y	
"	24	Alice Bamford, widow, fever, M., 30 y	
"	30	James Holden, cotton spinner, weakness, M., 47 y	
Apr	1	John s. Joseph & Sally [Sarah] Pimlott, tailor, weakness, M., 1 y 2 m	
"	2	Charles s. Samuel & Jane Higginbottom, weaver, small pox, M., 3 y	
"	2	Jenny [Jane] d. Robert & Christian Terynam, shoe maker, decline, M.,10m	
"	3	Mary w. Samuel Etchels, weaver, child bed, Failsworth, 42 y	
"	3	John s. Mary Eastwood, weakness, M., 1 y 9 m	
"	7	Thomas Threlwind, Joiner, weakness, M., 78 y	
"	7	James Tetlow, weaver, consumption, Newton, 35 y	
"	17	Robert Williams, blacksmith, consumption, M., 27 y	
"	19	Joseph s. Elias & Sarah Wild, weaver, weakness, Droylsden, 4 y	
"	20	Oliver s. Abraham & Hannah Heyes, weaver, fits, M., 2 y	

	20	John s. James & Alice Ogden, weaver, decline, Failsworth (*1799*)
"	20	John s. John & Jane Yates, weaver, decline, Hollinwood
"	21	William s. John & Barbara Burgess, labourer, consumn., M., 1 y
"	21	Betty [Elizth] d. James & Betty [Elizth] Clough, weaver, consumn., Failsworth, 17 y
"	21	John Slater, labourer, jaundice, Newton, 57 y
"	25	Betty [Elizth] Walker, widow, decline, Failsworth, 83 y 4 m
"	28	Sarah d. William & Sarah Aldridge, fever, M., 1 y 6 m
"	28	Mary d. John & Mary Willshaw, skinner, fever, M., 1 y
"	28	Mary Anne d. Henry & Anne Bullock, crofter, fits, M., 3 days
"	28	Joseph s. Joseph & Elizabeth Smith, weaver, fits, M., 6 days
May	1	Anne d. John & Anne McDowell, weaver, weakness, M., 1 y 6 m
"	2	Mary Newton, weakness, Failsworth, 8 y
"	2	Anne Nicholson, widow, M., 77 y
"	5	Samuel Heald, weaver, dropsy, Failsworth, 55 y
"	6	James Smith, weaver, decline, Failsworth, 52 y
"	7	George s. Thomas & Hannah Blackley, weaver, weakness, M., 3 m
"	10	John Waters, weaver, weakness, Failsworth, 48 y
"	12	Mary d. William & Mary Patten, brewer, decline, M., 19 y
"	13	Anne w. Edward Wrigley, weaver, dropsy, Failsworth, 57 y
"	16	Dolly w. John Isherwood, cotton spinner, consumpn., M., 49 y
"	17	Sally [Sarah] w. John Sutcliff Whittaker, weaver, consumpn., Failsworth, 30 y
"	19	Anne d. Patrick & Martha McGuire, M., 15 m
"	26	Anne w. John McDowell, weaver, weakness, M., 34 y
"	28	Alice w. Thomas Gorton, joiner, consumpn., Failsworth, 43 y
"	30	Maria d. John & Ellen Berry, weaver, fits, Failsworth, 1 m 21 days
Jun	2	James Townley, weaver, consn., Newton, 70 y
"	2	Sarah d. Thomas & Ann[e] Williams, cotton spinner, M., 1 y 11 m
"	3	Anne d. William & Mary Curley, labourer, fits, M., 5 m
"	3	Betty [Elizth] d. Edmund & Jane Allen, weaver, fits, Failsworth, 9 m
"	6	Mary Anne d. James & Rebecca Banks, schoolmaster, fits, M., 17 y
"	8	Anne w. William Evins, weaver, cons., M., 42 y
"	23	Rhoda w. William Friend, weaver, ch bed, M., 34 y
"	23	John s. John & Ann[e] Holdsworth, weaver, M.
"	30	Sarah w. Richard Lancaster, weaver, weakness, Moston, 47 y
Jul	7	Sarah d. Robert & Hannah Bentley, weaver, M., 3 y 3 m
"	9	Rebecca d. Thos. & Rebecca Hulme, warehouseman, consumn., M., 14y7m
"	9	Edward s. Henry & Margaret Foster, printer, conn., Newton, 9 y
"	10	Alice d. John & Hannah Allen, wheelwright, Droylsden, 2 y 1 m
"	10	Ellen d. James & Betty [Elizth] Townley, weaver, weakness, Newton, 15 y
"	16	Sarah d. Edw. & Ann[e] Wolstencroft, weaver, Droylsden, 11 y 4 m
"	16	Joseph s. Samuel & Mary Birtles, tailor, weakness, Failsworth, 14 days
"	21	Zaccheus s. William & Mary Lucas, labourer, small pox, M., 4 y 4 m
"	23	Esther d. Samuel & Mary Moss, weaver, weakness, M., 20 y 4 m

"	24	William s. Robert & Betty [Elizth] Robinson, millwright, fever, M., 13 y
"	24	Abraham Clegg, weaver, M., 50 y
"	28	Mary d. John & Nancy Coe, cotton carder, small-pox, M., 4 y
"	29	Robert s. Robert & Christian Robinson, weaver, small-pox, M., 9 m
Aug	7	Mary d. James & Phoebe Irvine, weaver, small-pox, M., 6 m
"	9	John s. John Larken, fits, M., 1 m 14 days
"	18	Elizabeth d. John & Elizh. Hughes, tailor, weakness, M., 3 m
"	18	Sarah d. James & Anne Cha[m]berlain spinner, small pox, M., 9 m
"	22	Samuel s. Saml. & Mary McDowell, weaver, small pox, M., 3 y 6 m
"	22	James s. John & Nancy Coe, cotton carder, small pox, M., 2 y 3 m
"	23	Lettuce d. James & Margt. Dannister, weaver, small pox, M., 7 m
"	24	John Travis, weaver, paral, Droylsden, 78 y
"	25	James Hall s. James & Anne Conner, spinner, small pox, M., 14 m
"	26	Mary d. Joseph & Martha Taylor, hatter, M., 2 y 11 m
"	28	Elizabeth d. Thos. & Anne Grimes, miller, decline, M., 6 y
"	29	Edmund Harrop, hatter, weakness, M., 47 y
Sep	1	William s. Robt. & Mary Calvert, weaver, meazles, M., 1 y
"	1	Hannah d. James & Sarah Whitehead, bricklayer, fits, Failsworth, 4 y 3 m
"	3	John s. Richard & Nancy Mallory, weaver, small pox, M., 2 y
"	4	Joseph s. Joseph & Martha Clayton, weaver, chin., M., 2 y 4 m
"	9	Robert s. William & Rhoda Friend, weaver, small pox, M., 10 y 6 m
"	10	James s. John & Anne Shuttleworth, weaver, small pox, M., 3 y
"	15	Anne d. James & Ann[e] Chamberlane, spinner, small pox, M., 3 y 3 m
"	15	Jonathan Scholfield, weaver, Cor Warr, Wood houses, 44 y
"	18	Joseph Taylor, smith, weakness, M., 36 y
"	22	Samuel Thomas, cotton spinner, decline, M., 44 y
"	29	William s. George & Sarah Firth, spinner, chinc, M., 7 y
"	29	Thos. s. Edwd. & Anne Jones, whitesmith, decline, M., 7 y
"	29	Jane d. Edwd. & Anne Jones, whitesmith, chin, M., 1 y
Oct	2	Nancy w. John Coe, weakness, M., 27 y
"	4	Elizh. d. Joseph & Susanna Hall, bricklayer, weakness, Newton, 33 y
"	6	David Jones, spinner, rheumatn., M., 37 y
"	6	Robert s. Robt. & Anne Mills, spinner, decline, M., 1 y 5 m
"	8	Elizabeth d. William & Alice Lane, innkeeper, small pox, M., 7 m
"	18	Jane d. Willm. & Jane Butterworth, weaver, fits, Failsworth, 3 y 1 m
"	18	Esther d. Richd. & Ann[e] Fletcher, fur cutr., decline, M., 14 y
"	20	Oliver s. William & Elizh. Boston, gardener, chin., M., 1 y 8 wks
"	27	Frances d. Robert & Mary Inman, joiner, small pox, M., 1 y 6 m
"	31	John s. John & Mary Lucas, warehouseman, weakness, M., 7 m
Nov	1	Robert s. John & Jane Pemberton, hatter, small pox, M., 2 y 3 m
"	3	Mary Anne d. Robt. & Elizabeth Wild, weaver, fits, M., 8 m
"	7	James s. Joseph & Anne Priestnall, cotton spinner, small pox, M., 2 y 8 m
"	7	Charles s. John & Martha Booth, shopkeeper, swelg lungs, Failsworth, 2 y
"	10	Mary d. Joshua & Sarah Etchels, weaver, weakness, M., 6 wks
"	12	Mary w. Samuel Berry, shoemaker, child b, Failsworth, 39 y

	13	Josiah s. James & Jane Wardley, weaver, swell, M., 11 y
"	14	James s. Richard & Anne Moloy, weaver, weakness, M., 9 m
"	17	Mary d. Michael & Margt. Leary, weakness, M., 8 y
"	19	Jane d. James & Mary Harlow, spinner, small pox, M., 2 y 7 m
"	21	Jonathan s. John & Elizabeth Fairclough, labourer, M., 1 y 1 m
"	21	Martha d. James & Dorothy Coe, cotton carder, ch., M., 1 y 9 m
"	21	Elizabeth d. William & Susanna Robinson, wheelwright, small pox, M., 3 y
"	24	William s. Henry & Mary Cryer, cotton spinner, meazles, M., 1 y 8 m
"	24	Samuel s. Samuel & Mary Roberts, dyer, meazles, M., 1 y 5 m
"	25	William s. George & Sarah Brook, M., 5 y
"	29	Joseph s. Matthew & Nancy Field, cordwainer, meazles, M., 11 m
Dec	1	John s. Joseph & Anne Horrocks, printer, small pox, M., 14 m
"	1	Sally [Sarah] d. Joseph & Sally [Sarah] Pimlott, tailor, swellg lungs, M., 4 y
"	3	Mary d. John & Mary Harrison, shopkeeper, meazles, M., 2 y
"	3	Mary Anne d. Willm. & Sarah Birchinall, spinner, small pox, 1 y
"	3	Margaret d. Richard & Betty [Elizth] Bibby, spinner, small pox, M., 1y 5m
"	3	Joseph s. John & Sally Ramsbotham, dyer, fits, Failsworth, 1 m
"	4	George s. Richard & Anne Bowden, cotton spinner, weakness, M., 25 y
"	4	Betty [Elizth] d. Robert & Mary Glossop, weaver, dropsy, Moston, 59 y
"	8	John Booth, weaver, rupture, Moston, 76 y
"	8	Alice w. Nathaniel Shelmerdine, weaver, consumpn., Newton, 43 y
"	11	Robert s. John & Betty [Elizth] Brown, surveyor, fever, M., 9 m
"	12	Nathan s. James & Sarah Boardman, weaver, small pox, M., 3 y 7 m
"	20	Catherine d. Joseph & Catherine Mather, weaver, small pox, Newton, 14 y
"	22	Sarah d. William & Esther Potter, cotton spinner, meazles, M., 9 m
"	27	Joseph s. Maria Allen, fever, Moston, 10 m
"	28	Richard Lancashire, weaver, weakness, Moston, 48 y
"	29	William s. Thomas & Hannah Ellanson, miner, fits, M., 2 m
"	29	Sarah d. Thomas & Betty [Elizth] Wood, husbandman, consum, M., 2 m 14 days

1800

Jan	1	Joseph s. John & Betty [Elizth] Whitwham, cotton spinner, small pox, M., 9 m
"	5	Edmund s. Edmund & Mary Newton, farmer, consump., Failsworth, 30 y
"	8	Mary d. James & Sarah Boardman, weaver, small pox, M., 5 y
"	9	Margaret d. William & Lydia Ireland, weaver, convul., M., 9 m
"	12	John s. Samuel & Margaret Utling, cabinet maker, small pox, M., 8 m
"	12	Mary d. James & Sarah Wild, weaver, weakness, Newton, 3 y
"	12	Sarah d. Thomas & Mary Barlow, weaver, consump., Failsworth, 39 y
"	13	John s. John & Mary Howarth, weaver, small pox, M., 1 y 9 m
"	14	Mary Pollitt (, widow *not in BT*), decline, Newton, 77 y
"	15	Thomas s. John & Mary Lee, weaver, small pox, M., 9 m
"	18	Margaret d. Robert & Anne Knight, weaver, small pox, M., 9 m

"	19	Robert s. James & Mary Walker, weaver, small pox, M., 1 y 1 m
"	19	William s. Richard & Jane Roberts, butcher, small pox, M., 3 y
"	19	Sarah d. Charles & Susanna Farrow, coal miner, M.
"	19	Thomas Howard Wignall, asthma, M.
"	20	John s. John & Amelia Hall, cotton spinner, small pox, M., 1 y
"	20	Edward s. Robert & Hannah Clayton, collier, small pox, M., 8 m
"	21	Susanna d. James & Anne Hull, coal miner, small pox, M., 1 y 2 m
"	22	John Walmsley, surveyor, Failsworth, 49 y
"	23	John s. James & Mary Hulme, warehouseman, small pox, M., 2 y
"	23	Sarah w. Thomas Bray, clothier, surfeit, M., 52 y
"	24	Thomas s. Samuel & Margaret Chetham, farmer, M., 1 y 3 m
"	25	Alice d. Robert & Alice Gaskell, husbandman, weakness, M., 24 y
"	30	Betty [Elizth] Etchels (, widow *not in BT*), Failsworth, 88 y
"	30	Richard s. John & Esther Morton, cotton spinner, decline, M., 1 y 6 m
"	31	John Pugh, husbandman, fever, Newton, 30 y
Feb	1	Robert s. Isaac & Sarah Fitton, weaver, consump., Failsworth, 20 y 2 m
"	2	Nancy d. Nathan & Ph(o)ebe Ashly, weaver, decline, M., 2 m 14 days
"	2	Charles s. Samuel & Hannah Robinson, weaver, weakness, Newton, 5 m
"	2	Rachel d. William & Alice Mar(r)[s], weaver, measles, M., 2 y 10 m
"	3	Jane d. John & Betty [Elizth] Hewit, husbansman, fits, M., 6 m
"	9	Matthew s. Thomas & Anne Bent, weaver, measles, M., 8 m
"	9	Jonathan [sp] s. Anne Wrigley, weak, Failsworth, 5 days
"	9	Philip s. John & Elizabeth Acton, cotton spinner, w. swellg., M., 12 y
"	10	Samuel Smith, weaver, consump., Failsworth, 50 y
"	10	Betty [Elizth] d. John & Elizabeth Ashworth, weaver, decline, Newton, 7y
"	12	Robert s. Robert & Betty [Elizth] Parry, miner, weakss., M., 1 y
"	13	Martha w. Joseph Ogden, manufacturer, consump., Failsworth, 58 y
"	14	Thomas s. Alice Kershaw, weak, Failsworth, 3 y
"	14	Sarah d. Jeremiah & Dorothy Buxton, butcher, measles, 7 m
"	17	Thomas Gibson, weaver, weak, M., 35 y
"	19	Betty [Elizth] d. Thomas & Jane Wilson, farmer, fever, Moston, 88 y
"	21	Martha Whittle, weak, Moston, 70 y
"	23	Thomas s. John & Anne Rudd, spinner, M., 1 y 6 m
"	25	Mary d. John & Alice Parry, collier, weakness, M., 1 y 10 m
"	28	John Smithels, weakness, Moston, 70 y
Mar	3	George Benison, weaver, decline, M., 31 y
"	5	Martha d. Willm. & Sarah Allen, bleacher, decline, M., 1 y 2 m
"	5	Mary w. William Smith, weaver, decline, Newton, 36 y
"	5	David Ogden, weaver, consump., Moston, 29 y
"	6	Robert s. Patrick & Esther Smiley, weaver, M., 3 m
"	9	Elizabeth d. John & Alice Parry, M., 1 m 7 days
"	9	Samuel s. Richard & Jane Grice, husbandman, small pox, M., 2 y 1 m
"	9	Joshua s. Ralph & Betty [Elizth] Syddal, collier, small pox, M., 2 m 2 days
"	13	Gowen Duncuff, labourer, consum., M., 75 y
"	13	Mary w. William Blackshaw, crofter, consum., Openshaw, 52 y

"	13	Betty [Elizth] w. John Blackshaw, cotton spinner, consum., Audenshaw, 28 y *(1800)*
"	16	Mary d. Elias & Anne Rayner, cotton spinner, small pox, M., 14 m
"	16	Charles s. Issachar & Anne Thorpe, printer, fever, Reddish Mill, 4 y
"	16	Thomas s. John & Sarah Booth, weaver, weakness, Failsworth, 21 days
"	16	Anne d. William & Martha Pickard, joiner, fever, M., 8 y
"	17	Matthew s. Peter & Alice Brindle, weaver, weakness, M., 3 y 10 m
"	18	Mary Ogden, widow, dropsy, Newton, 70 y
"	18	Alice w. John Perry, collier, decline, M., 21 y
"	18	Nancy w. William Rayner, weaver, weakness, M., 36 y
"	21	William s. James & Elizh. Trimble, weaver, weakness, M., 1 y 6 m
"	22	Lissey d. Richard & Mary Richardson, weaver, measles, Newton, 11 m
"	22	William s. Charles & Betty [Elizth] Garlick, weaver, measles, Failsworth, 1 y 6 m
"	25	James Wood, dropsy, M., 57 y
"	25	Susanna w. James Cardwell, weaver, weakness, M., 21 y
"	26	Jane Chapman, weakness, Moston, 80 y
"	27	John Brown sp. s. Mary Hardy, measles, Failsworth, 9 m
Apr	2	Esther d. Thomas & Hannah Gradwell, weaver, measles, M., 1 y 5 m
"	2	Helen d. Gilbert & Grace Mackay, staymaker, consump., M., 18 y
"	6	Anne d. Thomas & Elizabeth Plimmer, collier, measles, M., 1 y 1 m
"	6	Martha Warburton, weakness, M., 54 y
"	6	Daniel Wood sp. s. Sarah Peers, sw. lungs, Failsworth, 5 y 7 m
"	8	Hannah d. John & Elizabeth Taylor, warehouseman, worm fever, M,2y 8m
"	9	George Butterworth, weaver, weakness, Moston, 81 y
"	9	Joseph s. John & Esther Taylor, shoemaker, measles, Failsworth, 1 y 10 m
"	13	Robert s. Samuel & Mary McDowell, weaver, fever, M., 2 y
"	15	Joseph s. George & Betty [Elizth] Hardy, weaver, weakness, Failsworth, 10 y 8 m (*? - age faded*)
"	19	Margaret w. William Saunders, inflamation, M., 46 y
"	20	Samuel s. William & Frances Chatterton, confectioner, small pox, M., 1 y
"	24	Nancy d. James & Alice Lees, weaver, Failsworth, 1 day
"	24	Charles s. John & Catherine Morgan, spinner, fits, M., 6 m
"	28	Sarah d. Richard & Mary Bamber, cotton manr., measles, M., 1 y 6 m
"	29	Martha d. James & Margaret Howarth, weaver, weakness, Newton, 1 y 3 m
May	1	James s. Joseph & Anne Sutcliffe, weaver, fits, 2 m 24 days
"	1	Anne d. Ralph & Hannah Chatterton, shopkeeper, small pox, M., 1 y 3 m
"	1	Anne Stott, widow, consump., Failsworth, 66 y
"	4	Jonathan s. Daniel & Mary Sanders, farmer, dropsy, Failsworth, 5 y 11 m
"	5	John Barlow, cotton spinner, decline, M., 31y
"	5	Joseph s. John & Mary Smith, weaver, measles, Failsworth, 1 y 11 m
"	10	Frances Jackson, widow, Gorton, 75 y
"	20	George Booth, farmer, Failsworth, 83 y
"	20	Jenny d. Joshua & Betty [Elizth] Swift, weaver, Failsworth
"	22	Richard Downing, clockmaker, fever, M., 28 y

"	23	Peter s. Thomas & Anne Higson, weaver, fits, M., 4 m
"	25	Josiah s. Josiah & Ellen Ridgeway, hatbandmaker, weakness, M., 16 y
"	28	Mary d. John & Mary Holmes, clockmaker, teeth, M., 11 m
"	30	Jane d. John & Mary Blacklock, printer, convulsn., Prestwich, 1 y 1 m
Jun	1	Amey w. Philip Newall, joiner, weakness, M., 22 y
"	4	Mary d. John & Dorothy Costigin, machine maker, worms, M., 1 y 4 m
"	8	Sally [Sarah] d. James & Sarah Whitehead, bricklayer, weakness, Failsworth, 11 y 5 m
"	10	Mary d. Edwd. & Anne Campbell, warehouseman, small pox, M., 2 y
"	10	Jane d. Michael & Mary Smith, shoemaker, looseness, M., 2 m 29 days
"	12	Mary d. Jonathan & Martha Glossop, weaver, decline, Moston, 18 y
"	12	Maria d. James & Mary Hooly, farmer, swell-lungs, Failsworth, 8 m
"	16	Mary Ogden, widow, Failsworth, 39 y
"	25	William Clough, weaver, Failsworth, 84 y
"	29	Betty [Elizth] w. Samson Farrand, weaver, cancer, Failsworth, 56 y
Jul	1	John s. James & Isabel Ryley, weaver, M., 6 y (? - *age faded*)
"	6	Martha d. John & Alice Goulden, husbandman, small pox, Oldham, 4 m
"	9	Martha d. John & Mary Bates, cordwainer, small pox, Failsworth, 3 y 5 m
"	13	Maria d. John & Anne Mounsey, cordwainer, small pox, M., 3 y
"	22	Mary w. William Johnstone, joiner, weakness, M., 36 y
"	22	William Allen, dyer, decline, Salford, 27 y
"	22	Mary d. Philip & Emmy Newal, joiner, convul., M., 3 y 6 m
"	23	Elizabeth w. Thomas Plimmer, collier, weakness, M., 25 y
"	24	Charles Anderson, silk weaver, asthma, M., 48 y
"	24	Thomas Slater, M., 52 y
"	28	James Berry, farmer, paral., Failsworth, 57 y
Aug	3	Phoebe w. Samuel Ainsworth, hatter, Newton
"	3	Elizabeth d. Jacob & Mary Ogden, weaver, worm fever, M., 4 y
"	4	Rosanna d. Richard & Sarah Light, coal-miner, Chadderton, 16 y
"	5	Abel s. Thomas & Margaret Pearson, machine maker, fits, M., 7 m
"	11	James s. James & Elizabeth Moors, limegetter, small pox, M., 2 y
"	12	Isabel w. James Riley, weaver, dropsy, M., 26 y
"	13	Anne d. Arthur & Catherine Cardwell, weaver, worms, M., 7 y
"	14	Mary Anne d. Henry & Mary Birckill, cotton spinner, convuls, M., 7 m
"	15	James s. Henry & Anne Bullcock, crofter, weakness, M., 3 m
"	15	Thomas s. Thomas & Mary Marsh, farmer, Moston, 16 y
"	18	Sarah d. George & Margaret Clayton, hatter, fever, M., 13 y 4 m
"	19	Anne d. William & Anne Haynes, weaver, weakness, Newton, 2 y
"	20	Hannah w. Roger Richardson, weaver, fever, Newton, 60 y
"	20	Robert s. Robert & Jane Stott, manufacturer, worm fever, Failsworth, 1 y 3 m
"	22	Ellen d. James & Alice Thomas, bookkeeper, fever, M., 1 y 3 m
"	24	Ann[e] Lees, M., 43 y
"	27	Elizabeth d. John & Anne Mounsey, shoemaker, small pox, M., 1 y
"	29	Henry s. William & Alice Lomas, cotton spinner, convuls, M., 2 y 3 m

	31	David s. John & Anne Jones, pumpmaker, M., 3 y
Sep	1	Sarah d. Edward & Jane Tomlinson, labourer, small pox, M., 10 m
"	3	Richard Thomason, weaver, dropsy, Failsworth, 71 y
"	7	Richard s. Richard & Mary Copley, joiner, measles, M., 18 m
"	7	Hannah w. William McWilliam, weaver, childbed, M., 32 y
"	7	Richard s. James & Anne Milner, cordwainer, M., 9 y
"	9	Mary Anne d. James & Elizh. Moors, limegetter, small pox, M., 9 m
"	11	Elizabeth d. James & Esther Allen, weaver, fits, Newton, 5 m
"	15	Mary w. George Rise, clockmaker, decline, M., 54 y
"	16	Esther w. James Allen, weaver, decline, Newton, 22 y
"	17	Maria d. William & Mary Greenwood, weaver, fev., Newton, 1 y 6 m
"	faded[16]	John s. John & Sarah Norcross, shoemaker, fever, M., 2 y 11 m
"	faded[16]	William s. John & Sarah Norcross, shoemaker, M., 1 y 6 m
"	18	Henry Smith, weaver, M., 80 y
["	18	Hannah d. Geo. & Alice Robinson, Droylsden (entry in BT only)]
"	21	Joseph s. Samuel & Jane Thomas, cotton spinner, M., 13 y 4 m
"	26	Joseph s. Thomas & Sarah Cowell, whitesmith, M., 1 y 6 m
"	28	Matthew s. James & Anne Holden, cotton spinner, M., 1 y 6 m
Oct	3	George Lucas, whitster, fever, M., 54 y
"	5	Thos. s. Willm. & Elizh. Wainwright, shopkeeper, weakness, M., 3 m
"	9	Sarah d. William & Anne Lees, weaver, fever, M., 23 y
"	9	Joseph Peters, cotton spinner, weakness, M., 56 y
"	13	Hannah d. Robert & Anne Glossop, weaver, worm-fever, Failsworth, 3 y
"	19	Thomas s. John & Jane Berwick, joiner, consump., M., 8 y
"	19	Anne d. William & Sarah Ramsden, engineer, convul., M., 1 y 6 m
"	24	Richard s. John & Sarah Jones, locksmith, fits, M., 14 days
"	29	Mary sp. d. Grace Knott, fits, Failsworth, 1 m 7 days
"	30	John Howard, weaver, fever, M., 33 y
Nov	3	Harriet d. Thomas & Elizh. Plimmer, collier, consump., M., 3 y 6 m
"	9	Bold Eckersley, weaver, consump., Failsworth, 70 y
"	9	William s. John & Betty [Elizth] Howarth, print cutter, decline, Failsworth, 18 y
"	11	Sarah sp. d. Elizabeth Storey, small pox, M., 11 m
"	17	Sally [Sarah] d. James & Nancy Wolstencroft, crofter, decline, Failsworth, 2 y 4 m
"	21	Sarah d. John & Betty [Elizth] Berrington, tanner, Failsworth, 2 y 5 m
"	30	Alice w. James Baguley, blacksmith, weakness, M., 45 y
Dec	1	Mary w. Thomas Schofield, hatter, childbed, Failsworth, 22 y
"	4	William s. John & Mary Evans, weaver, weak, M., 9 m
"	7	Elizabeth Lees, dropsy, Droylsden, 35 y
"	8	Anne d. Robert & Anne Clayton, coalminer, fits, M., 21 days
"	9	Mary d. Thomas & Esther Hooley, bleacher, fever, Newton, 27 y
"	10	Jane d. Robert & Anne Blacklock, printer, small pox, Prestwich, 8 m
"	10	Mary d. Luke & Anne Smith, weaver, fever, Failsworth, 4 y 8 m
"	14	Thomas Hill, collier, fever, M., 44 y

"	14	John s. William & Sarah Daltry, farmer, Newton, 4 y
"	15	Mary sp. d. Sarah Mather, fits, Droylsden, 14 days
"	19	Dan Shepley, weaver, paral., Newton, 55 y
"	28	John (sp. *not in BT*) s. Margaret Souther, weakness, M., 6 m
"	28	John s. James & Martha Swift, weaver, consump., Failsworth, 35 y
[		This is a true Copy taken from the Register at Newton Heath Chapel]
[		A. Ashworth Minister]
[		William Brown James Kenyon Ch. Wardens]

1801

Jan	2	Anne Roden, widow, consump., M., 50 y
"	5	Frances d. Richard & Elizh. Hill, coalminer, weakness, M., 1 y 7 m
"	7	James s. James & Anne Fidian, decline, M., 7 y
"	8	Abraham Ogden, coalminer, accident, M., 50 y
"	11	Joseph s. Sally [Sarah] Mather, cons, Droylsden, 2 m 14 days
"	13	Thomas s. John & Mary Plimmer, collier, fever, M., 7 y
"	14	David s. William & Anne Whitehead, weaver, fever Failsworth, 5 y
"	15	Nancy w. Charles Moors, weaver, rheumatism, M., 42 y
"	20	James s. William & Elizabeth Haynes, worm fever, Failsworth, 7 y
"	27	John Wolstenholme, weaver, Newton, 66 y
Feb	2	Anne w. William Whitehead, weaver, fever, Failsworth, 34 y
"	8	Peter Scholes, weaver, decline, Failsworth, 68 y
"	8	John s. William & Sarah Anderton, spinner, chincough, M., 8 m
"	15	Anne Hill, cons., Droylsden, 68 y (*? - age faded*)
"	22	Thomas Higson, weaver, cons., M., 26 y
"	22	William s. Joseph & Mary Swallow, cotton spinner, swell lungs, M., 5y 6m
"	26	Samuel s. Richard & Elizh. Thomason, weaver, fever, Failsworth, 25 y
Mar	1	Dan s. James & Nancy Woolstencroft, bleacher, decline, Failsworth, 1y4m
"	4	Abraham s. Thomas & Anne Ogden, weaver, tooth fever, M., 9 m
"	8	Betty [Elizth] d. John & Mary Redman, weaver, cons., M., 14 m
"	8	Mary Bateman, widow, M., 82 y
"	8	Violet d. Joshua & Mary Smith, weaver, consump., Failsworth, 18 y
"	8	George s. William & Mary Brown, manufacturer, convul., M., 4 y
"	15	John s. John & Sarah Moors, weaver, convul., M., 11 m
"	17	Elizabeth d. Edmund & Rebecca Harrop, hatter, dropsy, Openshaw, 13 y
"	18	John Clough, weaver, paral., Failsworth, 68 y
"	22	John s. John & Jane Yates, weaver, convuls., Failsworth, 2 y (*? - age faded*)
"	22	Peter s. Matthew & Jane Wardley, weaver, tooth fever, M., 10 m
"	25	Thomas Hooley, bleacher, fever, Newton, 54 y
"	25	Joel sp. s. Betty [Elizth] Holt, fits, Failsworth, 2 m 14 days
"	29	Hannah d. John & Mary Robinson, weaver, small pox, Droylsden, 6 y
"	29	Sarah d. George & Anne Etchels, weaver, fever, Failsworth, 8 y

"	29	Jane w. Joseph Andrew, whitster, paral., M., 65 y	(1801)
"	29	John Bowler, carder, fever, M., 58 y	
"	31	Francis s. James & Barbara Broadley, weaver, worm fever, M., 3 y 9 m	
"	31	Robert Thorp, weaver, Moston, 86 y	
Apr	5	William s. Thomas & Elizh. Lewis, plasterer, weakness, M., 1 y 7 m	
"	5	Henry s. Samuel & Anne Hunsiton, currier, M., 2 y 6 m	
"	7	Sarah w. William Allen, labourer, fever, M., 38 y	
"	10	Robert Thorp, weaver, decline, M., 57 y	
"	11	Samuel s. Samuel & Martha Johnson, weaver, convul., M., 8 m	
"	12	William s. Joshua & Hannah Holroyd, blacksmith, convul., M., 3 days	
"	12	Ellen w. Samuel Rigby, engineer, weakness, Bradford, 48 y	
"	12	James s. Henry & Anne Chatterton, collier, fever, M., 12 y	
"	12	Ann d. William & Alice Gillibrand, weakness, Failsworth, 31 y	
"	12	Mary d. Abraham & Jane Pollit, fever, Failsworth, 21 y	
"	13	Sarah d. Joseph & Martha Ogden, manufacturer, decline, Failsworth, 27 y	
"	15	John s. John & Elizabeth Brownhill, farmer, fever, Openshaw, 22 y	
"	16	Anne w. Issachar Thorp, printer, decline, M., 38 y	
"	24	Mary Ogden, widow, fever, M., 58 y	
"	24	Samuel s. William & Anne Whitehead, weaver, fever, Failsworth, 1 y 5 m	
"	26	John s. William & Jane Atkinson, cotton spinner, decline, M., 1 y	
"	26	James Wardly, weaver, decline, M., 35 y 3 m	
"	29	Jeremiah s. Jeremiah & Martha Kemp, warper, fits, M., 1 y 8 m	
"	30	Mary Priestnall, widow, asthma, M., 50 y	
May	3	John s. Edward & Mary Williams, hatter, weakness, M., 14 m	
"	5	Elizabeth sp. d. Mary Wood, fits, Newton, 1 y 3 m	
"	6	Jonathan Booth, manufacturer, int. fever, Failsworth, 56 y	
"	6	Sarah d. John & Mary Lyon, hatter, chincough, M., 1 y 9 m	
"	8	William s. John & Mary Lucas, warehouseman, weakness, M., 6 m	
"	8	Alice d. James & Elizabeth Bythel, bleacher, fever, Newton, 9 m	
"	10	Henry s. John & Ellen Owen, potter, decline, M., 7 y	
"	10	Samuel Moss, crofter, M., 52 y	
"	13	William [sp] s. Sarah Clough, convul., M., 6 m	
"	17	Harriet d. Henry & Anne Jowell, joiner, convul., M., 6 m	
"	17	Sarah w. Peter Owen, shoemaker, weakness, M., 31 y	
"	17	James Holt, weaver, fever, M., 85 y	
"	17	Sarah d. Jonathan & Peggy [Margt] Grimshaw, weaver, weakness, Droylsden, 1 y	
"	17	Anne w. George Etchels, weaver, decline, Failsworth, 39 y	
"	18	Thomas Plimmer, coal-miner, fever, M., 30 y	
"	19	Sarah d. Abraham & Mary Ogden, miner, M., 27 y	
"	21	James s. Thomas & Judith Hancock, spinner, M., 1 m 14 days	
"	22	Mary w. Luke Weatherbed, spinner, childbed, M., 25 y	
"	22	Anne Wolstenholme, widow, consumption, 43 y	
"	26	Margaret d. John & Margaret Bridge, weaver, fever, M., 16 y	
"	30	Elizabeth w. William Finch, forgeman, fever, M., 52 y	

"	31	Elizabeth d. Samuel & Sarah Brickill, cotton spinner, decline, M., 13 y
Jun	2	John s. Thomas & Elizabeth Emlow, mason, consump., M., 14 y 6 m
"	3	Joseph s. William & Elizabeth Hibbert, weaver, consump., Newton, 22 y
"	6[7]	Alice d. John & Anne Rogers, weaver, consump., Newton, 27 y
"	6	Alice d. Elias & Jane Bythell, farmer, consump., Newton, 5 y
"	7	Mary d. Samuel & Martha Taylor, labourer, weakness, M., 1 y 3 m
"	8	John s. James & Anne Pilkington, cotton spinner, conv., M., 8 y
"	10	Elizabeth d. Samuel & Hannah Robinson, weaver, consump., Newton, 22 y 3 m
"	15	Martha w. William Pickard, joiner, fever, M., 35 y
"	16	Sarah w. Joseph Etchels, weaver, cons., M., 37 y
"	17	Betty [Elizth] d. Robert & Jane Stott, manufacturer, decline, Failsworth, 1 y 9 m
"	17	Thomas Smith, innkeeper, decline, Failsworth, 70 y
"	17	James Booth, shoemaker, fever, M., 44 y
"	18	Mary d. William & Fanny Toole, cotton spinner, chincough, M., 2 y 3 m
"	27	Elizabeth w. John Witwham, cotton spinner, consump., M., 25 y 3 m
"	28	James s. Richard & Sarah Hall, bricklayer, small pox, M., 1 y 6 m
"	28	John s. John & Mary Stansfield, hatter, weakness, Newton, 8 y
"	28	Simeon s. Levi & Mary Whitehead, writer, consump., M., 2 y 2 m
"	29	Elizabeth [sp] d. Hannah Lawrenson, sw. lungs, M., 6 m
"	30	George Hudson, cotton spinner, fever, M., 45 y
"	30	Martha d. George & Jane Hudson, cotton spinner, fever, M., 17 y
Jul	5	Richard s. Richard & Sarah Heywood, husbandman, decline, M., 24 y
"	5	Joshua Etchels, weaver, fever, M., 58 y
"	7	Mary d. Samuel & Mary Duggan, weaver, weakness, M., 1 y
"	8	Thomas s. James & Betty [Elizth] Hodson, calico printer, decline, M., 17y
"	9	Hannah w. Jeremiah Clayton, woolcomber, fever, M., 47 y
"	12	Jacob s. Samuel & Sarah Brickill, cotton spinner, decline, M., 1 y 3 m
"	14	James Crossley, weaver, weakness, Failsworth, 41 y
"	14	Martha d. Peter & Jane Ormrod, weaver, small pox, M., 4 y
"	15	Tacy d. William & Anne Coats, cotton spinner, fever, M., 27 y
"	16	Thomas s. Thomas & Mary [Sarah] Walmsley, farmer, infl., Failsworth, 1 m 21 days
"	16	Sarah w. William Thornley, shoemaker, cons., Droylsden, 65 y
"	21	Joseph Bardsley, weaver, fever, M., 60 y
"	22	John s. William & Mary Curley, porter, fits, M., 5 m
"	25	Jeremiah Clayton, woolcomber, fever, M., 46 y
"	26	Elizabeth d. Marlow & Mary Magill, weaver, weakness, M., 1 y 10 m
"	29	Mary w. James Hulme, warehouseman, infl., M., 33 y 2 m
Aug	2	Hannah d. William & Christian Taylor, smith, fits, M., 2 y
"	3	James s. James & Mary Thorp, weaver, chincough, Failsworth, 5 m 21 d
"	5	Betty [Elizth] w. John Etchels, weaver, fever, Failsworth, 44 y
"	6	Hannah d. John & Alice Kershaw, weaver, chincough, Failsworth, 1 y
"	8	Dorothy w. James Coe, cotton carder, fever, M., 37 y

"	9	Elizabeth d. Patrick & Martha McGuire, shoemaker, weakness, M., 1 y 6m
"	12	Jane w. Samuel Thomas, cotton spinner, con., M., 44 y *(1801)*
"	13	James Adcroft, collier, fever, M.
"	13	Hannah w. Robert Clayton, collier, fever, M., 26 y
"	16	Esther d. John & Betty [Elizth] Clough, weaver, chincough, Failsworth, 1y
"	18	Samuel s. Matthew & Nancy Field, shoemaker, M., 1 y 1 m
"	20	John Mather, manufacturer, consump., M., 29 y
"	21	Elias s. Jeremiah & Hannah Clayton, woolcomber, fever, M., 22 y
"	23	Martha w. Samuel Johnson, weaver, weakness, M., 33 y
"	24	Matthew s. Jacob & Anne Wolstencroft, weaver, weakness, M., 10 m
"	28	John s. John & Martha Berry, farmer, fever, Failsworth, 28 y 4 m
"	30	Alice Walmsley, widow, cons., Failsworth, 63 y
"	30	Sarah d. William & Sarah Aldridge, weaver, conv., M., 21 days
"	31	William s. William & Alice Lane, innkeeper, con., M., 13 m
Sep	1	Daniel Walker, weaver, fever, M., 39 y
"	5	Margaret w. John Bridge, weaver, fever, M., 62 y
"	13	Joseph s. William & Sarah Birchenall, spinner, weakness, M., 6 m
"	13	Anne sp. d. Alice Whitaker, weakness, M., 6 m
"	13	William s. John & Mary Waters, weaver, decline, Failsworth, 22 y
"	14	Jane d. James Pearson, colonel, decline, Taunton, 14 y
"	15	Amelia d. John & Elizabeth Butterworth, weaver, chincough, M., 14 m
"	19	Elizabeth w. John Lees, hatter, fever, M., 30 y
"	20	Alice d. Elijah & Anne Ashley, weaver, chincough, M., 2 m 21 days
"	21	George s. Benjn. & Mary Butterworth, weaver, fever, Moston, 10 y
"	22	Mary d. John & Elizabeth Fairclough, labourer, cons., M., 13 y
"	27	Henry s. James & Mary Crossley, weaver, small pox, Failsworth, 9 m
"	27	Thomas [sp] s. Martha Mather, small pox, Newton, 2 y 6 m
"	27	John s. John & Elizabeth Humphrey, weaver, weakness, M., 6 m
"	27	Jeremiah Buxton, butcher, fever, M., 41 y
"	28	Catherine d. John & Mary Bell, weaver, weakness, M., 11 m
"	30	Mary w. James Hooley, husbandman, dropsy, Failsworth, 35 y
Oct	1	Edmund s. Thomas & Mary Schofield, hatter, cons., Chadderton, 11 m
"	2	James Lees, weaver, decline, Rusholme, 70 y
"	4	Jane d. John & Elizabeth Lees, hatter, fever, M., 1 y
"	8	Sarah d. John & Judith Leigh, weaver, chinc., M., 2 y 6 m
"	16	Thomas s. James & Hannah Wilkinson, weaver, chinc., Failsworth, 9 m
"	16	Anne d. Thomas & Mary Whitehead, weaver, fever, Failsworth, 22 y
"	21	John s. Edward & Martha Whitehead, bricklayer, small pox, Droylsden, 15 m
"	23	George s. John & Mary Reynolds, machine maker, small pox, M., 1 y 5 m
"	25	Robert s. James & Anne Smith, spinner, M., 9 m
"	25	William s. Thomas & Hannah Pearson, small pox, M., 2 y 10 m
"	25	George s. Abraham & Margt. Johnson, machine maker, small pox, M., 8 m
"	27	Esther d. Joshua & Mary Taylor, farmer, decline, M., 60 y
"	28	Joseph s. Joseph & Mary Holland, bricklayer, small pox, Droylsden, 3y3m

"	29	Mary w. John Lucas, warehouseman, fever, M., 26 y
Nov	1	Mary w. John Mather, hatter, fever, M., 60 y
"	3	William s. James & Jane Charlton, weaver, small pox, M., 2 y 6 m
"	6	Ellen Crabtree, widow, fever, M., 73 y
"	8	Robert s. James & Sarah Boardman, weaver, fever, M., 2 y 7 m
"	8	William s. John & Mary Booth, cotton spinner, small., M., 1 y 6 m
"	8	Joseph s. James & Mary Holt, weaver, Failsworth, 7 days
"	9	Thomas s. James & Mary Hooley, labourer, weakness, Failsworth, 2 m
"	10	Mary w. John Williamson, collier, fever, M., 62 y
"	13	Samuel s. William & Mary Jenkinson, weaver, fever, M., 6 y
"	13	James Blackley, weaver, fever, M., 63 y
"	13	Anne w. James Blackley, fever, M., 65 y
"	13	Martha d. Robert & Mary Walmsley, farmer, weakness, Newton, 4 m 7 d
"	15	Hannah d. Samuel & Margaret Utting, cabinet maker, small pox, M.
"	17	Jonathan s. John & Elizh. Fairclough, labourer, teeth, M., 3 m 21 days
"	17	Thomas s. John & Esther Whitehead, weaver, fever, Failsworth, 22 y
"	17	Betty [Elizth] sp. d. Martha Green, small pox, M., 5 y
"	22	Anne d. Michael & Anne Russel, cotton spinner, small pox, M., 2 y 6 m
"	24	Anne d. Richard & Hannah Wolstencroft, fusn. cutter, small pox, M., 2 y 7 m
"	24	Nancy sp. d. Betty [Elizth] Sison, fever, M., 2 m
"	25	Margaret w. Thomas Horrocks, weaver, cons., Failsworth, 50 y
"	27	Jeremiah s. Jeremiah & Dorothy Buxton, butcher, small pox, M., 11 m
"	29	William s. Arthur & Catherine Cardwell, weaver, small pox, M., 1 y 6 m
"	30	Richard s. Richard & Margaret Rowley, fustian cutter, small pox, M., 2 y
Dec	1	John s. William & Bella Bolton, calico printer, small pox, Newton, 6 y
"	1	Mary Anne d. Robert & Elizabeth Wild, weaver, small pox, M., 1 y
"	1	Anne d. James & Hannah Johnson, weaver, tooth fever, M., 9 m
"	4	Thomas s. Samuel & Margaret Cheetham, innkeeper, weakness, M., 21 d
"	5	Harriet d. John & Margaret Whitehead, cabinet maker, small pox, M., 1 y 6 m
"	5	John s. John & Alice Brevitt, weaver, tooth fever, Newton, 2 y
"	8	Phoebe sp. d. Betty [Elizth] Rushton, small pox, M., 2 y
"	10	Patrick s. Arthur & Catherine Cardwell, weaver, small pox, M., 4 y
"	11	Frances Porter d. Thos. & Alice Stafford, collier, Bradford, 1 y
"	13	William Berry, weaver, cons., Failsworth, 70 y
"	15	Susanna d. Ralph Skinner, tailor, fever, M., 22 y
"	16	Alice d. John & Deborah Whitaker, weaver, surfeit, Failsworth, 51 y
"	17	Daniel Howarth, weaver, weakness, Salford, 66 y
"	18	Sarah d. John & Elizabeth Warrington, millwright, teeth, M., 20 m
"	20	James sp. s. Anne Reyner, tooth fever, Failsworth, 2 y
"	20	Mary d. John & Elizabeth Mather, manufacturer, cons., M., 1 y 5 m
"	21	Sarah d. Isaac & Ellen Beesley, printer, small pox, Failsworth, 1 y 7 m
"	21	Isabella d. Richard & Nancy Hall, print cutter, small pox, Newton, 2 y
"	23	Anne w. James Allen, weaver, cons., Failsworth, 36 y

"   25   William s. Charles & Mary Grime, weaver, chinc., M., 1 y 10 m
"   25   Richard s. Richard & Esther Blomeley, weaver, decline, M., 8 m
"   25   Mary d. William & Nancy Ormond, spinner, weakness, M., 11 y
"   27   Mary Anne d. Nathaniel & Catherine Dabzel, weaver, small pox, M., 3 y
"   27   Thomas s. William & Mary Jenkinson, weaver, fever, M., 13 y
"   29   Christiana w. James Babb, breeches maker, decline, M., 66 y
"   29   Margaret d. James & Rebecca Hardy, calenderer, tooth fever, M., 1 y 6 m
"   30   Frances d. John & Elizabeth Porter, bookkeeper, small pox, Bradford, 3 y
[The above is a true Copy taken from the Register at Newton Heath Chapel]
[William Brown James Kenyon John Moors Ch. Wardens   ]

Burials in 1802
[Burials at Newton Heath Chapel in the Year of Our Lord 1802]

Jan   1   William Walker sp. s. Alice Wood, fits, M., 20 days
"   1   Mary d. Luke & Anne Barnes, weaver, chin., M., 5 y 4 m
"   2   William s. Isaac & Ellen Beesley, printer, small pox, Failsworth, 4 y
"   3   John s. John & Anne Keymster, hatter, small pox, M., 1 y 7 m
"   5   Anne w. James Pilkington, spinner, childbed, M., 30 y
"   5   John s. Oliver & Anne Greenwood, weaver, M., 3 y 2 m
"   9   Betty d. William & Bella [Betty] Bolton, printer, swell. lungs, Newton,
            1 y 10 m
"   10   Richard s. James & Alice Thomas, bookkeeper, tooth fever, M., 1 y 3 m
"   10   Anne d. Luke & Anne Barnes, weaver, chinc., M., 2 y
"   10   John s. Thomas & Nancy Williams, spinner, worm fever, M., 7 y
"   12   Mary w. James Clough, weaver, fever, Failsworth, 22 y 10 m
"   12   Elizabeth w. John Faulkner, weaver, cons., Newton, 60 y
"   13   Richard s. William & Mary Fleetwood, watchmaker, fever, M., 3 y
"   17   Matilda d. John & Ellen Laverick, joiner, small pox, M., 1 y 8 m
"   17   William s. John & Elizabeth Moss, weaver, fits, Cheetham, 14 days
"   17   James s. John & Jane Talbot, collier, small pox, M., 3 y
"   20   William s. James & Anne Ridings, weaver, fever, Failsworth, 19 y 4 m
"   20   Uriah s. James & Anne Wroe, weaver, fever, Failsworth, 9 y
"   21   Anne d. Philip & Catherine Forshaw, joiner, chinc., M., 1 y 7 m
"   22   John s. Edward & Anne Eckersley, weaver, loose, Failsworth, 2 y 6 m
"   22   Hannah d. George & Betty Hardy, weaver, small pox, Failsworth, 2 y 2 m
"   23   Charlotte d. Thomas & Sarah Frost, cotton spinner, small pox, M., 1 y
"   24   John s. James & Elizabeth Trimble, weaver, worm-fever, M., 6 y 8 m
"   25   Martha d. George & Betty Hardy, weaver, small pox, Failsworth, 6 y
"   25   John s. James & Janette Renfrew, cotton spinner, chinc., M., 1 y 8 m
"   26   Thomas s. Thomas & Elizabeth Barlow, weaver, fits, Failsworth, 1 y
"   27   Sarah w. William Grimshaw, weaver, decline, M., 41 y
"   29   John s. James & Elizabeth Barrett, shopkeeper, small pox, M., 4 y 4 m
Feb   1   Charles s. John & Mary Plimmer, coal miner, small-pox, M., 1 y 3 m
"   7   Samuel Duggan, weaver, weakness, M., 38 y

"	7	William sp. s. Anne Holden, decline, M., 3 y 6 m
"	7	John s. William & Anne Smethurst, collier, small pox, M., 1 y 8 m
"	7	Mary d. Robert & Mary Inman, joiner, small pox, M., 10 m
"	9	James s. John & Anne Lindley, dyer, small pox, M., 2 y
"	12	William s. Robert & Anne Wilson, millwright, weakness, M., 23 y
"	13	Jane d. Robert & Christiana Robinson, weaver, measles, 1 y 8 m
"	14	Sarah d. William & Anne Smethurst, crofter, swell lungs, M., 9 y
"	14	Sarah w. William Aldridge, husbandman, decline, M., 34 y
"	14	Richard s. Henry & Anne Slater, clock maker, chinc., M., 8 m
"	16	William s. Isaac & Elizabeth Johnson, turner, chin., M., 9 m
"	16	Esther w. James Beswick, blacksmith, childbed, M., 38 y
"	21	Samuel sp. s. Anne Buckleton, M., 16 y
"	21	William Gillibrand, weaver, cons., Failsworth, 67 y
"	24	Archibald, s. Joseph & Ellen Birtles, weaver, chin., M., 2 m
"	25	Anne d. Robert & Mary Lees, bleacher, decline, Newton, 54 y
"	26	James s. Joseph & Elizabeth Wrigley, weaver, small pox, Failsworth, 8 m
"	28	Edward s. John & Mary Howarth, weaver, small pox, M., 1 y 1 m
"	28	George s. Luke & Mary Weatherby, spinner, chin., M., 10 m
"	28	Anne sp. d. Elizabeth Booth, inflam., Newton, 1 y 10 m
Mar	4	William s. John & Mary Wright, weaver, chin., M., 1 y 3 m
"	7	Anne d. Jonathan & Mary Shelmerdine, weaver, fits, Newton, 11 m
"	7	John Faulkner, weaver, paral., Newton, 67 y
"	8	Ellen d. William & Sarah Sudworth, coal miner, fits, M., 6 m
"	10	Betty d. Robert & Hannah Clayton, collier, fits, M., 5 y 3 m
"	13	George s. Robert & Martha Hirst, weaver, fever, M., 8 m
"	14	William s. Robert & Betty Parry, miner, chinc., M., 5 y 9 m
"	14	Sarah d. Jonathan & Mary Scholfield, weaver, weakness, Waterside [Ashton Parish], 11 y
"	14	Matthew Field, cordwainer, fever, M., 36 y
"	17	James s. John & Esther Moreton, spinner, chin., M., 6 y 4 m
"	17	Anne w. Thomas Worsley, weaver, dropsy, M., 27 y
"	18	William s. James & Elizabeth Hampson, weaver, swell lungs, M., 4 y 5 m
"	20	Elizabeth d. Edward & Jane Allen, weaver, weakness, Failsworth, 1 y 1 m
"	26	Sarah of [d.] Thomas & Frances Andrew, manufacturer, small pox, M., 3 y
"	26	Thomas Walmsley, farmer, weakness, Failsworth, 37 y
"	28	Anne w. Thomas Green, whitesmith, cons., M., 40 y
"	30	James s. Ralph & Betty Syddal, weaver, fits, M., 4 y
Apr	1	Harold s. William & Anne Harlow, tailor, tooth-fever, M., 9 m
"	4	Esther d. James & Esther Beswick, labourer, small pox, M., 3 y 3 m
"	6	Sarah d. John & Isabella Pugh, labourer, small pox, Newton, 2 y 2 m
"	6	Briant Lawrenson, weaver, decline, M., 38 y
"	6	Robert McGuire, navigator, inflam bowels, M., 57 y
"	27	Robert Hulme, weaver, cons, Newton, 67 y
"	29	John Mather, hatter, paral., M., 51 y

"	29	Elizabeth w. John McNeal, weaver, childbed, M., 43 y *(1802)*
"	30	Mary Swallow, widow, pleur., M., 47 y
May	2	Mary d. Robert & Mary Conlan, weaver, small pox, M., 15 m
"	2	Mary Boardman, cons, Hollinwood, 71 y
"	2	Hannah d. John & Lydia Dodd, tailor, decl, M., 29 y
"	2	Thomas Atkinson, cotton spinner, cons., M., 35 y
"	3	Betty d. Daniel & Mary Smith, weaver, cons, Failsworth, 11 y 4 m
"	5	James Brown, farmer, apoplex, Woodhouses, 67 y
"	9	Martha w. Jonathan Glossop, weaver, decline, Failsworth, 63 y
"	9	The Revd. [Reverend] George Mason, fever, Newton, 32 y
"	10	James s. Lawrence & Jane Riley, cooper, apoplexy, M., 36 y
"	11	Anne d. Thomas & Martha Hardy, printer, decline, Newton, 21 y 3 m
"	13	Betty d. Samuel & Betty Lees, blacksmith, weakness, Failsworth, 3 days
"	14	Richard Partington, collier, accident, M., 40 y
"	23	John s. John & Martha Shaw, clother, measles, M., 10 m
"	23	Anne d. Thomas & Sally Booth, weaver, fits, Moston, 4 y
"	24	Elizabeth w. Thomas Allen, wheelwright, fever, M., 56 y
"	24	James Travis, weaver, cons, Droylsden, 70 y
"	25	Saml. Grimshaw s. John & Mary Whitehead, innkeeper, Newton
"	25	John s. Patrick & Mary Wynne, cons., M., 6 y 3 days
"	27	Elizabeth w. James Smith, weaver, cons, Failsworth, 48(?) y
"	28	Mary d. Joseph & Anne Lomax, weaver, small pox, M., 13 m 2 days
"	30	Anne d. John & Jane Yates, weaver, fits, Hollinwood, 1 m
"	30	Mary d. James & Sarah Whitehead, bricklayer, decline, Failsworth, 17 y
Jun	8	John s. Samuel & Ellen Rigby, blacksmith, decline, Bradford, 16 y
"	9	John Wood, farmer, Newton, 87 y
"	13	Hannah d. Elizab[et]h Tomlinson, small, Moston, 1 y 8 m
"	20	George s. James & Anne Ashworth, cotton spinner, weakness, M., 10 y
"	21	Mary d. Briant [Brion] & Anne Lawrenson, weaver, worm fever, M., 10 y
"	22	Daniel s. John & Alice Syddal, collier, worm fever, M., 3 y
"	23	William s. William & Martha Gillaspie, weaver, rash fever, M., 1 y 9 m
"	23	Mary d. James & Alice Lees, weaver, fits, Failsworth, 21 days
"	25	Martha d. George & Mary Hall, cotton spinner, small pox, M., 1 y 2 m
"	29	John s. James & Elizabeth Whitehead, bleacher, accident, M., 19 y
Jul	1	Jane d. Joshua & Elizabeth Ogden, weaver, decline, Failsworth, 34 y
"	4	John s. John & Martha Shaw, clothier, measles, M., 10 m
"	4	Anne d. Thomas & Sarah Booth, weaver, fits, Newton, 4 days
"	5	Mary d. Matthew & Catherine Carol, weaver, weakness, M., 1 m 7 days
"	5	Maria d. John & Mary Smith, weaver, small pox, Failsworth, 2 y 3 m
"	5	Thomas s. Thomas & Margaret Pearson, turner, measles, M., 1 y 1 m
"	5	Jane d. John & Anne Lindley, dyer, Reddish, 4 y
"	11	Betty d. Robert & Anne Glossop, weaver, decline, Failsworth, 6 y
"	13	Martha d. Joseph & Sarah Ogden, weaver, weakness, Newton, 1 m 1 day
"	18	James Pilkington, cotton spinner, decline, M., 33 y
"	19	Thomas s. James & Anne Cha[m]berlain, cotton spinner, weakness M.,7m

"	20	William sp. s. Anne w. Joseph Tetlow, soldier, small pox, Failsworth, 2 y
"	25	Richard s. Ralph & Betty Burchell, weaver, small pox, Failsworth, 11 m
"	28	Mary d. Guy & Mary Bray, cotton spinner, M., 4 m
"	28	Sarah d. James & Phoebe Smethurst, weaver, measles, Failsworth, 3 y 6 m
"	31	George s. William & Mary Jenkinson, weaver, fits, M., 3 y
Aug	2	Joseph s. James & Anne Ashton, labourer, fever, M., 5 y
"	3	Nancey w. John Shuttleworth, weaver, fever, M., 49 y
"	4	Charles s. Benjamin & Elizh. Johnson, blacksmith, small, Heaton norris 2y
"	5	Joseph Tinker, weaver, dropsy, Moston, 48 y
"	6	John s. John & Hannah Williamson, labourer, swell lungs, Ashton Parish, 1 y 7 m
"	8	Mary d. Benj[amin] & Elizabeth Heywood, weaver, scar fever, M., 2 y 9 m
"	10	Daniel s. James & Mary Butterworth, weaver, weakness, M., 9 m
"	11	Aaron Maken [Maden], labourer, decline, M., 82 y
"	14	William Richards, labourer, fever, Newton, 23 y
"	14	Anne sp. d. Milly Gradwell, small pox, Newton, 9 m
"	16	John s. George & Sarah Etchels, weaver, small pox, Failsworth, 3 y 6 m
"	17	Robert s. Joseph & Tabitha Tinker, weaver, fever, Moston, 14 y
"	28	Martha sp. d. Margaret Thomason, weaver, fever, Failsworth, 12 y
"	29	John s. John & Ellen Owen, potter, decline, M., 4 y 3 m(*? - age faded*)
Sep	2	Martha w. John Leech, weaver, childbed, M., 20 y
"	2	James s. James & Mary Gradwell, weaver, small pox, Failsworth, 2 y 9 m
"	2	Alice d. James & Mary Gradwell, weaver, small pox, Failsworth, 2 y 9 m
"	5	Solomon Coe, weaver, decline, M., 65 y
"	5	Anne d. Edward & Mary Thornley, silk spinner, weakness, M., 2 y
"	8	Hannah d. Andrew & Anne Wilson, cotton spinner, small pox, M., 1 y 1m
"	12	James s. James & Elizabeth Moor[e]s, carter, scar. fever, M., 1 y 2 m
"	16	Sally d. Joseph & Sarah Berry, blacksmith, small pox, Failsworth, 7 m
"	16	Martha w. Abel Whitehead, white smith, weakness, M., 50 y
"	16	Mary w. James Butterworth, weaver, dropsy, M., 27 y
"	19	Hannah w. James Holt, weaver, cons, M., 82 y
"	21	Mary d. John & Martha Booth, shopkeeper, fever, Failsworth, 17 y
"	24	Mary d. John & Sarah Whitehead, manufacturer, swell throat, Failsworth, 7 m 14 days
"	24	Joseph s. John & Fanny Goodier, weaver, fever, Failsworth, 9 m
"	27	Anne d. Richard & Sarah Lancashire, weaver, fever, Moston, 10 y (*? - age faded*)
"	29	James s. John & Anne Hulton, weaver, small pox, Failsworth, 8 m
Oct	7	Mary d. Philip & Alice Dunkerly, weaver, small pox, Failsworth, 1 y 7 m
"	10	Robert s. James & Mary Milner, cotton spinner, small., M., 6 m
"	10	Anne d. William & Sarah Wood, gluemaker, fever, Newton, 5 m
"	15	William sp. s. Catherine Gradwell, weakness, M., 2 days
"	18	James s. John & Dorothy Wilkinson, labourer, chinc., M., 1 y
"	19	Samuel s. Samuel & Jane Thomas, cotton spinr., weakness, M., 17 y
"	19	Jonathan s. David & Nancy Burton, joiner, flux, M., 5 y 7 m

"	19	Joseph s. David & Nancy Burton, joiner, flux, M., 4 y 4 m
"	22	Elizabeth w. Richard Holt, weaver, decline, Failsworth, 57 y
"	24	Lissey d. John & Anne Eckersley, weaver, swell lungs, Failsworth, 1m 14d
"	24	Alice d. Abraham & Jane Ashworth, weakness, Newton, 5 days
"	27	Alice w. Jonathan Slater, weaver, inflam., Newton 63 y
"	28	Anne w. Thomas Bent, weaver, pleurisy, M., 42 y
"	31	John s. David & Nancy Burton, joiner, fits, M., 1 y 4 m
"	31	Mary d. George & Sarah Etchels, weaver, fever, Failsworth, 1 y 21 days
Nov	2	Alice d. Robert & Elizabeth Hall, weaver, fever, Newton, 9 y
"	3	John s. James & Mary Thorp, weaver, fever, Failsworth, 6 y 6 m
"	7	Sarah d. James & Mary Hulme, bricklayer, conv., M., 1 m 21 days
"	8	Thomas [Charles] s. Charles & Martha Plimmer, collier, fever, M., 19 y
"	14	Benjamin Hulton, weaver, paral, Failsworth, 65 y
"	14	Jane d. John & Frances Goodier, weaver, fever, Failsworth, 6 y
"	15	Esther d. George & Mary Brown, weaver, swell lungs, M., 5 m
"	16	Harriet d. Josiah & Ellin Ridgeway, hatband maker, M., 12 y
"	16	John Brown, husbandman, fever, M., 73 y
"	18	James s. James & Hannah Sanderson, weaver, fever, M., 3 y
"	21	Mary d. John & Sarah Marsh, weaver, chinc., M., 7 m
"	22	Henry McCullough, weaver, M., 80 y
"	23	Charles s. Thomas & Sarah Walmsley, weaver, fever, Failsworth, 19 y
"	28	Ellen d. William & Sarah Walker, weaver, fever, Newton, 3 y
"	30	Martha Turner, consump., Droylsden, 25 y
"	30	Anne w. Robert Milnes, cotton spinner, childbed, M., 32 y
Dec	1	Alice d. William & Mary Brown, manufacturer, fever, Newton, 7 y 9 m
"	5	James s. James & Sarah Boardman, weaver, scarl. fever, M., 4 y 8 m
"	6	Mary d. William & Rebecca Worral, fever, Failsworth, 5 y
"	7	Hannah d. John & Elizabeth Whitaker, weaver, fever, Failsworth, 5 m
"	7	Thomas Taylor [Thomas] s. George & Elizh. Mathewson, weaver, small pox, M., 2 y 9 m
"	8	Susanna w. William Cooper, weaver, dropsy, M., 40 y
"	8	Samuel s. William & Anne Clarke, weaver, fever, Newton, 3 y 4 m
"	8	James s. James & Deborah Whitaker, weaver, fever, Failsworth, 4 y 5 m
"	8	John Ogden, weaver, fever, Failsworth, 20 y
"	9	Jane d. Benjamin & Mary Hulton, weaver, fever, Failsworth, 23 y 3 m
"	11	Margaret d. Charles & Mary Bridge, weaver, weakness, M., 10 m
"	12	William s. Edward & Mary Howarth, innkeeper, fever, M., 3 y
"	14	Jemima d. Peter & Mary Weatherbed, sieve maker, chinc, M., 1 y 6 m
"	17	Robert sp. s. Jane [Alice] Walmesley, farmer, small pox, Failsworth, 3 y
"	19	Edmund s. Charles & Mary Watson, plasterer, small pox, M., 3 y
"	19	John Pollitt, weaver, fever, Failsworth, 30 y
"	19	Ophelia d. John & Abigail Winterbottom, weaver, fever, Failsworth, 21 y
"	23	John s. Matthew & Elizabeth Thorpe, weaver, fever, Moston, 3 y
"	23	John s. John & Elizabeth Robinson, slater, fever, Newton, 17 y
"	24	William Davies, Newton

"	25	John s. Robert & Mary Barlow, weaver, weakness, Failsworth, 7 m 2 days
"	26	Ellen d. William & Sarah Taylor, logwood miller, small., M., 1 y 11 m
"	26	Selena d. Robert & Martha Hurst, weaver, fever, M., 3 y
"	26	Mary d. James & Hannah Ashton, weaver, fits, Failsworth, 1 m 31days
"	30	Mary Haworth, weaver, consn., Newton, 32 y 5 m
"	31	Anne d. Benjamin & Violet Hulton, weaver, small pox, Failsworth, 11 m
"	31	Martha d. John & Martha Booth, shopkeeper, weakness, Failsworth, 10 m
[		A. Ashworth Minister]
[		James Kenyon William Brown Ch Wardens]

Burials in 1803
[Burials at Newton Heath in 1803]
(*each page in the BT for this year is signed* A. Ashworth Minister)

Jan	1	John Wyatt, weaver, consumpn., Newton, 44 y
"	2	William s. William & Mary Brown, Manufacturer, fever, M., 3 m
"	2	George s. Robert & Isabel Hulton, weaver, fever, Failsworth, 3 y
"	2	Hannah d. William & Anne Bottomly, husbandman, decl., M., 1 day
"	4	William sp. s. Martha McGuire, small pox, M., 4 m
"	4	Joseph s. Thomas & Sarah Cowell, whitesmith, weakness, M., 6 m
"	5	Mary d. John & Elizabeth Robinson, slater, fever, Newton, 19 y
"	6	Mary d. James & Mary Crossley, labourer, fever, Moston, 4 y 9 m
"	6	Martha d. John & Elizabeth Fairclough, labourer, fits, M., 5 m
"	6	James s. John & Elizabeth Coe, carder, weakness, M., 2 y 7 m
"	7	Anne d. Robert & Nancy Williamson, gardener, decline, M., 7 y
"	7	Alice d. John & Mary [Margt] Carter, printer, fits, Droylsden, 9 y
"	9	John s. Thomas & Sarah Walmsley, weaver, fever, Failsworth, 2 y
"	10	John s. John & Lissey Wilde, weaver, fever, Ashton Parish, 16 y
"	12	James s. Thomas & Nancy Whitaker, weaver, fits, M., 14 days
		(*The age has faded towards the end of the next two entries.*)
"	16	John s. Joseph & Mary Greenwood, collier, small pox, M., 3 m
"	16	John s. Thomas & Betty Holland, weaver, fever, Moston, 1 y 1 m
"	20	James s. James & Frances Fazakerly, warehouseman, decline, M., 10 m
"	28	Elizabeth d. John & Sarah Marsh, weaver, fits, M., 9 m
"	30	Margaret d. Thomas & Mary Beresford, weaver, weakness, M., 1 m 21 days
"	30	Thomas Kemp, weaver, paral., M., 68 y
Feb	2	Rachel w. John Gradwell, weaver, decline, Newton, 26 y
"	2	Alexander Simpson, weaver, paral., M., 78 y
"	5	Mary w. William Heywood, dyer, childbed, Newton, 33 y
"	6	James Hulme, collier, decline, M., 46 y
"	6	John sp. s. Betty Horrocks, decline, Newton, 21 y
"	8	Millicent d. Thomas & Sarah Cowell, whitesmith, fever, Pendleton, 2y 5m
"	10	James Andrew, printcutter, cons., Newton, 42 y
"	11	Jane d. Robert & Anne Glossop, weaver, fever, Failsworth, 10 m

"	13	Joseph Heath, tanner, fever, Newton, 36 y (*1803*)
"	13	James Hulme, warehouseman, decline, M., 35 y
"	13	Betty w. John Brownhill, labourer, erysipelas, Gorton, 49 y
"	13	Martha d. John & Jane Green, weaver, fever, M., 24 y
"	18	William Bradshaw, weaver, surfeit, M., 75 y
"	20	Mary w. Richard Stansfield, weaver, par & drop., Newton, 66 y
"	20	Samuel s. Jonathan & Mary Shelmerdine, weaver, fits, Newton, 1 m 1 day
"	21	Sarah d. Elias & Anne Rayner, cotton spinner, fits, M., 5 m
"	23	James s. James & Sarah Lomax, weaver, fits, Newton, 12 days
"	27	James sp. s. Hannah Rothwell, Waterside Ashton Parish
Mar	2	James Nicholson, hatter, M., 82 y
"	6	Thomas s. Patrick & Martha Hughes, weaver, M., 8 m
"	6	John s. John & Anne Lee, collier, fits, M., 2 m 7 days
"	8	Mary w. James Fullalove, cotton spinner, weakness, M., 55 y
"	9	John Oakes, bookkeeper, cons, M., 33 y
"	10	Elizabeth w. James Hampson, weaver, childbed, M., 24 y
"	11	Mary d. John & Sarah Burgess, weaver, tooth fever, M., 9 m
"	13	Margaret d. Michael & Mary Smith, shoemaker, conv., M., 8 m 11 days
"	13	George s. Samuel & Mary Kempster, cotton spinner, tooth fever, M., 8 m
"	13	Mary w. John Evans, weaver, childbed, M., 30 y
"	17	James Ogden, bleacher, M., 60 y
"	18	James s. John & Mary Anderton, weaver, fits, Moston, 7 days
"	20	Anne d. William & Anne Scholfield, weaver, fits, Droylsden, 8 m
"	20	Elizabeth d. John & Esther Moreton, cotton spinner, tooth fever, M., 6 y
"	22	Martha Hulme, M., 83 y
"	22	Mary sp. d. Alice Whittaker, fits, M., 8 m
"	25	Samuel s. James & Margaret Dennison [Dennistin], weaver, cons, M., 3 y
"	25	Mary d. Joseph & Anne Ravenscroft, labourer, fits, Newton, 13 days
Apr	1	Thomas s. John & Mary Costlow, weaver, small pox, M., 11 m
"	1	William s. John & Elizabeth Ward, weaver, inflamn., M., 5 m
"	1	Stanley s. James & Anne Winstanley, weaver, swell. lungs, M., 8 m
"	2	Frederick s. Abraham & Hannah Heyes, weaver, fits, M., 8 m
"	3	Richard s. John & Mary Booth, cotton spinr., swell. lungs, M., 6 y
"	7	Sarah w. William Wood, farmer, cons, Newton, 29 y
"	8	Margaret d. John & Esther Etchels, weaver, swell. lungs, Failsworth, 3 y
"	9	Richard Dean, farmer, fever, Newton, 46 y
"	10	Thomas Walmsley, weaver, fever, Failsworth, 56 y
"	10	Michael s. Henry & Mary Flood, labourer, decline, M., 8 y
"	11	Thomas s. Robert & Penelope Whitehead, weaver, swelling throat, Failsworth, 1 y 5 m
"	13	Joseph s. Samuel & Elizabeth Mather, weaver, decline, Levenshulme, 2 m
"	14	Thomas [spu] s. Betty Holt, swelg. lungs, Failsworth, 3 y
"	17	Hannah d. James & Mary Blackshaw, syer, small pox, M., 3 y 5 m
"	19	Thomas Aspinall, farmer, asthma, Bradford, 78 y
"	19	Martha d. John & Mary Broadhurst, dresser, cons., M., 15 y

"	20	Mary d. James & Mary Ridings, weaver, decline, Failsworth, 16 y
"	21	Esther d. John & Mary Walmsley, surveyor, decline, Failsworth, 17 y
"	22	Bartholomew s. Bartholow. & Bridget McCue, manufacturer, cons., M., 12 y 2 m
"	24	Thomas s. John & Sally Mason, bleacher, cons., Droylsden, 2 m 21 days
"	25	Jane d. John & Mary Pollit, weaver, cons., Newton, 7 m 2 days
"	26	Betty d. James & Mary Waters, weaver, weakness, Failsworth, 1 y 5 m
"	27	James s. Robert & Sally Bridgehouse, bleacher, surfeit, M., 23 y
May	1	Martha d. Charles & Mary Hulme, warehouseman, worm fever, M., 5 y 5 m (? - *age faded*)
"	1	Betty w. John Pollit, weaver, cons., Failsworth, 30 y
"	2	Hannah d. Nathaniel & Anne Thorley, weaver, fits, Failsworth, 21 days
"	2	Alice d. William & Mary Patten, weaver, decline. M., 17 y
"	3	Henry sp. s. Sarah Ashworth, worm-fever, M., 11 m
"	4	Lucy d. Samuel & Sarah Brickell, cotton spinner, conv., M., 4 m
"	5	Betty d. John & Betty Whitwam, cotton spinner, weakness, M., 1 m 14 d
"	9	James Baguley, smith, decline, M., 74 y
"	11	Mary d. Joseph & Mary Turner, slater, decline, Newton, 4 y 6 m
"	13	Elizabeth w. James Wood, cotton spinner, pl. fever, M., 59 y
"	13	Betty d. Thomas & Mary Smith, weaver, conv., Failsworth, 3 m 14 days
"	14	Betty d. Mattw. & Anne Gradwell, weaver, fits, Failsworth, 1 y 2 m
"	15	William Sephton, cordwainer, decline, M., 25 y
"	16	John Thorpe, weaver, decline, Moston, 26 y
"	18	Peter s. Peter & Mary Weatherbed, sievemaker, small pox, M., 5 y
"	22	Samuel s. James & Elizabeth Bradshaw, weaver, sc. fever, M., 4 y 2 m
"	25	Hannah d. Samuel & Hannah Robinson, weaver,decline, Newton, 5 y
"	29	Alice w. Richard Ditchfield, weaver, weakness, Failsworth, 57 y
"	30	Joseph Booth, shopkeeper, M., 81 y
Jun	3	Thomas Fitzsimmons, weaver, asthma, M., 36 y
"	5	Sarah d. John & Mary Oakes, cotton spinner, M., 7 days
"	7	William Radcliffe, weaver, cons., Failsworth, 47 y
"	7	Elizabeth d. Richd. & Mary Whittenstall, joiner, cons., M., 1 y
"	8	William s. Joshua & Alice Wyatt, weaver, fits, Newton, 1 day
"	14	William Cooper, weaver, pleurisy, M., 47 y
"	17	John Pollack, mason, fever, Preston, 47 y
"	20	George s. George & Catherine Tomkinson, joiner, tooth fever, M., 1 y
"	29	Thomas s. Thomas & Esther Tomkinson, hatter, tooth fever, Newton, 8 m 14 days
Jul	6	Esther d. Samuel & Mary Newton, drysalter, swellg. lungs, Ashton Parish, 1 y 2 m
"	7	John s. John & Mary Harrison, shopkeeper, decline, M., 11 y
"	7	Bernard McCloughlin, cordwainer, M., 76 y
"	10	William s. William & Mary Bird, weaver, weakness, M., 12 y 11 m
"	13	Ellen w. John Yarwood, labourer, weakness, M., 46 y
"	14	Mary w. John Knight, weaver, childbed, Newton, 22 y

"	17	John s. Samuel & Mary Boden, cotton spinner, weakness, M., 4 y
"	17	Betty w. John Smith, weaver, ch. bed, Failsworth, 29 y
"	25	John s. John & Betty Smith, weaver, conv., Failsworth, 21 days
"	26	Samuel s. James & Mary Andrew, printer, decline, Newton, 1 m 21 days
"	26	Mary d. Thomas & Elizabeth Jones, weaver, small pox, M., 2 m
"	31	Sarah d. Edward & Anne Jones, whitesmith, weakness, M., 3 m 7 days
Aug	3	Isabel d. Edward & Anne Eckersley, weaver, weakness, Failsworth, 1 y 6 m
"	3	William s. Samuel & Betty [Elizth] Mather, weaver, weakness, Levenshulme, 6 m
"	7	Jane w. George Lucas, bleacher, weakness, M., 61 y
"	7	William Pendleton, tailor, fever, Failsworth, 39 y
"	8	John s. Thomas & Martha Ashton, weaver, fever, Chadderton, 16 y
"	9	James Slater, mason, fever, Newton 21 y
"	12	Anne Mary w. Robert Wilson, millwright, apo., Salford, 57 y
"	17	Elizabeth w. Richard Bradley, labourer, cons, Bradford, 69 y
"	18	Thomas s. John & Alice Green, weaver, weakness, M., 4 m
"	19	Margaret d. Thomas & Fanny Cowling, weaver, cons, M., 2 m
"	23	Betty w. Joseph Bardsley, weaver, cons, Failsworth, 55 y
"	31	Alice w. Gowen Duncuff, labourer, M., 82 y
"	31	Harriet d. John & Mary Thorp, weaver, decline, Moston, 5 y 2 m
Sep	5	John s. John & Anne Kershaw, weaver, small pox, M., 6 m
"	6	James s. John & Mary Lyon, hatter, small pox, M., 1 y 6 m
"	7	Hannah d. John & Mary Lees, bricklayer, cons, M., 15 y
"	11	Joseph s. James & Martha Whitehead, weaver, weakness, Failsworth, 14 y 1 m
"	12	Charles s. George & Jane Hudson, spinner, cons., M., 20 y 7 m
"	20	Nancy w. James [Ralph] Smethurst, weaver, ch. bed, Failsworth, 36 y
"	20	Robert s. Robt. & Anne Milnes, cotton spinner, small pox, M., 9 m
"	22	Lucy d. John & Martha Shaw, shopkeeper, fits, M., 9 m
"	25	Margaret d. John & Elizabeth Bramall, weaver, swelling lungs, M., 5 y
"	25	John s. Peter & Hannah Lomax, dyer, weakness, Newton, 1 y
"	27	Joseph Stansfield, weaver, fever, Newton, 25 y
"	30	Thomas s. James & Elizabeth Jameson, weaver, small pox, M., 1 y
Oct	2	Peter s. Peter & Rebecca Baxendale, carder, small pox, M., 1 y 6 m
"	7	John s. James & Jane Thornley, weaver, fits, Droylsden, 5 days
"	16	Mary d. John & Margaret Aspinall, turner, M., 5 y 5 m
"	16	John s. Samuel & Elizabeth Procter, dyer, small pox, M., 1 y 2 m
"	16	William s. Thomas & Jane Smart, lamplighter, decline, M., 3 y
"	25	Anne d. Joseph & Anne Tetlow, weaver, cons., Newton, 30 y
"	26	Elizabeth d. Richd. & Elizth. Wilkinson, joiner, gang., Newton, 1 y 8 m
"	27	George s. John & Elizabeth Robinson, slater, decline, Newton, 8 m
Nov	2	Sarah sp. d. Anne Stafford, small pox, M., 5 m
"	6	James s. Joseph & Mary Butterworth, weaver, fits, M., 2 m 1 day
"	7	Sarah d. Joseph & Martha Clough, weaver, fits, Woodhouses, 3 m 21 days
"	9	Elizabeth Hulme, M., 87 y 6 m

"	10	Jane w. William Gorton, gardener, cons., Failsworth, 72 y
"	15	John s. Thomas & Nancy Whitaker, weaver, small pox, M., 10 m
"	16	George s. William & Elizabeth Jones, coal merchant, small pox, M. 2y 2m
"	16	John s. William & Martha Gillaspie, weaver, small pox, M., 1 y 4 m
"	17	Samuel Hall, bricklayer, fever, M., 64 y
"	20	Peter s. John & Mary Owen, weaver, cons., M., 17 y
"	23	John sp. s. Elizabeth Barlow, small pox, Newton, 1 y
"	26	Mary Anne d. William & Mary Hall, weaver, small pox, M., 6 y 5 m
"	29	James s. John & Elizabeth Fletcher, weaver, fits, Failsworth, 2 days
Dec	1	Mary Anne d. John & Ann Durker, bleacher, fits, M., 2 days
"	4	Abraham s. James & Sarah Ogden, collr., small pox, M., 10 m
"	4	Mary d. John & Mary Finney, cotton spinner, small pox, M., 3 y
"	4	Hannah d. Robert & Hannah Bentley, weaver, small pox, M., 9 m
"	7	Alice w. John Golding, labourer, cons., Werneth, 27 y
"	8	James Beswick, bleacher, Newton
"	11	Joseph [spu] s. Rebecca Bardsley, fits, M., 21 days
"	15	Elizabeth d. Samuel & Mary Booth, innkeeper, M., 1 y
"	18	Alice w. John Hulton, weaver, cons., Failsworth, 31 y
"	22	Mary d. John & Mary Barnes, pavier, small pox, M., 5 y
"	22	John Butterworth, weaver, accident, M., 41 y
"	25	Mary w. Ezekiel Sanderson, coal merchant, paral., M., 66 y
"	31	Elizabeth w. Bryan Rowlinson, weaver, fever, M., 51 y
[		A. Ashworth Minister]
[		Jas Kenyon William Brown John Moore Chapel Wardens]

Burials 1804
[Burials at Newton Heath Chapel Anno 1804]

Jan	1	Richard s. James & Mary Walker, weaver, small pox, M., 4 y 9 m
"	1	Thomas s. Thomas & Rebecca Kempster, weaver, small pox, M., 2 y 9 m
"	1	Robert s. Luke & Anne Smith, weaver, fits, Failsworth, 1 m 21 days
"	2	Catherine w. Aaron Meaden, tinplate worker, cons, M., 23 y
"	4	Mary d. Edward & Anne Wrigley, weaver, dropsy, Failsworth, 24 y
"	4	William s. John & Mary Simister, weaver, fits, Failsworth, 1 day
"	7	Ellen d. John & Ellen Taylor, printer, fits, Waterside, 5 m 21 days
"	8	Joseph Shelmerdine, weaver, gripes, Newton, 65 y
"	8	Margt. d. William & Sarah Lees, weaver, swellg lungs, M., 1 y 8 m
"	15	Anne d. Samuel & Mary Scholes, weaver, measles, Failsworth, 5 m
"	20	Eliz Betty [Betty] d. Ralph & Anne Mather, weaver, weakness, Droylsden, 6 m
"	22	Robert s. Robert & Mary Ryder, cotton spinner, small pox, M., 1 y 6 m
"	23	Alice sp. d. Elizabeth Eckersley, fits, Failsworth, 3 m 14 days
"	24	Elizabeth w. Joseph Whitaker, weaver, cons., Failsworth, 71 y
"	25	Thomas s. James & Martha Allen, weaver, fits, Newton, 2 days

"	31	Sarah d. Jonathan & Esther Slater, merchant, fits, M., 7 days (*1804*)
		(*see entry Feb 13*)
Feb	1	Thomas Hooley, calenderer, decline, M., 31 y
"	1	Sarah w. Richard Burchill, weaver, dropsy, M., 65 y
"	4	James s. James & Betty Jameson, weaver, cons., M., 4 y 6 m
"	5	Alice [sp] d. Betty Sidebotham, cons., M., 4 y 10 m
"	7	Hannah d. William & Sarah Smith, weaver, tooth fever, M., 7 m
"	12	Edward Allen, labourer, inflamn., M., 62 y
"	13	Thomas s. Jonathan & Esther Slater, merchant, fits, M., 21 days
"	15	John s. Richard & Anne Andrew, weaver, fits, Bradford, 10 m
"	15	James s. James & Mary Harlow, cotton spinr., small, M., 3 y 11 m
"	16	Moses Berry, farmer, cons., Failsworth, 23 y 10 m
"	19	Mary w. John Makin, weaver, Failsworth, 81 y 6 m
"	20	Charles s. John & Elizabeth Wilson, weaver, small pox, M., 1 y
"	22	Susannah d. John & Hannah Lord, dyer, fits, Waterside, 2 y
"	24	John Ridings [Rydings], weaver, jaundice, Failsworth, 71 y
Mar	3	John s. Samuel & Mary Holland, weaver, fits, Failsworth, 2 days
"	4	Mary d. Thomas & Martha Bower, gardener, fits, Newton, 5 m
"	7	Edmund s. Philip & Esther Houghton, farmer, cons, Newton, 8 m
"	11	Anne d. Robert & Mary Thorp, weaver, cons., M., 34 y
"	12	Mary Andrew, widow, cons., Newton, 30 y
["	12	A Female Child found dead in Newton (*entry in BT only*)]
"	13	Benjamin sp. s. Anne Jefferson, infl. of lungs, M., 3 y
"	16	John s. Robert & Anne Bleakley, warehouseman, weakness, M., 8 m
"	18	Hannah w. William Brown, weaver, Newton
"	25	Maria d. Joseph & Elizh. Seel, printer, cons, Newton, 3 m 14 days
"	26	Mary w. John Tully, weaver, dropsy, M., 54 y
"	28	William Clegg, joiner, dropsy, Failsworth, 35 y
"	29	Anne w. Ralph Mather, weaver, consn., Droylsden, 29 y
Apr	1	James s. Thomas & Hannah Blackley, weaver, small pox, M., 15 m
"	4	John s. Philip & Esther Houghton, farmer, conv., Newton, 10 y
"	5	Sarah d. William & Mary Berry, weaver, fever, Failsworth, 41 y
"	8	Mary d. Robert & Ellen Avenson, miller, conv, Moston, 4 m 14 days
"	8	John s. Timothy & Elizabeth Cave, printer, conv., Moston, 5 m
"	9	Luke s. William & Mary Sutcliffe, weaver, Rushworth, 14 y
"	10	John Wood, cottonspinner, consn., M., 31 y
"	13	Hannah w. James Wilde, weaver, consn., Droylsden, 20 y
"	15	Rosanna d. Richard & Sarah Light, collr., small pox, Ashton Parish, 15 m
"	15	Ellen d. Joseph & Ellen Caldwell, farmer, conv., Newton, 15 m
"	19	Elizabeth d. William & (*blank*) [Elizth] Ball, weaver, cons, Newton, 27 y
"	19	Samuel Robinson, weaver, cons, Newton, 49 y
"	19	Sarah d. Isaac & Ellen Beesly, printer, fits, Failsworth, 6 days
"	22	William s. Thomas & Mary Sephton, cordwainer, decline, M., 10 m
"	24	Ellen w. William Hibbert, weaver, decline, Failsworth, 32 y
"	26	William s. William & Mary Galloway, joiner, conv., M., 5 m

"	26	Peter s. James & Ellen Moorfield, cotton-spinner, chin., M., 11 m
"	29	Alice d. James & Mary Whitehead, collier, smallpox, M., 11 m
"	30	William s. William & Ellen Hibbert, weaver, fits, Failsworth, 1 m
May	1	John s. Thomas & Mary Portis, spinner, chin., M., 2 y 8 m
"	2	Samuel s. Mark & Mary Fisher, miner, tooth fever, Droylsden, 8 m
"	6	Sarah d. George & Mary Lucas, labourer, weakness, M., 1 y
"	6	James sp. s. Sarah Clough, fits, Failsworth, 1 y 2 m
"	8	Mary sp. d. Sarah Taylor, small pox, M., 1 y 1 m
"	13	Samuel Hardy, weaver, consn., M., 47 y
"	15	Abraham s. Ralph & Anne Mather, weaver, weakness, Droylsden, 2 y
"	17	John s. Joseph & Betty Wrigley, weaver, weakness, Failsworth, 1 y 5 m
"	20	William Thornley, shoemaker, consn., Droylsden, 71 y
"	20	Margaret Duckett, cons, M., 21 y
"	20	William s. James & Alice Mason, weaver, quincey, Newton, 1 y 8 m
"	23	Sarah w. James Berry weaver, pleurisy, Failsworth, 25 y
"	25	Samuel s. Robert & Mary Grimshaw, weaver, convs., Newton, 1 m 1 day
"	27	Noah s. John & Ellen Berry, weaver, fits, Failsworth, 21 days
Jun	3	Jane d. John & Sarah Ogden, weaver, fits, Failsworth, 8 m
"	3	Elizabeth d. Robert & Anne Downs, spinner, decline, M., 2 y 4 m
"	4	Judith w. John Lee, weaver, decline, M., 47 y
"	7	Charles s. Peter & Anne Lomax, dyer, fits, Newton, 2 m 25 days
"	8	Betty w. James Clough, weaver, cons., Failsworth, 52 y
"	10	Thomas Wilson, farmer, apopy., Failsworth, 68 y
"	12	Frances sp. d. Betty Ormrod, weakness, M., 1 y 6 m
"	14	William Lees, weaver, jaundice, M., 71 y
"	15	Martha w. John Berry, farmer, cons., Failsworth, 63 y
"	26	Sarah d. Thomas & Sarah Clegg, farmer, fits, M., 1 y
"	29	James sp. s. Mary Barlow, fits, Newton, 11 days
Jul	2	Mary d. John & Sarah Hulme, weaver, small pox, M., 1 y 7 m
"	4	Martha Wroe, pleurisy, Failsworth, 35 y
"	6	Betty d. James & Alice Schofield, collier, infla, M., 1 y 8 m
"	12	Elizabeth w. Thomas Shepley, manufacturer, cons., Failsworth, 30 y
"	16	Jane Taylor, cons, Failsworth, 63 y
"	19	Robert Stott, manufacturer, cons, Failsworth, 36 y
"	19	Eliza d. Thomas & Margt. Pearson, manufacturer, conv., M., 4 m
"	22	Mary w. James Barlow, weaver, cons., M., 37 y
"	22	Jane d. James & Hannah Sandels, weaver, infla, M., 3 y 11 m
"	23	Catherine d. Michael & Margt. Leary, weaver, hooping cough, M., 6 m
"	24	Fortunatus Brickill, manufacturer, consumption, M., 61 y
"	31	John s. James & Sarah Pearson, weaver, cons., M., 6 m
Aug	5	James Shaw, whitster, paral., Blackley, 36 y
"	6	James s. Launcelot & Mary Hulton, weaver, infl., Failsworth, 8 m
"	7	Martha d. Edward & Mary Williams, hatter, small pox, M., 5 y 9 m
"	10	Margaret d. James & Alice Thorpe, weaver, fits, M., 1 day
"	12	William s. Robert & Mary Calvert, weaver, chinc., M., 6 m

"	13	Elizabeth w. James Fletcher, labourer, Failsworth, 26 y
"	15	Roger s. Samuel & Sarah Leigh, warehouseman, cons., M., 5 m
"	19	Nancy d. Ralph & Nancy Smethurst, weaver, tooth fever, Failsworth, 11m
"	20	Thomas s. John & Rebecca Morley, hatter, fits, Droylsden, 6 days
"	30	John s. Richard & Mary Richardson, weaver, Newton, 1 day
"	31	William s. William & Alice Mars, weaver, teeth, M., 1 y 1 m
Sep	2	Anne d. John [& Sarah] Williams, reeler, decline, M., 22 y
"	2	Mary w. Joseph Holt, weaver, decline, Failsworth, 57 y
"	7	Mary d. Francis & Ellen Keating, weaver, fever, M.
"	9	Sarah d. James & Jane Brown, labourer, conv., Failsworth, 15 days
"	16	Sarah d. William & Sarah Lees, weaver, M., 10 m
"	20	William s. Samuel & Mary Robinson, slater, fits, Newton, 1 day
"	23	Betty w. James Needham, weaver, cons, Failsworth, 26 y
"	23	Catherina d. Israel & Elizabeth Shaw, spinner, chinc., M., 1 m
"	25	Mary d. John & Martha Unsworth, shopkeeper, fits, M., 14 days
"	27	William Ormond, spinner, cons., M., 36 y
"	28	Martha d. George & Anne Etchels, weaver, cons., Failsworth, 13 y
"	28	William s. James & Nancy Woolstencroft, whitster, decline, Failsworth 5m
"	30	Anne w. Robert Blackley, warehouseman, decline, M., 26 y
"	30	Mary w. Thomas Fallows, gardener, decline, Didsbury, 33 y
"	30	John s. Adam & Mary Dawson, dyer, chinc., Failsworth, 5 y
Oct	1	Catherine d. Richard & Jane Smith, weaver, cons, M., 16 y
"	7	Robert s. Aaron & Catherine Maden, tinplate worker, M., 15 m
"	7	Edwin s. Henry & Anne Cotes, bookkeeper, cons, M., 15 m
"	7	Margaret d. Thomas & Margt. Pearson, manufacturer, cons, M., 16 m
"	9	Ellen Heywood, widow, Newton, 60 y
"	10	Edward s. Edward & Anne Jones, whitesmith, cons, M., 14 y
"	10	Elizabeth sp. d. Betty Wilkinson, conv, M., 2 m
"	11	Samuel Wardley, weaver, conv, Failsworth, 76 y
"	14	George s. Rowland & Nancy Wilson, spinner, chinc, M., 4 m
"	16	Frances d. James & Anne Robinson, weaver, fever, M., 2 y 2 m
"	22	Mary d. John & Betty Whitehead, weaver, cons, Moston, 2 y
"	23	James s. Thomas & Mary Beresford, weaver, cons, M., 7 m
"	24	Jonathan Butterworth, weaver, fever, M., 41 y
"	25	Absalom s. William & Anne Wilson, weaver, Moston
"	28	Margaret w. James Dronsfield, weaver, cons., Failsworth, 30 y
"	31	Mary w. James Waters, weaver, cons., Failsworth, 29 y
Nov	7	Martha w. James McMayhan, weaver, cons., M., 29 y
"	7	Elizabeth d. Edward & Mary Williams, hatter, M., 2 y 4 m
"	11	Harriet d. John & Elizh. Butterworth, weaver, swell lungs, M., 7 m
"	15	Richard sp. s. Hannah Taylor, carder, M., 7 m
"	16	Benjamin s. John & Mary Wilkinson, weaver, chinc, Failsworth, 5 m
"	19	Mary d. William & Sarah Smith, weaver, cons, M., 13 y 6 m
"	20	Richard Birchinal, weaver, cons, M., 71 y
"	25	Joseph s. Philip & Lucy Berry, weaver, fever, Failsworth, 14 y

"	27	John s. Thomas & Mary Thorpe, weaver, conv., Failsworth, 10 days
"	28	James Horrocks [Horrex], husbandman, cons, Failsworth, 63 y
"	28	Thomas s. William & Mary Tomlinson, weaver, teeth, Moston (*no age*)
"	28	Benjamin s. Samuel & Mary Booth, innkeeper, small pox, M., 4 y 1 m
"	30	Margaret w. Samuel Duxbury, weaver, cons, M., 24 y
"	30	Maria d. Edward & Anne Jones, whitesmith, conv., M., 1 m
Dec	2	Ralph s. William & Anne Smethurst, whitster, cons, M., 2 y
"	2	Mary wdw. [w.] George Tomlinson, weaver, dysent, Moston, 66 y
"	4	Anne d. John & Elizabeth Beresford, weaver, cons., M., 1 y
"	5	Joseph Ferr, weaver, cons., M., 60 y
"	6	Betty d. George & Mary Tomlinson, weaver, dysent, Moston, 24 y
"	9	William s. John & Sarah Tomlinson, weaver, M., 4 y
"	9	Jane d. James & Mary Hulton, weaver, cons, Oldham, 21 y
"	9	David sp. s. Betty Holt, accdt., Failsworth, 1 y 3 m
"	12	Edward s. Henry & Sebre Smith, weaver, chinc, M., 2 m 1 day
"	16	Ellen d. John & Mary Lister, collier, fits, M., 1 m 14 days
"	18	Mary w. John Walmsley, farmer, cons., Failsworth, 47 y
"	23	Elizabeth d. Alice Butterworth, convul., M., 7 m
"	27	Anne w. Thomas Goodier, weaver, consn., Failsworth, 72 y
[		A. Ashworth Minister]

Burials in 1805
[Buried at Newton Heath Chapel in the year 1805]

Jan	1	Joshua Holroyd, blacksmith, consum, M., 49 y
"	1	John Wilkinson, weaver, consum, Failsworth, 29 y
"	8	Betty d. James & Betty Bottomly, blacksmith, swellg. lungs, Bradford, 2 m 7 days
"	9	Cornelius s. Charles & Sarah Thomson, baker, M., 1 y 1 m 1 day
"	9	Richard s. Richard & Mary Whittenstall, joiner, M., 3 m 21 days
"	12	Nancy d. Thomas & Frances Conolly, weaver, quin, M., 3 y
"	13	Thomas s. Robert & Anne Hobson, bleacher, consn., Droylsden, 8 y
"	14	Betty w. John Hallworth, printer, consn., Newton, 22 y
"	16	Edward Jones, whitesmith, cholera, M., 48 y
"	16	Alice d. John & Elizabeth Lees, bricklayer, inflam., M., 2 y
"	22	John s. Philip & Mary Rogerson, weaver, cons, M., 5 y
"	31	Mary Whalley, winder, Newton
Feb	4	Sarah w. Joseph Berry, blacksmith, paral, Failsworth, 43 y
"	5	Anne Makin, Failsworth, 68 y
"	6	Thomas s. John & Betty Royle, spinner, swell lungs, M., 5 m
"	6	David s. David & Elizabeth Potter, dyer, conv, Moston, 7 m
"	7	James Lees, bleacher, consn., Failsworth, 73 y
"	12	James s. James & Sarah Chadderton, consn., Failsworth, 72 y
"	15	Richard s. James & Mary Whitehead, miner, cons, M., 6 m
"	17	Ellen d. Joseph & Ellen Caldwell, farmer, conv, Newton, 2 m 14 days

"	19	Betty d. John & Alice Thorpe, weaver, Failsworth, 19 y (*1805*)
"	21	Martha w. Thomas Bower, gardener, childbed, Newton, 27 y
"	21	Alice d. Thomas & Martha Bower, gardener, conv, Newton, 3 days
"	25	William s. Thomas & Betty Hulton, weaver, cons, Moston, 60 y
"	27	Betty w. Joseph Booth, weaver, decline, M., 82 y
"	27	John Moores, weaver, decline, Failsworth, 58 y
Mar	3	Sarah d. Thomas & Betty Stirrup, weaver, hoopg. cough, M., 1 y
"	10	Jane w. Thomas Brown, bleacher, decline, Newton, 80 y (*?- age faded*)
"	17	Robert s. Zacchaus & Anne Gravel, weaver, cons., M., 7 m
"	17	Alice w. James Howarth, labourer, fever, Failsworth, 33 y
"	19	Thomas s. William & Mary Keighley, weaver, small pox, M., 2 m 7 days
"	30	Abel Tomlinson, weaver, decline, Failsworth, 36 y
Apr	6	Benjamin s. Benjamin & Violet Hulton, weaver, decline, Failsworth, 1y 1m
"	14	Michael s. Michael & Mary Smith, cordwainer, decline, M., 16 y
"	14	Fanny d. Jonathan & Peggy Grimshaw, weaver, decline, Droylsden, 1y 1m
"	16	James s. John & Martha Bell, barber, small pox, M., 4 y
"	18	Samuel Thomas, spinner, decline, M., 22 y
"	21	Nancy Chadwick, weaver, decline, Failsworth, 19 y
"	29	Hannah d. Joseph & Nancy Priestnal, spinner, decline, M., 5 y
May	9	Sarah d. John & Mary Whitehead, inn keeper, fits, Newton, 2 m 21 days
"	10	Ann w. Joshua Cordingly, weaver, decline, Failsworth, 45 y
"	12	Charlotte d. George & Mary Shore, labourer, decline, M., 13 y
"	15	Margaret w. William Turner, dyer, decline, Newton, 67 y
"	16	Charlotte d. John & Martha Jackson, labourer, decline, Newton, 5 y
"	17	William s. Charles & Elizabeth Mathewson, weaver, fever, M., 1 y 9 m
"	19	Ann w. William McCullough, joiner, decline, M., 52 y
"	20	Sarah d. Thomas & Betty Barlow, weaver, decline, Failsworth, 11 y
"	21	George s. Joseph & Nancy Priestnal, spinner, hooping cough, M., 1 y
"	22	Joseph Moors, weaver, dropsy, M., 64 y
"	22	Betty d. Thomas & Hannah Gradwell, weaver, swell lungs, M., 1 y 6 m
"	22	Alice w. Thomas Horrocks [Horrax], labourer, decline, Failsworth, 31 y
"	26	William s. William & Sarah Taylor, labourer, conv., M., 14 days
"	26	Esther w. Philip Houghton, farmer, decline, Newton
Jun	2	Nancy d. John & Ellen Jenkinson, spinner, small pox, M., 1 y 5 m
"	2	Eliza d. John & Alice Hughes, labourer, small pox, M., 1 y 3 m
"	2	Betty d. John & Betty Whitehead, miner, decline, M., 8 m
"	4	Richard s. William & Nancy Robinson, fits, Failsworth
"	5	Richard Lonsdale, spinner, lunacy, M., 36 y
"	5	Thomas s. Sarah Marsh, weaver, fits, M., 2 y
"	5	Ann w. Joseph Pollit, weaver, decline, Failsworth, 30 y
"	6	Philip Houghton, farmer, pleurisy, Newton, 41 y
"	7	Richard Whittlestone, joiner, decline, M., 30 y
"	9	Betty d. Thos. & Elizabeth Charlesworth, labourer, decline, M., 9 m
"	21	Mary d. Simeon & Ann Smith, weaver, childbed, Failsworth, 21 y
"	23	Hannah d. Henry & Mary Cryer, spinner, erysipelas, M., 2 y 1 m

"	25	Elizabeth d. William & Rebecca Boyden, weaver, decline, M., 4 m
"	27	Betty Ogden (, singlewoman *not in BT*), weaver, decline, Ashton Parish, 45 y
"	30	James s. William & Betty Burgess, spinner, decline, M., 1 y 3 m
Jul	1	Mary d. James & Mary Barlow, weaver, decline, Newton, 25 y
"	2	Martha d. William & Alice Mather, weaver, decline, Newton, 29 y
"	3	Elizabeth w. Edward Coltman, labourer, fever, Newton, 29 y
"	3	Jane d. Samuel & Betty Clough, weaver, decline, Failsworth, 7 y
"	4	Anne d. Joseph & Anne Lomax, weaver, small pox, M., 1 y 6 m
"	4	John s. Joseph & Elizabeth Wilshaw, weaver, fits, M., 14 days
"	5	Henry s. John & Anne Hamson, weaver, tooth fever, M., 7 m
"	8	George s. Samuel & Mary Robinson, slater, Newton
"	9	Robert Barlow, weaver, decline, Newton, 31 y
"	10	John s. Mary Kirkham, spinster, fits, M., 14 days
"	12	Anne w. James Thorpe, weaver, decline, Failsworth, 72 y
"	14	Thomas s. John & Ellen Laverick, joiner, small pox, 1 y
"	16	Hannah d. William & Betty Goodier, weaver, fever, Newton, 30 y
"	18	Jane d. John & Mary Wilkinson, weaver, decline, Failsworth, 2 y 6 m
"	22	Thomas s. Betty Wilson, reeler, small pox, M., 6 m
"	28	James Whitehead, weaver, decline, Moston, 72 y
"	28	Mary w. Jonathan Hooley, coachman, decline, Newton, 62 y
"	30	John s. John & Betty Whitehead, weaver, hooping cough, Newton, 9 m
Aug	2	Joseph Lock, stablegroom, dropsy, Newton, 60 y
"	6	Samuel Hyde, dyer, sudden death, Harpurhey, 63 y
"	9	James s. John & Martha Bell, barber, fits, M., 2 days
"	11	Betty d. James & Sarah Nuttal, dyer, fits, Newton, 2 m 21 days (*cross* X *in margin to this entry*)
"	15	Samuel s. John & Mary Plimmer, miner, accident, M., 2 y 2 m
"	15	Sarah w. John Mason, crofter, childbed, Droylsden, 26 y 9 m
"	20	Peter s. Luke & Elizabeth Sloan, weaver, small pox., M., 3 y
"	21	William s. Abel & Mary Tomlinson, weaver, decline, Failsworth, 1 y 6 m
"	28	Mary d. William & Mary Blackshaw, crofter, decline, Openshaw, 21 y
"	30	William Jenkins[on], weaver, decline, M., 42 y
Sep	1	John Williamson, miner, decline, M., 60 y
"	2	James s. John & Martha Shaw, porter, fits, M., 5 m
"	2	Mary w. Robert Thorpe, weaver, decline, M., 62 y
"	4	Andrew s. Samuel & Betty Clough, weaver, decline, Failsworth, 2 m 7 days
"	4	Obadiah Bradshaw, labourer, decline, Failsworth, 45 y
"	8	Deborah wdw. Joseph Moors, weaver, dropsy, M., 58 y
"	9	John s. John & Betty Leech, butcher, fits, M., 2 m
"	9	Marianne d. Michael & Magt [Mary] Leary, weaver, hoopg cough, M., 4 y 8 m
"	11	John s. George & Ann Brandon, smith, fits, Newton, 6 m 21 days
"	14	Betty d. John & Esther Fitton, weaver, fits, Moston, 2 m 21 days
"	17	Mary d. Richard & Sarah Overend, weaver, small pox, M., 1 y 6 m

"	17	Joseph s. Peter & Mary Wyld, waggoner, worried by a pig, Newton, 1m 1d
"	23	Anne d. Issachar & Betty Thorpe, weaver, fits, Failsworth, 2 m
"	23	Mary d. George & Mary Tomlinson, decline, Failsworth, 5 m
"	25	Ellen w. Thomas Ryder, crofter, lunacy, M., 47 y
"	27	Frances d. Sarah Whittlestone, sewing woman, decline, M., 1 m 7 days
"	30	George s. Barnet & Anne Nugent [Newgent], weaver, fits, M., 2 m 7 days
Oct	1	Harriet d. John & Mary Whitehead, joiner, small pox, M., 1 y
"	2	Thomas s. Daniel & Mary Smith, weaver, decline, Failsworth, 22 y
"	6	Michael s. Nicholas & Hannah Pritchard, decline, M., 3 m
"	7	William s. James & Betty Riddal, weaver, decline, Newton, 1 y 6 m
"	10	John s. Jonathan & Mary Hartley, miner, decline, M., 1 y 5 m
"	11	Alice Page, widow, decline, Newton, 85 y
"	13	Lydia Mather, widow, decline, M., 69 y
"	14	William s. James & Betty Bythel, crofter, hoopg cough, Droylsden, 1y 3m
"	15	Isaac s. Thomas & Anne Ogden, weaver, small pox, M., 11 m
"	16	Thomas s. Robert & Mary Hulme, crofter, accident, Droylsden, 12 y
"	18	John Buckelton, architect, inflam. on lungs, M., 59 y
"	20	Mary d. Michael & Anne Dermot, tailor, small pox, M., 1 y 4 m
"	20	Thomas s. James & Rebecca Hardy, calenderer, fits, M., 7 m
"	20	Mary d. William & Sarah Daltry, farmer, swell. lungs, Newton, 2 y 6 m
"	27	Sarah d. John & Mary Redmund, warehouseman, small pox, M., 1 y 13 d
"	27	David s. Elias & Jane Bythel, labourer, shot, Newton, 12 y
"	27	Elizabeth d. William & Mary Hall, weaver, hoopg. cough, M., 1 y
"	27	Elizabeth w. Samuel Clough, weaver, decline, Failsworth, 28 y
"	30	Richard Ditchfield, weaver, decline, Failsworth, 63 y
Nov	9	Harriet d. Richard & Elizh. Hill, miner, tooth fever, M., 8 m
"	10	Betty d. James & Anne Whitehead, weaver, worm fever, Failsworth
"	12	Robert s. William & Ellen Harrison, print cutter, fits, Newton, 3 y 14 days
"	12	Isaac Nixon, joiner, decline, M., 66 y
"	15	William s. William & Mary Jenkinson, weaver, decline, M., 5 m
"	18	Stephen s. John & Mary Redmund, warehouseman, small pox, M., 4 y
"	24	William s. Thomas & Mary Beresford, weaver, fits, M., 2 m
Dec	4	Mary Wardleworth, widow, weaver, decline, Moston, 82 y
"	5	Joseph s. Joseph & Mary Rogers, small pox, M., 3 y 4 m
"	5	Samuel s. Edward & Mary Thornley, silk spinner, small pox, M., 2 y 6 m
"	8	Thomas s. George & Mary Clark, dyer, inflam. lungs, M., 1 y
"	8	William s. Thomas & Ann Stafford, warper, tooth fever, M., 9 m
"	10	James Berry, weaver, decline, Failsworth, 65 y
"	13	Ann d. James & Elizh. Bradshaw, weaver, small pox, M., 1 y 3 m
"	16	Jane d. Ellen Cares[oft], sewing woman, small pox, M., 1 y 4 m
"	16	Maria d. Robert & Betty Perry, miner, hoop. cough, M., 1 y
"	16	Mary d. William & Martha Pickard, joiner, decline, M., 18 y
"	17	Samuel s. Joseph & Martha Taylor, hatter, small pox, M., 9 m
"	27	Sarah d. John & Betty Bardsley, weaver, hoopg. cough, Droylsden, 1 y 6 m
"	28	George s. Samuel & Susanna Coe, spinner, small pox, M., 5 m

" 28 Harriet d. Joseph & Sarah Wright, saddler, decline, M., 8 m

Burials in 1806
[Buried at Newton Heath Chapel in the year 1806]

Jan	1	William s. Mary Williamson, weaver, fits, M., 21 days
"	5	Thomas s. Anthony & Al[l]icia Ryan, baker, decline, M., 1 m
"	8	John Jenkinson, weaver, decline, M., 72 y
"	9	Mary w. James Thorp, weaver, decline, Failsworth, 34 y
"	10	Agnes w. James Hulton, weaver, decline, Failsworth, 69 y
"	12	Nancy d. George & Ann Etchels, weaver, decline, Failsworth, 18 y
"	21	William s. John & Sarah Hulme, weaver, decline, M., 6 m
"	22	Betty w. John Lees, bricklayer, decline, M., 41 y
"	22	Hannah d. Charles & Mary Partington, weaver, decline, M., 5 m
"	24	Betty d. James & Ann Thorp, weaver, decline, Failsworth, 34 y
"	26	Phebe Withington, weaver, decline, Salford, 84 y
"	26	Joseph s. John & Ellen Bird, weaver, hoop. cough, Ardwick, 4 y
"	29	Elizabeth d. Thomas & Jane Moors, weaver, small pox, M., 5 m
"	31	Betty (wdw. Moses *not in BT*) Berry, weaver, decline, Failsworth, 21 y
Feb	2	Ann w. Jacob Wolstencroft, weaver, decline, M., 24 y
"	4	Ann d. Luke & Ann Burn, weaver, hoopg. cough, M., 3 y 9 m
"	9	John s. James & Rosetta Maffin, mason, fits, M., 10 days
"	10	Ann w. Samuel Travis, weaver, decline, M., 68 y
"	14	Thomas Bentley, warehouseman, flux, Cheetham, 53 y
"	14	Esther w. Samuel Wyat, weaver, decline, M., 66 y
"	14	John Harrison, hawker, decline, M., 57 y
"	23	John s. John & Lydia Ingham, weaver, accident, Reddish
"	24	Hannah d. Sarah Berry, decline, Failsworth, 15 y
"	26	Samuel Smith, fever, Failsworth, 47 y
Mar	3	John s. Thomas & Alice Horridge [Orridge], weaver, decline, Failsworth, 5 m 21 days
"	5	Michael s. Frances & Ellen Keating, weaver, decline, M., 4 y
"	9	William s. William & Sarah Walker, weaver, decline, Newton, 11 m
"	9	Thomas Lancaster, weaver, decline, Failsworth, 56 y
"	12	Benjamin Garside, sawyer, dropsy, M., 58 y
"	13	Elizabeth d. Robert & Mary Anderson, joiner, decline, M., 1 y 6 m
"	19	Betty d. John & Dorothy [Deborah] Blomely, weaver, small pox, M., 1 y 2 m
"	19	Betty d. John & Betty Lees, bricklayer, fever, M., 6 y
"	23	Jane Hudson (, widow *not in BT*), spinner, inflam. bowels, M., 54 y
"	23	Mary Wilkinson (, widow *not in BT*), weaver, decline, Failsworth, 30 y
"	23	William s. James & Ann Croom, farmer, small pox, Newton
"	25	Mary d. Saml. & Jane Heginbottom [Higginbottom], weaver, small pox, M., 3 y

"	27	Thomas Johnson, cordwainer, decline, M., 23 y	(*1806*)

" 27 Thomas Johnson, cordwainer, decline, M., 23 y   (*1806*)

" 30 John s. Robert & Elizh. Wyld, weaver, small pox, M., 2 y 11 m

Apr 1 Sarah d. James & Hannah Saunders, weaver, decline, M., 10 y

" 2 Sarah d. Joseph & Sarah Walker, labourer, small pox, Droylsden, 1 y 1 m

" 4 Sarah w. Daniel Saunders, labourer, decline, Failsworth, 66 y

" 6 Elizabeth d. Mary Lomax, weaver, decline, Newton, 2 m

" 6 James s. William & Nancy Robinson, weaver, Failsworth

" 6 Michael s. Michael & Mary Smith, cordwainer, convul., M., 2 m

" 6 Thos. Dixon s. James & Isabella [Elizabeth] Fullalove, spinner, measles, M., 9 m

" 9 Joseph s. Richard & Mary Coffinson, miner, small pox, Bradford, 5 y

" 9 Harriet d. John & Betty Lees, bricklayer, fits, M., 5 m

" 11 Martha d. Henry & Jane Singleton, bricklayer, small pox, M., 2 y

" 11 Rosette d. Thomas & Jane Johnson, cordwainer, hoopg. cough, M., 2 y

" 13 Thomas s. John & Mary Robinson, tailor, rheuma. fever, Failsworth, 9 m

" 15 Thomas Cooper, farmer, decline, Newton, 74 y

" 17 Sarah d. John & Mary Whitehead, innkeeper, decline, Newton, 1 m 7 days

" 18 Elizabeth (wdw. Samuel *not in BT*) Schofield, joiner, decline, Ardwick, 47 y

" 20 Ann d. John & Alice Thomson, labourer, small pox, M., 12 y

" 20 Mary d. Robert & Mary Bolton, weaver, croup, M., 3 y 3 m

" 22 Thomas s. Richard & Mary Coffinson, miner, small pox, Bradford, 3 y

" 22 Alice d. George & Hannah Tattershall, spinner, small pox, M., 2 y

" 26 Mary w. Isaac Allridge, weaver, fever, Ardwick, 28 y

" 28 Mary d. Alexander & Mary McDonald, decline, M., 11 m

" 29 John Saxton, Soldier in the Guards, decline, M., 33 y

May 4 Benjamin s. Robert & Mary Bolton, weaver, small pox, M., 1 y

" 6 Oliver s. Oliver & Ann Greenwood, weaver, small pox, M., 4 y

" 9 John s. William & Rebecca Worral, manufacturer, fever, Failsworth 2y 6m

" 11 Richard Bonshall, weaver, consn., M., 57 y

" 11 John Lyon Birtles s. Joseph & Ellen Birtles, weaver, small pox, M., 1 y

" 11 Anne d. Oliver & Anne Greenwood, weaver, small pox, M., 1 y

" 11 William s. Charles & Betty McLough, weaver, consumpn., M., 2 y 4 m

" 15 Joseph Walmsley, shopkeeper, accident, Failsworth, 53 y

" 16 Jonas s. William & Mary Brown, manufacturer, measles, M., 1 y 10 m

" 18 James Dronsfield, weaver, pleurisy, M., 31 y

" 19 James Whitworth, whipmaker, consumpn., M., 47 y

" 19 Ellen w. John Taylor, calico printer, consumpn., Ashton Parish, 24 y

" 21 Jonathan s. James & Mary Thorp, weaver, consumpn., Failsworth, 1 y

" 21 Maria d. John & Elizabeth Edge, weaver, small pox, M., 1 y 2 m

" 23 Mary d. William & Mary Hulme, miner, small pox, M., 5 y 7 m

" 27 John s. John & Mary Slone, spinner, consumpn., M., 1 y 7 m

[" 31 Jane d. Samuel & Hannah Weaver, M. (*entry in BT only*)   ]

Jun 4 Sarah d. John & Sarah Leigh, weaver, convuln., M., 9 m

" 4 James s. James & Sarah Wilson, weaver drowned, Moston, 3 y

" 8 George s. William & Hannah Scowcroft, labourer, small pox, M., 3 y 6 m

"	8	Jane d. Richard & Frances Ledger, weaver, measles, M., 1 y 1 m (*1806*)
"	10	John s. Joseph & Elizabeth Seel, printer, dropsy, Newton, 9 y
"	11	Thomas s. Thomas & Ruth Booth, cloth dresser, swell lungs, Ardwick, 4 y 2 m
"	12	John s. James & Martha Kemp, weaver, small pox, M., 3 y 4 m
"	15	Hannah d. Robert & Mary Calvert, weaver, measles, M., 1 y 1 m
"	16	George s. James & Mary Ainsworth, weaver, small pox, M., 1 y 6 m
"	17	Mary d. John & Ellen Taylor, printer, decline, Ashton Parish, 1 y 8 m
"	17	Joseph s. Richard & Betty Wilkinson, joiner, fits, Oldham, 21 days
"	19	Anne d. Thomas & Phebe Winterbottom, weaver, decline, Failsworth, 19y
"	19	Mary d. Richard & Hannah Thicket, cordwainer, small pox, M., 10 m
"	19	Thomas Bower, gardener, fever, Newton, 36 y
"	20	Harriet d. Ralph & Hannah Chadderton [Chatterton], innkeeper, measles, [M], 4 y
"	23	Samuel s. Thomas & Frances Robinson, labourer, measles, Newton, 1y 6m
"	23	William (H. Atkinson *not in BT*) s. William & Jane Atkinson, hosier, decline, M., 2 y
"	24	Thos. s. Willm. & Sarah Bir(k)shenhead, spinner, decline, M., 1 y 3 m
"	25	Elizabeth w. John Hewit [Hewett], labourer, decline, M., 45 y
"	25	John Harlow, spinner, fever, M., 23 y
"	25	Philip s. John & Mary Tetlow, weaver, sw. lungs, Kirkmanshulme, 3y 10m
"	28	John Smith, silk manufacturer, pleurisy, M., 39 y
"	29	William Jackson, crofter, decline, M., 33 y
"	29	Jenny d. Richard & Anne Pollit, weaver, dysent, Failsworth, 1 y 3 m
"	29	John s. John & Mary Makin, gardener, small pox, M., 4 y
"	29	John s. Richard & Sarah Hartley, dyer, M., 3 days
Jul	2	Richard Coffinson, miner, suffocd. by damp, Bradford, 31 y
"	2	Mary d. John & Ann Clough, drawer, measles, M., 1 y 7 m
"	6	Joseph s. John & Betty Taylor, miner, sm. pox, M., 1 y 6 m
"	6	William s. Josiah & Mary Ingham, weaver, M., 1 y 3 m
"	6	Hannah d. Samuel & Mary Bowden, spinner, M., 1 y 9 m
"	7	Bernard s. Patrick & Ann Gillner, weaver, measles, M., 7 y
"	7	Andrew s. Thomas & Martha Goodier, weaver, fits, Failsworth, 1 m 7 days
"	11	James s. David & Betty Potter, dyer, decline, Failsworth, 1 y
"	13	William s. Henry & Mary Etchels, weaver, decline, Failsworth
"	13	William s. John & Mary Tetlow, weaver, sw. lungs, Kirkmanshulme, 1 y
"	13	William s. William & Frances Toole, cordwainer, measles, M., 1 y
"	14	Anne d. John & Lydia Dodd, taylor, decline, M., 21 y
"	20	Maria d. John & Ann Burgess, spinner, measles, M., 7 m
"	23	Anne w. Edward Campbell, warehouseman, decline, Salford, 49 y
"	27	Joseph s. Thomas & Agnes Jameson, joiner, fever, M., 13 y
"	29	Fanny d. William & Mary Hulme, miner, small pox, M., 11 m
"	29	Anne w. Edward O'Hara, weaver, decline, M., 38 y
"	29	Elizabeth w. John Clayton, miner, decline, M., 58 y
"	29	William (sp. *not in BT*) s. Mary Horrocks, weaver, fits, Failsworth, 2 m

"	29	Daniel s. James & Nancy Wolstencroft, bleacher, measles, Failsworth, 11m
"	30	Rebekah d. Mich[ae]l & Isabel(la) NSN, labourer, small pox, M., 1 y 10 m
Aug	3	Ralph s. Philip & Mary Rogerson, weaver, decline, M., 4 y 4 m
"	4	William s. Francis & Ellen Brown, weaver, decline, M., 4 m
"	15	Edmund Whitehead, weaver, decline, Ashton Parish, 58 y
"	17	Anne d. John & Sarah Norcroft, calenderer, decline, M., 2 y
"	17	Robert Wyld, weaver, decline, M., 50 y
"	20	William s. Thomas & Jane Moors, weaver, fits, M.
"	24	Mary d. Sarah Syddal, weaver, swell. lungs, M., 2 y 8 m
"	26	Sarah d. George & Margt. Taggart, weaver, fits, M., 3 m
"	28	James s. Martha Smith, weaver, convulsns., Failsworth, 3 y
"	31	Alice d. Henry & Elizh. Wood, spinner, fits, M., 2 m 14 days
Sep	3	Owen s. Patrick & Anne McWade, weaver, decline, M., 1 y .... (*remainder faded*)
"	3	William s. Thomas & Mary Dawson, dyer, tooth fever, Newton, 11 m
"	8	John Smith, gold nokler (*uncertain reading*), decline, Failsworth [Newton], 65 y
"	9	Mary d. James & Anne Allen, weaver, decline, Failsworth, 21 y
"	9	John s. James & Margaret Crossley, labourer, dysent, Harpurhey, 6 y
"	12	Esther Hulme, weaver, pleurisy, M., 53 y
"	13	Anne w. David Robinson, print cutter, childbed, Droylsden, 31 y
"	15	Peter s. Joseph & Anne Lomax, weaver, M., 1 y 5 m
"	15	Robert s. John & Mary Whalley, weaver, fits, M., 3 m 14 days
"	18	George s. George & Mary Brown, weaver, fits, M., 14 days
"	23	Thomas s. James & Bella Aspinal, printer, decline, M., 1 m 7 days
"	23	Hannah [sp] d. Sarah Singleton, weaver, fits, M., 1 y 6 m
"	23	Mary d. Samuel & Mary Siddal, miner, fits, M.
"	23	James [sp] s. Jane Kershaw, weaver, decline, M., 7 m
"	26	James Thorpe, weaver, drowned in canal, Failsworth, 24 y
"	28	James sp. s. Mary Greenwood, weaver, fits, M.
Oct	6	George Moore, bricklayer, flux, M., 28 y
"	14	James s. John & Sarah Moors, weaver, small pox, M., 8 m
"	14	James Beswick, crofter, decline, Newton, 48 y
"	20	William s. Francis & Matty Brown, farmer, fits, Woodhouses
"	22	Mary d. Henry & Sabre Smith, weaver, fits, M.
"	28	Mary w. Robert Ogden, weaver, decline, Newton, 27 y
"	31	Sarah Whitworth, innkeeper, palsy, Moston, 82 y
Nov	5	John s. Thomas & Anne Stanton, weaver, decline, M., 9 m
"	16	Betty d. Peter & Hannah Lomax, dyer, decline, Failsworth, 2 m 7 days
"	23	Alice d. James & Mary Byrne, weaver, decline, M., 23 y
"	27	Robert s. John & Alice Clough, weaver, Failsworth, 1 m
"	27	Ralph s. Joseph & Alice Taylor, weaver, hoopg. cough, M., 6 m 8 days (*see next entry; one entry only in BT*)
"	27	Ralph s. Joseph & Alice Taylor, weaver, hoopg. cough, M., 6 m 22 days (*see previous entry*)

"	30	Thomas Rilley, weaver, asthma, M., 55 y
"	30	Elizabeth d. Peter & Sarah Travis, miner, fever, M., 1 y 1 m
Dec	1	Sally d. James & Alice Howarth, carter, small pox, Failsworth, 8 y
"	10	Thomas s. James & Sarah Whitaker, weaver, fits, Failsworth
"	12	John Reaves, labourer, M., 32 y
"	18	Anne d. John & Sarah Tetlow, weaver, hoopg. cough, M., 2 y 8 m
"	21	Felix s. Anthony & Eliza Ryan, baker, scalded, M., 13 y 7 m
"	21	James s. John & Anne Whitaker, weaver, fits, Failsworth, 8 m 18 days
"	25	Anne w. Thomas Stanton, weaver, decline, M., 22 y
[		A. Ashworth Minister]
[		James Kenyon Joseph Bertenshaw William Brown John Moore Wardens]

Burials in 1807

Jan	2	John Houghton, innkeeper, dropsy, Newton, 33 y
"	4	Mary d. Charles & Mary Watson, plasterer, decline, Newton, 1 y 3 m
"	8	James s. George & Ruth Thorp, weaver, fits, M., 1 m 14 days
"	11	Mary d. Sarah Brevet, winder, fits, Newton, 21 days
"	15	James Wolstencroft, crofter, dropsy, Failsworth, 45 y
"	18	John s. Thomas & Sarah Neal, collier, .. of lungs, M., 1 y 6 m
"	18	Jane d. Joseph & Elizabeth Hough, cordwainer, Bradford, 10 y
"	19	Mary d. Richard & Margaret Fenner, weaver, hoop. cough, M., 4 m 14 d
"	20	Elizabeth d. Esther Taylor, weaver, fits, Failsworth, 1 m 7 days
"	22	John (sp. *not in BT*) s. Martha Etchels, weaver, Failsworth, 4 m 14 days
"	25	Sarah w. James Whitaker, weaver, decline, Failsworth, 36 y
Feb	2	John s. James & Anne Tully, weaver, decline, M., 12 y
"	5	Susanna d. Philip & Mary Haughton, weaver, fits, Droylsden, 14 days
"	8	Samuel Beswick, bleacher, decline, Levenshulme, 92 y
"	11	Alice wdw. Samuel Lees, weaver, fever, Failsworth, 71 y
"	11	Martha w. Jeremiah Hopwood, weaver, childbed, Newton, 18 y
"	13	Alexander s. James & Rebekah [Rebecca] Johnson, weaver, hoopg. cough, M., 10 m
"	13	John s. David & Anne Etchels, small pox, Failsworth, 2 y 2 m
"	15	John s. James & Betty Ogden, weaver, fits, Failsworth, 8 m
"	15	Thomas s. Thomas & Betty Stirrup, weaver, decline, M., 1 y
"	16	Nancy w. Edmund Travis, bleacher, decline, Newton, 59 y
"	22	Jonathan s. William & Hannah Winstanley, forgeman, M., 1 y 6 m
"	22	Thomas Williams, spinner, hurt (*uncertain reading*), M., 49 y
"	25	William s. David & Martha Ridgway, fur cutter, fits, M., 3 m
"	26	William McNear, weaver, decline, M., 43 y
Mar	1	Mary w. William Mather, weaver, decline, Droylsden, 51 y
"	3	Maria d. John & Mary Stansfield, hatter, fits, Newton, 7 m
"	8	Jonathan s. Edmund & Alice Walmsley, joiner, decline, M., 3 y 1 m
"	11	Mary d. John & Sarah Ryley, miner, hoopg. cough, M., 3 y

"	15	Thomas s. John & Sarah Ryley, miner, hoopg. cough, M., 1 y *(1807)*
"	15	Anne d. John & Anne Reaves, labourer, decline, M., 1 y 2 m
"	19	John s. Hugh & Margaret Carrol, weaver, decline, M., 1 y 3 m
"	19	Hannah w. John Rogers, weaver, decline, Newton, 50 y
"	19	Richard s. Philip & Mary Rogerson, weaver, decline, M., 1 y 5 days (*see entry Mar 31*)
"	24	Sarah Allen (wdw. Thomas Allen *not in BT*), labourer, palsy, Newton, 62 y
"	25	Thomas s. John & Mary Costlow, weaver, hoopg. cough, M., 1 y
"	30	George s. Samuel & Fanny Ogden, weaver, small pox, Failsworth, 3 y 1 m
"	31	James s. Philip & Mary Rogerson, weaver, fits, M., 1 y 17 days
"	31	Brunker Wilkinson, weaver, decline, Failsworth, 66 y
Apr	1	John s. John & Hannah Brennand, weaver, sw. lungs, Droylsden, 2 m 7 d
"	1	John s. Elizabeth Wood, weaver, tooth fever, M., 8 m
"	5	James Walker, collier, decline, M., 48 y
"	5	Jonathan s. Joshua & Betty [Elizth] Swift, weaver, hoopg. cough, Newton, 1 y 7 m
"	7	John s. John & Betty Clough, weaver, fever, Failsworth, 9 y
"	7	John s. William & Mary Brown, manufacturer, measles, M., 9 m
"	8	Mary d. Thomas Ogden, weaver, childbed, Moston, 21 y
"	10	Frederick s. Luke & Nelly [Ellen] Etchels, weaver, tooth fever, Failsworth, 9 m (*altered from* 6 m)
"	12	Hannah d. John & Mary Smith, warehouseman, decline, Newton, 5 m
"	12	Mary w. Nathan Thomson, weaver, decline, Chadderton, 80 y
"	16	Peter Faris, collier, drowned, Bradford, 30 y
"	17	Anne w. John Rudd, spinner, dropsy, M., 54 y
"	19	Jane w. Peter Ormrod, weaver, decline, Ardwick, 36 y
"	19	James s. James & Nancy Wolstencroft, crofter, fever, Failsworth, 1 y 5 m
"	22	John s. Joseph & Nancy Ogden, weaver, small pox, Failsworth
"	23	Jane w. John Johnson, weaver, M., 58 y
"	23	Betty d. Robert & Mary Clough, weaver, swell. lungs, Failsworth, 17 y
"	29	Hannah d. Samuel & Margt. Cheetham, innkeeper, hoopg. cough, M.
May	3	John Pollit, weaver, decline, Newton, 70 y
"	3	Jane w. John Leigh, weaver, decline, M., 39 y
"	3	John s. William & Hannah Greenwood, small pox, M., 9 m
"	5	Mary w. Robert Clough, weaver, decline, Failsworth, 61 y
"	6	Martha d. Joseph & Ellen Ackers, weaver, hoop. cough, M., 3 y 4 m
["	7	Mary d. Willm Tyme, M. (*entry in BT only*)]
"	11	John s. James & Anne Grindred, weaver, inflamn. head, Newton, 4 y
"	12	Eliza d. Thomas & Margt. Pearson, manufacturer, decline, Salford, 1y 1m
"	14	Robert s. Thomas & Jane Moors, weaver, fits, Newton, 1 day
"	20	Nancy w. James Hulton, weaver, decline, Failsworth, 32 y
"	22	George s. Jonathan & Esther Etchels, labourer, fits, Failsworth, 1 m
"	24	Joseph s. John & Betty Stott, manufacturer, small pox, Failsworth, 1y 6m
"	24	John s. Thomas & Abigail Holme, farmer, decline, 10 y

"	26	Mary d. James & Sarah Boardman, weaver, tooth fever, M., 1 y 1 m
"	27	George s. John & Mary Booth, weaver, decline, Failsworth
"	28	James s. Jane Ogden, weaver, tooth fever, Moston, 1 y
"	28	John s. Sarah Dunkerly, weaver, swell. lungs, Chadderton, 2 y 2 m
"	29	James s. John & Mary Billinge, hatter, convul., Newton, 1 day
"	29	Joseph s. Richard & Betty Thomason, weaver, decline, Failsworth, 19 y
Jun	1	Daniel Gillibrand, weaver, decline, M., 67 y
"	2	James Thorpe, weaver, rheu. fever, Failsworth, 70 y
"	3	William s. James & Sarah Nuttal, dyer, dysent., Newton, 5 m 14 days
"	14	Pharaoh s. James & Anne Taylor, collier, fits, M., 21 days
"	17	Anne d. James & Alice Thorp, weaver, fits, Failsworth, 1 y 1 m
"	21	Randal s. Randal & Hannah Alcock, husbandman, swell. lungs, Cheadle 12y
"	23	William s. James & Ann Gagger, collier, decline, M
"	24	George s. Willm. & Anne Shannor, weaver, fits, M., 10 m
"	26	Anne d. James & Mary Hulme, warehouseman, fever, M., 7 y 3 m
"	28	John Booth, shopkeeper, fever, Failsworth, 48 y
"	28	Thomas s. Mary Ogden, weaver, fits, Moston, 3 m
"	28	Charlotte d. John & Martha Shaw, decline, M., 9 m
Jul	6	Anne d. William & Anne McNair, weaver, decline, M., 6 m
"	10	Jonathan s. Thomas & Ann Whittaker, crofter, decline, Newton, 2 y 9 m
"	12	Alice d. James & Mary Lees, weaver, decline, Rusholme, 25 y
"	18	Samuel s. Jonathan & Peggy Grimshaw, weaver, decline, Droylsden, 10 m
"	26	Mary Whitehead, weaver, decline, Failsworth, 79 y
"	28	James s. James & Sarah Baron, labourer, fits, M., 3 m 21 days
"	29	Deborah w. James Walmsley, weaver, small pox, Failsworth, 28 y
Aug	2	Mary Grimshaw, widow, decline, Hurst, 67 y
"	3	Elizabeth d. George & Ann Brandon, sw. lungs, Newton, 11 m
"	4	James s. James & Alice Thomas, bookkeeper, decline, M., 2 y 6 m
"	14	Ellen d. William & Penelope Hughes, blacksmith, tooth fever, M., 1 y
"	20	Sarah d. John & Mary Gregory, spinner, small pox, M., 2 y 4 m
"	20	Ann d. John & Mary Gregory, spinner, small pox, M., 8 m
"	23	Henry Lee, husbandman, decline, M., 79 y
"	25	Barnet s. James & Ann Burne, weaver, accident, M., 2 y
"	26	Elizabeth d. Isaac & Elizabeth Hall, brewer, fits, M., 5 y
"	27	Robert s. Thomas & Elizabeth Wood, husbandman, convul., M., 7 days
"	30	Benjamin s. James & Sarah Ogden, weaver, inflam. lungs Failsworth 1y 4m
Sep	6	Ellen d. Samuel & Hannah Hulme, weaver, inflam. lungs, M., 11 m
"	6	Ann Hulme, weaver, decline, M., 42 y
"	6	Elizabeth d. John & Hannah Lord, weaver, small pox, M., 4 m 7 days
"	11	Richard Hulme, bleacher, decline, Droylsden, 87 y
"	16	Mary d. John & Mary Leicester, miner, dysent., M., 6 m
"	17	Ellen (wdw. James *not in BT*) Berry, farmer, decline, Failsworth, 63 y
"	18	Mary d. Isaac & Mary Alridge, weaver, decline, Ardwick, 5 y 5 m
"	20	Emma d. Thomas & Barbara Hughes, innkeeper, decline, Newton, 14 days
"	22	George s. George & Elizabeth Prince, warehouseman, fits, Newton, 1 day

"	22	Sarah d. George & Elizabeth Prince, warehouseman, fits, Newton, 1 day
"	23	Anthony Lane, farmer, decline, Newton, 64 y
"	27	Elizabeth (wdw. Dan *not in BT*) Shepley, weaver, decline, Newton, 61 y
Oct	7	Jonathan Hartley, engineer, decline, Newton, 68 y
"	13	John Bell, barber, decline, Newton, 38 y
"	16	John s. John & Betty [Elizth] Barrington, tanner, fever, Failsworth 5y 4m
"	18	Ann d. John & Mary Whitehead, weaver, decline, Moston, 25 y
"	21	Mary (sp. *not in BT*) d. Martha Ashton, weaver, decline, Failsworth, 14 d
"	22	Isabel (wdw. Bold *not in BT*) Eckersley, weaver, decline, Failsworth, 72 y
"	25	Martha d. Patrick & Martha Hughes, weaver, decline, M., 1 y 5 m
"	25	Mary w. John Smith, manufacturer, decline, Newton, 32 y
"	27	Joseph s. John & Mary Firth, spinner, hoopg. cough, M., 1 y 5 m
["	28	Time d. Mary Booth, M. (*entry in BT only*)]
Nov	5	Sarah d. James & Jane Fitton, spinner, scar. fever, M., 2 y 8 m
"	8	Ann d. Thos. & Elizth. Stuart, weaver, decline, M., 2 y 3 m
"	11	William Aldred, weaver, bl flux, M., 62 y
"	12	George s. Sarah Hudson, spinner, scar. fever, M., 3 y 10 m
"	12	Joseph s. Betty Pendleton, weaver, tooth fever, Failsworth, 9 m
"	17	Sarah d. John & Anne Ham[p]son, weaver, sc. fever, M., 7 y 10 m
"	19	Elizabeth d. Levi & Mary Whitehead, clerk, sc. fever, M., 3 y 2 m
"	23	Elizabeth w. Thomas Wood, labourer, sudden death, M., 47 y
"	23	John s. Richard & Ann Pollit, weaver, decline, Failsworth, 6 m
"	24	William s. John & Dorothea Blomely, weaver, sw. lungs, M., 6 m
"	30	Mary d. James & Phebe Irvine, weaver, wm. fever, Moston, 3 y 8 m
Dec	1	Rowland s. Rowland & Nancy Wilson, spinner, scar. fever, M., 5 y 2 m
"	5	Mary (wdw. Solomon *not in BT*) Coe, weaver, decline, M., 59 y
"	9	Mary d. James & Ann Wroe, weaver, decline, Failsworth, 19 y
"	9	Martha w. William Robinson, slater, decline, Newton, 62 y
"	13	Hiram s. John & Elizabeth Taylor, warehouseman, small pox, M., 2 y
"	13	James s. John & Elizabeth Wyat, weaver, fever, Newton, 11 m
"	13	John Jackson, labourer, decline, Newton, 45 y
"	13	John s. William & Mary Harrison, whitesmith, sw. lungs, M., 2 y 6 m
"	16	Hannah d. John & Ann Clayton, labourer, tooth fever, M., 1 y 3 m
"	18	Elizabeth d. Willm. & Elizh. Goodier, weaver, fits, Newton, 7 days
"	19	Lucy d. Joseph & Mary Berry, weaver, dysent, Failsworth, 11 m
"	20	Jane w. Cornelius Lyons, weaver, decline, M., 45 y
"	21	Anne d. Joseph & Tabitha Tinker, weaver, ch. birth, Failsworth, 23 y
"	23	James s. Elizabeth Hall, weaver, tooth fever, Newton, 1 y 1 m
"	24	Ellen d. Samuel & Martha Ax[t]on, labourer, consump., Droylsden, 21 y
"	27	Elizabeth d. Arthur & Ann (Borren *blank in BT*), weaver, burned, M., 5 y 3 m
"	27	Edwin s. Thomas & Barbara Hughes, innkeeper, fits, Newton, 4 m
"	29	Jane d. Edmund & Jane Whitaker, weaver, fever, M., 22 y
[		A. Ashworth Minister]
[		Jos'h Bertenshaw William Brown John Moore Chapel Wardens]

Burials in 1808
[Burials at Newton Heath Chapel in 1808]

Jan	14	James s. John & Mary Booth, weaver, decline, Failsworth, 18 y
["	16	Richard s. William & Lily Waredane, M. (*entry in BT only*)]
"	19	Jane d. John & Mary Blacklock, printer, M., 3 y
"	22	Isabel w. John Wolstencroft, weaver, decline, M., 64 y
"	25	William Etchels, weaver, accident, Droylsden, 62 y
"	25	Hannah d. John & Sarah Marsh, weaver, decline, M., 2 y 5 m
"	27	Mary w. John Etchels, weaver, childbed, Droylsden, 23 y
"	31	Alice d. Peter & Hannah Lomas, decline, Newton, 4 m
"	31	Anne d. William & Sarah Rydings, weaver, Failsworth, 16 y
Feb	2	John Clayton, miner, palsy, M., 70 y
"	7	Charles Moores, weaver, bl. flux, M., 58 y
"	11	Isabel d. James & Elizabeth Ashton, weaver, fits, Newton, 9 days
"	11	Hannah d. William & Ellen Hibbert, weaver, decline, Failsworth, 8 y
"	14	Susanna w. Samuel Coe, spinner, decline, M., 32 y
"	18	Rachel d. James & Elizth. Ashton, weaver, fits, Newton 14 days
"	18	Sally d. James & Hannah Hibbert, weaver, Newton, 7 y
"	21	Ann d. William & Elizth. Haynes, weaver, decline, M., 1 y 2 m
"	21	Daniel s. George & Betty Hulton, weaver, tooth fever, Failsworth, 10 m
"	26	Sarah d. John & Mary Bates, cordwainer, Failsworth, 1 day
Mar	2	James Berry, weaver, fever, Newton, 31 y
"	4	John s. John & Mary Walmsley, weaver, fever, Failsworth, 14 y
"	8	M. Anne [My. Ann] d. James & Martha Allen, weaver, fits, Failsworth 21d
"	9	Esther d. John & Esther Whitehead, weaver, decline, Failsworth, 20 y
"	10	Jane d. John & Mary Walmsley, fever, Failsworth, 19 y
"	13	Thomas s. William & Nancy Robinson, weaver, fits, Failsworth, 21 days
"	14	Nancy d. John & Mary Etchels, weaver, fits Droylsden, 2 m 7 days
"	20	Elizabeth (wdw. Thomas *not in BT*) Heywood, crofter, decline, Harpurhey, 71 y
"	20	Edward s. Betty Whitehead, weaver, fits, Failsworth, 7 days
"	21	Nathan s. Charles & Sarah Thom[p]son, baker, fever, [M.,] 7 y 7 m
"	22	Alice w. John Plimmer, miner, decline, M., 30 y
"	22	Hannah (wdw. Thomas *not in BT*) Smith, innkeeper, palsy, Failsworth, 74y
"	23	Miles Schofield, crofter, decline, Newton, 44 y
"	27	James s. James & Alice Thomas, book-keeper, fits, [M.,] 2 days
"	27	Ellen d. William & Isabella Atkinson, weaver, convuls, M., 3 m
"	27	Samuel s. William & Catherine Heap, weaver, fever, Droylsden
"	27	William s. William & Nancy Blomiley, labourer, looseness, Salford, 14 d
"	29	John s. William & Nancy McCullock, spinner, decline, M., 15 y
Apr	6	William s. David & Martha Ridgway, fusn. cutter, decline, M., 1 m 21 days
"	6	Mary d. Richard & Jane Smith, weaver, decline, M., 22 y
"	7	Milly d. William & Alice Smith, weaver, Newton, 1 y 2 m
"	14	Mary w. Thomas Hilton, weaver, rheumatism, Moston, 60 y

"	17	William s. John & Mary Isherwood, hatter, decline, M., 1 y 2 m (*1808*)
"	24	Thos. Shepley, victualler, decline, M., 31 y
"	24	Sarah d. Robert & Penelope Whitehead, weaver, w fever (*uncertain reading*), Failsworth, 4 m
"	27	Betty d. Ralph & Betty Burchil, weaver, Failsworth, 9 y
May	4	Henry Hartly s. Henry & Mary Cryer, spinner, decline, M., 3 y
"	4	Alice w. John Kershaw, weaver, decline, Failsworth, 44 y
"	6	Mary w. Robert Robinson, joiner, decline, M., 36 y
"	9	John Fletcher, labourer, palsy, Ardwick, 49 y
"	11	Mary d. James & Martha Kemp, weaver, decline, 7 y
"	19	John s. John & Elizabeth Harlow, spinner, decline, M., 1 y 10 m
"	21	James s. John & Betty Tarvin, labourer, decline, Newton, 8 y
"	22	Sarah d. Joseph & Ann [Sarah *struck through*] Lomas, weaver, fits, M. 21d
"	22	John Brennan(d), weaver, decline, Droylsden, 38 y
"	29	Abraham s. James & Mary Ainsworth, weaver, measles, M., 1 y 1 m
Jun	2	Esther d. Luke & Ann Smith, weaver, decline, Failsworth, 17 y
"	2	William s. Johnson & Betty Whitten, weaver, measles, M., 1 y 4 m
"	3	Charles s. Thomas & Sarah Shepley, innkeeper, decline, M.
"	13	John s. Eli & Sarah Whiteley, weaver, w. fever, Droylsden, 2 y 3 m
"	13	Hannah d. Daniel & Mary Smith, weaver, decline, Failsworth, 19 y
"	15	Sarah w. Thomas Cowell, whitesmith, decline, M., 31 y
"	16	Ellen d. Peter & Ann Farhurst, miner, measles, M., 1 y 2 m
"	26	Anne d. Mary Ormrod, weaver, drowned, Chadderton, 10 y
"	30	Martha d. William & Martha Gillesey, weaver, fits, M., 2 m 21 days
Jul	4	Anne d. James & Ann Robinson, weaver, sw. lungs, M., 1 y 5 m
"	10	Catherine s. John & Mary Fish, weaver, decline, M., 39 y
"	10	Mary d. James & Elizth. Bradshaw, weaver, fever, M., 6 y
"	10	Mary w. John Stansfield, hatter, childbed, Newton, 41 y
"	10	Richd. s. Richd. & Mary Richardson, weaver, measles, Newton, 1 y 7 m
"	11	Anne d. Jos'h [Joseph] & Lettice Tomlinson, weaver, decline, Failsworth, 9 y 9 m
"	17	Esther d. John & Mary Chadderton, miner, sw. lungs, M., 9 m
"	19	Margt. d. John & Ann Clough, print drawer, M.
"	24	Richard s. Thomas & Ellen Harris, dyer, fits, M., 1 m 21 days
"	24	Betty w. James Wolstencroft, inflamn., Failsworth, 62 y
"	30	Alice w. John Williamson, weaver, dropsy, Failsworth, 31 y
"	31	Marianne [My. Ann] d. Henry & Jane Singleton, bricklayer, decline, M., 1 m 14 days
Aug	7	Thomas s. Levi & Jane Hulton, weaver, fits, Failsworth, 5 m
"	7	Edmund s. Thomas & Sarah Gorton, joiner, fits, Failsworth, 10 m
"	7	Maria d. James & Elizth. Moors, labourer, fits, M., 1 m 7 days
"	10	James s. George & Margt. Taggart, weaver, decline, M., 2 m 14 days
"	17	Sarah d. James & Alice Ogden, weaver, dysent, Blackley, 1 y 4 m
"	17	Ann d. Benjamin & Betty Heywood, weaver, dysent, M., 4 m
"	21	William s. John & Betty Worsley, weaver, measles, Newton, 1 y 10 m

"	22	Marianne [My. Ann] d. Thos. & Hannah Allen, weaver, fits, Failsworth, 2 y 9 m
"	25	Ann d. James & Mary Radcliffe [Ratcliff], weaver, fits, Newton, 4 m
"	25	Edward Coe, carder, decline, M., 20 y
"	28	Hannah w. John Lees, weaver, decline, Failsworth, 40 y
"	28	Robert s. James [Jane] Whitaker, weaver, decline, M., 1 y 3 m
"	30	John s. James & Jane Brown, labourer, fever, Failsworth, 11 y
"	31	James s. John & Ann Hampson, weaver, decline, M., 4 m
Sep	4	Mary McMhan, weaver, apoplexy, M., 46 y (*1808*)
"	4	Lucy d. John & Alice Williamson, weaver, fits, Failsworth, 2 m
"	9	Ann d. Robert & Nancy Downs, spinner, flux, M., 1 y 3 m
"	11	John s. Ambrose & Mary Yates, weaver, decline, M., 3 m
"	17	Betty d. Jos'h [Joseph] & Betty Lees, weaver, fever, Failsworth, 17 y
"	18	Nancy d. John & Mary Stansfield, hatter, decline, Newton, 3 m
"	20	Thomas s. Edward & Mary Thornley, porter, decline, M., 4 m
"	26	Elizabeth d. George & Elizh. Turner, weaver, tooth fever, M., 9 m
Oct	3	Sarah d. James & Margt. Jackson, weaver, tooth fever, M., 16 m
"	7	James s. James & Ann Smith, silk spinner, decline, M., 13 m
"	9	James Ashworth, weaver, decline, M., 80 y
"	9	Jane d. John & Nancy Carr, weaver, decline, M., 18 y
"	9	Elizabeth d. Willm. & Martha Gillespie, weaver, decline, M., 6 m
"	9	Samuel Bullock, brazier, dropsy, M., 66 y
"	11	Anne d. Jonathan & Hannah Glossop, weaver, fits, Failsworth, 3 m
"	16	John Norcross, cordwainer, decline, M., 46 y
"	24	William s. Robert & Ann Downs, spinner, decline, M., 5 y 8 m
"	28	Nancy d. Samuel & Martha Clough, weaver, decline, Failsworth, 1 y 4 m (*? - age faded*)
Nov	4	Jonathan s. John & Mary Slater, manufacturer, fits, Newton, 9 days
"	4	Joseph s. Joseph & Jane Lees, schoolmaster, decline, M., 4 m 14 days
"	6	Anne w. Samuel Goodier, weaver, sudden, Newton, 63 y
"	13	Elijah s. Richard & Ann Pollit, weaver, Newton, 3 m 14 days
"	15	Betty sp. d. Sarah Ashworth, weaver, decline, M., 1 y
"	15	Rose w. James Etchels, weaver, palsy, Failsworth, 68 y
"	17	Jane wdw. Robert Hardy, husbandman, accident, M., 76 y
"	20	Edward s. Thomas & Mary Brown, weaver, fits, Newton, 6 m (*The age has faded towards the end of the next two entries.*)
"	21	Nehemiah s. Robt. & Penelope Whitehead, weaver, con., Failsworth, 9 y 3 m
"	21	Jane d. Abel & Betty Andrew, spinner, s. pox, Newton, 4 y 3 m
Dec	6	Henry Shackleton, weaver, drowned, Wadsworth Yorks., 19 y
"	14	Catherine d. Charles & Elizh. McCullough, fever, M., 2 y 10 m
"	16	Anne wdw. John Fogg, whitesmith, decline, M., 44 y
"	17	Josiah Gillibrand, weaver, decline, Failsworth, 66 y
"	25	Jane d. Edmd. & Ellen Whitehead, weaver, fits, Failsworth, 1 m
"	25	Catherine w. John Harrop, hatter, decline, Openshaw, 30 y

"   25   Sarah d. Thomas & Mary Farrand, weaver, fits, Ardwick, 2 m 7 days
[A true Copy from the Register of Newton Chapel from 14 Jany. to 28th
                 Decr. 1808 both inclusive   ]
[R.A. Singleton Curate   ]
[William Brown Jos'h Bertenshaw John Moore   ]

Burials in 1809
[Burials at Newton Heath Chapel in 1809]

Jan	8	James Kemp, weaver, palsy, M., 80 y 5 days
"	8	Ann w. Thomas Makin, weaver, decline, M., 60 y
"	9	John Antrobus, farmer, inflam lungs, Bradford, 64 y
"	16	Jonathan d. James & Mary Hooley, labourer, decline, Newton, 15 y
"	19	Martha w. John Hardy, velvet dresser, decline, M., 6 y
"	20	Jane [sp.] d. Sarah Bowker, weaver, decline, M., 6 y
"	20	Martha d. John & Frances Dome[l]o, weaver, decline, M., 2 y 5 m
"	25	Jonathan s. James & Mary Allen, weaver, fits, Failsworth, 2 m 14 days
"	29	Gabriel s. William & Frances Toole, cordwainer, hoopg. cough, M., 1y 9m
"	29	Ann w. John Wood, labourer, fever, Failsworth, 66 y
"	29	Richard Gorton, labourer, fever, Failsworth, 23 y
"	30	George s. Samuel & Mary Holland, weaver, fever, Failsworth, 2 y 10 m
"	30	Moses s. Samuel & Sarah Tonge, weaver, pl. fever, M., 24 y
Feb	1	John s. John & Martha Hardy, velvet dresser, fits, M., 1 m 21 days
"	4	Andrew s. George & Sarah Etchels, weaver, fever, Failsworth, 1 y
"	5	Henry s. Israel & Elizh. Shaw, spinner, convul, M., 1 m 7 days
"	8	Ann d. Henry & Ann Whaley, weaver, fits, M., 6 m
"	8	John [sp.] s. Martha Bailey [Bayley], reeler, fits, M., 8 m
"	9	Robert Downs, spinner, decline, M., 40 y
"	10	Jonathan Hartley, miner, decline, M., 33 y
"	10	Hannah d. John & Frances Dome[l]o, weaver, decline, M., 1 y 1 m
"	12	Hannah w. Thomas Moors, weaver, childbirth, M., 24 y
"	16	Christopher Pennal, blacksmith, inflamn., M., 62 y
"	19	Samuel s. James & Hannah Hibbert, labourer, small pox, Newton, 1 y 2 m
"	19	Sarah d. James & Sarah Anderton, weaver, fits, M., 5 m
"	22	John Dean, labourer, decline, Newton, 35 y
"	24	Fanny d. John & Ann Cadman, stay maker, small pox, M., 2 y
"	26	Ann w. William Etchels, weaver, fever, Failsworth, 23 y
Mar	1	Mary [sp.] d. Mary Hartley, fits, Newton, 1 y 1 m
"	9	Martha sp. d. Ann Andrew, weaver, fits, Newton, 9 days
"	20	Margaret d. John & Mary Barker, weaver, fits, M., 2 y 10 m
"	21	George Leech, weaver, fits, M., 27 y
"	22	Mary Rothwell, weaver, palsy, Failsworth, 81 y
"	26	George s. John & Sarah Marsh, weaver, decline, M., 2 y 2 m
"	26	Betty w. Robert Bowker, weaver, childbed, Droylsden, 36 y
"	26	Robert s. Robert & Betty Bowker, weaver, sw. lungs, Droylsden, 2 m

"	26	Philip s. Thomas & Mary Houghton, hatter, sc. fever, M., 3 y 8 m
"	28	Ellen d. Joseph & Margaret Meden, weaver, fits, Newton, 8 m
"	29	Richard Armstrong, weaver, palsy, Newton, 19 y
"	29	James Ashworth, weaver, fever, M., 44 y
Apr	2	Elizabeth w. Johnson Whitten, weaver, ch. bed, M., 28 y
"	4	William s. Richd. & Hannah Gorton, labourer, fever, Failsworth, 1 y 9 m
"	4	William Allen, labourer, Newton, 48 y
"	7	Thomas Etchels, weaver, decline, Failsworth, 54 y
"	11	Elizabeth d. Thomas & Mary Houghton, hatter, M., 3 y 8 m
"	23	Jenny wdw. William Clegg, innkeeper, Failsworth, 39 y (*? - age faded*)
"	27	James s. John & Ann Blackley, weaver, fever, Failsworth, 20 y
"	27	Richard s. William & Hannah Bottomly, decline, M., 9 m
May	3	Mary wdw. William Aldred, weaver, decline, M., 61 y
"	3	Robert s. John & Sarah Ogden, weaver, fits, Failsworth, 14 days
"	4	Hannah w. Thomas Blackley, weaver, decline, Salford, 29 y
"	4	Henry s. John & Sarah Clark, cordwainer, decline, Failsworth, 1 y
"	8	Penelope w. Robert Whitehead, weaver, consn., Failsworth, 38 y
"	10	Mary d. John & Esther Morton, book keeper, inflamn., M.
"	11	Ann w. James Smith, silk spinner, decline, M., 29 y
"	14	Mary Nailor [Naylor], serving woman, decline, M., 38 y
"	19	Fanny w. John Goodier, weaver, fever, Hollinwood [- near Oldham], 31 y
"	23	Sarah d. George & Sarah Hudson, cot. spinner, decline, M., 30 y
Jun	1	Jane w. James Thornley, weaver, decline, Droylsden, 28 y
"	2	William McGuire, hoptia (*uncertain reading*), M., 23 y
"	2	Mary d. William & Sarah Wood, farmer, decline, Newton 17 y
"	2	Joseph Tomlinson, weaver, decline, Failsworth, 42 y
"	2	Ann w. James Chamberlane, spinner, decline, M., 50 y
"	4	James s. Johnson & Elizabeth Whitten, weaver, decline, M., 3 m
"	5	Sarah d. James & Jane Fitton, cot. spinner, decline, M., 1 y 1 m
"	5	Mary wdw. James Berry, weaver, decline, Newton, 34 y
"	7	Joseph s. Thos. & Hannah Pearson, cot. spinner, nerv. fever, Salford, 8 y
"	9	Mary d. John & Betty Knight, weaver, decline, M., 21 days
"	11	Abraham s. James & Sarah Ogden, miner, small pox, M., 2 y 2 m
"	14	Sarah w. John Ogden, weaver, decline, Failsworth, 37 y
"	15	Sarah d. John & Sarah Norcross, cordwainer, decline, M., 1 y 6 m
"	18	Ann d. Joseph & Alice Taylor, weaver, small pox, M., 5 y
"	18	Peter Bent, weaver, decline, M., 68 y
"	20	James s. Robert & Penelope Whitehead, weaver, decline, Failsworth, 4 m
"	23	Edmund Walmsley, joiner, decline, M., 40 y
"	23	Mary d. John & Sarah Walmsley, labourer, decline, Failsworth, 10 m
"	25	George s. George & Ann Travis, weaver, decline, Newton, 2 m 21 days
"	25	William s. Isaac & Hannah Brindle, weaver, decline, Newton, 7 m
"	25	Joseph s. Thomas & Mary Thorpe, weaver, decline, Failsworth, 1 m 7 d
"	27	Ann wdw. Josiah Gillibrand, weaver, decline, Failsworth, 76 y
Jul	1	Mary d. John & Sarah Lee, pt. glazier, fits, M., 21 days

"	2	Jonathan s. Jonathan & Ann Whitaker, weaver, small pox, M., 1 y 1 m
"	3	Nancy d. James & Mary Broughton, weaver, convul, M., 14 days
"	3	Joseph s. James & Sarah Booth, weaver, decline, Failsworth, 1 y 6 m
"	9	James s. William & Alice Lane, innkeeper, small pox, M., 1 y 5 m
"	9	John [sp.] s. Sarah Ashworth, weaver, small pox, M., 1 y 8 m
"	24	William s. Thomas & Sarah Neal, coalminer, small pox, M., 4 m
"	25	James Howarth, weaver, dysent., Failsworth, 81 y
"	26	Ruth d. John & Ann Partington, coalminer, small pox, 7 m
"	28	Joanna d. Thomas & Margt. Pearson, manufacturer, decline, M., 3 m
"	28	Benjamin s. Samuel & Ellen Clough, weaver, decline, Failsworth, 1 y 2 m
"	28	John Clark, cordwainer, decline, Failsworth, 36 y
"	30	Daniel s. John & Elizabeth McNeal, weaver, accident, M., 10 y
"	30	James s. James & Anne Smith, silk spinner, decline, M., 3 m 14 days
"	30	Ann d. John & Elizh. Edge, weaver, convul., M., 2 y 6 m
"	30	William s. John & Elizh. Edge, weaver, convul., M., 4 days
"	30	Mary d. John & Sarah Kenyon, coal miner, small pox, M., 1 y 11 m
"	31	Esther d. Thomas & Mary Whitehead, weaver, childbed, Failsworth, 27 y
"	31	George s. John & Alice Clayton, miner, small pox, M., 10 m
Aug	2	John Gradwell, weaver, diabetes, Failsworth, 66 y
"	2	Sarah d. Thomas & Hannah Blakeley, dyer, hoopg. cough, Salford, 4 y
"	4	Anne d. James & Anne Winstanley, weaver, small pox, M., 3 y
"	4	Mary [sp.] d. Susanna Farrow, weaver, small pox, M., 3 y 4 m
"	6	Jane d. Charles & Mary Watson, plasterer, decline, M., 22 y
"	7	James Williamson, coalminer, accident, M., 21 y
"	7	Betty d. Joseph & Mary Butterworth, weaver, small pox, M., 7 m
"	8	James s. Peter & Hannah Lomas, dyer, decline, Newton, 2 m 14 days
"	9	John s. Simeon & Sarah Whitehead, warehouseman, decline, M., 27 y
"	11	William s. Jacob & Ellen Wolstencroft, weaver, small pox, M., 1 y
"	13	William s. Thomas & Elizth. Dimelow [Dumelo], hatter, small pox, M.5m
"	13	Samuel Pendleton, weaver, decline, Failsworth, 63 y
"	14	James s. James & Phoebe Smethurst, weaver, convul, Failsworth, 14 days
"	14	Stephen s. John & Mary Maken, gardener, fever, Cheetham, 5 y
"	16	John Bowker, cotton spinner, consn., M., 46 y
"	16	Ann d. Edmund & Nancy Travis, whitster, consn., Newton, 17 y
"	17	Alice d. John & Mary Gardner, gardener, consn., Newton, 9 y
"	20	William [sp] s. Mary Williamson, weaver, small pox, M., 1 y 3 m
"	20	James s. Alexander & Mary Swan [Sloan], cordwainer, fever, M., 7 y
"	25	Edmund s. Edmund & Alice Walmsley, joiner, small pox, M., 14 m
"	27	Martha Andrew widow, washerwoman, decline, M., 52 y
"	27	Hannah d. Samuel & Margt. Cheetham, small pox, M., 1 y 9 m
Sep	6	John sp. s. Mary Etchels, weaver, fever, Failsworth, 2 m 7 days
"	7	Jane d. James & Betty Bethel, weaver, tooth fever, Droylsden, 1 y 1 m
"	12	Sarah w. Abraham Mather, rheumsm., Droylsden, 72 y
"	19	William s. Anthony & Mary Lane, innkeeper, small pox, M., 4 m
"	22	Mary d. Samuel & Betty Clough, weaver, measles, Failsworth, 7 y

"	26	Samson s. Thomas & Mary Farrand, weaver, measles, Ardwick, 11 m
Oct	1	Richard s. Thomas & Ellen Tully, weaver, measles, M., 1 y 10 m
"	2	Mary w. James Miller, decline, Droylsden, 26 y
"	3	Mary d. John & Ann O'Brines, labourer, measles, Salford, 2 y 9 m
"	4	Mary d. Thomas & Elizh. Greenwood, hatter, measles, Newton, 5 y
"	8	John s. John & Ann O'Brines, labourer, measles, Salford, 9 m
"	9	Mary d. Francis & Ellen Brown, weaver, measles, M., 13 y 6 m
"	12	Richard Mather, weaver, inflamn., Stockport, 67 y
"	17	William s. John & Mary Smith, weaver, measles, M., 2 y 2 m
"	17	Josiah s. John & Ellen Davies, labourer, fever, Failsworth, 5 y
"	19	John s. Andrew & Betty Beard, weaver, measles, M., 2 y
"	20	James Booth s. Betty Pendleton, weaver, convul., Failsworth, 9 m
"	22	Sarah [sp.] d. Alice Butterworth, weaver, measles, M., 1 y 8 m
"	22	Hannah d. James & Sarah Pearson, spinner, small pox, Salford, 6 m
"	27	Robert s. John & Sarah Walmsley, labourer, decline, Failsworth, 4 y 6 m
"	30	Catherine w. William Heap, weaver, dropsy, Droylsden, 48 y
"	31	Kempfield Dimelow [Domelo], hatter, decline, M., 64 y
Nov	1	John s. John & Jane Smith, weaver, measles, Failsworth, 7 y
"	3	Ann d. Thos. & Anne Beswick, weaver, measles, Failsworth, 3 y
"	4	Thomas s. Joseph & Mary Horrocks [Horrox], weaver, measles, Failsworth, 1 y 9 m
"	5	Jonathan s. Samuel & Ann Etchels, measles, Failsworth, 4 y 4 m
"	5	Jane d. John & Peggy Lees, warehouseman, measles, Failsworth, 1 y 6 m
"	5	Ann d. William & Betty Pickles, cordwainer, measles, Failsworth, 1 y 3 m
"	10	Betty [sp.] d. Betty Burgess, sewing woman, fits, Failsworth, 3 m
"	12	Mary d. James & Ann Mills, weaver, fits, M., 10 m
"	12	William Henry s. Levi & Sarah Whitehead, clerk, measles, M., 1 y
"	13	Elizabeth d. David & Mary Hening, weaver, tooth fever, M., 10 m
"	16	Jane d. John & Ann Hewit, hatter, fits, M., 1 y 1 m
"	19	Mary d. John & Sarah Ogden, weaver, measles, Failsworth, 2 y 9 m
"	20	Phoebe d. John & Martha Turner, weaver, measles, Failsworth, 9 m
"	24	Mary d. John & Phoebe Taylor, weaver, measles, Moston, 3 y 4 m
Dec	1	Mary Ann s. David & Martha Massey, cordwainer, measles, Failsworth, 2 y 10 m
"	1	William s. George & Margt. Tagat, weaver, decline, M., 3 m
"	6	John s. Thomas & Ruth Booth, cloth dresser, infl. lungs, Ardwick, 17 m
"	7	Samuel s. Ashton & Sarah Buckley, book keeper, fever, M., 3 y 4 m
"	10	Elizh. wdw. Joseph Ogden, weaver, decline, Failsworth, 92 y
"	10	Mary w. James Walker, weaver, decline, M., 32 y
"	10	Sarah d. James & Rebecca Johnson, weaver, measles, M., 2 y
"	11	Charles s. John & Ann Butterworth, brewer, measles, M., 10 m
"	17	Thomas Shepley, musician, decline, M. [Failsworth late of M.], 75 y
"	17	William s. John & Mary Ann Robinson, weaver, decline, Droylsden, 3 y 11 m
"	20	Thomas s. Thomas & Jane Wagstaff, breadbaker, measles, Ardwick, 2 y

"	21	Elizabeth d. Robert & Mary Walmsley, farmer, dysent, Newton, 24 y 10 m
"	22	James s. John & Mary Slater, manufacturer, decline, Newton, 3 m 21 days
"	24	Jane w. Thomas Wagstaff, breadbaker, dysent, Ardwick, 29 y
"	24	John s. John & Ellen Morison, fustian dresser, measles, M., 2 y 6 m
"	28	Sarah d. Samuel & Mary Hill, coalminer, fits, M., 1 m
"	29	Edward s. Ashton & Mary Shepley, manufacturer, fits, Newton, 4 m

[A Copy of all the Burials from the Burials Register of the Chapel of Newton in the Parish of Manchester in the County of Lancaster, in the Diocese of Chester, from the 8th of Januy. 1809 to the 29. Dec. 1809 both inclusive.   ]

[R.A. Singleton Curate   ]

[Jos'h Bertenshaw Warden William Brown John Moore John Stott]

Burials in 1810

Jan	5[4]	Mary d. Thomas & Sarah Chadwick, weaver, measles, M., 3 y 4 m
"	9	Maria d. James & Rebecca Hardy, measles, M., 11 m
"	17	John Robinson, slater, decline, Newton, 51 y
"	21	Hannah Jacobs, weaver, decline, Newton, 39 y
"	21	Dionysius Varley, weaver, decline, Newton, 42 y
"	21	Mary w. John Wilson, weaver, decline, Oldham P., 2 y
"	21	Martha wdw. Peter Bent, weaver, dropsy, M., 47 y
"	28	Jane d. Richard & Hannah Briscoe, cal. printer, fits, Newton, 21 days (*see entry Feb 3*)
"	28	Ann w. Richard Bo(w)den, gardener, decline, M., 75 y
Feb	2	Robert s. Robert & Penelope Whitehead, weaver, hoopgcough, Failsworth, 3 y 8 m
"	3	Elizabeth d. Richard & Hannah Briscoe, cal. printer, fits, Newton, 25 days
"	7	Mary w. John Whitehead, weaver, decline, Moston, 71 y
"	11	George s. James & Ann Croom, farmer, worm fever, M., 3 y
"	12	Nancy sp. d. Mary Smith, weaver, fits, Failsworth, 6 m
"	13	Joseph s. Benjn. & Elizabeth Johnson, smith, Heaton Norris, 1 y 6 m
"	13	Robert sp. s. Sarah Thorpe, weaver, hoopg. cough, Failsworth, 1 y 2 m
"	13	Sarah Linney, weaver, Newton
"	18	Betty w. Jonathan Partington, weaver, ch. bed, Blackley, 19 y
"	19	Mary w. John Stafford, labourer, decline, Newton, 60 y
"	21	Alice w. William Smith, weaver, decline, Newton, 34 y
"	23	William s. James & Rebekah [Rebecca] Hardy, calenderer, measles, Salford, 3 y 5 m
"	25	John sp. s. Ann Wroe, weaver, hoopg. cough, Failsworth, 2 y 7 m
Mar	1	Ellen w. James Morefield, cot. spinner, decline, M., 41 y (*altered from* 21 y)
"	1	James Swift, weaver, decline, Failsworth, 69 y
"	4	James s. John & Bridget Coe, spinner, decline, M., 4 m
"	5	Amos Ogden, weaver, asthma, Failsworth, 75 y

"	6	John s. William & Hannah Marshal, weaver, inflam. head, M., 18 y
"	8	Robert s. Jonathan & Betty Partington, weaver, decline, Blackley, 1 m
"	9	John Stafford, labourer, decline, Newton, 73 y (age altered)
"	11	Hannah d. Thomas & Mary Brown, weaver, fits, Newton, 21 days
"	16	Elizabeth d. Jonathan & Martha Glossop, weaver, Failsworth, 35 y
"	18	Margaret w. John Collins, weaver, decline, M., 21 y
"	25	Bridget w. John Coe, cot. spinner, decline, M., 21 y
"	25	Thomas s. James & Sarah Hill, miner, small pox, M.
"	25	Betty w. John Whitehead, miner, decline, M., 34 y
"	27	William s. Patrick (& Mary not in BT) Quinn, weaver, burned, M.
"	27	Betty w. Joseph Tomlinson, weaver, decline, Levenshulme, 65 y
Apr	1	James s. John & Ellen Jenkinson, soldier, hoopg. cough, M., 2 m
"	2	Lettice wdw. Thomas Whitaker, weaver, decline, Failsworth, 69 y
"	5	Mary d. Richard & Jane Robert, butcher, hoopg. cough, M., 9 m
"	6	Hannah wdw. James Wolstencroft, whitster, decline, Failsworth, 92 y
"	8	Elizabeth w. Peter Boardman, weaver, decline, Droylsden, 29 y
"	9	Henry s. Samuel & Mary Birtles, tailor, fits, Failsworth, 1 m 14 days
"	10	John s. Elijah & Sally Whitehead, weaver, fits, Failsworth, 1 day
"	11	Harriet d. Willm. & Elizh. Hibbert, weaver, hoopg. cough, Failsworth, 1 y 6 m
"	12	Elizabeth (d. blank in BT) James & Mary Thorp, weaver, fever, Failsworth, 10 y
"	12	Sophia d. James & Rebecca [Rebecka] Jones, joiner, decline, M., 24 y
"	13	Maria d. John & Mary Hulton, weaver, decline, Failsworth, 2 y
"	15	John s. George & Mary Hall, decline, M., 2 y 6 m
"	15	Samuel Wyat, weaver, sudden death, Failsworth, 74 y
"	20	Nancy d. Thos. & Elizh. Barlow, weaver, inf. lungs, Failsworth, 1 y 5 m
"	24	Jonathan Etchels, weaver, decline, Failsworth, 28 y
"	24	Elizh. sp. d. Matty Bell, hairdresser, decline, M., 11 m
"	25	Catherine w. Thos. Hardy, printer, decline, Newton, 63 y
"	25	Joseph Andrew, bleacher, decline, M., 78 y
"	25	John Ogden, weaver, dropsy, Failsworth, 51 y
"	29	John s. John & Jane Smith, labourer, fits, Failsworth, 21 days
"	30	Samuel s. Samuel & Martha Clough, weaver, hoop. cough, Failsworth, (age faded)
"	30	Mary d. William & Martha Walker, manufacturer, decline, M., 20 y
May	1	Emma d. James & Ann Winstan[d]ley, weaver, hoop. cough, M., 11 m
"	4	Robert Holroyd, labourer, inflam. bowels, Newton, 44 y
"	9	Charlotte d. John Ireland, weaver, hoop. cough, M., 1 y
"	10	Alice d. John & Betty Bardsley, weaver, fits, Droylsden, 13 m
"	18	Hannah w. Thos. Walker, cal. printer, dropsy, Newton, 31 y
"	21	Edward s. Edward & Martha Whitehead, builder, sw. lungs, Droylsden 2 y 6 m
"	21	Hannah d. Thomas & Betty Holland, weaver, fits, Failsworth, 21 days
"	22	Ann wdw. William Hibbert, cordwainer, decline, Failsworth, 80 y

"	27	Edward Wrigley, weaver, dropsy, Failsworth, 70 y
"	29	Henry s. Henry & Jane Singleton, builder, hoop. cough, M., 11 m
Jun	3	Ann d. Henry & Ann Bullock, dyer, hoopg. cough, Hulme, 11 m
"	4	Betty d. Thomas & Ann Hamer, weaver, fits, Droylsden, 11 days
"	5	Isaac s. Isaac & Betty Hall, hawker, M., 4 y
"	11	Mary Ann d. John & Mary Isherwood, hatter, hoop. cough, M., 1 y 4 m
"	17	Mary d. George & Hannah Nicholson, hatter, decline, M., 1 y 6 m
"	17	John s. Amos & Sarah Butterworth, miner, fits, M., 14 days
"	17	Mary d. Thos. & Mary Dawson, dyer, fits, Newton, 5 m
"	19	Ann w. Richard Pollit, weaver, decline, Failsworth, 25 y
"	24	Miranda d. John & Martha Turner, weaver, fits, Failsworth, 2 m
"	25	James Lees, weaver, fever, Failsworth, 51 y
"	26	Thomas Hulme, warehouseman, decline, M., 73 y
"	26	Mary d. Richd. & Ann Kenyon, c. printer, hoop. cough, 11 m
Jul	2	Joseph s. John & Esther Taylor, cordwainer, drowned, Failsworth, 3y 10m
"	8	James s. William & Ellen Bateman, weaver, cons., Newton, 7 y
"	10	Rosina d. James & Nancy Ridings, weaver, tooth fever, Failsworth, 11 m
"	15	Mary Ann wdw. James Lyon, velvet dresser, inflam. stomach, Stockport, 66 y
"	19	Ellen d. Henry & Mary Cryer, spinner, burned, M., 2 y 6 m
"	21	Esther d. Esther Whitehead, weaver, hoop. cough, Failsworth, 11 m
"	22	John s. Richard & Sarah Hartley, dyer, decline, M., 10 m (? - *age faded*)
"	22	Mary w. Peter Wyld, waggoner, ch. bed, Newton, 31 y
"	24	John Wolstencroft, weaver, decline, M., 64 y
"	24	Jonathan Glossop, weaver, decline, Failsworth, 75 y
"	25	Hannah d. Ann Pollit, weaver, dysent, Failsworth, 4 y 3 m
"	27	Helen w. John Berry, weaver, ch. bed, Failsworth, 32 y
"	27	Charles s. William & Jane Allen, weaver, fits, Failsworth, 4 m
"	27	Alice w. John Dawson, cordwainer, ch. bed, Moston, 28 y
"	30	Elizh. d. John & Alice Dawson, fits, Moston, 7 days
"	31	Jane d. Revd. Abrah. & Jane Ashworth, minister of Newton, decline, Newton, 10 y
Aug	5	George s. John & Mary Redman, warehouseman, hoop. cough, M., 1 y 1 m 7 days
"	12	Henry s. John & Mary Redman, warehouseman, hoop. cough, M., 1 y 1 m 14 days
"	13	Jonah [Josiah] s. Henry & Nancy Kearsley, bleacher, blood vessel .., Newton, 8 y
"	24	Ann d. Richard & Ann Pollit, weaver, hoopg. cough, Failsworth, 4 m
Sep	1	Luke s. James & Martha Swift, weaver, hoopg. cough, Failsworth, 13 m
"	2	William s. George & Betty Turner, weaver, fits, M., 2 m 21 days
"	5	Robert s. John & Elizh. Smith, silkspinner, fever, M., 18 y
"	6	Sarah wdw. William Clough, weaver, decline, Failsworth, 73 y
"	9	Jeremiah s. Peter & Hannah Lomas [Lomax], dyer, fits, Newton, 21 days
"	16	Elizabeth w. Samuel Ainsworth, hatter, decline, Newton, 57 y

"	25	Mary wdw. Abraham Ogden, miner, decline, M., 60 y
Oct	3	Joseph s. George & Mary Tomlinson, weaver, hoopg. cough, Failsworth, 1 y 5 m
"	7	Mary d. Francis & Ellen Keating, decline, M., 4 m
"	8	Alice d. William & Mary Wyld, weaver, fits, Droylsden, 5 m
"	9	Ann d. John & Elizh. Thorp, weaver, decline, M., 23 y
"	24	Richard Holt, weaver, decline, Failsworth, 61 y (*or* 64 y *faded*)
"	29	Joseph Bailey, coal miner, fever, M., 55 y
Nov	14	Mary w. John Arnold, whitster, decline, Failsworth, 30 y
"	18	Richard Wolstencroft, fustian cutter, asthma, M., 55 y
"	19	John Jones, weaver, decline, M., 69 y (*? - age faded*)
"	25	Sarah d. Betty Diggles, weaver, fits, Newton, 2 m 14 days
"	25	William Gorton, gardener, sudden, Failsworth, 79 y
"	26	John s. Mary Scholes, weaver, burned, Failsworth, 7 y
"	30	David s. John & Phebe Taylor, weaver, hoopg. cough, Moston, 9 m
Dec	2	Samuel s. Thomas & Amelia Heald, weaver, fits, Newton, 9 m
"	2	William s. Ambrose & Mary Yates, weaver, fits, M., 9 m
"	7	Thomas Roberts, miner, sudden, M., 57 y
"	13	John Thorp, weaver, decline, M., 22 y
"	13	Elizabeth d. Thomas & Mary Whitehead, decline, Failsworth, 33 y
"	16	Ralph Benson s. William & Martha Long, excise officer, fits, Newton, 21 days (*altered from* 2 m)
"	17	Maria d. Sarah Parker, inflam lungs, M., 2 y 2 m
"	23	Agnes d. William & Martha Long, excise officer, fits, Newton, 2 m
"	25	Mary w. William Greenwood, weaver, decline, M., 65 y
"	25	Ann w. Arthur Doran, weaver, inflam bowels, M., 40 y
"	30	Thomas s. Francis & Ann Fairclough, spinner, fits, M., 2 m 7 days
"	30	William Walker, manufacturer, decline, M., 48 y
"	31	William s. Willm. & Lily Dean, weaver, fits, M., 21 days
[		A True Copy from the Burial Register of Newton Chapel in the Parish of Manchester & Diocese of Chester for the year 1810]
[		R.A. Singleton Curate]
[		Joseph Bertenshaw William Brown Tho. Hulton Wardens]

Burials in 1811

Jan	6	William s. John & Mary Mitchel, labourer, decline, M., 11 m
"	6	Jonathan s. John & Ann Clayton, labourer, fits, M., 9 days
"	9	Jonathan s. Robert & Jane Edwards, engineer, decline, M., 14 y
"	9	Sarah w. James Clough, weaver, decline, Failsworth, 31 y
"	13	Jane wdw. Robert Stott, manufacturer, decline, Failsworth, 42 y
"	16	Margaret Oldham, weaver, decline, Newton, 85 y
"	19	Sarah d. Richard & Alice Mills, labourer, fits, Newton, 1 m
"	23	Ralph s. Philip & Sarah Acton, fits, M., 11 m
"	31	Robert Bowker, weaver, decline, Droylsden, 76 y

Feb	5	John s. Jonathan & Esther Etchels, weaver, fits, Failsworth, 21 days
"	11	Martin s. Nicholas & Hannah Pritchet, labourer, hoopgcough, M., 10 m
"	11	Matthew s. Matthew & Ann [Nancy] Gradwell, weaver, small pox, Failsworth, 9 m
"	20	Alice Clegg, decline, M., 60 y
"	20	Sarah wdw. James Anderton, painter, decline, M., 22 y
"	28	Richard Hardy, velvet dresser, dropsy, M., 56 y
Mar	1	John s. Thomas & Hannah Allen, weaver, decline, Failsworth, 2 y 6 m
"	3	Thomas s. John & Betty Robinson, weaver, fits, M., 3 m
"	6	Henry Chatterton, coalminer, decline, M., 71 y
"	6	Robert s. John & Martha Hulme, weaver, burned, Droylsden, 2 y
"	6	Sarah d. Christopher & Sarah Mellor, labourer, fits, Newton, 3 y
"	12	Hannah d. John & Peggy [Margarette] Lees, weaver, fever, Failsworth 20y
"	21	Betty d. David & Ann Etchels, weaver, decline, Failsworth, 11 m
"	24	Esther w. John Mor[e]ton, bookkeeper, childbed, M., 37 y
"	27	Peggy wdw. James Horrocks, labourer, fever, Failsworth, 68 y
Apr	2	Elizabeth d. Willm. & Elizabeth Haynes, smith, fits, M., 2 m 21 days
"	3	Betty d. Willm. & Betty Hibbert, weaver, decline, Newton, 29 y
"	7	John Tomlinson, weaver, decline, M., 66 y
"	12	Mishal [Myshall] d. Philip & Sarah Schofield, weaver, decline, Droylsden, 6 y
"	14	Hannah d. Willm. & Frances Toole, cordwainer, decline, M., 14 y
"	14	Alice d. James & Esther Heywood, dyer, inflam lungs, M., 14 m
"	14	James s. William & Mary Wallcroft, weaver, fits, Newton, 9 m
"	17	Mary wdw. Samuel Beswick, bleacher, decline, Levenshulme, 82 y
"	25	Mary w. Robert Whitehead, weaver, decline, Failsworth, 65 y
"	28	Martha d. Rigby & Susanna Stanton, calenderer, fits, Newton, 1 day
"	30	Mary w. William Allen, surgeon, decline, Failsworth, 71 y
May	5	James s. Benjn. & Betty Heywood, decline, M., 3 m
"	7	Ann d. John & Hannah Lord, weaver, fits, Droylsden, 3 m
"	15	Mary wdw. William Berry, weaver, decline, Failsworth, 76 y
"	22	Alice d. Thomas & Mary Fallows, gardener, decline, Withington, 18 y
"	23	Sarah w. Jonathan Lilly, clothier, decline, Saddleworth, 95 y
"	24	Richard s. Richd. & Margt. Burgess, weaver, fits, M., 14 days
"	28	James Shepley, gentleman, inflamn., M., 53 y
"	30	Hannah (sp. *not in BT*) d. Jane Chadwick, weaver, fits, M., 1 m (*altered from* 6 m)
Jun	2	David s. John & Betty Clough, weaver, fits, Failsworth, 2 m
"	4	Helen[a] d. John & Mary Bates, cordwainer, fits, Failsworth, 14 days
"	10	Joseph Berry, blacksmith, decline, Failsworth, 58 y
"	11	Thomas s. George & Martha Hall, bricklayer, tooth fever, M., 9 m
"	12	Mary w. John Hooley, whitster, decline, Droylsden, 60 y
"	19	John s. John & Mary Leigh, weaver, nerv. fever, M., 6 y
"	19	Martha w. John Crossley, labourer, decline, Newton, 43 y
"	23	Jane d. John & Mary Chadwick, weaver, decline, M., 24 y

"	24	Sarah wdw. Samuel Smith, weaver, fever, Failsworth, 60 y *(1811)*
"	30	Margaret d. George & Margt. Tagart, weaver, fits, M., 3 m 21 days
"	30	Thomas s. John & Mary Ashton, weaver, fits, Failsworth, 2 m 21 days
Jul	3	William Lombard, sailor, decline, Newton, 23 y
"	4	Peter s. Nancy Renshaw, weaver, fits, Failsworth, 8 m
"	15	Mary d. Willm. & Hannah Winstanley, forger, fever, M., 8 y
"	16	Ann d. James & Jane Allen, weaver, inflamn., Newton, 8(?) y 14 days
"	24	Mary d. Joseph & Nancy Ogden, weaver, fits, Failsworth, 13 m
"	29	Ann d. William & Mary Booth, innkeeper, decline, Newton, 23 y
Aug	2	William s. James & Betty Riley, labourer, fits, M., 4 m
"	2	Elizabeth d. Edmund & Ellen [Helena] Whitehead, weaver, fits, M., 9 m
"	6	Edward Walker, weaver, palsy, Failsworth, 73 y
"	9	Thomas s. Thomas & Jane Smith, weaver, fits, Failsworth, 9 m
"	25	Esther d. John & Esther Morton, bookkeeper, decline, M., 3 m
"	27	Mary d. Nathaniel & Ann Thorley, gardener, inflamn., Failsworth, 24 y
"	28	George s. George & Mary Hall, cotton spinner, decline, M., 6 y 3 m
"	29	John Newton, hatter, ner. fever, M., 31 y
"	30	Hannah d. James & Hannah Berry, blacksmith, decline, Failsworth, 3y 3m
"	30	Sarah d. Thomas & Margt. Piearson, gent., fits, M.
Sep	12	Mary w. Thomas Whitehead, weaver, decline, Failsworth, 55 y
"	15	Ellen d. William & Betty Pegge, surgeon, fits, Newton, 2 y
"	16	James Grimshaw, weaver, decline, M., 48 y
"	29	William s. Charles & Elizabeth Walmsley, labourer, infln., Newton, 6 m
Oct	6	Elizabeth d. John & Mary Harrison, shopkeeper, dropsy, M., 9 y
"	6	George s. Thomas & Jane Yates, bleacher, fits, Newton, 21 days
"	10	John Butterworth, labourer, manslaughter, M., 22 y
"	10	Mary d. Thomas & Ruth Booth, clothdresser, decline, M., 2 y
"	20	Martha d. Henry & Jane Singleton, bricklayer, accident, M., 5 y
"	31	Heritage s. Samuel & Mary Holland, weaver, decline, Failsworth, 4 m 21 d
"	31	Mary Jones, widow, decline, Newton, 55 y
Nov	10	Jane wdw. Richd. Burchel, weaver, decline, M., 46 y
"	17	Edward s. Benjamin & Sarah Priest, spinner, decline, M., 3 m 21 days
"	18	Joseph s. John & Mary Slater, manufacturer, decline, Newton, 8 y 4 m
"	24	Alice d. Thomas & Alice Stafford, miner, accident, Droylsden, 5 y 8 m
"	24	Joseph Clough, weaver, dropsy, Newton, 67 y
"	26	Jane d. John & Martha Bell, barber, decline. M., 13 y
Dec	1	William s. James & Alice Mason, weaver, sudden death, M., 2 y 9 m
"	3	Ann w. Thomas Meaden, cal. printer, decline, M., 24 y
"	8	William s. Jeremiah & Hannah Thom[p]son, soldier, decline, Newton, 18y
"	10	Rachel d. Robert & Elizh. Clayton, miner, decline, M., 9 m
"	12	George s. George & Elizh. Turner, weaver, fits, M., 3 m
"	25	John s. John & Mary Whitehead, soldier, decline, M., 11 m
"	29	Edward Whitehead, weaver, decline, Failsworth, 91 y
"	29	Esther d. William & Mary Wyld, fits, Droylsden, 3 days

[A. Ashworth Minister   ]
[Joseph Bertenshaw John Brundrett Wardens   ]

Burials in 1812

Jan	1	Margt. d. Edward & Ann Tagan, weaver, decline, Newton, 3 m 21 days
"	8	Jane d. Richard & Lydia Downing, victualler, decline, M., 13 y
"	19	Joseph Whittaker, weaver, decline, Failsworth, 82 y
"	20	John s. Willm. & Elizh. Domelow, hatter, inflam., M., 3 m
"	26	Ann d. Daniel & Mary Smith, weaver, decline, Failsworth, 37 y
"	26	Violet w. Benjamin Hulton, weaver, decline, Failsworth, 30 y
"	29	George s. James & Elizh. Tetlow, warper, fits, Failsworth, 2 m 2 days
Feb	2	Elizh. d. Willm. & Hannah Marshall, tailor, fits, M., 6 m
"	5	Mary w. John Whitehead, cabinet maker, decline, M., 31 y
"	7	Richard s. Richd. & Jane Smith, weaver, decline, M., 18 y
"	9	Mary w. William Wallcroft, weaver, childbirth, Newton, 33 y
"	9	John sp. s. Sarah Brewitt, winder, decline, Newton, 6 m
"	9	Ann d. Thomas & Mary Smith, weaver, tooth fever, Failsworth, 1 y 7 m
"	18	Thomas s. Philip & Sarah Berry, labourer, decline, Droylsden, 23 y
"	21	Mary w. Thurstan Smethurst, weaver, dropsy, Failsworth, 41 y
"	23	Jane w. William Allen, weaver, consumpn., Failsworth, 30 y
"	23	Helena d. Robt. & Alice Whitehead, weaver, Woodhouses, 9 m
"	27	Samuel Etchels, weaver, decline, Failsworth, 54 y
Mar	1	Randel s. John & Elizh. Fairclough, labourer, quinsey, M., 7 y 9 m
"	2	Richard s. Thos. & Ann Horrocks, labourer, dropsy, Failsworth, 1 y 5 m
"	5	Thomas s. James & Mary Morrison, weaver, small pox, M., 2 y 8 m 10 d
"	6	Elizh. d. James & Jane Fitton, spinner, small pox, M., 8 y 6 m
"	8	Mary d. James & Mary Morrison, weaver, small pox, M., 3 y 3 m 10 days
"	15	Nancy d. John & Alice Jackson, weaver, consumpn., Newton, 19 y
"	16	John Burgess, decline, M., 37 y
"	18	Mary wdw. Benjamin Hulton, weaver, decline, Failsworth, 74 y
"	22	Daniel Smith, weaver, consumpn., Failsworth, 60 y
"	22	James s. James & Mary Hulton, weaver, consumpn., Oldham, 24 y
"	26	William s. John & Elizh. Bowler, spinner, fits, M., 16 m
"	27	Mary Ann d. James & Jane Fitton, spinner, small pox, M., 4 y 10 m
"	27	Henry s. David & Helena Wilmot, engineer, fits, Newton, 1 y
"	30	Catherine d. Alexandr. & Isabel Galshan, weaver, scrofula, Failsworth, 16 y
		(*see baptism same date*)
Apr	2	John Ridge, tailor, decline, M., 78 y
"	6	John s. Benj. & Violet Hulton, weaver, decline, Failsworth, 2 m 21 days
"	7	Jane d. James & Mary Taylor, joiner, fits, M., 15 m
"	12	Millicent w. John Salt, cal. printer, decline, Newton, 58 y
"	14	Nancy d. John & Sarah Marsh, weaver, fits, M., 2 y
"	14	William s. John & Ann Kay, coal miner, measles, M., 11 m
"	21	Sarah d. Willm. & Maria Hamner, labourer, fever, Failsworth, 6 y

"	26	Sarah d. Richd. & Ann Johnson, labourer, measles, Ardwick, 3 y 3 m
"	26	George s. Joseph & Rachel Yarwood, soldier, fever, M., 18 m
"	26	Robert s. Robt. & Mary Abraham, joiner, measles, M., 17 m
"	26	Margt. d. George & Margt. Montgomery, weaver, measles, M., 18 m
"	29	Lucy d. John & Betty Robinson, weaver, fits, M., 4 m 21 days
May	4	Sampson s. Thos. & Mary Farrand, weaver, inf. bowels, Ardwick, 11 m
"	10	William s. Betty Taylor, weaver, decline, M., 13 m
"	10	Ann d. Jonathan & Elizh. Bythel, labourer, decline, Newton, 1 y
"	10	John s. Joseph & Rachel Yarwood, soldier, r fever, M., 3 y 2 m
"	11	Helena d. Robert Bowker, weaver, water in head, M., 5 y 3 m
"	13	William s. Richd. & Ann Kenyon, printer, r fever, Newton, 1 y
"	17	William s. James & Mary Etchels, weaver, small pox, Failsworth, 4 y
"	22	Mary wdw. James Pendleton, tailor, decline, Failsworth, 85 y
"	24	Ann d. Esther Wolstenhulme, weaver, measles, M., 2 y
"	24	William Gradwell, weaver, decline, Newton, 79 y
"	28	Mary w. John Booth, weaver, decline, Failsworth, 49 y
Jun	3	Robert McMaghan, weaver, decline, M., 44 y
"	6	Hannah w. Joseph Tetlow, mariner, decline, Newton, 47 y
"	10	William s. James & Elizh. Trimble, weaver, measles, M., 4 y 9 m
"	14	Henry s. John & Sarah Tetlow, warehouseman, fits, Newton, 10 m
"	17	Josiah Hyde, coal miner, fever, M., 25 y
"	18	Mary d. John & Sarah Walmsley, labourer, fits, Failsworth, 15 m
"	21	John s. John & Phoebe Taylor, weaver, decline, Moston, 11 y
"	22	Hannah w. Isaac Taylor, coal miner, fever, M., 21 y
"	23	Thomas s. James & Elizh. Birch, dyer, small pox, M., 2 y 4 m
"	25	William Kenyon, blue dyer, rheu fever, Newton, 22 y
"	28	Mary d. Ann Fairclough, spinner, fits, M., 2 m 14 days
"	28	Philip s. William & Martha Acton, tinplateworker, fits, M., 2 m
Jul	5	Betty wdw. John Butterworth, weaver, fever, M., 50 y
"	5	James s. John & Betty Butterworth, weaver, fits, Newton, 21 days
"	5	Esther d. John & Grace Blackshaw, blacksmith, small pox, Failsworth, 1 y 1 m
"	6	Joseph s. Josiah & Ann Hyde, coal miner, measles, M., 1 y 1 m
"	6	Mary d. James & Bridget O'Conner, weaver, fits, M., 1 m 31 days (*sic*)
"	9	Hannah w. Thos. Gradwell, weaver, decline, M., 47 y
"	11	Thomas s. Thos. & Ann Maddocks, labourer, fits, M., 2 m 21 days
"	20	Robert Chadderton, weaver, rupture, Failsworth, 72 y
"	21	John Whitaker, weaver, decline, Failsworth, 46 y
"	21	John s. Saml. & Mary Robinson, slater, white swell., Newton, 6 y 1 m
"	23	James s. William & Sarah Smith, weaver, fever, M., 16 y
"	26	Elizh. d. Thomas & Rebecca Borras, weaver, fits, M., 10 m
"	28	John s. James & Susanna Byrom, bleacher, fits, Failsworth, 2 y
"	29	Joseph Cook, slater, decline, Newton, 38 y
"	30	Edward Walker, labourer, decline, Newton, 81 y
Aug	2	David s. William & Mary Bentley, cal. printer, rash fever, Newton, 5m 3d

"	2	Charles s. John & Bridget Waring, coal miner, rash fever, Droylsden, 7 m
"	5	Jeremiah Smith, weaver, dropsy, M., 21 y
"	9	Margaret w. Isaac Dean, serving man, rupture, Failsworth, 58 y
"	19	Jenny w. George Hulton, weaver, consump., Failsworth, 31 y
"	21	Hannah w. John Haslam, weaver, consump., Failsworth, 42 y
"	24	Samuel Rigb[e]y, joiner, consump., Bradford, 61 y
"	27	Samuel sp. s. Alice Etchels, weaver, consump., Failsworth, 5 m
"	27	James s. Samuel & Mary Robinson, slater, small pox, Newton, 1 y 9 m
"	30	Charles s. Michael & Ann Russel, cotton spinner, measles, M., 18 m
Sep	2	William Greenwood, weaver, consump., M., 64 y
"	2	Samuel s. Sarah Wood, weaver, measles, M., 19 m
"	9	John Wilshaw, cotton spinner, consumpn., M., 55 y
"	12	James Sykes s. John & Mary Thorley, weaver, rash fever, Failsworth 2 y 6 m
"	15	William s. late Wm. & Sarah Allen, labourer, small pox, Newton, 12 y
"	16	Joseph s. John & Mary Thorley, weaver, rash fever, Failsworth, 6 y 11 m
"	18	Ann w. John Preston, dealer & chapman, pleurisy, Failsworth, 50 y
"	20	Nancy d. James & Mary Thorp, weaver, rash fever, Failsworth, 9 y
"	20	Betty d. Richard & Mary Thorp, weaver, consn., Wood houses, 39 y
"	24	Sarah d. John & Sarah Tetlow, weaver, infl. lungs, M., 4 m
"	28	Mary d. James & Martha [Sarah] Tetlow, weaver, small pox, M., 2 y
"	29	William Sudworth, coal miner, pleurisy, M., 53 y
Oct	1	Daniel s. James & Martha Wild, labourer, rash fever, Newton, 2 y
"	5	Elizabeth d. James & Mary Holt, weaver, rash fever, Failsworth, 9 y
"	7	Lucy d. John & Betty Tarvin, labourer, small pox, Newton, 5 y
"	11	Richard Hall, bricklayer, dropsy, Failsworth, 63 y
"	18	Joseph Shaw, weaver, consumpn., M., 28 y
"	18	Mary d. James & Mary Broughton, weaver, small pox, M., 3 y 5 m
"	21	Elizabeth w. James Chadderton, weaver, consum., Failsworth, 54 y
"	21	Margaret w. Thomas Welsh, calenderer, sudden, Newton, 64 y
"	22	Mary d. James & Betty Ogden, weaver, r. fever, Failsworth, 1 y 9 m
"	22	Margaret d. John & Betty Tarvin, labourer, r. fever, Newton, 1 m 7 days
"	25	James Leech, weaver, dropsy, Newton, 42 y
"	26	Mary d. John & Grace Blackshaw, blacksmith, fits, Failsworth, 3 y 6 m
"	28	Nancy w. James Morris, cal. printer, Newton, 56 y
"	28	Mary w. John Leigh, weaver, childbed, M., 40 y
"	29	Mary d. John & Mary Ramsbottom, dyer, cons, Failsworth, 18 y
"	29	James Berry sp. s. Alice Berry, weaver, small pox, Failsworth, 1 y 6 m
Nov	5	Mary d. James & Sarah Clough, weaver, drowned, Failsworth, 12 y 10 m
"	9	William s. Joseph & Martha Clough, weaver, fits, Woodhouses, 6 y
"	12	Thomas Brown, currier, ner fever, M., 41 y
"	19	Susanna d. Elias & Sarah Whiteley, labourer, infl. lungs, Droylsden, 6 m
"	22	Samuel s. James & Alice Mason, weaver, small pox, M., 1 y 4 m
"	22	Jane d. George & Hannah Nic(h)olson, hatter, fits, M., 9 m
"	22	Bryant [Brian] Luvrison, weaver, decline, M., 79 y

"	26	Edward sp. s. SH *or* IH & Hannah Wrigley, servant, fits, Newton, 2 m
		(*BT reads:* Edward spu. s. Hannah Wrigley, servant, Newton)
"	29	Mary d. Richd. & Mary York, weaver, convul., M., 5 m
"	29	Joseph Leech, weaver, decline, M., 71 y
"	30	Thomas Booth, weaver, dropsy, Moston, 51 y
Dec	3	James s. James & Mary Ridings, weaver, r fever, Failsworth, 3 y
"	6	James s. John & Mary Tetlow, weaver, water in head, Failsworth, 10 m
"	18	Henry sp. s. Betty Ditchfield, weaver, sc. fever, Failsworth, 15 m
[		The above is a true Copy taken from the Register at Newton Heath Chapel]
[		A. Ashworth Minister]
[		Robert Berry James Tetlow Wardens]

(*new register commences: volume 8 - George Rose format*)

1813
(*BT faded; most entries cannot be verified upto February 16*)

Jan	1	Robert Thorp, Manchester, 10 m
"	3	Eliza Whitehead, Failsworth, 1 y 5 m
"	6	Mary Whitehead, Manchester, 5 y
"	10	Christina Galashan, Failsworth, 14 y
"	10	William Grimes, Manchester, 4 y 6 m
"	10	Anne Shenston, Manchester, 9 m
"	13	William Bell, Manchester, 1 y 3 m
"	17	Mary Ball, Manchester, 5 y
"	17	Joseph Morris, Newton, 31 y
"	24	Anne Hartley, Manchester, 1 y 5 m
"	24	Jane Williamson, Woodhouses, 10 wks
"	24	Sarah Sudworth, Manchester, 36 y
"	25	John Etchels, Failsworth, 15 y
"	27	Alice Etchels, Failsworth, 21 y
"	31	Robert Smith, Oldham, 32 y
Feb	7	John Andrew, Manchester, 12 m
"	9	James Wood, Manchester, 1 m
"	10	Robert Whitehead, Manchester, 7 y
"	14	John Clayton, Manchester, 11 wks
"	16	Anne Etchels, Failsworth, 13 days
"	21	Joshua Cordingley, Failsworth, 72 y
"	17	Samuel Moss, Manchester, 67 y
"	21	Charles Ashworth, Manchester, 87 y
"	21	Jonathan Clough, Newton, 3 y
"	21	Samuel Wyld, Droylsden, 4 wks
"	26	John Salt, Salford, 60 y
Mar	1	Thomas Brown, Failsworth, 5 y

"	7	David Cryer, Manchester, 8 days	*(1813)*
"	7	John Lees, Manchester, 2 y	
"	15	Moses Brown, Manchester, 6 m	
"	16	Joel Wyld, Droylsden, 3 wks	
"	17	Betty Brown, Failsworth, 10 m	
"	21	Daniel Wallcroft, Newton, 14 m	
"	21	Thomas Stafford, Droylsden, 14 m	
"	23	Andrew Sudworth, Manchester, 1 y	
"	28	Margaret Bailey, Manchester, 14 m	
"	28	Catharine Obrines, Manchester, 2 y 8 m	
"	29	Hannah Hulton, Failsworth, 17 y	
"	31	Mary Tetlow, Failsworth, 25 y 11 m	
"	31	Maria Crossley, Manchester, 6 m	
"	31	Hannah Holland, Failsworth, 2 days	
Apr	7	Samuel Mason, Newton, 26 y	
"	11	Joseph Wyld, Openshaw, 25 y	
"	11	Mary Wyld, Openshaw, 27 y	
"	12	Elizabeth Goodier, Newton, 72 y	
"	13	Daniel Whitehead, Failsworth, 8 m	
"	13	Mary Butterworth, Manchester, 6 m	
"	18	Thomas Wainwright, Newton, 50 y	
"	18	Elizabeth Lane, Manchester (*age blank in PR & BT*)	
"	20	Mary Hill, Manchester, 2 y 2 m	
"	22	Emanuel Smith, Failsworth, 2 days	
"	22	Mark Howles, Newton, 2 y 2 m	
"	25	Martha Gillibrand, Manchester, 67 y	
"	25	Lucy Hardy, Manchester, 3 y	
"	25	Richard Bee, Manchester, 9 m	
"	25	Elizabeth Chapman, Manchester, 6 m	
"	29	Hannah Bottomley, Manchester, 77 y	
May	2	Harriot Heyes, Manchester, 11 m	
"	2	Mary Smith, Failsworth, 61 y	
"	3	Charles Brown, Manchester, 17 m	
"	4	Margery Trimble, Manchester, 12 y	
"	7	William Smith, Manchester, 19 y	
"	11	Walter Hughes, Newton, 2 m	
"	12	Sarah Molloy, Manchester, 9 y	
"	13	Hannah Gradwell, Newton, 27 y	
"	14	Mary Bee, Manchester, 3 y	
"	16	Anne Birch, Manchester, 62 y	
"	16	Jane Peters, Manchester, 59 y	
"	23	Mary Pollet, Newton, 43 y 4 m	
"	30	Jonathan Winstanley, Manchester, 5 m	
"	30	Esther Taylor, Failsworth, 25 y	
"	30	Ann Eckersley, Failsworth, 37 y	

Jun	1	Margaret Grimes, Manchester, 16 y	*(1813)*
"	4	John Hulme, Manchester, 34 y	
"	6	Jonathan Butterworth, Manchester, 74 y	
"	6	Mary Butterworth, Manchester, 9 m	
"	8	Thomas Harris, Manchester, 10 wks	
"	9	Joseph Clough, Newton, 7 y	
"	20	Helena Andrew, Manchester, 4 y 6 m	
"	27	Ann Wyld, Newton, 9 m	
"	30	Elizabeth Shone, Newton, 21 y	
"	30	James Allanson, Newton, 11 wks	
Jul	4	Jane Whitaker, Manchester, 60 y	
"	11	Hannah Walmsley, Failsworth, 22 y	
"	11	Lucy Taylor, Failsworth, 21 y	
"	16	James Taylor, Manchester, 10 y	
"	21	David Etchels, Failsworth, 37 y	
"	26	Emanual Stafford, Newton, 2 m	
"	29	Mary Davis, Manchester, 71 y	
Aug	1	Robert Etchels, Failsworth, 22 y	
"	3	Eliza Hulton, Failsworth, 2 wks	
"	10	Ann Marsden, Newton, 7 m	
"	15	Ezekiel Sanderson, Manchester, 77 y	
"	24	Sarah Whalley, *(abode blank in PR & BT)*, 17 y	
"	27	Joseph Seel, Newton, 1 y 6 m	
"	29	George Clayton, Salford, 39 y	
"	29	Mary Whitehead, *(abode blank in PR & BT)*, 4 y 4 m	
"	31	Rachel Galmori, Newton, 15 y	
"	31	John Ogden, Failsworth, 76 y	
Sep	1	Edward Kenyon, Manchester, 70 y	
"	7	James Smith, Failsworth, 26 y	
"	7	Zacariah Seel, Newton, 26 y	
"	8	James Woolstencroft, Manchester, 1 y 6 m	
"	15	Thomas Moors, Manchester, 8 y	
"	20	Simeon Whitehead, Failsworth, 2 days	
"	22	Hannah Barrows, Manchester, 17 days	
"	26	Thomas Barlow, Failsworth, 71 y	
"	26	James Boardman, Manchester, 9 m [71 y]	
"	27	Charles Clough, Failsworth, 9 y 6 m	
"	27	John Holland, Newton, 15 m	
"	30	Thomas Robinson, Newton, 18 y	
Oct	6	John Heywood, Newton, 38 y	
"	10	Edward Redman, Manchester, 15 m 1 wk	
"	10	Hannah Slater, Newton, 8 m 3 w	
"	10	Anne Wylde, Droylsden, 71 y	
"	17	John Basley, Newton, 7 m	
"	24	David Rowcroft, Manchester, 9 m	

"	24	Elizabeth Eckersley, Newton, 19 y	
"	31	Margaret Horrox, Openshaw, 3 y 4 m	
"	31	Sarah Oaks, Manchester, 10 y	
Nov	3	Mary Dawson, Newton, 2 y 5 m	
"	8	James Caurrie, Newton, 1 y 1 m	
"	14	James Tetlow, Failsworth, 26 y	
"	14	Margaret Ogden, Manchester, 3 y 8 m	
"	17	William Edge, Manchester, 1 y 5 days	
"	19	Richard Barlow, Manchester, 71 y	
"	21	Elizabeth Robert, Manchester, 14 y	
"	24	Edward Tompson, Manchester, 2 y	
"	30	Sarah Brown, Newton, 32 y	
Dec	1	Martha Kershaw, Failsworth, 32 y	
"	1	Joseph Pollet, Failsworth, 14 y	
"	3	Mary Gradwell, Blackley, 23 y	
"	5	Esther Garlick, Failsworth, 82 y	
"	5	James Whitaker, Failsworth, 62 y	
"	7	Jane Rydings, Failsworth, 1 y 6 m	
"	16	Sarah Smith, Failsworth, 25 y	
"	19	Robert Walmsley, Newton, 58 y	
"	19	John Moreton, Manchester, 52 y	
"	25	John Crossby, Manchester, 49 y	
[		A. Ashworth Minister	]
[		Joseph Barker Warden	]

1814
[Newton Heath Burials 1814]

Jan	3	Sarah Bolton, (*abode blank in PR & BT*), 11 m 9 days
"	4	Elizabeth Rogerson, Manchester, 2 y 8 m
"	4	Esther Barsnett, Manchester, 44 y
"	9	John Windstandley, Manchester, 7 m
"	13	John Wyatt, Manchester, 4 y
"	16	Abraham Taylor, Manchester, 63 y
"	16	Isabella Smith, Failsworth, 17 y
"	16	Jane Wilson, Failsworth, 77 y
"	16	Elizabeth Tomlinson, Moston, 1 y 7 m
"	16	John Etchels, Failsworth, 12 y
"	19	William Hulme, Manchester, 1 y 3 wks
"	20	Betty Ashworth, Manchester, 79 y
"	23	James Taylor, Manchester, 70 y
"	23	Sarah Travis, Newton, 76 y
"	23	Gowin Duncuff, Manchester, 14 y
"	27	Nancy Aldred, Newton, 8 m
"	30	John Holland, Failsworth, 75 y

"	30	Betty Allowell, Newton, 11 y
Feb	2	James Hulme, Droylsden, 25 - (*same in BT*)
"	6	Sarah Billinge, Manchester, 3 y 5 m
"	6	Jonathan Etchels, Failsworth, 5 m
"	7	Sarah Etchels, Failsworth, 9 m
"	9	Elizabeth Ashton, Failsworth, 55 y
"	9	William Sudworth, Manchester, 3 m
"	11	William Billinge, Manchester, 9 y
"	11	Sarah Tetlow, Manchester, 6 m
"	12	Mary Ann Grimes, Manchester, 1 y 8 m
"	13	Meredith Convall, Manchester, 51 y
"	14	John Ward, Manchester, 8 wks
"	16	James Windstanley, Manchester, 9 m
"	20	Elizabeth Hardy, Manchester, 1 y 8 m
"	21	James Berry (James *in BT*) Makin, Failsworth, 14 m
"	27	Mary Billinge, Manchester, 1 y
"	27	John Preston, Failsworth, 2 m
Mar	2	Frederick Etchels, Failsworth, 2 y
"	3	Ann Hamlet, Manchester, 69 y
"	6	Mary Tetlow, Newton, 56 y
"	6	Thomas Meden, Manchester, 2 y
"	6	Martha Taylor, Manchester, 53 y
"	10	Hannah Leigh, Manchester, 1 y 5 m
"	13	John Hardy, Manchester, 5 y 3 m
"	13	Jane Lees, Manchester, 11 m
"	15	Hannah Smith, Manchester, 3 y 9 m
"	17	William Booth, Newton, 63 y
"	17	Martha Lomas, Newton, 62 y
"	20	John Heath, Newton, 11 y
"	20	Mary Hampson, Manchester, 16 y
"	20	John Booth, Newton, 4 y
"	20	James Ashton, Failsworth, 34 y
"	20	Sarah Pilling, Moston, 6 wks
"	22	James Roberts, Manchester, 3 y
"	24	Hannah Wilmot, Manchester, 1 wk
"	25	Samuel Smethurst, Manchester, 3 y 6 m
"	27	Mary Hill, Manchester, 17 wks
Apr	1	Nanny Hulton, Failsworth, 1 y 6 m
"	3	Anne Potter, Failsworth, Failsworth, 3 wks
"	5	Mary Wardley, Manchester, 33 y
"	6	James Ashworth, Manchester, 4 y
"	6	Esther Whitehead, Manchester, 59 y
"	6	Joseph Ogden, Newton, 57 y
"	10	Mary Booth, Failsworth, 18 y
"	12	Sarah Lord, Manchester, 1 y 10 m

"	15	James Jones, Manchester, 70 y
"	17	James Chadderton, Hollinwood, 73 y
"	18	James Smith, Hollinwood, 5 m
"	24	Sarah Daltry, Oldham, 10 m
May	1	Elizabeth Simister, Failsworth, 2 y 5 m
"	1	John Worrall, Failsworth, 5 wks
"	2	Daniel Knott, Failsworth, 64 y
"	2	Henry Crossley, Failsworth, 20 m
"	5	Jane Smethurst, Failsworth, 1 y 9 days
"	5	William Wardley, Manchester, 6 y
"	9	Rebecca Cassedy, Manchester, 33 y
"	10	Joseph Whittaker, Failsworth, 3 y 2 m
"	10	Mary Farrand, Newton, 52 y
"	10	Samuel Smith, Manchester, 42 y
"	13	John Marsden, Newton, 4 y 1 m
"	16	Nancy Ingham, Newton, 80 y
"	17	Sarah Lee, Manchester, 5 m
"	20	Mary Whittaker, Failsworth, 20 y
"	22	John Wolstencroft, Manchester, 9 y 10 m
"	24	Squire Mason, Manchester, 1 y
"	26	Elizabeth Smith, Manchester, 18 y
"	27	Esther Rosina Hulton, Failsworth, 2 y 6 m
"	28	Christiana Hulton, Failsworth, 10 m 2 wks
"	29	Joseph Ogden, Failsworth, 1 y
"	29	Betty Smith, Newton, 11 y 11 m
Jun	2	Anne Pollet, Newton, 21 y
"	3	Martha Tetlow, Manchester, 4 y
"	5	Matty Timmis, Failsworth, 1 y
"	5	Martha Lane, Failsworth, 1 y 3 m
"	12	Mary Anne Hunt, Manchester, 1 y 6 m
"	14	Mary Owen, Manchester, 3 m
"	16	Jeremiah Kemp, Manchester, 44 y
"	21	Bridget Cardwell, Salford, 4 y 6 m
"	21	James Brown, Manchester, 7 y 5 m
"	22	Anne Allen, Failsworth, 1 y 6 m
"	22	Nancy Stott, Newton, 30 y
"	29	Betty Wilson, Hollinwood, 2 y 8 m
Jul	3	Maria Makin, Manchester, 26 y
"	14	Margaret Moors, Manchester, 2 y 10 m
"	17	Richard Johnson, Ardwick, 42 y
"	17	Henry Walton, Newton, 10 m
"	24	Catharine Whitaker, Manchester, 13 y
"	24	Sarah Brown, Manchester, 2 y 9 m
"	24	George Brown, Manchester, 3 wks
"	29	Maria Acton, Manchester, 2 y 3 days

"	31	Betty Livsey, Manchester, 1 y 4 m	*(1814)*
Aug	3	George Gradwell, Blackley, 1 y 4 m	
"	5	John Whitaker, Newton, 2 y 9 m	
"	7	John Septon, Manchester, 74 y	
"	14	Mary Jackson, Manchester, 55 y	
"	15	James Tetlow, Failsworth, 19 wks	
"	17	Mary Kemp, Newton, 62 y	
"	21	Mary Roberts, Manchester, 54 y	
"	21	Joseph Roberts, Manchester, 25 y	
"	23	George Fairclough, Manchester, 16 wks	
"	23	Thomas Ryley, Manchester, 5 y 8 m	
"	28	Elizabeth Blacklock, Salford, 2 y 3 m	
Sep	14	Louisa Hamner, Manchester, 2 y 2 m	
"	18	John Slater, Manchester, 1 day	
"	18	Mary Slater, Manchester, 1 day	
"	18	Lavinia Whitehead, Droylsden, 1 y 6 m	
"	25	Joseph Lomax, Manchester, 7 m 17 days	
"	28	Andrew Gorton, Failsworth, 7 m	
"	29	Mary Andrew, Manchester, 4 y	
Oct	23	James Cooper, Manchester, 7 y	
"	23	John Cooper, Manchester, 3 y	
"	30	Daniel Heywood, Manchester, 73 y	
"	30	Matthew Howles, Newton, 1 y 2 m	
"	31	Maria Makin, Manchester, 6 m	
Nov	1	John Smith, Failsworth, 5 m	
"	6	Mary Smethurst, Manchester, 33 y	
"	6	Elizabeth Thorpe, Moston, 64 y	
"	6	Sarah Fallows, Withington, 12 y 9 m 14 days	
"	17	Hannah Barlow, Middleton, 66 y	
"	21	Catharine Hibbert, Manchester, 2 y 2 m	
"	27	John Rudd, Manchester, 61 y	
Dec	1	Benjamin Jones, Newton, 9 - *(same in BT)*	
"	7	David Taylor, Newton, 1 y 3 wks	
"	8	Mary Wild, Droylsden, 45 y	
"	8	Jebaz Thompson, Manchester, 1 y 5 m	
"	14	Daniel Ashton, Failsworth, 57 y *(order thus in PR & BT)*	
"	12	Sam Rydings, Failsworth, 9 m	
"	12	Elizabeth McKenna, Newton, 33 wks	
"	15	Alice Whitehead, Failsworth, 1 y 2 m	
"	15	Mary Hulme, Manchester, 9 wks	
"	18	William Morrison, Manchester, 5 y	
"	18	Samuel Livsey, Manchester, 26 y	
"	21	Joseph Nicholson, Manchester, 32 y	
"	21	Robert Preston, Newton, 2 y 3 m	
"	25	Joseph Wright, Manchester, 6 wks	

	26	James Kay, Manchester, 1 y 5 m
	29	John Wroe, Newton, 19 y
	29	John Haslem, Failsworth, 10 days

1815

Jan	1	Mary Newton, Manchester, 83 y
"	5	Robert Clayton, Manchester, 41 y
"	8	John Walton, Manchester, 7 m
"	8	Mary Groves, Manchester, 55 y
"	16	Susanna Etchels, Failsworth, 21 y
"	20	Benjamin Rydings, Failsworth, 2 wks
"	22	Esther Aldred, Woodhouses, 56 y
"	22	John Arnold, Newton, (*age blank in PR & BT*)
"	24	Joseph Turner, Newton, 5 m
Feb	2	William Hardman, Manchester, 10 m
"	5	Alice Booth, Salford, 88 y
"	6	Betty Yates, Newton, 10 y
"	7	Phebe Wilson, Failsworth, 45 y
"	7	George Wilkinson, Failsworth, 13 m
"	8	James Farrand, Manchester, 9 m
"	10	Jonathan Buckley Newton, Manchester, 33 y
"	10	Jonathan Andrew, Failsworth, 75 y
"	12	Robert Hulton, Failsworth, 47 y
"	14	Frances Toole, Manchester, 41 y
"	14	Elizabeth Hardy, Manchester, 1 y 8 m
"	26	Sarah Bithell, Failsworth, 35 y
Mar	2	John Etchels, Failsworth, 81 y
"	5	Hannah Toole, Manchester, 2 y 4 m
"	5	Isabella Whitehead, Failsworth, 18 y 3 m
"	5	Jane Yates, Manchester, 2 y 2 m
"	5	Jane Savage, Newton, 72 y
"	15	Elizabeth Greenwood, Newton, 17 wks
"	19	Betty Haslem, Failsworth, 24 y
"	19	Luke Burns, Manchester, 63 y
"	26	John Lee, Manchester, 6 wks
Apr	2	Richard Sutcliffe, Manchester, 2. 3 days (*same in BT*)
"	2	Jane Boyne, Newton, 1 day
"	4	James Hulton, Failsworth, 82 y
"	4	Hannah Heath, Newton, 12 hours
"	5	Abraham Nicholson, Manchester, 5 y
"	5	Mary Lee, Manchester, 5 - (*same in BT*)
"	9	Sarah Taylor, Manchester, 2 m
"	9	Josiah Ingham, Manchester, 44 y
"	12	John Thorpe, Manchester, 3 wks

"	14	Julia Seele, Failsworth, 18 y
"	18	James Boardman, Manchester, 55 y
"	23	James Taylor, Manchester, 4 y 5 m
"	25	Catharine Cros[s]ley, Manchester, 12 y
"	26	Richard Jackson, Manchester, 1 wk
"	27	Maria Grindrod, Manchester, 1 y 4 m
"	30	Joseph Tomlinson, Failsworth, 18 y 11 m
"	30	William Cook, Manchester, 15 y
May	2	David Wylde, Droylsden, 4 y 1 m
"	3	Charles Welch, Newton, 7 wks
"	7	Charles Syddal, Clayton, 6 m
"	7	Jonathan Hooley, Manchester, 3 y
"	11	John Holt, Failsworth, 72 y
"	14	John Jackson, Manchester, 3 wks
"	15	Robert Clegg, Failsworth, 39 y
"	19	Anne Livsey, Manchester, 9 m
"	21	Anne Robinson, Failsworth, 8 m
"	24	Elizabeth Turner, Manchester, 12 wks 1 day
"	28	Betty Haslem, Manchester, 67 y
"	30	Elizabeth Wild, Droylsden, 20 y
"	30	Samuel Townley, Manchester, 4 y 4 m
Jun	1	Mary Hulton, Failsworth, 6 y
"	1	Anne Anderton, Moston, 1 y
"	4	Sarah Kemp, Manchester, 10 y
"	17	Sidney Smith, Failsworth, 4 y 4 m
"	22	John Plimmer, Manchester, 34 y
Jul	9	Elizabeth Winstanley, Manchester, 33 - (*same in BT*)
"	9	Anne Rogers, Failsworth, 1 y 10 m
"	13	George Dean, Failsworth, 47 y
"	16	Jonathan Winstanley, Manchester, 8 m
"	16	Mary Harrison, Manchester, 1 y
"	18	John Ryley, Manchester, 43 y
"	19	Thomas Stafford, Droylsden, 6 hours
"	20	Anne Winstanley, Manchester, 2 y 2 m
"	20	William Slater, Manchester, 18 y
Aug	3	Hannah Winstanley, Manchester, 6 m
"	9	Elizabeth Ogden, Manchester, 38 y
"	9	George Eckersley, Failsworth, 4 y
"	13	Anne Makin, Manchester, 3 y
"	15	Benjamin Pritchard, Newton, 3 m
"	20	Maria Lord, Manchester, 6 y 11 m
"	31	Charles Cooper, Manchester, 1 y
Sep	4	William Isherwood, Manchester, 4 y 5 m
"	10	Amelia Wade, Newton, 2 y 6 m
"	10	Oliver Whitley, Droylsden, 14 days

"	10	Anne Marsh, Manchester, 1 y
"	11	Thomas Davies, Manchester, 70 y
"	11	Jane White, Newton, 4 m
"	17	William Smith, Manchester, 1 y 5 m
"	18	Rachel Atkinson, Manchester, 59 y
"	18	Mary Isherwood, Manchester, 1 y 4 m
"	24	Alice Syddal, Manchester, 7 wks 1 day
"	26	Ellen Berry, Failsworth, 23 wks
"	28	Anne Dilworth, Manchester, 18 y
"	29	William Lomax, Newton, 65 y
Oct	1	John Tervin, Newton, 47 y
"	1	Mary Bowler, Manchester, 21 y
"	9	James Tomlinson, Newton, 84 y
"	18	Elizabeth Shaw, Failsworth, 2 wks
"	19	John Dawson, Droylsden, 29 wks
"	23	Alice Whitaker, Manchester, 10 y
Nov	2	John Allen, Duckinfield, 50 y
"	2	Ellen Rudd, Manchester, 21 y
"	5	William Mars, Manchester, 18 y
"	5	Mary Rogers, Manchester, 10 wks
"	8	Thomas Hall, Newton, 7 m
"	19	Richard Wilkinson, Failsworth, 6 y
"	26	John Whitehead, Moston, 77 y
"	26	Richard Kershaw, Manchester, 4 m
"	27	Elizabeth Jones, Manchester, 8 m
"	27	Samuel Booth, Manchester, 55 y
Dec	4	Nehemiah Dimelow, Manchester, 36 y
"	10	John Howarth, Failsworth, 67 y
"	11	Anne Harding, Salford, 10 wks
"	12	Nancy Etchels, Failsworth, 3 y 3 m
"	17	John Burgess, Manchester, 70 y
"	17	Elizabeth Wardle, Manchester, 19 days
"	18	William Harrison, Oldham, 94 y
"	18	James Etchels, Ashton, 3 days
"	24	Oliver Etchels, Ashton, 9 days
"	24	Isabel Eckersley, Failsworth, 15 y 6 m
"	29	Henry Mills, Manchester, 7 m
"	31	Charles Hulme, Manchester, 50 y
"	31	James Mills, Medlock Vale, 9 wks
"	31	Edwin Winstanley, Manchester, 9 m
[		Signed John Piccop]

1816

Jan	3	Mary Tinker, Failsworth, 1 y 7 m
"	3	Martha Lees, Manchester, 21 y
"	7	Ellen Morrison, Manchester, 32 y
"	9	John Brickhill, Manchester, 7 m
"	14	Martha Pollit, Newton, 39 y
"	21	Sarah Aldred, Manchester, 38 y
"	22	James Hampson, Manchester, 9 m
"	22	Josiah Slater, Newton, 1 day
"	26	Michael Cheetham, Manchester, 9 m
"	28	Alice Smith, Failsworth, 65 y
"	28	Jane Walmsley, Manchester, 1 y 1 m
"	30	Sarah Ramsbottom, Failsworth, 55 y
"	31	Alice Clayton, Manchester, 3 days
"	31	Mary Crossley, Failsworth, 57 y
Feb	1	Philip Whitehead, Manchester, 8 m
"	4	Elizabeth Wild, Wood Houses, 56 y
"	4	Mary Barlow, Failsworth, 16 y
"	4	William Robinson, Newton, 72 y
"	7	Joseph Clough, Failsworth, 6 wks 5 days
"	12	Jane Smith, Manchester, 51 y
"	13	Mary Butterworth, Moston, 57 y
"	13	James Whitehead, Failsworth, 2 wks
"	14	Jonathan Hulme, Droylsden, 19 y
"	14	Joseph Allen, Failsworth, 23 wks
"	18	Jane Fletcher, Manchester, 9 m
"	18	Joseph Stansfield, Newton, 10 m
"	18	Hannah Brown, Manchester, 1 y 2 m
"	20	John Wylde, Failsworth, 33 y
"	21	Alice Billinge, Manchester, 7 y
"	22	Mary Gradwell, Blackley, 3 m
"	25	Jane Makin, Failsworth, 8 wks
"	26	Thomas Clough, Failsworth, 14 wks
"	27	William Thorpe, Failsworth, 20 y
"	27	Elizabeth Smith, Newton, 63 y
"	28	Mary Smith, Manchester, 55 y
Mar	3	Hannah Timmis, Failsworth, 34 y
	4	Mary Wroe, Failsworth, 1 y 10 m 14 days
"	6	Rebecca Barton, Newton, 1 y 3 m
"	10	Sarah Ramsden, Newton, 1 y 4 m
"	10	William Livsey, Manchester, 1 y 4 m
"	12	James Beswick, Newton, 46 y
"	14	Ellen Morrison, Manchester, 1 y 7 m
"	14	Elizabeth Butterworth, Manchester, 1 y 1 m

"	15	William Wild, Failsworth, 88 y	(*1816*)
"	17	Mary Taylor, Manchester, 1 y 1 m	
"	17	Robert Smith, Failsworth, 4 days	
"	18	John Willshaw, Manchester, 3 y 6 m	
"	19	Sarah Hoyle, Manchester, 2 y 11 m	
"	20	Edwin Thompson, Manchester, 10 m	
"	27	Henry Turner, Failsworth, 11 wks 3 days	
"	28	Abraham Dawson, Newton, 12 y 6 m	
"	31	Elijah Ashley, Manchester, 5 y 6 m	
"	31	John Jones, Manchester, 3 y	
Apr	1	Mary Kemp, Manchester, 83 y	
"	7	Mary Barker, Newton, 45 y	
"	7	Jane Hill, Manchester, 11 m	
"	8	Mary Worsley, Manchester, 57 y	
"	8	Thomas Willshaw, Manchester, 1 y 4 m	
"	10	Samuel Howles, Newton, 7 y	
"	21	Martha Dean, Droylsden, 76 y	
"	21	Mary Greenwood, Droylsden, 41 y	
"	21	Anne Hewitt, Manchester, 29 y	
"	21	Jane Hewitt, Manchester, 4 m	
"	21	William Hooley, Newton, 12 y	
"	21	Elizabeth Whitham, Manchester, 14 wks	
"	21	Anne Burton, Manchester, 35 y	
"	23	John Bentley, Cheetham, 4 wks	
"	28	Abraham Nicholson, Manchester, 9 y 6 m	
"	28	Anne Hardy, Manchester, 1 y 2 m	
May	7	William Whitehead, Newton, 10 m	
"	9	George Hall, Manchester, 18 days	
"	24	Margaret Bentley, Cheetham, 27 y	
"	26	Thomas Carr, New Malton Yorks[hire], 5 y	
Jun	2	George Hall, Manchester, 10 m	
"	7	Sarah Wyld, Newton, 17 y	
"	11	Anne Jackson, Manchester, 5 wks	
"	13	Eliza Quin, Manchester, 6 y	
"	13	Sarah Berry, Failsworth, 27 y	
"	16	Elizabeth Williams, Manchester, 3 days	
"	16	Martha Hall, Ardwick, 27 y	
"	19	Phebe Irwin, Manchester, 37 y	
"	23	Rachel Hough, Newton, 36 y	
"	23	Robert Whitehead, Failsworth, 71 y	
"	23	Richard Partington, Manchester, 6 y	
"	27	John Yates, Newton, 6 y	
"	30	William Irwin, Manchester, 3 m	
"	30	George Duncuft, Manchester, 27 y	
Jul	7	Mary Syddall, Droylsden, 30 y	

"	7	Richard Foden, Newton, 6 days	*(1816)*
"	7	Edward Birch, Manchester, 8 m	
"	9	Anne Knott, Broughton, 1 y 7 m	
"	10	William Moores, Collyhurst, 73 y	
"	10	Samuel Hampton, Manchester, 9 m	
"	10	William Lawrinson, Manchester, 21 y	
"	14	Jonathan Wroe, Failsworth, 22 y	
"	14	Thomas Powdger, Newton, 1 y 3 m	
"	15	Joseph Johnson, Reddish, 46 y	
"	15	John Lee, Manchester, 52 y	
"	18	Richard Wolstencroft, Manchester, 22 y	
"	25	Roger Richardson, Newton, 80 y	
"	26	Margaret Quinn, Manchester, 3 y	
"	28	James Hough, Newton, 6 wks	
Aug	1	Joseph Hamner, Newton, 12 y	
"	11	Martha Booth, Manchester, 60 y	
"	11	Jane Dawson, Newton, 9 m	
"	14	Joshua Smith, Manchester, 54 y	
"	18	Elizabeth Taylor, Moston, 20 y	
"	24	John Mills, Failsworth, 2 days	
"	30	William Ashton, Failsworth, 23 y	
Sep	5	Woman unknown found in Rochdale Canal Newton	
"	12	John Heywood, Manchester, 47 y	
"	17	*(altered from* 14) [17] Anne Moss, Newton, 67 y	
"	24	John Wild, Newton, 56 y	
"	29	Anne Morris, Manchester, 2 y	
Oct	3	Patrick Hughes, Manchester, 37 y	
"	9	Oliver Duxbury, Manchester, 12 y	
"	16	George Waine, Clayton, 25 y	
"	17	Mary Chadwick, Manchester, 72 y	
"	22	Mary Siddal, Clayton, 4 m	
"	24	William Quinn, Manchester, 1 y	
"	27	Jane Nixon, Manchester, 15 m	
"	28	Hannah Rothwell, Manchester, 7 m	
Nov	3	Alice d. Betty Stansfield, Manchester, 18 wks	
"	3	Mary d. John & Mary Roch, Newton, 7 days	
"	6	James Rydings, weaver, Failsworth, 78 y	
"	17	Samuel Hyde, crofter, Gorton, 55 y	
"	17	James Coe, carder, Manchester, 51 y	
"	17	Thomas s. John & Hannah Duncuft, Manchester, 25 y	
"	20	Sydney s. Samuel & Mary Robinson, Newton, 11 m	
"	21	Alice d. Joseph & Rosa Tinker, Failsworth, 1 m	
"	26	Elizabeth w. William Tomlinson, Moston, 65 y	
"	27	Ambrose Birch, Manchester, 50 y	
Dec	1	Edward s. Edward & Mary Fairfield, Manchester, 14 y	

"	1	James Kemp, musician, Newton, 49 y
"	1	Edward Pulison, Newton, 32 y
"	1	Henry s. Henry & Elizabeth Brickill, Manchester, 25 days
"	6	John s. Elizabeth Sheldon, Moston, 8 m
"	8	Henry s. Dennis & Ellen Ramsbottam, Newton, 27 y
"	8	William s. William & Lilly Dean, Manchester, 13 m
"	15	Martha w. Thomas Allen, Hollinwood, 36 y
"	16	Ann w. Richard Molloy, Manchester, 44 y
"	16	Ann d. James & Mary Chatterton, Manchester, 18 m
"	17	George Garlick, Failsworth, 89 y
"	19	Betty d. John & Mary Booth, Failsworth, 18 y
"	22	Elizabeth d. James & Mary Taylor, Manchester, 6 m
"	22	Thomas s. Thomas & Betty Welch, Newton, 4 m
"	25	Betty w. James Taylor, Failsworth, 69 y
"	25	Frederick s. Levi & Elizabeth Booth, Newton, 6 m
"	25	Thomas Brown, crofter, Newton, 93 y
"	29	Betty w. Robert Taylor, Failsworth, 54 y
[		Signed John Piccop]

1817

Jan	2	Alice w. John Clayton, Manchester, 24 y
"	5	Ellen w. William Greenhalgh, Failsworth, 32 y
"	5	Richard s. Robert & Elizabeth Hall, Newton, 8 m
"	5	Grace d. Richard & Anne Kenyon, Newton, 14 days
"	7	Ann w. John Austin, Newton, 69 y
"	12	Richard Boden, Manchester, 72 y
"	15	George s. Thomas & Ann Shaw, Newton, 39 y
"	19	Maria d. Peter & Nancy Travis, Manchester, 9 m
"	25	Andrew Berry, Bradford, 59 y
"	31	William s. Mary Anne Rawlinson, Ashton Parish, 17 wks
Feb	2	Elizabeth w. John Fairclough, Manchester, 49 y
"	2	Mary d. Jonathan & Phoebe Hindley, Clayton, 2 y
"	2	Ann d. Joseph & Ann Ogden, Manchester, 25 y
"	3	Ann d. Samuel & Sarah Livesey, Manchester, 2 y
"	5	Ann d. William & Frances Toole, Manchester, 7 y
"	9	Nancy d. John & Elizabeth Taylor, Newton, 7 wks
"	16	Margaret w. James Pollet, Hollinwood, 53 y
"	16	James s. Peter & Ann Colling, Failsworth, 10 m
"	23	James Rothwell, Manchester, 31 y
Mar	4	Sarah d. William & Elizabeth Jones, Manchester, 5 y
"	4	William s. James & Betty Taylor, Moston, 7 m
"	4	John s. Joseph & Sarah Rogers, Failsworth, 13 m
"	7	Hannah w. Samuel Smith, Hollinwood, 25 y
"	9	Solomon s. Edward & Jane Tipton, Clayton, 9 m

	10	Nathaniel Clough, Failsworth, 76 y
"	11	Emma d. George & Emma Metcalf, Manchester, 3 y
"	16	Elizabeth d. John & Margaret Whitehead, Manchester, 11 m
"	23	Esther d. Thomas & Elizabeth Monks, Manchester, 5 y
"	23	William Hamnet, Manchester, 20 y
"	25	William Whitehead, Newton, 53 y
"	25	Betty d. John & Betty Bardsley, Droylsden, 6 wks
Apr	1	Margaret d. William & Ann Oakes, Manchester, 15 (*incomplete in PR & BT*)
"	5	Sarah d. John & Ann Wild, Ashton, 2 y
"	6	James s. James & Jane Kemp, Newton, 10 days
"	6	Josias Rowe, Failsworth, 27 y
"	8	Edwin Stott, natural child, Failsworth, 3 m
"	20	Lettice Whitehead d. Robert & Betty Clough, Failsworth, 13 wks
"	24	Esther w. Jacob Bamford, Manchester, 81 y
"	25	Mary Ann w. George Travis, Newton, 32 y
"	27	Harriet d. Thomas & Jane Smith, Failsworth, 18 m
"	29	Sarah d. Thomas & Mary Berry, Failsworth, 9 m
"	30	John Whitehead, Moston, 59 y
"	30	Elizabeth d. Thomas & Mary Brown, Newton, 2 m
May	5	Thomas s. John & Sarah Schofield, Manchester, 20 y
"	11	Elizabeth d. John & Mary Barnes, Ardwick, 27 y
"	12	John s. Philip & Margaret Grimshaw, Droylsden, 2 m
"	18	William Roberts, Manchester, 79 y
"	18	Joseph s. Joseph & Mary Tetlow, Oldham, 21 m
"	19	Thomas Cornes, Newton, 40 y
"	21	Jane d. Richard & Jane Travis, Newton, 6 m
"	22	Sarah w. William Crossley, Failsworth, 24 y
"	25	Lydia w. James Lord, Manchester, 73 y
"	25	George s. George & Mary Ann Travis, Newton, 1 m
Jun	1	Reuben s. Samuel & Martha Clough, Failsworth, 15 m
"	3	Thomas Horrocks, Failsworth, 50 y
"	3	Abraham s. Josias & Jenny Pollit, Failsworth, 2 y
"	4	John s. David & Betty Whitaker, Newton, 13 m
"	5	Edwin s. John & Mary Thorley, Failsworth, 3 y
"	10	John Taylor, Newton, 35 y
"	12	Joseph Barker, Chapel Warden of Newton, Newton, 54 y
"	13	Hannah d. William & Elizabeth Valentine, Newton, 22 m
"	15	Mary d. Ann Smethurst, Failsworth, 10 m
"	18	Ann d. Thomas & Isabella Smith, Newton, 2 y
"	22	John Walton, Manchester, 64 y
"	23	Francis s. Joseph & Rebecca Hulton, Failsworth, 13 wks
"	24	William Smith, Manchester, 68 y
"	25	William s. Jacob & Matilda Jackson, Manchester, 8 m
"	25	Mary w. Joseph Brown, Failsworth, 39 y

"	26	Sarah w. James Whitehead, Failsworth, 63 y
"	29	Ann d. John & Sarah Jones, Manchester, 5 y
Jul	5	Joseph Wild, Cheetwood, 63 y
"	6	Sarah d. Joseph & Mary Brown, Failsworth, 3 wks
"	13	Frederick s. Thomas & Betty Shepley, Newton, 21 y
"	13	James Hulton, Hollinwood, 68 y
"	16	Mary d. Edmund & Anne Whitehead, Newton, 12 wks
"	16	Jane w. William Butterworth, Failsworth, 49 y
"	22	John Farrow, Manchester, 76 y
"	29	Joseph s. Richard & Sarah Rogers, Manchester, 4 y
"	30	Emmanuel s. John & Martha Etchells, Droylsden, 2 y 10 m
Aug	17	James Whitehead, Failsworth, 63 y
"	24	William s. William & Mary Owen, Manchester, 6 wks
"	27	Jonathan s. William & Esther Greyson, Manchester, 1 day
"	27	John s. John & Mary Smith, Manchester, 18 days
"	30	James s. John & Ellen Chapman, Manchester, 11 y
"	31	Elizabeth w. Ralph Birchell, Failsworth, 55 y
Sep	8	Hannah d. Abraham & Martha Pollit, Faiklsworth, 1 y
"	9	William s. Egerton & Nancy Smith, Newton, 37 y
"	9	William s. John & Ann Burgess, 14 y
"	14	Anne w. James Ogden, Manchester, 40 y
"	14	Luke Etchells, Failsworth, 36 y
"	16	John Tetlow, Newton, 47 y
"	16	Alice w. George Smith, Failsworth, 37 y
"	25	John s. James & Emma Bowker, Manchester, 11 y
"	29	William s. Oliver & Martha Ogden, Failsworth, 30 wks
"	30	Jane d. James & Mary Leigh, Newton, 9 y
Oct	1	John s. John & Martha Whitehead, Newton, 30 y
"	2	Eliza d. William & Elizabeth Hardman, Manchester, 11 m
"	3	Jane d. Thomas & Mary Ashton, Failsworth, 3 y
"	5	Mary d. Thomas & Mary Brown, Newton, 9 m
"	5	James Blake, Failsworth, 32 y
"	23	Richard Wood, Manchester, 66 y
"	31	Hannah d. Robert & Sarah Branton, Newton, 1 m (*see entry Nov 6*)
Nov	2	George s. Joseph & Susannah Brierley, Clayton, 6 wks
"	5	John s. William & Susannah Proctor, Manchester, 3 y 2 m
"	6	Mary d. Robert & Sarah Branton, Newton, 5 wks
"	19	Betty d. John & Hannah Lelshaw, Manchester, 1 y
"	23	Mary w. James Harlow, Manchester, 51 y
"	25	Violet d. Samuel & Ann Pollit, Failsworth, 6 m
"	27	Elizabeth d. Joseph & Sarah Lees, Failsworth, 2 y
"	30	Mary d. Joseph & Hannah Williamson, Newton, 15 m
"	30	John Holt, Failsworth, 62 y
Dec	4	Betty wdw. Jonathan Booth, Failsworth, 68 y
"	7	Mary d. Thomas & Mary Shone, Manchester, 1 y

"	8	Joseph s. Jonathan & Ann Glossop, Failsworth, 2 m
"	11	Susannah w. Charles Farron, Manchester, 40 y
"	11	John Hulton, Failsworth, 71 y
"	15	John s. John & Catharine Shuttleworth, Droylsden, 3 wks
"	16	Sarah w. Daniel Whitehead, Failsworth, 37 y
"	28	William Rowcroft, Manchester, 56 y
"	28	Joseph s. Hannah Chappel, Clayton, 2 y
[		Signed John Piccop]

1818

Jan	4	Rowland Wilson, Manchester, 55 y
"	4	Elizabeth d. Nathaniel & Mary Stansfield, Manchester, 33 y
"	6	Azariah s. Joseph & Alice Robinson, Newton, 1 y
"	6	Betty wdw. Joshua Collinson, Failsworth, 79 y
"	7	John Jones, Manchester, 44 y
"	8	James Smith, Newton, 31 y
"	11	Elizabeth d. William & Martha Acton, Manchester, 3 y
"	14	Dorcas d. James & Mary Lees, Manchester, 50 y
"	15	Mary d. James & Betty Boardman, Manchester, 1 m
"	18	Abraham s. Levi & Elizabeth Booth, Newton, 12 days
"	21	Sarah d. Samuel & Mellicent Simister, Failsworth, 15 days
"	23	Robert s. James & Betty Marsden, Newton, 11 m
"	23	James s. William & Betty Valentine, Newton, 3 wks
"	28	Hannah d. James & Elizabeth Clough, Manchester, 8 m
Feb	1	Jane d. Samuel & Ann Benyon, Manchester, 10 m
"	1	George s. Joseph & Fanny Tartington, Manchester, 13 days
"	1	William s. George & Martha Hall, Manchester, 5 y
"	1	Mary d. Daniel & Sarah Whitehead, Failsworth, 10 m
"	4	Elizabeth w. Samuel Proctor, Manchester, 56 y
"	5	Thomas s. Morris & Lydia Williams, Manchester, 7 y
"	5	Joseph s. Thomas & Jane Wild, Newton, 13 m
"	8	James s. Thomas & Ellen Harries, Manchester, 1 y
"	8	Harriot d. William & Betty Hibbert, Manchester, 9 m
"	8	Peter s. David & Elizabeth Marsden, Newton, 27 y
"	8	Mary d. Joseph & Maria Arrondale, Droylsden, 6 m
"	9	Charles s. John & Elizabeth Whitaker, Failsworth, 7 m
"	11	Mary d. Garside & Alice Blomeley, Newton, 7 m
"	15	Harriot d. William & Jane Atkinson, Manchester, 3 y 6 m
"	15	Ann d. Thomas Spencer & Mary Williamson, Manchester, natural child, 7 y [6 m]
"	15	Martha d. Samuel & Mary Robinson, Newton, 6 m
"	16	Nancy d. Peter & Mary Wildblood, Newton, 11 y
"	18	Martha d. Samuel & Susannah Thornely, Manchester, 10 m
"	19	William Haddocks, Failsworth, 65 y

"	20	Thomas Tomkinson, Failsworth (Newton *rubbed out*) [Failsworth], 63 y
"	22	Joseph Ogden, Failsworth, 77 y
Mar	1	John s. Adam & Alice Mortin, Manchester, 17 y
"	3	Betty wdw. James Brown, Little Moss in the Parish of Ashton under Lyne, 80 y
"	5	Elizabeth d. Abraham & Mary Horrocks, Woodhouses in the Parish of Ashton under Lyne, 8 m
"	6	Amelia w. John Taylor, Failsworth, 27 y
"	8	Ralph s. Adam & Alice Mortin, Manchester, 9 m
"	10	John Mills, Medlock Vale, 22 y
"	13	James Austen, Newton, 38 y
"	13	Mary d. George & Rachel Livsey, Manchester, 18 m
"	15	George s. George & Ann Shone, Manchester, 13 m
"	15	Harriot d. Peter & Nancy Travis, Manchester, 2 y
"	15	Sarah w. James Swift, Failsworth, 30 y
"	15	James s. Thomas & Mary Smith, Manchester, 9 m
"	15	Alice d. Thomas & Sarah Gorton, Failsworth, 8 m
"	16	Joseph s. Edmund & Ann Tetlow, Failsworth, 3 y 8 m
"	20	Benjamin Priest, Manchester, 26 y
"	22	Sarah d. James & Elizabeth Brownhill, Ardwick, 8 m
"	22	Sarah w. William Wilkinson, Manchester, 32 y
"	24	Mary Thorp, Moston, 82 y
"	25	Elizabeth d. John & Sarah Marsden, Newton, 1 y
"	26	Thomas s. John & Mary Hoyle, Manchester, 7 y 9 m
"	31	Mary Wood, Newton, 58 y
Apr	5	John Thorp, Moston, 54 y
"	5	James s. Robert & Mary Allen, Newton, 13 days
"	6	Mary d. Thomas & Sarah Roberts, Manchester, 17 m
"	12	Elizabeth d. Charles & Mary Partington, Manchester, 11 m
"	12	Sarah d. John & Elizabeth Hill, Manchester, 8 y
"	17	Elizabeth d. William & Mary Walker, Manchester, 8 days
"	19	Esther d. John & Sarah Houlton, Manchester, 6 m
"	22	Mary d. John & Sarah Mills, Manchester, 18 m
"	28	Grace d. John & Elizabeth Bowler, Manchester, 2 y 10 m
May	1	Sarah w. William Wallcroft, Newton, 26 y
"	3	Anne d. Mary Mather, Newton, 2 y 9 m
"	5	Mary d. Joseph & Sarah Rogers, Failsworth, 14 wks
"	6	James Shores, Manchester, 81 y
"	6	Betty wdw. Richard Thomason, Failsworth, 77 y
"	6	Charlotte d. James & Mary Taylor, Manchester, 6 m
"	10	Hugh s. James & Hannah Tomlinson, Newton, 3 y
"	10	Amelia d. James & Hannah Tomlinson, Newton, 3 m
"	10	Elizabeth d. William & Hannah Kay, Manchester, 15 m
"	12	Jonathan s. Thomas & Alice Smith, Manchester, 6 m
"	15	James s. John & Susan Johnson, Newton, 13 m

"	15	Edward Fletcher, Manchester, 33 y	*(1818)*
"	15	John Taylor, Manchester, 31 y	
"	17	Olive d. Isaac & Amelia Moors, Manchester (*illegible placename crossed through*) [Manchester], 1 y 9 m	
"	17	Benjamin s. Benjamin & Mary Hulton, Failsworth, 1 y 19 wks	
"	24	James s. Thomas & Alice Smith, Manchester, 2 y 9 m	
"	24	Samuel s. Ashton & Sarah Buckley, Hollinwood, 8 m	
"	24	Samuel s. Samuel & Mary Harrison, Manchester, 7 y	
"	27	Martha d. Mary Allen, Failsworth, 3 y 6 m	
Jun	2	Josias Howard, Manchester, 78 y	
"	3	Alice w. Elisha Knott, Failsworth, 30 y	
"	3	Mary wdw. Robert Lees, Failsworth, 92 y	
"	5	James s. James & Alice Schofield, Manchester, 15 m	
"	5	John s. Martha Berrington, Moston, 3 days	
"	7	Sarah w. William Rydings, Failsworth, 64 y	
"	9	Elizabeth d. John & Esther Smith, Manchester, 2 y	
"	10	Betty d. William & Mary Booth, Failsworth, 1 y 3 m	
"	14	Sarah d. William & Martha Ogilvie, Manchester, 9 m	
"	14	Jane wdw. Richard Dawson, Newton, 76 y	
"	15	Jane w. Elias Bythill, Newton, 61 y	
"	16	Charles Farrar, Manchester, 45 y	
"	16	Hannah d. Thomas & Grace Sunderland, Manchester, 15 m	
"	21	William Brown, Newton, 70 y	
"	25	Edward s. John & Hannah O'Brine, Salford, a Roman Catholic, 7 m	
"	25	Richard s. Phillip & Mary Rogerson, Manchester, 7 y	
"	26	John s. William & Betty Valentine, Newton, 6 m	
"	28	Margaret d. William & Agnes Dinnington, Manchester, 15 m	
"	28	Thomas s. Robert & Esther Walmsley, Manchester, 14 y	
"	28	Mary w. James Kershaw, Kirkmanshulme in Newton, 80 y	
"	29	James s. William & Elizabeth Lees, Manchester, 19 m	
"	29	Sarah d. James & Mary Whitehead, Manchester, 1 y	
Jul	3	Thomas Walker, Manchester, 21 y	
"	10	George s. Thomas & Mary Robinson, Manchester, 13 m	
"	15	Charles s. Arthur & Anne Done, Manchester, 19 y	
"	15	Joseph s. Henry & Anne Booth, Failsworth, 28 y	
"	19	Mary d. George & Mary Hall, Manchester, 7 y	
"	21	William Winstanley, Manchester, 63 y	
"	23	Alice d. Robert & Mary Gorton, Hollinwood, 18 m	
"	26	John s. Joseph & Sarah Riley, Manchester, 18 y	
"	26	Edward s. James & Mary Shepley, Newton, 5 m	
"	26	Mary w. James Morrison, Manchester, 42 y	
"	29	Thomas s. Thomas & Jane Yates, Newton, 10 m	
"	29	John s. Solomon & Elizabeth Coe, Manchester, 2 y 9 m	
Aug	2	William s. Nancy Cheetman, Manchester, 6 wks	
"	6	Mary d. James & Mary Morrison, Manchester, 2 m	

"	6	Anne d. Catharine Tomlinson, Newton, 3 y
"	11	William s. John & Anne Bayley, Manchester, 11 wks
"	13	John s. James & Mary Barlow, Manchester, 5 m
"	16	Mary d. Isaac & Elizabeth Hall, Manchester, 7 y
"	18	Samuel s. Samuel & Mellicent Simister, Failsworth, 7 m
"	19	Richard s. Alice Dean, Newton, 2 y
"	19	Rev. Abraham Ashworth, Clerk, M.A., Incumbent of Newton, 62 y
"	19	Isabel d. Thomas & Mary Berry, Failsworth, 6 m
"	20	George s. Elizabeth Pickup, Bradford, 9 y
"	23	Anne w. John Duckworth, Manchester, 57 y
"	23	Samuel s. William & Susannah Proctor, Manchester, 7 y 10 m
Sep	1	Anne d. Francis & Jane Burton, Newton, 3 y 11 m
"	1	Joseph s. Samuel & Elizabeth Barlow, Ashton, 7 m
"	1	Hannah d. Jonathan & Martha Leech, Newton, 1 y
"	14	Maria d. Luke & Hannah Etchels, Thornham in the Parish of Rochdale 9y
"	16	Hannah d. Elisha & Sarah Whitehead, Failsworth, 10 m
"	18	Joseph s. Thomas & Betty Tetlow, Newton, 33 y
"	20	Mary Anne d. John & Alice Ashworth, Manchester, 15 m
"	21	James s. John & Jane Bottomley, Manchester, 1 m
"	21	Michael s. Thomas & Mary Smith, Manchester, 2 y 10 m
"	24	Thomas s. John & Anne Holt, Failsworth, 2 y 7 m
"	28	Fanny d. John & Martha Thomason, Failsworth, 1 y 9 m
Oct	5	Hannah w. James Wright, Manchester, 30 y
"	7	Elizabeth d. William & Margaret Hall, Manchester, 15 wks
"	7	Jane d. James & Anne Kershaw, Manchester, 13 wks
"	11	Samuel Ogden, Failsworth, 84 y
"	13	William s. John & Anne Haslam, Failsworth, 2 y 10 m
"	13	James s. Daniel & Hannah Birtles, Manchester, 10 m
"	14	Joseph s. James & Hannah Wright, Manchester, 4 y
"	16	Elizabeth w. William Hibbert, Manchester, 36 y
"	16	Elizabeth w. James Pollit, Failsworth, 68 y
"	23	Hannah wdw. John Berry, Newton, 81 y
"	25	Isaac Hall, Manchester, 66 y
Nov	1	Susannah wdw. James Kemp, Manchester, 78 y
"	2	Ruth d. Thomas & Mary Brown, Newton, 3 wks
"	3	Susannah d. James & Mary Nuttall, Failsworth, 19 y
"	5	Mary d. Edmund & Mary Clough, Failsworth, 66 y
"	11	Sarah d. Ralph & Mary Newton, Failsworth, 3 days
"	18	John s. John & Sarah Wild, Newton, 2 y
"	18	William s. John & Mary Fenton, Woodhouses in Ashton Parish
"	22	Joseph Turner, Newton, 55 y
"	27	James s. James & Ellen Whitehead, Manchester, 4 m
"	27	Sarah w. John Tetlow, Manchester, 37 y
"	29	Charles Watson, Manchester, 64 y
Dec	2	Robert s. Robert & Nancy Downs, Manchester, 19 y

"   2   William s. Abraham & Elizabeth Mather, Failsworth, 5 m
"   7   John s. Samuel & Mary Holland, Failsworth, 9 m
"   9   Betty w. Robert Whitehead, Failsworth, 46 y
"   11   Abraham Henry s. Abraham & Hannah Marshall, Newton, 18 wks
"   13   William Wallcroft, Manchester, 29 y
"   16   Joseph s. William & Mary Berry, Failsworth, 50 y
"   20   Jane d. John & Sarah Madin, Failsworth, 2 y
"   20   Edward s. William & Mary Fletcher, Manchester, 3 y 6 m
"   20   Timothy s. Samuel & Mary Houghton, Manchester, 17 wks
"   27   John s. John & Ann Beswick, Manchester, 26 days
"   30   Hannah d. James & Hannah Andrew, Manchester, 18 m
"   31   Ann w. James Smith, Newton, 30 y
[Signed. Thos Gaskell, Incumbent of Newton   ]
[Witness My Hand Jas Hough Chapelwarden of Newton   ]

1819

Jan   10   John s. William & Elizabeth Livesey, Manchester, 13 y
"   11   Ann w. James Whitehead, Failsworth, 44 y
"   12   Mary d. James & Martha Swift, Failsworth, 11 m
"   15   James Schofield, Manchester, 40 y
"   15   Charles Swindels, Newton, 72 y
"   20   James Waters, Failsworth, 70 y
"   24   Alice w. James Rowe, Failsworth, 75 y
"   24   Mary d. Hannah Gorton, Failsworth, 6 m
Feb   7   John Wyld, Manchester, 52 y
"   7   Joseph s. Joseph & Jemima Roberts, Manchester, 4 y
"   7   Betty d. Thomas & Ann Horrocks, Newton, 14 m
"   7   Henry s. Abraham & Betty Mather, Failsworth, 3 y
"   7   William Bateman, Newton, 60 y
"   10   Betty w. David Ogden, Failsworth, 33 y
"   10   Nancy d. Betty Allen, Failsworth, one m
"   18   James s. Thomas & Margaret Hill, Manchester, 7 y
"   23   John s. Thomas & Sarah Chadwick, Manchester, 11 y
"   24   Esther d. Charles & Ellen Brown, Manchester, 12 m
"   26   Charlotte d. Joseph & Charlotte Greenwood, Failsworth, 22 y
Mar   3   Harriet d. John & Sarah Nadin, Failsworth, 4 y
"   4   Mary d. Austin & Mary Chadwick, Manchester, one y
"   5   Betty w. Joseph Garlick, Failsworth, 36 y
"   7   Elizabeth d. George & Margaret Tomlinson, Moston, 7 wks
              (New Grave *is written in the margin against the next 9 entries in the PR*)
"   10   Ednea d. John & Ann Slater, Manchester, 4 m
"   10   William s. John & Hannah Benson, Manchester, 11 m
"   11   George s. George & Sarah Wilkeson, Manchester, 18 y
"   13   Ellen w. Dennis Ramsbottom, Newton, 73 y

"	14	Sally d. Thomas & Mary Wroe, Failsworth, 26 y	*(1819)*
"	17	Samuel s. Garside & Alice Blomely, Newton, 7 wks	
"	21	James Whitehead, Failsworth, 43 y	
"	25	Hannah w. George Nicholson, Manchester, 29 y	
"	25	Elizabeth w. John Harding, Newton, 74 y	
Apr	4	George s. James & Elizabeth Duncuft, Manchester, 2 y 6 m	
"	6	Hannah w. Charles Swindels, Manchester, 61 y	
"	8	James s. Sarah Charlesworth, Failsworth, 13 m	
"	13	John Thorp, Moston 66 y	
"	14	Eliza d. Ellen Graham, Droylsden, 14 y	
"	15	Martha w. Isaac Rowe, Failsworth, 70 y	
"	18	James s. Thomas & Ann Hamer, Newton, 7 y	
"	18	Ashton s. Elizabeth Clegg, Failsworth, 17 days	
"	18	John s. Thomas & Catherine Walmsley, Manchester, 6 m	
"	18	Mary Ann d. Thomas & Elizabeth Robinson, Manchester, 11 m	
"	21	Peter s. James & Mary Whitehead, Bradford, 12 y	
"	25	John Fairclough, Manchester, 63 y	
"	25	Elizabeth d. James & Elizabeth Turner, Newton, 9 m	
"	25	Ann Booth, Failsworth, 62 y	
"	28	James s. David & Betty Ogden, Failsworth, 6 m	
"	28	William Smith, Failsworth, 65 y	
"	28	Michael s. William & Elizabeth Vine, Hartland County of Devon, 23 y	
"	29	Martha w. John Hulton, Failsworth, 71 y	
"	29	Martha w. James Bradbury, Manchester, 24 y	
May	3	Martha w. James Ogden, Openshaw, 75 y	
"	9	William Booth, Hollinwood, 33 y	
"	10	Sarah d. Joseph & Mary Hampson, Manchester, 3 y 5 m	
"	13	Alice w. Thomas Crossley, Droylsden, 70 y	
"	13	Maria w. William Brundritt, Droylsden, 31 y	
"	16	Mary Ann d. James & Elizabeth Clough, Manchester, 19 days	
"	16	Robert s. Robert & Betty Brierly, Failsworth, 8 wks	
"	16	Martha w. James Swift, Newton, 79 y	
"	18	Thomas Hewitt, Manchester, 29 y	
"	26	Zechariah Partington, Manchester, 63 y	
"	27	Mary w. Thomas Hulton, Failsworth, 46 y	
"	27	Isaac Butterworth, Moston, 87 y	
"	27	Harriet d. William & Hannah Terrent, Newton, 4 m	
"	29	James s. Austin & Mary Chadwick, Manchester, 8 y	
"	31	Edward s. James & Martha Bradbury, Manchester, 5 wks 4 days	
Jun	4	George s. Mary Thorpe, Failsworth, 11 days	
"	6	Sarah w. George Etchels, Failsworth, 47 y	
"	6	Thomas s. Charles & Mary Partington, Manchester, 9 wks	
"	8	Hannah d. Robert & Alice Stansfield, Newton, 3 m	
"	8	Ann w. William Whitehead, Failsworth, 54 y	
"	8	Francis s. Samuel & Mary Holland, Failsworth, 11 m	

"	10	James Clough, Failsworth, 66 y	(*1819*)
"	13	John Wilson, Failsworth, 53 y	
"	17	Mary w. Nathaniel Clough, Failsworth, 78 y	
"	17	Robert s. Nathaniel & Elizabeth Taylor, Failsworth, 13 m	
"	23	Margaret w. James Jackson, Manchester, 35 y	
"	24	Thomas s. Jacob & Sarah Simpson, Newton, 5 y	
"	29	John Frith s. William & Martha Ogilvie, Manchester, 4 y	
Jul	4	Benjamin s. Benjamin & Sarah Butterworth, Manchester, 6 wks	
"	7	John s. Joseph & Nancy Ambler, Newton, 17 y	
"	12	Margaret d. James & Margaret Jackson, Manchester, 3 wks	
"	12	Ann d. James & Margaret Jackson, Manchester, 3 wks	
"	12	Mary d. Robert & Nancy Ridings, Failsworth, 8 m	
"	23	Isabella d. Richard & Isabella Dennington, Manchester, 19 y	
Aug	2	Esther d. John & Amelia Turner, Failsworth, 3 y 7 m	
"	4	Nancy w. William Robinson, Failsworth, 31 y	
"	9	James s. Joseph & Ann Etchels, Hollinwood, 2 y	
"	13	Thomas Beswick, Manchester, 29 y	
"	15	Jane d. Robert & Elizabeth Wilson, Newton, 25 y	
"	16	Betty w. Joseph Wrigley, Manchester, 48 y	
"	20	William s. William & Sarah Heywood, Droylsden, 19 y	
"	22	Eliza d. Thomas & Nancy Hewitt, Manchester, 9 m	
"	27	John s. Thomas & Sarah Lamb, Newton, 14 m	
"	28	James s. John & Alice Hardman, Manchester, 10 wks	
"	29	Joseph s. Joseph & Mary Buller, Manchester, 10 wks	
Sep	1	James s. John & Ann Beswick, Manchester, 9 m	
"	3	Robert s. Ralph & Martha Wyld, Manchester, 3 wks	
"	5	Martha d. John & Mary Livesey, Manchester, 19 y	
"	5	Ann w. Thomas Hamer, Newton, 34 y	
"	12	William Prince, Newton, 75 y	
"	19	Thomas s. Joseph & Maria Ogden, Manchester, one y	
"	19	Ellen d. Joseph & Maria Ogden, Manchester, one y	
"	21	Ann w. Thomas Whitehead, Manchester, 61 y	
"	26	Martha w. John Whitehead, Newton, 73 y	
Oct	1	Frances d. William & Mary Brown, Manchester, 4 m	
"	3	Ellen d. John & Margaret Turner, Newton, 9 m	
"	6	Joseph Whittaker, Failsworth, 53 y	
"	6	Wright s. Peter & Elizabeth Boardman, Manchester, 6 y	
"	12	Samuel s. Joseph & Mary Horrocks, Failsworth, 10 m	
"	13	Marianne d. William & Lydia Thornycroft, Newton, one y four m	
"	21	Robert s. Thomas & Jane Taylor, Manchester, 5 y	
"	22	Hannah d. Thomas & Betty Monks, Manchester, two y	
"	26	James s. Richard & Margaret Whitehead, Failsworth, 4 y 10 m	
"	26	Thomas s. Christopher & Sarah Mellor, Newton, 14 m	
"	27	Mary d. Thomas & Jane Taylor, Manchester, one y	
Nov	2	Mary w. John Whitehead, Moston, 60 y	

"	7	Joshua Smith, Hollinwood, 64 y
"	7	John s. John & Mary Smith, Newton, 18 m
"	14	John s. Joshua & Sarah Swift, Manchester, 10 m
"	15	Martha d. Edward & Ann Whitehead, Newton, 25 y
"	28	George s. Samuel & Ann Butterworth, Manchester, one m
"	30	Elizabeth d. George & Charlotte Smethurst, Newton, one m
Dec	2	Elizabeth d. Joseph & Mary Porter, Bradford, 4 y 9 m
"	3	Samuel s. Samuel & Mary Robinson, Newton, 9 m
"	3	Samuel s. Thomas & Ann Shaw, Newton, 23 y
"	5	Ann d. Joseph & Priscilla Fletcher, Newton, 10 m
"	9	Ann d. Thomas & Jane Wood, Newton, 20 m
"	10	Thomas s. Elizabeth Barlow, Failsworth, 28 y
"	12	Mary w. Joseph Scholfield, Failsworth, 41 y
"	12	John Makin, Manchester, 48 y
"	12	Ann w. John Eckersley, Failsworth, 54 y
"	13	William s. Samuel & Ann Butterworth, Manchester, 3 y 9 m
"	19	John s. Peter & Nancy Travis, Manchester, 2 y
"	20	Ellen d. James & Elizabeth Hamson, Manchester, 9 y
"	21	Sarah d. Joseph & Hannah Smith, Newton, 3 m
"	21	Elizabeth w. John Smith, Manchester, 49 y
"	22	Caroline w. John Wood, Newton, 23 y
"	24	Ann d. Ann Simister, Failsworth, 12 y
"	26	Maria d. Peter & Nancy Travis, Manchester, 9 m
"	26	James s. Abraham & Mary Horrocks, Ashton Parish, 9 m
[		Thos Gaskell, Incumbent of Newton]
[		Jas Hough Chapelwarden of Newton]

1820

Jan	2	Peggy w. John Lees, Failsworth, 50 y
"	4	Mary w. John Livesey, Manchester, 55 y
"	9	Joseph s. Ann Drinkwater, Moston, one y
"	9	Ann w. William Simister, Failsworth, 71 y
"	10	Mary w. William Booth, Newton, 71 y
"	13	Mary d. Thomas & Margaret Hill, Manchester, 8 days
"	14	John s. Thomas & Sarah Charlesworth, Manchester, 9 m
"	20	Frederic s. George & Elizabeth Parkinson, Failsworth, one y
"	23	Charles Thomson, Manchester, 20 y
"	23	Sarah d. Thomas & Jane Wood, Newton, 4 y 8 m
"	26	Elizabeth d. James & Mary Radcliffe, Newton, 5 y 6 m
"	28	Jessica w. James Eyres, Liverpool, 53 y
"	30	Sarah d. George & Ann Morris, Ashton Parish, 3 y
"	31	George s. Elizabeth Worral, Moston, 2 wks
Feb	3	William Whitehead, Failsworth, 54 y
"	6	Thomas s. Thomas & Sarah Charlesworth, Manchester, 3 y

"	7	Martha w. James Newton, Moston, 64 y
"	8	William s. William & Martha Ogilvie, Manchester, 10 m
"	11	Marianne d. Maria Kershaw, Failsworth, 14 wks
"	13	Esther d. Levi & Elizabeth Booth, Newton, 11 y
"	16	Ann d. Edward & Hannah Radcliffe, Manchester, 7 m
"	18	Mary d. Robert & Mary Walmesley, Manchester, 14 wks
"	20	William s. Josiah & Sarah Howard, Manchester, one m
"	20	Mary w. James Barlow, Failsworth, 70 y
"	20	Sarah w. William Prince, Newton, 75 y
"	23	Hannah d. James & Ann Mills, Manchester, 2 y
"	24	Margaret d. William & Ellen Caldwell, Newton, 20 y
"	24	Joseph s. William & Phoebe Jacks, Clayton, 9 m
"	27	Sarah d. Charles & Mary Gardner, Manchester, 6 wks
"	28	Thomas Hulton, Failsworth, 57 y
Mar	3	Elizabeth d. William & Mary Daltry, Oldham, 3 days
"	5	Thomas Whitehead, Failsworth, 66 y
"	5	Ellen d. John & Marianne Smith, Newton, one day
"	5	Thomas s. James & Ann Mills, Manchester, 5 wks
"	5	James s. Isaac & Elizabeth Hall, Manchester, 18 y
"	6	Thomas s. James & Mary Wardle, Chorlton, 10 y 11 m
"	7	Alice w. John Etchels, Failsworth, 85 y
"	8	William s. John & Hannah Williamson, Ashton Parish, 10 m
"	9	Samuel s. William & Sarah Bradshaw, Newton, 17 y
"	10	John Mold, Manchester, 60 y
"	13	Joel s. Joseph & Mary Brown, Little Moss, 19 y
"	22	Alice w. James Lees, Failsworth, 60 y
"	23	Esther d. George & Elizabeth Smith, Droylsden, 1 y 9 m
"	25	Mary d. Thomas & Sarah Walmsley, Failsworth, 19 y 11 m
"	25	Adam Dodson, Newton, 50 y
"	27	Mary d. James & Ann Taylor, Failsworth, 1 m
"	27	Joseph s. Joseph & Elizabeth Higham, Newton, 5 m
Apr	2	Christopher Mills, Newton, 47 y
"	2	Joseph s. Thomas & Ann Stanton, Manchester, 7 m 9 days
"	10	Sarah w. Henry Rogerson, Newton, 21 y
"	10	James s. James & Sarah Simister, Newton, 2 y
"	14	Mary w. James Kenyon, Failsworth, 71 y
"	14	Simeon Whitehead, Manchester, 72 y
"	23	Elizabeth d. John & Hannah Livesey, Manchester, 2 y 11 m
"	23	Mary d. Mary Walmsley, Failsworth, 3 m
"	24	Mary d. Robert & Jane Stott, Failsworth, 23 y
"	24	William s. James & Mary Lees, Failsworth, 8 m
"	25	Abraham s. John & Elizabeth Allen, Manchester, 1 y
"	25	Elias s. Adam & Margaret Horrocks, Droylsden, 1 wk
"	30	Sarah d. Richard & Martha Lees, Manchester, 16 wks
"	30	Robert Walmsley, Manchester, 76 y

May	1	Martha Stott, Newton, 40 y
"	3	Robert Ridings, Failsworth, 38 y
"	3	Charles Charlesworth, Salford, 30 y
"	4	Elizabeth d. Samuel & Mary Riley, Manchester, 11 m
"	4	Elizabeth d. George & Elizabeth Smith, Droylsden, 3 wks
"	7	Mary d. John & Elizabeth Knight, Manchester, 9 y
"	8	John Brown, Newton, 56 y
"	10	Jane d. Francis & Elizabeth Hubbart, Manchester, 11 y
"	11	Joseph Smith, Newton, 77 y
"	15	Anne d. Samuel & Elizabeth Taylor, Failsworth, 10 m
"	21	Charles s. Philip & Mary Rogerson, Manchester, 4 m
"	23	Joseph s. Abraham & Nancy Lee, Manchester, 3 m
"	28	Jonathan Hooley, Newton, 78 y
"	30	Rachel d. Edmund & Martha Buckley, Newton, 4 y
"	30	John Harrison, Newton, 57 y
"	31	Mary w. George Tomlinson, Failsworth, 48 y
Jun	2	Hannah d. James & Margaret Crossley, Moston, 18 y
"	4	William s. Joseph & Mary Robinson, Manchester. 11 m
"	4	Jonathan Slater, Newton, 81 y
"	11	Sarah w. John Moors, Salford, 53 y
"	11	Joseph s. Joseph & Sarah Greenwood, Clayton, 9 m
"	19	John s. Joseph & Rose Tinker, Failsworth, one y
"	25	Sarah d. John & Elizabeth Ball, Manchester, 5 y
"	28	Elizabeth d. John & Charlotte Whitehead, Manchester, 11 m
Jul	4	Robert s. Richard & Sarah Hartley, Manchester, 9 m
"	5	James s. William & Ann Rowcroft, Manchester, 12 y
"	9	James s. Joseph & Fanny Partington, Manchester, 18 m
"	16	Ann d. George & Ellen Barlow, Salford, 6 y
"	16	Thomas s. Joseph & Sarah Tomlinson, Newton, 11 m
"	18	John s. George & Margaret Tomlinson, Moston, 6 m
"	20	Hannah w. John Barton, Newton, 45 y
"	20	Mary w. Wright Cranshaw, Newton, 31 y
"	22	Mary d. William & Lucy Seal, Newwton, 18 wks
"	23	Betty d. James & Martha Wild, Droylsden, 8 y
"	23	Hannah d. William & Elizabeth Ashworth, Manchester, 7 y
"	25	John Makin, Moston, 61 y
"	27	Elizabeth d. William & Mary Aldred, Manchester, 15 wks
"	30	George Ramscar, Manchester, 73 y
"	31	Jane d. James & Hannah Swindels, Manchester, 1 y 10 m
Aug	1	Robert s. Edward & Elizabeth Wild, Manchester, 6 m
"	7	Nathan Ashley, Manchester, 25 y
"	9	John Smith, Chadderton, 75 y
"	11	John Thomason, Failsworth, 39 y
"	11	Ellen d. William & Mary Pendleton, Newton, 2 y
"	13	John s. Robert & Ann Leeds, Manchester, 7 y

"	13	Jane w. Abraham Dawson, Newton, 35 y
"	13	Elizabeth d. Samuel & Phoebe Travis, Newton, 14 m
"	16	Elizabeth w. Joseph Higham, Newton, 28 y
"	20	Robert s. James & Mary Broughton, Manchester, 6 m
"	21	William s. Thomas & Jane Yates, Newton, 15 m
"	21	Alice d. Betty Clough, Failsworth, 3 days
"	27	Sarah d. William & Mary Butterworth, Failsworth, 1 day
"	29	William s. William & Jenny Bethel, Failsworth, 2 wks
"	31	Deborah w. James Whittaker, Failsworth, 17 y
Sep	6	Mary w. William Butterworth, Failsworth, 36 y
"	12	Martha w. John Mills, Manchester, 68 y
"	21	Betty d. Thomas & Isabella Smith, Newton, 14 y
"	22	James Cheetham, Failsworth, 71 y
"	24	James s. George & Mary Anne Horrocks, Manchester, 14 days
"	27	Jane w. Joseph Heath, Manchester, 62 y
"	27	Ann w. Richard Kenyon, Manchester, 47 y
Oct	1	George s. Michael & Mary Hubbert, Manchester, 11 m
"	1	Sophia d. James & Mary Tagg, Newton, 35 y
"	3	Peter Walker, Failsworth, 60 y
"	4	Ralph s. William & Mary Rutter, Newton, 10 m
"	9	John Nicholson, Manchester, 61 y
"	15	John s. Martha Garlick, Failsworth, 23 wks
"	16	Lettice w. Thomas Ottley, Newton, 60 y
"	19	Thomas Tetlow, Newton, 59 y
"	23	Alice w. John Makin, Moston, 58 y
"	25	Phoebe d. Joseph & Lettice Tomlinson, Failsworth, 31 y
"	13	Thomas Blomely, Manchester, 38 y
"	28	James s. Mary Gould, Moston, 18 m
Nov	1	Jane w. John Smith, Failsworth, 50 y
"	1	Mary d. Abraham & Sarah Mather, Droylsden, 40 y
"	8	Richard Makin, Moston, 27 y
"	8	Joseph s. John & Alice Makin, Moston, 20 y
"	14	Sarah d. Richard & Betty Makin, Moston, 1 y 8 m
"	14	Alice d. Sarah Makin, Moston, one y 8 m
"	14	William s. Joseph & Mary Aldred, Newton, 2 m
"	23	Martha d. Elijah & Charlotte Hulton, Failsworth, 2 y
"	29	Mary w. Henry Etchels, Failsworth, 79 y
Dec	3	John Thorpe, Manchester, 16 y
"	4	John Fildes, Newton, 28 y
"	14	Stephen s. James & Margaret Higham, Failsworth, 11 wks
"	19	James s. John & James Smith, Failsworth, 4 y
"	22	Mary w. John Robinson, Macclesfield, 49 y
"	24	Mary w. John Smith, Manchester, 27 y
"	24	Thomas s. James & Martha Swift, Failsworth, one y 3 m
"	28	William Allen, Failsworth, 83 y

" 31 Samuel s. Thomas & Hannah Dunkerly, Failsworth, 4 y
[Signed, Thos Gaskell, Incumbent of Newton   ]
[(*blank*) Chapelwarden   ]

1821

Jan	2	Eliza d. Joseph & Ann Houghton, Manchester, 14 m
"	2	Marianne d. Thomas & Alice Crossley, Moston, 29 y
"	3	Susannah w. Thomas Etchels, Failsworth, 54 y
"	7	Jane w. James Andrew, Woodhouses, 32 y
"	7	Charles s. John & Mary Billinge, Manchester, 9 m
"	7	Marianne d. Elijah & Charlotte Hilton, Failsworth, 9 m
"	8	Jonathan s. Jonathan & Ann Glossop, Failsworth, 1 y 7 m
"	12	Mary w. Richard Richardson, Newton, 49 y
"	12	Edwin s. Joseph & Hannah Smith, Newton, 5 days
"	15	Betty d. William & Mary Whittaker, Manchester, 2 y
"	16	Ann d. John & Sarah Wylde, Newton, 10 m
"	17	Betty w. Robert Whitehead, Failsworth, 30 y
"	24	William s. Moses & Clarissa Gradwell, Newton, 1 y
"	25	William Ridings, Failsworth, 61 y
"	25	Leah s. Leah & Mary Foden, Newton, 8 y
Feb	11	William s. Thomas & Margaret Hill, Manchester, 5 y 6 m
"	11	Charles s. James & Mary Taylor, Manchester, 5 m
"	21	Samuel s. Thomas & Ann Hamer, Newton, 18 m
"	21	Nathaniel Burns, Manchester, 23 y
"	23	Joseph s. Jane Berry, Failsworth, 14 m
"	25	Richard Blomiley, Manchester, 66 y
"	27	Mary d. John & Margaret Crompton, 3 y 8 m
Mar	4	Thomas s. Joseph & Susanna Brierly, Droylsden, 5 days
"	6	James s. Sarah Makin, Newton, one wk
"	13	Samuel Wyat, Manchester, 36 y
"	14	Sarah Anne d. Lauchlin & Mary Boyn, Newton, 15 y
"	18	Ann d. James & Sarah Greenwood, Manchester, 11 m
"	20	David s. David & Eleanora Chapman, Manchester, 4 y
"	20	Esther w. Isaac Tetlow, Kirkmanshulme, 28 y
"	23	Thomas s. William & Betty Lee, Newton, 2 y
"	24	Joseph s. John & Mary Wilkinson, Failsworth, one day
"	25	Thomas Barker, Bubnel near Bakewell Derbyshire, 28 y
"	26	Martha d. Samuel & Maria Wyatt, Manchester, 12 y
"	28	James s. James & Ellen Walmsley, Newton, 11 y
"	30	John Porter, Newton, 27 y
Apr	3	John Shepley, Newton, 21 y
"	3	James s. John & Mary Porter, Newton, 16 m
"	8	Ann d. James & Esther Lyon, Manchester, 3 y 2 m
"	8	Martha Ashton, Failsworth, 58 y

"	13	George s. Henry & Alice Holden, Newton, 7 y
"	15	John s. Richard & Betty Bee, Manchester, 6 y
"	15	Hodgson s. Thos. & Elizabeth Brown, Manchester, 8 days
"	18	Thos. Joseph s. Charles & Alice Taylor, Newton, 2 y 9 m
"	18	Esther d. John & Hannah Lord, Manchester, 2 m
"	18	Mary w. Elijah Knott, Failsworth, 21 y
"	19	James Unsworth, Newton, 37 y
"	29	Thomas s. Joseph & Mary Buller, Manchester, 4 y
May	3	Mary w. Thomas Fallows, Withington, 57 y
"	4	Hannah d. Thomas & Mary Berry, Failsworth, 1 y 10 m
"	6	Hannah w. William Yarwood, Manchester, 68 y
"	6	David s. Elijah & Mary Knott, Failsworth, 25 wks
"	7	John Williamson, Woodhouses, 61 y
"	8	James Hampson, Manchester, 46 y
"	10	Elizabeth w. John Brammal, Manchester, 44 y
"	12	Sarah d. Charles & Alice Taylor, Newton, 6 m
"	13	Thomas Booth, Manchester, 53 y
"	13	Esther w. Jonathan Naylor, Newton, 17 y
"	13	Robert s. Sarah Booth, Manchester, 15 y
"	18	John s. Thomas & Anne Wilson, Woodhouses, 6 m
"	20	Joseph s. Samuel & Mary Hoyle, Droylsden, one y
"	20	Mary d. James & Sarah Hill, Manchester, 17 y
"	21	Elizabeth d. James & Eliza Gillibrand, Ardwick, 17 days
"	21	Mary d. John & Ann Stafford, Droylsden, 14 m
"	22	Mary w. John Clough, Failsworth, 63 y
"	22	Susanna Whitehead, Failsworth, 85 y
"	23	Charlotte Scholes d. James & Betty Aspel, Newton, 10 m
"	27	Abigail w. Robert Hulme, Failsworth, 50 y
"	28	Issachar s. William & Nancy Whittaker, Newton, 2 y 11 m
"	29	Joseph s. John & Ann Broughton, Manchesr., 14 days
Jun	3	Hannah d. Ralph & Sarah Ogden, Failsworth, 1 y 7 m
"	10	James s. Jonathan & Phoebe Handley, Droylsden, 13 m
"	12	George s. Jonathan & Anne Glossop, Failsworth, 5 m
"	13	John Wroe, Blackley, 89 y
"	30	John s. John & Elizabeth Fildes, Newton, 4 m
Jul	1	Mary Ridings, Failsworth, 81 y
"	5	Robert Johnson, Failsworth, 32 y
"	11	Sarah w. John Tomlinson, Manchester, 49 y
"	12	Hannah Ridings, Failsworth, 35 y
"	15	William s. Martha Jackson, Failsworth, 10 m
"	18	Ann d. Nathaniel & Anne Thorley, Failsworth, 19 y
"	18	George s. John & Alice Jackson, Newton, 19 y
"	19	James s. James & Alice Mills, Medlock Vale, 5 y
"	22	Selina d. Sarah Yarwood, Manchester, 2 y 5 m
"	22	John s. John & Nancy Halliwell, Newton, 10 y

"	24	Betty d. Betty Clayton, Manchester, 18 y
"	24	Thomas s. James & Ann Holden, Manchester, 21 y
"	26	John s. Thomas & Mary Entwisle, Manchester, 47 y
"	29	Henry Etchels, Failsworth, 71 y
Aug	3	Mary w. James Broughton, Manchester, 45 y
"	6	James Robinson, Manchester, 52 y
"	8	Ann w. John Jones, Manchester, 80 y
"	10	Robert s. Joseph & Hannah Williamson, Newton, 4 m
"	12	James s. Thomas & Sarah Brundritt, Failsworth, 4 y
"	13	Jane d. Carrol & Jane Allen, Failsworth, 7 m (*see entry Aug 21*)
"	14	Jane d. John & Mary Wilson, Hollinwood, 7 y
"	21	Ann d. Carrol & Jane Allen, Failsworth, 7 m
"	21	John Harding, Ardwick, 40 y
"	26	John Ogden, Failsworth, 51 y
"	28	Ellen w. Isaac Dean, Gorton, 67 y
Sep	3	Jane d. Sarah Knott, Failsworth, one y
"	4	Daniel s. John & Sarah Jones, Manchester, 15 days
"	9	John Collins, Manchester, 80 y
"	13	Mary w. James Whitehead, Failsworth, 60 y
"	13	Jonas Whalley, Manchester, 28 y
"	14	Joseph s. James & Martha Swift, Failsworth, 7 y
"	23	Ann w. Henry James, Manchester, 56 y
"	23	Alice w. Thomas Hall, Manchester, 53 y
"	24	Esther d. Peter & Alice Brindle, Manchester, 17 m
"	27	Usilla d. Richard & Mary York, Manchester, one y
"	27	James s. Joseph & Rose Tinker, Failsworth, 6 m
"	28	Ann w. Henry Chadderton, Manchester, 73 y
Oct	1	Abraham s. James & Ellen Clough, Failsworth, 16 days
"	1	John Howarth, Droylsden, 81 y
"	9	Elizabeth Atkinson, Failsworth, 51 y
"	9	Mary w. Jonas Stafford, Droylsden, 25 y
"	10	Jane Lloyd d. Griffith & Jane Humphreys, Manchester, 9 m
"	11	Sarah d. George & Margaret Tomlinson, Moston, 11 wks
"	14	Emma d. James & Elizabeth Clough, Manchester, 27 days
"	15	Samuel s. Thomas & Hannah Plant, Manchester, 9 m
"	16	George s. Sarah Ravenscroft, Manchester, 10 m
"	16	Sarah w. James Wilson, Moston, 29 y
"	28	Thomas s. Thomas & Alice Calvert, Manchester, 2 y
"	28	Rebekah Hulme, Manchester, 74 y
"	30	Elizabeth d. David & Anne Clark, Manchester, 11 m
"	31	Thomas s. Job & Mary Tetlow, Hollinwood, 14 m
"	31	Ellen d. James & Jane Fitton, Manchester, 16 m
Nov	7	Richard s. Ralph & Hannah Mather, Manchester, 18 m
"	7	Sarah Anne d. Peter & Nancy Travis, Manchester, 15 m
"	8	Jane w. John Bottomly, Manchester, 24 y

"	11	Mary d. Samuel & Anne Bottomly, Manchester, 5 m
"	11	Abraham s. George & Anne Wyld, Droylsden, 1 y 8 m
"	18	Thomas s. George & Anne Syddal, Manchester, 16 m
"	20	Anne d. Thomas & Catherine Walmsley, Manchester, 1 y 9 m
"	24	Elizabeth Burns, Manchester, 29 y
"	25	James Barnes, Ardwick, 28 y
"	27	Anne w. James Thorpe, Failsworth, 32 y
"	27	Charles s. James & Anne Kershaw, Manchester, 9 m
Dec	2	William s. Sarah Allen, Manchester, 10 m
"	3	Elizabeth w. Samuel Lees, Manchester, 56 y
"	6	Benjamin s. James & Hannah Whitehead, Newton, 9 m
"	6	Sarah d. George & Mary Robinson, Newton, 11 m
"	9	Edmund s. Thomas & Mary Dawson, Newton, 5 wks
"	9	Samuel s. John & Anne Grindrod, Manchester, 9 m
"	10	William s. Daniel & Sarah Clayton, Manchester, 2 y 4 m
"	23	Eliza d. William & Mary Pratt, Manchester, 10 wks
"	24	Betty Mills, Medlock Vale, 25 y
"	24	Ellen d. Betty Mills, Medlock Vale, 10 wks
"	26	Joseph Robinson, Manchester, 40 y
[		T. Gaskell, Incumbent of Newton]
[		James Hough Chapelwarden]

1822

Jan	1	Mary d. Ambrose & Mary Yates, Manchester, 8 m
"	1	Elizabeth d. Joseph & Susan Brierly, Droylsden, 3 y
"	2	Joseph s. James & Sarah Wood, Newton, 6 wks
"	2	Emma w. John Heywood, Manchester, 54 y
"	6	Betty d. Samuel & Anne Lowe, Manchester, 2 y 7 m
"	7	Anne w. Simeon Smith, Failsworth, 77 y
"	8	Hannah d. Daniel & Hannah Barrington, Manchester, 7 m
"	9	Thomas s. Charles & Mary Partington, Manchester, 15 m
"	10	Mary d. Samuel & Anne Lowe, Manchester, 14 m
"	10	James s. James & Anne Beswick, Manchester, 9 m
"	12	Elizabeth d. John & Ruth Cheetham, Newton, 3 y 10 m
"	16	Ann d. James & Phoebe Smethurst, Failsworth, 26 y
"	17	Richard Roberts, Manchester, 55 y
"	20	Martha d. Henry & Tebra Smith, Manchester, 3 y
"	20	Jane w. William Holdby Atkinson, Salford, 43 y
"	22	George s. William & Martha Ogilvie, Manchester, 1 y
"	22	Elizabeth d. Peter & Esther Boardman, Newton, 4 y
"	25	Isaac s. Isaac & Mary Whitehead, Manchester, 13 m
"	27	Rachel d. Edmund & Matty Buckley, Newton, 3 wks
"	27	George John Duckworth s. John & Mary Duckworth, Failsworth, 2 y
"	27	Elizabeth d. Willm. & Catherine Gradwell, Failsworth, 10 y

"	29	James s. James & Jane Aldred, Newton, 19 m	(*1822*)
"	29	Mary d. Samuel & Alice Johnson, Newton, 7 wks	
"	30	Sarah w. John Smith, Newton, 44 y	
Feb	3	James Whitehead, Manchester, 70 y	
"	10	Edward s. Joseph & Susanna Brierly, Droylsden, 2 wks	
"	14	James Tomlinson, Levenshulme, 37 y	
"	14	Samuel Pollitt, Newton, 78 y	
"	15	John s. Jonathan & Anne Chadwick, Newton, 10 m	
"	20	Richard s. James & Hannah Blomily, Manchester, 14 y	
"	21	Samuel s. Isaac & Mary Whitehead, Manchester, 3 y	
"	21	Betty d. Thomas & Jane Robinson, Newton, 17 y	
"	25	Eliza d. Thomas & Sarah Hartley, Manchester, 14 m	
Mar	5	Susan d. Joseph & Ellen Barton, Newton, 21 y	
"	7	Elizabeth d. Peter & Rebecca Lee, Newton, 2 y	
"	12	Sarah d. Patrick & Mary Quinn, Manchester, 8 m	
"	14	John Caldwell, Newton, 29 y	
"	17	John Coe, Manchester, 33 y	
"	17	John s. John & Anne Holt, Failsworth, 10 days	
"	17	Hannah d. John & Anne Blackley, Failsworth, 21 y	
"	19	William s. Robert & Martha Croft, Manchester, 3 y	
"	20	Samuel s. Garside & Alice Blomily, Newton, 1 y 11 m	
"	24	Sarah w. John Harrison, Newton, 66 y	
"	24	George Livesey, Manchester, 25 y	
"	26	Thomas s. Thomas & Alice Smith, Manchester, 8 m	
"	29	Eliza d. Anne Wroe, Newton, 1 m	
"	31	Elizabeth Sydebotham, Manchester, 63 y	
Apr	2	Phoebe w. Samuel Clough, Failsworth, 56 y	
"	3	John Buxton, Manchester, 33 y	
"	7	Alice d. Samuel & Mary Etchels, Failsworth, 14 days	
"	9	Philip s. Henry & Tebra Smith, Manchester, 10 m	
"	9	James Fitton, Manchester, 42 y	
"	13	Anne d. John & Mary Berry, Newton, 7 m	
"	14	Matilda d. Robert & Catherine Howarth, Newton, 3 m	
"	14	Nancy d. John & Betty Bardsley, Droylsden, 8 m	
"	14	William Brownhill, Manchester, 41 y	
"	17	Eliza d. Thomas & Mary Fallows, Withington, 23 y	
"	17	John s. Alice Mills, Moston, 5 y	
"	17	Elizabeth Clough, Manchester, 31 y	
"	18	Joseph Berry, Failsworth, 50 y	
"	21	William Hulme, Manchester, 63 y	
"	21	Sarah d. John & Elizabeth Bowling, Manchester, 6 m	
"	24	Sarah d. John & Betty Whitehead, Manchester, 15 m	
"	25	Ann d. Thomas & Sarah James, Manchester, 13 m	
May	2	Elizabeth Madin, Manchester, 85 y	
"	2	John s. William & Anne Winn, Newton, 5 days	

"	5	William Yarwood, Manchester, 55 y	*(1822)*
"	5	Benjamin s. William & Fanny Cocker, Newton, 7 m	
"	5	Alice w. Peter Kershaw, Failsworth, 74 y	
"	6	Thomas s. Thomas & Sarah Booth, Moston, 20 y	
"	7	Elizabeth d. John & Sarah Bentley, Woodhouses, 3 days	
"	12	Robert Clough, Failsworth, 83 y	
"	14	Isabella Unsworth, Newton, 35 y	
"	17	Richard Wood, Droylsden, 29 y	
"	19	Hannah d. Jane Pollitt, Failsworth, 13 m	
"	21	Charles s. John & Alice Hartley, Manchester, 5 m	
"	26	Esther Hooley, Newton, 85 y	
"	27	Sarah w. James Townley, Manchester, 38 y	
"	27	Mary d. Thomas & Mary Duxbury Fish, Manchester, 1 y	
"	29	Sarah w. William Entwisle, Manchester, 26 y	
Jun	3	Catherine w. John Makin, Failsworth, 67 y	
"	5	Peter Pilling, Newton, 36 y	
"	5	Samuel Barton, Newton, 67 y	
"	9	Hannah d. James & Betty Marsden, Salford, 15 m	
"	13	William s. George & Mary Ramscar, Manchester, 11 y 8 m	
"	13	William s. William & Phoebe Heap, Newton, 36 y	
"	13	James s. Robert & Elizabeth Hall, Newton, 24 y	
"	25	Marianne d. Thomas & Elizabeth Walker, Manchester, 17 m	
"	25	Elizabeth w. William Philips, Manchester, 40 y	
"	26	James Barlow, Manchester, 52 y	
"	26	Edward s. John & Hannah Gough, Manchester, 16 m	
"	26	George s. James & Sarah Townley, Manchester, 6 wks	
"	28	Hannah w. James Knowles, Manchester, 45 y	
"	30	Robert Clough, Failsworth, 45 y	
"	30	William s. Thomas & Ellen Harris, Manchester, 9 m	
"	30	Esther d. George & Jane Hilton, Failsworth, 10 y	
Jul	4	Thomas Mason, Newton, 75 y	
"	7	Henry s. Thomas & Mary Heaton, Manchester, 8 m	
"	8	Henry s. Samuel & Anne Dawson, Failsworth, 13 m	
"	14	Mary w. Joseph Bardsley, Failsworth, 26 y	
"	23	James s. Samuel & Mellicent Simister, Failsworth, 9 y	
"	23	John Lees, Failsworth, 52 y	
"	28	Charles s. George & Sarah Garlick, Hollinwood, 12 days	
"	28	Mary d. John & Anne Gardner, Droylsden, 3 m	
"	31	Rebekah Jones, Manchester, 79 y	
Aug	1	Thomas Houlton, Manchester, 53 y	
"	2	Alice d. Charles & Hannah Haywood, Newton, 6 y	
"	4	Sarah d. Robert & Mary Calvert, Manchester, 5 m	
"	4	James Lees, Manchester, 68 y	
"	5	Martha Allen, Newton, 31 y	
"	5	Sarah w. James Smith, Newton, 39 y	

"	5	Joseph s. James & Sarah Smith, Newton, 5 wks
"	6	John s. John & Mary Crompton, Manchester, 8 m
"	18	John Brownhill, Salford, 69 y
"	21	Hannah d. William & Anne Johnson, Sheffield, 15 y
"	25	Charles s. William & Anne Johnson, Manchester, one y
"	25	Philip s. James & Lucy Berry, Newton, 12 y
"	27	Ann d. William & Phoebe Jacks, Droylsden, 1 y 7 m
"	27	Thomas Allen, Droylsden, 73 y
"	30	Matthew s. Matthew & Mary Eaton, Manchester, 4 y
Sep	9	Anne d. Mary Stafford, Manchester, 14 m
"	12	Thomas s. William & Esther Summers, Manchester, 5 m
"	15	Hannah d. James & Anne Mills, Manchester, 13 m
"	15	John Thorpe, Failsworth, 31 y
"	22	Elizabeth d. John & Mary Wilkinson, Failsworth, one wk
"	22	Jonathan s. James & Mary Whittaker, Manchester, 15 m
"	25	Marianne d. Rose Etchels, Failsworth, 13 days
"	27	Betty wdw. Robert Clegg, Failsworth, 44 y
"	27	Sarah d. John & Mary Hoyle, Manchester, 2 y 9 m
"	29	Sarah w. James Hill, Manchester, 42 y
"	29	William Barnett, Manchester, 56 y
Oct	2	Elizabeth d. Roger & Elizabeth Williamson, Manchester, 5 y
"	3	John s. John & Mary Royle, Manchester, 6 m
"	3	Sarah w. Thomas Chadwick, Manchester, 36 y
"	9	Eliza d. John & Jane Clough, Manchester, 2 days
"	13	Daniel s. Samuel & Mary Walker, Manchester, 17 days
"	14	Fanny wdw. Meredith McConvil, Manchester, 63 y
"	16	Catherine Cheetham, Failsworth, 75 y
"	18	Maria d. Jonathan & Hannah Schofield, Droylsden, 3 wks
"	23	Samson Ferrand, Newton, 83 y
"	28	Betty Demilow, Manchester, 75 y
Nov	1	William s. Joseph & Anne Falkner, Droylsden, 9 m
"	1	John Gillibrand, Ardwick, 46 y
"	8	Martha Ogden, Failsworth, 57 y
"	10	Jane Wood, Woodhouses, 54 y
"	10	Margaret Holt, Failsworth, 75 y
"	10	William s. Thomas & Mary Thorpe, Failsworth, 22 y
"	11	Eliza d. Edward & Elizabeth Ferns, Manchester, 7 y
"	12	Sarah Anne d. John & Sarah Rothwell, Newton, 5 y
"	17	Levi s. Thomas & Rachel Sudworth, Manchester, 1 y
"	17	Martha wdw. Anthony Lane, Manchester, 72 y
"	24	Peter Sydebotham, Manchester, 22 y
"	24	William s. John & Martha Consterdine, Newton, 6 m
"	26	Mary w. Abraham Lee, Manchester, 29 y
"	27	William s. James & Mary Tetlow, Newton, 25 y
"	27	Joseph s. William & Sarah Shelmerdine, Newton, 14 days

Dec	8	William s. Peter & Sarah Travis, Manchester, 15 y
"	9	Benjamin s. Ralph & Mary Darbyshire, Droylsden, 3 m
"	12	Jenny w. Thomas Allen, Newton, 35 y
"	17	Hannah d. Robert & Betty Clayton, Manchester, 19 y
"	18	Hannah d. John & Nancy Holt, Bradford, 10 y
"	19	Benjamin Hill, Manchester, 48 y
"	22	Thomas Whitehead, Manchester, 28 y
"	25	Elizabeth Jane d. Joseph & Mary Anne Telford, Manchester, 6 m
"	25	Jane d. John & Anne Wyld, Ashton Parish, 6 y
"	29	Anne w. Robert Naylor, Manchester, 69 y
[		T. Gaskell, Incumbent of Newton]

1823

Jan	5	Richard Clayton, Manchester, 75 y
"	5	Mary w. George Booth, Failsworth, 67 y
"	5	Anne wdw. John Buckleton, Manchester, 78 y
"	6	Mary d. Joseph & Mary Berry, Failsworth, 8 wks
"	6	Thomas Walker, Manchester, 41 y
"	7	Jane Bentley, Manchester, 60 y
"	9	Alice w. John Hartley, Manchester, 22 y
"	12	Ann Goodier, Failsworth, 81 y
"	12	Robert Wolstenholme, Newton, 46 y
"	12	Andrew Lane, Manchester, 32 y
"	12	Dan s. Ashton & Mary Shepley, Newton, 21 y
"	19	Robert s. Robert & Mary Anne Blacklock, Manchester, 3 m
"	19	Mary w. James Cooke, Manchester, 42 y
"	19	Thomas s. William & Elizabeth Porter, Bradford, 3 y 7 m
"	20	William s. John & Jane Crossley, Ashton Parish, 1 day
"	26	James s. James & Anne Livesey, Manchester, 5 m
"	26	Nanny w. Matthew Gradwell, Blackley, 51 y
"	27	Violet d. Samuel & Millicent Simister, Failsworth, 7 m
"	28	Thomas Worsley, Manchester, 54 y
Feb	5	Sarah Goodier, Newton, 50 y
"	9	Jane w. George Eaton, Failsworth, 28 y
"	12	Richard s. Richard & Mary York, Manchester, 9 m
"	13	Hannah Tomlinson, Moston, 60 y
"	16	Thomas s. Thomas & Ellen Greenhalgh, Newton, 9 m
"	16	David s. James & Anne Fideham, Manchester, 19 y 9 m
"	16	Luke s. Jonathan & Mary Hooley, Newton, 9 m
"	16	Elizabeth d. James & Anne Coe, Manchester, 1 y 9 m
"	17	Sarah d. Marianne Gould, Moston, 3 wks
"	19	James Taylor, Woodhouses, 84 y
"	19	Mary Thorp, Moston, 64 y
"	20	Ashton s. George & Elizabeth Ripley, Newton, 18 y

"	21	Alice w. James Eckersley, Failsworth, 60 y *(1823)*
"	23	Abraham Townend, Moston, 65 y
"	25	Harriet d. James & Anne Reed, Failsworth, 22 y
"	25	Hannah d. William & Elizabeth Ashworth, Manchester, 6 m
"	26	Sarah w. John Kenyon, Manchester, 45 y
"	27	Hannah w. Randle Alcock, Cheadle Parish, 70 y
Mar	2	William Adshead, Manchester, 70 y
"	2	Sarah wdw. William Bragg, Manchester, 53 y
"	12	Anne d. Joshua & Sarah Eckersley, Failsworth, 3 m
"	13	Mary w. Patrick Quinn, Manchester, 41 y
"	13	Alice d. Thomas & Jane Allen, Newton, 14 wks
"	14	Matilda d. Joseph & Mary Brown, Ashton Parish, 1 y 5 m
"	14	Nathaniel Thorley, Failsworth, 66 y
"	17	William Atkin, Manchester, 75 y
"	17	Anne d. Thomas & Margaret Hill, Manchester, 1 y 2 m
"	19	John s. Thomas & Mary Duxbury, Manchester, 6 y 10 m
"	23	Elizabeth w. James Muggleston, Droylsden, 38 y
"	26	Elizabeth d. David & Anne Clarke, Manchester, 6 m
"	28	Dorothy d. Thomas & Elizabeth Brown, Manchester, 7 m
"	30	Mary d. Elizabeth Allen, Failsworth, 21 y
"	30	Ellen d. George & Jane Eaton, Failsworth, 6 m
"	30	Betty d. Elijah & Sarah Whitehead, Failsworth, 3 y 9 m
"	30	William s. John & Esther Dewhurst, Hollinwood, 9 m
Apr	2	James s. Leah & Mary Foden, Newton, 9 y 7 m
"	3	Thomas Hardy, Newton, 67 y
"	6	Sarah d. Abraham & Mary Lee, Manchester, one y
"	15	Abraham s. Abraham & Mary Lee, Manchester, 4 y 6 m
"	16	William Harding, Stockport, 69 y
"	17	Robert spurious s. Betty Barlow, Failsworth, 2 y 5 m
"	17	Jonas s. Mary Whalley, Manchester, 1 y 7 m
"	21	Jane wdw. John Antrobus, Manchester, 83 y
"	24	Mary d. Samuel & Jane Bethel, Newton, 1 y 8 m
"	29	Hannah d. Thomas & Jane Wyld, Newton, 5 m two wks
May	2	Thomas Moore, Manchester, 40 y
"	4	William s. John & Anne Bentham, Newton, 17 m
"	7	James s. Thomas & Sarah Pearson, Manchester, 2 y 5 m
"	9	Phoebe d. William & Phoebe Fishwick, Newton, 10 wks
"	14	John s. John & Sarah Partington, Manchester, 7 wks
"	18	Ann wdw. Joseph Newton, Manchester, 96 y
"	20	William s. William & Phoebe Fishwick, Newton, 3 m
"	20	Sarah w. George Frith, Manchester, 62 y
"	23	John s. James & Jane Schofield, Newton, 11 days
"	25	Joseph s. Thomas & Sarah Charlesworth, Manchester, two y
"	25	Elizabeth w. William Moss, Manchester, 37 y
"	25	James s. Richard & Esther Brown, Manchester, 1 y 9 m

"	25	Richard s. Richard & Mary Walker, Newton, 4 y 6 m	*(1823)*
"	25	George s. Samuel & Mary Holland, Failsworth, 9 m	
"	26	Isabella w. Ralph Ramshaw, Newton, 60 y	
"	28	William Barnes, Newton, 73 y	
"	29	Thomas s. Thomas & Anne Moss, Manchester, 7 wks	
Jun	5	Charles Roberts s. Joseph & Anne Hooley, Newton, 21 y	
"	12	Sarah w. William Hall, Newton, 35 y	
"	13	Simeon Smith, Failsworth, 79 y	
"	15	Emma d. Samuel & Alice Johnson, Manchester, 4 m	
"	17	Sarah d. Thomas & Sarah Hewit, Manchester, 2 y 9 m	
"	17	Sarah w. John Goodier, Newton, 26 y	
"	18	John s. Joseph & Mary Porter, Bradford, 14 y	
"	10	Daniel s. John & Sarah Syddal, Manchester, 15 y *(order thus in PR & BT; see entry in Baptisms)*	
"	18	James s. Nancy Brown, Manchester, 15 wks	
"	19	Samuel s. Joseph & Nancy Ogden, Failsworth, 7 y	
"	19	Anne d. William & Lucy Poppleton, Manchester, 9 m	
"	22	James s. John & Betty Kay, Failsworth, 5 m	
"	22	Robert s. Benjamin & Jane Hulton, Failsworth, 1 day	
"	23	Ellen d. Charles & Ellen Brown, Manchester, 20 m	
"	24	Eliza d. Samuel & Elizabeth Stafford, Bradford, 12 days	
"	26	Betty w. William Crompton, Manchester, 31 y	
"	26	Jane w. George Marsh, Manchester, 23 y	
"	27	James s. George & Martha Leigh, Manchester, 22 m	
"	29	Margaret d. John & Alice Ogden, Droylsden, 3 y	
"	29	Peter s. Peter & Anne Sydebotham, Manchester, 7 m	
"	30	Amelia d. Adam & Anne Shore, Salford, 13 m	
Jul	2	Joseph Nicholson, Manchester, 75 y	
"	2	Mary w. Robert Abraham, Manchester, 46 y	
"	4	Henry s. John & Mary Whalley, Manchester, 1 day	
"	4	Martha d. Andrew & Hannah Clegg, Failsworth, 19 y	
"	7	Joseph s. James & Ellen Ogden, Failsworth, 10 days	
"	7	Hannah d. William & Maria Winstanley, Manchester, 3 m	
"	10	Francis Murray, Newton, 50 y	
"	13	Anne d. Alice Robinson, Manchester, 17 wks	
"	13	Henry Booth, Failsworth, 62 y	
"	16	Catherine w. John Smith, Hollinwood, 52 y	
"	17	William s. George & Martha Leigh, Manchester, 7 m	
"	21	Elizabeth d. John & Sarah Madin, Manchester, 3 y 3 m	
"	22	James s. Betty Hulme, Manchester, 9 m	
"	23	Joseph s. Hannah Hardy, Manchester, 11 m	
"	27	Betty d. William & Betty Crompton, Manchester, 1 m	
"	27	John s. William & Hannah Kay, Blackley, 4 y	
"	29	John s. Leah & Mary Foden, Newton, 5 y 10 m	
"	30	Abraham s. Joseph & Sarah Mather, Newton, one y	

"	30	William Shaw, Failsworth, 90 y *(1823)*
Aug	3	Robert s. George & Anne Syddal, Manchester, 11 m
"	6	Peggy d. Thomas & Mary McIlvenna, Newton, 23 y
"	10	Lucy d. Benjamin & Lucy Cocker, Newton, 10 wks
"	11	Henry s. Ann Gradwell, Manchester, 17 m
"	17	Edward s. Joseph & Mary Hampson, Manchester, 5 y 7 m
"	22	William s. George & Anne Hall, Manchester, 3 y 9 m
"	24	Sarah d. William & Anne Leigh, Manchester, 2 y

(New register commences: volume 10)

"	25	Charles s. William & Mary Counsel, Newton, 8 y 6 m
"	27	Joseph Sutcliffe, Manchester, 54 y
"	28	Christopher s. Joel & Elizabeth Stafford, Manchester, 17 m
"	29	David Ogden, Manchester, 50 y
Sep	3	Thomas s. James & Mary Cooke, Manchester, 8 m
"	7	William Robinson, Newton, 38 y
"	7	Mary d. Alice Hobson, Newton, 3 y
"	7	Edward Williams, Manchester, 56 y
"	7	Enoch s. William & Mary Cliffe, Newton, 1 y 9 m
"	10	Martha d. Richard & Elizabeth Hill, Manchester, 15 y
"	11	Elijah s. John & Henrietta Smith, Manchester, 16 m
"	14	Mary d. Thomas & Sarah James, Manchester, 6 m
"	14	Anne d. George & Anne Yates, Newton, 4 m
"	19	Andrew s. Daniel & Hannah Etchels, Failsworth, 1 y 10 m
"	21	Mary d. Benjamin & Sarah Brammal, Manchester, 4 y
"	25	Alice w. Joseph Tetlow, Manchester, 30 y
"	26	Anne d. Thomas & Nancy Ogden, 4 y 4 m
"	28	James s. Alice Berry, Manchester, 18 m
"	28	James s. John & Mary Hoyle, Manchester, 15 y 4 m
"	30	William s. William & Agnes Allen, Failsworth, 14 m
Oct	1	Catherine d. Charles & Mary Coyle, Manchester, 8 m
"	2	Mary d. Robert & Esther Wylde, Manchester, 3 y one m
"	3	John s. Charles & Sarah Clough, Manchester, 1 y 10 m
"	5	Maria d. William & Sarah Robinson, Newton, 26 y
"	7	Alice d. William & Elizabeth Moss, Manchester, 16 m
"	9	Thomas s. William & Ellen Caldwell, Manchester, 21 y
"	10	William Mather, Droylsden, 68 y
"	12	Hannah w. Thomas Dunkerly, Failsworth, 40 y
"	12	Anne d. Nathaniel & Betty Taylor, Failsworth, 1 y 4 m
"	14	Harriet d. John & Anne Hamson, Manchester, 7 m
"	15	Betty d. James & Betty Ogden, Failsworth, 2 y 3 m
"	15	Betty w. William Heaton, Failsworth, 20 y
"	19	Henry s. Edward & Nancy Robinson, Failsworth, one y
"	21	Mary d. John & Anne Wood, Ashton Parish, 10 wks

"	21	Sarah d. Thomas & Mary Robinson, Manchester, 10 m
"	22	Martha d. Mary Corns, Newton, 8 m
"	22	James s. Thomas & Elizabeth Coupe, Droylsden, one y
"	26	Eliza d. Joseph & Anne Sutcliff, Manchester, 4 y
"	27	James s. Joseph & Mary Davies, Newton, 14 m
"	28	Charles James s. Charles & Ellen Brown, Manchester, 3 m
"	28	Ellis s. William & Sarah Hall, Manchester, 11 m
"	29	Alice d. William & Betty Valentine, Manchester, 17 m
"	31	Mary d. James & Hannah Sykes, Newton, 14 m
Nov	1	Eliza d. Ellis & Sarah Whittaker, Newton, 2 y 5 m
"	2	Richard s. John & Martha Owen, Blackley, 21 m
"	2	Michael s. John & Mary Smith, Newton, one y
"	2	James s. James & Sarah Dunstan, Manchester, 2 y 2 m
"	4	Jane d. William & Alice Walton, Failsworth, 2 y
"	5	John Monks, Manchester, 76 y
"	6	John s. James & Rebecca Wyld, Newton, 2 y
"	9	Mary Anne d. James & Sarah Simister, Newton, 18 m
"	12	Hannah d. Joseph & Mary Butterworth, Manchester, 2 y
"	13	Elizabeth d. William & Elizabeth Johnson, Manchester, 7 wks
"	14	Elizabeth d. John & Esther Smith, Manchester, 2 y 6 m
"	16	Hannah d. Robert & Anne Ridings, Failsworth, 2 y 6 m
"	16	Hannah d. Samuel & Phoebe Travis, Newton, 2 y 1 m
"	16	Richard s. John & Elizabeth Williams, Manchester, 21 y
"	23	Thomas s. Hamlet & Elizabeth Lowe, Manchester, 1 y 11 m
"	23	Marianne d. Richard & Hannah Etchels, Failsworth, 10 m
"	23	Margaret d. Adam & Margaret Horrocks, Droylsden, 2 y 2 m
"	24	William s. Thomas & Sarah Bruce, Manchester, 4 y 3 m
"	24	John s. Thomas & Mary Hilton, Failsworth, 2 wks
"	24	Elizabeth d. Ashton & Anne Shepley, Newton, 4 y
"	26	Ellen w. William Jackson, Newton, 76 y
"	30	Esther d. John & Mary Wolstencroft, Manchester, 4 y 11 m
"	30	William s. James & Ellen Ogden, Failsworth, 7 y
"	30	James s. Betty Taylor, Droylsden, 9 m
Dec	1	John s. Thomas & Mary Hall, Manchester, 2 y 8 m
"	4	John Robinson, Failsworth, 63 y
"	5	Elizabeth d. James & Anne Taylor, Failsworth, 17 m
"	5	Robert s. Robert & Betty Taylor, Failsworth, 10 m
"	7	Joseph Chadderton, Failsworth, 81 y
"	7	Joshua s. William & Martha Cordingly, Failsworth, 2 y
"	7	James Hooley, Manchester, 51 y
"	8	Alice d. Wright & Mary Cranshaw, Newton, 4 y 10 m
"	9	Margaret d. Peter & Anne Tanny, Ireland, 11 days
"	9	Maria d. Joseph & Betty Mills, Medlock Vale, 2 y
"	11	Anne wdw. Joseph Clough, Newton, 63 y
"	14	Henry Whittaker, Newton, 35 y

"	14	Thomas s. Robert & Bathsheba Boardman, Manchester, 12 y
"	14	Eliza d. George & Margaret Tomlinson, Moston, 14 wks
"	15	Hannah d. Thomas & Elizabeth Hatfield, Droylsden, 15 m
"	17	James s. John & Joice Maize, Manchester, one wk
"	17	Anne d. Eleanor Yielding, Newton, 2 y
"	19	Hannah w. William Bowker, Manchester, 35 y
"	21	Anne d. John & Dinah Tonge, Failsworth, 18 m
"	21	Eliza d. Hannah Hamlet, Newton, 4 y 3 m
"	22	Mary d. Joel & Hannah Bradley, Manchester, 7 m
"	25	Charles s. John & Mary Godridge, Manchester, 3 m
"	25	Betty Smith, Failsworth, 76 y
"	31	Sarah d. John & Sarah Emmerson, Newton, 9 m
"	31	Joseph Pollitt, Newton, 71 y
"	31	James Wyld, Moston, 78 y
[		T. Gaskell, Incumbent of Newton]

1824

Jan	1	Ambrose s. Ambrose & Mary Yates, Manchester, 1 y
"	1	Samuel Berry, Failsworth, 68 y
"	1	Anne d. Joshua & Martha Bertenshaw, Manchester, 1 y 9 m
"	1	Alice d. Luke & Catherine Eckersley, Failsworth, 6 m
"	2	Peter s. Thomas & Betty Fotheringham, Newton, 10 m
"	2	Sarah w. George Bardsley, Newton, 49 y
"	6	John s. Mary Pollitt, Failsworth, 17 m
"	7	Ellen d. William & Hannah Bowker, Manchester, 4 m
"	7	Frances d. Robert & Mary Jackson, Manchester, 18 m
"	8	Sarah d. Thomas & Sarah Moores, Manchester, 13 m
"	8	Elizabeth w. John Greenwood, Manchester, 27 y
"	8	Andrew s. James & Anne Kershaw, Manchester, 11 m
"	8	Richard Thorpe, Moston, 74 y
"	9	Esther w. James Ogden, Moston, 70 y
"	12	William Smethurst, Manchester, 59 y
"	13	Elizabeth d. Richard & Hannah Briscoe, Manchester, 5 y 10 m
"	13	Esther wdw. Zechariah Partington, Manchester, 75 y
"	15	Ellen d. George & Mary Etchels, Newton, 14 m
"	18	Amelia d. Matthew & Rebecca Shaw, Newton, 2 y
"	10	Alice d. Nancy Gradwell, Blackley, 18 wks
"	18	Ann d. Sarah Fletcher, Newton, 11 m
"	18	Anne wdw. James Wroe, Failsworth, 60 y
"	21	Nancy d. Robert & Nancy Percival, Manchester, 3 y 3 m
"	22	Anne d. Edmund & Elizabeth Shaw, Newton, 6 y
"	22	Charles s. James & Charlotte Wolstencroft, Manchester, 1 y 3 m
"	25	Sarah d. James & Ellen Travis, Manchester, 1 y 6 m
"	25	Mary Hooley, Newton, 41 y

"	27	John Johnson, Newton, 25 y
"	28	Elizabeth w. Thomas Thorpe, Manchester, 65 y
"	29	Marianne d. John & Charlotte Whitehead, Manchester, 2 y 7 m
"	29	Samuel s. Henry & Elizabeth Kirk, Newton, 2 y
"	30	John s. James & Sarah Bradbury, Newton, 2 y
Feb	1	Marianne d. Benjamin & Sarah Priest, Manchester, 10 y
"	1	Mary d. John & Alice Ogden, Droylsden, 2 y
"	3	Hannah d. Benjamin & Nancy Worsick, Droylsden, 14 m
"	4	John s. John & Mary Billinge, Manchester, 6 y
"	5	Hannah wdw. Richard Wolstencroft, Manchester, 63 y
"	5	Thomas s. Thomas & Mary Kay, Newton, 5 wks
"	6	Jane d. James & Betty Wilson, Newton, 11 m
"	8	Hannah d. Thomas & Martha Whitelegg, Manchester, 13 m
"	8	Robert s. Edward & Grace Allen, Manchester, 1 y 7 m
"	9	Henry s. Betty Hardy, Failsworth, 5 m
"	9	Francis s. William & Anne Middleton, Failsworth, 9 m
"	11	John s. John & Mary Linley, Newton, 3 days
"	11	Sarah w. John Corns, Failsworth, 29 y
"	13	Mary w. John Clough, Ashton Parish, 72 y
"	15	Henry s. Samuel & Mary Holland, Failsworth, 8 m
"	18	Olive d. James & Sarah Bradbury, Newton, 5 m
"	20	Mary d. Thomas & Nancy Ogden, Failsworth, 3 y
"	22	Alice d. George & Rachel Livesey, Manchester, 3 y
"	22	Margaret d. Joseph & Alice Partington, Manchester, 6 m
"	22	Thomas s. George & Nancy Travis, Newton, 13 y
"	22	Elizabeth d. John & Alice Chadwick, Newton, 2 y
"	23	Ralph Smethurst, Failsworth, 59 y
"	23	Mary Wolstenham, Failsworth, 79 y
"	25	Samuel s. Joseph & Jane Berry, Newton, 10 m
"	25	Robert s. James & Isabella [Isabel] Carr, Moston, 8 y 9 m
"	29	James Kenyon, Manchester, 84 y
"	29	Mary d. John & Anne Isherwood, Manchester, 17 m
"	29	William Lee, Manchester, 36 y
Mar	2	Marianne d. John & Esther Butterworth, Newton, 3 wks
"	9	James s. Thomas & Mary Hall, Manchester, 9 m
"	14	Sarah w. James Robinson, 33 y
"	14	Elizabeth d. William & Martha Leigh, Manchester, 6 m
"	14	James s. William & Sarah Bradshaw, Manchester, 18 y
"	14	Thomas Collinson, Newton, 37 y
"	14	David s. David & Mary Peet Chapman, Failsworth, one wk
"	14	John s. Abel & Mary Horrocks, Ashton Parish, 5 wks
"	17	Samuel s. George & Martha Stafford, Droylsden, 2 y
"	18	Samuel Heath, Newton, 70 y
"	22	Mary d. Betty Lee, Manchester, 8 y
"	24	Mary d. James & Sarah Houghton, Newton, 16 days

"	24	Thomas Jameson, Manchester, 62 y	*(1824)*
"	24	John Crossley Travis s. Mary Crossley, Harpurhey, 14 m	
"	25	Ellen d. William & Anne Ward, Newton, 5 y	
"	28	Sarah d. William & Mary Greenhalgh, Manchester, 9 m	
"	28	Isabel Holt, Failsworth, 67 y	
"	29	Elizabeth d. William & Sarah Ridings, Failsworth, 17 wks	
"	31	Thomas s. Anne Crawford, Manchester, 10 m	
"	31	Samuel s. Thomas & Alice Smith, Manchester, 14 m	
Apr	4	Betty w. Samuel Pollitt, Failsworth, 29 y	
"	4	Joseph s. John & Mary Edwards, Newton, 11 m	
"	7	Jane d. Robert & Anne Ridings, Failsworth, 7 m	
"	9	Sarah w. John Wilson, Manchester, 38 y	
"	11	George s. Nanny Gradwell, Blackley, 4 y	
"	13	Anne d. John & Alice Ishwerwood, Manchester, 3 y 5 m	
"	15	Betty wdw. John Thorp, Moston, 77 y	
"	18	Hannah w. James Burgess, Manchester, 19 y	
"	19	Sarah wdw John Riley, Manchester, 86 y	
"	19	John Hartley, Manchester, 54 y	
"	20	Mary d. Richard & Anne Isherwood, Manchester, 4 y 4 m	
"	21	Joseph s. Thomas & Ellen Harris, Manchester, 9 m	
"	22	Henry s. Thomas & Mary Hulton, Failsworth, 3 y	
"	22	John s. Joseph & Alice Tetlow, Manchester, 1 y 10 m	
"	22	Mary Hardy, Newton, 40 y	
"	23	Anne d. Robert & Mary Hulme, Droylsden, 19 y	
"	24	Hannah d. Thomas & Betty Hayes, Failsworth, two wks	
"	25	Mary w. Robert Grimshaw, Manchester, 41 y	
"	28	James s. Hannah Berry, Failsworth, 3 days	
"	30	Samuel s. James & Anne Wright, Newton, 11 m	
May	2	Luke Eckersley, Failsworth, 24 y	
"	2	Sarah d. Jonathan & Betty Taylor, Hollinwood, 7 y	
"	2	Maria d. Thomas & Ellen Harris, Manchester, 5 y	
"	3	Philip s. John & Sarah Houghton, Failsworth, 4 y	
"	4	Martha Buxton, Manchester, 37 y	
"	5	John s. Samuel & Anne Hunston, Manchester, 1 y 10 m	
"	7	James s. James & Isabella Carr, Moston, 3 y	
"	9	Edward Riley, Manchester, 27 y	
"	9	Samuel Wyatt, Manchester, 64 y	
"	11	Sarah d. William & Mary Lomas, Worsley, 18 m	
"	12	Anne d. Richard & Anne Launder, Manchester, 18 m	
"	13	James Robinson, Manchester, 55 y	
"	16	Amelia d. John & Hannah James, Manchester, 2 y	
"	16	Mary w. Joseph Berry, Failsworth, 42 y	
"	16	James s. John & Mary Hall, Manchester, 6 y	
"	17	Jane d. John & Mary Blackley, Newton, 2 y 4 m	
"	18	Thomas s. Ratcliff & Elizabeth Fielding, Droylsden, 13 m	

	20	Mary d. George & Alice Smith, Failsworth, 21 y	(*1824*)
"	21	Mary d. Samuel & Sarah Syddal, Droylsden, 9 y 8 m	
"	27	James Whitehead, Salford, 52 y	
"	28	Elizabeth d. Thomas & Rachel Bottomley, Bradford, 2 y 6 m	
"	30	Robert Richardson, Hollinwood, 24 y	
"	30	James s. John & Sarah Partington, Manchester, 13 y	
"	31	Betty d. Thomas & Mary Thorpe, Failsworth, 18 y	
Jun	1	Susanna Hall, Harpurhey, 83 y	
"	3	Mary d. David & Anne Etchels, Failsworth, 21 y	
"	6	Sally d. William & Betty Worral, Failsworth, 6 y	
"	7	Charlotte w. John Duncuft, Bolton, 43 y	
"	11	John s. Samuel & Anne Bottomley, Manchester, 1 y 9 m	
"	11	Harriet d. Joseph & Sarah Wright, Newton, 9 y 6 m	
"	11	Hannah d. Samuel & Margaret Cheetham, Newton, 6 m	
"	17	Thomas Wood s. Thomas & Mary Chown, Manchester, 3 y	
"	19	Mary d. John & Anne Gardner, Droylsden, one y	
"	20	Samuel s. Thomas & Milly Yeald, Failsworth, 8 y	
"	20	Thomas s. James & Susanna Roberts, Manchester, 8 y 6 m	
"	20	James Whitehead, Macclesfield, 41 y	
"	21	John Bowker, Newton, 29 y	
"	22	George Curry, Manchester, 58 y	
"	22	James s. Edmund Whitehead, Droylsden, 22 y	
"	23	John s. James & Sarah Robinson, Newton, 11 m	
"	23	Abraham s. John & Esther Fitton, Manchester, 12 y	
"	27	Joshua s. Joseph & Mary Sykes, Manchester, 10 m	
"	29	Nancy d. Nathan & Phoebe Ashley, Manchester, 20 y	
Jul	1	Anne d. James & Ellen Lindley, Newton, 3 y	
"	4	Richard s. William & Alice Dixon, Manchester, one y	
"	4	Mary w. Ambrose Yates, Manchester, 36 y	
"	4	Sarah d. William & Elizabeth Boardman, Manchester, 8 m	
"	5	Andrew s. Samuel & Phoebe Travis, Newton, 13 y	
"	8	Sarah w. John Whitehead, Droylsden, 58 y	
"	11	Maria d. William & Elizabeth Scott, Manchester, 10 m	
"	18	Martha d. Matthew & Sarah Brown, Newton, one y	
"	18	Robert s. James & Alice Rhodes, Manchester, 3 m	
"	18	Jane d. John & Martha Consterdine, Newton, 8 m	
"	22	Mary d. James & Mary Walmsley, Newton, 19 y	
"	22	Elizabeth d. George & Esther Wood, Newton, 11 m	
"	23	Sarah d. Daniel & Hannah Smethurst, Manchester, 1 y 6 m	
"	25	Issachar Thorpe, Moston, 42 y	
"	27	Robert Branton, Newton, 29 y	
"	28	Joshua Ogden, Failsworth, 79 y	
"	29	William Allen, Failsworth, 44 y	
"	29	Sarah wdw. Simeon Whitehead, Manchester, 76 y	
"	30	William s. William & Lucy Poppleton, Manchester, 2 m	

"	30	Thomas s. George & Betty Taylor, Newton, 7 y
Aug	1	Jane w. John Slater, Moston, 38 y
"	3	Betty w. Joseph Grimshaw, Newton, 87 y
"	3	Catherine d. William & Anne Paul, Newton, 7 m
"	6	William Fletcher, Manchester, 54 y
"	8	James s. Betty Allen, Newton, 16 m
"	10	Margaret w. James Clough, Failsworth, 57 y
"	11	Sarah w. John Wyld, Newton, 29 y
"	11	Emma d. John & Jane Blackshaw, Newton, 15 wks
"	13	Thomas s. David & Anne Ogden, Failsworth, 18 wks
"	15	Elizabeth wdw. James Heap, Manchester, 98 y
"	29	Betty Thorpe, Manchester, 60 y
Sep	5	Nathaniel Stansfield, Manchester, 71 y
"	6	Letitia d. Thomas & Susan Brown, Openshaw, 14 m
"	9	Elizabeth d. John & Mary Billinge, Manchester, 10 m
"	14	John s. Eli & Jane Swift, Failsworth, 11 m
"	19	John Porter, Bradford, 76 y
"	22	A Person unknown (*struck through and does not appear in BT*) Joshua Blundall, Warwickshire found drowned in the Rochdale Canal (*age blank in PR & BT*)
"	22	Jane wdw. William Robinson, Manchester, 70 y
"	23	Rachel d. James & Mary Nuttal, Mottram, 23 y
"	24	Robert s. Thomas & Mary Duxbury, Manchester, 1 y 10 m
"	26	Mary w. William Hooten, Manchester, 38 y
"	26	Olive w. Joseph Needham, Failsworth, 20 y
Oct	1	James s. John & Sarah Wyld, Newton, 10 m
"	3	Anne d. Betty Bardsley, Failsworth, 8 m
"	5	Sarah w. John Drinkwater, Manchester, 22 y
"	6	Frances w. Jeremiah Hopwood, Newton, 44 y
"	10	Betty d. Bathsheba Boardman, Manchester, 11 m
"	10	Jane wdw. James Bowker, Manchester, 78 y
"	10	Isaac s. John & Betty Wilson, Manchester, 18 m
"	17	Harriet d. Charles & Martha Tomlinson, Newton, 14 days
"	18	Oliver Tinker, Manchester, 58 y
"	19	Mary w. James Shepley, Newton, 28 y
"	20	William Stanley s. Charles & Eliza Eckersley, Newton, 2 y
"	26	Joshua s. Levi & Marianne Lomax, Manchester, 2 y 3 m
Nov	4	Zeno s. Charles & Anne Wilson, Newton, 5 wks
"	5	John s. Anne Bradshaw, Failsworth, 4 m
"	7	Edward s. Luke & Jane Wharmby, Newton, 8 days
"	7	Jane d. Samuel & Martha Podmore, Manchester, 4 y
"	9	George Whittingham, Priest in Shropshire drowned in the Rochdale Canal, 22 y
"	9	Edward s. Emma Young, Newton, one m
"	18	Ellis s. Robert & Anne Crompton, Manchester, 18 m

	21	Betty wdw. James Andrew, Manchester, 85 y
"	21	Richard s. Joseph & Mary Hamson, Manchester, 9 m
"	21	Sarah d. John & Sarah Wilson, Manchester, 7 m
"	25	Elizabeth d. Ellen Hardman, Manchester, 4 m
"	30	James s. Samuel & Mary Riley, Manchester, 2 days
Dec	1	James s. Robert & Jane Railson, Droylsden, 2 y 7 m
"	7	Hannah d. John & Betty Taylor, Manchester, 6 y
"	7	Mary d. Samuel & Mary Hoyle, Droylsden, 7 m
"	8	Elizabeth d. Anne Drinkwater, Moston, 14 wks
"	8	Abraham Pollitt, Failsworth, 76 y
"	13	Mary w. John Barnes, Ardwick, 69 y
"	15	Samuel s. James & Mary Lees, Failsworth, 3 days
"	19	Mary d. George & Esther Wood, Newton, 3 y
"	19	Philip s. Thomas & Martha Goodier, Chadderton, 29 y
"	19	William s. James & Jane Bent, Manchester, 26 y
"	19	Robert Moon, Manchester, 56 y
"	26	Elizabeth w. Joseph Turner, Manchester, 33 y
"	26	Robert s. Isaac & Betty Heapy, Droylsden, 1 y 7 m
"	29	Lucy d. John & Eliza Withnal, Manchester, 3 y
"	30	Maria d. George & Ellen Bruce, Manchester, 7 wks

1825

Jan	2	Thomas s. John & Catherine Shuttleworth, Droylsden, 9 y
"	7	John s. Robert & Sarah Wyld, Manchester, 8 m
"	9	Jane Thorpe, Manchester, 78 y
"	11	Jane d. Isaac & Mary Whitehead, Manchester, 10 m
"	12	Mary w. George Brown, Manchester, 55 y
"	13	Thomas Finney, Newton, 86 y
"	13	John s. James & Hannah Burgess, Manchester, 15 m
"	16	Sarah w. Henry Burns, Manchester, 20 y
"	16	Dennis Ramsbottom, Newton, 80 y
"	17	Mary w. Robert Hulme, Droylsden, 62 y
"	23	George s. Anne Gildart, Manchester, 15 wks
"	23	Sarah d. James & Mary Shepley, Newton, 18 wks
"	25	Samuel s. Samuel & Martha Hulton, Moston, 3 y
"	26	Mary d. Joshua & Sarah Eckersley, Failsworth, 6 y 10 m
"	30	William s. James & Elizabeth Brown, Manchester, 7 wks
"	30	Martha d. Luke & Sarah Cordwell, Manchester, 8 y
Feb	1	Joseph Aldred, Manchester, 41 y
"	14	John Walker, Manchester, 52 y
"	15	Joseph s. Joseph & Olive Needham, Failsworth, 10 m
"	15	John Mills, Manchester, 69 y
"	18	Sarah d. John & Nancy Holt, Bradford, 4 y 3 m
"	20	Elizabeth w. James Birch, Manchester, 41 y

"	21	Elizabeth w. John Ridge, Ardwick, 86 y *(1825)*
"	22	Thomas Duxbury, Manchester, 70 y
"	24	Mary Anne d. Joseph & Sarah Wright, Newton, 23 y
"	27	John Shaw, Newton, 48 y
"	27	Sarah Ogden, Failsworth, 78 y
Mar	1	Anne Galashan, Failsworth, 20 y
"	3	Isabel w. Robert Hulton, Failsworth, 60 y
"	6	Laura d. Henry & Sarah Burns, Manchester, 14 m
"	6	John s. Samuel & Mary Holland, Failsworth, 11 m
"	6	Ann Wilkinson, Failsworth, 34 y
"	7	James s. David & Esther Walmsley, Manchester, 2 y 6 m
"	8	John s. John & Mary Thornley, Failsworth, 2 wks
"	10	Nancy d. Abraham & Betty Mather, Failsworth, 13 y 10 m
"	11	Catherine d. Samuel & Alice Thorp, Newton, 14 y
"	15	Anne w. William Middleton, Failsworth, 26 y
"	16	Thomas Crossley, Moston, 77 y
"	16	Henry s. Philip & Elizabeth Schofield, Newton, 14 m
"	17	Alice wdw. George Robinson, Droylsden, 74 y
"	20	John s. Richard & Esther Brown, Manchester, 2 y
"	20	Anne wdw. John Hall, Failsworth, 97 y
"	21	Frances Tinker, Manchester, 35 y
"	22	Nancy w. John Whittaker, Failsworth, 42 y
"	23	Joseph Tomlinson, Levenshulme, 83 y
"	28	Maria w. Reuben Heywood, Manchester, 24 y
"	29	Marianne d. Jane Whitehead, Manchester, 2 y 8 m
"	31	Betty w. David Booth, Chadderton, 28 y
Apr	1	William s. Joseph & Mary Davies, Newton, 8 m
"	1	Robert Lord, Newton, 32 y
"	3	James s. Peter & Margaret Later, Moston, one m
"	9	James s. Sarah Wood, Newton, 3 m
"	10	John s. Samuel & Hannah Robinson, Failsworth, 8 m
"	10	Robert s. James & Anne Allen, Failsworth, 19 wks
"	12	Mary w. Michael Leary, Manchester, 23 y
"	13	Thomas s. Edmund & Alice Walmsley, Failsworth, 19 y
"	17	John Crossley, Bradford, 74 y
"	17	George Jandrill, Newton, 28 y
"	17	Edwin s. Anthony & Mary Lane, Manchester, 3 days
"	21	Dorothy wdw. John Mitchel, Manchester, 79 y
"	24	Peggy wdw. Joseph Smith, Newton, 78 y
"	24	Thomas Taylor, Manchester, 38 y
"	27	John s. John & Anne Hesford, Manchester, 10 wks
"	28	Anne d. Thomas & Sarah Travis, Failsworth, 8 m
"	29	Elizabeth Maskiter, Blackley, 54 y
May	2	Mary w. Thomas Cannon, Manchester, 47 y
"	5	Margaret d. James & Jane Holland, Manchester, 13 m

"	6	Elizabeth w. David Whittaker, Newton, 33 y	*(1825)*
"	10	Mary d. Mary Berry, Failsworth, 9 m	
"	11	Revd. Joseph Charles Frederick Whitehead, Preston, 42 y	
"	15	William Worral, Failsworth, 56 y	
"	25	William Jackson, Newton, 76 y	
"	26	Thomas s. Thomas & Betty Coupe, Droylsden, 7 m	
"	26	John s. Charles & Anne Syddal, Manchester, 11 m	
"	27	George s. John & Esther Butterworth, Staleywood, 2 m	
"	28	Jane w. Benjamin Butterworth, Blackley, 82 y	
"	29	Mary w. William Partington, Manchester, 27 y (*a cross appears in the margin against this entry in the PR*)	
"	30	Elizabeth d. George & Anne Syddal, Manchester, 11 m	
Jun	6	James s. Thomas & Ann Moss, Manchester, 9 m	
"	7	Robert s. Anne Hulton, Failsworth, 5 y	
"	14	John s. Samuel & Martha Johnson, Manchester, 30 y	
"	14	Robert s. James & Mary Burton, Newton, 1 y 9 m	
"	15	Susanna d. John & Elizabeth Howles, Newton, 7 m	
"	16	Betty w. Thomas (James *struck through*) [Thomas] Walsh, Newton, 50 y	
"	20	Margaret d. James & Sarah Dunstan, Manchester, 11 m	
"	22	John Shepley, Newton, 25 y	
"	22	John Pollitt, Newton, 70 y	
"	22	William s. James & Sarah Houlton, Newton, 19 days	
"	29	John Walmsley, Newton, 67 y	
"	30	Edward s. Edward & Jane Tipton, Droylsden, one y	
Jul	3	Hannah d. Joseph & Mary Butterworth, Manchester, 14 m	
"	3	Joel s. William & Hannah Hulme, Newton, 2 y 2 days	
"	4	Thomas s. Thomas & Alice Rider, Medlock Vale, 5 wks	
"	6	Sarah d. William & Lucy Seel, Newton, 1 y 10 m	
"	13	Sarah d. Thomas & Elizabeth Jones, Harpurhey, 17 y	
"	17	Sarah d. Peter & Elizabeth Fletcher, Manchester, 19 m	
"	25	Mary w. John Lyon, Manchester, 57 y	
"	27	James s. Samuel & Mary Bradshaw, Droylsden, 11 wks	
"	27	William s. Francis Hooton, Droylsden, 12 y	
Aug	3	Esther Hyde, Gorton, 26 y	
"	3	Esther d. James & Mary Dyson, Newton, 17 m	
"	9	Edmund Lee s. Thomas & Elizabeth Walker, Manchester, 3 wks	
"	17	William Lane, Manchester, 55 y	
"	21	James Walkden, Manchester, 50 y	
"	23	Celia d. John & Betty Clayton, Manchester, 9 wks	
"	24	Mark s. Edmund & Martha Buckley, Manchester, 10 wks	
"	29	James s. George & Harriet Gaskell, Newton, 6 m	
"	31	Sarah Anne d. Marianne Kershaw, Newton, 3 m	
Sep	1	William s. Ashton & Esther Boardman, Manchester, 18 m	
"	4	Jane d. James & Elizabeth Bamford, Newton, 9 wks	
"	7	Eliza d. William & Sarah Thorley, Manchester, 6 y	

"	8	John Schofield, Failsworth, 48 y
"	11	James Mills, Newton, 67 y
"	11	Mary d. Joseph & Anne Whitehead, Failsworth, 18 m
"	11	Joseph Grimshaw, Newton, 89 y
"	13	Robert s. Obadiah & Alice Bradshaw, Manchester, 6 m
"	13	Anne wdw. William Moores, Collyhurst, 81 y
"	13	Hannah w. William Hulme, Newton, 24 y
"	15	Richard s. William & Esther Whitehead, Failsworth, 1 y 7 m
"	16	James s. Richard & Susanna Thomas, Manchester, 3 y 3 m
"	18	James s. John & Nancy Broughton, Manchester, 1 y 10 m
"	18	Margaret d. Thomas & Mary Ogden, Manchester, 16 m
"	18	Jane d. Austin & Mary Chadwick, Manchester, 4 m
"	22	John s. John & Nanny Gradwell, Newton, 6 m
"	25	John Haines, Manchester, 48 y
"	25	Thomas s. Joseph & Maria Arrandale, Droylsden, 5 m
Oct	3	James s. Robert Walmsley, Manchester, 1 y 4 m
"	4	William Syddal, Manchester, 28 y
"	6	Benjamin Butterworth, Newton, 61 y
"	6	Alice d. Joshua & Alice Wyatt, Newton, 27 y
"	6	James Lomax, Manchester, 51 y
"	9	Alice d. Robert & Anne Ridings, Failsworth, 6 wks
"	11	James s. David & Elizabeth Whittaker, Newton, 8 m
"	13	William s. Thomas & Sarah Ogden, Newton, 13 m
"	16	John s. Samuel & Mary Lord, Failsworth, 7 m
"	16	Eliza d. Thomas & Ellen Greenhalgh, Newton, 6 m
"	19	Edmund s. Joseph & Anne Etchels, Hollinwood, 9 m
"	25	Oswald s. Adam & Anne Shore, Salford, 14 y
Nov	1	Elizabeth d. William & Sarah Sudworth, Manchester, 14 m
"	2	John Knight, Manchester, 65 y
"	2	Mary Anne d. Mary Goodier, Chadderton, 1 y 10 m
"	6	Mary d. James & Jane Brough, Manchester, 18 m
"	6	James s. Thomas & Ellen Greenhalgh, Newton, 16 y
"	13	Elizabeth d. Richard & Elizabeth Bee, Manchester, 7 days
"	15	Anne wdw. Richard Wood, Manchester, 72 y
"	15	Mary wdw. John Wilshaw, Manchester, 66 y
"	16	Hannah d. Edward & Hannah Radcliffe, Manchester, 10 wks
"	17	Alice d. Jane Valentine, Manchester, 18 m
"	17	Sarah w. Thomas Ogden, Newton, 25 y
"	20	Margaret d. Elijah & Anne Ashley, Manchester, 19 y
"	20	Mary wdw. Samuel Ogden, Moston, 90 y
"	27	Alice wdw. Edward Fairfield, Droylsden, 65 y
Dec	4	John Clough, Failsworth, 74 y
"	9	Matthew Walmsley, Manchester, 55 y
"	10	A Person drowned in the Canal from Littleborough, Littleborough near Rochdale

"   14   Edward s. John & Sarah Roberts, Newton, 7 m
"   15   Joseph Walker, Droylsden, 60 y
"   20   Betty wdw. Thomas Tetlow, Newton, 60 y
"   27   Anne d. Robert & Elizabeth Whitehead, Failsworth, 24 y
"   28   William Turvin, Newton, 29 y
[T. Gaskell, Incumbent of Newton   ]
[Attested by Jas Hough Chapelwarden   ]

1826
[Register of Baptisms & Burials at Newton in the Parish of Manchester for the Year
1826. Missent & lately recovered.]

Jan   1   Mary Johnson, Manchester, 27 y
"   3   Luke s. John & Sarah Harrison, Newton, 17 y
"   2   Robert s. Joseph & Mary Davies, Newton, 7 days
"   4   John & Mary twin children of John & Mary Schofield, 14 days
"   8   George s. George & Mary Ramscar, Manchester, 10 wks
"   11   Philip Walker, Failsworth, 80 y
"   13   Joseph Moores s. James & Phoebe Hulme, Newton, 20 y
"   15   Mary Lees, Manchester, 58 y
"   18   Sarah d. John & Sarah Moores, Salford, 25 y
"   22   George s. John & Grace Bradshaw, Manchester, 2 y
"   22   Martha d. William & Anne Booth, Manchester, 11 m
"   23   John s. Michael & Mary Hubbert, Manchester, 4 y 8 m
"   24   Jane d. Samuel & Sarah Oakesley, Droylsden, 2 m
"   24   Frances d. Susan Mills, Medlock Vale, 10 m
"   24   Hannah w. John Ridings, Failsworth, 61 y
"   25   Thomas s. William & Deborah Davies, Medlock Vale, 3 wks
"   26   Richard Andrew, Manchester, 57 y
"   29   John Rogers, Newton, 80 y
"   30   John s. William & Martha Scott, Newton, 16 m
"   31   Robert s. Betty Barlow, Failsworth, 4 days
Feb   2   Mary d. Dan & Hannah Hulton, Newton, 12 y
"   3   Benjamin Lake, Stockport, 41 y
"   5   Joseph s. Thomas & Ellen Caldwell, Newton, 3 y
"   5   James Gradwell, Newton, 37 y
"   7   Joseph Taylor, Failsworth, 80 y
"   7   Rachel d. John & Hannah Gough, Duckenfield, 9 m
"   8   Jane w. John Schofield, Manchester, 62 y
"   9   Amy wdw. Andrew Berry, Manchester, 56 y
"   12   Thomas s. Sarah Travis, Failsworth, 2 wks
"   12   William s. James & Betty Leatherbarrow, Newton, 6 wks
"   20   Thomas Southwell s. Henry Joseph & Martha Saul, Manchester, 7 m
"   21   Hannah w. William Booth, Chadderton, 28 y
"   26   Thomas Stafford, Droylsden, 64 y

| " | 26 | William s. Benjamin & Jane Howarth, Droylsden, 1 y 7 m | (1826) |

"   26   William s. Benjamin & Jane Howarth, Droylsden, 1 y 7 m   (*1826*)
"   27   John s. James & Hannah Berry, Failsworth, 10 y
Mar   4   William s. Nicholas & Margaret Edge, Failsworth, 2 wks
"   5   Margaret wdw. John Hoyle, Manchester, 72 y
"   5   William s. John & Hannah Horrocks, Newton, 13 days
"   8   Edward s. Joseph & Mary Tetlow, Manchester, 1 y 7 m
"   8   Margaret wdw. John Holt, Failsworth, 70 y
"   8   William s. John & Eliza Billington, Manchester, 7 m
"   8   Mary wdw. Robert Westwick, Manchester, 42 y
"   12   Robert s. Edward & Betty Wyld, Manchester, 2 y 6 m
"   12   John Stansfield, Manchester, 75 y
"   12   Betty d. Nathaniel & Betty Taylor, Failsworth, 19 m
"   14   Selina d. James & Sarah Tweedale, Newton, 14 m
"   15   John s. Joseph & Maria Ogden, Salford, 17 y
"   17   Peter Joseph Buxton, Manchester, 28 y
"   19   Sarah d. Samuel & Mary Walker, Manchester, 13 m
"   19   Philip Smith, Failsworth, 70 y
"   26   Thomas s. John & Phoebe Taylor, Newton, 22 y
"   26   Lydia d. John & Mary Hoyle, Manchester, 9 wks
"   26   Matty d. James & Betty Ogden, Failsworth, 9 days
"   28   James Philips, Manchester, 22 y
"   30   Susan w. James Mills, Medlock Vale, 71 y
Apr   2   Sarah wdw. Thomas Barlow, Newton, 85 y
"   4   Martha d. Thomas & Mary Hudson, Manchester, 4 y
"   4   Richard s. Richard & Sarah Rogers, Newton, one y 10 m
"   5   Robert s. James & Alice Mills, Medlock Vale, 10 m
"   5   Betty wdw. John Porter, Bradford, 74 y
"   8   Elizabeth d. Ralph & Betty Gardner, Failsworth, one m
"   9   Anne d. Launcelot & Mary Hilton, Newton, 19 y
"   10   Martha w. Francis Brown, Failsworth, 47 y
"   11   John s. Margaret Turner, Manchester, 8 m
"   11   George Blackmore, Openshaw, 28 y
"   12   Ellen d. James & Sarah Whittaker, Failsworth, 4 y
"   13   Samuel Tonge, Manchester, 73 y
"   16   William Hibbert, Newton, 54 y
"   16   Mary d. Samuel & Susanna Bagnal, Newton, 5 y
"   16   Robert s. Samuel & Susanna Bagnal, Newton, 7 m
"   21   William s. David & Anne Clarke, Manchester, 2 y 8 m
"   23   Jane wdw. Abram Pollitt, Failsworth, 78 y
"   23   William s. William & Hannah Winn, Manchester, 5 y 9 m
"   26   Frederick s. Edward & Marianne Fisher, Manchester, 2 y 9 m
"   30   Martha wdw. John Walmsley, Newton, 65 y
"   30   Henry s. David & Anne Ogden, Newton, 10 m
"   30   Margaret d. Anne Whitehead, Manchester, 7 m
May   3   Robert Hulton, Failsworth, 70 y

"	4	Charlotte d. Joseph & Sarah Swift, Manchester, 3 y *(1826)*
"	10	Maria d. Mary Worthington, Newton, 14 y
"	14	Elizabeth d. Richard & Margaret Burgess, Manchester, 17 m
"	15	Anne w. Richard Wardleworth, 21 y
"	16	Mary w. George Wolstenholme, Newton, 43 y
"	21	Mary d. Thomas & Nancy Ridings, Failsworth, 15 m
"	22	William s. Lee & Mary Foden, Newton, 6 y 8 m
"	22	Elizabeth w. Aaron Pearson, Manchester, 75 y
"	24	Mary d. Joseph & Mary Kailey, Manchester, 3 y
"	26	Elizabeth d. Richard & Mary Whitehead, Manchester, 2 y 4 m
"	28	Anne d. John & Anne Brown, Manchester, 21 y
"	28	Jane d. Sarah Robinson, Newton, 10 wks
"	30	Charles s. George & Anne Syddal, Manchester, 3 wks
"	30	Emanuel s. Jonathan & Mary Hooley, Newton, 10 y
Jun	1	Joseph s. Dan & Hannah Hulton, Newton, 19 y
"	1	Hannah w. John Benson, Manchester, 42 y
"	4	Charlotte w. James Dukes, Droylsden, 26 y
"	4	Samuel s. Richard & Alice Evans, Manchester, 18 m
"	9	Thomas s. Phoebe Whitehead, Failsworth, 8 y
"	12	Jonathan Leech, Newton, 49 y
"	12	Betty d. Betty Wolstenholme, Newton, 2 y
"	14	Anne w. William Lees, Manchester, 43 y
"	18	David s. David & Elizabeth Horrocks, Manchester, 13 m
"	21	Anne w. Thomas Wilson, Chadderton, 28 y
"	27	Joseph Schofield, Failsworth, 84 y
"	27	James s. David & Sarah Taylor, Failsworth, 14 days
"	27	John s. Mary Butterworth, Newton, 3 y
"	28	John Beever s. James & Harriet Pownal, Manchester, 7 m
Jul	2	Edmund Travis, Pendleton, 80 y
"	3	Frederick s. James & Anne Taylor, Newton, 1 y
"	3	Thomas s. William & Mary Entwisle, Manchester, 14 m
"	7	Samuel Ogden, Droylsden, 24 y
"	9	Samuel s. James & Anne Clough, Newton, 6 m
"	10	Sarah d. William & Alice Thorpe, Failsworth, 2 y 6 m
"	10	Joseph s. Sarah Wolstenholme, Newton, 2 y
"	18	Mary w. William Brown, Failsworth, 21 y
"	20	Anne w. James Clough, Newton, 26 y
"	23	Phillis d. Samuel & Olive Wilson, Newton, 20 m
"	23	Marianne d. James & Elizabeth Bamford, Newton, 4 y 3 m
"	23	John Whittaker, Failsworth, 48 y
"	26	Henry s. John & Alice Pilkington, Failsworth, one y
"	30	Sarah d. William & Anne Ward, Collyhurst, 11 m
Aug	1	Reuben s. Abraham & Mary Horrocks, Newton, 1 y
"	3	Samuel Heath, Newton, 37 y
"	4	Robert Abrahams, Manchester, 52 y

"	6	James Smith, Newton, 44 y
"	7	Mary d. Thomas & Mary Bagnal, Manchester, 13 wks
"	10	Isaac s. Samuel & Catherine Taylor, Manchester, two m
"	10	Elizabeth w. James Wilson, Newton, 45 y
"	10	Nathan Hibbert, Failsworth, 75 y
"	13	Jane d. Thomas & Elizabeth Hadfield, Newton, 9 days
"	20	William s. John & Sarah Gaskell, Manchester, 10 days
"	23	Edward Leech, Manchester, 41 y
"	25	James Etchels, Failsworth, 85 y
"	27	Mary d. John & Ellen Taylor, Failsworth, one y
"	28	John s. Martha Lancashire, Newton, 5 y
"	30	Thomas s. Septimus & Mary Hibbert, Manchester, one wk
"	31	John Whitehead, Droylsden, 55 y
"	31	James s. Thomas & Betty Littlefore, Manchester, 15 y
Sep	3	Jane w. Henry Singleton, Manchester, 53 y
"	8	Henry Wilkinson, Droylsden, 29 y
"	10	Jane w. Christopher Ratcliff, Newton, 52 y
"	12	Sarah d. John & Sarah Mason, Droylsden, 21 y
"	13	Thomas s. William & Harriet Cooper, Failsworth, 4 m
"	13	Joseph s. Thomas & Hannah Taylor, Newton, one y
"	15	Catherine w. Joseph Fletcher, Newton, 37 y
"	17	Samuel s. Thomas & Margaret Hill, Manchester, 16 y
"	20	John s. John & Sarah Marsden, Newton, 19 m
"	21	John s. John & Sarah Bowker, Manchester, 10 days
"	21	Phoebe w. James Smethurst, Failsworth, 54 y
"	24	James Ogden, Newton, 72 y
"	24	William s. George & Elizabeth Brookes, Newton, 6 days
"	24	Marianne d. John & Anne Stott, Manchester, 13 m
"	27	Elizabeth d. David & Jane Burton, Manchester, 3 m
"	29	Anne w. Patrick Sloan, Manchester, 60 y
"	29	Isaac s. Richard & Martha Lees, Stayley Bridge, 9 m
Oct	8	John s. James & Jane Schofield, Manchester, 2 y 4 m
"	12	Patrick Sloan, Manchester, 54 y
"	12	John Barns, Ardwick, 78 y
"	15	Robert Bolton, Manchester, 73 y
"	15	Samuel Travis, Newton, 31 y
"	17	Martha w. Charles Ellison, Manchester, 57 y
"	18	Peter Thorpe, Moston, 26 y
"	20	John Lees, Manchester, 43 y
"	22	Hannah w. Cornelius Lomas, Manchester, 21 y
"	22	Ralph Mather, Droylsden, 55 y
"	22	Jane d. James & Jane Townley, Manchester, 6 m
"	23	Jane w. William Robinson, Failsworth, 19 y
"	24	Martha wdw. William Roberts, Newton, 94 y
"	25	Anne d. Robert & Mary Grimshaw, Manchester, 5 y

	25	Samuel Gudgeon, Newton, 26 y
"	29	James s. William & Hannah Drinkwater, Newton, 5 m
Nov	2	Mary d. Samuel & Mary Holland, Harpurhey, 10 m
"	5	William s. James & Anne Taylor, Failsworth, 7 m
"	7	William Counsel, Manchester, 63 y
"	8	James Fiddeham, Manchester, 87 y
"	9	Samuel s. George & Hannah Heath, Salford, 9 m
"	9	John s. William & Ruth Anderson, Manchester, 9 m
"	12	William s. Thomas & Anne Potter, Newton, 14 m
"	22	Jane d. Samuel & Anne Benyon, Manchester, 2 y 6 m
"	23	Margaret d. John & Sarah Partington, Manchester, 5 y 11 m
"	24	Mary w. Thomas Bagnal, Manchester, 39 y
"	26	Hannah d. Joseph & Anne Rayner, Manchester, 9 m
"	28	Mary w. John Thorley, Failsworth, 45 y
"	30	James Ogden, Openshaw, 88 y
"	30	William s. Thomas & Sarah Bruce, Manchester, 2 y 8 m
Dec	1	Mary w. Thomas James, Droylsden, 72 y
"	3	Maria d. Edward & Hannah Radcliffe, Manchester, 5 wks
"	5	Margaret d. Thomas & Sarah Ratcliff, Denton, 6 m
"	7	Amelia w. Thomas Heald, Failsworth, 45 y
"	7	Anne wdw. Henry Booth, Failsworth, 61 y
"	8	Mary w. John Wolstencroft, Manchester, 53 y
"	9	Joseph s. John & Anne Holt, Failsworth, 6 m
"	10	William s. John & Anne Grindrod, Manchester, 5 m
"	11	Elizabeth w. John Wilson, Manchester, 36 y
"	13	Elizabeth w. George Ripley, Collyhurst, 63 y
"	14	Caroline d. George & Ellen Bruce, Manchester, 10 wks
"	17	Thomas Ankiers, Failsworth, 53 y
"	17	Charlotte d. John & Margaret Turner, Newton, 5 y
"	17	John s. John & Anne Halliwell, Manchester, 4 m
"	19	Charles Syddal, Manchester, 80 y
"	20	Jane d. John & Phoebe Anderson, Manchester, 22 y
"	20	John Clough, Ashton Parish, 83 y
"	22	James Kenyon, Failsworth, 81 y
"	24	Esther d. Robert & Elizabeth Whitehead, Failsworth, 22 y
"	27	Thomas s. William & Betty Sutcliff, Newton, one y 10 m
"	29	Luke Cordwell, Manchester, 46 y
"	31	Ellen d. James & Ellen Travis, Manchester, 8 m

1827

Jan	2	Jane w. Alexander Cairns, Newton, 46 y
"	4	Anne d. Thomas & Jane Yates, Newton, 11 y
"	7	Sarah d. Edward & Mary Hill, Manchester, 10 y
"	7	Andrew s. James & Anne Barnes, Newton, 1 y 9 m

"	8	Hannah Kemp, Newton, 81 y	*(1827)*
"	9	Thomas s. James & Betty Moston, Moston, 17 wks	
"	9	Henry s. John & Frances Holt, Newton, 11 y	
"	17	Robert s. Thomas & Jane Horne, Droylsden, 2 y	
"	18	Rachel wdw. William Taylor, Newton, 65 y	
"	19	Anne wdw. Joseph Timperley, Failsworth, 77 y	
"	21	Charlotte d. Joseph & Sarah Swift, Newton, 7 m	
"	21	William s. William & Mary Greenhalgh, Failsworth, 7 m	
"	22	Nancy d. James & Hagar Radcliffe, Droylsden, 10 m	
"	23	Sarah d. Richard & Hannah Hulme, Droylsden, 6 y	
"	23	John s. Thomas & Sarah Ratcliff, Droylsden, 2 y 6 m	
"	24	Anthony s. John & Margaret Ward, Manchester, 17 y	
"	28	Mary wdw. William Hulme, Manchester, 62 y	
"	28	Anne d. William & Sarah Gorton, Manchester, 6 y	
"	28	Henry s. John & Prudence Hughes, Newton, 2 y	
"	28	George s. Joshua & Sarah Swift, Ratliff, 6 y	
"	28	Abraham s. Abraham & Martha Whitehead, Chadderton, 4 y	
"	31	Michael Smith, Manchester, 70 y	
Feb	1	Elizabeth d. John & Martha Turvin, Hollinwood, 1 y 9 m	
"	4	Alice wdw. Daniel Haywood, Manchester, 83 y	
"	4	Jonas s. Joseph & Sarah Greenwood, Droylsden, 2 y 8 m	
"	7	Robert s. John & Betty Clayton, Duckinfield, 3 wks	
"	11	Martha wdw. James Shaw, Newton, 70 y	
"	14	Margaret w. William Stocks, Newton, 27 y	
"	21	Rosetta d. John & Alice Ridings, Newton, 2 y 6 m	
"	21	Martha w. Thomas Lancashire, Moston, 68 y	
"	25	William s. John & Jane Farral, Salford, 21 y	
"	27	Ellen w. William Spencer, Manchester, 75 y	
"	27	John s. William & Jane Robinson, Failsworth, 5 m	
Mar	4	Hannah w. Joseph Thornley, Failsworth, 36 y	
"	4	Mary w. Charles Coyle, Manchester, 32 y	
"	6	Thomas Charlesworth, Manchester, 42 y	
"	11	Rachel d. Charles & Mary Watson, Sale Cheshire, 21 y	
"	11	Samuel Bradshaw, Newton, 38 y	
"	13	Peter s. John & Betty Abbot, Newton, 11 m	
"	15	William Smith, Failsworth, 30 y	
"	18	Thomas Sim[m], Failsworth, 73 y	
"	25	James Mills, Medlock Vale, 70 y	
"	25	Anthony s. Thomas & Elizabeth Fleming, Manchester, 8 m	
"	25	Mary w. Richard Whitehead, Manchester, 22 y	
"	28	John s. Charles & Mary Hulton, Manchester, 1 y 8 m	
Apr	3	John s. Richard & Mary Whitehead, Manchester, one m	
"	4	James s. John & Anne Broughton, Manchester, 9 m	
"	4	William Grimshaw, Manchester, 67 y	
"	4	Betty w. George Hardy, Failsworth, 58 y	

"	10	John Pollitt, Newton, 29 y	*(1827)*
"	11	Ellen d. Samuel & Betty Hardman, Newton, 11 m	
"	11	Mary w. John Thornley, Failsworth, 31 y	
"	13	Mary w. Samuel Wardley, Manchester, 34 y	
"	15	Charity wdw. Edmund Priest, Manchester, 73 y	
"	17	Joseph s. William & Alice Crompton, Manchester, 18 m	
"	17	Sarah wdw. Robert Chadderton, Newton, 79 y	
"	18	Alice w. James Turner, Newton, 35 y	
"	18	Philip Newham, Manchester, 39 y	
"	18	Joseph s. Joseph & Betty Mills, Failsworth, 15 wks	
"	18	Samuel Lees, Failsworth, (*age blank in PR & BT*)	
"	22	Thomas s. James & Hannah Sykes, Manchester, 9 m	
"	22	Joseph s. Joseph & Anne Etchels, Hollinwood, 4 y	
"	25	Anne d. Edward & Jane Tipton, Droylsden, 7 m	
"	27	James Shepley, Newton, 34 y	
May	1	Hannah w. Andrew Clegg, Failsworth, 48 y	
"	2	Hannah d. Charlotte Eastwood, Manchester, (*age blank in PR & BT*)	
"	2	Joseph s. Richard & Mary York, Manchester, 3 y 4 m	
"	2	Betty d. David & Betty Booth, Chadderton, 11 m	
"	3	James s. John & Mary Whitehead, Failsworth, 2 y	
"	6	Martha d. Charles & Ellen Brown, Manchester, 6 m	
"	8	James Cooke, Failsworth, 41 y	
"	9	Richard Stansfield, Newton, 92 y	
"	13	James Leigh, Manchester, 30 y	
"	13	Elizabeth Dawson, Droylsden, 37 y	
"	14	John s. John & Elizabeth Taylor, Failsworth, 1 y 8 m	
"	15	Ruth w. George Higson, Newton, 30 y	
"	15	Marianne d. John & Alice Chadwick, Newton, 16 m	
"	16	Sarah Anne d. Joseph & Sarah Kenyon, Newton, 7 wks	
"	20	Marianne d. Matthew & Mary Eaton, Manchester, 6 y	
"	20	Thomas s. Robert & Alice Duncuft, Manchester, 6 wks	
"	20	Jane w. Andrew Diamond, Manchester, 35 y	
"	21	George Etchels, Newton, 55 y	
"	21	George Senior, Manchester, 46 y	
"	22	Elizabeth Whittaker, Newton, 43 y	
"	24	Elijah s. William & Elizabeth Livesey, Manchester, 4 m	
"	24	Frederick s. Samuel & Mary Leech, Manchester, 10 y	
"	24	Sarah Ann d. Isaac & Mary Whitehead, Manchester, 3 m	
"	24	Samuel Hardy, Manchester, 22 y	
"	25	Benjamin s. William & Mary Howarth, Newton, 5 y	
"	27	Jane d. Joseph & Martha Walmsley, Failsworth, 2 y	
"	27	William Simister, Failsworth, 85 y	
"	27	Anne Barlow, Woodhouses, 53 y	
"	28	Robert Hall, Newton, 64 y	
Jun	3	Mary d. Charles & Alice Brown, Manchester, 11 days	

"	3	Hannah d. William & Sarah Pollitt, Failsworth, 1 y 11 m	*(1827)*
"	6	Anne d. James & Anne Howarth, Newton, 8 m	
"	7	Thomas Blackshaw, Failsworth, 75 y	
"	8	Mary wdw. Edmund Hilton, Failsworth, 70 y	
"	10	John Chadwick, Manchester, 78 y	
"	11	Job Tetlow, Oldham, 34 y	
"	17	Ellen d. James & Anne Howarth, Newton, 8 m	
"	17	Anne wdw. James Bamford, Manchester, 94 y	
"	19	Hannah d. John & Anne Hilton, Failsworth, one y 4 m	
"	20	William s. William & Sophia Lithgo, Manchester, one y 5 m	
"	21	Mary d. Betty Boardman, Newton, *(age blank in PR & BT)*	
"	23	Henry s. Willm. & Esther Grimshaw, Newton, 16 m	
"	24	Luke Sloan, Manchester, 66 y	
"	29	Robert s. James & Mary Hilton, Newton, 6 y	
"	29	Nancy d. Thomas & Nancy Johnson, Failsworth, 1 y 9 m	
Jul	1	Esther d. James & Phoebe Whitehead, Manchester, 5 y	
"	1	Joseph Sharpe, Moston, 72 y	
"	1	Alice d. Thomas & Alice Crossley, Moston, 43 y	
"	2	Joseph s. Sarah Knott, Failsworth, 17 y	
"	3	Robert s. Joseph & Hannah Williamson, Newton, 11 m	
"	3	Isabella w. Isaac Bradshaw, Failsworth, 34 y	
"	4	Mary wdw. William Adshead, Manchester, 70 y	
"	6	Jonathan s. James & Sarah Whittaker, Failsworth, 16 m	
"	10	Rebekah w. Matthew Shaw, Newton, 46 y	
"	18	Joseph s. George & Sarah Hulton, Newton, 6 y	
"	25	Anne d. Thomas & Sally Brundritt, Failsworth, 5 y	
"	25	Henry Whalley, Manchester, 69 y	
"	26	Mary d. Thomas & Ellen Greenhalgh, Newton, 6 m	
"	26	Daniel s. Daniel & Hannah Berrington, Newton, 2 y	
"	29	Job s. James & Jane Jackson, Manchester, 6 m	
"	30	William s. Elizabeth Mills, Newton, 1 y 6 m	
Aug	5	Jane d. Margaret Williams, Newton, 19 y	
"	7	William s. Harriet Parry, Manchester, 14 m	
"	9	Anne d. William & Sarah Barlow, Newton, 2 y	
"	13	Richard s. John & Martha Owen, Blackley, 6 wks	
"	13	Richard Pollitt, Newton, 66 y	
"	16	Rebecca wdw. Joseph Moores, Failsworth, 83 y	
"	19	Mary d. John & Jane Clough, Manchester, 1 y 7 m	
"	19	Mary w. William Bowker, Manchester, 31 y	
"	21	Mary d. Ellen Berry, Failsworth, 4 m	
"	22	Anne d. Samuel & Mary Etchels, Newton, 20 m	
"	28	William Mason, Manchester, 61 y	
Sep	2	Hannah w. James Ogden, Manchester, 23 y	
"	5	John s. Miles & Marianne Mason, Failsworth, 10 y	
"	10	Thomas Glynn, Newton, 17 y	

"	12	Jane d. Samuel & Sarah Anderson, Manchester, 3 m *(1827)*
"	16	Hannah d. John & Mary Tipton, Openshaw, 5 y
"	19	William s. Aaron & Ellen Syddal, Manchester, 18 m
"	19	Richard s. John & Mary Tipton, Openshaw, 2 y
"	21	Esther Hampson, Manchester, 21 y
"	23	John s. Jeremiah & Mary Weatherils, Manchester, one m
"	26	Elizabeth wdw. Daniel Knott, Failsworth, 81 y
"	27	Alice w. Thomas Massey, Newton, 48 y
"	29	John Matthews, Manchester, 55 y
Oct	1	Thomas s. John & Betty Robinson, Newton, 18 m
"	3	Alice d. Elijah & Mary Hardy, Manchester, 17 m
"	5	Samuel s. Ashton & Betty Ashton, Failsworth, 9 m
"	10	Ellen w. George Leigh, Manchester, 67 y
"	11	John s. Betty Bailey, Failsworth, 10 w
"	14	Anne d. David & Jane Wolstencroft, Manchester, 2 y 6 m
"	15	Grace wdw. John Bowler, Manchester, 79 y
"	17	Mary w. James Wardle, Hebden Bridge Yorkshire, 40 y
"	18	Anne w. John Wood, Failsworth, 28 y
"	19	Anne d. William & Nancy Whittaker, Newton, 15 y
"	22	Thomas s. Hamlet & Elizabeth Lowe, Newton, 11 m
"	28	Joshua Dunkerley, Hollinwood, 71 y
"	28	Esther w. Jonathan Schofield, Moston, 46 y
"	28	Thomas Turner, Newton, 23 y
"	31	Anne wdw. William Smethurst, Manchester, 57 y
Nov	1	John s. Reuben & Maria Heywood, Manchester, 4 y 5 m
"	1	Betty Goodier, Denton, 57 y
"	2	Mary d. Benjamin & Betty Lees, Failsworth, 18 m
"	2	John Hardinge, Newton, 79 y
"	4	Hannah d. Sarah Wyatt, Failsworth, 7 m
"	4	Nancy d. John & Mary Thornley, Denton, 7 m
"	7	Sarah w. John Hulme, Newton, 46 y
"	9	Hannah d. Andrew & Hannah Clegg, Failsworth, 16 y
"	11	Frances d. John & Mary Whitehead, Manchester, 23 y
"	14	David s. Thomas & Mary Goddard, Manchester, 3 m
"	15	James Barker, Manchester, 29 y
"	16	Mark s. William & Alice Tinker, Manchester, 13 m
"	18	Abraham s. Thomas & Anne Ogden, Manchester, 6 m
"	18	Joseph s. William & Elizabeth Livesey, Manchester, 2 y 7 m
"	18	Elizabeth d. Joseph & Frances Lane, Newton, 2 y
"	25	George s. William & Alice Walton, Newton, 21 m
"	29	John s. John & Anne Tennant, Newton, 3 y
Dec	2	Sarah d. Matthew & Sarah Brown, Newton, 11 y
"	3	Rachel d. Sarah Hooley, Woodhouses, *(age blank in PR & BT)*
"	3	Sarah Whittaker, Failsworth, 45 y
"	5	James Simister, Droylsden, 77 y

"	7	James s. John & Hannah Hilton, Failsworth, 1 day
"	9	Joseph s. John & Martha Higham, Newton, 7 m
"	9	Alice wdw. John Sephton, Manchester, 79 y
"	11	Joseph Wright, Newton, 54 y
"	16	Sarah wdw. James Tomlinson, Newton, 98 y
"	16	Alice d. Samuel & Mary Hoyle, Droylsden, 2 y
"	19	Sarah d. James & Jane Whitehead, Manchester, 11 wks
"	19	Susannah d. Robert & Frances Mills, Gorton, 25 y
"	23	Philip s. Robert & Sarah Whitehead, Newton, 8 wks
"	23	William Tomlinson, Moston, 73 y
"	23	John s. John & Sarah Wolstencroft, Manchester, 8 m
"	25	Marianne d. Edward & Elizabeth Hancock, Newton, 2 days
"	25	Sarah d. Mark & Millicent Gradwell, Manchester, one wk
"	25	Elizabeth w. William Williamson, Manchester, 62 y
"	25	Martha d. Thomas & Alice Smith, Manchester, 13 m
"	28	Nathaniel s. James & Sarah Dunstan, Manchester, 10 m
"	30	Betty w. Benjamin Lees, Failsworth, 23 y
"	30	Garratt Brown, Newton, 33 y
[		Thos Gaskell, Incumbent of Newton]

1828

Jan	1	Elizabeth d. Robert & Anne Howard, Newton, 3 y nine m
"	2	Andrew s. Anthony & Mary Lane, Manchester, 6 y
"	2	Anne d. John & Martha Hartley, Manchester, 3 wks
"	4	Elizabeth d. Peter & Margaret Later, Newton, 13 wks
"	6	Thomas s. William & Elizabeth Johnson, Manchester, 3 y 3 m
"	7	Sarah wdw. Charles Hooley, Ashton Parish, 23 y
"	8	John Nuttal, Hadfield Glossop Parish, 38 y
"	8	Shadrack s. James & Mary Kenyon, Openshaw, 4 y
"	9	John s. John & Jane Blackshaw, Newton, 12 y
"	13	Anne d. Thomas & Mary Whitehead, Manchester, 1 y 7 m
"	13	Isaac s. John & Anne Wilkinson, Newton, 19 m
"	13	Robert s. Robert & Sarah Wyld, Manchester, 5 y 6 m
"	15	Sarah d. Thomas & Margaret Horrocks, Failsworth, 5 y
"	15	Thomas s. Thomas & Margaret Horrocks, Failsworth, one y
"	16	John s. William & Elizabeth Johnson, Manchester, 9 m
"	20	Samuel Goodier, Newton, 79 y
"	20	Thomas Barlow, Failsworth, 61 y
"	23	Elizabeth d. John & Jenny Etchels, Newton, 16 y
"	25	Mary d. Charles & Ellen Brown, Manchester, 11 y
"	26	Thomas Taylor, Failsworth, 22 y
"	27	Margaret d. John & Frances Smith, Newton, 5 wks
"	30	Charles s. Jonathan & Rebekah Thomson, Manchester, 18 m
"	30	Elizabeth d. Richard & Sarah Rogers, Newton, 24 y

Feb	3	Sarah wdw. Jonathan Butterworth, Manchester, 69 y
"	3	James s. Joseph & Susan Hilton, Moston, 8 m
"	5	Richard s. William & Sarah Wolstencroft, Manchester, 2 y 10 m
"	6	Samuel Berry, Failswsorth, 52 y
"	10	James s. James & Ellen Higson, Manchester, 10 m
"	10	Hannah w. John Allen, Newton, 26 y
"	10	Hannah d. Henry & Mary Walton, Manchester, 17 wks
"	13	Anne d. Edward & Martha Allen, Failsworth, 8 m
"	16	Charles Stott, Droylsden, 82 y
"	14	Olive d. James & Mary Butterworth, Newton, 4 y
"	17	Amelia d. John & Alice Worsick, Failsworth, 14 m
"	17	Mary d. John & Mary Berry, Newton, 4 m
"	18	James & Rebekah s. & d. Ashton & Sarah Worral, Failsworth, 3 days
"	19	Mary w. Thomas Mons, Manchester, 55 y
"	22	Sarah w. John Gaskell, Manchester, 28 y
"	24	James s. James & Ellen Hulton, Failsworth, 8 m
"	26	Joseph Fletcher, Newton, 42 y
"	27	Marianne d. Daniel & Hannah Smethurst, Manchester, 1 y
"	28	Charlotte d. John & Hannah Barton, Newton, 15 y
Mar	2	Sarah d. Elizabeth Rogers, Newton, 8 m
"	2	Eliza d. John & Rebekah Chadwick, Manchester, 16 m
"	3	Emma d. John & Jane Blackshaw, Newton, 1 y 9 m
"	4	Anne d. John & Eliza Withnal, Manchester, 6 wks
"	5	Sarah w. James Goodier, Manchester, 35 y
"	7	Sarah w. John Pilling, Manchester, 21 y
"	9	Samuel Winstanley, Newton, 35 y
"	9	Joel s. Joseph & Mary Brown, Ashton Parish, 18 m
"	9	Samuel Procter, Manchester, 67 y
"	10	Hannah d. John & Elizabeth Smith, Newton, 3 y 6 m
"	11	Martha wdw. Thomas Blomiley, Manchester, 62 y
"	12	Dorothy wdw. Jeremiah Buxton, Manchester, 70 y
"	13	Joseph Lees, Chadderton, 79 y
"	13	Robert s. Robert & Bella Murphy, Newton, 1 y 9 m
"	16	Peter s. John & Margaret Jones, Moston, 6 wks
"	16	Charlotte wdw. John Stansfield, Manchester, 74 y
"	16	Elizabeth d. William & Mary Hulton, Failsworth, 1 y 9 m
"	19	Mary d. Catherine Hartley, Manchester, 18 m
"	19	Nancy w. James Ridings, Newton, 60 y
"	23	Anne d. Peter & Mary Done, Manchester, 13 m
"	23	James Thomas s. James & Anne Mills, Manchester, 8 m
"	24	Hannah d. Charles & Anne Winstanley, Manchester, 11 m
"	25	Thomas Lancashire, Moston, 69 y
"	25	Samuel s. Samuel & Anne Lowe, Manchester, 2 y 3 m
"	30	Lucy d. Richard & Nancy Naylor, Newton, 7 m
"	30	Mary d. Luke & Isabella Smith, Failsworth, 8 m

"	30	Mary d. Samuel & Anne Chadderton, Droylsden, 10 y	*(1828)*
Apr	2	Betty Smith, Failsworth, 44 y	
"	4	Nancy d. Henry & Mary Cowburn, Newton, 24 y	
"	6	John s. Thomas & Alice Smith, Manchester, 3 y 5 m	
"	9	James s. Esther Butterworth, Manchester, 20 m	
"	11	John Littlefair, Manchester, 19 y	
"	13	Sarah Anne d. John & Sarah Wolstencroft, Manchester, 3 y 3 m	
"	13	William s. Thos. & Mary Mayall, Ardwick, 3 m	
"	15	Joseph s. Robert & Alice Stansfield, Newton, 20 m	
"	15	Phoebe Maria d. John & Mary Gaskell, Newton, 2 m	
"	17	William s. Samuel & Elizabeth Moors, Manchester, 3 y 4 m	
"	20	Hannah d. James & Anne Livesey, Manchester, 4 y	
"	20	Nathan Ashley, Manchester, 60 y	
"	20	William Lithgoe, Manchester, 44 y	
"	20	Isaac s. John & Mary Tipton, Openshaw, 2 y	
"	21	Heber s. Heber & Elizabeth Whittingham, Manchester, 11 m	
"	24	James s. Joseph & Sarah Kenyon, Newton, 18 days	
"	27	Hannah d. Samuel & Elizabeth Moore, Manchester, 13 m	
"	27	John s. John & Elizabeth Barton, Manchester, 4 y	
"	30	John s. Nicholas & Margaret Edge, Failsworth, one y	
May	1	John s. John & Juliana Fairfield, Manchester, 20 y	
"	1	Margaret w. William Harrison, Manchester, 20 y	
"	4	Jane d. George & Hannah Heath, Salford, 3 m	
"	4	Elizabeth d. Samuel & Susanna Bagnal, Newton, one y	
"	4	George s. Samuel & Mary Holland, Harpurhey, 7 m	
"	6	Mary Booth, Failsworth, 41 y	
"	7	Betty wdw. John Mould, Newton, 72 y	
"	8	James s. George & Anne Grimshaw, Oldham, 11 m	
"	11	William s. Lucy Walker, Newton, 9 m	
"	11	Martha d. Jacob & Hannah Etchels, Newton, 28 y	
"	12	George s. James & Anne Livesey, Manchester, 9 m	
"	13	Frances wdw. John Porter, Bradford, 77 y	
"	13	Sarah wdw. Samuel Berry, Failsworth, 55 y	
"	14	James s. Matthew & Harriet Broadbent, Failsworth, 8 days	
"	14	John Bentley, Newton, 22 y	
"	15	James s. James & Elizabeth Jackson, Manchester, one y 11 m	
"	15	Anne d. Robert & Betty Taylor, Failsworth, 11 m	
"	16	Lydia Seddon d. Thomas & Jane Wylde, Newton, 19 m	
"	18	John s. John & Rachel Wylde, Manchester, 2 y 10 m	
"	18	Sarah d. Robert & Alice Duncuft, Manchester, 3 wks	
"	25	George s. Charles & Margaret Lee, Manchester, 3 wks	
"	25	Rebekah wdw. John Hawthornthwaile, Manchester, 62 y	
"	25	Joel s. Thomas & Alice Brown, Hollinwood, 6 m	
"	27	Randle Alcock, Cheadle, 77 y	
"	29	Joel s. William & Sarah Prescott, Newton, 11 wks	

"	30	George s. Samuel & Anne Lowe, Manchester, 4 y 5 m *(1828)*
Jun	1	Anne d. Alice Robinson, Manchester, 3 y
"	6	Anne w. John Whitehead, Failsworth, 23 y
"	12	Mary Marsh, Newton, 25 y
"	15	Anne w. Thomas Fletcher, Newton, 57 y
"	15	Hannah w. Samuel Hulme, Manchester, 67 y
"	17	Elizabeth d. James & Isabel Lomas, Newton, 10 wks
"	17	Susanna d. James & Hannah Stansfield, Manchester, 9 m
"	20	Hannah d. John & Alice Howarth, Droylsden, 4 days
"	22	Alice d. John & Elizabeth Whitehead, Manchester, 1 y 8 m
"	23	Joseph s. William & Sarah Shelmerdine, Newton, 5 y
"	25	William s. William & Mary Wood, Droylsden, 12 y
Jul	3	Emma d. Charles & Grace Sedgewell, Manchester, 15 days
"	13	Edward s. Edward & Jane Leech, Manchester, 3 y
"	15	Sarah d. Edmund & Sarah Walmsley, Failsworth, one day
"	20	Matthew s. Matthew & Mary Marrs, Manchester, 14 y
"	20	William s. William & Maria Eastwood, Newton, 9 wks
"	21	Mary w. Daniel Bent, Manchester, 29 y
"	27	Betty wdw. William Clough, Newton, 89 y
"	29	Thomas Brundritt, Failsworth, 35 y
"	31	Launcelot Hilton, Newton, 47 y
Aug	1	Edward s. Charles & Mary Gardner, Manchester, 3 wks
"	1	Thomas s. John & Mary Hartley, Manchester, 1 y 10 m
"	8	William s. George & Martha Leigh, Manchester, 10 m
"	8	John s. Thomas & Frances Hepworth, Manchester, 3 y
"	8	Elizabeth d. Robert & Susanna Marsden, Newton, one m
"	17	Hannah d. Thomas & Elizabeth Walton, Manchester, 6 m
"	17	Thomas Jemison, Manchester, 24 y
"	21	Hannah d. Elijah & Mary Hardy, Manchester, 8 y 4 m
"	22	John Schofield, Manchester, 77 y
"	31	John s. John & Hannah Davies, Manchester, one m
Sep	7	James s. Anne Hardy, Manchester, 11 m
"	14	Philip s. Anne Smith, Manchester, one y 5 m
"	14	Benjamin s. John & Alice Hulton, Failsworth, 34 y
"	15	Anne d. Benjamin & Mary Hulton, Failsworth, 11 m
"	21	John s. Anthony & Elizabeth Lane, Manchester, 16 m
"	21	Joseph s. William & Mary Entwisle, Manchester, 15 m *(see entry Sep 29)*
"	21	Henry Kearsley, Newton, 62 y
"	29	John s. William & Mary Entwisle, Manchester, 15 m
"	29	Samuel Johnson, Manchester, 65 y
Oct	3	Hannah d. Thomas & Sarah Dean, Newton, 5 m
"	5	James s. Charles & Elizabeth Morris, Droylsden, 6 wks
"	5	Samuel s. Josiah & Jane Garlick, Failsworth, 17 wks
"	6	James s. John & Anne Bailey, Manchester, 2 y
"	9	Charlotte w. Matthew Wolstenholme, Harpurhey, 19 y

"	14	Benjamin Heywood, Manchester, 53 y
"	16	Betty wdw. William Hibbert, Newton, 54 y
"	21	Maria Winstanley, Manchester, 28 y
"	21	Maria w. George Hall, Failsworth, 34 y
"	26	Alice d. John & Anne Hamer, Manchester, 3 y 5 m
"	28	James s. John & Anne Clough, Failsworth, 19 y
"	29	Joseph s. Isaac & Mary Whitehead, Manchester, 20 wks
"	29	Sarah d. Joshua & Alice Wyatt, Newton, 42 y
"	30	James s. William & Mary Whittaker, Manchester, 2 y
Nov	2	Eliza d. Thomas & Anne Brookes, Newton, 18 m
"	2	Mary w. James Etchels, Failsworth, 60 y
"	4	Thomas s. Robert & Sarah Lewis, Manchester, 4 m
"	6	Elizabeth w. Thomas Madders, Newton, 55 y
"	6	Robert s. John & Anne Berry, Newton, one y
"	16	Robert Wroe, Manchester, 43 y
"	16	Hannah d. John & Anne Wilshaw, Manchester, 2 y 10 m
"	16	Peter Kershaw, Manchester, 81 y
"	17	Anne w. James Livesey, Manchester, 43 y
"	19	Betty d. John & Sarah Harrison, Newton, 46 y
"	20	Mark s. Elizabeth Buckley, Manchester, 3 wks
"	23	Alice w. Richard Evans, Manchester, 21 y
"	25	Edward s. John & Sally Whitehead, Newton, 2 m
"	25	Samuel s. Abraham & Mary Moore, Failsworth, one day
"	26	Esther w. John Whitehead, Droylsden, 65 y
"	28	Margaret w. William Waters, Manchester, 30 y
"	29	Joseph Porter, Bradford, 40 y
"	30	John s. John & Mary Rogers, Newton, 4 m
"	30	James s. Thomas & Jane Heywood, Newton, 10 m
Dec	3	Esther d. James & Sarah Houlton, Newton, 2 wks
"	7	Sarah wdw. John Ogden, Hollinwood, 76 y
"	14	Thomas s. James & Ruth Whitehead, Failsworth, 3 y
"	14	Joseph Allen, Manchester, 65 y
"	16	Margaret d. John & Betty Whitehead, Manchester, 4 y
"	17	Edwin s. Thomas & Esther Berry, Moston, 5 m
"	18	Esther Tomkinson, Failsworth, 39 y
"	21	John s. William & Lucy Seel, Newton, 11 m
"	21	Hannah w. Daniel Smethurst, Manchester, 25 y
"	22	Benjamin s. George & Anne Yates, Newton, 7 m
"	28	Nathan s. Leigh & Mary Foden, Newton, 1 y 9 m
"	30	Sarah d. Charles & Sarah Thomson, Manchester, 19 y

[Thos Gaskell   ]

1829

Jan	4	Sarah wdw. John Tomlinson, Manchester, 66 y
"	11	Robert s. Joseph & Betty Seel, Failsworth, 5 y 6 m
"	11	John s. James & Eliza Gradwell, Newton, 18 m
"	11	Maria d. Edward & Emma Ratliff, Manchester, 13 m
"	11	Joseph s. Hugh & Hannah Booth, Ashton Parish, 11 m
"	15	Betty wdw. Samuel Pendleton, Failsworth, 87 y
"	16	Thomas s. James & Sarah Greenwood, Manchester, 13 m
"	18	William s. William & Elizabeth Welsh, Newton, 7 m
"	18	Alice d. Samuel & Anne Hunston, Manchester, 1 y 11 m
"	20	Simeon s. George & Sarah Garlick, Hollinwood, 11 m
"	21	Moses s. Francis & Ellen Brown, Manchester, 15 y
"	25	Thomas Goodier, Failsworth, 88 y
"	27	Sarah w. William Lupton, Manchester, 64 y
"	27	James s. John & Hannah Allen, Failsworth, 17 m
"	29	Mary w. Jonathan Tong, Hollinwood, 77 y
"	29	John Twimlow, Newton, 32 y
"	30	William Hibbert, Failsworth, 73 y
Feb	2	William Tinker, Manchester, 37 y
"	3	Thomas s. Thomas & Sarah Handley, Manchester, 18 m
"	8	John s. Robert & Alice Stansfield, Newton, 7 y
"	8	Mary wdw. Charles Ashworth, Manchester, 89 y
"	8	John Harrison, Newton, 78 y
"	8	Thomas s. Robert & Alice Whitehead, Newton, 9 y
"	8	James s. John & Ellen Taylor, Failsworth, 5 y
"	9	Betty w. Thomas Hayes, Failsworth, 26 y
"	10	Marianne d. Thomas & Charlotte Hall, Newton, 4 wks
"	15	Elizabeth w. Edward Wyld, Manchester, 32 y
"	15	Mary d. John & Anne Hilton, Failsworth, 22 y
"	15	Stephen s. John & Betty Redfern, Newton, 5 m
"	15	Elijah s. John & Eliza Withnal, Manchester, 10 y
"	16	Jane d. Thomas & Sarah Bruce, Manchester, 2 y 8 m
"	18	Mary w. John Rogers, Newton, 25 y
"	18	John Syddal, Manchester, 59 y
"	22	Elizabeth d. Joseph & Ellen Clough, Manchester, 11 m
"	22	Anne d. John & Mary Blakeley, Newton, one y
"	24	John Butterworth, Manchester, 60 y
"	24	Richard s. Thomas & Mary Thorp, Failsworth, 26 y
"	25	Ruth d. John & Elizabeth Bramwell, Manchester, 20 y
"	27	Richard s. Samuel & Anne Dawson, Failsworth, 10 m
Mar	1	David s. James & Elizabeth Boardman, Manchester, 14 m
"	3	Susanna d. James & Sarah Mills, Ashton Parish, 3 days
"	4	John Hind, Manchester, 23 y
"	8	Mary d. George & Sarah Wyatt, Droylsden, 1 y 8 m

"	15	Joseph s. Thomas & Hannah Allen, Failsworth, one y *(1829)*
"	15	Andrew s. Samuel & Phoebe Travis, Newton, 18 wks
"	15	Sarah d. James & Sarah Swift, Manchester, 16 y
"	18	Hannah d. Joseph & Alice Whitehead, Failsworth, 14 wks
"	22	William s. John & Sarah Wood, Failsworth, 3 wks
"	29	Elizabeth d. Maria Riley, Failsworth, 5 m
"	29	John s. John & Mary Lindley, Newton, 3 y
"	29	Jane d. Thomas & Isabel Vaughan, Newton, one m
"	29	Mary d. James & Betty Barlow, Newton, 7 m
"	29	John Dimelo, Manchester, 44 y
"	31	James s. Joseph & Maria Arrandale, Droylsden, 10 days
"	31	Lydia wdw. John Bruce, Manchester, 80 y
Apr	5	Thomas s. Thomas & Betty Hodgson, Newton, 8 m
"	5	Samuel Bardsley, Failsworth, 8 m
"	5	Thomas s. John & Sarah Twimlow, Newton, 2 y 5 m
"	7	George s. John & Sarah Partington, Manchester, 7 m
"	12	Martha d. Anthony & Mary Lane, Manchester, 15 y
"	12	Betty wdw. Edmund Whitehead, Ashton Parish, 81 y
"	15	James Whitehead s. Isaac & Elizabeth Heapy, Droylsden, 4 m
"	17	Thomas s. Samuel & Mary Leech, Manchester, 10 y
"	19	John s. John & Nancy Holt, Bradford, one y
"	19	James s. Joseph & Alice Robinson, Failsworth, 3 wks
"	19	William s. Margaret Horrocks, Failsworth, 17 y
"	20	Anne d. Mary Dean, Gorton, 20 y
"	21	John s. Adam & Betty Doodson, Newton, 3 y
"	22	James Hough, Newton, 52 y
"	22	James s. James & Sarah Worral, Failsworth, 5 wks
"	23	Sarah d. Richard & Alice Evans, Manchester, 2 y 6 m
"	23	Anne d. Mary Whitehead, Failsworth, 4 m
"	27	James s. Thomas & Elizabeth Rogers, Openshaw, 2 y
"	28	Jane d. Richard & Elizabeth Richardson, Newton, 9 m
"	29	James s. William & Martha Ogilvie, Manchester, 4 y
May	1	Thomas s. Thomas & Mary Whittaker, Manchester, 8 m
"	3	Joseph Hibbert, Manchester, 26 y
"	3	Sarah w. Samuel Howard, Failsworth, 38 y
"	3	Margaret w. James Crossley, Harpurhey, 59 y
"	3	Susan d. Thomas & Anne Wilson, Moston, 3 y
"	5	William s. Thomas & Ellen Greenhalgh, Manchester, 6 m
"	7	William s. John & Mary Makin, Moston, 3 days
"	10	Abner s. Robert & Mary Keymer, Droylsden, 24 y
"	10	David s. William & Hannah Brindley, Newton, 7 wks
"	10	Margaret d. William & Margaret Harrison, Newton, 20 m
"	10	Thomas s. Charles & Alice Coyle, Manchester, 3 m
"	12	Sarah Anne d. John & Frances Tattersett, Manchester, 10 m
"	15	George s. George & Esther Wood, Newton, 5 days

"	17	Elizabeth w. Richard Hinks, Droylsden, 25 y	(*1829*)
"	19	Mary wdw. John Oaks, Manchester, 67 y	
"	20	Betty d. Nicholas & Jane Bentley, Newton, 19 y	
"	27	Martha d. Thomas & Nancy Ogden, Newton, 3 y	
"	27	Robert Smith, Newton, 44 y	
"	28	John Greenwood, Newton, 38 y	
"	31	George s. Richard & Jane Travis, Newton, 9 y	
Jun	3	Frederick James s. Marianne Loyd, Manchester, 9 m	
"	5	Marianne d. Sarah Taylor, Newton, 5 y	
"	9	Jane w. John Smith, Failsworth, 48 y	
"	10	Jenny d. Thomas & Alice Brown, Moston, 18 days	
"	12	Edward s. James & Ruth Whitehead, Failsworth, 6 m	
"	14	Thomas Whitehead, Failsworth, 23 y	
"	19	Alice w. James Thomas, Manchester, 54 y	
"	21	Isabel d. Martha Whittaker, Newton, 17 days	
"	23	Ellen d. Joseph & Mary Moseley, Newton, 12 y	
"	26	Edwin s. John & Anne Clough, Failsworth, 10 y	
"	28	James s. Samuel & Sarah Anderson, Manchester, 10 m	
"	28	Edmund Walmsley, Failsworth, 45 y	
"	28	Jeremiah s. James & Hannah Kemp, Manchester, 11 m	
"	28	Edward s. Christopher & Sarah Mellor, Newton, 18 y	
"	29	Alice d. James & Anne Thorpe, Failsworth, 11 y	
"	30	Anne wdw. James Harrison, Manchester, 71 y	
Jul	1	Jane w. Charles Harrison, Manchester, 27 y	
"	8	Sarah d. Thomas & Anne Brookes, Newton, 16 y	
"	8	Robert Whitehead, Newton, 47 y	
"	9	Martha w. James Kemp, Manchester, 66 y	
"	12	Marianne d. William & Lucy Seel, Newton, 3 wks	
"	19	James Kenyon, Droylsden, 26 y	
"	26	James s. John & Esther Schofield, Droylsden, 7 y	
"	28	John Oldham, Newton, 51 y	
Aug	3	Joseph s. Elizabeth Schofield, Manchester, 4 y	
"	5	Robert s. Thomas & Isabel Walmsley, Failsworth, 3 m	
"	9	George Bardsley, Newton, 60 y	
"	10	Marianne d. John & Anne Berry, Manchester, 9 m	
"	11	Nancy Ridings, Moston, 66 y	
"	18	Anne d. Edward & Martha Allen, Failsworth, 10 m	
"	23	Emma d. Samuel & Martha Hulton, Failsworth, 3 m	
"	23	Mary Abrahams, Manchester, 22 y	
"	25	Robert s. Robert & Bathsheba Boardman, Newton, 12 m	
"	28	Nancy w. William Whittaker, Newton, 46 y	
Sep	1	James Warrant, Manchester, 79 y	
"	1	Dolly w. John Knott, Newton, 37 y	
"	3	Mary w. Alexander Greaves, Failsworth, 74 y	
"	4	Mary d. Oliver & Hannah Morris, Manchester, 17 m	

"	6	John s. James & Alice Fletcher, Newton, 17 wks
"	10	Isabel w. Thomas Walmsley, Failsworth, 23 y
"	13	Samuel s. Robert & Mary Hulme, Droylsden, 30 y
"	17	Abraham s. William & Anne Whitehead, Chadderton, 19 days
"	20	Henry s. John & Anne Tonge, Newton, 9 wks
"	22	Sarah d. James & Sarah Fildes, Manchester, 2 y 5 m
"	25	Susanna d. William & Kitty Morgan, Newton, 14 wks
"	27	Isabel d. Benjamin & Jane Hulton, Failsworth, 18 m
"	29	William Harrison, Ardwick, 33 y
"	30	Ellen w. Samuel Clough, Failsworth, 45 y
Oct	4	Catherine w. William Gradwell, Failsworth, 51 y
"	11	Abel s. Mary Tomlinson, Moston, 11 m
"	12	William s. Joseph & Betty Smithurst, Newton, 3 y
"	13	William s. James & Sarah Greenwood, Manchester, 4 y
"	13	William s. David & Sarah Hulton, Newton, 11 m
"	14	Jonas s. Joseph & Hannah Thornley, Failsworth, 18 y
"	15	Mary Anne d. Abraham & Elizabeth Mather, Failsworth, 16 y
"	15	Anne d. Benjamin & Elizabeth Bruce, Manchester, 16 m
"	20	Samuel s. John & Harriet Simpson, Newton, 6 m
"	23	William s. James & Ophelia Berrington, Newton, 5 wks
"	25	Ellen d. Samuel & Mary Higginbotham, Manchester, 17 m
"	25	Nancy d. George & Betty Hilton, Failsworth, 1 y 8 m
"	27	Mary d. James & Hannah Rothwell, Newton, 2 days
"	27	William s. Thomas & Anne Cordingly, Failsworth, 2 m
"	29	Joseph s. Samuel & Betty Jones, Newton, 5 y
Nov	1	Richard s. John & Esther Dichfield, Newton, 3 wks
"	1	Richard Pollitt, Newton, 83 y
"	4	Elizabeth d. James & Hannah Pilkington, Newton, 10 m
"	8	William s. Uriah & Hannah Booth, Ashton under line, 2 wks
"	11	Elizabeth d. Sam[ue]l & Elizabeth Sudlow, Newton, 4 y
"	15	Jane w. John Ridings, Failsworth, 54 y
"	15	Betty w. James Ogden, Failsworth, 47 y
"	15	Thomas s. John & Margaret Jones, Droylsden, 3 y 3 m
"	15	John Makin, Failsworth, 57 y
"	19	Mary d. Elijah & Sarah Whitehead, Failsworth, 6 m
"	19	Anne d. John & Anne Horrocks, Newton, 9 m
"	22	Anne d. Thomas & Mary Mayo, Ardwick, 3 m
"	22	Anne d. Joseph & Mary Hamson, Manchester, 7 wks
"	22	Matthew s. George & Dorothy Hibbert, Manchester, 20 y
"	24	Henry s. Josiah & Jane Garlick, Failsworth, 18 wks
"	24	Walter s. Jane Stott, Newton, (*age blank in PR & BT*)
"	26	Sarah Pendleton, Newton, 75 y
"	26	John s. James & Sarah Fildes, Newton, 11 wks
"	29	Samuel s. Joseph & Mary Hamson, Manchester, 8 wks
"	30	James s. Joseph & Betty Smithurst, Newton, 13 m

Dec	3	George s. Fanny Etchels, Droylsden, 9 days
"	3	Francis McAuley, Failsworth, 52 y
"	3	Thomas Dawson, Failsworth, 57 y
"	3	Betty w. Joseph Mills, Failsworth, 39 y
"	8	John s. Samuel & Anne Butterworth, Manchester, 6 m
"	9	Sarah w. James Fildes, Newton, 24 y
"	10	Olive d. Robert & Betty Wroe, Failsworth, 2 y 4 m
"	13	Nancy Wolstencroft, Newton, 65 y
"	13	Alice w. John Thorpe, Failsworth, 69 y
"	13	Jonathan Shelmerdine, Manchester, 73 y
"	14	Sarah d. John & Betty Royle, Hollinwood, 15 wks
"	14	Maria w. Benjamin Thornley, Droylsden, 25 y
"	15	Jane d. William & Nancy Whittaker, Newton, 8 y
"	17	Martha d. John & Anne Grindrod, Manchester, 7 y
"	20	Elizabeth d. Charles & Lydia Walker, Gorton, 5 m
"	27	Maria d. William & Maria Eastwood, Manchester, 4 m
"	27	Marianne Byron d. Richard & Eliza Byron Cherry, Manchester, 4 m
"	27	Esther w. John Whitehead, Failsworth, 82 y
"	29	Anne Lees, Failsworth, 30 y
"	29	John s. John & Jane Nightingale, Newton, 10 m
[		Thos Gaskell]

1830

Jan	3	Sarah d. Joseph & Betty Mills, Failsworth, 2 y
"	5	George s. William & Martha Eyre, Failsworth, 9 m
"	7	Jane d. John & Betty Abbot, Failsworth, 14 m
"	10	Edwin s. David & Harriet Hilton, Failsworth, 15 m
"	11	John s. William & Elizabeth Porter, Bradford, 5 y 4 m
"	15	Joseph Grimshaw, Newton, 60 y
"	17	Jane wdw. John Rogers, Newton, 59 y
"	17	Betsey d. Thomas & Elizabeth Brown, Manchester, 10 days
"	17	Elizabeth Council, Manchester, 21 y
"	17	Jane w. Joseph Ogden, Stayley Bridge, 43 y
"	20	Joseph s. Charles & Eliza Eckersley, Manchester, 13 m
"	20	Mary d. Philip & Elizabeth Leigh, Ashton Parish, 13 m
"	24	Anne d. William & Harriet Cooper, Failsworth, 6 m
"	25	William s. John & Sarah Whitehead, Failsworth, 18 m
"	26	Hannah d. Luke & Rachel Hilton, Failsworth, 2 y 3 m
"	31	Anne wdw. John Shannon, Newton, 40 y
"	31	Anne wdw. NXN Downs, Manchester, 72 y
"	31	Thomas Gradwell, Newton, 27 y
"	31	Sarah d. Samuel & Betty Berry, Failsworth, 15 m
Feb	2	Elizabeth d. William & Eleanor Philpot, Newton, 11 m
"	2	Mary w. Thomas Ogden, Hollinwood, 29 y

"	7	Robert Pollitt, Newton, 33 y	(*1830*)
"	7	James s. William & Esther Hall, Newton, 4 days	
"	7	Sarah w. Richard Hall, Manchester, 67 y	
"	7	Elizabeth d. Richard & Ellen Hill, Manchester, 14 wks	
"	9	James s. Josiah & Jane Pollitt, Failsworth, 16 y	
"	14	Mary w. James Lees, Failsworth, 34 y	
"	14	Milly wdw. John Gradwell, Newton, 87 y	
"	16	Robert Hulme, Failsworth, 56 y	
"	16	Alice d. Thomas & Susan Hibbert, Failsworth, 1 y 8 m	
"	19	Alice wdw. Joseph Grimshaw, Newton, 63 y	
"	21	Charles Shore, Newton, 66 y	
"	21	Thomas s. Henry & Mary Rogerson, Newton, 2 y 4 m	
"	28	Maria d. Joseph & Margaret Barlow, Newton, 15 y	
Mar	1	James Boardman, Newton, 33 y	
"	5	William Brown, Failsworth, 52 y	
"	7	Samuel s. George & Martha Leigh, Manchester, 11 m	
"	7	Frederick s. John & Anne Tonge, Newton, 7 m	
"	7	William s. John & Mary Plummer, Manchester, 1 y 11 m	
"	9	Margaret d. William & Elizabeth Price, Newton, 13 m	
"	9	William Walter s. David & Anne Ogden, Newton, 8 m	
"	10	Sarah d. Charles & Martha Tomlinson, Newton, 1 y 10 m	
"	10	Luke s. Joseph & Anne Higham, Newton, 15 m	
"	10	George s. Samuel & Mary Holland, Failsworth, 2 y	
"	14	John Holt, Failsworth, 49 y	
"	14	Elias s. Samuel & Jane Bethell, Newton, 6 y	
"	16	James Aldred, Newton, 50 y	
"	16	Lemuel s. William & Mary Smith, Failsworth, 13 y	
"	21	Mary w. George Smith, Failsworth, 66 y	
"	22	Mary w. John Higham, Newton, 58 y	
"	25	Edward s. John & Alice Heap, Newton, one day	
"	28	Anne w. John Tonge, Newton, 27 y	
"	28	Philip s. John & Anne Davies, Manchester, 4 y 11 m	
Apr	4	John s. John & Lydia Barlow, Newton, 7 m	
"	8	George s. Abraham & Mary Horrocks, Newton, 8 m	
"	8	Thomas s. Adam & Margaret Horrocks, Droylsden, 12 y	
"	8	Caroline d. Thomas & Nancy Johnson, Failsworth, 12 y	
"	11	Sarah d. Richard & Sarah Tetlow, Newton, 13 m	
"	11	Sarah d. Joseph & Jane Ogden, Staley Bridge, 3 m	
"	11	James s. Thomas & Catherine Madders, Manchester, 11 m	
"	11	James Aldred, Woodhouses, 91 y	
"	11	Robert s. John & Hannah Allen, Failsworth, 5 y 4 m	
"	16	Hannah d. James & Mary Lees, Failsworth, 7 y	
"	18	Anne d. Hamlet & Elizabeth Lowe, Newton, 18 m	
"	22	James s. Charles & Alice Brown, Manchester, 14 m	
"	22	Elizabeth d. Thomas & Alice Ferns, Newton, one m	

"	22	Elizabeth d. Daniel & Hannah Berrington, Newton, 2 y 7 m	*(1830)*
"	23	James s. John & Mary Smith, Newton, 14 m	
"	25	Jane d. Robert & Alice Whitehead, Newton, 15 y	
"	25	James s. James & Jane Hesketh, Failsworth, 15 m	
"	25	Nancy d. Thomas & Alice Collinson, Newton, 15 y	
"	25	Elizabeth d. Thomas & Elizabeth Holland, Failsworth, 22 y	
"	25	Esther w. John Jackson, Failsworth, 78 y	
"	28	James Dunstan, Manchester, 55 y	
"	29	Samuel s. John & Anne Smith, Newton, 3 y	
May	2	Job s. William & Mary Daltry, Oldham, 18 wks	
"	2	William s. Jonah & Betty Goodier, Newton, 5 y	
"	6	William s. William & Hannah Ackers, Newton, 15 m	
"	6	Margaret wdw. William Thomas, Manchester, 77 y	
"	6	Margaret w. John Ward, Manchester, 44 y	
"	7	Richard Hill, Manchester, 55 y	
"	9	Joseph s. Richard & Anne Hulme, Harpurhey, 19 y	
"	9	Martha d. Edward & Harriet Shirley, Newton, 14 m	
"	12	Grace d. Thomas & Jane Jackson, Manchester, 2 y 5 m	
"	12	Abraham s. Samuel & Mary Chadderton, Newton, 10 m	
"	19	Martha wdw. Thomas Shaw, Failsworth, 83 y	
"	20	Sarah w. Thomas Moores, Manchester, 44 y	
"	23	George Garlick, Failsworth, 42 y	
"	23	Samuel s. John & Sarah Sydebotham, Newton, 13 m	
"	23	Thomas s. Mary Pollitt, Failsworth, 18 m	
"	24	Ellen wdw. William Caldwell, Newton, 66 y	
"	25	Daniel s. Joseph & Mary Tetlow, Newton, 3 y 4 m	
Jun	1	William s. John & Nancy Holt, Newton, 3 days	
"	1	Sarah Birkett, Newton, 50 y	
"	2	Jonathan Philips, Newton, 74 y	
"	4	Joseph Bardsley, Failsworth, 37 y	
"	4	Hannah d. Richard & Alice Whitehead, Manchester, 18 m	
"	6	Jane d. John & Esther Linley, Newton, 14 m	
"	6	James Kemp, Manchester, 72 y	
"	9	Margaret d. John & Anne Holt, Failsworth, 10 wks	
"	16	Thomas s. Thomas & Sarah Brundritt, Failsworth, 2 y 3 m	
"	16	Mary d. William & Anne Aldred, Droylsden, 15 m	
"	18	Paul Hemmons, Winscomb near Axbridge Somerset, 65 y	
"	20	Elizabeth d. Mary Smith, Manchester, 15 m	
"	20	Luke Smith, Failsworth, 71 y	
"	20	Charles s. John & Martha Ivison, Newton, 18 m	
"	20	Mally w. John Whitehead, Failsworth, 30 y	
"	22	John s. Thomas & Alice Pollitt, Newton, 15 m	
"	27	Ralph s. Thurston & Jane Smethurst, Hollinwood, 10 m	
"	27	Marianne d. James & Sarah Blaze, Droylsden, 11 m	
"	27	Sam[ue]l Scholes, Failsworth, 31 y	

Jul	4	Emma d. John & Jenny Etchels, Failsworth, one y
"	6	Harriet d. John & Anne Whittaker, Failsworth, 18 y
"	8	Esther d. James & Anne Allen, Failsworth, 2 y
"	18	Rebekah w. Joseph Barratt, Newton, 46 y
"	21	Elizabeth d. William & Jane Lomax, Failsworth, one y
"	22	Marianne d. John & Betty Allen, Failsworth, 15 wks
"	25	Matthew s. John & Mally Whitehead, Failsworth, 13 wks
"	27	John s. Esther Simister, Newton, 16 wks
"	29	Ashton Shepley, Newton, 33 y
Aug	1	John s. Thomas & Mary Ogden, Hollinwood, 17 m
"	1	Mary Ellen d. Joseph & Mary Smethurst, Newton, 6 y
"	2	Betty d. James & Hannah Etchels, Failsworth, 3 y
"	6	Samuel s. Samuel & Mary Lord, Failsworth, 5 wks
"	18	Thomas s. James & Ophelia Berrington, Newton, 3 wks
"	19	Betty wdw. Edmund Whitehead, Failsworth, 70 y
"	22	Alice d. John & Eliza Withnal, Manchester, 19 m
Sep	6	Betty d. George & Alice Smith, Failsworth, 24 y
"	12	Richard Hall, Salford, 66 y
"	15	Hannah w. Benjamin Taylor, Failsworth, 20 y
"	19	John Haslam, Failsworth, 58 y
"	19	Martha d. Charles & Hannah Heywood, Failsworth, 16 y
"	26	Amelia d. Thomas & Alice James, Manchester, 6 m
"	27	Anne d. Robert & Margaret Taylor, Hollinwood, 18 m
"	27	Sarah w. John Taylor, Newton, 54 y
"	29	Thomas s. Joseph & Mary Dean, Manchester, 4 y 9 m
Oct	8	Elizabeth d. John & Mary Gradwell, Newton, one y
"	10	George s. James & Sarah Simister, Newton, 18 y
"	14	Anne w. John Burgess, Harpurhey, 47 y
"	20	Anne wdw. Joseph Walmsley, Failsworth, 83 y
"	26	Joseph s. Robert & Alice Whitehead, Newton, 14 y
"	26	Thomas Eckersley, Failsworth, 21 y
"	31	Betty w. James Dean, Chadderton, 51 y
"	31	Ellen d. Henry & Delilah Clegg, Newton, 2 y
Nov	4	George s. Michael & Mary Hibbert, Manchester, 4 y 9 m
"	7	Jane d. John & Martha Tetlow, Newton, 3 y 11 m
"	9	Sarah d. James & Betsey Moston, Moston, 9 days
"	9	William s. Thomas & Betty Davies, Newton, 3 m
"	10	Richard s. Joseph & Mary Barratt, Newton, 14 m
"	14	Thomas s. William & Martha Eyre, Failsworth, one day
"	17	William s. Thomas & Mary Pollick, Manchester, 3 y 4 m
"	17	Joseph s. Joseph & Hannah Williamson, Newton, 9 wks
"	17	Sarah d. Joseph & Mary Collinson, Failsworth, 1 y 8 m
"	18	James s. John & Mary Thorpe, Moston, 14 y
"	18	John Richardson, Failsworth, 62 y
"	23	Joseph s. Thomas & Martha Whitelegg, Salford, 9 y

"	26	George Heaton, Ashton Parish, 54 y
Dec	5	Edna d. Charles & Margaret Swift, Manchester, 6 m
"	5	Joseph s. Mary Hooley, Newton, 17 m
"	8	William s. Joseph & Sarah Swift, Manchester, 2 wks
"	8	Elizabeth w. Samuel Sidlow, Newton, 42 y
"	12	Hannah w. Joseph Williamson, Newton, 41 y
"	12	Jane d. John & Anne Bateman, Newton, one m
"	13	Mary Cheetham, Failsworth, 48 y
"	19	Ellen w. James Horatio Nelson Hulton, Failsworth, 31 y
"	21	James s. William & Mary Waterfield, Droylsden, 2 y
"	26	Sarah w. John Thorley, Failsworth, 64 y
"	26	Thomas Wood, Manchester, 38 y
"	29	Sarah McClement, Bolton, 64 y, murdered
"	29	Samuel Pollitt, Failsworth, 74 y
[		Thos Gaskell, Incumbent of Newton]
[		(*blank*) Chapelwardens]

1831

Jan	2	William s. James & Anne Taylor, Failsworth, 3 m
"	5	Hannah w. William Hilton, Newton, 46 y
"	6	William s. Daniel & Jenny Jackson, Failsworth, 7 wks
"	9	James s. James & Margaret Smith, Failsworth, 11 m
"	9	Eliza d. James & Marianne Barber, Newton, 15 wks
"	10	Mary w. James Buckley, Hollinwood, 53 y
"	14	Thomas s. Thomas & Anne Hamson, Moston, 19 y
"	16	Edward s. Richard & Mary Hughes, Manchester, 11 m
"	18	Edwin s. Joseph & Betty Halliwell, Droylsden, 1 y 11 m
"	20	Sarah Anne d. James & Elizabeth Walmsley, Newton, 11 wks
"	23	Midry d. John & Esther Smith, Manchester, 1 y 9 m
"	31	Alice w. Joshua Wyatt, Newton, 67 y
Feb	1	Anne d. Dan & Martha Hilton, Newton, 18 wks
"	2	William s. Sarah Hasledine, Newton, 7 wks
"	3	Phineas s. John & Alice Makin, Failsworth, 14 y
"	6	Anne w. Oliver Greenwood, Manchester, 63 y
"	9	Samuel s. Elijah & Mary Hardy, Manchester, one y
"	10	Hannah d. James & Nancy Ridings, Newton, 35 y
"	11	John s. Samuel & Martha Rosthern, Newton, 7 wks
"	13	John s. Levi & Ellen Clough, Newton, 6 y 10 m
"	13	Mary w. John Thorpe, Moston, 58 y
"	13	Moses s. Thomas & Catherine Walmsley, Manchester, 2 wks
"	13	Sarah Gradwell, Newton, 20 y
"	13	Wright s. Peter & Esther Boardman, Newton, 10 y
"	17	John Whitehead, Newton, 79 y
"	18	John Wood, Newton, 86 y

"	27	John s. James & Lucy Heyes, Failsworth, 7 days	*(1831)*
"	27	John Council, Manchester, 18 y	
"	28	Mary d. James & Eliza Gradwell, Droylsden, 2 y	
"	28	Richard Walmsley, Failsworth, 19 y	
Mar	6	Eliza d. Charles & Anne Siddal, Manchester, 16 m	
"	6	Betty wdw. John Ogden, Failsworth, 70 y	
"	6	Sarah Anne d. Joseph & Betty Consterdine, Newton, 18 m	
"	7	James Wroe, Moston, 68 y	
"	7	George s. Hugh & Janet Jemison, Newton, 8 m	
"	9	Sarah d. Richard & Anne Rose, Manchester, 1 y 6 m	
"	9	Hannah d. William & Hannah Brindley, Failsworth, 3 wks	
"	11	Elizabeth d. Thomas & Mary Cheetham, Manchester, 2 m	
"	13	Richard Ormrod, Newton, 27 y	
"	14	Alice Ogden, Ashton Parish, 69 y	
"	14	Anne d. Eli & Sarah Swift, Failsworth, 2 y 11 m	
"	17	Sarah wdw. Samuel Tonge, Manchester, 82 y	
"	22	William s. James & Mary Hilton, Newton, one y	
"	27	Moses Ogden, Droylsden, 26 y	
"	28	James s. Samuel & Jane Bethel, Newton, 2 y	
"	30	Thomas s. David & Anne Ogden, Newton, 7 wks	
Apr	3	George s. George & Mary Clay, Newton, 5 y	
"	3	Robert s. John & Betty Wolstenholme, Failsworth, 5 m	
"	6	Joseph s. George & Betty Hardy, Failsworth, 21 y	
"	15	Edwin s. Samuel & Olive Taylor, Newton, 1 y 7 m	
"	17	Edward Marsh, Newton, 74 y	
"	17	Mary w. John Duxbury, Newton, 26 y	
"	19	Robert & Joseph ss. Luke & Rachel Hilton, Failsworth, Robt 6 y & Joseph 8 m	
"	19	Betty w. Joseph Hilton, Failsworth, 24 y	
"	21	Martha w. Abraham Pollitt, Failsworth, 47 y	
"	24	Jane d. Joseph & Mary Taylor, Droylsden, 4 y 4 m	
"	27	James s. Thomas & Mary Mayo, Manchester, 6 m	
"	28	George s. Joseph & Betty Seel, Failsworth, 14 y	
"	29	Betty d. Joseph & Mary Whitehead, Failsworth, 4 y	
May	4	Richard Hill, Manchester, 30 y	
"	8	Betty d. William & Jane Shepley, Newton, 15 m	
"	12	Margaret w. Robert Taylor, Failsworth, 25 y	
"	12	Henry s. Jonathan & Mary Ratliffe, Newton, one y	
"	15	James s. Anne Gillibrand, Newton, 14 m	
"	22	Rebecca d. John & Mary Etchels, Failsworth, 18 y	
"	22	Charles s. Horatio & Anne Ridings, Newton, one m	
"	23	William s. William & Sarah Stansfield, Newton, 2 y	
"	24	Lettuce wdw. Joseph Tomlinson, Failsworth, 70 y	
"	24	William s. William & Phoebe Jacks, Hollinwood, 7 m	
"	29	John s. James & Hannah Wrigley, Droylsden, 13 m	

Jun	2	Sarah Anne d. William & Alice Walton, Newton, 5 m	*(1831)*
"	2	Thomas s. William & Sarah Walmsley, Failsworth, 2 wks	
"	3	William s. Thomas & Nancy Ogden, Failsworth, 9 m	
"	3	Sarah d. Nathaniel & Betty Taylor, Failsworth, 21 y	
"	5	James s. Joseph & Betty Hilton, Failsworth, 10 wks	
"	5	Mary Anne d. John & Sarah Mather, Newton, 12 days	
"	5	Elizabeth d. Thomas & Alice Brown, Moston, one y	
"	5	Susan d. Hugh & Janet Jemison, Newton, 2 y	
"	7	Mary w. Robert Heywood, Ashton Parish, 40 y	
"	7	Anne Carter d. Jeremiah & Mary Weatherill, Manchester, 2 y 5 m	
"	8	John s. John & Alice Howarth, Droylsden, 11 m	
"	9	Samuel s. Joseph & Mary Grimshaw, Newton, 20 y	
"	9	Lucy d. John & Elizabeth Travis, Failsworth, 4 y	
"	12	Dolly wdw. James Kenyon, Manchester, 79 y	
"	12	Joseph Taylor, Manchester, 59 [y]	
"	12	Barbara w. George Robinson, Newton, 54 y	
"	12	Samuel Clough, Failsworth, 61 y	
"	14	Jonathan s. James & Sarah Whittaker, Failsworth, 11 m	
"	15	Martha d. Thomas & Jane Jackson, Newton, 14 m	
"	15	Marianne d. William & Sarah Hall, Manchester, one y 9 m	
"	16	Betty w. Elias Whittaker, Failsworth, 27 y	
"	16	George s. Nicholas & Jane Simister, Newton, 18 m	
"	16	Henry s. James & Mary Yates, Newton, 2 y 5 m	
"	17	Walter s. David & Anne Ogden, Newton, 18 wks	
"	19	Elizabeth Grimshaw, Manchester, 64 y	
"	19	Marianne d. Thomas & Jane Jones, Newton, 14 m	
"	19	Ellen d. Peter & Sarah Lee, Newton, 3 y 7 m	
"	23	Betty wdw. John Robinson, Newton, 76 y	
"	26	John s. William & Elizabeth Ashworth, Manchester, 2 y 11 m	
"	26	Edwin s. James & Sarah Mather, Newton, 9 m	
"	29	Charles s. Philip & Elizabeth Schofield, Newton, 9 y	
"	29	Sarah d. Samuel & Betty Berry, Failsworth, one m	
Jul	3	Mary d. Joseph & Anne Boon, Newton, 4 y 8 m	
"	4	Jane d. John & Margaret Turner, Newton, 15 m	
"	5	Andrew Ward, Manchester, 20 y	
"	7	Lucy d. James & Ellen Howarth, Newton, 15 y	
"	8	Mary d. John & Sarah Marsden, Newton, 11 y	
"	10	Anne Allen, Failsworth, 40 y	
"	10	Jane d. Joseph & Nancy Gardner, Newton, 1 y	
"	10	Betty Booth, Newton, 36 y	
"	10	Martha d. Samuel & Mary Holland, Newton, 17 y	
"	14	Anne d. John & Margaret Murphy, Newton, 13 m	
"	17	George Leigh, Manchester, 36 y	
"	17	Sarah w. Richard Edwards, Manchester, 61 y	
"	19	Thomas s. John & Mary Crawford, Manchester, 5 m	

	20	John s. Charles & Sarah Holland, Failsworth, 3 y 3 m
"	20	John s. Charles & Sarah Holland, Failsworth, 3 y 3 m
"	24	Elizabeth d. Martha Berrington, Moston, 18 y
"	24	Mary d. George & Sarah Wyatt, Droylsden, 16 m
"	24	Thomas s. Abraham & Catherine Dawson, Manchester, 5 m
"	24	John s. Joseph & Anne Etchels, Hollinwood, 15 y
"	24	Joseph s. John & Sarah Ridings, Failsworth, 12 wks
"	26	Alice d. Joel & Betty Taylor, Failsworth, 20 days
"	31	John Thorpe, Failsworth, 71 y
Aug	1	Joseph s. John & Grace Ridings, Failsworth, 6 wks
"	5	Mary w. Henry Cowburn, Newton, 59 y
"	9	Alice d. George & Anne Siddal, Manchester, 5 wks
"	9	Thomas Rider, Medlock Vale, 59 y
"	15	Joseph Basnet, Manchester, 23 y
"	15	Thomas Allen, Failsworth, 23 y
"	19	Thomas s. John & Alice Hyde, Moston, 13 m
"	22	Robert Hughes, Manchester, 21 y
"	22	Hannah d. Sarah Ogden, Newton, 17 wks
"	23	Thomas s. Matthew & Sarah Smith, Newton, 19 m
"	24	Anne w. Charles Faulkner, Newton, 30 y
"	28	Mary d. Luke & Nancy Etchels, Newton, 2 y 10 m
"	28	John s. John & Anne Pattison, Newton, 2 y 6 m
"	30	Robert s. Betty Hulme, Droylsden, 4 m
"	30	Martha Stafford d. Ratliffe & Elizabeth Fielding, Droylsden, 7 m
"	30	Matthew s. John & Violet McNamee, Newton, 4 y 2 m
"	31	James s. Alice Livesey, Manchester, 17 m
Sep	4	James s. Elizabeth Rowcroft, Manchester, one m
"	7	Marianne d. Joseph & Anne Ogden, Newton, 11 m
"	9	Elizabeth d. John & Elizabeth Billington, Newton, 15 m
"	9	Anne w. James Thorpe, Newton, 54 y
"	11	Sally wdw. George Garlick, Failsworth, 31 y
"	11	Maria d. William & Anne Hilton, Newton, 10 days
"	19	Martha wdw. John Thomason, Failsworth, 49 y
"	20	Matthew s. John & Hannah Wyatt, Newton, 7 wks
"	21	Jane w. James Allen, Newton, 65 y

(New register commences: volume 12)

"	22	William s. Thomas & Martha Whitelegg, Manchester, 17 m
"	25	Jane d. James & Eliza Swift, Failsworth, 16 m
"	28	Samuel s. George & Hannah Hall, Manchester, 2 y 7 m
"	29	Thomas Sutton, Newton, 51 y
"	30	Ruth w. John Cheetham, Manchester, 37 y
Oct	2	John s. James & Hagar Ratliff, Droylsden, 17 y
"	2	Ellen d. Thomas & Alice Pollitt, Newton, 7 m
"	2	James s. Benjamin & Jane Howarth, Droylsden, 8 m

"	4	Henry Hargreaves, Manchester, 36 y
"	6	Robert s. Thomas & Betty Coupe, Newton, 14 wks
"	9	John Booth, Oldham, 40 y
"	9	Ellen d. John & Sarah Wrench, Newton, 17 m
"	9	Henry s. Betty Holland, Failsworth, 3 wks
"	16	Henry s. John & Esther Linley, Newton, 10 y
"	16	Joseph s. John & Anne Walker, Newton, 5 y
"	20	Isabella Ormrod, Newton, 49 y
"	20	Sarah Anne d. Richard & Martha Lees, Staley Bridge, 6 m
"	23	Mary Heywood, Manchester, 79 y
"	23	John s. Joseph & Isabel Grimshaw, Failsworth, 7 m
"	24	Amelia d. Charles & Anne Faulkner, Newton, 3 y
Nov	1	Isabella d. James & Isabella Carr, Moston, 18 y
"	3	James Morris, Failsworth, 78 y
"	8	Anne d. Charlotte Crossley, Harpurhey, 4 y
"	8	Joseph s. Joseph & Ellen Telford, Manchester, 3 m
"	10	Thomas s. Joseph & Susanna Brierly, Droylsden, 9 m
"	13	Hannah w. James Hibbert, Manchester, 52 y
"	15	John s. Charles & Hannah Heywood, Failsworth, 23 y
"	17	Betty w. John Whittaker, Failsworth, 52 y
"	20	Eliza d. Samuel & Elizabeth Bradshaw, Failsworth, 18 y
"	24	Betty d. James & Esther Keen, Newton, 33 y
"	27	Mary w. Jonas Stafford, Droylsden, 41 y
"	27	Betty Hulme, Droylsden, 31 y
"	27	Susan w. Thomas Hibbert, Failsworth, 27 y
Dec	4	Alice w. Edward Preston, Hollinwood, 74 y
"	5	Harriet d. Thomas & Alice Rider, Medlock Vale, 15 y
"	12	Anne wdw. John Kay, Manchester, 91 y
"	14	Robert s. Jane Hibbert, Failsworth, 11 y
"	18	Anne d. John & Mary Brierly, Failsworth, 15 y
"	19	Elizabeth w. Charles Walmsley, Newton, 55 y
"	20	Ellen Johnson, Manchester, 23 y
"	25	Ellen w. Edmund Whitehead, Failsworth, 60 y
"	25	James s. Reuben & Sarah Holt, Droylsden, one y
[		T. Gaskell. Incumbent of Newton]

1832

Jan	1	William Whitehead, Chadderton, 80 y
"	1	Sarah d. James & Hannah Hibbert, Failsworth, 2 y 3 m
"	1	Alice d. John & Hannah Lord, Manchester, 17 y 3 m
"	3	Richard s. Joseph & Anne Etchels, Failsworth, one y
"	6	Betty w. Patrick Carrol, Newton, 68 y
"	8	Emma d. John & Anne Dean, Newton, 2 y 11 m
"	8	Fanny d. John & Esther Schofield, Failsworth, 13 m

"	9	Edwin s. Frances Dimilow, Manchester, 3 m	(1832)
"	10	Rachel d. William & Anne Philips, Manchester, 11 m	
"	11	Sarah wdw. William Smith, Manchester, 69 y	
"	12	Mary d. Thomas & Sarah Thornley, Failsworth, 2 y 5 m	
"	12	Mary d. Hannah Ogden, Failsworth, one y	
"	18	Margaret d. John & Esther Butterworth, Newton, 2 wks	
"	19	Mary d. George & Sally Garlick, Failsworth, one y 9 m	
"	22	Mary w. Joseph Whitehead, Failsworth, 42 y	
"	22	Alexander s. John & Mary Crawford, Manchester, 7 y 11 m	
"	24	Thomas Booth, Failsworth, 65 y	
"	26	Jane d. Joseph & Sarah Ogden, Failsworth, 6 m	
"	29	James s. John & Sarah Arrandale, Droylsden, 5 m	
"	29	James s. Joseph & Alice Whitehead, Failsworth, 7 m	
"	29	Isabel d. Betty Coupe, Failsworth, 3 y 6 m	
Feb	5	John s. Joseph & Mary Barratt, Droylsden, 5 m	
"	5	Joseph s. Luke & Nancy Etchels, Newton, 11 m	
"	5	Joseph Ogden, Failsworth, 39 y	
"	5	Dorothy d. John & Dorothy Plummer, Manchester, 30 y	
"	12	Samuel s. Samuel & Mary Holland, Failsworth, 12 wks	
"	15	Samuel s. John & Margaret Jones, Droylsden, 7 m	
"	16	James s. John & Betty Bardsley, Droylsden, 20 y	
"	19	James s. Catherine Higginbotham, Newton, 16 m	
"	19	Nancy d. Joseph & Mary Smethurst, Hollinwood, 8 y	
"	19	Richard Hulme, Droylsden, 48 y	
"	23	James Hill, Manchester, 60 y	
"	26	Esther wdw. William Haddock, Failsworth, 74 y	
"	26	Ellen d. Hannah Gradwell, Newton, 5 days	
"	26	James Dawson, Failsworth, 61 y	
"	29	Mary w. John Batty, Newton, 41 y	
Mar	1	Sally wdw. Thomas Booth, Newton, 71 y	
"	4	James s. William & Harriet Allen, Newton, 5 y	
"	4	Bridget d. Anne Kennedy, Ashton Parish, 23 y	
"	4	Nicholas Pritchard, Ardwick, 66 y	
"	7	John s. Francis & Elizabeth Bowler, Newton, 5 m	
"	11	John s. Jeremiah & Anne Hopwood, Newton, 20 y	
"	12	Mary d. John & Mary Simister, Failsworth, 12 y	
"	13	Mary d. James & Mary Singleton, Manchester, 5 m	
"	15	Anne d. Nathaniel & Anne Wolstencroft, Droylsden, 9 m	
"	15	Mary w. Benjamin Lees, Failsworth, 32 y	
"	18	Betty d. John & Anne Hibbert, Newton, 8 m	
"	19	Thomas s. William & Elizabeth Makin, Newton, 6 y	
"	20	Sabrin w. Hohn Hyde, Newton, 86 y	
"	21	Sarah Anne d. Benjamin & Mary Hulton, Failsworth, 9 m	
"	25	Anne wdw. Joseph Walker, Manchester, 25 y	
"	25	John s. John & Anne Bailey, Manchester, one y 8 m	

"	26	William Walker, Droylsden, 25 y
"	27	Anne d. John & Betty Barlow, Manchester, one y
Apr	1	William s. Robert & Jane Taylor, Failsworth, 10 m
"	1	Hannah Ainsworth, Manchester, 39 y
"	1	Margaret d. Frances Porter, Bradford, 1 y 8 m
"	1	Joseph s. Joseph & Nancy Ogden, Failsworth, 8 y 4 m
"	1	John James s. Samuel & Elizabeth Ogden, Droylsden, 3 y 3 m
"	3	Thomas s. Thomas & Anne Bancroft, Manchester, 10 m
"	3	George s. John & Charlotte Ramsbotham, Newton, 10 m
"	12	George Booth, Failsworth, 77 y
"	12	Robert s. Samuel & Anne Hunstan, Manchester, 15 m
"	15	Thomas s. William & Deborah Bentley, Newton, 18 m
"	15	William Etchels, Newton, 26 y
"	17	Robert Arrandale, Droylsden, 56 y
"	18	Mary w. William Heywood, Sale Cheshire, 68 y
"	23	John s. Philip & Sarah Dunkerley, Failsworth, one y 9 m
"	24	Jane d. Thomas & Anne Drinkwater, Manchester, 1 y 7 m
"	29	Thomas s. Thomas & Elizabeth Walmsley, Newton, one day
May	1	Horsefall s. Joseph & Elizabeth Tomkinson, Newton, 11 wks
"	3	John s. John & Sarah Marsden, Newton, 2 y 4 m
"	3	Esther d. Thomas & Mary Leigh, Droylsden, 3 y 3 m
"	6	Mary d. William & Elizabeth Reid, Newton, 9 m
"	9	Thomas Pollitt, Failsworth, 82 y
"	9	John Fitton, Moston, 82 y
"	13	Hannah w. William Wrench, Manchester, 51 y
"	13	John s. John & Elizabeth Billington, Newton, 3 y 4 m
"	13	Nancy Gradwell, Blackley, 30 y
"	13	Sarah d. Samuel & Phoebe Travis, Newton, 1 y 9 m
"	14	Marianne d. Joseph & Sarah Kenyon, Newton, 6 m
"	20	Thomas Jones, Manchester, 37 y
"	20	Daniel s. John & Ruth Bottomley, Bradford, 2 y
"	21	Andrew s. Joseph & Mary Berry, Failsworth, 20 y
"	24	Richard Stansfield, Newton, 27 y
"	24	Sarah w. Joseph Hatfield, Chadderton, 30 y
"	24	Oliver Greenwood, Manchester, 60 y
"	27	Margaret d. George & Ellen Bruce, Manchester, 1 y 7 m
"	27	John Thorpe, Moston, 59 y
"	29	Thomas Thorpe, Moston, 82 y
"	31	Edward Allen, Chadderton, 67 y
Jun	3	John s. James & Anne Campbell, Manchester, one y
"	5	Sarah w. Thomas Stanney, Manchester, 51 y
"	6	Richard s. Isaac & Mary Whitehead, Manchester, 3 m
"	10	Henry s. Robert & Mary Heywood, Ashton Parish, 2 y 2 m
"	10	James Caldwell, Droylsden, 27 y
"	10	Hannah d. James & Sarah Williamson, Droylsden, 12 y

"	17	Elizabeth Hardinge, Newton, 49 y (*1832*)
"	17	Hannah d. James & Susan Forshaw, Newton, 13 y
"	19	Jane d. James & Sarah Howarth, Newton, one y
"	20	Mary d. William & Esther Whitehead, Failsworth, 9 y
"	24	Thomas Clarke s. Thomas & Esther Kershaw, Manchester, one y
"	25	Joseph s. Joseph & Mary Harrison, Newton, 3 m
"	25	Mary d. Joseph & Mary Harrison, Newton, 3 m
"	28	William s. Uriah & Hannah Booth, Newton, 2 days
Jul	1	Betsey d. Joshua & Margaret Bent, Droylsden, 4 y 3 m
"	1	Thomas Gorton, Failsworth, 76 y
"	1	Sarah Etchels, Failsworth, 40 y
"	4	Anne d. Thomas & Mary Grime, Manchester, 15 m
"	4	Samuel s. William & Jenny Bethel, Failsworth, 3 m
"	4	Marianne d. Thomas & Martha Whitelegg, Manchester, 14 wks
"	8	William Blackshaw, Openshaw, 87 y
"	10	Mary w. James Dyson, Newton, 29 y
"	11	Robert s. Abraham & Agnes Mills, Medlock Vale, 2 y
"	15	Joseph Partington, Manchester, 85 y
"	15	Thomas Greenhalgh, Manchester, 48 y
"	22	Sarah d. John & Elizabeth Whitehead, Manchester, 11 y
"	22	Anne w. James Tomlinson, Newton, 42 y
"	24	Joseph Clough, Failsworth, 59 y
"	25	Mary d. James & Elizabeth Barker, Manchester, 10 y
"	29	Sarah d. William & Nancy Bailey, Droylsden, 14 m
Aug	5	Robert s. Peter & Nancy Travis, Manchester, 14 m
"	10	Jane d. Sarah Kershaw, Manchester, 14 m
"	13	James Fildes, Newton, 28 y
"	13	James s. Thomas & Anne Hamson, Moston, 5 y
"	15	Biddy d. Biddy Kennedy, Medlock Vale, 5 m
"	16	William s. John & Sarah Gammel, Droylsden, 24 y
"	19	Robert s. Harriet Blomily, Manchester, 2 y 11 m
"	21	Thomas s. James & Anne Ogden, Failsworth, 4 y 8 m
"	21	Sarah w. Edward Thomson, Newton, 56 y
"	23	John Billinge, Manchester, 52 y
"	26	Elizabeth d. Robert & Catherine Brooks, Manchester, 11 m
"	28	Jane w. Thomas Lancashire, Droylsden, 55 y
"	28	Thomas Leigh, Droylsden, 28 y
"	30	Jane wdw. Joseph Nicholson, Manchester, 86 y
"	30	Harriet w. Richard Wood, Droylsden, 18 y
"	30	Margaret d. Thomas & Marianne Clarke, Droylsden, 7 y
"	31	James Cardwell, Manchester, 66 y
Sep	1	Thomas Green, Droylsden, 60 y
"	2	Anne wdw. Luke Smith, Failsworth, 71 y
"	2	Alice d. John & Jane Blackshaw, Newton, 11 m
"	3	Anne Wrigley, Droylsden, 63 y

	4	Martha w. George Stafford, Droylsden, 40 y	*(1832)*
	4	John Ogden, Openshaw, 65 y	
"	4	John Ball, Openshaw, 38 y	
"	7	Sarah w. Samuel Syddal, Droylsden, 36 y	
"	7	Anne d. Thomas & Mary Leigh, Droylsden, 6 m	
"	7	Charles s. Charles & Ellen Brown, Manchester, 7 y 11 m	
"	8	James s. Arthur & Ellen Cardwell, Openshaw, 9 y 7 m	
"	9	Samuel Grimshaw s. James & Elizabeth Johnson, Manchester, 6 wks	
"	10	Jacob s. William & Elizabeth Livesey, Manchester, 4 m	
"	12	Anne d. Robert & Jane Ralston, Newton, 17 y	
"	13	William Fildes, Newton, 79 y	
"	15	Mary w. Edward Wood, Droylsden, 48 y	
"	16	Hannah Hepworth, Manchester, 25 y	
"	19	Betty d. James & Martha Bell, Failsworth, 17 m	
"	23	John s. Thomas & Mary Taylor, Failsworth, 9 y	
"	27	Margaret w. Joseph Bennet, Droylsden, 54 y	
Oct	1	William s. John & Catherine McClaskey, Manchester, 4 y	
"	3	James Pollitt, Failsworth, 86 y	
"	5	Henry s. Reuben & Sarah Holt, Droylsden, one day	
"	8	Betty d. Elizabeth Taylor, Manchester, 8 m	
"	14	Maria d. John & Anne Wyld, Woodhouses, one y	
"	21	Charles Partington, Manchester, 50 y	
"	21	James Stansfield, Oldham, 26 y	
"	23	Anne w. William Hibbert, Failsworth, 26 y	
"	23	Martha w. Thomas Goodier, Chadderton, 73 y	
"	23	Joseph Aldred, Chadderton, 39 y	
"	25	John Blackley, Failsworth, 70 y	
"	28	Mary Lees, Failsworth, 76 y	
"	31	Isaac s. John & Mary Egerton, Newton, 6 y	
"	31	Emma d. Maria Royle, Failsworth, 7 y	
Nov	4	William s. Charles & Mary Partington, Manchester, 6 y	
"	4	James s. Joseph & Jenny Thornley, Failsworth, 6 y	
"	6	John Eckersley, Failsworth, 67 y	
"	7	Jane d. Michael & Elizabeth Waring, Newton, 19 y	
"	8	John s. Robert & Elizabeth Wilkinson, Failsworth, 3 y	
"	12	Joseph s. David & Anne Ogden, Newton, 3 m	
"	14	Eliza w. John Wyatt, Newton, 23 y	
"	14	Robert s. John & Mary Moon, Manchester, 7 m	
"	15	Sarah d. William & Ellen Summersgill, Hollinwood, 14 y	
"	18	Alice d. Elizabeth Schofield, Droylsden, 6 wks	
"	25	Eliza d. James & Anne Pomfrit, Newton, 21 wks	
"	26	Robert s. Thomas & Alice Whitehead, Failsworth, 7 m	
"	29	Marianne d. Thomas & Martha Kemp, Newton, 5 y	
Dec	2	Sarah wdw. John Harrison, Newton, 65 y	
"	2	Ellen d. Francis & Sarah Blackley, Manchester, 9 y	

"	2	Charles s. George & Betty Hilton, Failsworth, 21 y
"	2	Mary w. Daniel Howarth, Manchester, 35 y
"	4	Andrew s. Thomas & Jane Nelson, Newton, 2 y 9 m
"	9	Nancy w. Joseph Hare, Newton, 71 y
"	10	Violet d. Thomas & Anne Thorpe, Failsworth, 6 m
"	12	Henry s. Samuel & Betty Taylor, Failsworth, 9 m
"	16	Mary w. John Ashton, Failsworth, 46 y
"	16	John s. Thomas & Margaret Horrocks, Failsworth, 6 m
"	16	John s. Thomas & Elizabeth Monks, Manchester, 2 y 10 m
"	16	William s. Samuel & Betty Kay, Newton, 16 m
"	17	Alice w. Joseph Berry, Newton, 63 y
"	21	Bridget Susanna d. Thomas & Jane Nelson, Newton, 6 m
"	23	William s. James & Sally Tweedale, Newton, 7 wks
"	23	Caroline d. Thomas & Nancy Johnson, Manchester, 2 y 7 m
"	25	Mary d. Benjamin & Nancy Worsick, Droylsden, 7 m
"	25	Anne Whitehead, Failsworth, 84 y
"	27	John Brown, Failsworth, 37 y
"	30	John Hyde, Newton, 83 y
"	30	Mary w. Benjamin Lees, Failsworth, 59 y

1833

Jan	1	Stephen s. Thomas & Anne Brookes, Newton, 18 m
"	6	Anne d. Joseph & Jane Smith, Failsworth, 6 m
"	6	Elizabeth d. John & Esther Schofield, Failsworth, 2 m
"	7	Elizabeth w. James Woodward, Manchester, 58 y
"	9	Esther Hooley, Newton, 55 y
"	11	Lemuel s. Elias & Nancy Whittaker, Failsworth, 5 m
"	13	Charles s. John & Mary Egerton, Newton, 4 y 2 m
"	13	Martha d. Edward & Elizabeth Taylor, Manchester, 12 y
"	15	Nancy w. Richard Travor, Newton, 29 y
"	20	George Clough, Manchester, 21 y
"	23	John Allen, Newton, 74 y
"	25	Jane w. James Taylor, Newton, 36 y
"	28	Joseph Grimshaw s. James & Elizabeth Johnson, Manchester, 2 y 9 m
"	30	John Whitton, Manchester, 67 y
"	31	Clarissa d. Joseph & Ellen Dawson, Failsworth, 13 m
Feb	1	William s. John & Mary Whitehead, Moston, 6 m
"	3	Ellen d. Joseph & Mary Ramsbotham, Newton, 19 y
"	6	Thomas Wood, Manchester, 70 y
"	7	James Bottomley, Bradford, 72 y
"	8	James Houlton, Newton, 31 y
"	10	Anne w. John Beswick, Chorlton row, 49 y
"	14	Jonathan Hooley, Newton, 53 y
"	17	Sarah w. Thomas Ratliff, Manchester, 34 y

"	17	Mary d. James & Anne Etchels, Droylsden, 13 y
"	20	Elizabeth w. Samuel Moore, Manchester, 40 y
"	21	Mark Edward s. Mark & Millicent Gradwell, Manchester, 8 m
"	28	Richard s. James & Anne Stansfield, Manchester, 15 m
Mar	3	William s. Jonathan & Mary Hooley, Newton, 19 y
"	4	James s. Mary Whitehead, Chadderton, 14 m
"	4	Elizabeth w. Thomas Davies, Newton, 38 y
"	7	Dinah d. William & Alice Walton, Newton, 5 m 2 wks
"	17	Jane d. William & Alice Walton, Newton, 9 y
"	17	John Hall, Newton, 20 y
"	18	Thomas s. Joseph & Priscilla Fletcher, Newton, 12 y
"	19	Sarah Whitehead, Failsworth, 49 y
"	21	James s. Thomas & Alice Rothwell, Moston, 9 m
"	24	Thomas s. William & Hannah Brindley, Failsworth, 7 m
"	24	James s. William & Elizabeth Bentley, Manchester, 3 y
"	24	Thomas s. Thomas & Esther Mills, Moston, 7 y
"	24	Sarah w. Joshua Eckersley, Failsworth, 34 y
"	25	Nancy wdw. Peter Travis, Manchester, 43 y
"	26	Alice w. Thomas Collinson, Newton, 61 y
"	26	James Allen, Hollinwood, 75 y
"	27	James s. Thomas & Mary Kay, Failsworth, 11 y
"	27	Patrick Carrol, Newton, 61 y
"	28	Jane d. John & Jenny Roe, Failsworth, 6 m
"	31	Martha d. John & Elizabeth Warburton, Newton, 4 m
"	31	Nathan s. William & Mary Thomson, Manchester, 4 m
Apr	3	Alice d. Isaac & Mary Whitehead, Manchester, 3 y 6 m
"	4	Charlotte w. Richard Atkinson, Droylsden, 39 y
"	5	Samuel Bythell, Newton, 34 y
"	7	Jacob Haslam, Manchester, 39 y
"	9	Sarah d. William & Mary Dawson, Failsworth, 3 y
"	9	Sarah d. John & Isabella Morris, Failsworth, 3 y
"	12	Elizabeth d. Joseph & Anne Copeland, Failsworth, 9 wks
"	14	Edmund s. Edmund & Mary Jackson, Newton, 7 m
"	17	James s. George & Anne Robinson, Failsworth, 6 y 10 m
"	18	Jane d. George & Anne Morris, Ashton Parish, 11 y 10 m
"	19	Esther d. Richard & Betty Ditchfield, Moston, 14 y
"	21	Anne w. John Walsh, Newton, 65
"	21	Martha d. Thomas & Elizabeth Hadfield, Newton, 14 m
"	22	Mary w. Michael Hubbert, Manchester, 36 y
"	23	William Wood, Newton, 64 y
"	24	John s. Richard & Charlotte Atkinson, Droylsden, 7 wks
"	28	James s. George & Sarah Watson, Manchester, 3 y
"	29	Ellen d. George & Martha Leigh, Manchester, 2 y 10 m
"	30	Mary d. Benjamin & Mary Lees, Failsworth, 1 y 10 m
"	30	Joseph s. Joseph & Anne Etchels, Failsworth, 4 y

"	30	John s. George & Jane Robinson, Failsworth, 14 m *(1833)*
"	30	Thomas Hamson, Moston, 57 y
May	5	Sarah d. Joshua & Sarah Eckersley, Failsworth, 2 m
"	5	Catherine d. Peter & Dorothy Glover, Hollinwood, 2 y 10 m
"	5	William s. James & Abigail Blackshaw, Failsworth, 9 y
"	8	Sarah d. Luke & Ellen Etchels, Failsworth, 24 y
"	8	John Schofield, Failsworth, 47 y
"	9	Sarah w. John Ramsey, Failsworth, 40 y
"	10	William s. Benjamin & Jane Hulton, Failsworth, 2 y 6 m
"	10	Margaret d. Thomas & Ellen Moss, Newton, 4 y
"	12	Margaret Wardle, Manchester, 22 y
"	12	Joseph s. Joseph & Mary Dean, Manchester, 13 m
"	12	Frances Stafford, Droylsden, 26 y
"	14	Eliza d. Thomas & Jane Wild, Newton, 2 y 6 m
"	14	William s. John & Betty Bennet, Manchester, 15 y
"	19	James Smith, Manchester, 59 y
"	19	Mary d. William & Anne Entwisle, Newton, 2 y
"	19	Jesse s. Thomas & Elizabeth Massey, Newton, 7 y
"	26	Anne wdw. Nathan Thorley, Manchester, 73 y
"	28	Mary d. William & Harriet Willcock, Newton, 9 wks
Jun	2	Benjamin s. Edward & Maria Hulton, Failsworth, 10 days
"	4	Phoebe w. William Smethurst, 32 y
"	5	George s. Thomas & Hannah Sumner, Openshaw, 17 m
"	5	Margaret d. James & Eliza Gradwell, Failsworth, 10 m
"	5	Moses s. Thomas & Anne Bancroft, Manchester, 6 m *(see entry Jun 18)*
"	5	Mary w. Ashton Shepley, Newton, 65 y
"	7	Elizabeth w. George Brown, Manchester, 40 y
"	12	Jane wdw. Thomas Taylor, Manchester, 47 y
"	16	Adam Moston, Manchester, 58 y
"	18	Aaron s. Thomas & Anne Bancroft, Manchester, 6 m
"	20	David s. Samuel & Anne Williamson, Bradford, 7 wks
"	23	Anne w. James Forest, Newton, 28 y
"	25	Rachel w. Thomas Sudworth, Manchester, 49 y
"	27	John s. John & Esther Butterworth, Newton, 18 days
"	30	Mary d. Alice Etchels, Failsworth, 15 wks
"	30	Samuel Timmis, Failsworth, 28 y
"	30	John s. James & Sarah Wilson, Moston, 12 y
"	30	Mary Butterworth, Newton, 42 y
Jul	1	Samuel North, Derbyshire, found in the Rochdale Canal, *(age blank in PR & BT)*
"	7	Betty Consterdine, Newton, 46 y
"	7	John s. James & Sarah Worral, Failsworth, 14 y
"	12	Anne w. George Wyld, Droylsden, 42 y
"	12	Emanuel s. Abraham & Martha Pollitt, Failsworth, 14 y
"	17	Elizabeth d. James & Ophelia Berrington, Newton, 20 days

	17	Mary w. William Hayes, Newton, 27 y	(*1833*)
	18	Austin Chadwick, Manchester, 50 y	
	19	Charles s. Charles Travis & Anne Faulkner, Moston, 5 y	
	19	Betty w. James Johnson, Failsworth, 67 y	
	28	Mary Lilley, Openshaw, 24 y	
Aug	4	Mary wdw. John Metcalf, Manchester, 85 y	
	4	Samuel Sidlow, Failsworth, 56 y	
	4	Jane w. James Taylor, Droylsden, 53 y	
	7	Richard s. Samuel & Betty Boden, Manchester, 8 m	
	11	Anne d. James & Anne Forest, Newton, 8 m	
	12	Alice w. John Lees, Newton, 35 y	
	12	Joseph s. Thomas & Jane Wilkinson, Newton, 17 m	
	15	Alice d. John & Hannah Gough, Duckenfield, 4 y	
	16	Edward Pimlot, Failsworth, 60 y	
	18	David Winstanley, Manchester, 38 y	
	19	John s. Joseph & Mary Grindrod, Manchester, 15 m	
	23	Joseph s. Joseph & Betty Tomkinson, Newton, 5 wks	
	25	James Butterworth, Manchester, 59 y	
	25	David s. David & Sarah Makin, Newton, 8 m	
	27	Elizabeth d. William & Lucy Seel, Newton, 6 m	
	27	Joseph Harrison, Newton, 29 y	
Sep	1	William Eckersley, Failsworth, 34 y	
	3	Marianne d. Martha Kershaw, Manchester, 6 m	
	8	Thomas s. Robert & Alice Simpson, Newton, 2 m	
	8	Henry s. William & Sarah Bardsley, Newton, 2 y 5 m	
	12	Phoebe w. James Hulme, Newton, 61 y	
	13	James Eckersley, Failsworth, 77 y	
	15	Esther w. John Nield, Newton, 52 y	
	22	Jane d. John & Anne Beswick, Hollinwood, 4 y	
	22	Thomas s. George & Sarah Watson, Salford, 7 wks	
	29	Mary w. Thomas Cole, Failsworth, 38 y	
	29	Willliam Hulme, Manchester, 54 y	
Oct	2	Elizabeth d. Peter & Mary Wyld, Failsworth, 4 y 6 m	
	3	Nancy d. Samuel & Anne Chadderton, Droylsden, 27 y	
	6	Anne Whitehead, Moston, 88 y	
	8	Elizabeth w. William Stile, Newton, 45 y	
	9	John s. John & Sarah Ramsey, Moston, 6 m	
	13	Henry s. John & Sarah Marsden, Newton, 15 m	
	13	Mary w. Thomas Smith, Failsworth, 57 y	
	15	George Ingham, Newton, 43 y	
	20	John Schofield, Failsworth, 35 y	
	23	Mary d. Richard & Mary Richardson, Manchester, 22 y	
	27	William Bardsley, Droylsden, 20 y	
	30	Laughlen Boyne, Newton, 60 y	
Nov	1	John s. Charles & Charlotte Berry, Moston, 9 m	

"	3	Sarah w. William Ridings, Hollinwood, 25 y
"	7	Thomas Dawson, Newton, 20 y
"	10	John Taylor, Chadderton, 55 y
"	10	Caroline d. Daniel & Mary Knott, Ashton Parish, 10 wks
"	12	James Aspell, Newton, 47 y
"	13	George s. Simon & Martha Williams, Newton, one y five m
"	24	Elizabeth w. William Scott, Harpurhey, 28 y
Dec	1	Lilless w. Thomas Garner, Newton, 55 y
"	1	Richard s. Richard & Martha Lees, Staley bridge, 5 wks
"	1	John s. Isaac & Elizabeth Heppy, Droylsden, 14 wks
"	1	Mary d. John & Frances Dimilo, Manchester, 17 y
"	3	John s. William & Susan Wain, Newton, 13 m
"	5	Richard Bee, Manchester, 46 y
"	8	Alice d. Thomas & Mary Grime, Manchester, 10 m
"	8	Anne w. David Ogden, Newton, 35 y
"	9	Sarah Mills, Medlock Vale, 49 y
"	11	Alice d. Wright & Martha Cranshaw, Newton, 4 y 6 m
"	13	Anne w. Charles Siddal, Manchester, 30 y
"	16	Thomas Fallows, Withington, 69 y
"	19	Maria d. William & Elizabeth Stile, Newton, 16 wks
"	20	Mary d. John & Hannah Roe, Newton, 2 y 2 m
"	22	Esther w. John Lindley, Newton, 42 y
"	22	Joseph Kershaw, Failsworth, 36 y
"	23	Sarah d. Anne Bardsley, Newton, 11 y
"	24	Thomas s. William & Sarah Prescot, Newton, 8 y
"	25	James s. James & Mary Butterworth, Manchester, 16 m
"	28	Sarah w. William Prescot, Newton, 29 y
"	29	Hannah d. William & Nancy Bailey, Droylsden, 3 m
[		Thos Gaskell, Incumbent of Newton]
[		Attested by A. Briscoe Chapelwarden of Newton]

1834

Jan	2	Lucy d. Esther Robinson, Newton, 2 y
"	5	Maria d. Garside & Alice Blomily, Newton, 2 y 3 m
"	5	Ellen d. John & Elizabeth Robinson, Newton, 6 m
"	5	James s. Samuel & Elizabeth Berry, Hollinwood, 8 wks
"	10	Amelia d. William & Elizabeth Porter, Bradford, 5 m
"	11	George Joseph Skilbeck, Manchester, 42 y
"	12	James s. Joseph & Betty Mills, Newton, 16 m
"	16	William Wylde, Denton, 64 y
"	19	William Riley, Failsworth, 19 y
"	19	John Whitehead, Moston, 73 y
"	22	William James s. Aaron & Hannah Johnson, Manchester, 2 y
"	22	Jane w. John Heys, Newton, 65 y

"	23	Jane d. Richard & Alice Whitehead, Manchester, 10 m
"	28	Sarah w. James Blomiley, Newton, 78 y
"	30	Alice d. Rolando & Alice Collinson, Newton, 7 m
Feb	5	Henry s. John & Sarah Mills, Manchester, 11 m
"	9	James s. Charles & Lavinia Barnes, Newton, 3 y 1 m
"	9	John s. Joseph & Betty Needham, Failsworth, 5 wks
"	11	Mary w. Adam Dawson, Failsworth, 69 y
"	13	Mary w. William Smith, Failsworth, 47 y
"	16	Elizabeth w. William Goodier, Newton, 56 y
"	16	Anne d. Thomas & Mary Thorpe, Failsworth, 22 y
"	16	Jonathan s. Thomas & Mary Thorpe, Failsworth, 20 y
"	16	Judith d. Matthew & Mary Marsden, Newton, 13 y
"	16	Mary d. Abraham & Sarah Knott, Failsworth, 20 wks
"	16	Sarah d. Abraham & Sarah Knott, Failsworth, 3 y
"	18	John Whitehead, Failsworth, 88 y
"	18	Rowenna d. Mary Arrandale, Droylsden, 14 m
"	19	Mary d. Phineas & Mary Makin, Newton, 2 wks
"	20	Jane d. Robert & Mary Allen, Newton, 22 y
"	23	Mary d. William & Harriet Blaze, Droylsden, 13 m
"	23	Anne d. Joseph & Sarah Wyld, Newton, 6 y
"	23	Mary wdw. John Fishburn, Manchester, 79 y
"	26	Anne w. William Anderton, Manchester, 55 y
"	27	Margaret w. Daniel Hall, Manchester, 27 y
"	27	Henry s. William & Mary Pendleton, Newton, 13 y
Mar	2	Ralph Wheldon, Newton, 89 y
"	2	Robert Bennet, Manchester, 27 y
"	4	Jane d. James Horatio & Anne Hilton, Failsworth, 10 m
"	9	Sarah d. Richard & Sarah Tetlow, Newton, 10 m
"	11	William s. Robert & Bathsheba Boardman, Newton, 2 y 8 m
"	11	Sarah w. John Ogden, Failsworth, 28 y
"	12	Mary w. James Ratliff, Newton, 48 y
"	12	James Morris, Failsworth, 26 y
"	12	Susanna d. Samuel & Mary Lord, Failsworth, 5 y
"	13	Matthew s. John & Maria Berry, Manchester, 18 wks
"	16	Robert s. Robert & Mary Harrison, Collyhurst, 6 m
"	16	Thomas s. George & Ellen Bruce, Manchester, 8 m
"	16	Alice d. Thomas & Margaret Horrocks, Ashton Parish, 14 y
"	19	Esther w. William Hall, Newton, 48 y
"	19	Robert s. Walter & Margaret Davy, Newton, 2 y 4 m
"	20	Alice d. James & Emma Moseley, Newton, 3 y
"	20	Sarah w. James Whitehead, Moston, 24 y
"	23	Richard Hall, Newton, 51 y
"	23	Robert s. Jonathan & Betty Hilton, Failsworth, 11 wks
"	23	Thomas Hill, Manchester, 56 y
"	23	Esther d. John & Esther Lindley, Newton, 3 m

"	23	Esther d. George & Mary Ashworth, Newton, 2 y 9 m	*(1834)*
"	24	Alice d. James & Alice Lees, Harpurhey, 9 m	
"	26	Mary w. Benjamin Howarth, Droylsden, 73 y	
"	26	Eliza d. Samuel & Hannah Bottomley, Manchester, 5 wks	
"	30	Sarah w. John Tomlinson, Moston, 41 y	
"	30	Elizabeth w. Robert Taylor, Failsworth, 31 y	
"	31	Charles s. Betty Clough, Failsworth, 3 days	
Apr	1	Mary wdw. Richard Thorpe, Failsworth, 84 y	
"	1	Edward s. John & Anne Stafford, Droylsden, one y	
"	2	Thomas s. James & Jane Smethurst, Manchester, 4 y 9 m	
"	3	Betty w. Jonah Goodier, Newton, 37 y	
"	3	Kezia wdw. Samuel Ogden, Moston, 64 y	
"	5	Peter Crossley, Manchester, 54 y	
"	6	Thomas Blackshaw, Failsworth, 45 y	
"	6	James Allen, Newton, 63 y	
"	13	John s. John & Anne Bailey, Manchester, 8 m	
"	14	Joseph s. John & Sarah Tomlinson, Moston, 3 wks	
"	15	Betty wdw. Robert Brierly, Failsworth, 47 y	
"	15	Joseph s. Samuel & Eliza Smith, Failsworth, 2 m	
"	16	George Worral, Failsworth, 40 y	
"	18	William Booth, Manchester, 30 y	
"	20	John Smith, Newton, 62 y	
"	20	Edmund Whitehead, Newton, 36 y	
"	22	John William s. Sarah Schofield, Droylsden, 1 y 7 m	
"	23	James Pollitt, Newton, 68 y	
"	27	Mary d. Henry & Sarah Jackson, Manchester, 2 y 4 m	
"	27	John Kershaw, Manchester, 79 y	
"	27	Isaac Dean, Oldham, 74 y	
May	4	Hannah d. Mary Smith, Manchester, 9 m	
"	4	Hannah w. George Duncalf, Manchester, 72 y	
"	4	James s. Robert & Mary Whittle, Newton, 6 wks	
"	11	James s. Joseph & Mary Roberts, Manchester, 2 y	
"	11	Mary d. Luke & Elizabeth Williamson, Moston, 1 day	
"	14	Edward s. Giles & Mary Howarth, Droylsden, 11 m	
"	16	Thomas s. Robert & Mary Walmsley, Failsworth, 4 y	
"	18	Robert s. James & Alice Lees, Harpurhey, 11 m	
"	18	Francis Isdale, Newton, 50 y	
"	18	Thomas Fisher, Newton, 43 y	
"	21	Mary d. Joseph & Betty Smethurst, Newton, 9 y	
"	23	Mary Anne d. Isaac & Mary Whitehead, Manchester, 13 m	
"	25	Joseph Hooley, Salford, 53 [y]	
"	25	Thomas Robinson, Newton, 65 y	
"	25	John Ogden, Hollinwood, 67 y	
"	25	James s. John & Betty Whittaker, Droylsden, 29 y	
"	26	Sarah d. Thomas & Sarah Barlow, Failsworth, 2 y	

Jun	1	William s. James & Alice Lees, Harpurhey, 3 y
"	1	Mary w. Joseph Horrocks, Newton, 53 y
"	4	George Brown, Newton, 29 y
"	4	James s. George & Mary Brown, Newton, 11 m
"	4	Richard s. Richard & Elizabeth Pendlebury, Droylsden, 1 wk
"	6	Hannah w. Oliver Morris, Manchester, 28 y
"	6	Lucy w. William Peppleton, Manchester, 42 y
"	8	Mary w. William Davies, Manchester, 23 y
"	10	John s. Tho[ma]s & Elizabeth Rogers, Openshaw, 2 y 5 m
"	11	William Kay, Manchester, 44 y
"	15	John Hatton, Droylsden, 25 y
"	18	Ann Pimblet, (*abode blank in PR & BT*), 53 y
"	18	Olive d. John & Mary Egerton, Manchester, 10 m
"	22	Elizabeth w. Joseph Seele, Failsworth, 32 y
"	22	Robert Glossop, Moston, 71 y
"	22	Joseph Ravenscroft, Newton, 70 y
"	25	Daniel s. George & Ann Clarke, Manchester, 6 y 6 m
"	25	Sarah Wilburn, Newton, 65 y
Jul	1	Robert Duncufet, Manchester, 29 y
"	4	Walter Beck, Newton, 36 y
"	6	Jeremiah s. James & Mary Ann Kemp, Manchester, 15 m
"	7	Mary d. Abraham & Jane Ashworth, Newton, 46 y
"	7	Betty w. James Walmsley, Newton, 36 y
"	13	Mary w. Tho[ma]s Berry, Moston, 50 y
"	17	Mary Ann d. James & Elizabeth Duncalf, Bradford, (*age blank in PR & BT*)
"	20	Thomas s. Thomas & Ann Poster, Manchester, 10 m
"	23	Jane w. Rich[ar]d Travis, Newton, 53 y
"	27	George s. George & Mary Clay, Manchester, 16 m
"	27	Margaret d. Thomas & Mary Whitehead, Manchester, (*age blank in PR & BT*)
"	31	Peter Gollifer, Newton, 43 y
"	31	Anne d. James & Mary Ann[e] Fideham, Manchester, 9 m
Aug	1	Thomas Hulme s. Rob[er]t & Mary Anne Hulme, Newton, 4 m
"	1	Richard Naylor, Newton, 70 y
"	3	Richard Nelson, Newton, 21 y
"	4	Hannah w. William Brindle, Failsworth, 38 y
"	5	Alice d. Ratcliff & Elizabeth Fielding, Droylsden, 6 y
"	5	Emma d. Thomas & Sarah Rogers, Newton, 23 m
"	8	William Poppleton, Manchester, 48 y
"	9	John s. James & Mary Wardle, Yorkshire, 9 y
"	13	Ellen d. John & Maria Heywood, Newton, (*age blank in PR & BT*)
"	14	William s. Joseph & Jane Berry, Newton, 6 m
"	16	Sarah Hall, Newton, 49 y
"	17	John Hogg, Newton, days - (*sic; same in BT*)

"	17	Adam Dawson, Failsworth, 73 y
"	19	John Lindley, Newton, 43 y
"	20	Sarah d. John & Esther Lindley, Newton, 17 y
"	24	Jane d. Edward & Elizabeth Taylor, Manchester, (*age blank in PR & BT*)
"	28	Samuel George Ridgeway, (*abode blank in PR & BT*), 5 wks
"	29	Mary Taylor, Newton, 43 y
"	31	Thomas Robinson, Failsworth, 76 y
"	31	James Corns, Newton, 32 y
Sep	5	William Lees, Grange, 52 y
"	5	Caroline Shaw, (*abode blank in PR & BT*), 8 days
"	6	Elizabeth Shaw d. Hugh & Margaret Shaw, Manchester, 9 days
"	14	Wright Kearsley, Newton, 32 y
"	14	James Ellensworth, (*abode blank in PR & BT*), 58 y
"	23	Thomas Watson, Newton, 19 y
"	28	Charles s. Joseph & Susan Hulton, Failsworth, 13 m
"	28	Jane d. Rob[er]t & Jane Mills, Failsworth, 16 m
"	29	William Ashworth, Manchester, 41 y
"	29	Thomas s. Mary Beswick, Chadderton, 2 y
Oct	5	Elizabeth d. Peter & Esther Boardman, Manchester, 7 y
"	9	Thomas s. William & Betty Worrall, Failsworth, 20 y
"	10	John s. Edward & Hannah Radcliffe, Miles Platting, 9 wks
"	10	James Bardsley s. Thomas & Nancy Johnson, Manchester, 5 y
"	7	Henry s. Frederick & Doretta Goos, Manchester, 14 m (*the word 'misplaced' appears in the margin of both the PR & BT*)
"	8	Sarah w. Charles Thompson, Manchester, 58 y
"	12	James Blomeley, Newton, 78 y
"	12	Sarah Ann d. John & Hannah Connor, Manchester, 5 y
"	14	James s. Andrew & Hannah Wilkinson, Newton, 8 m
"	14	Peter Boardman, Manchester, 50 y
"	14	Thomas s. James & Sarah Robinson, Newton, 4 m
"	19	Mary d. William & Alice Walton, Newton, 6 m
"	19	Martha w. James Bell, Hollingwood, 31 y
"	23	Emma d. George & Ann Morris, Ashton, 8 m
"	24	Elizabeth w. James Edward Hancock, Newton, (*age blank in PR & BT*)
"	26	Lydia w. Charles Shore, Manchester, 65 y
"	29	John Clayton, Manchester, 64 y
Nov	2	Maria d. Richard & Martha Richardson, Newton, 11 m
"	2	Mary Dean, Failsworth, 44 y
"	3	Joseph Allen, Failsworth, 1 y 11 m
"	3	Sally Sandiford, Failsworth, 2 y 6 m
"	3	James Berry, Newton, 51 y
"	3	Betty Bell, Hollingwood, 11 m
"	4	Phebe Nichols, Failsworth, 4 y
"	6	Joseph Wylde, Newton, 68 y
"	10	Joseph s. John & Francis Bertenshaw, Newton, 6 m

"	11	Sarah d. James & Elizabeth Wilson, Mostyn, 9 y
"	12	Mary w. Anthony Lane, Manchester, 48 y
"	12	Sarah d. John & Sarah Sidebothom, Newton, 18 m
"	12	Jane Still d. John & Elizabeth Bradford, Newton, 9 m
"	16	George Young, Newton, 19 y
"	16	Ann d. Joseph & Betty Nichols, Hollingwood, 15 m
"	17	Charles Henry s. Charles & Lavinia Barnes, Newton, (*age blank in PR & BT*)
"	19	Thomas Whitehead, Harpurhey, 85 y
"	20	John Blomeley, Manchester, 2 y 10 m
"	21	Alice d. Thomas & Ann Thornley, Droylsden, 2 y 10 m
"	23	Margaret Ainsworth Widow, Failsworth, 67 y
"	23	Luke s. Joel & Mary Smith, Failsworth, 15 m
"	24	Martha w. Richard Richardson, Newton, 48 y
"	27	Eliza Hardy, Newton, 2 y 2 m
"	27	Margaret w. Benjamin Allen, Manchester, 24 y
"	28	James s. John & Betsey Holt, Newton, 3 y
"	30	James Glossop, Failsworth, 58 y
"	30	William s. Thomas & Mary Ormrod, Manchester, 3 y
"	30	Ann d. Robert & Hannah Hardman, Manchester, 1 y 7 m
"	30	Samuel Edward s. Samuel & Susanna Bagnall, Chorlton on Medlock, 7 m
"	30	Elizabeth d. Thomas & Sarah Holt, Newton, 2 y 8 m
Dec	3	William s. Samuel & Elizabeth Ogden, Failsworth, 8 m
"	3	Robert Taylor, Failsworth, 24 y
"	3	Ann d. Charles & Alice Brown, Manchester, 1 y 9 m
"	3	Esther Monks, Manchester, 83 y
"	4	Ann d. William & Sarah Walmesley, Failsworth, 5 wks
"	7	Jane d. John & Betsey Holt, Newton, 14 m
"	7	William s. Joseph & Ann Copeland, Failsworth, 8 m
"	7	James s. Reuben & Mary Holt, Failsworth, 5 m
"	9	John s. James & Isabella Lomas, Newton, 3 y 9 m
"	9	Mary Ann d. John & Sarah Wilson, Manchester, (*age blank in PR & BT*)
"	9	Alice d. Abraham & Ann Collinge, Manchester, 4 y 11 m
"	9	Susanna d. John & Mary Siddall, Newton, 7 m
"	11	(*entry blank and struck through; blank in BT*)
"	11	Sarah Boardman, Newton, 79 y
"	11	Margaret d. James & Sarah Farrand, Ashton, 7 m
"	14	Hannah Winstanley, Manchester, 74 y
"	14	John s. John & Martha Servin, Newton, 15 m
"	14	Margaret d. Robert & Alice Whitehead, Newton, 22 y
"	14	Thomas s. George & Alice Lane, Hollingwood, 4 y 3 m
"	14	Joseph s. John & Mary Tetlow, Newton, 9 m
"	14	James s. John & Mary Tetlow, Newton, 2 y
"	15	Willey Booth, Newton, 45 y
"	21	Jonas s. Thomas & Elizabeth Brown, Manchester, 2 y

"	21	Selina d. George & Mary Whitaker, Failsworth, 14 m
"	21	Mary d. John & Violet MacNamee, Newton, 10 m
"	21	George s. Robert & Alice Duncuft, Manchester, 2 y 5 m
"	22	Emma Stott, Newton, 3 y 6 m
"	24	Esther d. John & Mary Smith, Newton, 1 y 8 m
"	24	Hannah d. David & Sarah Froggatt, Newton, 2 y
"	25	William s. Thomas & Mary Greenwill, Chorlton on Medlock, 3 m
"	28	James s. William & Ann Heald, Newton, 5 m
"	29	Mary Lees, Newton, 13 y 9 m
"	29	Joseph s. Samuel & Mary Etchings, Newton, 3 m
[		April 20 1835 Willm Hutchinson Incumbent of the Chapelry of Newton]
[		Witness Abraham Taylor Chapel Warden]

1835

Jan	1	Sarah Jane d. Elizabeth Kaye, Newton, 15 m
"	2	Ann d. William & Elizabeth Stansfield, Manchester, 7 m
"	2	Ann d. Hamlet & Elizabeth Lowe, Newton, 2 y 5 m
"	4	Eliza d. George & Ellen Whitmore, Manchester, (*age blank in PR & BT*)
"	4	William s. Joseph & Sarah Chadderton, Newton, 9 m
"	4	Hannah Blackshaw a Widow, Newton, 83 y
"	4	John Grey s. Robert & Hannah Ermeston, Newton, 3 y
"	4	Ellen d. John & Ann Hibbert, Moston, 1 y 11 m
"	4	Hannah Blackshaw, Newton, 24 y
"	4	John Ingram, Newton, 35 y
"	6	Elizabeth d. John Joseph & Mary Skelmerdine, Manchester, (*age blank in PR & BT*)
"	6	Samuel s. Robert & Sarah Wylde, Manchester, (*age blank in PR & BT*)
"	7	Mary d. James & Mary Schofield, Failsworth, 4 m
"	7	Robert s. Edwin & Mary Travis, Newton, 10 m
"	8	Jane w. Benjamin Hulton, Failsworth, 34 y
"	8	Ann d. James & Ophelia Berrington, Newton, 7 m
"	10	Isaac s. Isaac & Maria Jones, Newton, 1 y 9 m
"	11	Hannah d. George & Sarah Brown, Manchester, 5 wks
"	11	Sarah d. Jonathan & Elizabeth Somerscales, Manchester, 15 m
"	11	Mary d. Andrew & Sarah Smith, Failsworth, 15 m
"	11	Nanny d. James & Betsey Terratt, Manchester, 7 wks
"	14	Jonathan s. William & Sally Lane, Failsworth, 15 m
"	14	Mary d. Robert & Sarah Hulme, Manchester, 6 y
"	18	Emma d. Hannah Haigh, Newton, 7 m
"	18	Samuel s. Joseph & Ann Copeland, Failsworth, 4 y
	(*1835*)	
"	18	Robert s. Joseph & Martha Walmesley, Failsworth, 10 m
"	18	Samuel s. James & Rosa Taylor, Failsworth, 1 y 10 m
"	18	Joel s. William & Mary Berry, Failsworth, 1 y 10 m

"	18	Edward s. Robert & Jane Taylor, Failsworth, 16 m
"	18	John Farrand, Droylsden, 70 y
"	19	Thomas s. Tho[ma]s & Sarah Barlow, Failsworth, 10 m
"	19	Jane d. William & Mary Swindells, Newton, 15 m
"	21	Phebe d. James & Mary Johnson, Mostyn, 17 m
"	23	Robert s. George & Mary Bardsley, Newton, 5 m
"	25	Solomon Coe, Manchester, 42 y
"	25	Thomas Wilson, Failsworth, 77 y
"	25	Thomas Etchells, Failsworth, 3 y
"	25	William Wylde, Newton, 2½ y
"	29	Maria w. John Haslam, Failsworth, 27 y
"	29	Sarah d. Tho[ma]s & Betty Wylde, Failsworth, 29 y
"	29	Mary w. Edwin Travis, Newton, 26 y
"	26	Josiah s. Samuel & Mary Leech, Manchester, 6 wks
"	26	Ann d. James & Rosa Taylor, Failsworth, 4 y 9 m
Feb	1	Hamlet s. Tho[ma]s & Betty Marsden, (*abode blank in PR & BT*), 18 m
"	1	Sarah d. John & Martha Shadwick, Failsworth, 2 y
"	1	Robert s. William & Lucy Seel, Newton, 3 m
"	1	George s. Will[ia]m & Sarah Drinkwater, Newton, 18 m
"	1	Ann w. John Greenwood, Failsworth, 52 y
"	1	Sarah w. Samuel Wardley, Manchester, 44 y
"	8	Reuben s. Hannah Tomlinson, Failsworth, 5 wks
"	8	Joseph s. Joseph & Ann Copeland, Failsworth, 5½ y
"	13	Mary Ann d. John & Ann Hilton, Mostyn, 1 y
"	15	Emma d. Nathan & Ellen Dale, Failsworth, 3 m
"	15	Mary w. Joseph Pollitt, Failsworth, 40 y
"	16	Robert Tomlinson, Newton, 15 y
"	18	Sarah w. Rob[er]t Whitehead, Droylsden, 36 y 11 m
"	22	Ellen d. Matthew & Hannah Howarth, Newton, 17 m
"	24	James Boardman, Newton, 71 y
"	25	Ellen d. James & Ellen Ogden, Failsworth, 2 y 2 m
"	27	Sally d. William & Mary Berry, Failsworth, 3 y 4 m
Mar	4	James s. James & Betty Jones, Newton, 1 y 9 m
"	8	Ann d. Jane Wilkinson, Failsworth, 1½ y
"	8	James s. John & Alice Parkinson, Newton, 12 m
"	8	Mary Mills, Spinster, Moston, 25 y
"	12	John s. John & Hannah Traver, Newton, 6 m
"	12	Sarah Dean Widow, Newton, 51 y
"	13	John s. William & Hannah Barlow, Failsworth, 18 m
"	15	George Henry s. Henry & Sarah Jackson, Manchester, 11 m
"	18	Hannah d. James & Martha Robinson, Failsworth, 18 m
"	19	James s. Thomas & Ann Bancroft, Manchester, 9 m
"	22	Joseph s. Sarah Haseldine, illegitimate (*abode not given in PR & BT*), 5 m
"	22	Richard Norcross, Manchester, 31 y
"	22	Joseph s. John & Sarah Clough, (*abode blank in PR & BT*), 12¾ y

"	24	Isabella d. Betty Clough, Failsworth, 14 m (*1835*)
"	25	William Shepley, Newton, 29 y
"	26	William s. William & Elizabeth Livesey, Manchester, (*age blank in* PR & BT)
"	31	Thomas Simpson, Failsworth, 27 y
Apr	3	Matilda Berry Audenshaw, 18 y
"	5	Ann d. Levi & Alice Whitehead, Failsworth, 1 y 11 m
"	12	Lucy Berry, Audenshaw, 21 y
"	12	Henry s. William & Elizabeth Bentley, Manchester, 7 y 8 m
"	12	Elizabeth w. Peter Johnson, Droylsden, 39 y
"	15	Jane w. William Charles Ridings, Newton, Newton, 26 y
"	16	Jane d. John & Elizabeth Robinson, Newton, 1 y 8 m
"	19	Rob[er]t Hall, Manchester, 25 y
"	25	John Knowton, Newton, 19 y
"	29	Joseph s. Isaac & Ann Barratt, Newton, 4 y
May	10	Mary w. W[illia]m Barker, Newton, 42 y
"	11	Esther Haddock, Failsworth, 41 y
"	13	Mary w. Rob[er]t Jackson, Manchester, 54 y
"	13	Thomas s. Samuel & Hannah Taylor, Failsworth, 8 m
"	17	Joseph s. Peter & Lucy Maria Holroyd, Failsworth, 7 wks
"	17	Mary Ann w. James Procter, Blakeley, 22 y
"	24	Sarah w. George Watson, Salford, 33 y
"	24	Elizabeth d. John & Harriot(t) Thorpe, Manchester, 8 wks
"	26	John Whitehead, Moston, 27 y
"	26	John Hulton, Failsworth, 66 y
"	26	William s. Francis & Esther Broadbent, Newton, 2 y
"	27	Matthew s. Thomas & Mary Ormrod, Newton, 9 m
"	28	Alice d. James & Richard Whitehead, Failsworth, 10 m
"	31	Elizabeth d. James & Margaret Burgess, Manchester, 15 m
Jun	2	James Gradwell, Failsworth, 2 y 10 m
"	2	Mary d. John & Margaret Murphy, Newton, 3 m
"	7	John Livesey, Manchester, 73 y
"	10	Esther Blomeley, (*abode blank in* PR & BT), 80 y (85 *struck through*) [80 y]
"	11	John s. Thomas & Alice Rothwell, Newton, (*age blank in* PR & BT)
"	14	Emma d. John & Elizabeth Whitehead, Moston, 2 y
"	16	Elizabeth w. John Robinson, Newton, 36 y
"	21	Mary Hall, Failsworth, 86 y
"	24	Martha d. Ann Timmis, illegitimate (*abode not given in* PR & BT), 17 w
"	24	Samuel s. Samuel & Sarah Traver, Ashton, 6 wks
"	25	Catherine d. James & Mary Andrew, Newton, 5 m
Jul	5	Mary d. Alice Etchells, illegitimate (*abode not given in* PR & BT), 15 wks
"	5	William Wright s. Matthew & Hannah Gradwell, Newton, 10 m
"	12	James Taylor, Droylsden, 57 y

"	15	Thomas s. Edmund & Sarah Walmesley, Failsworth, 2 days (*age blank in BT*)
"	15	Edmund Whitehead, Newton, 46 y
"	17	James s. Thomas & Sarah Thorneley, Failsworth, 15 m
"	21	George s. James Small & Jane Thornl[e]y Surgeon, Newton, 1 m
"	27	Hannah d. Thomas & Alice Whitehead, Failsworth, 10 m
"	31	Nancy w. Will[ia]m Hilton, Moston, 18 y
Aug	2	Isabella w. Tho[ma]s Smith, Newton, 60 y
"	6	Sarah Ann d. Isaac & Ann Johnson, Ardwick, 6 m
"	9	John Jones, Droylsden, 21 y
"	12	Betty w. Andrew Brewster, Droylsden, 39 y
"	16	Jane Beswick, Spinster, Manchester, 35 y
"	16	James Rowe, Newton, 69 y
"	21	Margaret d. John & Helen Bentley, Manchester, 2 m
"	27	William Henry s. Charles & Mary Hulton, Manchester, 5 m
"	30	Ann d. Thomas & Mary Cartman, Manchester, 18 days
Sep	9	Phebe d. Jonathan & Hannah Chadderton, Failsworth, 8¾ y
"	10	John Walter s. William & Mary Butterworth, Manchester, 2 m
"	13	Sarah d. James & Sarah Whittaker, Failsworth, 1 y 4 m
"	13	Alice d. William & Alice Thorpe, Failsworth, Inft
"	24	Giles Eckersley, Failsworth, 73 y
"	27	Mary Mather, Newton, 62 y
"	29	George s. Charles & Margaret Gorty, Droylsden, 12 y 10 m
Oct	4	Abraham Knott, Newton, 56 y
"	5	Esther Whitehead, Failsworth, 20 y
"	7	John Bentley, Newton, 35 y
"	14	John Goodier, Denton, 62 y
"	18	James Roe, Manchester, 27 y
"	19	John Hulme, Salford, 75 y
"	25	Eliza d. Peter & Mary Moyle, Newton, 11 m
"	29	Robert Walmesley, Newton, 46 y
"	30	Elizabeth d. Hetty Hogg, illegitimate, Newton, 5 wks
Nov	2	Alice w. Philip Dunkerley, Failsworth, 70 y
"	4	Richard s. Samuel & Elizabeth Ogden, Failsworth, 3 y
"	8	George s. Robert & Alice Duncuft, Manchester, 10 m
"	9	(8 *struck through*) [9] Mary d. William & Ann Barker, Manchester, 13 m
"	8	(9 *struck through*) [8] George s. Richard & Sarah Hall, Newton, 3 y
"	11	Edward Jones, Droylsden, 21¾ y
"	11	Thomas s. Thomas & Elizabeth Brown, Manchester, 11 m 10 days
"	15	Betty d. Samuel & Elizabeth Ogden, Failsworth, 2 wks
"	15	Mary Ann d. William & Harriett Blakeley, Ashton under line, 1 y 11 m
"	16	Mary w. Thomas Thorpe, Failsworth, 62 y
"	18	Hannah Ford Widow, Newton, 75 y
"	18	Sarah w. James Williamson, Droylsden, 55 y
"	22	Emma d. George & Mary Rogers, Newton, 5 y

"	22	John s. Thomas & Sarah Simpson, Failsworth, 1 y 3 m
"	24	George s. Nancy Gradwell, illegitimate, Blakeley, 8 y
"	25	Betty w. Thomas Chadderton, Woodhouses, 79 y
"	29	James s. George & Hannah Darbishire, Manchester, 1 y 8 m
"	30	Alice w. Obadiah Bradshaw, Manchester, 32 y
Dec	2	Alice d. Thomas & Ann Crosby, Newton, 18 days
"	3	Thomas s. Joseph & Frances Leaver, Newton, 3½ y
"	3	Benjamin Howarth, Droylsden, 76 y
"	3	Joseph s. John & Judith Baxter, Newton, 4 y
"	6	Elizabeth d. Robert & Mary Allen, Newton, 6 y 10 m
"	10	Abraham Mather, Droylsden, 90 y
"	10	Mary w. Job Travis, Newton, 36 y
"	13	Joseph Jamieson, Manchester, 9 y 4 m
"	14	Philip Dunkerley, Failsworth, 71 y
"	17	William s. Samuel & Ann Lowe, Manchester, 6 y 5 m
"	17	Thomas s. Joseph & Sarah Wylde, Newton, 5 y
"	20	George Hibbert, Failsworth, 71 y
"	23	Richard s. Richard & Hannah Kenyon, Manchester, 14 m
"	25	Alice d. Joseph & Mary Grindrod, Manchester, 17 m
"	27	Charles s. John & Grace Bradshaw, Manchester, 4 y 4 m
[		W. Hutchinson Incumbent of Newton]
[		Abraham Taylor Chapel Warden]

1836

Jan	1	Hannah d. Samuel & Ann Lowe, Manchester, 3 y
"	2	Sarah d. John & Grace Bradshaw, Broughton, 6 y 3 m
"	3	Charlotte d. Joseph & Mary Holme, Newton, 1 m
"	3	Thomas s. William & Hannah Ingham, Failsworth, 15 m
"	3	Thomas Whittaker, Newton, 63 y
"	3	Sarah d. Philip & Rebecca Lancashire, Moston, 5 days
"	3	Sarah w. Ellis Whittaker, Newton, 55 y
"	6	Thomas s. Joshua & Nancy Robinson, Newton, 13 m
"	7	Mary Skelmerdine Widow, Ashton, 72 y
"	10	Elizabeth d. William & Mary Minshull, Newton, 9 m
"	10	Jonathan Lees, Failsworth, 76 y
"	17	John s. Joseph & Harriett Lees, Newton, 11 wks
"	17	George s. George & Sarah Watson, Manchester, 5½ y
"	21	George Fildes, Newton, 75 y
"	22	Martha Kemp, Manchester, 78 y
"	24	James Horatio s. John & Ellen Taylor, Failsworth, 5 y
"	25	Ashton Shepley, Newton, 66 y
"	31	Martha Bethel d. John & Rachel Bethel, Failsworth, 24 y
"	31	John Turner, Newton, 47 y
Feb	7	Richard Jackson, Newton, 42 y

"	10	Hannah w. Edward Durbin, Manchester, 37 y
"	14	Robert Lee, Manchester, 43 y
"	14	James Bowers, Manchester, 75 y
"	20	Joseph Nuttall, Failsworth, 44 y
"	21	John Knott, Manchester, 46 y
"	21	Higham s. Job & Mary Travis, Newton, 2 y
"	24	Ann Dawson Widow, Manchester, 88 y
"	28	Samuel Clark, Chorlton upon Medlock, 18 y
"	28	Mark s. James & Mary Darbyshire, Failsworth, 9 m
"	28	Louisa d. Job & Mary Travis, Newton, 1 y
"	28	James s. Samuel & Martha Hulton, Newton, 13 m
"	29	Mary d. Jonathan & Esther Dawson, Failsworth, 8 m
Mar	6	Thomas s. John & Sarah Sidebotham, Newton, 7 m
"	6	Sarah Smith, Manchester, 90 y
"	8	Robert s. Robert & Sarah Whitehead, Droylsden, 1 y
"	8	William s. Joseph & Mary Roberts, Manchester, 2¼ y
"	10	Jane d. Thomas & Jane Taylor, Newton, 11 m
"	13	Dorothy w. Rob[er]t Lees, Newton, 55 y
"	13	Sarah Ann d. William & Sally Lane, Failsworth, 12 m
"	13	Richard s. Rob[er]t & Alice Stansfield, Newton, 6 wks
"	16	John s. Israel & Sarah Clough, Failsworth, 3 y
"	16	Betty w. Rich[ar]d Rostron, Droylsden, 25 y
"	17	Martha w. John Taylor, Failsworth, 63 y
"	18	Ann d. John & Mary Gradwell, Pendleton, 1¾ y
"	20	John Marvill, Droylsden, 33 y
"	20	Ellen d. John & Mary Jones, Newton, 11 m
"	21	James s. John & Elizabeth Hulme, Newton, 6 m
"	22	Abraham s. Hannah Arundale, illegitimate, Droylsden, 8 y
"	23	Joseph s. William & Ann Entwistle, Newton, 7 y
"	23	Mary d. James & Ann Tomlinson, Newton, 4¾ y
"	27	James Brown, Moston, 70 y
"	27	Martha d. Peter & Hannah Calland, Newton, 10 wks
Apr	3	Mary d. Henry & Betty Brown, Newton, 6 m
"	4	Harriett d. James & Betty Whitehead, Failsworth, 3 y 10 m
"	7	George Mills, Newton, 29 y
"	7	James s. James & Betty Barlow, Failsworth, 8 m
"	10	John s. Thomas & Ann Wilson, Ashton under line, 2 y
"	10	Thomas Allinson, Newton, 51 y
"	10	Thomas s. John & Elizabeth Smith, Manchester, 10 m
"	10	Thomas s. Israel & Sarah Clough, Failsworth, 9 m
"	14	Solomon s. John & Betty Redfern, Stockport, 18 wks
"	14	William Cliff, Newton, 43 y
"	16	Catharine Ashworth, Newton, 30 y
"	17	George s. Nathaniel & Ann Wolstencroft, Openshaw, 17 m
"	17	Sarah Ann d. William & Mary Barker, Newton, 1 y 11 m

"	19	James s. Edward & Alice Entwistle, Droylsden, 3 y (*1836*)
"	24	William s. Peter & Lucy Maria Holroyd, Failsworth, 2 m
"	24	Joseph s. James & Mary Ogden, Droylsden, 15 m
"	29	Alice d. William & Elizabeth Thornley, Droylsden, 3 wks
May	4	Samuel Ford, Newton, 43 y
"	8	Mary Ann Whitehead, Moston, 25 y
"	10	Sarah d. Samuel & Susan Bagnall, Chorlton on Medlock, 18 y
"	10	Jane d. Thomas & Catherine Walmesley, Manchester, 1½ y
"	10	Nancy d. Rob[er]t & Elizabeth Whittaker, Newton, 10 m
"	10	Mary Ann d. William & Elizabeth Lindley, Newton, 6 wks
"	11	Edward s. John & Hannah Goff, Manchester, 14 m
"	12	Henry s. George & Ellen Whitmore, Manchester, 18 m
"	13	Mary Ann d. James & Mary Ann Arundale, Ashton, 2 y
"	15	Harriett d. John & Sarah Goodier, Newton, 7 wks
"	19	Elizabeth d. Betty Grayson, Newton, 10 y
"	19	William s. Samuel & Mary Harrison, Manchester, 22 y
"	22	Mary w. John Whitehead, Failsworth, 36 y
"	25	Sarah wdw. Tho[ma]s Shepley, Failsworth, 61 y
"	26	John s. Jonas & Mary Thornton, Newton, 5 m
"	31	Hannah w. Rob[er]t Edmeston, Newton, 35 y
Jun	1	John Ridings, Failsworth, 70 y
"	2	John Greenhalgh, Salford, 25 y
"	7	Susanna d. Joseph & Mary Roberts, Manchester, 5 m
"	8	Joseph s. John & Ann Hulme, Newton, 7 m
"	9	Abraham Horrocks, Newton, 55 y
"	9	James Bent, Manchester, 58 y
"	14	Oliver Whitehead, Failsworth, 23 y
"	14	John s. John & Ann Roberts, Newton, 5 m
"	15	Eliza d. William & Prudence Lockit, Failsworth, (*age blank in PR & BT*)
"	17	Susanna d. Arthur & Ellen Cardwell, Manchester, (*age blank in PR & BT*)
"	21	William s. John & Sarah Houlton, Newton, (*age blank in PR & BT*)
"	26	James s. James & Alice Lees, Harpurhey, 14 m
"	28	William Harrison, Colly hurst, 27 y
"	29	Mary d. John & Ann Gradwell, Newton, 4 y
"	30	Betty Heald, Culcheth, 27 y
Jul	2	Edward s. Edward & Mary Hill, Manchester, 4 days
"	3	Thomas s. Thomas & Ann Rothwell, Newton, (*age blank in PR & BT*)
"	3	Jonathan s. William & Alice Butterworth, Manchester, 1 y 8 m
"	6	Matthew Cummins, Newton, 55 y
"	8	Mary w. Geo[rge] Clay, Manchester, 32 y
"	8	Mary w. James Andrew, Newton, 38 [y]
"	13	James Whitehead, Droylsden, 57 y
"	14	Thomas s. Francis & Sarah Blakely, Newton, 10 y
"	22	Elizabeth d. Thomas & Hannah Sumner, Openshaw, 10 m
"	25	Jane w. John Roe, Failsworth, 30 y

"	27	Jane Lees, Tong Prestwich, 86 y	(*1836*)
"	27	Mary d. John & Mary Whitehead, Failsworth, 10 wks	
"	28	Catharine d. Thomas & Elizabeth Hadfield, Newton, 1 y 7 m	
"	31	Ellen w. Francis Brown, Manchester, 66 y	
Aug	3	Noah s. Ellen Berry, Failsworth, 3 m	
"	4	Hannah d. Daniel & Jenney Jackson, Failsworth, 2 y	
"	10	Elizabeth d. James & Hannah Berry, Failsworth, 26 y	
"	10	Mary w. Abednego Ashton, Droylsden, 53 y	
"	11	Maria d. Charles & Ann Walton, Manchester, 15 days	
"	14	Jane d. William & Ellen Lees, Manchester, 8 y	
"	14	Thomas s. John & Mary Yates, Newton, 1 m	
"	14	Joseph Heath, Newton, 55 y	
"	18	Henry James, Manchester, 50 y	
"	21	Thomas s. Daniel & Mary Davis, Failsworth, 12 m	
"	25	Samuel Wylde, Droylsden, 49 y	
"	31	Edward s. William & Elizabeth Lees, Salford, 10 y	
"	31	Ann w. John Thornley, Droylsden, 44 y	
Sep	8	Ann w. Thomas Stanton, Manchester, 53 y	
"	15	Sarah w. Tho[ma]s Pointon, Manchester, 38 y	
"	18	Elizabeth d. David & Hannah Taylor, Newton, 5 m	
"	21	Elizabeth d. William & Jane Berry, Manchester, 1 y 7 m	
"	21	Elizabeth d. Daniel & Harriett Ashton, Newton, 5 m	
"	27	Thomas Poynton, Manchester, 40 y	
Oct	1	Laurence Castels, Droylsden, 60 y	
"	2	Edward s. Will[ia]m & Mary Dealtry, Oldham, 9 y	
"	5	George Robinson, Newton, 55 y	
"	5	Peter Johnson, Newton, 38 y	
"	5	John s. Joseph & Elizabeth Holland, Failsworth, 8 y	
"	9	Jabez s. William & Ann Williams, Newton, 10 wks	
"	11	Samuel s. John & Elizabeth Lloyd, Droylsden, 9 m	
"	16	John s. Thomas & Sarah Chadwick, Manchester, 15 y	
"	16	Mary d. John & Ann Tarrant, Newton, 16 days	
"	20	Matthew s. Mary Thorp, Moston, 6 y	
"	23	Charles s. John & Alice Heald, Newton, 15 m	
"	28	Mary d. Arthur & Ann Trevor, Failsworth, 3 wks	
Nov	1	Mary d. William & Harriett Wharton, Collyhurst, 19 wks	
"	6	John Connor, Salford, 42 y	
"	7	Daniel s. John & Mary Smith, Salford, 32 y	
"	13	John Hulton, Failsworth, 70 y	
"	13	Ellen w. John Baron, Salford, 66 y	
"	14	Caleb s. Joseph & Mary Barker, Ardwick, 27 y	
"	15	Alice d. John & Elizabeth Johnson, Failsworth, 2 y	
"	17	George s. James & Margaret Barlow, Manchester, 3 wks	
"	18	A woman found drowned name unknown, in Failsworth, about 30 y	
"	20	Sarah relict of Rich[ar]d Moss, Clayton, 65 y	

"	21	John s. James & Mary Blomeley, Newton, 11 m
"	23	George s. George & Mary Clay, Newton, 2 y 11 m
"	23	Michael s. George & Mary Mills, Failsworth, 15 m
"	27	Henry s. Joseph & Alice Whitehead, Newton, 6 m
"	27	Elizabeth Stafford, Manchester, 20 y
"	27	Ellen d. Tho[ma]s & Mary Wilkinson, Droylsden, 8 m
"	27	Mary Ann d. Edward & Alice Berry, Hollinwood, 3 y 7 m
"	29	William Hooley, Newton, 54 y
"	29	Margaret Duxbury, Manchester, 26 y
Dec	1	John s. John & Mary Plummer, Manchester, 2 y 4 m
"	4	James Avison, Moston, 54 y
"	4	John s. Thomas & Susanna Siddall, Manchester, 13 m
"	4	Thomas s. Edw[ar]d & Alice Berry, Hollinwood, 18 m
"	4	Sarah d. Mary Ridings, Failsworth, illegitimate, 17 m
"	6	Jonathan Whitehead, Manchester, 54 y
"	7	Robert s. Rob[er]t & Nancy Arundale, Droylsden, 17 y
"	7	Mary d. John & Ann Holt, Newton, 15 m
"	11	(*altered from* 9) [11] Moses Steel, Newton, 66 y
"	9	Samuel Lees, Manchester, 73 y
"	11	Mary d. John & Mary Plummer, Manchester, 8 m
"	9	(*altered from* 11) [9] Mary w. Tho[ma]s Duxbury, Manchester, 62 y
"	16	Ellen d. John & Ann Brown, Manchester, 12 y
"	16	Jane d. Adam & Sarah Horrocks, Newton, 2 y
"	18	Elizabeth d. Samuel & Olive Taylor, Newton, 20 y
"	18	Rebecca d. John & Ann Hulme, Newton, 6 m
"	18	Thomas s. Jane Wylde, Newton, 7 days
"	20	George Young, Newton, 50 y
"	21	Samuel s. Tho[ma]s & Hannah Hogg, Newton, 14 days
"	21	David s. John & Sarah Wylde, Newton, 15 y
"	25	Harriott d. Aaron & Mary Lilly, Openshaw, 24 y
"	25	Charles s. Will[ia]m & Elizabeth Lees, Droylsden, 4 y
"	25	Jane Edge Widow, Failsworth, 28 y
"	25	Elias Bethell, Failsworth, 86 y
[		To the Registrar of the Diocese of Chester.
		Abraham Taylor Chapel Warden Newton]

1837

Jan	1	Samuel s. Samuel & Olivia Taylor, Newton, 18 days
"	1	Job Travis, Newton, 36 y
"	1	Mary d. Eliz[abe]th Robinson, Oldham, illegitimate, inft.
"	4	Samuel John s. John & Mary Siddall, Clayton, 13 m
"	4	Ellen d. John & Mary Harrison, Manchester, 2 y 9 m
"	4	Barbara Barns, Manchester, 49 y
"	8	Alice Potts, Culcheth, 48 y

"	8	Elizabeth d. Launcelot & Ann Hogg, Droylsden, 2 m
"	8	William s. Will[ia]m & Phebe Jacks, Hollinwood, 8 m
"	8	Joseph Hesford, Newton, 27 y
"	10	Hannah d. Tho[ma]s & Mary Ann Barrett, Newton, 1 y 11 m
"	12	Samuel s. Sarah Hardman, Failsworth, 7 y
"	12	Ann d. Elijah & Sarah Whitehead, Failsworth, 25 y
"	15	John s. Joseph & Sarah Bentley, Newton, 7 wks
"	15	Margaret d. Rich[ar]d & Margaret Thorpe, Failsworth, 17 y
"	15	William s. John & Sarah Parkinson, Culcheth, 24 y
"	15	John Joseph & Nancy Garner, Newton, 11 m
"	15	Betty w. Ab[raha]m Mather, Newton, 61 y
"	15	John s. Rob[er]t & Ann Hulme, Newton, 5 y 8 m
"	15	John s. John & Betty Ramsbotham, Newton, 3 wks
"	16	Robert s. Thomas & Mary Ogden, Failsworth, 9 m
"	16	James s. Jonas & Mary Thornton, Newton, 3 y 3 m
"	20	Mary d. Willey & Nancy Booth, Newton, 8 y
"	20	Mary Ann d. Amelia Royle, Newton, illegitimate, 12 m
"	20	Ralph Siddall, Manchester, 64 [y]
"	24	Samuel Lees, Manchester, 90 y
"	26	Hannah Wilkinson Widow, Newton, 46 y
"	29	Ashton Ashton, Failsworth, 56 y
"	29	Margaret d. Seth & Jane Blackburn, Manchester, 10 y
"	29	John s. Ab[raha]m & Nancy Taylor, Newton, 11 wks
"	29	Elizabeth d. Thomas & Esther Kershaw, Manchester, 1 y 7 m
"	29	David s. Peter & Hannah Calland, Newton, 3 y 2 m
"	30	Henry s. Will[ia]m & Mary Pendleton, Failsworth, 14 days
"	31	Sarah Ann d. Will[ia]m & Hannah Wylde, Droylsden, 3 wks
Feb	2	James Johnson, Failsworth, 68 y
"	2	Sarah w. Samuel Arrowsmith, Manchester, 48 y
"	3	Margaret d. John & Martha Higham, Newton, 5 m
"	3	Ann w. Joseph Higham, Newton, 45 y
"	3	James Tweedale, School Master, Newton, 41 y (*entry inserted at a later time; entry not in BT*)
"	5	Isabella Harking Widow, Culcheth, 65 y
"	5	Daniel s. Daniel & Hannah Birtles, Manchester, 15 m
"	5	Ellen Horridge Widow, Manchester, 83 y
"	5	Elizabeth w. Geo[rge] Parkinson, Droylsden, 59 y
"	5	Mary Chadwick Widow, Manchester, 77 y
"	6	James Whitehead, Failsworth, 70 y
"	7	Hannah d. Richard & Ann Rose, Manchester, 2 y 8 m
"	8	Eliza d. Elizabeth Robinson, Failsworth, 3 m
"	8	Elizabeth w. Will[ia]m Johnson, Manchester, 49 y
"	9	John Bates, Failsworth, 68 y
"	12	Eliza w. Will[ia]m Wylde, Newton, 24 y
"	12	Mary w. Geo[rge] Hall, Manchester, 59 y

"	12	John Jones, Newton, 51 y	*(1837)*
"	12	Ann w. James Williams, Newton, 38 y	
"	12	James s. Robert & Eliza Thompson, Oldham, 3 y	
"	12	Abraham s. Samuel & Jane Mather, Newton, 19 y	
"	15	Samuel Arrowsmith, Manchester, 51 y	
"	15	Christopher Hindle, Newton, 72 y	
"	16	Jacob Fletcher, Clayton, 72 y	
"	16	Hannah Brown, Moston, 12 y	
"	19	Anne Tomlinson, Newton, 5 y	
"	19	Lydia Tomlinson, Newton, 8 m	
"	19	Betty Littlefair, Manchester, 52 y	
"	20	Joseph Richardson, Droylsden, 18 y	
"	21	Esther w. John Butterworth, Newton, 40 y	
"	21	Ann w. Geo[rge] Siddall, Manchester, 48 y	
"	21	Sarah Ann d. Samuel & Ann Lowe, Manchester, 6 m	
"	22	Edwin s. James & Frances Newton, Newton, 1 y	
"	23	Thomas Bentley s. Mary Prince, Cheetham, 2 y 11 m	
"	23	Ellen w. John Axton, Manchester, 64 y	
"	28	Frances d. John & Elizabeth Tipton, Clayton, 3½ y	
Mar	2	Hannah d. Edward & Hannah Ratcliffe, Manchester, 10 m	
"	3	Jane w. John Greenhalgh, Manchester, 57 y	
"	3	Philip s. Thomas & Mary Dunkerley, Newton, 7 m	

(next 8 entries altered from February to March; March in BT)

"	5	Enoch s. Thomas & Mary Hopwood, Newton, 2 y
"	5	Edward Preston, Failsworth, 80 y
"	8	John Fideham, Manchester, 28 y
"	8	Joseph s. David & Betty Booth, Newton, 8 y
"	9	Samuel Etchells, Droylsden, 28 y
"	9	Abraham Briscowe s. James & Jane Thornley, Newton, *(age blank in PR & BT)*
"	12	John s. William & Martha Butterworth, Manchester, 2 y
"	13	Mary Glossop, Failsworth, 43 y
"	13	Betty w. John Robinson, Newton, 55 y
"	16	Martha w. John Dawson, Culcheth, 22 y
"	19	John Lees, Failsworth, 74 y
"	22	Mary Whitehead Widow, Chadderton, 81 y
"	23	Mary w. Philip Taylor, Failsworth, 44 y
"	28	Alice d. Thomas & Nancy Sandiford, Manchester, 7 y
"	29	James s. James & Jane Taylor, Newton, 7 y
"	29	William s. John & Elizabeth Barlow, Manchester, 16 m
"	31	Mary d. Thomas & Sarah Brundrett, Failsworth, 16 y
Apr	2	Harriett d. William & Elizabeth Southwell, Manchester, 16 y
"	2	Hannah d. Edward & Alice Berry, Hollinwood, 1 y 10 m
"	2	George s. James & Frances Howarth, Newton, 7 wks
"	9	Alice d. David & Hannah Harrison, Newton, 7 m

"	9	James William s. James & Margaret Burgess, Salford, 8 m	*(1837)*
"	9	Joseph s. Joseph & Betty Smethurst, Newton, 9 m	
"	9	Sarah d. Adam & Hannah Lomas, Moston, 9 m	
"	9	Jinney w. Eli Smith, Failsworth, 52 y	
"	11	Eliza d. Joseph & Mary Smethurst, Hollinwood, 5 y	
"	12	Thomas Charlesworth, Newton, 80 y	
"	12	Mary d. William & Mary Smethurst, Failsworth, 4 y	
"	13	Nancy w. Rob[er]t Percival, Manchester, 61 y	
"	14	Robert s. William & Alice Thorpe, Failsworth, 12 wks	
"	14	Jane d. John & Jane Ramwell, Moston, 5 y	
"	16	John s. John & Nanny Gradwell, Newton, 2 y	
"	16	Priscilla d. John & Frances Bertenshaw, Newton, 18 m	
"	16	Jane w. Isaiah Crossley, Newton, 28 y	
"	17	John s. Laurence & Grace Waring, Newton, 2½ y	
"	18	Isaac Steel, Clayton, 32 y	
"	19	Thomas Taylor, Manchester, 28 y	
"	23	Ann w. Robert Glossop, Failsworth, 77 y	
"	28	Jinney d. Thomas & Alice Brown, Moston, 9 m	
"	30	Rachel Rhodes relict of John Rhodes, Manchester, 72 y	
May	1	Abraham Clough, Failsworth, 33 y	
"	2	Samuel s. John & Ann Hilton, Harpurhey, 5 y	
"	7	Jane d. James & Nancy Anderson, Manchester, 3 y	
"	7	Joseph Booth, Failsworth, 75 y	
"	8	William Greenhalgh, Failsworth, 45 y	
"	9	James Ogden, Manchester, 58 y	
"	11	Sarah d. Charles & Ann Harcroft, Manchester, 8 m	
"	16	Charles s. Aaron & Alice Booth, Manchester, 14 m	
"	20	James Moore Ross, patient out of Asylum at Newton, 36 y	
"	21	Mary w. George Lane, Failsworth, 36 y	
"	21	James Barrett, Newton, 23 y	
"	21	James Gorton, Blackley, 86 y	
"	21	James s. Edward & Harriett Shirley, Newton, 2 y	
"	21	Ann d. Peter & Ann Whitehead, Droylsden, 16 days	
"	23	William s. Samuel & Elizabeth Duxbury, Manchester, 18 wks	
"	24	John s. William & Sarah Marsden, Newton, 2 y 4 m	
"	25	John s. Jane Lees, Newton, 13 wks	
"	28	Ann Millar, Newton, 24 y	
"	28	Elizabeth d. James & Ann Anderson, Failsworth, 1 y	
"	31	Martha d. John & Harriett Simpson, Newton, 3 wks	
"	31	Betty d. Edmund & Betty Anderson, Manchester, 2 y 3 m	
"	31	Ellen d. Sophia Lithgo, Manchester, 2 y 9 m	
Jun	2	Joseph Seel, Newton, 18 y	
"	2	Robert s. John & Ann Heywood, Droylsden, 10 m	
"	2	Richard Whitehead, Failsworth, 60 y	
"	3	Mary Ross, Clayton Vale, 25 y	

"	4	Edward Smith, Clayton, 9 y
"	4	Esther Stansfield, Newton, 62 y
"	5	Sarah Hannah d. William & Helen Dawson, Newton, 5 wks
"	5	George Hardy, Failsworth, 76 y
"	6	James s. Joseph & Ellen Clough, Newton, 15 m
"	8	Jane d. William & Ann Scott, Newton, 1 y
"	9	Thomas s. Joshua & Mary Bent, Droylsden, 2 y 5 m
"	11	Elizabeth w. James Hall, Newton, 41 y
"	12	Sarah d. Thomas & Jane Hall, Manchester, 13 m
"	15	Margaret Cox, Droylsden, 60 y
"	19	A man name unknown: found drowned in the Canal, Failsworth, 50 y
"	22	Margaret d. Ann Turner, Newton, 5 m
"	24	Eliza d. Thomas & Sarah Poynton, Newton, 16 y
"	25	John s. James & Maria Turner, Newton, 16 wks
"	29	James Turner, Newton, 43 y
"	30	James s. Joseph & Elizabeth Selby, Droylsden, 14 m
Jul	2	Rachel d. John & Jane Clough, Manchester, 1 y 10 m
"	2	Margaret d. Richard & Esther Brown, Manchester, 3 y 8 m
"	2	Jane d. John & Jane Wroe, Failsworth, 14 m
"	5	Matthew s. John & Hannah Trevor, Newton, 14 m
"	6	Diana Wellock, Newton, 76 y
"	7	Daniel Holroyd, Manchester, 58 y
"	15	Ann w. William Spence, Clayton, 30 y
"	16	Mary d. John & Alice Riley, Newton, 9 m
"	16	Hannah d. Joseph (John *struck through in PR*) & Hannah Bardsley, Droylsden, 4 m
"	16	John Thornley, Failsworth, 18 y
"	16	Hannah d. Henry & Elizabeth Kirke, Manchester, 3 y
"	16	Elizabeth w. Joseph Holden, Newton, 33 y
"	18	Harriett w. Absalom Hilton, Failsworth, 22 y
"	18	Mary Ann d. Martha Stewart, Newton, 6 m
"	21	Sarah w. James Smith, Newton, 30 y
"	21	Margaret d. William & Esther Whitehead, Failsworth, 5 y
"	25	John Halliwell, Colley hurst, 55 y
"	26	Joseph Entwistle, Manchester, 70 y
"	27	Violet w. John MacNamee, Newton, 30 y
"	31	John Ousey, Clayton, 14 y
"	31	Thomas s. Seth & Lydia Blackburn, Manchester, 12 m
Aug	4	John s. Alexander & Mary Cowburn Cairns, Culcheth, 2 wks
"	15	Isabella d. Mark & Ann Smith, Newton, 6 m
"	20	Thomas s. William & Catharine Murdy, Newton, 1 y 10 m
"	20	Ann d. Edwin & Mary Hilton, Manchester, 15 m
"	23	Sarah d. John & Margaret Berry, Failsworth, 13 wks
"	23	Eliza d. David & Alice Williamson, Droylsden, 2 y 10 m
"	26	Thomas Allen, Newton, 23 y

"	28	Ellen Wroe, Failsworth, 58 y *(1837)*
Sep	6	William s. George & Sarah Hardman, Failsworth, 1 y 7 m
"	7	Veturia w. R[ichar]d Fishwick, Newton, *(age blank in PR & BT)*
"	8	Martha d. James & Alice Robinson, Newton, 4 y
"	10	Sidney s. William & Sarah Smith, Failsworth, 20 y
"	12	Charles s. John & Sarah Sidebottom, Newton, 6 m
"	13	George s. Anne Travis, Newton, 7 wks
"	13	John Walker, Manchester, 56 y
"	16	Levi Hedley, Newton, 27 y
"	17	Amelia d. James & Esther Barnes, Newton, 1 y 8 m
"	17	Elizabeth d. Jonathan & Sarah Goodier, Newton, 9 wks
"	19	George Hibbert, Manchester, 53 y
"	22	Ann Kershaw, Failsworth, 38 y
"	24	William Harris, Failsworth, 44 y
"	24	John s. Thomas & Mary Cartman, Manchester, 8 m
"	24	Ann d. Joshua & Mary Smith, Newton, 14 m
"	28	Ann Travis, Manchester, 47 y
"	29	Betty d. James & Betty Ogden, Failsworth, 13 y
Oct	1	Ann Thomason, Newton, 33 y
"	2	Charles Thorpe, Failsworth, 24 y
"	3	William Henry s. Henry & Lydia Haughton, Newton, 2 y
"	4	Robert s. Absalom & Harriett Hulton, Failsworth, 9 m
"	4	John Sharples, Ashton, 29 y
"	4	Sarah d. Jeremiah & Lucy Thompson, Manchester, 8 m
"	4	Robert Hulme, Droylsden, 80 y
"	6	Benjamin s. John & Alice Heald, Newton, 1 m
"	6	Sarah d. Joseph & Sarah Kenyon, Newton, 3 y
"	8	James s. John & Hannah Grundy, Newton, 10 wks
"	8	Betty Butterworth Widow, Manchester, 74 y
"	13	Elizabeth Smith, Manchester, 32 y
"	13	Jane w. John Hulme, Colley hurst, 26 y
"	19	Hannah w. Geo[rge] Robinson, Salford, 25 y
"	20	Thomas s. Jesse & Hannah Johnson, Newton, 3 y
"	22	Ann d. John & Sarah Barrow, Newton, 1 m
"	22	Joseph s. John & Jane Hulme, Newton, 3 wks
"	22	Mary Hulton, Failsworth, 40 y
"	24	Samuel s. Jane Heath, Newton, 9 m
"	29	Dinah d. Betty Goodier, Newton, 9 m
"	31	William s. John & Sarah Mather, Newton, 13 y
Nov	5	Harriett d. Will[ia]m & Mary Walker, Newton, 7 y
"	5	Joseph s. Joseph & Betty Halliwell, Droylsden, 12 y
"	8	Thomas s. Thomas & Charlotte Collyer, Failsworth, 5 y
"	9	Esther Hannah d. George & Margaret Lee, Newton, 18 m
"	10	Martha d. John & Betty Wolstenholme, Failsworth, 6 m
"	12	George Etchells, Failsworth, 78 y

"	12	John Greenwood, Failsworth, 54 y	*(1837)*
"	12	Betty Hampson, Manchester, 60 y	
"	15	Joseph Stott, Manchester, 21 y	
"	16	Mary w. James Rydings, Failsworth, 69 y	
"	21	John Spekeman, Manchester, 52 y	
"	24	James s. John & Ellen Mills, Ashton, 3 y	
"	26	James Thomas s. Thomas & Mary Ann Mayo, Ardwick, 3 m	
"	26	James Pollitt, Failsworth, 23 y	
"	30	Mary w. Amaziah Holland, Manchester, 64 y	
Dec	3	James s. James & Ann Etchells, Failsworth, 1 y 10 m	
"	3	Elizabeth w. Will[ia]m Booth, 62 y	
"	3	James s. Jesse & Hannah Johnson, Newton, 1 y 7 m	
"	5	Thomas Duxbury, Manchester, 39 y	
"	6	Mary Ann d. Charles & Elizabeth Hesford, Clayton, 15 m	
"	13	Samuel s. James & Sarah Mather, Newton, 5 m	
"	17	George Howe s. James & Sarah Deane, Newton, 2 y	
"	17	Elizabeth Isdell Widow, Newton, 54 y	
"	17	Eliza d. John & Parnell Cordwell, Newton, 1 y 8 m	
"	18	Ann d. Reuben & Mary Holt, Failsworth, 14 m	
"	18	Mary d. Joseph & Elizabeth Smethurst, Newton, 3 wks	
"	19	Robert s. Charles & Mary Cordey, Droylsden, 3 y	
"	19	Ann d. Rob[er]t & Mary Hulme, Culcheth, 3 y	
"	23	Michael Wareing, Turton, 50 y	
"	24	William Hulme, Newton, 36 y	
"	24	Mary Dawson Widow, Failsworth, 57 y	
"	31	Samuel Ainsworth, Failsworth, 73 y	

Index 1

Names

The computer has been programmed to use the following abbreviations in the index of names for Christian names and their variations.

Aa Aaron; Abi Abigail; Abr Abraham; Aga Agatha; Agn Agnes; Alex Alexander; Alf Alfred; Ali Alice; Amb Ambrose; Ame Amelia, Amy; And Andrew; Ann Anne, Nancy, Nanny; Anbl Annabel; Ant Anthony; Arbl Arabella; Arn Arnold; Art Arthur; Aug Augustus; Bar Barbara, Barby; Bart Bartholemew; Ben Benjamin; Ber Bernard; Eliz Betty, Elizabeth; Bri Brian; Brid Bridget; Car Carol(ine); Cat Catherine; Cbl Christabel; Cec Cecily; Chas Charles; Chat Charlotte ; Chn Christian; Chr Christopher; Clem Clement; Cor Cornelius; Cut Cothbert; Dan Daniel; Dav David; Deb Deborah; Den Denis; Di Diana; Dor Dorcas; Dot Dorothy; Dud Duseldley; Ebe Ebenezer; Edg Edgar; Edm Edmund; Edw Edward; Edn Edwin; Elnr Eleanor; Eli Elijah, Elias; Eliz Elizabeth, Betty; Els Elisha; Ell Ellen, Helen; Emm Emmeline; Eno Enoch; Est Esther, Hester ; Fer Ferdinand; Fres Frances; Fris Francis; Fred Frederick; Gab Gabriel; Gef Geoffrey Jeffery; Geo George; Ginny Ginney; Gra Grace; Greg Gregory; Ham Hamlet; Han Hannah Anna; Har Harriet; Hea Henrietta; Hen Henry, Harry; Hum Humphrey; Isa Isaac; Isb Isabel; Ish Isiah; Isr Isreal; Jab Jabez ; Jac Jacob; Jam James; Jan Janet; Jer Jeremy; Jn John, Jno, Ino; Jon Jonathan; Jos Joseph ; Josh Joshua; Josi Josiah; Jud Judith; Lan Lancelot; Law Lawrence; Leo Leonard; Let Lettice; Lnl Lionel; Lyd Lydia ; Mab Mabel; Ma Magdaline;Mgt Margaret, Peggy; Mgy Margery ; Mar Martha; Mat Matthew; Mic Michael; Mil Miles; Mor Mordecai; Mos Moses; My Mary, Maria; Nat Nathan Nathaniel; Ne Nehemiah; Nel Nelly; Nic Nicholas; NXN no Christian name; Oli Oliver; Olv Olive; Pat Patrick; Pen Penelope; Pet Peter; Phe Phebe ; Pru Prudence; Phi Philip; Pho Phoebe; Pri Priscilla; Rac Rachel; Ral Ralph; Ran Randal; Reb Rebecca; Reu Reuben; Ric Richard; Rob Robert; Rog Roger; Ros Rosomund; Row Roland Rowland; Sal Sally Salley; Sam Samuel;Sar Sarah; Sil Silas; Sim Simeon; Sol Solomon; Sop Sophia; Ste Steven; Sue Susan(nah); Tab Tabitha; Thz Thirza; Theo Theophilus; Tho Thomas ; Thon Thomasin; Thu Thurstan; Tim Timothy; Tit Titus; Uri Uriah; Urs Ursula; Wat Walter; Wilf Wilfred; Wm William; Win Winifred; Zach Zachariah

(When a name occurs more than once on the same page, the number of times is shown in parentheses. The merging of surnames in this index should not be taken to indicate a belief that they are necessarily the same name.)

256

Atkinson, Chat 301(2); Eliz 29,250; Ell
205; H 199; Harriot 237; Isb 205; Jane
176,199,237,251; Jn 176,301; My 29;
Rac 230; Ric 301(2); Tho 182; William
Holdby 251; Wm 29,176,199(2),205,
237

Austen (Austin), Ann 234; Jam 238; Jn
234

Avison (Avenson, Ivison), Chas 289; Ell
22,190; Jam 318; Jn 289; Mar 289; My
22,190; Rob 22,190

Axton, Ell 204,320; Jn 320; Mar 204;
Sam 204

Ayres (Eyre, Eyres, Haire, Hare), Ali 143;
Ann 76,129,300; Ben 36; Dav 56; Eliz
103; Geo 25,30,36,50,56,66,76,85,112,
287; Jam 244; Jessica 244; Jn 50,93; Jos
300; Josh 66; Mar 93,103,112,129,143,
287,290; Mgt 25,30,36,56,66,76,85;
My 50; Sar 85,101; Sarah Anne 101;
Tho 25,101,290; Wm 30,93,103,112,
129,143,287,290

B

Babb, Christiana 180; Jam 180

Bagnall (Bagnal), Ali 146; Annabella 146;
Eliz 103,280; Jn 146; My 78,270,
272(2),273; Rob 270; Sam 103,270(2),
280,309,316; Samuel Edward 309; Sar
316; Sue 103,270(2),280,309,316; Tho
78,272,273; Wm 78

Baguley, Ali 174; Eliz 57; Jam 174,187;
Jos 57; Tho 57

Bailey (Bayley), Ann 56,71,81,97,106,
110,240, 281,296,298,304,306; Ben
56,71,81; Eliz 277; Han 304; Isa 97;
Jam 106,281; Jane 164; Jn 97,106,110,
164,208,240,277,281,296(2),306(2);
Jos 215; Mar 208; Marianne 81; Mgt
222; Sar 164,298; Tryphena 71; Wm
56,110,240,298,304

Baker, Eliz 104; Jane 104,112; Jn 104(2),
112; Marianne 112

Ball, Eliz 190(2),246; Jn 246,299; My
221; Sar 246; Wm 190

Bamber, My 172; Ric 172; Sar 172

Bamford, Ali 167; Ann 276; Eliz 267,
271; Est 235; Jac 235; Jam 267,271,
276; Jane 267; Marianne 271

Bancroft, Aa 302; Ann 297,302(2),311;
Jam 311; Mos 302; Tho 297(2),302(2),
311

Banks, Ann 48,50; Ell 48; Jam 168; Jn
50; Mary Anne 168; Reb 168; Rob 48,
50

Barber, Dav 84; Eliz 291; Ell 84; Hen
156; Jam 291; Jesse 84; Jn 156(2);
Marianne 291; My 156(2); Thamar 156

Bardsley (Barsley), Ali 109,123,152,213;
And 65,143; Ann 64,78,117,152,252,
264,304; Car 121; Edn 117; Eliz 2,11,
47,60,64,72,78,83,109,119,121,138,
188,196,213,235(2),252,264,296; Elnr
91; Geo 2,7(2),87,97,109,114,121,129,
138,149,260,285,311; Han 43,47,55,
87,113,117,119,136,153(2),322(2);
Helena 109; Hen 122,303; Jam 16,60,
72,91,109(2),121,123,126,149,152,
296; Jane 136; Jn 43,64,109(2),116,
126,138,151,196,213,235,252,296,
322; Jos 11,16,22(2),46,55,65,78(2),
87,113,117,119,129,136,143,153,
177,188,189,253,289,322; Leonora
121; Mar 46,65,116; My 11,14,16,22,
78(2),87,97,109(2),121,129,138,143,
149,253,311; Olv 116,126,138,151(2);
Reb 189; Rob 133,138,311; Sam 14,
123,284; Samuel Thomason 14; Sar 2,7,
72,87(2),113,114,122,133,143(2),
152(2),196,260,303,304; Sarah Anne
91; Tho 83; Wm 46,60,97,114,122,
133,143,152,303(2)

Barker, Ann 3,7,313; Caleb 317; Eliz 75,
81,90,298; Jam 75,81,90,277,298;
Jemima 141; Jn 3,90,208; Jos 75,224,
235,317; Kezia 141; Mgt 7,208; My 81,
141,208,232,298,312,313,315,317;
Sam 3,7; Sarah Ann 141,315; Sue 141;

Tho 248; Wm 141,312,313,315
Barlow, Ali 33,41,47,58,153; Ann 40,58,
96,108,213,246,275, 276,297; Eliz
7(2),13,20(2),28,31,33,40,57,76,81,
94(2),108,119,122,127,135,159,167,
180,189,194,213,240,244,256,269,
284,297,315,320; Ell 122,246; Geo 60,
159,246,317; Han 38,107,116,124,
133,135,144,145,227,311; Isa 58; Jam
3,7,57,81,119(2),124,127,159,165,
191(2),195,240,245,253,284,315(2),
317; Jane 9,47; Jn 12,16,24,60,108,
114(2),133,159,167,172,185,189,240,
288(2),297,311,320; John Williams
127; Jos 41,135,144,153,240,288;
Lavinia 102; Lyd 57,108,114,288; Mar
24,38,47,145; Mary Anne 28; Mgt 288,
317; My 3(2),7,9,12,16,22,58(2),60,
108,118,165(2),167,170,185,191(2),
195(2),231,240,245,284,288; Nancy
Maria 58; Olv 108; Phe 153; Ric 122,
224; Rob 7,16,22,33,41,47,58,76,107,
185,195,256,269; Sam 94(3),107,108,
240; Sar 47,81,83,96,102,107,108,118,
135,170,194,270,276,306(2),311;
Sarah Ann 144; Tho 7,13(2),20,40,47,
102,108,116,118,135(2),170,180(2),
194,213,223,244,270,278,306,311(2);
Wm 22,31,83(2),94,96,107(2),116,
133,145,276,311,320
Barnes (Barns), Ali 11; Ame 145,323;
And 273; Ann 14,30,71,77,78,86(2),91,
102,137,139,180(3),273; Anne Buckley
131; Bar 318; Cat 11; Charles Henry
137,309; Chas 113,121,128,137,144,
154,305,309; Edn 154; Eliz 11,78,102,
235; Est 137,145,154,323; Han 144;
Jam 24,77,91,102,121,137,145,154,
251,273,305,323; James Hall 71; Jn
130(2),139,189,235,265, 272; Jos 24,
131; Lavinia 113,121,128,137,144,
154(2),305,309; Luke 180(2);
Marianne 71; Mat 30; My 24,71,82,
100,180,189(2),235,265; Phillis 130,
139; Robert Newton 137; Sam 71,78,86;

Sar 91,131; Sarah Anne 100; Tho 11,
113,137; Wm 14,71,77,82(2),100,128,
257
Barnett, Wm 254
Barns - see Barnes
Baron, Ell 317; Jam 203(2); Jn 317; Sar
203
Barratt (Barrat, Barret, Barrett, Barritt),
Ann 12,96,107,140,312; Ben 63; Eliz
3,11(2),12,21,180; Fres 21; Fris 21;
Han 39,67,141,319; Hen 152; Isa 96,
107,140,312; Jam 12,21,180,321; Jane
39; Jn 69,180,296; Jos 63,67,69,78,87,
146,290(2),296,312; Mary Ann 141,
152,319; Mgt 87,142; My 3,146,290,
296; Reb 63,69,78,87,107,290; Ric 96,
290; Rob 142,146; Sam 39,67,78,146;
Sar 142,146(2); Sarah Ann 140; Tho
141,152,319; Wm 3,11
Barrington, Caleb 137; Dan 137,251; Eliz
12,31,204; Han 137,251(2); Jam 31; Jn
12,31,204(2); Mar 68; Mgt 12; Wm 68
Barritt - see Barratt
Barrow (Barrows), Ann 46,60,120,323;
Ben 13,46(2),50,54,60,85; Eliz 27,46,
49,54,58,71; Han 37,48,53(2),71,223;
Hen 42; Isa 120; Jam 3; Jane 3,8,13,21,
35,44; Jenny 27,42; Jn 44,46,49(2),58,
323; Jos 21,120,155; Mar 35; My 46,
50(2),54,58,60,85,155; Ric 37,48(2),
53,71; Sal 8,37; Sar 8,323; William
Bland 155; Wm 3,8,13,21,27,35,42,44,
85
Barsley - see Bardsley
Barsnett - see Basnet
Barton, Chat 279; Eliz 107(2),280; Ell
252; Han 246,279; Jam 68; Jn 107,246,
279,280(2); Jos 252; Mar 68; Reb 231;
Sam 68,253; Sue 252
Barwick, Jane 167; Jn 167; My 167
Basley - see Beesley
Basnet (Barsnett), Est 224; Jos 294
Bateman, Ann 95,140,291; Chas 140;
Eliz 95; Ell 214; Emma 95; Jam 214;
Jane 291; Jn 95,140,154,291; Lucy 154;

320; Hen 59,146; Isb 240; Jam 9,10,18,
21,22,23,24,31,38,47,52,58(2),63,83,
87,93,95(2),97(2),98(2),116,130,173,
191,196,203,205,209,217,220,254,
258,262,270,304,308,317; Jane 10,15,
34,61,73,88,146,151,248,261,307,317;
Janet Martha 98; Jn 7,8,11,17,26,27,
28,29,32,34,43,52(2),58,63,64,66,
75,82,85,89,93,96,105(2),110,116(2),
126,130,157,161,168,178(2),191(2),
214,240,252,270,279,282,285,303,
305,322; Joel 138,146,153,310; John
Clare 58; Jos 1,7,16,21,23,26(2),29,
33(2),38,41,43,46,53,58,61,67,73(2),
83,88,93,97,126,132,144,153,161,163,
183,192,193,204,216,241,248,252,
255,261,262,297,300,307; Lucy 33,53,
63,192,204,254,312; Mar 21(2),42,52,
81,115,151,178,191; Marianne 110,
131,285; Mary Ann 318; Mary Gee 130;
Mat 305; Matilda 67,312; Mgt 322;
Mos 10,20,43,190,197; My 1,8,9(2),20,
21,31,33,38(2),43,46,53,61,64,67,73,
80,83(2),85,89,91(2),95(2),96,103,
111,116,125,127,138,143,145,146,
168,169,190,204,209,216,235,240,
241,249,252,255(2),262,267(2),276,
279(2),297,305,307,310,311; Noah
146,191,317; Olv 33,85; Phi 10,15,23,
28,33,83,87,96,97,116,127,146,161,
192,218,254; Rob 3,11,18,27,34,49,54,
55,66,89,93,95,101,145(2),221,282; Sal
125,183,311; Sam 1,9,22,28,36,42,88,
143,153,163,169,260,261,279,280,
287,293,304; Sar 3,7,9,11,16(2),17,
18(2),21,22,26,27,28,34(2),36,55,76,
81,91,115,145,161,163,183,190,191,
193,197,218,232,235,280,287,293,
322; Sarah Ann 153; Tabby 28; Tho 10,
15,23,32,38,42,43,51,58,59,61,73,75,
80,95,127,144,218,235,240,249,282,
307,318; Tho Whitehead 76; Violet 73;
Wm Philip 145; Wm 17,18,115,125,
151,179,190,216,241,307,310,311,317
Bertenshaw, Alf 78; Ann 78,260; Fres

321; Fris 308; Jn 308,321; Jos 33,40,42,
44,46,201,204,208,212,215,218,308;
Josh 260; Mar 78,260; Pri 321
Berwick, Jane 174; Jn 174; Tho 174
Beswick, Abr 7,18; Ann 7,22,34(2),137,
211(2),241,243,251,300,303; Eliz 59,
163; Ell 59; Est 15,162,181(3); Han
59(2); Jam 15,162(2),163,181(2),189,
200,231,243,251(2); Jane 7,15,18,303,
313; Jn 22(2),137,164,241(2),243,300,
303; Jos 137; Mgt 56; My 164,216,308;
Sam 18,56,164,201,216; Tho 211,243,
308; Tho Wroe 34; Wm 56
Bethell (Bethel, Bithel, Bithell, Bythel,
Bythell, Bythill), Ali 12,18,61,176,177;
Ann 89,98,219; Dav 29,196; Eli 7,89,
177,196,239,288,318; Eliz 12,16,25,32,
40,80,176,196,210,219; Ell 128; Jam
12,16,25,32(2),40,111,176,196,210,
292; Jane 7,40,61,73,79,89,98,111,
128,135,177,196,210,239,256,288,
292; Jenny 80,89,102,247,298; Jn 18,
29,73,102,314; Jon 219; Mar 314; My
16,79,256; Rac 18,29,314; Sam 7,73,
79,89,98,111,128,256,288,292,298,
301; Sar 228; Wm 25,61,80,89,102,
135(2),196,247(2),298
Bibby, Eliz 170; Mgt 170; Ric 170
Bickley, Hugh 2; Jane 2; Tho 2
Billinge (Billenge), Ali 231; Chas 248;
Eliz 264; Jam 35,203; Jn 27,35,203,
248,261(2),264, 298; My 27,35,203,
225,248,261, 264; Sar 225; Wm 27,225
Billington, Eliz 270,294(2),297; Jn 270,
294,297(2); Wm 270
Bine, Looklean 30; My 30; Sarah Anne
30
Birch, Amb 233; Ann 130,222; Edw 233;
Eliz 38,219,265; Jam 38,219,265; Jn
130,149; Mar 149; My 38; Sar 149; Tho
219; Wm 130
Birchal (Birchell, Birckill, Burchel,
Burchell, Burchil, Burchill), Ali 119;
Eliz 2,15,162,183,206(2),236; Hen 173;
Jane 217; Josh 2,162; Mary Anne 173;

Broadhurst, Jn 186; Mar 186; My 186
Broadley, Bar 176; Fris 176; Jam 176
Bromhead, Ann 146; Sam 146; Tho 146
Brook (Brooke, Brookes, Brooks), Ali 54;
  Ann 54,113,122,131,282,285, 300; Cat
  134,298; Chas 131; David Hague 83;
  Eliz 110,272,282,298; Geo 170,272;
  Jam 113; Jn 83; Marianne 110; Rob
  110,134,298; Sar 83,170,285; Ste 122,
  300; Tho 54,113,122,131,134,282,
  285,300; Wm 170,272
Brough, Jam 268; Jane 268; My 268
Broughton, Ann 210,249,268,274; Jam
  210,220,247,250,268,274; Jn
  249,268,274; Jos 249; My
  210,220(2),247,250; Rob 247
Brown, Ali 4,9,10,74,118,119,140,152,
  184,275,280,285,288,293,309,321;
  Ann 68,117,129,142,154,257,271(2),
  309,318; Ashton 31,117,129,142; Bart
  119; Bart John 140; Betsey 287; Cat 2,
  9,16,25,32; Charles James 259; Chas
  222,241,257,259,275(2),278,288,
  299(2),309; Dot 256; Edn 126; Edw 38,
  46,207; Eliz 2,10,16(2),23,24,31,39,
  43,48,54,60,86,106,117,118,123,129,
  133(2),134,139,143,152,165,170,222,
  235,238,249,256,265,287,293,302,
  309,313,315; Eliza Whittaker 119; Ell
  200,211,241,257(2),259,275,278,283,
  299,317,318; Eno 101; Est 35,112,184,
  241,256,266,322; Frank 78; Fres 243;
  Fris 36,44,48,53,63,200(2),211,270,
  283,317; Garratt 278; Garrick 101; Geo
  2,16,25,175,184,200(2),226,265,302,
  307(2),310; Han 4,10,39,40,69,108,
  117,119(2),126,137,190,213,231,310,
  320; Har 123; Hen 23,117,123,133,143,
  152,315; Hodgson 249; Isb 101; Jam 2,
  9,16,22,25,32,86,87,117,119,139,152,
  155,182,192,207,226,238,256,257,
  265,288,307,315; Jane 5,86,192,194,
  207; Jenny 285; Jinney 321; Jn 2,4,9,
  10,19,24,25,30,31(2),32,36,56,60,68,
  154, 165,170,172,184,202,207,246,

266,271,300,318; Joel 13,68(2),115(2),
  245,279,280; John Brundritt 119; Jon
  88; Jonas 24,198,309; Jos 9,13,16,17,
  22,30,31,38,44,48(2),54,63,90,117,
  126,127,137,235,236,245,256,279;
  Josh 35(2); Josi 10,16,23,31,39,43,60;
  Let 264; Mar 9,36,48,53,63,68,78,86,
  142,155,263,270,275; Mark 106,134;
  Mary Ann 152; Mary Anne 54,74; Mat
  16,17,23,31,40,45,50,56,61,70(2),86,
  98,112,152, 263,277; Matilda 256;
  Matty 200; Mgt 10,24,31(2),33,322;
  Mos 222,283; My 2,5,8,10,12,13,
  16(2),18,19,22,23,24,25,29,30,31,
  33(2),38(2),44,46,48,50,63,78(2),90,
  115,143,155,166(2),175,184(2),185,
  198,200,202,207,211,213,235(2),
  236(3),240,243,245,256,265,271,275,
  278,279,307,315; Olv 154; Phe 12,88;
  Phillis 127; Ric 18,43,127,134,166,256,
  266,322; Rob 117,170; Ruth 240; Sal
  16; Sam 100; Sar 17,23,31,40,45,50,56,
  61(2),63(2),69,70,86,87,98,100,112,
  117,134,137,139,192,224,226,236,
  263,277(2),310; Sarah Matilda 152; Sue
  2,264; Sue Barker 2,165; Tho 5,8,12,18,
  19,25,29,33,38(2),45,46,53,68,90,106,
  118,140,152,194,207,213,220,221,234,
  235,236,240,249,256,264,280,285,
  287,293,309,313(2),321; Wm 2(2),8,
  10(2),16,18,24,29,31,33,40,42,44,
  78(2),88,98,100,108(2),119,152,
  175(2),180,184,185(3),189,190,198,
  200(2),201,202,204,208,212,215,239,
  243,265,271,288
Brownhill (Brownells), Eliz 151,176,186,
  238; Jam 238; Jn 151,176(2),186,254;
  Ric 151; Sar 238; Wm 252
Bruce, Ann 286; Ben 286; Car 273; Eliz
  286; Ell 265,273,297,305; Geo 265,
  273,297,305; Jane 283; Jn 284; Lyd
  284; Mgt 297; My 265; Sar 259,273,
  283; Tho 259,273,283,305; Wm
  259,273
Brundrett (Blundret, Brundret, Brundrit,

Mos 142; My 64,80,88(2),99,142,153,
251; Sarah Ann 153; Wm 64
Dudson - see Dodson
Duggan, My 177(2); Sam 177,180
Dukes, Chat 271; Jam 271
Dummelow - see Dimelow
Duncalf (Duncufet, Duncuff, Duncuft),
Ali 188,275,280,310,313; Chat 263;
Eliz 242,307; Geo 232,242,306,310,
313; Gowen 171,188,224; Han 233,306;
Jam 242,307; Jn 233,263; Mary Ann
307; Rob 275,280,307,310,313; Sar
280; Tho 233,275
Dunkerley (Dunkerly), Abi 88; Ali 3,10,
18,38,98,165,183, 313; Ann 3,39(2),
88,110; Eliz 38; Geo 8; Han 45,52,248,
258; Harriett 39; Isa 52; Jam 39; Jn 45,
104,118,165,203,297; Josh 277; My 8,
98,104,110,129(2),149, 183,320; Phi 3,
10(2),18,108,118,149(3),165,183,297,
313,314,320; Ruth 8; Sam 248; Sar 108,
118,149,203,297; Tho 18,39,45,52,98,
104,108,110,129,149,248,258,320
Dunkerly - see Dunkerley
Dunn, Gra 162,164; Hen 162,164; My
164
Dunstan, Jam 259(2),267,278,289; Mgt
267; Nat 278; Sar 259,267,278
Durbin, Edw 315; Han 315
Durker, Ann 189; Jn 189; Mary Anne 189
Dutton, Aa 121; Jn 121; My 121
Duxbury, Eliz 321; Jn 256,292; Mgt
193,318; My 256,264,292,318; Oli 233;
Rob 264; Sam 193,321; Tho 256,264,
266,318,324; Wm 321
Dyson, Est 267; Jam 109,117,267,298; Jn
117; Jos 43; My 43,109,117,267,298;
Sar 43,109

E

Eastwood, Chat 275; Han 275; Jn 167;
My 167,281,287(2); Wm 281(2),287
Eaton, Ann 105; Eliz 84,95,105; Ell 256;
Geo 255,256; Jam 84; Jane 255,256;

Jn 84,95,105; Marianne 275; Mat
254(2),275; My 254,275; Rob 95
Eckersley, Ali 5,11,24,118,162,189,256,
260; Alice Thorpe 87; Ann 6,9,11,15,
18,24,31,32,42,50,118,120,162,180,
184,188,222,244,256; Ben 50; Bold
174,204; Cat 87,260; Chas 72,83,264,
287; Edm 15; Edw 9,15,24,32,42,50,
180,188; Eliz 48,72,83,122,189,224,
264,287; Ell 74; Geo 96,229; Giles 11,
48,313; Han 95,103; Hen 31,120,
137(2); Isb 11,15,118,188,204,230;
Jam 5,11,108,162,256,303; Jane
Townsend 72; Jn 6,9,18,31,116,162,
180,184,244,299; Jos 96,103,287; Josh
66,74,108,118,129,256,265,301,302;
Lissey 18,184; Luke 11,87,95,260,262;
Mar 116,122,145; My 48,66,120,137,
145,265; Rob 32,116,122,145; Sal 96;
Sar 66,74,108,118,129(2),162,256,
265,301,302(2); Tho 42,162,290;
William Stanley 83,264; Wm 5,6,95,
103,118,137(2),303
Edge, Ann 6,210; Eliz 167,198,210(2);
Ell 167; Jane 6,131,318; Jn 104,198,
210(2),280; Mgt 104,114,124(2),131,
155,270,280; My 198; Nic 104,114,
124,131,155(2), 270,280; Sar 114; Tho
167; Wm 210,224,270
Edmondson (Edmeston, Edmiston), Ann
135; Han 127,135,316; John Grey 127;
Rob 127,135,316
Edwards, Anne Eliza 51; Jane 215; Jn 262;
Jon 215; Jos 262; Mary Anne 51; My
262; Ric 293; Rob 215; Sar 293
Egerton, Ann 115,124,134; Chas 113,
300; Isa 299; Jn 113,132,299,300,307;
Marianne 115,132; My 113,299,300,
307; Olv 132,307; Sam 134; Tho 124;
Wm 115,124,134
Ekersley, Chas 68; Eliz 68; Geo 68
Ellanson - see Allinson
Ellensworth, Jam 308
Ellinson - see Allinson
Ellison, Chas 272; Jn 78; Job 78;

Sar 284; Wm 120,168,174

Eyre, Eyres - see Ayres

F

Fairclough, Ann 215,219; Eliz 170,178, 179,185,218,234; Fris 215; Geo 227; Jn 170,178,179,185,218,234, 242; Jon 170,179; Mar 185; My 178,219; Randel 218; Tho 215

Fairfield, Ali 268; Edw 233(2),268; Jn 280(2); Juliana 280; My 233

Fairhurst (Farhurst, Faris, Ferries), Ann 34,206; Ell 34,206; Jam 134; Pet 34, 202,206; Sar 134; Tho 134

Falkner - see Faulkner

Fallows, Ali 87,216; Eliz 8,87,101,252; Jam 87,101; Jn 2,101; My 2,8,192,216, 249,252; Sar 227; Tho 2,8,192,216, 249,252,304

Farhurst - see Fairhurst

Faris - see Fairhurst

Farmer, Car 148; Hen 148; Ric 148

Farral, Jane 274; Jn 274; Wm 274

Farrand (Ferrand, Ferrent), Ali 37; Eliz 37,173; Han 69; Har 69; Jam 145,228, 309; Jn 311; Mgt 145,309; My 208,211, 219,226; Samson 37,173,211,219,254; Sar 13,145,208,309; Tho 208,211,219; Wm 13,69

Farrar, Chas 239

Farron, Chas 237; Sue 237

Farrow, Chas 171; Jn 236; My 210; Sar 171; Sue 171,210

Faulkner (Falkner), Amc 295; Ann 254, 294,295,303; Charles Travis 303; Chas 294,295,303; Eliz 180; Jn 180,181; Jos 254; Wm 254

Fazakerly, Fres 185; Jam 185(2)

Featherstone, Ali 65; Tho 65; Wm 65

Fegan, Isb 161; Pet 161

Fenner, Mgt 201; My 201; Ric 201

Fenton, Ali 98; Jam 81; Jane 106; Jn 64, 240; Marianne 106; My 64,81,89,98, 240; Sar 89; Wm 64,81,89,98,106,240

Fernon, Ell 167; Jn 167; Rob 167

Ferns, Ali 288; Edw 254; Eliz 254(2),288; Tho 288

Ferr, Jos 193

Ferrand, Ferrent - see Farrand

Ferries - see Fairhurst

Fiddeham (Fideham, Fidian, Phathain), Ann 175,255,307; Dav 255; Hen 149; Jam 175(2),255,273,307; Jn 320; Mary Anne 307; Mat 149; My 149

Field, Ann 16,170,178; Eliz 16,159; Jos 170; Mat 16,159,170,178,181; Sam 178

Fielding, Ali 307; Alice Stafford 123; Eliz 123,130,262,294,307; Marianne 130; Martha Stafford 294; Ratcliff 123,130, 262,294,307; Tho 262

Fildes, Ann 9,16,24,25,33,40,46,52(2), 70,134; Eliz 25,70,77,249; Geo 314; Jam 24,103,286(2),287,298; Jn 49,70, 77(2),148,247,249(2),286; Jos 9,16, 24,33(2),40,46,52, 70(2); My 43,49,70, 134,148; Olv 43; Rob 16; Sar 46,103(2), 286(3),287; Tho 40,134,148; Wm 9, 299

Finch, Ali 135,160; Eliz 160,176; Hen 160; Rob 160; Thomas Henry 135; Wm 135,160,176

Finley, Fres 79; Jam 79

Finney, Jn 189; My 189(2); Tho 265

Firth, Geo 159(2),169; Jn 204; Jos 204; My 204; Sar 159,169; Wm 169

Fish, Cat 206; Jn 206; Jos 162; Mary Duxbury 253; My 158,162,206,253; Sar 162; Tho 253; Wm 158

Fishburn (Fishburne), Jn 157,305; My 157,305; Rob 157

Fisher, Ann 149; Edw 270; Ell 149; Fred 270; Marianne 270; Mark 191; My 191; Sam 191; Tho 306; Wm 149

Fishwick, Barnard 119; Ber 128,139; Han 150; Hen 128; Jn 119; My 119,128,139, 150; Phe 256(3); Ric 154,323; Rob 139; Veluria 154; Veturia 323; Wm 150,154, 256(3)

Fitton, Abr 263; Eliz 22,195,218;

Mary Anne 11; Mgt 167,180; My 11,
172,212,262,277,281, 291; Reb 180,
196,212(2); Ric 167,216; Rob 5,166,
207; Sam 48,129,152,191,275,291; Sar
152; Tho 182,196,213,256; Wm 17,99,
116,121,129,143, 212
Hare - see Ayres
Hargreaves, Harriett 145; Hen 295; Jane
145
Harking, Isb 319
Harlow, Ann 161,167,181; Eliz 206;
Harold 181; Jam 167,170,190(2),236;
Jane 170; Jn 199,206(2); My 170,190,
236; Rhoda Anne 161; Wm 161,167,
181
Harris (Harries), Ann 20; Eliz 20,155(2);
Ell 206,237,253,262(2); Emma 155;
Geo 20; Jam 237; Jos 262; My 155(3),
262; Ric 206; Tho 206,223,237,253,
262(2); Wm 155(3),253,323
Harrison, Ali 150,320; Ann 81,91,102,
113,285; Chas 14,285; Dav 6,83,97,
113,150,320; Eliz 217,282; Ell 196,
318; Elnr 28; Geo 163(2); Han 83,97,
150,320; Horatio 38; Jam 91(2),162,
285; Jane 102,113,285; Jn 6,14,29,
113(2),162,170,187(2),197,204,217,
246,252,269,282,283,299,318; Jos
298(3),303; Luke 269; Mgt 280,284(2);
My 29,97,162,170(2),187,204,217,
229,239,298(3),305,316,318; Ric 23,
83; Rob 28,196,305(2); Sam 239(2),
316; Sar 6,14,23(2),29,38,163,252,
269,282,299; Tho 23; Wm 23(2),28,
38,81,102,113,196,204,230,280,284,
286,316(2)
Harrop, Ann 126; Cat 13,24,207; Edm
169,175; Eliz 175; Jane 24,126; Jn
13(2),24,207; John Owen 126; Reb 175
Hartley, Ali 253,255; Ann 221,278; Cat
279; Chas 253; Eliz 252; James
Rutherford 22; Jn 196,199,214,253,255,
262, 278,281; Jon 196,204,208; Mar
278; My 22,196,208(2),279,281; Ric
22,199,214,246; Rob 246; Sar 199,214,

246,252; Tho 252,281
Haseldine (Hasledine), Jos 311; Sar 291,
311; Wm 291
Haslam (Haslem), Ann 8,58,67,240;
Cyrus 140; Dan 67; Eliz 126,144,146,
228,229; Ell 107; Han 59,103,220; Jac
301; Jam 107,140; Jn 8(2),58,59,67,
103,130,146,160,220,228,240,290,
311; Jos 59; My 311; Pru 130,140;
Richard Corns 107; Sam 126,144(2),
146; Syers 130; Wm 58,126,240
Hasledine - see Haseldine
Haslem - see Haslam
Hatfield - see Hadfield
Hatton, Jn 307
Haughton, Hen 323; Lyd 323; My 68,74,
201; Phi 201; Sam 68,74; Sar 74; Sue
201; Tim 68; William Henry 323
Haworth, Jn 52(2); My 185; Rosanna 52;
Sar 52(2); Wm 52
Hawthornthwaite, Jn 280; Reb 280
Hay, Ann 89; Eli 75; Eliz 110,125,129;
Han 67; Jam 124,125,136,148; Jane
118,124,129,140,150; Jn 67,75,89,99,
110,121,140; Jos 136; Lucy 125,136,
148; Mark 99; My 67,75,89,99,110,
121,148; Sam 121; Sar 118; Tho 118,
124,129,140,150(2)
Haycock, Ali 42; Eliz 42; Jn 42
Hayes (Heyes, Heys), Abr 167,186; Eliz
85,262,283; Fred 186; Han 167,186,
262; Harriot 222; Jam 292; Jane 304;
Jn 292,304; Lucy 292; My 303; Oli 167;
Tho 85,262,283; Wm 85,303
Haynes - see Haines
Haywood - see Heywood
Heald, Ali 134,317,323; Ame 43,215,
273; Ann 310; Ben 323; Chas 317; Eliz
36,316; Jam 310; Jn 134,317,323;
Milley 36; Sam 43,134,168,215; Tho
36,43,215,273; Wm 310
Healey, Charity 61; Eliz 61; Tho 61
Heap, Ali 66,74,123,139,288; Cat 205,
211; Edw 288; Eliz 264; Geo 123; Han
66; Jam 264; Jn 66,74,123,139(2),288;

John Michael 103,111; Kezia 111
Higginson, Agn 98; Han 98; Ric 98
Higham, Ali 86; Ann 59,79,86,94,102,
    111,122,141(2),152,288,319; Edm 94;
    Eliz 50,54,59,64,73,87,90,111,245,
    247; Est 2,59,87; Geo 87; Han 9,102,
    116; Jam 59(2),66,80,90,100(2),112,
    118,129,138,247; Jn 2,9,18(2),54,59,
    80,88,94,104,111,116,152,278,288,
    319; Jos 50,54,59,64,73(2),79,86,94,
    102,104,111,122,138,141,245(2),247,
    278,288, 319; Luke 111,288; Mar 88,
    111,116,278,319; Matty 94,104; Mgt
    59,66,80,90,100,112,118,129,138,247,
    319; My 2,9,18,50,66,94,129,152,288;
    Sam 118; Sar 79,88; Ste 247; Tho 64;
    Wm 122; Wright 112
Higson, Ann 159,167,173; Eliz 159; Ell
    279; Geo 275; Jam 279(2); Pet 173;
    Ruth 275; Tho 159,167,173,175; Wm
    167
Hill, Ali 126; Ann 140,175,256; Ben 255;
    Edw 273,316(2); Eliz 175,196,238,258,
    288; Ell 121,288; Fres 175; Har 108,
    196; Jam 140,213,241,249,254,296;
    Jane 126,232; Jn 238; Josh 108; Mar
    258; Mgt 241,244,248,256,272; My
    212,222,225,244,249,273,316; Ric
    121(2),175,196,258,288,289,292; Sam
    212,272; Sar 108,212,213,238,249,254,
    273; Tho 174,213,241,244,248,256,
    272,305; Wm 140,248
Hilton, Abr 129; Absalom 42,322; Ali 92;
    Ann 44,50,102,104,107,108,112,126,
    130,133,139(2),148,270,276,283,286,
    291,294,305,311,313,321,322; Ben 42,
    130; Chas 45,300; Chat 60,67,80,85,95,
    102,111,127,248; Dan 102,133,291;
    Dav 65,152,287; Edm 276; Edn 148,
    287,322; Eli 60,67,80,85,95,102(2),
    111,127,248; Eliz 34,41,45,50,92(2),
    108(3),111,112,121,128,134(2),139,
    141,149,286,292,293,300,305; Est 253;
    Geo 41,45,77,92(2),102,108(2),126,
    253,286,300; Han 105,112,125,137,

276,278,287,291; Har 104,287;
    Harriett 322; Hen 81,111,126,134; Isa
    52; Jam 47,78,104(2),107(2),121,
    130(2),276,278,279,292, 293; James
    Berry 85; James Horatio 305; Jane 43,
    110,130(2),253,305; Jane Elizabeth
    111; Jn 34,43,44,47,50,52,65,102,104,
    112,125,126,137,139,152,259,276,
    278,283,311,321; Jon 44,128,134,139,
    305; Jonas 102; Jos 77,80,100,107,112,
    119,120,121(2),124,141,149,279,
    292(2),293; Lancelot 65,109(2),125,
    270, 281; Lavinia 95; Luke 81,95,105,
    119,139,287, 292; Mar 44(2),67,133,
    291; Marianne 248; Mary Ann 311; My
    41,65,78,100,107(2),109(3),120,128,
    137,148,205,259,270,276(2),283,292,
    294,322; Phe 139; Rac 81,95,105,119,
    141,287, 92; Reb 121(2); Ric 120; Rob
    65,78,95,110,111,124,134,139,149,
    276,292,305; Sal 60; Sam 19(2),126,
    321; Sar 19,34,43,47,52,65,77,92,102,
    109,110,124,126,129,139,152; Sue 104,
    112,279; Tho 205,259; Violet 42;
    William Berry 127; Wm 100,129,291,
    292,294,313
Hind, Jn 283
Hindle, Chr 320
Hindley, Jon 234; My 234; Phe 234
Hinks, Eliz 285; Ric 135,147,285; Sar
    147; Sarah Ann 135,147; Tho 135
Hirst - see Hurst
Hobson, Ali 258; Ann 193; My 258; Rob
    193; Tho 193
Hodgen (Hodgin), Ali 11; Ann 104; Eliz
    97; Jam 97,104; Jn 11,104; Pru 11;
    Tho 97
Hodgson (Hodson), Eliz 177,284; Hen
    115; Jam 177; Jane 66; Jn 115(2); Joel
    66; My 54; Rac 115; Sar 54; Tho 177,
    284(2)
Hogg, Ann 122,129,155,319; Eliz 155,
    313,319; Est 129; Han 128,155,318;
    Hetty 313; Jn 307; Lancelot 122,129,
    155,319; Sam 318; Sarah Anne 128;

Tho 122,128,155(2),318

Holcroft, Jam 146(2); Lucy Maria 146(2); Pet 146(2)

Holden (Holding), Ali 249; Ann 174,181, 250; Eliz 322; Geo 249; Hen 249; Jam 167,174,250; Jane 90; Jn 90; Jos 322; Mat 174; Mgt 25; Sam 90; Sar 25; Tho 25,250; Wm 181

Holdroyd, Ben 167; Han 167; Josh 167

Holds, Eliz 101; Geo 101; Jn 101

Holdsworth, Ann 168; Jn 168(2)

Holland, Ali 91; Amaziah 324; Ann 46, 68; Chas 294; Eliz 29,52,116,153,185, 213,289(2),295,317; Ell 46; Fris 67, 242; Geo 38,208,257,280,288; Han 89, 213,222; Hen 29,38,43,48,261,295; Heritage 217; Jam 59,266; Jane 266; Jn 9,24,46,47,48,52,59,68,74,185,190, 223,224,241,266,294,317; Jos 38,47, 74,178(2),317; Mar 43,47,55,68,293; Matty 52,59; Mgt 266; Mos 91; My 29, 38(2),43,48,55,57(2),67,89,116,178, 190,208,217,241,242,257,261,266, 273(2),280,288,293,296, 324; Ophelia 153; Phe 91; Sam 9,38,55,57,67,89, 116,190,208,217,241,242,257,261, 266,273,280,288,293,296(2); Sar 9, 24(2),74,294; Tho 185,213,289

Holme, Holmes - see Hulme

Holroyd, Dan 322; Han 176; Jam 146; Jos 141,312; Josh 176,193; Lucy Maria 118,141,146,312,316; Maria Lucy 128; My 29; Pet 29,118,128,141,146,312, 316; Rob 29,118,213; Sar 128; Wm 176,316

Holt, Ann 50,54,60,68(2),86,136,153, 240,252,255,265,273,284,289(2),318, 324; Betsey 123,132,309(2); Charles Francis 105; Dav 19,193; Eliz 12,13,19, 20,147,175,184,186,193,220,309; Elizabeth Ellen 91; Ell 110; Est 136; Esther Emma 142; Fres 274; Geo 127; Han 183,255; Hen 274,299; Isb 262; Jam 20,30,54,123,161,176,179,183, 220,295,309(2); Jane 132,309; Jn 30,

50,54,60,68,86,109,123,132,147,150, 161,229,236,240,252(2),255,265, 270,273,274,284(2),288,289(2), 309(2),318; Joel 13,175; John Thomas 147; Jos 179,192,273; Josi 95,105,110, 125,142,152; Josiah Borlase 152; Mar 101; Mary Ann 153; Mary Anne 91, 109; Mary Barnes 95,105,110,125,142, 152; Mary Jane Shepley 95; Mgt 161, 254,270,289; My 20,30,101,127,179, 192,220,309,318,324; Reu 50,134,150, 295,299,309, 324; Ric 184,215; Sam 134; Sar 134,150,265,295,299,309; Tho 12,60,86,136,186,240,309; William Henry Vincent 125; Wm 91, 101,109,127,153,289

Hooles, My 124; William Rostern 124

Hooley (Hooly), Ann 66,96,257; Betsey 52; Charles Roberts 85,257; Chas 278; Chat 135,141,154; Dav 39; Eliz 42; Emanuel 271; Est 174,253,300; Han 135; Jam 3,9,15,96,173,178,179,208, 259; Jn 42,55(2),216; Jon 23,31,39, 103,195,208,229,246,255,271,300, 301; Jos 31,135,257,291,306; Josephina Anne 85; Luke 255; Mar 29,39,44,52, 66,141; Mary Jane 135; My 3,9(2),15, 23(2),31,39(2),42,55,103,173(2),174, 178,179,195,208,216,255,260,271, 291,301; Rabbina 103; Rac 277; Reb 96; Sar 44,85,135,277,278; Tho 15,29,39, 44,52,66,154,174,175,179,190; Wm 3,29,135,141,154,232,301,318

Hooten (Hooton), Fris 267; My 264; Wm 264,267

Hope, Jn 114; Jos 6,24(2); My 6,24,114; Rob 114; Sue 6

Hopwood, Ann 296; Eno 140,320; Fres 264; James Richard 33; Jane 122; Jer 33, 201,264,296; Jn 296; Mar 33,201; My 122,129,140,320; Tho 122,129,140, 320; Thz 129

Horne, Jane 274; Rob 274; Tho 274

Horrax, Horrex - see Horrocks

Horridge (Orridge), Ali 29,197(2);

32,112; Wm 11,95

Hoyle, Ali 278; Eliz 2,14; Est 2; Jam 14,
258; Jn 98,238,254,258,270(2); Jos
249; Lyd 98,270; Mgt 270; My 98,238,
249,254,258, 265(2),270,278; Sam 2,
14,249,265,278; Sar 232,254; Tho 238

Hubbart (Hubbert), Eliz 246; Fris 246; Geo
247; Jane 246; Jn 269; Mic 247,269,
301; My 247,269,301

Hudson, Cat 38; Chas 188; Dav 38; Eliz
17,38,132; Geo 17(2),165,177(2),188,
204,209; Jane 165,177,188,197; Jenny
165; Jn 165; Mar 177,270; My 132,270;
Sar 204,209(2); Tho 132,270

Hughes (Hughs), Ali 194; Ann 108; Bar
36,46,203,204; Barbara Jane 122; Edn
36,204; Edw 3,291; Eliz 132,169(2),
194; Ell 203; Emma 36,203; Hen 274;
Jn 94,108,122,132,146,169,194,274;
Mar 186,204(2); My 3(2),94,108,122,
132,146(2),291; Pat 186,204,233; Pen
203; Pru 274; Ric 291; Rob 46,294;
Tho 36,46,94,186,203,204; Wat 222;
Wm 203

Hull, Ali 138; Ann 171; Edw 138; Jam
171; Sue 171; Wm 138

Hulme (Holme, Holmes), Abi 202,249;
Ali 5,12(2),18,27,34,41(2), 46; Ann 2,
34,47,68,76,83(2),126,136,138,147,
166(2),203(2),262,289,316,318,319,
324; Art 64; Cat 130,138,146; Chas
187,230; Chat 314; Dan 131; Eliz 3,5,
14,92,116,144,148,188,257,294,295,
315; Ell 203; Est 27,37,200; Fanny 199;
Han 68,95,127,203,267,268, 274,281;
Hannah Haigh 150; Har 125,131; Hen
138; Horsefall 87; Isr 161; Jam 2,8,14,
19,27,35(2),41,102,144,161,164,
166(2),171,177,184,185,186,203,225,
257,269,303;315; Jane 132,144,155,
323(2); Jn 3,12(2),19,35,46,58,125,
126,131,132,138,144(2),147,148,155,
171,173,191,197,202,216,223,277,
313,315,316,318,319,323(2); Joel 95,
267; Jon 231; Jos 5(2),12,18,27,34,

41(2),46,47,116,144,150,155,164,289,
314,316,323; Joseph Moores 27,269;
Mar 35,58,146,186,187,216; Marianne
87; Mary Ann 148,307; Mgt 56,64,83;
My 3,5,12(2),14,37,58,92,113,138,
150,158,164,166,171,173(2),177,184,
187,191,196,198(2),199,203,227,262,
265,274,286,310,314,324; Phe 2,8,14,
19,27,35,41,132, 161,269,303; Reb
147,168(2),250,318; Ric 47,68,76,
83(2),203,274,289,296; Rob 8,14,18,
37,87,102,113,126,127,130,136,144,
181,196,216,249,262,265,286, 88,
294,307,310,319,323,324; Sam 5,12,
203,281,286; Sar 76,102,113,127,144,
184,191,197,274,277,310; Tho 35,
56(2),64,83,125,130,136,138,146,168,
196,202,214,307; Wm 12,14,95,144,
166,197,198,199,224,252,267,268,
274,303,324

Hulton, Absalom 128,151,323; Agn 4,18,
28,35,65,74,197; Alf 93; Ali 1,4,9,
12(2),14,19(2),36,62,86,96,164,189,
281; And 30,86; Ann 4(2),8(2),9,11,14,
15,19,23,30,33,36,37,46,49,55,69,74,
75,92,96,106,128,155,183,185,202,
225,267,281; Anne Heathcot 123;
Ashton 55; Ben 22,26,28,35,52,62(2),
71(2),80,93(2),106,123,135,184(2),
185,194(2),218(3),239(2),257,281(2),
286,296,302(2),310; Chas 19,39,104,
274,308,313; Chat 55,74,247;
Christiana 50,226; Dan 26,34,39,51,60,
69,84,205,269,271; Dav 8,24,28,32,74,
112,124,136,139,286; Edn 53,60,77;
Edw 14,92,100,107,115,123(2),135,
145,147,302; Eli 55,247; Eliz 8,17,26,
28,34,49,50(2),54,55(3),65,75,95,100,
101,107,119,135,139,147,194,205,
223,279; Ell 74,85,279,291; Ellis 95;
Els 74; Emma 113,285; Est 11,18,47,
84,119,121; Esther Rosina 46,226; Fris
63,68,235; Geo 5,28,34,47,49,54,55,62,
65,70(2),75,90(2),185,205,220,276;
Han 11,26,27,32,39,51,60,62,69,84,

204; Phe 169,204; Sam 4(2),9; Thomas
Morris 9
Irwin, Phe 232; Wm 232
Isdale (Isdell), Eliz 324; Fris 306
Isherwood (Ishwerwood), Ali 262; Ann
261,262(2); Dolly 168; Eliz 2; Jane 2;
Jn 168,206,214,261,262; Mary Ann
214; My 206,214,230,261,262; Ric
262; Rob 2; Wm 206,229
Ivison - see Avison

J

Jacks, Ann 76,158,254; Jn 158; Jos 245;
Phe 76,85(2),245,254,292,319; Tho
158; Wm 76,85,245,254,292(2),319(2)
Jackson, Ali 148(2),218,249; Amos
Ezekiel 156(2); Ann 32,71,218,232,
243; Chat 194; Dan 291,317; Edm
301(2); Edw 17,25,32,42; Eliz 13,280;
Ell 125,259; Est 289; Fres 172,260;
Geo 125,249; Geo Henry 311; Gra 289;
Han 317; Hen 306,311; Jac 235; Jam
25,71(2),207,243(3),276, 280(2); Jane
276,289,293; Jenny 291,317; Jn 13,24,
86,194,204,218,229, 249,289; Job 276;
Jos 71; Mar 194,249,293; Mary Ann
152; Matilda 235; Mgt 71(3),207,
243(4); My 17,24,125,137,148,152,
227,260,301,306,312; Phe 71; Reu 148;
Ric 229,314; Rob 125,137,152,260,312;
Ruth 13,24; Sal 86; Sar 17,25,32,42,
156,207,306, 311; Sidney 148; Tho
137,289,293; Wm 42,71,148,199,235,
249,259,267,291
Jacobs, Han 212
James, Ali 290; Ame 262,290; Ann 250,
252; Han 262; Hen 250,317; Jn 262;
My 258,273; Sar 252,258; Tho 252,
258,273,290
Jameson (Jamieson, Jamison, Jammenson,
Jemison), Agn 159,199; Ali 109; Eliz
157(2),188,190; Geo 292; Hugh 292,
293; Jam 157,188,190(2); Jan 292,293;
Jos 199,314; My 109,159; Sue 293;

Tho 109,159,188,199,262,281
Jandrill, Geo 266
Jefferies (Geofrey, Jeffries), Ann 44,93;
Chr 91,93; Eliz 91; Han 91,93; My 44
Jefferson, Ann 190; Ben 190
Jeffries - see Jefferies
Jellashan, Alex 47; Isb 47; Wm 47
Jemison - see Jameson
Jenkinson, Ann 194; Ell 194,213; Geo
183; Jam 213; Jn 194,197,213; My 179,
180,183,196; Sam 179; Tho 180; Wm
179,180,183,195,196(2)
Jenning, Eliz 28; Sar 28
Jinks, My 73; Sar 73
Johnson (Johnstone), Aa 304; Abr 178;
Alex 201; Ali 252,257,317; Ann 2,
12(2),22,32,54(2),55(2),87,98(2),
106,140,179,219,254(2),276(2),
288,300,308,313; Ben 183,212; Car
288,300; Chas 183,254; Edw 140; Eliz
2,12,20,29,110,113,116,120,130,181,
183,212,259(2),278(2),299,300,303,
312,317,319; Ell 295; Emily 140;
Emma 257; Geo 178; Han 179,254,304,
323,324; Isa 181,313; Jam 12,20,29,
132,142,155,179,201,211,238,299,
300,303,311,319,324; James Bardsley
106, 308; Jane 198,202; Jesse 323,324;
Jn 29,113,116,130,202,238,261,267,
278,317; Jos 113,120(2),150,212,233;
Joseph Grimshaw 300; Mar 32,165,176,
178,267; Mary Elizabeth 142; Matilda
78; Mgt 178; My 12,78,130,132,142,
155(2),173,252,269,311; Pet 312,317;
Phe 22,132,311; Reb 201,211; Ric 2,
12,22,32,54,55,219,226; Rob 116,249;
Rosette 198; Sam 165(2),176(2),178,
252,257,267,281; Sam Grimshaw 299;
Sar 110,150,211,219; Sarah Ann 313;
Sue 238; Tho 20,78,98,106,110,198(2),
276,278,288,300,308,323; William
Cooper 87; William James 304; Wm
87,173,181,254(2),259, 278(2),319
Jones, Ann 79,164,169(2),174,188,
192,193,236,250; Ben 227; Cat 160;

Wm 110

Lowe, Agn 9; Ann 71,103,144,251(2),
279, 281,288,310,314(2),320; Eliz 71,
251,259,277,288,310; Geo 281; Ham
259,277,288,310; Han 144,314; Jam
28; Jn 9(2); My 28,251; Sam 28,71,
103(2),144,251(2),279(2),281,314(2),
320; Sarah Ann 320; Tho 259,277;
Wm 314

Loyd - see Lloyd

Lucas, Geo 174,188,191; Jane 188; Jn
169(2),176,179; My 168,169,176,179,
191; Sar 191; Wm 168,176; Zac 168

Lupton, Sar 283; Wm 283

Luvrison, Bryant 220

Lyon (Lyons), Ann 248; Cor 204; Est
248; Jam 188,214,248; Jane 204; Jn
176,188,267; Mary Ann 214; My 176,
188,267; Sar 176

Lytle - see Little

M

MacInvenna, Ann 153; Jn 153; Mar 153

Mack, Jn 135; My 135; Violet 135

Mackay (McKay), Chas 160; Edm 160;
Ell 172; Gil 159,172; Gra 172; Greswell
159; Jan 159

MacNamee (McNamee), Han 114; Jn
94,103,114,123,294,310, 322; Mar
123; Mat 103,294; My 310; Sar 94;
Violet 94,103,114,123,294,310, 322

Madders, Cat 288; Eliz 282; Jam 288;
Tho 282,288

Maddocks, Ann 219; Tho 219(2)

Maden (Madin, Meaden, Meden), Aa 183,
189,192; Ann 217; Cat 189,192; Eliz
252,257; Ell 209; Jane 241; Jn 241,257;
Jos 209; Mgt 209; Rob 192; Sar 241,
257; Tho 217,225

Maffin, Jam 197; Jn 197; Rosetta 197

Magill, Eliz 177; Jn 165; Marlow
165,177; My 165,177

Maize, Jam 260; Jn 260; Joice 260

Makin (Maken), Aa 183; Ali 2,3,10,70,

247(3),291; Ann 154,162,193,208,229;
Cat 253; Chas 79; Dav 10,89,100,109,
131(3), 303(2); Edm 119; Edn 154; Eliz
61,70,79,84,96,105,119, 247,296; Ell
162; Han 61; Jam 2,37,84,162,225,248;
James Berry 225; Jane 231; Jn 3,10,109,
190,199(2),210,244,246,247(2),253,
284,286,291; Jos 10,84,100,247; Mar
84; Marianne 89,105; Mgt 37; My 84,
190,199,210,226,227,284,305(2);
Phineas 3,291,305; Ric 61,70,247(2);
Sal 89,100,109; Sar 70(2),131(3),
247(2),248, 303; Ste 210; Tho 96,208,
296; Wm 37,79,84,96,105,119,154,
284,296

Mallory, Ann 169; Jn 169; Ric 169

Maloney, Car 146; Sarah Ann 146; Wm
146

Manfield, My 159; Tho 159; Wm 159

Manley, My 118; Wm 118(2)

Marrs (Mars), Ali 171,192; Mat 281(2);
My 281; Rac 171; Wm 171,192(2),230

Marsden, Ann 61,77,139,223; Dav 237;
Edw 152; Eliz 54,62,69,77,116,134,
147,237(2),238,253,281,311; Ell 83;
Emma 136; Est 109; Ham 134,311;
Han 79,253; Hen 126,152,303; Jam
54(2),61,62,69,77,105, 116,237,253;
Jn 31,37(2),54,73,83,94(2),98,105,
109,116(2),126,136,139,152,226,238,
272(2),293,297(2),303,321; Jos 69;
Jud 305; Lyd 31,37(2); Mar 145; Mary
Ann 147; Mat 305; Milley 31; My
37(2),73,109,115,116,293, 305; Pet
61,237; Rob 62,79,83,91,98,115,123,
133,145,237,281; Sar 54,73,83,94,105,
116,126,133,136,152(2),238,272,293,
297,303,321; Sarah Anne 83; Sue 79,83,
91,98,115,123,133,145,281; Tho 91,
134,147,311; Wm 54,123,139,152, 321

Marsh, Ali 165; Ann 218,230; Edw 292;
Eliz 185; Geo 208,257; Han 205; Hum
165; Jane 257; Jervis 165; Jn 184,185,
205,208,218; My 173,184,281; Sar 184,
185,194,205,208,218; Tho 173(2),194

McMayhan, Jam 192; Mar 192
McMhan, My 207
McNair, Ann 203(2); Wm 203
McNamee - see MacNamee
McNeal, Dan 210; Eliz 182,210; Jn
	182,210
McNear, Wm 201
McVenom, Ann 79; Eliz 79; Mgt 72; Rob
	72
McWade, Ann 200; Owen 200; Pat 200
McWilliam, Ephraim 165; Han 165,174;
	Wm 165,174
Meaden, Meden - see Maden
Medcalf - see Metcalf
Mellor, Chr 216,243,285; Edw 285; Eliz
	108; Jn 50; Mary Anne 20; Mgt 50; My
	5,20; Sam 5(2),20; Sar 216(2),243,285;
	Sarah Anne 108; Tho 243; Wm 108
Mercer, Car 96,102; Catherine Anne 102;
	Har 96; Jn 96,102
Mercey, Dav 33; Mar 33; Mary Anne 33
Metcalf (Medcalf), Emma 235(2); Geo
	235; Jn 159,303; My 159(2),303
Middleton, Alton 113; Ann 8,261,266;
	Eliz 132,133; Ell 123; Fris 261; Han 21;
	Jam 123,132,145; Jane 123,132,145;
	My 133; Sal 113; Sar 21,145; Wm 8(2),
	21,113,133,261,266
Miller (Millar), Ann 321; Chas 23; Chat
	154; Chn 25; Chr 37,60(2),69; Dav 154;
	Han 23; Jam 23,25,63,211; James
	Bishop 154; Jn 63; Mgt 63; My 211; Sar
	25,37(2),60,69; Tho 69
Mills, Abr 23,92,102,118,124,298; Agn
	124,298; Agnes Younge 118; Ali 29,47,
	48,60,75,77,81(2),84,96,103,116,128,
	129,146,160,164,215,249,252, 270;
	Ann 24,32,42,92,102(2),129,169,211,
	245(2),254,279; Chas 24,103; Chr 245;
	Edm 32; Eliz 29,58,67,70,80,102,107,
	160,161,251(2),259,275,276,287(2),
	304; Ell 128,251,324; Est 301; Fres 18,
	23,36,42,50,56,63,71,269,278; Geo
	129,143,315,318; Han 71,245,254;
	Hen 65,67,230,305; Isb 59,65; Jam 10,

58,75,77(2),84,96,103,116,129(2),
	146,211,230,245(2),249(2),254,268,
	270(2),274,279,283,304, 324; James
	Thomas 279; Jane 71,77,151,308(2);
	Jenny 48,84,107; Jn 24,32,42,50,59,
	60,65,124,128,160,161,233,238(2),
	247,252,265,305,324; Jos 58,67,70,80,
	84,102(2),107,259,275(2),287(2), 304;
	Mar 247; Mary Ann Jane 146; Mary
	Holmes 92; Mary Wilson 151; Mic 143,
	318; My 10,42(2),56,59,80,129,143,
	211,238,259,311,318; Phi 71; Rac 36;
	Ric 29,48,81,215; Rob 18,23,36,42,47,
	50,56,63(2),71(2),77,84,96,107(2),
	118,151,169(2),270,278,298,308; Sam
	47; Sar 75,107,215,238,283,287,304,
	305; Sarah Wilson 84; Sue 10,18,269,
	270,278,283; Tho 116,245,301(2);
	Wm 70,276
Milner, Ann 174; Eliz 138; Jam 138,174,
	183; Jane 89; Jos 89; My 183; Ric 174;
	Rob 183; Tho 138
Milnes, Ann 184,188; Rob 184,188(2)
Minshull, Eliz 314; Jn 151; Mar 152; My
	151,152,314; Rob 152; Wm 151,314
Mitchel, Dot 266; Jn 215,266; My 215;
	Wm 215
Mold (Mould), Eliz 280; Jn 245,280
Molloy (Moloy), Alexander Newall 61;
	Ann 61,170,234; Jam 170; Ric 61,170,
	234; Sar 222
Monks, Eliz 235,243,300; Est 235,309;
	Han 243; Jn 259,300; Tho 235,243,300
Mons, My 279; Tho 279
Montgomery, Eliz 158; Geo 219; Jam
	158; Mgt 158,219(2)
Moon, Jn 299; My 299; Rob 265,299
Moore, Abr 117,282; Ann 108; Eliz 30,
	119,280,301; Fred 150; Geo 200; Han
	280; Jn 13,19,33,40,42,77,189,201,
	204,208,212; Jos 86; Mar 117; My 19,
	36,77,86,108,117,119, 150,282; Sam
	13,36,77,86,108,119,150,280,282,301;
	Sar 30; Sue 13,19; Tho 30,36,256
Moores (Moors), Abr 147; Ame 66,

Matilda 146; Marianne 109; Olv 90,264, 265

Nelson, And 117,151,300; Bridget Susanna 300; Emma 136; Jane 107,117, 136,151,300(2); Reb 107; Ric 307; Tho 107,117,136,151,300(2)

Newall (Newal), Ame 158; Amey 173; Emmy 173; My 173; Phi 158,173(2); Wm 158

Newham, Phi 275

Newton, Ann 256; Cat 79; Chat 131; Edm 170(2); Edn 320; Eliz 74; Est 187; Fres 320; Jam 83,92,101,113,131,143,167, 245,320; Jn 74,75,78,98,113,217; Jonathan Buckley 228; Jos 256; Josh 78; Mar 143,245; Maria Albiston 79; Marianne 83; Mat 98; My 40,75(2),83, 92,98,101,113,131,143,167,168,170, 187,228,240; Ral 240; Sam 40,92,167, 187; Sar 74,78,101,240

Nicholls (Nichols), Ann 133,309; Ben 143; Eliz 113,121,133,309; Jam 143; Jane 143; Jn 113; Jos 113,121,133,146, 309; Phe 121,146(2),308

Nicholson, Abr 228,232; Ann 168; Geo 214,220,242; Han 214,220,242; Jam 186; Jane 220,298; Jn 247; Jos 227,257, 298; My 214; Sar 65; Sue 65

Nield (Neal), Est 303; Jn 201,303; Sar 201,210; Tho 201,210; Wm 210

Nightingale, Car 120; Jane 112,120,130, 287; Jn 112(2),120,130(2),287(2); Pet 34(2); Rac 34

Nixon, Cat 158; Edw 158; Isa 196; Jane 233; Wm 158

Noble, Alex 26; Geo 26; Mgt 26

Norcroft, Ann 200; Jn 200; Sar 200

Norcross, Jn 174(3),207,209; Ric 311; Sar 174(2),209(2); Wm 174

North, Sam 302

NSN, Eliz 34,57; Fres 34; Isb 200; Mic 200; Reb 200; Sam 34; Sar 28

Nugent, Ann 196; Barnet 196; Geo 196

Nuttall (Nuttal), Ann 149; Eliz 28,36,90, 149,195; Est 67; Jam 28,34,195,203,

240,264; Jn 278; Jos 90,149,315; Mgt 36; My 240,264; Rac 264; Sar 28,34, 195,203; Sue 67,90,240; Tho 36; Wm 34,203

O

O'Brian (O'Brine, O'Brines, Obrines), Ann 211(2); Cat 222; Edw 159,239; Han 239; Jn 211(3),239; My 211

O'Conner, Brid 219; Jam 219; My 219

O'Hara, Ann 199; Edw 199

O'Neal (O'Nield, O'Neale, O'Neile), Ali 159; Ell 87,90,154; Jn 87(2),90,154; Mar 154; My 90

Oakes (Oaks), Ali 130,138; Ann 235; Jn 186,187,285; Mgt 235; My 130,187,285; Sam 130,138; Sar 187,224; Wm 138,235

Oaksley (Oakesley), Jane 269; My 103; Sam 103,269; Sar 103,269

Obrines - see O'Brian

Ogden, Abr 40,71,84,103,114,161(2), 175(2),176,189,209,215, 277; Alex 122; Ali 1,14,17,26,39(2),45,56,139, 168,206,257,261,292; Amb 53; Amos 212; And 121; Ann 31,34,48(2),49(2), 55,56,58,67,69,70,71(2),73,77(2),78, 84(2),88(2),89(2),90,96,98,99,100, 103(3),104,107,109,110,114,118, 122(2),126,130,134,139,145,146, 148(2),151,152,156,161,175,196,202, 217,234(2),236,257,258(2),261,264, 270,277,285,288,292,293(2),294, 297,298,299,304; Beky 113; Ben 31, 93,148,152,203; Caleb 49; Car 98; Chas 23,136; Chat 32; Dav 3,7,9,18,21, 38,43,50,52,55,57,68,73,77,84,90,96, 104,114,171,241,242,258,264,270, 288,292,293,299, 304; Edm 33; Eliz 1, 7,14(3),17,19,23,26,31,32,35,36,38, 43,45(2),47(2),49,50(2),55,56(2),57, 59,60,62,68,78,81(2),84,91,106,130, 155,156,173,182,195,201,211,220, 229,241,242,258(2),270,286,292,297,

66,74,80

Potter, Ann 58,89,225,273; Dav 25(2),
58,67,193(2),199; Edw 89; Eliz 25,58,
67,193,199; Est 170; Jam 199; Mar 67;
Sar 170; Tho 89,273; Wm 170,273

Potts, Alf 87; Ali 318; Geo 45; Han 55;
Jn 33; Jos 33,36; My 33; Ratcliffe 36,
45,55,87,96; Rosanna 96; Sar 36,45,55,
87,96

Powdger, Tho 233

Pownal, Har 271; Jam 271; John Beever
271

Poynton (Pointon), Eliz 322; Sar 317,
322; Tho 317(2),322

Pratt, Eliz 251; My 251; Wm 251

Prenton (Printon), Ben 89; Eliz 101; My
40,89,101; Ric 40; Tho 40,89,101

Prescot (Prescott), Joel 280; Sar 100,280,
304(2); Tho 100,304; Wm 100,280,
304(2)

Prest, Esther Maria 153; Mar 153; Tho
153

Preston, Ali 23,295; Ann 52,60(2),165,
220; Edw 16,295,320; Eliz 16,23,25,57;
Han 52; Jn 57,165,220,225; Mos 16,23,
57; Rob 227; Sar 25,165; Wm 52,60

Price, Eliz 288; Mgt 288; Wm 288

Prichard - see Pritchard

Priest, Ben 217,238,261; Charity 275;
Edm 275; Edw 217; Marianne 261; Sar
217,261

Priestnal (Priestnall), Ann 159,169,
194(2); Geo 159,194; Han 194; Jam
169; Jos 159,169,194(2); My 176

Prince, Eliz 16,27(2),39,45,203,204; Geo
16,27,39,45,203(2),204; Han 45; Jn 24;
Lyd 16; My 24,320; Sar 24,204,245;
Tho 39; Wm 243,245

Printon - see Prenton

Pritchard (Prichard, Pritchet), Ben 229;
Eliz 11; Han 1,11,28,196,216; Martin
216; Mic 196; Nic 196,216,296; Sam
28; Wm 1(2),11,28

Procter (Proctor), Ann 166; Eliz 166,
188,237; Jam 141,312; Jn 141,188,236;

Mary Ann 141,312; Sam 166,188,237,
240,279; Sue 236,240; Wm 236,240

Pugh, Isb 11,181; Jn 11,171,181; Sar 11,
181

Pulison, Edw 234

Q

Quinn (Quin), Eliz 232; Est 67; Jam 67;
Mgt 233; My 213,252,256; Pat 213,
252,256; Sar 252; Wm 213,233

R

Raby, Eliz 150; Hen 143,150; Mgt 143,
150; Sarah Ann 143

Radcliff, Radcliffe - see Ratcliff

Radford, Sar 114(2)

Ralston (Railson, Railston), Ann 299; Ell
92; Har 82; Jam 82,265; Jane 82(2),92,
265,299; Rob 82(2),92,265,299

Ramsbottom (Ramsbotham,
Ramsbottam), Ali 20; Ann 17; Brid 162;
Chat 121,127,297; Den 134,234,241,
265; Eliz 62,89,143,319; Ell 20,234,
241,300; Ellen Adelah 141; Geo 62,89,
121,143,297; George Abraham 120;
Hen 127,234; Jam 162; Jn 17,20,121,
127,170,220, 297,319(2); Jos 120,134,
141,170,300; My 62,120,134,141,143,
220(2),300; Sal 170; Sar 89,231

Ramscar, Geo 246,253,269(2); My 253,
269; Wm 253

Ramsden, Ann 62,95,118,174; Eliz 147;
Jam 121(2); Jn 95,106,118,130,147;
Mary Ann 62; My 95,106,118,121,130,
147; Rob 62; Sar 71,130,174,231; Wm
71(2),106,174

Ramsey, Jn 302,303(2); Sar 302,303

Ramshaw, Ann 31; Eliz 31; Isb 20,257;
Ral 20,31,257; Wm 20

Ramwell, Jane 321(2); Jn 321

Randles, Mar 158; Sar 158; Tho 158

Ratcliff (Radcliff, Radcliffe, Ratcliffe,
Ratliff, Ratliffe), Ali 4,13; Ann 4,9,20,

Sidebottom (Sidebotham, Sidebothom, Sydebotham), Ali 190; Ann 134,257; Chas 84,98,106,120,134,151, 152,323; Eliz 84,98,106(2),120,134,151,190, 252; Jn 113,121(2),131,143,151,152, 289,309,315,323; Mar 84; My 25(2), 33,98; Pet 254,257(2); Sam 113,289; Sar 113,120,121,131,143,152,289, 309(2),315,323; Sarah Anne 131; Tho 25,33(2),143,315

Sidlow, Eliz 291; Sam 291,303

Simister (Simmester), Alf 62; Ali 136; Ann 16,34,45,56,94,117, 244(3); Dan 106; Edm 43,77; Eliz 26,46,49,52,64, 138,139, 226; Emma 139; Est 6,19,38, 68,290; Fris 50; Geo 114,115,290,293; Han 24,45,121; Hen 134; Jam 4,7,15, 17,24,41,43(2),68(4),81,134,138,140, 165,245(2),253,259,277,290; Jane 4,7, 12,38,43,49,52,59,68,77,85,94,106, 115,293; Jenny 121; Jn 17,26,38,45, 50,56,64,68,80(2),189,290,296; Jos 38, 140,141; Lucy 59; Marianne 81; Mary Anne 259; Mgt 134,140; Millicent 50, 65(2),237,240,253,255; Milly 32,45,46, 59,82; My 7,15(2),17,24,26,38,43,45, 50,56,59,64,80,114(2),141,165,189, 296(2); Nic 38,43,47,49,52,59,68,77, 85,94,106,115,123,293; Ric 6,10,19, 26,34,41,47,68; Rosa 117,123; Rose 138(2); Sal 62; Sam 32,45,46,50,59, 65(3),82,165,237,240(2),253,255; Sar 6,10,12,19,26(2),34,41,47,65,68(3), 81,141,237, 245,259,290; Violet 16,50, 82,136,255; Wm 10,32,85,117,121, 123,138(2),189,244,275

Simm, Tho 274

Simmester - see Simister

Simpson, Alex 185; Ali 303; Ell 165(2); Har 113,286; Harriett 321; Jac 54,66, 243; Jn 66,113,138,286,314,321; Mar 321; Rob 303; Sam 113,286; Sar 54,66, 138,243,314; Tho 54,138,165,243, 303,312, 314

Singleton, Han 200; Hen 198,206,214(2),

217,272; Jam 296; Jane 198,206,214, 217,272; Mar 198,217; Marianne 206; My 296(2); NXN 67; RA 40,42,44,208, 212,215; Sar 200

Sison, Ann 179; Eliz 179

Skelmerdine, Eliz 310; John Joseph 310; My 310,314

Skilbeck, George Joseph 304

Skinner, Ral 179; Sue 179

Slater, Agn 13,19,36,55; Ali 14,64,184; Ann 13,25,167,181,241; Annis 36; Ednea 241; Eliz 19,20(2),35(2); Est 1, 73,190(2); Han 127,141,223; Hen 82, 167,181; Jam 5,188,212; Jane 67,73, 82,127,264; Jn 12,14,20,25,32,67,73, 82,127,141,168,207,212,217,227,241, 264; Jon 1,184,190(2),207,246; Jos 13, 19,36,55,64,217; Josi 231; Mar 5; Mgt 99; Miles 20(2),35; My 12,14,20,25,32, 207,212,217,227; Pet 99; Ric 181; Sar 12,36,190; Sop 141; Sue 55,64; Tho 5, 173,190; Wm 1,32,67,99,167,229

Sloan (Sloane, Slone), Alex 163,210; Ann 164,167,272; Ber 167; Brid 164; Elnr 163; Eliz 195; Ell 163; Jam 210; Jn 164, 198(2); Luke 195,276; My 198,210; Pat 167,272(2); Pet 195

Small, Geo 313; Jam 313

Smaller, My 160; Ric 160; Wm 160

Smart, Jane 165,188; Ric 165; Tho 165, 188; Wm 188

Smethurst (Smithurst), Ali 27,34; Ame 82; Ann 3,10(2),13,15,21(3),87,113, 121,126,130,181(2),188,192(2),193, 235,251,277,296; Chat 64,88(2),98, 244; Dan 110,263,279,282; Eliz 5,72, 82,113,126,131,152,244,286(2),306, 321(2),324; Geo 64,88(2),98,244; Han 35,64,76,95,98,110,263,279,282; Jam 13,21,27,35,44,50,59(2),98,103, 110,183,188,210(2),251,272,286,306; Jane 26(2),34,39,45,50,82,103,116, 122,226,289,306; Jn 16,88,113,130, 181; Jos 5,10,15,87,95,126(2),152(2), 286(2),290,296, 306,321(3),324; Mally

𝕴𝖓𝖉𝖊𝖝 2

𝕻𝖑𝖆𝖈𝖊𝖓𝖆𝖒𝖊𝖘

(Where a name occurs more than once on the same page, the number of times is shown in parentheses. There are many variations of spelling in the text, which have been collected together under one spelling in the index.)

Index 3

Miscellaneous Items

(Where an item occurs more than once on the same page, the number of times is shown in parentheses. There are many variations of spelling in the text, which have been collected together under one spelling in the index.)